From Participation
to Deliberation
A Critical Genealogy
of Deliberative Democracy

Antonio Floridia

© Antonio Floridia 2017

First published by the ECPR Press in 2017

Translated by Sarah De Sanctis from the Italian edition, *Un'idea deliberativa della democrazia*, published by La Società editrice il Mulino

The translation of this work has been funded by SEPS
Segretariato Europeo Per Le Pubblicazioni Scientifiche

Via Val d'Aposa 7 – 40123 Bologna – Italy
seps@seps.it – www.seps.it

The ECPR Press is the publishing imprint of the European Consortium for Political Research (ECPR), a scholarly association, which supports and encourages the training, research and cross-national co-operation of political scientists in institutions throughout Europe and beyond.

ECPR Press
Harbour House
Hythe Quay
Colchester
CO2 8JF
United Kingdom

Typeset by Lapiz Digital Services

Printed and bound by Lightning Source

British Library Cataloguing in Publication Data

A catalogue record for this book is available from the British Library

HARDBACK ISBN: 978-1-785522-42-0
PAPERBACK ISBN: 978-1-785522-75-8
PDF ISBN: 978-1-785522-76-5
EPUB ISBN: 978-1-785522-77-2
KINDLE ISBN: 978-1-785522-78-9

www.ecpr.eu/ecprpress

Table of Contents

List of Figures

Acknowledgements

This book wouldn't have been possible without the discussions I've had over the years with friends and scholars who share an interest in the topics addressed here. In particular, some of them have read and commented on a preliminary version of this text, encouraging me about the usefulness of my work while also helping me make it better: Luigi Bobbio; Alessandro Ferrara; Alfio Mastropaolo; Jürg Steiner; and Nadia Urbinati. I thank Jane Mansbridge for suggestions on wording in the English translation.

A special thanks goes to Valeria Ottonelli and Enrico Biale, who organised and co-ordinated a seminar on the first version of this text: it was held in Turin on 22 September 2014 and involved Silvano Belligni; Luigi Bobbio; Laura Cataldi; Alfio Mastropaolo; Valentina Pazè; Mauro Piras; Gianfranco Pomatto; Stefania Ravazzi; and Chiara Testino. The valuable debate that took place on this occasion gave me ideas to improve and enrich my work.

First Dario Castiglione and then the editor of ECPR Press, Ian O' Flynn, have given me valuable advice on how best to realise this work. Deborah J. Savage, the ECPR copy-editor, has done an excellent job in improving the stylistic quality and clarity of my text.

The dialogue with other friends and scholars over the years has stimulated me and concretely helped me deepen my knowledge, both as a whole or about specific topics and authors: Umberto Allegretti; Giovanni Allegretti; Marco Almagisti; Fabrizio Barca; Roberto Cartocci; Ilaria Casillo; Giulio Citroni; Pierangelo Isernia; Anna Loretoni; Alberto Magnaghi; Giovanni Mari; Giovanni Moro; Massimo Morisi; Giancarlo Paba; Luigi Pellizzoni; Andrea Pillon; Walter Privitera; David Ragazzoni; Luca Raffini; and Iolanda Romano.

Special thanks to Ilvo Diamanti, for the precious conversations we have had all these years, especially on the work of Bernard Manin (also on the occasion of an honorary degree that the University of Urbino awarded him in 2015).

With some friends, the discussion has focused on specific aspects of my job: I am grateful for the constant dialogue I had with Luca Corchia, an expert on Habermas (on whom he edited a valuable bibliography, fundamental to navigating the stormy waters of the translations of his works).

Camilla Perrone gave me some essential bibliographic indications on the literature about theory and practice of urban and territorial planning.

My friend Mauro Imbimbo, with whom I shared my early philosophical training, has read and commented on first versions of the text with wit and irony.

Irene Lorieri has been a precious help in the editorial work on this edition of the book.

The translator, Sarah De Sanctis, has done an excellent job. Her work has often allowed me to clarify and improve my text.

None of this would have been possible without the Library of Social Sciences at the University of Florence: the rich catalogue, the availability of online access to a great number of international journals, and the efficiency of the inter-library lending service have been a really precious tool for me.

A preliminary version of Chapter Two was published in *Rivista Italiana di Scienza politica* (2014, n. 3, pp. 299–326) under the title "Beyond participatory democracy, towards deliberative democracy: elements of a possible theoretical genealogy".

Finally, special gratitude goes to the institution I work for: Tuscany Region. I couldn't have been dealing with deliberative democracy and participatory democracy for all these years if, in 2006, I hadn't been made responsible for a new sector – that of 'policies for participation'. If I hadn't been able to see the topics of this book from this particular perspective, I wouldn't have been able to experience directly the connection between theory, political culture and social and institutional practices that lies at the heart of my critical reconstruction.

Introduction

In a passage of his 2006 book, published during the beginning of the campaign that would lead him to the White House, Illinois Senator Barack Obama wrote:

> What the framework of our constitution can do is organize the way in which we argue about our future. All of its elaborate machinery – its separation of powers and checks and balances and Federalist principles and Bill of Rights – are designed to force us into a conversation, a 'deliberative democracy' in which all citizens are required to engage in a process of testing their ideas against an external reality, persuading others of their point of view, and building shifting alliances of consent.[1]

This excerpt comes from a chapter in which Obama explains his view of the American constitution and the ideal of democracy embodied by US institutions. This paragraph could perhaps be regarded as a milestone: the notion of 'deliberative democracy' here appears for the first time in the public discourse of a key figure of international politics. Yet the idea of deliberative democracy expressed by Obama's words might seem unusual or surprising in the light of the prevailing image of deliberative democracy today.

In this book, I will try to reconstruct the theoretical genesis of this deliberative idea of democracy and the steps that have led to a fully formed *theoretical field*, characterised both by common assumptions and a growing internal articulation. In this reconstruction, a key role will be played by a comparison of deliberative democracy with another notion: that of *participatory democracy*.

The present work therefore aims to be an essay in the 'history of ideas', that is, an attempt to understand deliberative democracy starting from its *theoretical genealogy*: its first theoretical formulations, the reasons behind its elaboration, and

---

1. Barack Obama (2006: 92). In Chapter Three I will outline the roots of political culture and the intellectual affiliation that may help elucidate Obama's words.

the conceptual (but also historical and political) core that can be found throughout its development and further articulation. My analysis will focus on the comparison with the idea (and practice) of participatory democracy for two reasons: first, to achieve a more complete critical and historical reconstruction; second, and above all, to contribute to an ongoing theoretical and political debate on these two adjectives (*participatory* and *deliberative*) that are frequently used to describe democracy and yet often left indeterminate or, worse, mistaken for one another.

I must warn the reader: I am not aiming for a systematic reconstruction of these two models of democracy, nor will I be able to offer an exhaustive critical review of the massive literature on the subject. It is not my goal to offer here a comprehensive presentation of what deliberative democracy means *today*. My purpose is more limited: to unearth the origins of this theoretical model and to reconstruct the phases of its development, hoping to offer a useful contribution to the contemporary theoretical and political debate on these topics. At the same time, a genealogic reconstruction of this model may help bring out its conceptual core better than a (rather difficult) systematic presentation of it. I shall only devote the final chapter to the analysis of the most recent developments in deliberative theory, outlining a possible 'map' of its current configuration.

Thus, my choice has been to offer a *historical-genetic* presentation rather than a *logical-systematic* one. In this regard I must make another preliminary clarification: usually the thinkers taken to be the 'fathers' of deliberative democracy are Jürgen Habermas and John Rawls. The choice of a systematic presentation would have implied starting from the analysis of the theoretical foundations on which these two authors built their different views of deliberative democracy. Instead, however, I have chosen to reconstruct the many steps through which the idea of deliberative democracy has come to be, with reference to various intellectual traditions and disciplinary approaches. I have decided to see how the authors engaged with this notion have drawn on Habermas and Rawls, dedicating Part III of this work to the analysis of the way in which these two prominent philosophers directly defined deliberative democracy in the early 90s.

Therefore, what the terms deliberative (and participatory) democracy mean will gradually emerge throughout the present book – a preliminary definition is not needed here. However, I wish to clarify why I chose to propose this sort of 'parallel history': why is the critical comparison with participatory democracy so important to understanding the deliberative model?

The studies devoted to deliberative democracy often claim that we can distinguish between an initial phase (in which a theoretical and an ideal model are defined), and a later phase (in which specific operative and methodological proposals are made, or specific institutions are conceived with the aim of testing the strict normative theoretical assumptions in practice). I think it is impossible to separate these two moments sharply, because – as we shall see – the first phase also entailed an experimental dimension. However, we can still roughly distinguish these two steps, particularly because in this evolution some misunderstandings happened. In fact, deliberative democracy has sometimes been simply identified with a series of institutions or methodologies (Deliberative Polling®, citizen juries, or the several models proposed and tested over the last twenty years). At other times, the idea of deliberative democracy has been overlapped with the complex set of theoretical and practical views related to the idea of participatory democracy; finally, it has sometimes been understood as a variation or a subset of the latter.

These are surely inappropriate views but there has undoubtedly been an objective reason for them: the new deliberative practices presented themselves – and could be taken also as – *participatory practices*. In other words, they proposed new models through which to promote citizens' participation in a more inclusive or effective way compared to the past. Nevertheless, the overlapping of deliberative and participatory democracy is also a *reductive* definition, because it overshadows the specific nature of the former as a *deliberative theory of democracy* (and not only as a *theory of democratic deliberation*). I wish to show that this distinction is, in fact, also crucial to a better understanding of the internal articulation of the 'deliberative constellation': that is, to comprehend how it can be taken as a *theoretical paradigm* which can be extended and adapted to a wide range of phenomena and thematic/disciplinary fields, as I will illustrate in the final chapter of this work.

The theoretical development of deliberative democracy has gone hand in hand with the growth and diffusion of new forms and institutions of democratic participation, as well as new models of *participatory governance* – the latter is the object of vast critical literature and is generally interpreted as a symptom or an effect of the so-called 'crisis' of democracy. It would be a mistake to emphasise the role of these new forms of participation, given the continuing importance of traditional mechanisms of government and, mainly, given other (very different and opposed) tendencies characterising contemporary democracies – I shall talk about this in the Conclusion of this book. It would also be a mistake to find a direct causal connection between what happened in theory and practical developments. As Bernard Manin (2002: 41–2) has noted, the spread of new participatory practices should be interpreted not only as an effect of the related theories: rather, these are new social and institutional practices, which need new theoretical paradigms to be understood. Therefore, there are theories seeking a practical translation as well as practices seeking a theoretical explanation.

However, if it would be wrong to overestimate the role of these new practices and models of participation, it would also be wrong to underrate it, even just as a sign of potential directions that contemporary democracies might take. Also for this reason, it is necessary to provide a rigorous definition of the theoretical assumptions behind the practices and models. Therefore, as we shall see, I think it is more correct to speak of *participatory models of the deliberative matrix* (or, more precisely, of the forms and means of participation inspired by a theoretical model of democratic deliberation). Such a definition makes it possible to consider many other participatory forms and practices that may rest on different normative assumptions; it also allows us to grasp the relationship between these different sources of inspiration.

The very diffusion of these new forms of participatory and/or deliberative governance has brought (and still brings) our attention to the relationship between such practices and the political sphere in a dual sense: both as a sphere of public policies and as a sphere of politics. I will not be able to address this topic directly or in depth here, as this would involve an analysis of all that *today* constitutes the theoretical field of deliberative democracy and its relation to one or more models of participatory democracy. It would also imply extending the timeframe of the analysis so as to include everything that has been produced over the past twenty years. A task of this magnitude is beyond the scope this book but I think the present critical reconstruction of the theoretical genealogy of these two paradigms may act as a basis for further analysis of the various approaches available today: that is, of how the ideas and practices of deliberative democracy can also help us to rethink the models of contemporary policy-making and the possible forms of democratic governance in our age.

As we shall see in Part I, the origins of participatory democracy can be found in the 1960s in the United States: it is then that a model of participatory democracy was born, drawing on the youth uprisings, the struggles for civil rights, the feminist movement and the protests of that decade; it was then given a theoretical synthesis in various texts by authors I shall analyse. At the same time, this wave drew on a revival of some topics and attitudes that had their roots in the Progressive Era. The constitutive traits of this model included the radical rejection of representation, or at least a sharp distinction or opposition between participation and representation (even though some authors argue for their potential coexistence): this rejection rested on the fact that representation was seen as mere *delegation*, which leads to the atrophying of people's political agency as well as to apathy and passivity. As an antidote to all that, participatory democracy exalted the potential virtues of active citizenship that should and could be educated and nourished with direct forms of empowerment: the (even partial) exercise of direct responsibility and the practice of autonomy and self-rule. This core of political culture, inspired by the social movements of the 1960s, would ignite the following attempt to translate these principles into institutions and all the aspects of social life (from families, to school, up to the workplace). This theoretical and political approach weakened around the mid 1970s and disappeared entirely in the 1980s and 1990s. However, it left a deep impression on the ideas of democracy to come, especially as it connects to feminist theoretical culture. Overall, 1960s participatory democracy has left a legacy of ideas and values that still inspires, or at least affects, contemporary democratic theory.

The term 'participatory democracy' came back into popularity in the early 2000s: part of Chapters Seven and Eight and Chapter Thirteen are devoted to how this return took place and the modes of its (sometimes problematic) encounter with the deliberative approach. Suffice it to say here that participatory democracy is today generally a very broad reference term indicating a set of practices embedding the *active* involvement of citizens *within* institutional decision-making processes. In this sense, 'participatory democracy' evokes a conception of democracy that stresses, valorises and (normatively) 'wishes for' processes of political decision-making *directly* involving citizens. On the one hand, this view implies or aims for some form of sovereignty to be directly exercised by the citizens; on the other, it privileges the active education of citizens that is provided by participatory practices. From this perspective, participation is the tool through which citizens gain critical awareness of their condition and regain control over the decisions affecting their lives.

Deliberative democracy tells us another story: it certainly has ancient roots and several antecedents but the idea first properly took shape in the early 1980s, developing from some specific intellectual traditions and disciplinary fields. This idea soon expanded and became a theoretical field with a variety of interpretations, especially with the decisive contributions of Jürgen Habermas and John Rawls in the early 1990s. Thus deliberative democracy has come to constitute an *ideal* but also a *theoretical model* of democracy and, finally, an actual *paradigm*, able to influence many spheres of knowledge and to inspire new social and institutional practices.

Ideal; theoretical model; paradigm: these are all different ways of understanding deliberative democracy and, in what follows, I will look at how these different definitions have been elaborated and developed. For now, though, it might be worth answering the question: what do we mean exactly by 'deliberation' (and therefore by 'deliberative' democracy)? In order to avoid some common misunderstandings, let me point out that the term (which is often fully assimilated to that of 'decision' in languages like French and Italian) should be understood in the light of its etymology, which, in English, has retained its original and separate meaning.

'To deliberate' originally means to weigh the pros and cons of the potential solutions to a problem, finding and supporting the reasons for a practical choice while criticising unconvincing ones, acknowledging persuasive arguments and rejecting those that are not. To 'deliberate' is to acquire a considered judgment on what is 'right' or 'wrong', 'good' or 'bad'; but *not* on what is 'true' or 'false'. A deliberation leads to 'being convinced' of something, not to 'demonstrating' something. It can take place in an individual's *inner forum*, but it also has a more or less *public* dimension through an exchange of ideas and arguments (the latter case is of greater interest, of course, when speaking of democracy). *Public deliberation* rests on the assumption that our opinions and judgments are not given and unchangeable but are formed and transformed in dialogue and communication, by listening to other people's views and assessing them. Finally, *public* deliberation is also *democratic* if it is configured as an *inclusive* process of the *discursive* formation of citizens' ideas, opinions, judgments and wills – provided that the citizens are *free* and *equal*. In other words, deliberation is democratic if it *includes* (directly or indirectly, through some form of representation) all those that have 'something to say' on a public matter and the right to say it.

This first synthetic definition – which I will discuss in the light of all the authors that have contributed to shaping it – allows us to identify immediately what deliberative democracy is set *against*: that is, all the views that, in one way or another, imply a *rejection of mediation*. A deliberative conception of democracy therefore opposes *both* the idea of *direct* democracy (which can be practised without 'deliberation') *and* any *plebiscitary* idea or practice of democracy (which, too, is direct and immediate). It also opposes any 'technocratic' view in which there is no space for choice and dialogue and there are just 'obligatory', technically 'correct' choices that only require the 'right' or 'most competent' person to make them. However, this idea of deliberative democracy is also different from versions of participatory democracy in which citizens are 'directly' given decision-making 'power'. This is one of the decisive points that will emerge in this book.

To clarify these issues, I thought it would be helpful to start from a reconstruction of what in the 1960s (for participatory democracy) and 1980s (for deliberative democracy) has become the theoretical structure of these two models of democratic thought. My analysis will show, first of all, that these are *two different histories*, starting in different times and based on profoundly different theoretical and political reasons. These paths have *some points of intersection* but these crossroads should not cause us to overlook the deep differences between the two.

However, I'll anticipate here on what ground there has been some overlap between participatory and deliberative democracy. 'Participation' is a very broad term, more indeterminate than 'deliberation'. Participation means 'taking part' in something, but also 'being part' of something in regard to many possible phenomena: participation can be differentiated according to the *sphere* (political, social, economic and so forth) in which it takes place and the *forms* it assumes. Ideally, such forms can be placed on a continuum that has conflictual social and political practices on the one side and social co-operation (through which people solve collective problems and deal with the common good, in a dimension related to the principle of *subsidiarity*) on the other. In between those two poles there is a very varied series of potential forms of participation: protest, denunciation, advocacy, claim, negotiation and so forth – there can also be, of course, hybrids and overlapping forms. Within these potential participatory expressions there can also be *a deliberative dimension*. Therefore, not all forms of participation are deliberative; not all forms of deliberation imply participation; and not all forms of deliberation are democratic: forms of *public and democratic deliberation* can be seen as *specific* forms of participation.

It is on this ground that the theoretical paths of deliberative and participatory democracy have crossed – but not without misunderstandings and problems. Often when we talk talking of participatory democracy (as we shall see), it is not only or not so much to various practices in which political and social participation find expression that we refer but rather to a properly *decisional* dimension: it is believed that participation is the specifically *democratic* mode of decision-making. This is its main point of difference from deliberative democracy. Participatory democracy is based on the *direct* action of citizens, who exercise decisional power; deliberative democracy, on the other hand, mainly points to the argumentative exchange and the public discussion *preceding* decision, regarding deliberation as a *phase* of a process of dialogic construction of decisions pertaining to legitimate democratic institutions. Of course, any private association or a group of people can make their decisions through deliberative procedures. However, when the sphere of *political* decisions comes into play, deliberation is a *phase* or a *dimension* of a process legitimated by institutional democratic procedures.

At this point, the crucial issue (which, as we'll see, has been tackled by many authors) becomes *public and inclusive deliberation as a source of democratic legitimacy*. Also, as Habermas put it with his idea of deliberative politics, there is the issue of the *double source of legitimacy* that may ground a democratic decision. The first is the *discursive* one produced in the public sphere, based on citizens' ability or potential to express a *communicative power* – that is, the potential power of *influence* the deliberative practice has over the political and decisional process. Next to it, there is another source of legitimacy that cannot be ignored: that of the institutional dimension that is proper to a democratic rule-of-law state, regulated by democratic procedures based on a constitution. Between these two levels there can be convergence and mutual strengthening but also – and often– tension and conflict. The theme of the forms and modes of democratic legitimation is one of the main threads of my analysis. In the Conclusion of this book I will try to show that this is the area in which deliberative democracy can offer valid solutions to the crisis and the transformation of contemporary democracies.

The book is divided into four Parts and a Conclusion. Part I is dedicated to participatory democracy in the 1960s and 1970s as well as to the related debate that took place in the early 1980s. In Chapter One, I will reconstruct the origins of this idea of democracy, which had its peak in the 1960s and 1970s: a very particular historical climate, marked by struggles for human rights and student movements born in the US. I will look at some of the first documents testifying to early approaches to the idea of participatory democracy; my analytical focus will be on how this idea was theoretically elaborated in those two decades by authors – such as Pateman, Macpherson and Arnstein, among others – who are still well known today as well as by others who are now less frequently recalled.

In Chapter Two, I will focus on a sort of 'transitional phase'. I will analyse two 1980s texts that go beyond participatory democracy: Jane Mansbridge's *Beyond Adversary Democracy* (1980) and Benjamin Barber's *Strong Democracy* (1984). These works were very much still tied to the discussion on participatory democracy but, at the same time, they helped move the debate on to the next phase. They (and Mansbridge's in particular) were the first texts to point to a possible passage to a deliberative view of democracy, even though the latter isn't yet explicitly referred to.

In the second part I will tell another story, one that begins and continues in full independence from the former: in the 1980s there were the first elaborations of a *theoretical model* (or, in other versions, an *ideal*) of deliberative democracy. The third chapter is devoted to an essay by Joseph M. Bessette, 'Deliberative democracy: the majority principle in republican government' (1980), which is today unanimously considered the birthplace of the term. I will then look at some works by constitutionalist and philosopher of law Cass R. Sunstein: such works are less often cited in this perspective but offered many suggestions for later and more complete elaborations of the deliberative model. Another constitutionalist and philosopher of law who contributed crucially to the first phase of deliberative democracy is Frank I. Michelman: I will deal with his work in Chapter Nine, through Habermas's discussion of his theses. When talking about Fishkin (section 7.3), I will also address the positions of another great scholar of American constitutionalism, whose views are different from Sunstein's and Michelman's: Bruce Ackerman. As we shall see, his work contributed to a particular line of evolution of the new theoretical field of deliberative democracy. Bessette's, Sunstein's, Michelman's and Ackerman's texts belong to a context that at first might seem very far from that of deliberative democracy as it is understood today: they tackle diverging interpretations of the idea of democracy embodied by the American constitution – a debate that was then very much alive in the US, also because of its approaching bicentennial anniversary.

My reconstruction of the genealogy of the new model will then dwell on some of the contributions in this area that appeared in the second half of the 1980s: Jon Elster's works (*Sour Grapes*, 1983; 'The market and the forum: three varieties of political theory', 1986) in Chapter Four; an essay by Bernard Manin, 'On legitimacy and political deliberation' (1987) in Chapter Five and, finally, a work by Joshua Cohen, 'Deliberation and democratic legitimacy' (1989) in Chapter Six. These texts represent a crucial moment in the development of the new deliberative theoretical field: as they start outlining it they also show the first areas of tension inherent to it.

Chapter Seven makes things more complicated, showing the *intersections*, *confluences* and *new developments* that define and enrich the deliberative constellation between the 1980s and the early 1990s, expanding towards new disciplines and overlapping with the tradition of participatory democracy. As a particularly relevant example of this phase, I will analyse the development of the theories and practices of *planning* (urban and regional planning and, more generally, public-policy planning), taking as an example the work of John Forester. I will also look at the work of John S. Dryzek, as an example of a 'critical-radical' approach to deliberative democracy, which will be relevant to the future development of the new model.

In particular, I will analyse the contributions made by political science and political theory: in 1991, James S. Fishkin published *Democracy and Deliberation: New directions for democratic reforms*, in which he formulated for the first time the proposal of Deliberative Polling®. This paved the way for another line of development in deliberative democracy: a focus on the places, methods and conditions that favour deliberation understood as the formation of informed opinions. This is a central strand in deliberative democracy that is sometimes mistakenly considered to be the only one; however, it is but one of the many strands in the development of the deliberative model between the 1980s and 1990s.

Overall, my reconstruction aims to show how, within a few years, authors coming from many different perspectives and disciplines first defined the 'critical' frontiers of the new paradigm and then consolidated its content. These authors acted independently at first but then started to exchange views and elaborate their ideas in different directions. In Chapter Eight, I will provide a general assessment of the 'constitutive phase' of deliberative democracy, also trying to answer some questions about the new model as it was developed and the tradition of participatory democracy: can the relationship between them be described in terms of *continuity* (as some claim), *contiguity* or *break*?

In the background of this first phase (and *only* in the background) are two figures that have deeply marked the political philosophy of our time: John Rawls and Jürgen Habermas. In different ways, all the authors mentioned thus far (apart from Fishkin, who mainly draws on the work of Robert Dahl) take some essential elements from Habermas and Rawls – especially Cohen, who should be considered fully Rawls's pupil – and discuss their theses. However, as we will see, they mostly look at the works Rawls and Habermas had produced *till then*: Rawls's first edition of *Theory of Justice* (1971)[2] and a series of 1970s works by Habermas, only partly considering his later *Theory of Communicative Action* (1981) and *Moral Consciousness and Communicative Action* (1983).

When reconstructing a history of ideas, *dates matter*; and the story of deliberative democracy shows a singular overturning of perspectives. Rawls and Habermas, who are today regarded as the forerunners of this new version of democracy, have certainly been essential theoretical references for those who first tried to elaborate it (as we shall see, this sometimes involved both criticisms and misunderstandings). However, only *after* the term 'deliberative democracy' had been introduced did they strengthen its theoretical and philosophical grounds with their 1990s works: *Between Facts and Norms* by Habermas (1992); *Political Liberalism* by Rawls (1993). With their different approaches, these two major works opened the door to different lines of development and theoretical elaboration. In a way, the circle was thus closed and, since then, deliberative democracy can be considered fully as a *theoretical, critical* and *normative model* on the one hand and as an *ideal model* on the other. Both types of model are still very influential on today's democratic thought, producing a massive number of contributions to the literature and operating as a *paradigm* within many disciplines and social practices (both new and old).

Part III of the book is therefore devoted to Habermas and Rawls and a description of the theoretical foundations of deliberative democracy they proposed. Chapter Nine is focused on Habermas and his notion of 'deliberative politics' (and not 'deliberative democracy' – a crucial distinction, as we shall see). Such a notion is proposed in *Between Facts and Norms*: I will especially focus on the pages in which Habermas engages in critical dialogue with the very authors I discuss in the previous chapters (Michelman, Sunstein, Ackerman, Elster, Cohen, Manin), who had outlined the early theoretical field of deliberative democracy. Here, Habermas also addresses the views of Robert Dahl, who proposed his own normative theory of democracy and indirectly influenced the definition of the new model.

In Chapter Ten I will complete my analysis of Habermas, focusing on the relations between deliberative politics and the public sphere, civil society and the state. In this regard I will look at Habermas's criticism of Joshua Cohen and the latter's response, in which he proposes (together with Charles Sabel) a model of deliberative governance and democratic experimentalism. I believe this

---

2. As we shall see, in Cohen's case, also Rawls's Tanner Lecture 'The basic liberties and their priority' (1982), which was then published and revised as Lecture VIII of *Political Liberalism* (1993).

critical exchange brings out one of the fundamental conflicts within the theoretical field of deliberative democracy, which is also one of its most promising lines of development.

Chapter Eleven will be dedicated to Rawls and especially his idea of 'public reason'. Rawls comes to talk about deliberative democracy explicitly rather late: he addresses it with (relative) breadth mainly in 'The idea of public reason revisited' (1997). However, the originality of his contribution is such that it significantly affected the developments of the deliberative theoretical field. In retrospect, many elements of his earlier theoretical path can be reread in a deliberative light: thus it has become usual practice to speak of a 'Rawlsian approach' within the intellectual community that deals with deliberative democracy (in the same way, there has been talk of a 'Habermasian approach'). Chapter Twelve is devoted to the direct dialogue between Rawls and Habermas in 1995: this exchange – which is regarded as one of the peaks of the philosophical debate of the past few decades – naturally touches on a wide range of issues that appear in their work; here, though, I will try to grasp the implications that mainly affect their way of understanding a deliberative conception of democracy.

My reconstruction stops at the end of the 1990s: I will not analyse what happened afterwards. Nevertheless, in the concluding chapter, I will propose a few hypotheses on how we might make a possible 'map' of today's complex deliberative field. I will look at some of its branches, noting how they cannot be only traced back to Rawls and Habermas; I will also investigate the so-called *empirical turn* of deliberative democracy, proposing to complete this notion with the expression '*policy-oriented turn*'.

I have tried to reconstruct the internal logic of the various positions analysed as well as the debate between them, trying to avoid (as much as possible) imposing critical judgments that might appear biased. However, in the last section of Chapter Thirteen, I will present what was recently described as a 'systemic approach' to deliberative democracy, illustrating why I believe that such an approach is the most promising and convincing for the future of this democratic model. In the Conclusion I will try to *explain* the affirmation and diffusion of deliberative democracy as a democratic ideal and as a theoretical model. I will mainly focus on the historical and political factors that, in my view, make such a model *credible* as an answer to the transformations and tensions affecting the very idea of democracy today.

To conclude, I wish to make a few more personal remarks. This work is rooted not only in my theoretical interest but also in my first-hand experience. In the past few years, I happened to hold an administrative position that has allowed me to follow one of the most significant trials of the above-mentioned participatory practices: a law of the Tuscany Region on participation that, in the view of many external observers, can be considered one of the first attempts to institutionalise a deliberative *and* participatory view of *policy-making*.[3] Throughout this experience,

---

3. *See*, for instance, Jürg Steiner 2012: 26–31, 249. I have analysed the successes and failures of the Tuscan experiment elsewhere (Floridia 2008, 2012, 2013). On the Tuscan law, *see also* Lewanski 2013.

I have confirmed and strengthened a specific viewpoint: models of political theory are not vague ideas belonging to the empyrean of concepts but are very often *implicit* in political and institutional practices as well as in the related political culture. These ideas can guide and inspire such practices; practices, in turn, test the concepts that interpret them.

In my work I have had firsthand experience with deliberative and participatory democracy. My job experience has entailed daily discussions with politicians, administrators, exponents of civic associations, experts and professionals in the field, researchers and scholars, and the most active as well as the most disillusioned citizens. I was a privileged witness and an external observer of, but also an active participant in, the public discourse in Tuscany (and in other Italian regions and cities). This experience made me aware that there was *some idea of democracy* affecting (sometimes spontaneously and unreflectively) the social, intellectual, political and institutional *practices*. And these *ideas*, these forms of political culture, these elements of 'normative self-understanding' (as Habermas would put it) have consequences: political discourse, the words it uses, the ideas and concepts it expresses are also *actions* intervening in reality, born out of *intentions* and following *goals*. 'Jeffersonian and Hamiltonian political ideas' – which John Dewey mentioned as an example in the introduction of his *The Public and its Problems* (1927) – 'are not merely theories dwelling in the human mind remote from facts of American political behaviour': they are 'forces which have shaped those facts and which are still contending to shape them in the future this way and that'. So, more generally,

> ... there is more than a speculative difference between a theory of the state which regards it as an instrument in protecting individuals in the rights they already have, and one which conceives its function to be the effecting of a more equitable distribution of rights among individuals. For the theories are held and applied by legislators in Congress and by judges on the bench and make a difference in the subsequent facts themselves (Dewey 1984: 240–1).

The ideas presented and discussed in this book are not, so to speak, mere 'academic exercises'. Reconstructing the genealogy and structure of a theoretical model means not only retracing its origins and links to earlier ideas and understanding the meaning that a given author grants it in dialogue or polemic with others. It also means understanding the historical reasons behind the emergence of an idea and, especially, the real processes that are self-understood through such an idea.

Such ideas (and the languages by which they are expressed) act in a given historical context – we *do things* with them and through them we think of politics in its very making (Austin 1962; Searle 1969; Skinner 1969, 1972). Nevertheless, they are also core concepts that can *transcend* their origins and can be used, modified and elaborated in order to understand and orientate different contexts of action. The history of the 'highest' peaks of political thought, and the study of the texts in which these ideas find their most refined expression, cannot avoid the task of interpreting the meaning they acquire as steps of a historical process in which different perspectives clash. We must not forget that these ideas are interpretations of reality *in fieri* as well as discourses on *possible* reality. Nevertheless, the non-contingent power of these peaks can best be measured precisely when they also manage to speak outside the context from which they emerged.

In the first chapters of this work I will try to show how, in the 1960s and 1970s, the idea of participatory democracy emerged from a historical period of intense change and turmoil, as the conscience of that time and as a tool of interpretation that itself tried to favour historical change. In the Conclusion – after reconstructing its origin and contents – I will try to understand why *a deliberative idea of democracy* has emerged over the past thirty years; why it seems to be plausible to many thinkers; how it constitutes (or may aspire to be) an effective way to understand the ways in which contemporary democracy could, potentially, be transformed; and how these ideas can serve as an alternative to currently dominant democratic ideas, practices and trends.

PART I

THE RISE AND FALL OF PARTICIPATORY
DEMOCRACY IN THE 1960s AND 1970s

Chapter One

Participatory Democracy in the 1960s and 1970s: The Origins of a Model

1. The background and the scene: participatory democracy in political and theoretical debates in the United States in the 1960s

Participatory democracy, both as a theoretical model and as a model of political culture, emerged in the United States in the 1960s, finding its first and perhaps best-known theoretical systematisation in the work of Carole Pateman (1970). However, to understand the evolution of this strand of democratic thinking, it is necessary to look at the intense political-theoretical debate that constitutes its context and background.[1] I believe it is accurate to say that 'participatory democracy' originated, first of all, within the intense movements of ideas and opinions and the socio-political processes that characterised the 1960s. Only afterwards were theoretical models elaborated that, on the one hand, offered an interpretive framework for such movements and, on the other, helped to nourish, motivate and enrich them. It is possible here to pinpoint some dates that have come to symbolise an entire political era. Later, in the early 1980s, Jane Mansbridge (1983: 376, note 1) would remember this phase, arguing that the term 'participatory democracy'

> ... came into widespread use after 1962, when SDS [Students for a Democratic Society] gave it a central place in its founding Port Huron Statement. What the term meant then was unclear, and it became less clear afterward, as it was applied to virtually every form of organization that brought more people into the decision-making process. In the actual organizations of the New Left, however, the term came to be associated quite quickly with the combination of equality, consensus, and face-to-face assembly.

The author is referring to the first meeting – on 11–15 June 1962 at Port Huron, Wisconsin – of the most important and well established student-based organisations of the American New Left: a central player in the struggle for

---

1. An overview of the first phase of participatory democracy can be found in Held 2006[1987] and Cunningham 2002: 123–41. On the '*histoire et généalogie*' of '*démocratie participative*', see Bacqué and Sintomer 2011. A text from that period which makes sense of the positions that were in conflict at the time is Keim 1975.

civil rights and in the protest movement that accompanied the escalation of the Vietnam War.[2]

The text of the Port Huron Statement is one well worth remembering, because it contained conceptual models that would recur in subsequent years, sometimes with more theoretical elaboration. In fact, it contained many of the ideas underpinning participatory discourse and practice as it developed in Western democracies from then until the mid-1970s and, intermittently, later.[3] These elements are:

a) An optimistic picture of human beings, focused on their potential for self-development, and a rejection of the idea that individuals are inherently 'incompetent,' incapable of governing their collective life or dealing with the issues of their own lives in a forward-looking way:

> We regard men as infinitely precious and possessed of unfulfilled capacities for reason, freedom, and love. In affirming these principles we are aware of countering perhaps the dominant conceptions of man in the twentieth century: that he is a thing to be manipulated, and that he is inherently incapable of directing his own affairs. We oppose the depersonalization that reduces human beings to the status of things – if anything, the brutalities of the twentieth century teach that means and ends are intimately related, that vague appeals to 'posterity' cannot justify the mutilations of the present. We oppose, too, the doctrine of human incompetence because it rests essentially on the modern fact that men have been 'competently' manipulated into incompetence – we see little reason why men cannot meet with increasing skill the complexities and responsibilities of their situation, if society is organized not for minority, but for majority, participation in decision-making.

b) The ideals of the self-determination, autonomy and independence of individuals and, at the same time, a valorisation of the individual that did not merely amount to an 'egoistic individualism':

> Men have unrealized potential for self-cultivation, self-direction, self-understanding, and creativity. It is this potential that we regard as crucial and to which we appeal, not to the human potentiality for violence, unreason, and submission to authority. The goal of man and society should be human independence ... This kind of independence does not mean egoistic individualism – the object is not to have one's way so much as

---

2. A journalistic/historical reconstruction can be found in Miller, J. 1987. Sale (1973: 69) says that the Port Huron Statement was 'the most widely distributed document of the American Left in the Sixties'. On this period of American history, see Foner 1998, chapter 12.

3. The first draft of the text was by Tom Hayden, president of SDS in 1962–3; he was later an active protagonist in the fight for civil rights and the protests against the Vietnam War and then Democratic Senator from California between 1992 and 2000. The text can easily be read in full online.

it is to have a way that is one's own. Nor do we deify man – we merely have faith in his potential. Human relationships should involve fraternity and honesty. Human interdependence is contemporary fact; human brotherhood must be willed, however, as a condition of future survival and as the most appropriate form of social relations.

c) The idea that decision-making processes on issues that have social consequences and collective implications needs to be carried out in a public and participatory way; collective problems are to be confronted in such a way as to identify concrete solutions, clarifying the terms of such solutions by comparing alternative, conflicting visions, in a manner that is capable of translating and reframing personal aspirations and private interests in the context of a more general vision:

> As a social system we seek the establishment of a democracy of individual participation, governed by two central aims: that the individual share in those social decisions determining the quality and direction of his life; that society be organized to encourage independence in men and provide the media for their common participation. In a *participatory democracy* [my emphasis], the political life would be based in several root principles:
>
> - that decision-making of basic social consequences be carried on by public groupings;
> - that politics be seen positively, as the art of collectively creating an acceptable pattern of social relations;
> - that politics has the function of bringing people out of isolation and into community, thus being a necessary, though not sufficient, means of finding meaning in personal life;
> - that the political order should serve to clarify problems in a way instrumental to their solution; it should provide outlets for the expression of personal grievance and aspiration; opposing views should be organized so as to illuminate choices and facilities the attainment of goals; channels should be commonly available to relate men to knowledge and to power so that private problems from bad recreation facilities to personal alienation are formulated as general issues.

These ideas had a peculiar historical setting and a 'militant' genealogy but they were subsequently taken up and theoretically elaborated in various ways. Some of these themes would later acquire great importance in the political culture of 1960s youth movements (in particular, the themes of alienation and reification). However, it is worth underlining that such a vision of participatory democracy – democracy as a way to realise human potentialities and individual liberty, moral autonomy, as well as the belief in oneself and in one's capacities – had its deepest roots in the political culture of 'democratic individualism' that is so crucial to American history and, especially, in John Dewey's view of democracy. 'Perhaps nowhere did

Dewey's ideals echo more resoundingly' – as Westbrook noted (1991: 549) – 'than in the "Port Huron Statement" (1962) of the Students for a Democratic Society.'[4]

On the theoretical level, the context in which these orientations matured and developed was one marked by an intense debate between diametrically opposed visions. On the one hand was an elitist-competitive conception of democracy and the powerful 'pluralist' school, which was, in those years, at the peak of its influence (along with the view of participation that, in various ways, this approach presented or presupposed). On the other hand, various thinkers tried to contest the hegemony of these approaches, proposing an ideal of democracy that would give a greater role to citizens's participation.

Although the term 'participatory democracy' would go on to become well known through the generational uprising of the 1960s, it also became a significant presence in academic and theoretical debate. Jane Mansbridge, immediately after the passage cited above, remembered in a footnote how the term 'was coined, apparently' in 1960 in an essay by Arnold S. Kaufman[5] called 'Human nature and participatory democracy', which appeared in *Responsibility*, one of the first issues of the series NOMOS (edited by Carl J. Friedrich).[6]

Kaufman's essay focused especially on the first of the points outlined above, which was among those that would later appear in the Port Huron Statement, namely, a discussion of 'human nature' and the constraints it can impose on a vision of democracy as the capacity for the self-determination and self-governance of individuals in the political sphere. Kaufman started with the assertion that 'some theorists have argued that because man's nature is what it is a democracy of

---

4.   On 'democratic individualism' and its roots and expressions in American political culture, see Kateb 1992 and Urbinati 2009. It is a tradition born of nineteenth-century philosophical 'transcendentalism', from thinkers like Emerson, Whitman and Thoreau, and culminates in Peirce's, James's, and Dewey's pragmatism. From this tradition, comes the idea of the *self-reliant* individual as Emerson defined it, as well as Walt Whitman's idea of 'perfect individualism': 'underneath the fluctuations of society', as he wrote in *Democratic Vistas* (1871), 'we see, steadily pressing ahead and strengthening itself, ... this image of completeness in separation of individual personal dignity, of a single person, either male or female, characterized in the main, not from extrinsic acquirements or positions, but in the pride of himself or herself alone; ... the simple idea that the last, best dependence is to be upon humanity itself, and its own inherent, normal, full-grown qualities ...' (Whitman 1949: 15). On the 'pragmatic turn' in contemporary philosophy, see Bernstein 2010.

5.   Kaufman is not often cited today but his name deserves to be recalled because he played an important role in the political and cultural context of those years. Born in 1927 and dying in an aeroplane accident in 1971, he was Professor of Political Philosophy, first at the University of Michigan – where he was significantly involved in the protests against the Vietnam War and one of the protagonists of the famous first teach-in held in that university in 1965 – and, from 1969 on, in California, at UCLA. J. Miller (1987: 44, 94–5) relates how Tom Hayden, who would draft the Port Huron manifesto, had, as a student, followed courses in political philosophy given by Kaufman at the University of Michigan in Ann Arbor and (*ibid.*: 111) how Kaufman himself would later be invited to lecture during the Port Huron convention.

6.   Kaufman's text would later be reprinted and presented along with a note ('Participatory democracy: ten years later') in a volume edited by William E. Connolly called *The Bias of Pluralism* (1969a), which developed a position that was strongly critical of pluralist theory, presenting the contributions of thinkers like Peter Bachrach and Morton S. Baratz, Theodore Lowi and Brian Barry.

participation is undesirable or even "impossible"'. (1969: 178). His aim, he added, was to 'weaken the hold that certain sceptical dogmas have on the minds of those who might otherwise be inclined to take more seriously the task of increasing the participatory element in modern industrial societies' (*ibid.*).

The arguments commonly raised against the idea of a participatory democracy, in Kaufman's analysis, were of two types: some were of a moral nature (positing the intrinsic 'wickedness' of humankind); others focused instead on a constitutive cognitive deficit that limits the intellectual capacities of individuals, as well as on the 'irrational' nature of their behaviour and choices.[7] The thinkers that he deemed emblematic of such a sceptical, pessimistic vision of human nature were Walter Lippmann and, later – after an excursus into psychoanalysis – Joseph Schumpeter, the latter of whose arguments received special attention (*ibid.*: 186). According to him, Schumpeter confused the potential role of 'direct participation' with the functions of a representative system in an institutional setting of checks and balances:

> ... the main justifying functions of the free competition for leadership are maintenance of order, protection against the tyrannical exercise of power, and fulfilment of actual human preferences without unduly sacrificing the value of efficient decision and expert opinion. The main justifying function of participation is development of the man's essential powers – inducing human dignity and respect, and making man responsible by developing their powers of deliberate action (*ibid.*: 198).

As we can see, a certain dualism was prefigured here between, on the one hand, the institutions that 'protect' human rights and ensure social order and, on the other, participation understood as the moment of development of the human potential for self-determination. The anti-Schumpeterian polemic set itself against a reductive vision of such potential: the development of participatory institutions had the precise aim of creating spaces and occasions where individuals could acquire 'direct responsibility for a certain range of decisions' and, in so doing, overcome the 'parochial barriers' that otherwise characterised their lives (*ibid.*: 189). The second target of his criticism of Schumpeter was the role played by leadership in Schumpeter's thought; here, Kaufman resorted to an argument that would recur in the work of other authors: even if we assign as much importance to leadership as Schumpeter did, what would ensure that irrational and incompetent individuals are capable of choosing a wise leadership? Actually, as Kaufman observed (*ibid.*: 190), 'the most important condition of the emergence of good leadership in modern industrial societies is, for the great mass of human beings, direct responsibility through participation'.

The relevance of Kaufman's essay today can be found in a question he posed at the end: 'can an empirical case be made for participation?'. That is, can we find

---

7. These positions were already present in American debate in the twenties: see Westbrook 1991: 280–6.

good, empirical evidence in support of this positive vision of participation? 'This is not a question', he added, 'that the great advocates of participatory democracy have ever faced seriously enough'. Although there was some consensus on the idea that participation could 'contribute to the development of the individual', what had been missing, even in thinkers like G. D. H. Cole and John Dewey, was an 'empirical defense' of this claim. 'An adequate philosophy of participatory democracy demands a more systematic approach to the problem'. However, as the author himself acknowledged, even his own text merely offered 'a few suggestions' about how to do this (*ibid.*: 191).[8]

Rereading now, more than a half-century later, these pages certainly present much of interest; above all, they offer a clear view of the difficulties that such an approach had to face. The author himself was well aware of these limits. In the postscript 'Ten years later', published in 1969, Kaufman recalled how his piece appeared 'at a time when few Americans defended participatory democracy', stating, instead, how 'ten years later the concept and the cause had been moved to the center stage'. How could this have happened? Kaufman relates this very strongly to American history: the promises of American democracy and, in particular, the concrete evolution of the pluralist model that Madison had put at the centre of the American constitutional design.

> James Madison provided a scheme for just the kind of system that has evolved: a political society composed of many groups which combine into unstable, shifting coalitions that, partly because of the political instability of the component coalitions, produces a transcendent social stability (*ibid.*: 201–2).

But all this opened up new contradictions: the goals of well-being and wealth that were achieved by American society

> … have been secured in a way that has had a most oppressive impact, economically and politically, on a vast portion of the population. Large segments have been excluded from equal access to, or participation in, the benefits of the system (*ibid.*)

As we shall see in other thinkers, these themes owe much to an analysis offered by Theodor Lowi, in those same years, of the reasons for the 'end of liberalism' and on the role played in this respect by the growing influence of powerful interest-groups. And many texts cited a famous statement by E. E. Schattschneider (1960:

---

8. It is curious to observe how the search for this 'empirical defense' of a 'participatory democracy' would lead Kaufman (and Pateman, too) to find possible support in new theories of shared, inclusive industrial management, that were beginning to consider the overcoming of Fordism and Taylorism. Kaufman, in particular, cited a symposium held in 1956 on Workers' Participation in Management, as part of the meeting of the International Sociological Association, the proceedings of which were published in the *International Archives of the Sociology of Cooperation* 2 (1957): 106–120.

35): 'The flaw in the pluralist heaven is that the heavenly chorus sings with a strong upper-class accent'.[9]

Kaufman thus underlined the anti-egalitarian and anti-democratic implications that the evolution of the Madisonian model was bringing to light: 'in the game of coalition politics, some interest groups have been more equal than others'. Hence the search for a 'participatory' answer, one rooted in the proposition that individuals and groups which are deprived of power and influence tend to 'demand a more participatory control over their destinies'. As we'll see in other versions and theories of participatory democracy, this is the key to this political and theoretical approach: participation is seen as the power of direct control over one's own life, and so as self-determination, and the enabler of the construction of one's own capacities for autonomy and self-governance. The starting point of all this, in theoretical terms, was a different conception of human development and its potential: 'in demanding something radically different, advocates of participatory democracy have tried to replace Madison's pessimistic assumptions (on which he reared his constitutional proposals) with an affirmation of man's potentialities for creative, moral existence' (Kaufman 1969: 203).[10]

That said, a self-consciously critical note was already emerging in this work by Kaufman. Even if participation could offer 'many answers', it could not respond to each and every problem. The reason for this is that assuming a conception of participation as the direct exercise of power by citizens means that participation could only occur in limited contexts in a modern industrial society, and that some conditions would 'sometimes make it undesirable even to try to bring decisions under direct control' (*ibid.*: 204).

[P]articipatory democracy is one of the ways to decentralize decision-making, but like other forms of decentralized control, it may function tyrannically. It may be necessary, therefore, to apply more centralized counterpower to devolved, participatory power. Certain Southern communities have a greater element of participation than one encounters in the North. But because white men constitute a decisive, tyrannical majority, black men in those same communities may understandably be a bit cynical about the blessings of Southern grass-roots democracy (*ibid.*: 205).

In short, the Madisonian problem of the tyranny of the majority could not be done away with.

---

9. It is significant to note that, in the same volume edited by William E. Connolly in which Kaufman's text reappeared (Connolly 1996b), the essay by Theodore J. Lowi, 'The public philosophy: interest-group liberalism' (1967), also appeared. This essay would later become the first chapter of the best-known work of this period of scientific production by Lowi, *The End of Liberalism*, an important work that would have two editions, in 1969 and in 1979.

10. At this point, Kaufman cites precisely those passages of the Port Huron Statement that I have quoted.

Ultimately, what emerged was what Kaufman defined as 'the paradox of participatory democracy': if it is true that what justifies participation is primarily its capacity to develop individuals' potential and to make them more competent and responsible (*ibid.*: 206), nothing at all guarantees *a priori* that 'good' or 'wise' decisions will issue. In fact, 'before participatory decisions can be sound, they will be unsound – necessarily' (*ibid.*). Furthermore, it is significant that a writer like Kaufman, who had experienced first-hand the protest movements of the 1960s, would, at the end of the decade, pen a critical reflection centred on the role of leadership and representation. The only way out of this paradox is to recognise that, in any given 'participatory group', an 'appropriate modification of the institutions of participatory democracy' is possible, so that 'the likelihood of calamitous decisions can be diminished'. '[I]n particular, participators should learn to appreciate the fact that, even within predominantly participatory arrangements, there is a place for leadership and representation' (*ibid.*: 207).[11]

It was the concrete experience of groups of 'young radicals' – the sites of 'small participatory democracies', as Jane Mansbridge would describe them a decade later (*see* Chapter Two, Section 2 in this volume) – that invited theoretical reflection on the limits of a radically egalitarian ('naive', we could say now) vision of participatory democracy. Participatory democracy was here understood as the exercise of direct power in the making of decisions affecting various aspects of social life but it can also simply have to do with a self-organising 'collective' in accordance with defined political aims. Well, in the consciousness of its protagonists – Kaufman wrote – this conception seemed dominated by the fear of reproducing the mechanisms and logic of 'leadership and authority', to the point of condemning their own political action to ineffectiveness.[12] At its core, there was also 'a wholly unanalyzed, undifferentiated conception of the nature of participatory democracy' (*ibid.*: 209). Kaufman here refers to an article by Michael Walzer,[13] in which the author echoed a famous line attributed to Oscar Wilde: 'the trouble with socialism' (or, in this context, participatory democracy) 'is that it takes up too many evenings'.[14] The classic problem of the intensity

---

11. On Kaufman, and his 'paradox of participatory democracy', *see also* Mansbridge 2003a: 176–7.

12. These young radicals 'knew that the effectiveness of their actions depended on drawing the distinction between competence and incompetence, upon investing those who clearly possessed greater competence than others with non-coercive authority. Nevertheless, they so feared that they would commit the Great Sins – being manipulative or authoritarian – that they frequently sacrificed the effectiveness of their program for the sake of "moral purity"' (Kaufman 1969: 208).

13. M. Walzer, 'A day in the life of a socialist citizen', *Dissent*, May–June 1968: 243–7.

14. The description of those who lived their participative commitment 'full time' is very vivid and restores to us the whole flavour of the era: if, for some, participation took 'too many evenings', other activists, 'with great personal sacrifice', chose instead to 'attend *all* the meetings, thus coming to think that they are the vanguard of good citizenry of the future' and to consider themselves 'as the political incarnation of the General Will'... 'The proprietary attitude some activists develop toward the organizations in which they participate has to be experienced to be believed', Kaufman caustically observed (*ibid.*: 209).

and frequency which individuals would need to commit to their participatory duties is addressed by recalling the inevitability of the recourse to processes and mechanisms of representation. And yet, though, certainly, 'participation is no panacea', Kaufman concluded, 'beyond any critical thrust lies a basic conviction, that vast enlargement of the sphere of participation is one essential condition of a decent society' (*ibid.*: 211).

So, 'ten years later,' an intellectual who had been one of the central figures of the movement embracing the ideal of 'participatory democracy' diagnosed it as worn out and self-contradictory. However, not all was lost. On the practical level, these experiences certainly demonstrated all the limitations of this model and, on the theoretical level, there was some weakness and roughness to its initial form; nevertheless, the debate over forms of democracy was alive and well and would go on through the whole of the 1960s. At the centre of the discussion were 'elitist theories of democracy' and the approach proposed by the pluralist school.

2. The critique of elitist theories of democracy and the meaning of the pluralist approach

In 1966, the authoritative journal *American Political Science Review* hosted a heated debate between a young academic from the University of Michigan, Jack L. Walker,[15] and someone who had already established himself as one of the leading exponents of American political science: Robert Dahl. At the centre of this debate was Walker's article 'A critique of the elitist theory of democracy' (1966).[16] This confrontation was, in various ways, unbalanced: Dahl's response, no doubt, struck quite a blow against Walker's conjectures. From the present point of view, it is relevant mostly to show the arguments that were central to Walker's critique. The authors he grouped together as embracing an 'elitist theory of democracy' – Schumpeter, first and foremost, but also Berelson, Lipset, Key, Milbrath and, especially, Dahl himself (in *A Preface to Democratic Theory* in 1956 and the subsequent *Who Governs?* in 1961)[17] – were perpetrators of an 'attack' on the 'concept of an active, informed, democratic citizenry'.

Walker structured his critique on two levels. On the empirical level, the elitist approach emphasised the absence, in Western democracies, of a real, diffuse presence of citizens, corresponding to the ideal of active civic behaviour proper to a 'classical' theory of democracy. On the normative level, this theoretical approach also underlined the dangers issuing from an undifferentiated and

---

15. J. L. Walker (1935–90), Professor of Political Science, would also become director of the Institute of Public Policy Studies of the University of Michigan as well as Chair of the Department of Political Science.

16. An essay by Quentin Skinner (1973) extensively cited the debate between Walker and Dahl, as well as many other debates of those years: at its core, we find the theme of the presence (or lack thereof) of normative and ideological assumptions in the empirical political sciences and in the very definition of 'democracy' offered by them. Carole Pateman (1974) discusses Skinner's analysis, too.

17. Berelson, Lazarsfeld and McPhee 1954; Lipset 1960; Key 1961; Milbrath 1965; Dahl 1956, 1961.

uncritically positive vision of mass participation, one that wholly ignored the risks tied to demagogy and to the 'tyranny' of the majority. It is on the 'normative implications' (Walker 1966: 286) of this elitist vision that Walker concentrated his attention. The classical tradition assumed that 'the most important prerequisite for a stable democracy was general agreement among the politically active (those who vote) on certain fundamental policies and basic values and widespread acceptance of democratic procedures and restraints on political activity'. Political leaders, then, should not violate these fundamental notions, lest 'an otherwise passive public' should revolt and mobilise against them. 'Elitist theorists argued instead that agreement on democratic values among "the intervening structure of elites", the very elements which had been seen earlier as potential threats to democracy, is the main bulwark against a breakdown in constitutionalism' (*ibid.*: 286–7).

It was precisely the 'fear of participation' that inspired this conception of democracy: 'a successful (that is, stable) democratic system depends on widespread apathy and general political incompetence' (*ibid.*). Starting from these presuppositions, the so-called 'elitist theorists have transformed democracy from a radical into a conservative political doctrine, stripping away its distinctive emphasis on popular political activity so that it no longer serves as a set of ideals toward which society ought to be striving' (*ibid.*: 288). In particular, what had been lost was the distinctive trait of the democratic ideal: the idea that the participation of a citizen in political life, his 'taking part in the affairs of his society', could actually allow him to acquire a greater knowledge and understanding of common problems, which could enable the rise of 'a deeper sense of social responsibility, and broaden his perspective beyond the narrow confines of his private life' (*ibid.*).

This is the core of a normative definition of democracy: the idea that it should promote 'human development' and thus exalt all the 'opportunities which existed in political activity to realize the untapped potentials of men and to create the foundations of a genuine human community' (*ibid.*).[18] This emphasis on the development of human potential tied to a participatory vision of democracy, according to Walker, was completely absent in the various contemporary versions of the elitist vision. In fact, the emphasis was altogether placed on the demands of systemic stability and the efficiency of government action. Thus, from this point of view, the active participation of citizens – especially once it crossed certain limits – was anything but desirable. It was precisely apathy that influential

---

18. As would later be the case with Pateman and Macpherson, Walker, too, referred to John Stuart Mill, citing a passage from 'Considerations on representative government' (1861): 'the most important point of excellence which any form of government can possess is to promote the virtue and intelligence of the people themselves. The first question in respect to any political institutions is, how far they tend to foster in the members of the community the various desirable qualities, ... moral, intellectual, and active' (Mill 1977 [1861]: 390). On Mill's political thought, see Urbinati 2002; Holmes 1995: 178–201; and the essays in Urbinati and Zakaras 2007, especially Zakaras 2007, on the conception of participation.

political scientists of the time, especially Lipset (1960), regarded as a sign of consensus.[19]

It is not necessary here to reiterate Walker's subsequent arguments, which were tied to political events and to an analysis of American society in the 1950s and 1960s; rather, what is of interest is the quite harsh, at times even sarcastic, answer that Robert Dahl gave his interlocutor (Dahl 1966). Walker had reprimanded the elitist theory for producing a conservative distortion of the democratic ideal and for elevating to normative status empirical observations on the low level of citizens' political participation, making it a requisite of the stability of democratic systems. Dahl completely reversed this criticism: for him, it was Walker who was guilty of having taken as normative some assumptions that were, in fact, descriptive analyses of contemporary democracies (*ibid.*: 298). Dahl denied that all the thinkers mentioned by Walker could accurately be grouped under the heading of 'elitist theorists' and, in particular, he denied that his own position could be defined in those terms or related to a conservative vision. This is a point on which it is worth dwelling. In fact, defending his own pluralist and polyarchic vision of democracy, Dahl strenuously denied that his position implied a poor or reductive vision of participation, or that it did not take into account a possibly wide level of political activity and citizens' participation.

Through a long series of self-citations, in particular from a work co-authored with Charles Lindblom (*Politics, Economics, and Welfare*, 1953), Dahl acknowledged the empirical fact that there are, of course, generally low levels of political participation but contended that there are or can be a great variety of situations and conditions characterised by and favouring citizens' political activity. Dahl also offered some significant claims that had a normative character:

[T]he question, then, is not so much whether citizens are active but whether they have the opportunity to exert control through activity when they wish to do so ... . Therefore the problem is not so much one of insuring that every citizen is politically active on every issue as it is one of insuring that all citizens have approximately equal opportunity to act, using 'opportunity' in a realistic rather than legalistic sense ... . Equal opportunity to act is not, however, a product merely of legal rights. It is a product of a variety of factors that make for differences in understanding the key points in the political process, access

---

19. William Connolly, in the chapter that served as introduction to his essay collection on 'pluralist bias' (Connolly 1969a), recalled this discussion between Walker and Dahl and critically observed how Dahl 'limits participation to government and views it primarily as a vehicle for channelling existing grievances to governmental arenas'. Another tradition of pluralist thought – Tocqueville's view of 'voluntary associations' – more directly links participation to the *development* of citizen capacities to translate problems into political issues and the production of wise political decisions. Connolly also argues that a viable political pluralism requires the expansion of participation beyond government to 'the family, the church, business, and the school': 'such a "social democracy" is necessary, in John Dewey's view, "from the standpoint both of the general welfare and the full development of human beings as individuals". These claimed linkages are clearly not the focus of Dahl's analysis' (Connolly 1969b: 10–11). The Dewey quotation is from *School and Society* (1937).

to them, methods of exploiting this access, optimism and buoyancy about the prospect of success, and willingness to act. (Dahl 1966: 302).

Having moved the debate to this level, Dahl concluded by welcoming the principal aspiration that emerged from Walker's essay: the construction of a 'better normative democratic theory' (*ibid.*: 305). However, he added, only with great difficulty could one think that there was such a thing as 'the' normative theory of democracy:

> Despite the frequency and confidence with which the 'classic theory of democracy' is often described, there has never been such a theory. Between Aristotle and Paine, as between Rousseau and Mill, there are universes of difference. Along with other people, theorists who believe in popular government have never agreed wholly on the goals or values to be maximized … Disagreement with respect to these basic assumptions is not going to disappear. We should therefore expect that in the future as in the past there will be not one but a number of differing normative theories of democracy. But I agree with Professor Walker: It is time to get on with the job (*ibid.*).

Dahl thus refuted the accusation that his pluralist position was elitist or was hostile in principle to participation. Nevertheless, the 'challenge to pluralist theory' (the title of an essay by Connolly from 1969) would remain alive in the theoretical debate of those years and would focus the attention on the oligarchic results that the pluralist order of American democracy tended to produce: 'many latent concerns – those which might well interest wide segments of society if they were publically articulated as issues – are not identified or sharply defined by the prevailing system of issue formation' (Connolly 1969b: 18).

The contest between a participatory vision and an elitist conception of democracy was a feature of political debate throughout the 1960s. In 1967, Peter Bachrach published a book dedicated to the 'theory of democratic elitism'. '[A]ll elite theories', Bachrach wrote, 'are founded on two basic assumptions: first, that the masses are inherently incompetent, and second that they are, at best, pliable, inert stuff or, at worst, aroused, unruly creatures possessing an insatiable proclivity to undermine both culture and liberty' (Bachrach 1967: 2).[20]

These two fundamental assumptions necessitated trusting in an educated, wise, and forward-looking elite, capable of sustaining the governance of the community.

---

20. Peter Bachrach (1919–2008) had already published, along with Morton S. Baratz, two essays that were significant attacks on the approach of the pluralist school: 'Decisions and nondecisions' (1963), a classic of policy analysis; and 'Two faces of power' (1962) – reissued, along with the former essay, in *Power and Poverty: Theory and practice* (1970). Bachrach, in 1970, on the occasion of a meeting that marked a striking rupture within the American Political Science Association, was the presidential candidate – he lost, but had much support – who expressed the most radical position, critical toward the compromises that certain sectors of the American academic world had made with respect to the political and military establishment. The same debate between Walker and Dahl can be understood as internal to this broader political and ideological fracture that traversed the community of American political scientists in this period.

But even in Bachrach's work, the real, decisive interlocutor was the pluralism represented by Dahl: his 'polyarchical' vision of democracy offered a more complex theoretical framework that was able to escape the simplifications of the most unsubtle elitist visions. In Dahl, Bachrach wrote (*ibid.*: 8),

> ... to be sure, the ordinary man still plays a role in the system since he has the freedom to vote, to bring pressure on the political elites, and to attempt himself to rise to an elite position. But by and large he does, and is expected to, remain relatively passive – in fact the health of the system depends upon it. For if he becomes more active, too much aroused in politics, awakening the alienated, the apathetic masses of the cities and the rednecks of rural communities, political equilibrium is thrown out of balance and the demagogue finds greater opportunity to challenge successfully the power of established elites.

On the contrary, 'the democratic ideal encourages the greatest utilization of the capabilities of individuals in the interest of the community, but in sharp contrast to elite theory, each individual's judgment is given weight equal with all others' (*ibid.*: 3).

Against an elitist vision of democracy, then, the value of participation was reaffirmed – following in the footsteps of John Stuart Mill – as a means to increase human intellectual and moral faculties, thus broadening people's horizons. '[T]he emphasis in classical democratic theory upon citizen participation in all aspects of public affairs is based on the premise that such involvements is an essential means to the full development of individual capacities' (*ibid.*: 4).

Bachrach dedicated a great part of his book to a critical analysis of elitist theory, starting from the scholars he considered its 'precursors', namely, Gaetano Mosca and Joseph Schumpeter; from the present point of view, however, it is more worth focusing on some passages from a chapter entitled 'The Revolt from the masses'. Bachrach here proposed his own reading of the debate that once divided the Founding Fathers (a terrain into which, as we will see in the coming chapters, many other writers would subsequently venture). In particular, Bachrach valorised the positions of Jefferson and of the Anti-Federalists, underlining how their adherence to the constitutional structure of 'checks and balances' (which, in the vision of the 'Madisonian democracy' offered by Dahl in his 1956 *Preface*, had been read in a 'pluralist' and 'polyarchical' way) was not suggested 'as it was in the *Federalist Papers*, by fear of the majority tyranny of the people, but by fear of the minority tyranny of the ruling elite' (*ibid.*: 27), as well as by a wish to protect the principle of the rule of the majority.

Needless to say, in this Jeffersonian vision, it was always possible that 'the people [be] corruptible, but it was assumed that the source of corruption was faulty political, economic, and social institutions' (*ibid.*), and that therefore it was possible to rely on the educational virtues of participation: 'thus what was called for was more, not less, democracy' (*ibid.*). And the nineteenth century, as well as the 'first thirty-five years of the twentieth century' – note the precise positioning in time – describe how the struggle for 'a continued extension and growth of democracy was the best assurance of preservation of constitutional liberalism' (*ibid.*), starting from popular struggles for the extension of suffrage and the affirmation of political rights. Thus, 'Jefferson was basically right: that, in the last analysis, it is the mass of the people, not the elite, who are the true guardian of liberty' (*ibid.*: 28).

Nonetheless, Bachrach noted how the advent of Nazism and the threat of Communist totalitarianism changed the perspective of democratic thought, shaking 'the confidence of liberals in the cause of democracy' (*ibid.*: 8).[21] The situation led, he claimed, to a reversal of the classical prospective of democratic thought:

> ... it is the elite, not the common man, who is looked upon as the chief guardian in the system. The revolt from the masses has led to a second shift in theory: the emphasis is no longer upon extending or strengthening democracy, but upon stabilizing the established system (*ibid.*: 32).

In the present day, he wrote, 'the focus, in short, is upon protecting liberalism from the excesses of democracy rather than upon utilizing liberal means to progress toward the realization of democratic ideals' (*ibid.*). This statement bears emphasising, because here we see a normative re-evaluation of participation resting centrally on the claim of a liberal ideal of autonomy and individual self-determination.

In Bachrach's work, as well as in other thinkers discussed in this chapter, central political and theoretical concerns emerged from the attempt to find a convincing position capable of reacting to a dual critical perspective. On the one hand, the social and political sciences of the era noted a widespread lack of interest in politics and the apathy and indifference of the so-called 'common' citizen.[22] On the other hand, there were recent historical experiences with a totalitarian vision of participation (or rather 'mobilisation') of the masses. In such conditions, it seemed like an congenial time for theorists of a vision that 'protected' the political order *from* democracy rather than one with a trusting, optimistic vision *of* democracy. In such a context, wrote Bachrach, 'the political passivity of the great majority of the people is not regarded as an element of democratic malfunctioning, but, on the contrary, as a necessary condition for allowing the creative functioning of the elite' (*ibid.*).

Faced with this, how was it possible to demonstrate faith in the virtue of participation or to affirm a participatory conception of democracy? On what basis

---

21. 'Liberals generally became disinclined toward the traditional criticism of American institutions ... and began to emphasize the danger of majority tyranny and extol the virtues of judicial review, checks and balances, and the pluralist system, characterized by compromise and government by consensus. The authority of social science has in recent years increasingly supported this position' (Bachrach 1967: 30–1).

22. A work of fundamental importance from this perspective, also discussed by Bachrach, was the one edited by Berelson, Lazarsfeld, and MacPhee, *Voting: A study of opinion formation in a presidential campaign* (1954), a classic of electoral studies. Among the writers who founded their vision of democracy on a radical lack of faith in the capacity or possibility that masses could truly contribute to a good government, Bachrach placed even Giovanni Sartori and his 1962 work, *Democratic Theory*.

could a democratic ideal be embraced that would not abandon the principle of political participation? A possible strategy was uniting a firm normative vision with a critical position that both should and could discover empirical foundations. From this point of view, a good line of attack could be found in the demonstration that, in reality, the pluralist condition theorised by Dahl turned out to be altogether illusory: 'a pluralism of elites does not necessarily produce a competitive situation among elites' (*ibid.*: 37).

Another point of criticism was provoked by the very notion of 'interest'. A requirement of democracy was that it should correspond to the 'interests' of the people, but in what sense? One could conceive of it in a minimal way, altogether compatible with an idea of civic passivity, but one could also affirm a broader conception, one that could not be reduced to the search for 'gains in material well-being power or status' (*ibid.*: 38) but, rather, would grasp more fully the objective of the 'personal satisfaction and growth attained from active engagement in the political process' (*ibid.*).

After dedicating significant space to the positions of various thinkers,[23] Bachrach devoted his concluding chapter to arguing for an alternative to elite theory. His approach affirmed an essential character of the normative dimension of democracy: democracy must always be considered, above all, an ideal to be inspired by, a goal to strive towards. At the foundation of this ideal, there were certain concepts or principles, ones that found their greatest expression in the Declaration of Independence. Humans are created equal and have an equal right to influence decisions that concern their lives and democracy is the ideal in which this right is instantiated in the equal distribution of political power among all the members of a given political community.

This normative projection of the democratic ideal – Bachrach noted – nonetheless appeared to the theorists of democratic elitism as no longer sustainable in modernity. Therefore, according to Dahl, it was not possible to realise the ideal of the equal distribution of power but only that of an of *opportunity to have access to* the exercise of power. However, to consider a political principle as never fully realisable did not mean to altogether devalue it. 'I see no reason why a principle, serving both as an ideal to strive for and as standard for judging the progress of a political system toward the achievement of the ideal, must be realizable in practice to perform its function' (*ibid.*: 86). A 'realistic' attitude, or rather a cynical one, would not negate the regulative value of an ideal, as a 'spur to a more humane

---

23. The authors considered are Truman (1951); Berle (1959); and Lasswell and Kaplan (1950). Particularly interesting is the analysis of the famous text by Wright Mills, 'The power elite' (1956), where he proposed his famous analysis of the dominance of the 'military–industrial complex' in American politics. In fact, Bachrach noted, Wright Mills was not thinking that the elite could be overthrown, being deeply pessimistic about the state of civic engagement in America: 'throughout his writings he was insistent that genuine publics, in John Dewey's meaning of the term, are rapidly becoming extinct in America' (Bachrach 1967: 38). After all, Wright Mills' position was a form of elitism, too, one that was supported by a rationalist approach that ended up entrusting only to intellectual elites the critical task of controlling the political elites (*ibid.*: 88–96). Cornel West's observations on Mills go in the same direction (West 1989: 124–38).

society' (*ibid.*). Dahl asserted that adopting an openly utopian principle actually led to its opposite, that is, cynicism regarding democracy.[24] On the other hand, to adopt the principle of equality of power as an integral part of democracy – Bachrach observed – contributed greatly to the affirmation of democracy and would play a historically significant role in broader democratisation.

Even the other side of Dahl's thesis – that 'key governmental decisions,' in big enough societies, cannot help but be made by the few – was contested by Bachrach. It is obvious enough that those decisions would be the prerogative of the few, 'but why must the criterion be limited to governmental decisions?' (*ibid.*: 87). Dahl himself, Bachrach noted, defined the dimension of the 'political' broadly. This being the case, then, this concept of equality of opportunity of access had to be applied even to non-governmental political institutions and, more generally, within the subsystems of the social and political body – in particular, in the economic sphere, in the democratisation of the structure of corporations (*ibid.*: 88) – and to all those structures of social life in which some form of power is exercised, or where decisions are made affecting collective life. Thus, Bachrach concluded,

> ... the crucial issue of democracy is not the composition of the elite ... Instead, the issue is whether democracy can diffuse power sufficiently throughout society to inculcate among people of all walks of life a justifiable feeling that they have the power to participate in decisions which affect themselves and common life of the community, especially in the immediate community in which they work and spend most of their waking hours and energy (*ibid.*: 92).

In these words, we find a key to the critical debates of those years. Those who upheld a 'participatory' vision of democracy did not try (in general, though Macpherson was an exception) to imagine an alternative model that depended on a different institutional structure. It was rather a matter of not 'lowering one's guard' on the ideological level (expressed, sometimes, in rather paternalistic terms, with verbs like 'to inculcate'). Today, Bachrach wrote, 'there is a general theory of democracy which is supported by most leading theorists ... It is a theory largely explanatory rather than normative in approach, directed toward clarifying on-going democratic systems rather than suggesting how they ought to operate' (*ibid.*: 93). Such a theory, Bachrach added, is rather benevolent in terms of actual structures of power and shows some 'impatience' towards phrases like 'the will of the people', 'grass-roots democracy' and 'the dignity of the common man'; thus, this theory

> ... purports to be above ideology but is in reality deeply rooted in an ideology, an ideology which is grounded upon a profound distrust of the majority of

---

24. A similar position was articulated by Sartori against what he referred to as 'perfectionism' (Sartori 1962: 51).

ordinary men and women, and a reliance upon the established elites to maintain the value of civility and the 'rules of the game' of democracy (*ibid.*: 93–4).

However, even though it defended the principles of liberalism, such a theory was marked by the substantial surrender of the normative premise of any democratic theory: faith in the people and in its potential for self-determination and self-governance. Democracy, then, became merely a 'method', one that would not have an 'overriding objective, such as enhancing the self-esteem and development of the individual' (*ibid.*: 94). To reduce democracy to a method for the competitive selection of the elite means accepting and legitimising the actual structure of the relationship between elite and mass, proposing a 'restrictive' vision of all that needs to be understood as the 'interest' of the people. In this way, Bachrach noted, 'the democratic elitist implicitly rejects the contention of the classic theorists that interest also include the opportunity for development which accrues from participation in meaningful political decisions' (*ibid.*: 95).

In the concluding pages, we find a synthesis of Bachrach's position, which can be taken as representative of the core theoretical claims of participatory democracy.

I believe that the theory of democracy should be based upon the following assumptions and principles: the majority of individuals stand to gain in self-esteem and growth toward a fuller affirmation of their personalities by participating more actively in meaningful community decisions; people generally, therefore, have a twofold interest in politics – interest in the results and interest in the process of participation; benefits from the latter interest are closely related to the degree to which the principle of equality of power is realized (*ibid.*: 101).

This idea of participation as a space in which a principle of equality of power can be expressed and exercised would be at the centre of later theoretical proposals for participatory democracy, which would emphasise participation as a process of empowerment, and as the *direct exercise* of equal power, in order to enrich and nourish the faculties and potential of individuals. But such an exercise of power cannot avoid being partial, temporary and, above all, local:

... political education is most effective on a level which challenges the individual to engage cooperatively in the solution of concrete problems affecting himself and his immediate community. In the past this task was ideally performed in the New England town meeting – in twentieth-century America it can effectively be performed in the factory community (*ibid.*: 103).

Consequently, even in this text by Bachrach, there is a fundamental weakness, one that would also be found in all the subsequent conceptions of participatory democracy. All these conceptions opposed to the institutional political structure of contemporary democracies, hoping to address the low levels of participation that characterised them, had in common was a vision of the constitutive terms of the democratic ideal. The proposed solution was a strategy of democratisation in all spheres of social and economic life (which can, nonetheless, be considered 'political,' insofar as they are shot through with power relations). In this way, participatory democracy was translated into the search for social spaces, neither state-based nor, even strictly speaking, 'governmental', in which diffuse and egalitarian forms of democratic power could be exercised. This was done, however, without having a full-fledged view of how these spaces would co-exist with representative institutions. This was a dilemma that other writers and other theoretical positions would also not be able to escape.

3. Participatory democracy as a new form of democracy: Pateman and Macpherson

Participatory democracy, then, was born in the political and cultural climate of the 1960s in America, against the background of the turmoil of ideas and conflicts that characterised this time. In these years, a debate within political theory developed, in which certain thinkers tried to delineate the foundations of a different model of democracy, based on a normative approach opposed to the dominant elitist vision. Such an approach was set against the view of democracy as the competitive selection of leadership, as well as the specific conception of American constitutional design that had been (and continued to be) proposed by the pluralist tradition. At the centre of this (both theoretical and political) project was a view of democracy based on two principles: first, the wide and diffuse participation of citizens as the exercise and expansion of the capacity for self-determination of individuals; and second, a view of participation as the direct exercise of *equal power*, that is, the idea that every individual would have to weigh in on the control and self-governance of the spheres of social life that affect her existence.

This approach made the theoretical view of participatory democracy congruent with the social movements which, in those years, attacked existing power structures. For some of these movements, the idea of 'participatory democracy' could blend more or less organically with a direct political perspective, thus becoming the ideological and programmatic content of a movement critical of capitalism that overlapped with certain ideas of 'socialism' – fundamentally, the idea of an expansion of democracy not limited to the sphere of institutional power and capable of affecting the structure and balance of socio-economic power.[25]

In countries like France and Italy, the wave of political mobilisation at the end of the 1960s would become strongly linked (even with regard to the presupposed or proposed idea of democracy), to the ideological framework offered by various versions of the Marxist tradition (from more orthodox to more heretical ones). In American progressive culture, the goal was instead to create a critical perspective not reducible to the canons of orthodox or heterodox Marxism. For certain authors,

---

25. See, for example, the retrospective testimonials of Joshua Cohen (2009a: 9; *see* Chapter Six, Section 2 in this volume). *See also* Hayat 2011: 106.

in fact, this critical perspective openly posited a conception of democracy capable of presenting itself as the 'heir' of the most authentic liberal tradition.

As we have seen, certain texts and thinkers could be considered precursors of this strand of thought: nonetheless, the works of Carol Pateman and, later, Crawford Brough Macpherson came especially to be deemed the most important theoretical contributions of this phase. The first and perhaps most influential work that proposed a more complete elaboration and 'model' of participatory democracy was Carol Pateman's *Participation and Democratic Theory* (1970).

For Pateman, too, the starting point was the criticism of mainstream contemporary democratic theory and the elitist-competitive vision that characterised it, both in Schumpeter's original and extremely influential version and in the subsequent elaborations of Berelson, Lazarsfeld and McPhee (1954), Dahl (1956), Sartori (1962) and Eckstein (1961). Pateman's first criticism of these thinkers was that they moved from the descriptive and analytical level to the normative one: in such theories, participation became a potential factor of instability in democracy and the apathy of citizens was not a pathology to recover from. Rather, apathy was taken as 'normal' and even desirable, protecting the system against the danger of 'overload', in which it would be paralysed by an excess of political claims and demands and by subsequent popular mobilisation. Indeed, as Pateman noted (1970: 1), not only did the concept of participation play 'a minimal role' in the democratic theories most accepted in those days, but they also placed great 'emphasis ... on the dangers inherent in wide popular participation in politics'.

Of particular interest, in this context, is the critical attention that Pateman directed to the work of Giovanni Sartori, whose most important quoted text, as with Bachrach, was *Democratic Theory* (1962).[26] Pateman judged Sartori's work, fundamentally, to be 'an extension of Dahl's theory of democracy as polyarchy' but also 'the most extreme version of the revision of earlier theories of democracy' (1970: 10). Pateman critically underlined that 'the emphasis that Sartori places on the danger of instability' also derived from the 'disillusion' that an idealised, mythological and 'perfectionist' vision of democracy can induce. Nonetheless, Pateman gave Sartori credit for being 'one of the very rare theorists of democracy who actually poses the question "How can we account for the inactivity of the average citizen?"'. However, 'his answer is that we do not have to account for it' (*ibid.*: 11). According to Sartori, it was important to acknowledge that, for the majority of citizens, interest in politics is limited or circumscribed to issues that are relevant to their experience; and it is impossible, or even dangerous, to think that anyone could force this condition in some way, in order to overcome the apathy of the ordinary citizen. And it is also useless to find explanations in the low level of culture or in misinformation or poverty: 'Sartori concludes', Pateman

---

26. *Democratic Theory* was published in the USA in 1962 as the translation and the expanded edition of the volume *Democrazia e definizioni*, published in Italy in 1957 and reissued in a second edition in 1958.

noted, that 'the apathy of the majority is nobody's fault in particular, and it is time we stopped seeking scapegoats' (*ibid.*).[27]

However, the key point of Pateman's approach was a vision of participatory democracy as the making of collective decisions that are not reducible to the exclusive domain of state institutions. 'The theory of representative government is not the whole of democratic theory' (*ibid.*: 20). Democracy can and must express itself in all spheres of social life; whenever some 'structure of authority' comes into action, it can be entrusted to an active process involving citizens, one that 'democratises' its operation, allowing citizens to 'control' the social forms and spheres in which their lives take place, thereby guaranteeing their equal condition.

So, participatory democracy, finally, is configured as a form of power, control and self-government, one that individuals would engage with *directly* in various areas of their social life, at the heart of the decision-making processes affecting their lives. It is understandable then, that from this perspective, workplaces would be one of the primary areas in which one could (and should) exercise real 'mastery' over one's own living conditions. It is therefore understandable that Pateman placed such emphasis – which today can seem dated – on the work of G. D. H. Cole and on his vision of an associational and co-operative socialism ('Guild Socialism'). The merit of John Stuart Mill and, later, of Cole, with respect to Rousseau (according to Pateman), was that of having moved the participatory theory of democracy 'out of the context of a city state of peasant proprietors [into that of a] modern political system' (*ibid.*: 27).

Democracy cannot be reduced to a 'method' or an institutional procedure: it is a direct taking part in decision-making, starting with the dimension of social life of which an individual has immediate, daily experience. It was, then, the whole social order that had to be regarded as democratic: participatory democracy, in this view, is a full and authentic realisation of the democratic ideal, which should not be reduced merely to the institutional sphere and/or to procedural political representation. Thus, we cannot properly speak only of democratic institutions, but rather (above all) of a democratic society as a participatory society (*ibid.*: 20, 35).

The search for a theoretical genealogy of this thesis brought Pateman to identify in Rousseau ('the theorist par excellence of participation … it is in his theory that the basic hypotheses about the function of participation in a democratic polity can

---

27. Sartori's words (1962: 87–90) are from chapter 5 of his book ('Governed democracy and governing democracy'), from a section in which Sartori especially emphasised his sceptical vision of the critical and participatory potential of the majority of citizens (1962: 88). Twenty-five years later, in *The Theory of Democracy Revisited* (1987), Sartori significantly expanded this chapter. Though the diagnosis remained the same ('apathy still looms large, with no detectable, long-range trend of change for the better'; 1987: 104), it became more complex, taking into account all the research that, since 1962, had analysed the processes and channels by which public opinion is formed. In particular, Sartori took on the answer that had been given to the problem of apathy by what was referred to as the 'revival' of the ideal of participatory democracy – a 'new rallying symbol' that deserved a new and autonomous treatment – in the context of chapter 6 ('Vertical democracy'). In this chapter, a great deal of writing was dedicated to 'Anti-elitism revisited', with particular reference to Bachrach's work, deemed to be 'the representative writing' of this tradition (*ibid.*: 178, 64), while Pateman's work only received a passing mention.

be found'; *ibid.*: 22) and, later, in John Stuart Mill, the inspirational origins of this vision of democracy. This was mainly because these thinkers did not only have in mind a 'protective' function for participation, as did Locke (or even Bentham and James Mill),[28] but rather a constitutive educational function in the broader sense: the herald of a full valorisation of the potential of human development in all things. 'The central function of participation in Rousseau's theory', noted Pateman, 'is an educative one, using the term "education" in the widest sense. Rousseau's ideal system is designed to develop responsible, individual social and political action through the effect of the participatory process' (*ibid.*: 24–5).

A participatory democracy and society can only be founded on the virtuous circle of the self-reproduction of the educational effects of participation. Thus, a 'participatory system' is 'self-sustaining' (*ibid.*: 42) insofar as the qualities required of citizens are the same as those that the process of participation itself would develop and nourish. '[T]he more individuals participate, the better able they become to do so' (*ibid.*). In all this, according to Pateman's interpretation of Rousseau, one sees the effective liberty of an individual. 'The individual's actual, as well his sense of, freedom is increased through participation in decision making because it gives him a very real degree of control over the course of his life and the structure of his environment' (*ibid.*: 26).

The potential beneficial effects of participation are to be found, therefore, essentially in the process of formation of an active and well informed citizenship: this was the crucial dimension that, from this perspective, would characterise participation, even though – but Pateman devoted only a fleeting mention to this aspect – it is also capable of operating as a source of legitimacy (collective decisions taken in a participatory manner would be both accepted and shared to a greater degree) and as a factor of integration and social cohesion (*ibid.*: 27).

It is clear that, in this vision of democracy and democratic society (even prior to a set of democratic institutions), it is at the local and communitarian level that one can and should exercise – and self-reproduce in a cumulative way – the individual and collective capacity for self-government. The workplace and the local community were the two pillars on which to build a democratic and participatory society. What seemed crucial, in particular, was the sphere of local self-government: it is through participation at the local level that the individual

---

28. Pateman asserted that 'the notion of a "classical theory of democracy" is a myth' (*ibid.*: 17) and scolded the first critics of the elitist-competitive vision – including Walker and Bachrach – for having accepted the flawed picture that Schumpeter had outlined of this supposedly 'classical doctrine'. Among the democratic theorists who could be described as 'classical' (in particular, Rousseau, Bentham, James Mill and John Stuart Mill (Pateman 1970: 18), there were stark differences in the role and vision of participation was described. On the basis of the broadly utilitarian approaches of Bentham and James Mill, Pateman noted, participation 'had a purely protective function, it ensured that the private interest of each citizen were protected (the individual interest being merely a sum of individual interest)'. Nonetheless, 'their theories can be classified as "democratic" because they thought that the "numerous classes" only were capable of defending the universal interest and thus advocated the participation (voting and discussion) of all the people'. This differentiates them from others like Locke ('who was far from being a democrat') and from their exclusively protective vision of participation (*ibid.*: 20).

'learns democracy', Pateman observed, quoting the famous words of John Stuart Mill: 'we do not learn to read or write, to ride or swim, by being merely told how to do it, but by doing it, so it is only by practicing popular government on a limited scale that the people will ever learn how to exercise it on a larger' (*ibid.*: 31).[29]

Pateman devoted much of her book to the issue of industrial democracy (indeed, three of five chapters, including one entirely dedicated to the experiences of self-management in Tito's Yugoslavia); these pages certainly give one a sense of the climate of that time. It would be unfair to assess these chapters only 'in hindsight' but today they surely seem characterised by a generous yet insufficiently robust intent, namely, 'proving' the practicality or plausibility of a particular model of participatory democracy.

From the present perspective, it is worth noting how the concrete operations of the process of self-government, though ideally extendable to all areas of social life, were left completely undefined. How to take part in decision-making? Through which rules, procedures, and institutions? How to adjust the dynamics of an assembly? The model of the participatory process that Pateman outlined was, as such, 'participation in the making of decisions' (*ibid.*: 24); a properly deliberative dimension – that is, the role of public discussion and argumentative exchange – was completely lacking.[30]

This vision of participation and democracy was summarised as follows by Pateman – 'in the participatory theory "participation" refers to (equal) participation in the making of decisions and "political equality" refers to equality of power in determining the outcome of decisions' (*ibid.*: 43). The core of this definition is the equality of power exercised by individuals within a decision-making process. Neither the issue of public discussion nor that of argumentative exchange comes into play: what matters is 'decision-making' and the ability to do so in conditions of equality, thus immediately affirming one's will. But how this could happen and, especially, how citizens' would form political judgments, were questions left completely undetermined.

---

29. This is a quote that Pateman cites from J. S. Mill, *Essays on Politics and Culture*, New York: Doubleday, 1963, p. 186.

30. It is beyond the present scope to offer an analysis of the correctness or completeness of the interpretation of Rousseau proposed by Pateman in this text. That said, she does seem to follow (at least regarding certain aspects) the internal logic of Rousseau's thought: the formation of the will of each individual is configured as a wholly inner and individual dimension with which 'no organized group' (Pateman, 1970: 25) can interfere, since such interference would distort the search for the common good. On these aspects of Rousseau's thought, see Urbinati 2006: 'Rousseau's model of political institutions is consistent with a delegated (as non deliberative) democracy versus a representative (as deliberative) democracy. It is based on popular sovereignty as a unitary act of the will the citizens perform either by electing law-redactors or lawmakers with instructions or by voting on the laws directly' (*ibid.*: 61–2). 'It is a commonplace', writes Urbinati (*ibid.*: 76), 'to think that Rousseau countered representation with direct participation': in Rousseau, the only form of 'participation' is that of the immediate expression of the will, of *ratification* (*ibid.*: 80–1), on the basis of a 'predetermined will' (Manin 1987: 345–6) that is not publically formed and that, actually, has to be preserved against the effects of rhetoric and of demagogy. On Manin's analysis of Rousseau, *see* Chapter Five, Section 1 in this volume.

Pateman's work assumed a view of democracy as a critique of the power structures of capitalism and, as such, it was fuelled by a radical and socialist sentiment. On the other hand, the subsequent work of Macpherson suggested a model of participatory democracy that was rather explicitly defined as a 'model of liberal democracy' (1977: 114). At the centre of this theoretical and political strategy was the possibility and desirability of a split between liberal democracy and capitalist development, laying the foundation of a possible different future for democracy and promising the possibility of actualising the 'central ethical principle of liberalism – the freedom of the individual to realize his or her human capacity' (*ibid*.: 2). Only by overcoming capitalism could the liberal vision of the autonomy and 'self-development' of individuals fully unfold.

Now, forty years later, what is most striking is the theoretical naivety of this political-cultural project. If, in the early parts of his work, Macpherson outlined an interpretive synthesis of 'models of democracy' destined to be taken up by others – in particular, the distinction between 'protective democracy' and 'developmental democracy,' crucial to David Held's seminal *Models of Democracy*, the first edition of which appeared in 1987 – the model of 'participatory democracy' that the Canadian scholar outlined in the final part of his work was characterised by a weak voluntaristic attitude. Such an element appealed to the political and social struggles of those years to see the signs and the 'proof' of the feasibility of this different model of democracy. In particular, as in Pateman's work, 'movements of democratic participation in decision-making at the workplace' (Macpherson 1977: 104) were valorised.

Most importantly for today, however, this participatory model was configured to combine, at its fundamental level, the basic forms of direct democracy and, at higher levels, forms of delegated democracy. This model entailed council-based democracy in places of work and study and in local communities; with a structure that was openly described as 'pyramidal' (*ibid*.: 109), democracy would be articulated at higher levels through forms of delegation and would reach some accommodation with electoral democracy and the enduring role of political parties (*ibid*.: 114). In this model, any concept of political representation, as well as any idea of public deliberation, was completely absent. What is essential, in this vision of participatory democracy, is 'substantial citizen participation in government decision-making' (*ibid*.: 93). The antidote to the 'apathy' that characterised 'the ordinary person in the formal political process' was offering citizens the possibility of some effective 'experience of participation', capable of forming and enriching their 'participatory competence' (*ibid*.: 106). 'Some significant amount of direct democracy', Macpherson thus openly concluded, 'is necessary for anything you might call participatory democracy' (*ibid*.: 112).

With the wide exposure they had, works such as those of Macpherson and Pateman contributed directly to, and also interpreted, a common political culture expressed by the processes of social and political mobilisation that characterised the 1960s and early 1970s. We can find in these works the theoretical and ideological matrix of a conception of participation that, while particular to its time, had important influence on future theorising. It was this vision that inspired theories of and political strategies for the gradual expansion of spaces in which citizens could and should participate in forms of self-management and self-government, in the creation of democratic 'counter-powers', and so on. This vision of participatory democracy was soon abandoned and then, at least for a few years, was largely forgotten. But some issues, some interpretive schemes, turned out to be quite persistent. Among these, one that seems particularly enduring and influential is the notion that 'real' participation (participation that is 'truly effective') is tied to the decision-making nature of the participatory process.

Even without fully committing to such a simplification, it is quite common in today's 'common sense', and also in the most theoretically aware literature to find the idea that the level of efficacy of a participatory device or institution must be commensurate with the decision-making powers attributed to it. This identification of participation with decision belongs not only to the theoretical and political tradition properly definable as 'participatory democracy'. When the new theoretical field of 'deliberative democracy' began to be delineated, proposing anew the theme of 'empowerment', this source of tension and confusion was still there.

4. Levels and forms of participation: Sherry R. Arnstein's 'ladder'

A very clear example of an idea of participation as empowerment is in the famous and successful systematisation found in a brief essay by Sherry R. Arnstein called 'A ladder of citizen participation' (1969).[31] This seminal work has been abundantly cited, even to this day, thanks especially to the effective image of the 'ladder' with rungs, through which we can distinguish different possible levels of citizens' participatory involvement.

The success (but also the ambiguity) of this image originated in an implicit assumption, first in early theories and then in the 'common sense' that developed around the notion of participatory democracy, that 'real' participation is what confers or attributes 'power' to participants. Arnstein's short essay contains a condensation of ideas destined to be circulated widely in future, such as the polemical juxtaposition of a participatory 'empty ritual' and the 'real power' at the outcome of the process: 'there is a critical difference between going through the empty ritual of participation and having the real power needed to affect the outcome of the process' (Arnstein 1969: 216). As Blondiaux and Fourniau noted

---

31. When she wrote her article, which appeared in the *Journal of the American Institute of Planners*, Sherry R. Arnstein (1930–97) was the director of a research non-profit centre, Community Development Studies for the Commons of Washington and Chicago, and then held a number of management and consulting positions in many projects and initiatives of the government. This experience is reflected extensively in her text, for the examples she made as well as for her criticism of various US federal programmes (and their 'participatory rituals'), which, in the 1960s, put forward inclusive strategies – often of a paternalistic character – towards the poorer sections of the population or ethnic minorities. On the role of 'Arnstein's ladder' in the American theoretical debate of those years over planning theories, see Healey 1997: 22–7) and Chapter Seven, Section 1.

(2011: 11), the reasons for the '*étonnante postérité*' of Arnstein's article resides in its having proposed for the first time a '*geste de recherche*' that would later come close to being a conditioned reflex: to 'try to evaluate the real impact of participatory devices on decision, proposing to classify them on a ladder in function of their degree of effectiveness and conformity to an ideal of real participation of citizens'.

On Arnstein's ladder (see Figure 1.1), each rung corresponds to a level of 'extension of the power of citizens' and their capacity and opportunity to determine a plan or programme. On the two lowest steps of the ladder, we find two forms of non-participation: manipulation and then what Arnstein calls 'therapy', which is the most 'arrogant and dishonest' form of manipulative strategy, explicitly aimed at 'curing' discomfort – even mental and behavioural discomfort – and the 'pathologies' of the poorest sections of the populace (Arnstein 1969: 218–9). The third and fourth steps are characterised as levels of 'tokenism', the practice of making minimal concessions to someone, or to some minority group, only as an outward symbolic gesture. Forms of tokenism are 'information' (third rung); 'consultation' (fourth rung); and, finally (fifth rung), 'placation', described as 'higher level tokenism because the ground rules allow have-nots to advise, but retain for the power holders the continued right to decide' (*ibid.*: 217).

Figure 1.1: Arnstein's 'ladder' of citizen participation

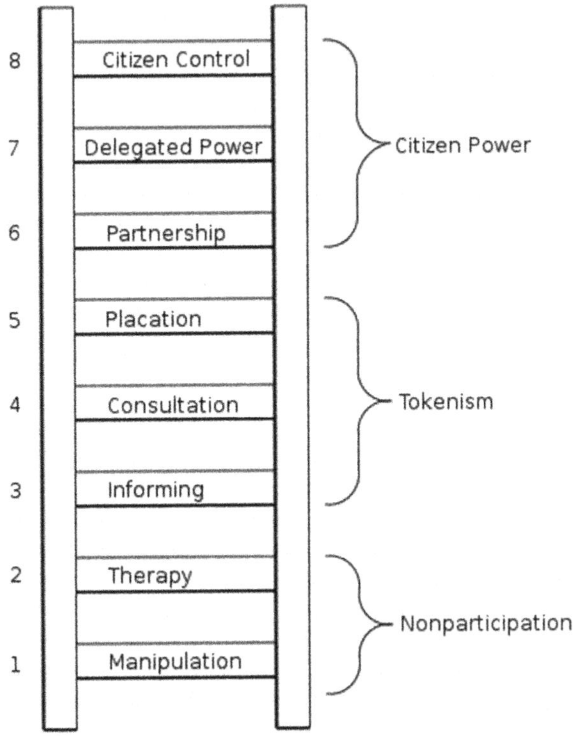

Source: Arnstein 1969: 217.

It is worth noting how information and consultation, characterised by a top-down flow, without a feedback channel (*ibid.*), were seen as very weak levels of participation because they did not provide any direct form of empowerment: 'when they are proffered by power-holders as the total extent of participation, citizens may indeed hear and be heard. But under these conditions they lack the power to insure that their views will be heeded by the powerful' (*ibid.*). In this framework, consultation, that is, 'inviting citizens, like informing them, can be a legitimate step toward their full participation. But if consulting them is not combined with other modes of participation, this rung of the ladder is still a sham since it offers no assurance that citizen concerns and ideas will be taken into account' (*ibid.*). Here, one finds quite a familiar expression that recurs even in some of the more recent analyses of participatory and/or deliberative processes: participation as a window-dressing ritual.

Finally, from the sixth to the eighth rungs, forms of participation are characterised by various 'levels of citizen power': 'partnership', with power being 'redistributed through negotiation between citizens and powerholders' (*ibid.*: 221); 'delegated power' (some decision-making power, formally defined, is delegated to citizens); and, finally, 'citizen-control' (citizens exercise full power over the decision or management of an area of policy). In the last three cases, the 'levels of citizen power', as Arnstein wrote, endow citizens 'with increasing degrees of decision-making clout': from forms of negotiation and co-management to the fullest direct exercise of power.

Texts have their own destiny and it is not always helpful or possible to presume that we can read them in a way that reveals their original context and intent. However, re-read today, Arnstein's article bears obvious marks of the political climate of the US in the 1960s: Johnson's Great Society; federal programmes to combat poverty and marginalisation; and urban-regeneration programmes based on a strategy (or goal) of community control – policy areas within which the author had worked directly, from which she drew all her examples and on which, with this essay, she proposed to act. The protagonists of Arnstein's vision, those who had to laboriously climb the rungs of the ladder, were first of all the so-called 'have-nots' and the 'powerless'; it was understandable, then, that the theme of participation as empowerment would predominate as an instrument of redemption from poverty, marginalisation and ignorance, and that the prevailing idea was the educational function of participation, specifically as a means for the construction and broadening of democratic citizenship. This was a difficult path, which would have to overcome many 'roadblocks', as Arnstein herself wrote, not least of which, she said, originated with the poor and powerless themselves: due to the 'inadequacies of the poor community economic infrastructure and knowledge-base, plus the difficulties of organizing a representative and accountable citizens' group in the face of futility, alienation, and distrust' (*ibid.*: 217).

Arnstein's work can also be located within an older democratic tradition of the United States, however. The theme of community control, in particular, entered American politics and culture during the Progressive Era, in the late nineteenth century: in the face of radical changes brought about by the development of industrial capitalism and the impact that it had on urban realities – poverty, social marginalisation, degradation and segregation, and the difficult integration of new waves of immigration from southern and eastern Europe[32] – the Progressive Movement identified this terrain as an essential area of intervention. This attempt was also supported by recent directions taken by the social sciences, oriented toward empirical investigation and reformist action, and by the philosophical approaches coming from the pragmatism of William James and John Dewey. According to this view, reformist actions could only take place through the concrete involvement of individuals and of local communities or 'neighbourhoods', animating an educational process that would allow the development of democratic 'control' by citizens over their own environment and life.[33]

Because of these characteristics, Sherry Arnstein's essay retains a high historical and documentary value and it is significant that her 'ladder' metaphor is still widely referenced – and even when not cited, it is often used as the prevailing interpretative schema or evaluation tool of current participatory processes and devices. The reason for its persistence is the strength, but also the ambiguities, inherent in the concept of empowerment and in its so-common identification with the idea of decision-making.

---

32. On this period and these aspects of American history, between the end of the nineteenth century and the First World War, and on the political culture of the Progressive Movement, see Wiebe 1995: chapters 5 and 7.

33. In *Creating a Democratic Public – The struggle for urban participatory democracy during the Progressive Era* (Mattson 1998; *see also* Mattson 2011), Kevin Mattson studied, in particular, the 'social centres' movement which, from initial local experiments, underwent a remarkable expansion to national level, only to cease in the climate created by the US intervention in the First World War. This movement included many scholar-activists and journalists (such as Herbert Croly), who can be considered forerunners of 'participatory democracy'; but, among these figures, that of Mary Parker Follett (1868–1933) especially deserves to be remembered. A graduate in political science from Harvard in 1898, she was linked to the group of the progressive magazine *New Republic*. Close to the thought of John Dewey and the pluralist ideas of British political scientist and Labour politician Harold Laski, Follett worked first as a social worker and activist in the urban slums of Boston. She proposed then, in the twenties, a new approach to management science, one that was sensitive to conflict in industrial societies, to methods of consensual resolution of conflicts, and to the role of groups and voluntary associations as places of education for active democratic citizenship. Benjamin Barber ('M. P. Follett as a democratic hero') and Jane Mansbridge ('M. P. Follett: feminist and negotiator') each penned heartfelt tributes to Mary P. Follett, in their Preface to the new edition (1998 [1918]) of one of her major works, *The New State, Groups, Organizations: The solution of popular government*. More recently, Mansbridge wrote that M. P. Follett can be considered the first to have theorised integrative forms of negotiation, 'win–win' forms that creatively produce new solutions, with respect to the initial state of the interests and objectives of the actors involved (Mansbridge 2009: 15–16). Even the work of Follett, however, carries with it a strong sign of the 'anti-partyism' typical of the Progressive Era. Her emphasis on groups and associations, on the formation of an 'independent' individual, and on non-partisan civic participation, were bound to the rejection of parties that characterised the Progressive Movement. On this issue, see the discussion of Follett's ideas by Nancy Rosenblum (2008: 188–9, 261–2). On M. P. Follett see Drucker 1995; Graham 1995; Baritono 2001; and Dorf and Sabel 1998: 415–18, note 468.

Chapter Two

Beyond Participatory Democracy:
The Debate in the 1980s

The social and political practices inspired by the theoretical model of 'participatory democracy', as it was elaborated between the 1960s and 1970s, rapidly declined under the onslaught of the conservative revolution of the following decade. Nevertheless, attempts to theorise an idea of participation that sought to counter the hegemony of the competitive-elitist vision of democracy and the dominant paradigms of democratic theory continued. Ultimately, this response would find an innovative expression in the development of a deliberative conception of democracy. First, however, there was a transitional phase, during which the idea of 'deliberative democracy' *per se* didn't appear: rather, attempts were made to open up new perspectives on democratic theory. Despite their work being rooted in earlier reflections on participatory democracy, these theorists were fully aware of the limitations (and failures) of the previous model.

To illuminate this theoretical transition, I will consider two works in particular: Benjamin Barber's *Strong Democracy* (1984) and Jane Mansbridge's *Beyond Adversary Democracy* (1983 [1980]).[1]

1. Benjamin Barber: searching for a 'strong democracy'

Compared to the works by Pateman and Macpherson discussed in Chapter Two, Barber's 1984 volume seems to be theoretically much more solid. Compared to Mansbridge's book, however, it is less innovative, in that it appears to be trying to 'rehabilitate' the basic points of the participatory model. From a philosophical point of view, its roots are mostly 'pragmatist', with frequent references to William James, Charles S. Peirce and John Dewey:[2] the tone could well be described as

---

1. At present, Benjamin Barber (born in 1939) is Senior Fellow of the Fordham University Urban Consortium and is also Walt Whitman Professor Emeritus at Rutgers University, NJ. Jane Mansbridge (also born in 1939) is Adams Professor of Political Leadership and Democratic Values at the John F. Kennedy School of Government in Harvard.

2. 'Democratic politics is a form of human relations, and does not answer to the requirements of truth. My task in this book has been to try to find an approach to democracy suitable to human relations rather than to truth. I have been much helped by the tradition of American pragmatism' (Barber 1984: xii). Barber devotes much space to critique of the liberal paradigm's frames, particularly the pre-conceptual and epistemological ones and their cognitivist and rationalist character (*ibid*.: 59–60): 'Politics do not rest on justice and freedom: it is what makes them possible. The object of democracy is not to apply independently grounded abstractions to concrete situations, but rather to extrapolate working abstractions from concrete situations. In a word, politics is not the application of Truth to the problem of human relations but the application of human relations to the problem of truth. Justice then appears as an approximation of principle in a world of action where absolute principles are irrelevant' (*ibid*.: 64–5).

communitarian and 'republican'. Also, in comparison with C. B. Macpherson, Barber's opposition to the liberal tradition is much stronger.

However, it should be noted that Barber – with greater theoretical and political caution – avoids openly theorising a form of 'participatory democracy' as a fully defined democratic system, as opposed to a liberal and representative one. He did not even use the expression 'participatory democracy', preferring to present his own vision of democracy as 'politics in the participatory mode'. Still, the fact that the very definition of this participative model, or mode, was entirely based on the opposition of two rather generic adjectives – *strong* and *thin* as alternate visions of democracy – indicates the difficulties of this theoretical strategy. And although Barber's criticism of the liberal paradigm was strong, well argued and passionate, his alternative paradigm seemed to emerge only by means of a 'negative' definition, as a criticism of the inadequacies and limitations of liberalism. Such a paradigm could not be defined as other than 'strong' compared to all that appears 'thin'.

In both theoretical and political terms, the defining characteristic of Barber's position is his radical criticism of representation, a position inspired by Rousseau. According to Barber, the mechanisms of 'delegation' intrinsic to forms of political representation – which were created to make democracy 'feasible' in the modern conditions of a large national state – ended up radically weakening the ideals and reality of democracy itself: today, representative democracy guarantees efficiency and accountability but at the cost of citizens' active participation in politics. To reduce the role of citizens – as Schumpeter and then Downs proposed – to that of voters who limit themselves to a periodical evaluation of their governors' performance entails a dramatic impoverishment of democracy.

According to Macpherson, participatory democracy could be posited as a fulfilment of the ideal premises and normative assumptions of liberalism (the ideal of a free and autonomous citizen), thus helping to separate the destiny of liberalism from that of capitalistic society. Barber instead believed that the ties between democracy and liberal theory must be broken: 'the survival of democracy therefore depends on finding for it institutional forms that loosen its connection with liberal theory' (*ibid.*: xiv). But what are the institutional forms that could revitalise democracy? How can we achieve active and conscious civic participation?

This is the stumbling block for these conceptions of democracy. Pateman tried (a little hopelessly, one might say with hindsight) to find a solution in co-operative, associative or self-management practices; Macpherson designed a new, but not very credible, participatory institutional structure. Barber's answer – despite being more solid on the theoretical level – appears today to be surprisingly 'minimalist', notwithstanding its self-proclaimed radical nature: 'strong democracy tries to revitalize citizenship without neglecting the problems of efficient government by defining democracy as a form of government in which all the people govern themselves in *at least some* public matters *at least some* of the time' (*ibid.*: xiv, my emphasis).

Later, in the conclusion of his book, he makes the following statement:

I have insisted that strong democracy entails both the intimacy and the feasibility of local participation and the power and responsibility of regional and national participation ... This is not to say that strong democracy aspires to civic participation and self-government on all issues at all times in every phase of government, both national and local. Rather, it projects some participation *some of the time* on selected issues. If all of the people can participate *some of the time in some of the responsibilities of governing*, then strong democracy will have realized its aspirations (*ibid.*: 267, my emphasis).

Thus, democracy mainly means self-rule; however, seeing as it is practically impossible to expect that such self-rule can be expressed by *all*, *everywhere*, on *all* matters and *constantly*, the conditions for this to happen at least on *some* issues and at least for *some of the* time need to be put in place. It is necessary that self-rule can be practised by all citizens on at least some of the matters of common interest: only through this participative practice, Barber argued, is it possible to keep alive 'the meaning and function of citizenship' (*ibid.*: xiv), which would be destined to atrophy if participation were entrusted only to the electoral mechanisms of legitimation and delegation.

'People', writes Barber, 'are apathetic because they are powerless, not powerless because they are apathetic' (*ibid.*: 272). When we delegate, not only do we cede power: we also lose the very sense of our civic autonomy. While the liberal view understands man as 'inactive, nonparticipating, isolated, uninterfering with, privatized, and thus free' (*ibid.*: 36), 'strong' democracy entails considering freedom as a full manifestation of the individual's autonomy (and thus of their power) within a dimension of collective and communitarian life. Freedom, therefore, is self-ownership, self-determination and self-realisation of one's potential.

The inspiration here can be traced back to a classic author of twentieth-century democratic thought, John Dewey, who viewed democracy as a shared way of life and 'politics as a way of living' (*ibid.*: 117):

... autonomy is not the condition of democracy, democracy is the condition of autonomy. Without participating in the common life that defines them and in the decision-making that shapes their social habitat, women and men cannot become individuals. Freedom, justice, equality, and autonomy are all products of common thinking and common living: democracy creates them. ... Our most deeply cherished values are all gifts of law and of the politics that make law possible. We are born in chains, slaves of dependency and insufficiency, and acquire autonomy only as we learn the difficult art of governing ourselves in common: we are born inferior or superior as measured by natural endowment or hereditary status: we acquire equality only in the context of socially sanctioned arrangements that spread across naturally unequal beings a civic mantle of artificial equality (Barber 1984: xv).

It is only by experiencing this self-rule, even if only partially and temporarily, that individuals can acquire autonomy and the ability to express and formulate political judgements and discuss them publicly; and thus participate in decisions affecting their lives.

The background against which this vision is offered is that of contemporary democracy, which is characterised by apathy, alienation, and estrangement: '... from the time of de Tocqueville, it has been said that an excess of democracy can undo liberal institutions. I will try to show that an excess of liberalism has undone democratic institutions' (*ibid.*: xi). The 'pervasive apathy' (*ibid.*: xiii) that is undermining democracy is due to the dominance of delegation and representation mechanisms that have numbed any sense of active citizenship and overshadowed the most authentic sense of democracy as self-rule and of participation as a civic duty. The destiny of freedom must therefore be saved from the clutches of liberalism. Barber concludes that:

> To be free, we must be self-governing: to have rights we must be citizens. In the end, only citizens can be free. The argument for strong democracy, though at times deeply critical of liberalism, is thus an argument on behalf of liberty (*ibid.*: xvi).

> ... if democracy entails the right to govern ourselves rather than to be governed in accordance with our interests, then liberal democratic institutions fall short of being democratic (*ibid.*: xiv–xv).

Thus, in Barber's work, the aim of revitalising civic culture appears to be even more central than in other authors, and this objective is not combined with any other politically oriented ends (that is, ends more or less traceable back to a socialist ideal, as in Pateman, or to radical liberalism, as in Macpherson). Barber is deeply rooted in the American democratic tradition; and the forms of 'workplace democracy' (so significant for the authors mentioned above) here assume an entirely secondary role. His proposed institutional innovations (*ibid.*: 261–311) for enriching the quality of the 'participatory mode' of democracy are also very 'American': such innovations range from the revival of New England's traditional town meetings to all the forms of neighbourhood assemblies – which were all tried and tested, or anyway feasible, in the heart of the United States (in the quiet hills of Vermont, certainly not in Tito's Yugoslavia or in G. D. H. Cole's utopian Guilds, as in Pateman's view).

Nevertheless, the impression that ultimately emerges, again, is the political and programmatic nature of the theoretical proposal of 'strong democracy':

> ... the innovative institutions described in this chapter should provide a concrete starting point for those who wish to reorient democracy toward participation. Yet strong democracy practice requires not just a political program but a political strategy. Neither ideas nor institutions are self-implementing. They demand a base: *a political movement composed of committed democrats* who understand themselves to have an interest in the realization of strong democracy. This fact means first of all that strong democracy must offer a systematic program of institutional reforms rather than a piecemeal package of particularistic, unrelated modifications (*ibid.*: 263, my emphasis).

Therefore, the sharper the theoretical opposition to the liberal model, the more prudent and realistic was the strategy for a progressive and gradual introduction of a 'politics in participatory mode' and of 'participatory ingredients' into the fabric of liberal democracies, so as to reverse the increasing democratic impoverishment of representative institutions:

> We might more quickly realise the strong democratic program by first removing certain liberal obstacles: representation, the party system, single-member legislative districts, and the separation of powers come immediately to mind. But the prudent democrat reforms by adding participatory ingredients to the constitutional formula, not by removing representative ingredients. The objective is to reorient liberal democracy toward civic engagement and political community, not to raze it – destroying its virtues along with its defects (*ibid.*: 308–9)

The call to 'abolish parties' is acknowledged as wholly unrealistic – '[t]o call for the abolition of parties is to call for utopia' (*ibid.*) – but the fact that Barber takes the idea of abolishing parties seriously, without doubting or questioning its desirability if it were feasible, is clearly meaningful. Here, it is possible to grasp the author's deep adhesion to one of the most rooted traditions of American political culture, which regards parties as *factions*.[3]

Rather – Barber posited – we should leverage the constitutive features of the 'American system' (which are also found in other established constitutional systems) to develop strong democracy: such a system, in fact, 'survives by evolving and evolves by accreting new institutional layers that conform to the contours of a historically tested practice even as they alter the system's dimension and centre of gravity'. In short, 'strong democracy is a complementary strategy that adds without removing and reorients without distorting'. '[T]here is no other way', Barber concludes, adopting an obviously realistic and gradualist tone (*ibid.*: 309).

Here we can clearly see the gap between some very critical and radical theoretical issues and a much less ambitious, short-term political project that was openly characterised as cautious by its author. It is likely that, in the 1980s, this distance between the two was widened by the failures and disappointments entailed by the backflow of the participatory wave of the previous two decades. Yet, leaving this political element aside, it is still necessary to highlight some points of connection with the subsequent deliberative turn as well as the gap between Barber's work and this theoretical position to come.[4]

---

3. On the topic of 'antipartyism' in the American tradition, see Rosenblum 2008. *See also* Sartori 2005.

4. Rainer Forst (2001: 356–8, 2012) takes Barber's work as an example of a 'communitarian model' of deliberative democracy. In my view it is perhaps premature to speak of 'deliberative democracy' as such in connection with Barber, but Forst's analysis of the communitarian dimension of his claims is surely convincing in the way it underlines their 'republican' character compared to other versions of communitarianism.

Specifically, the discursive dimension began to assume a crucial role: that is, 'public talk' comes to be understood as one of the key elements of a vibrant democracy. However, such talk could not be take place in isolation or in an exclusive way. In fact, Barber considers public talking to be closely related to the other two phases of democratic and participative politics: decision-making and action, that is, respectively, the specific process by which decisions are made and their implementation or realisation. Moreover, in Barber's account, *public talk* is a broad term, which also includes deliberation, along with agenda-setting, listening and 'empathy' (*ibid.*: 266).

In Barber's view, democracy in the participatory mode entails that all three moments (public talk, decision-making, action) are conceived as very strongly connected; therefore, the link should be not only between the discussion of public issues and the formation of opinions in the public sphere but also – essentially and at the same time – between the decision and the action taken to put that choice into practice. 'Strong democracy', thus, entails not only public discussion but also the direct assumption and exercise of a decisional role and, later, direct engagement and involvement in the implementation of choices.

It is unavoidable that giving citizens such a direct decisional function, accompanied by executive and operative ones, would privilege local and communitarian dimensions. And although Barber often stresses the need to avoid parochialism, it is nevertheless clear that those dimensions remain the basis for any further democratic development – both because of the citizen-learning implications entailed as the initial step of civic engagement at the local and community level and as the context within which participative training could begin to show its beneficial effects.

Indeed, the design of the new institutions that Barber proposes in the final chapter of his book also provides for moments of *common policy-making, common work* and *citizen service*, that is, moments of the self-organisation of communal life, in which citizens not only talk and discuss but also directly engage (or are induced to engage) in the realisation of common decisions. Such a dimension may be characterised (using a term often evoked in Europe today) as corresponding to the *principle of subsidiarity*. Furthermore, Barber devotes much attention to the forms of a national citizen service, which might even be non-voluntary, which is described with an openly 'republican' tone, also to avoid the risks of communitarian localism (*ibid.*: 302).[5]

Finally, we must note that Barber devotes considerable space (*ibid.*: 291–2) to participative arrangements inspired by the principle of random selection (which would receive much attention from deliberative theorists in later years). Yet, we must also note that Barber does not think of these arrangements as creating a

---

5. 'Almost all of the proposals examined in this chapter focus on local citizenship and therefore have the effects of parochialism. Universal citizen service thus becomes a crucial instrument of national citizenship and the instrument of choice for opening up neighbourhoods and overcoming localism' (Barber 1984: 302).

representative micro-cosmos[6] but rather as assigning – on a random basis, and by turns – the functions and roles of communitarian government. Free and equal citizens are able to exercise administrative functions for which no special, or particularly specialised, competence is necessary: all individuals can be – at the same time, on certain issues – both governors and governed. Thus, it is possible to entrust the choice of those called upon to hold local offices to the egalitarian criterion *par excellence* – the drawing of lots.[7]

Therefore, even in Barber's position, 'participation' essentially means taking part in a decision-making process, or rather possessing and exercising the power of decision-making. In this way, as much as his theoretical reflection may be more solid than previous (1960s and 1970s) versions of participatory democracy, Barber cannot escape the difficulties of finding an effective alternative to the model it sought to challenge (ambiguously defined as 'liberal'). In my opinion, these difficulties are caused by a weak and unsustainable theoretical approach, that is, by an undue identification of *representative* democracy and *liberal* democracy: the strong and well argued criticisms of the liberal paradigm and its philosophical and anthropological foundations, to which Barber devotes several pages of heated discussion (see, for example, *ibid.*: 32–5), lose force and credibility when used to support a full-on attack on the principles and institutions of democratic political representation and an openly dismissive attitude towards political parties (*ibid.*: 34–5).[8]

The relationship between participation and representation is the real Achilles' heel of this participatory vision of democracy, both when the relationship is understood in terms of an opposition and when it rests on a weaker and unarticulated juxtaposition of the two. Any participatory process and institution, no matter how well it might work as a place where a new and vital civic culture forms, is inevitably destined to clash with the principle of the democratic legitimacy of decisions. This conception of democracy in the participatory mode then faces a dilemma: either the narrow and rigid connection between public talk, decision-making and action manages to be credible and effective, but only (if anything) on

---

6. For discussion of the concept of 'microcosm' in Fishkin, *see* Chapter Seven, Section 3 in this volume. On the democratic significance of the rotation of offices entrusted to lot in Athenian democracy, and for the interpretations that have been given, see Manin 1997: 25–41. Manin's work identifies the reasons why, when modern representative government was born, the principle of drawing lots as a method of selection of rulers – a method that even Montesquieu and Rousseau considered to be the democratic and egalitarian principle *par excellence* – was abandoned. This classic principle leaves the stage – making way for the 'triumph of elections' – because it cannot secure another foundational principle of modern democracy: the act, or procedures, of consensus that authorise and legitimise representative government (Manin 1997: 79–93). On this subject, *see also* Sintomer 2007.

7. Barber suggests the suitability of some local offices that are typical of American local communities: 'some or even all members of the board of assessors, the school committee, the registrar of voters, the planning board, the zoning board, the conservation commission, the housing authority, and the licensing board' (*ibid.*: 292).

8. This critical point was emphasised by Jane Mansbridge in her review of Barber's book (Mansbridge 1987).

a micro-community scale; or, when envisaged on the large scale, the participatory mode inevitably ends up giving way to 'traditional' institutions.

It is because of this dilemma that, at the end of his work, as we have seen, Barber is forced to go for a sort of 'tactical retreat' that ends up being a recognition of the force and credibility of the 'liberal' model. And the effect is paradoxical: he acknowledges many positive aspects of the model but he does not acknowledge the, potentially, fully democratic nature of institutions of political representation; nor does he leave any room for a potential participative (and deliberative) dimension *within* representative institutions and their relation to the citizens. His failure to recognise this potentially fully democratic and deliberative dimension of representation ends up weakening any argument in favour of a participatory dimension of democracy, exposing it to an irremediable deficit of legitimacy and legitimation.

In conclusion, we can say that Barber's work marks a particularly complex moment in the development of democratic theory, after the passing of the season of 'participatory democracy', (weak in its theoretical foundations; well meaning but often also unrealistic in its practical projections). Critics of the liberal paradigm and of elitist-competitive models of democracy were in search of new terrains of elaboration and a more solid theoretical anchorage. A new framework was needed, one that would be capable of accounting for the enduring vitality (or the difficulty of replacing) democratic arrangements based on electoral democracy and political representation but also, at the same time, capable of indicating other possible conceptions or dimensions of democracy. In this context, the peculiarity and value of Barber's contribution are to be found in his valorisation of an approach typical of the American democratic tradition, to which pragmatism offered solid philosophical and theoretical foundations.

It was a view of democracy as a shared 'form of life', as self-rule and the self-realisation of human potential, as self-determination through the formation of civic attitudes and the taking of civic responsibilities and even though public talk, as a co-operative search for common, consensus-based solutions (as opposed to solutions based on the acknowledgement of irremediably diverse interests). If, in the 1970s, this democratic ideal had cross-fertilised with new youth political movements and was strongly imbued with radical (or even socialist or revolutionary) tones, for Barber, this ideal was organically embedded in a context that exalted a specific American tradition of communitarian self-rule. Yet, his fierce criticism of the 'thin' model of liberal democracy ultimately leads only to juxtaposition or possible coexistence between diverse democratic logics, without providing any effective solution to the problem of the feasibility of integrating political participation and political representation.

2. Jane Mansbridge: 'unitary democracy' and 'adversary democracy'

As we have seen, the first scholars of participatory democracy (Arnstein, Pateman, Macpherson) first matured their positions in a cultural climate characterised by intense social and political mobilisation: however, I have also noted how even an author like Barber, in a text published in 1984, showed the influence of a changing political environment. If, on the one hand, the theoretical opposition between diverse 'modes' of democracy became more radical, on the other, from a political point of view, the aim was to gradually affirm a 'more participative' view of democracy that would approach its goals in a gradual and realistic way.

Another significant work, Jane Mansbridge's *Beyond Adversary Democracy* (published in 1980 and reprinted in 1983, with a new and important Preface) can also be fully comprehended only if read in the light of its particular historical background: the crisis of the participative conception following the events of the 1960s and early 1970s. In fact, from several points of view, Mansbridge's book also sought to review that period and to interpret at least some of the reasons for the crisis. However, this work, although linked to that time, also marked a break with the previous participatory model and prefigured some elements of the deliberative theoretical paradigm to come.

Furthermore, Mansbridge's approach can be placed on a different level in relation to the other works I have analysed. It did not draw on the traditional conceptual opposition that defined normative models of democracy (between direct and representative democracy, a crucial dichotomy in earlier participatory theories) but rather suggested a new pair of theoretical categories – *unitary* versus *adversary* democracy – that 'cut through' the old definitions and reformulated their terms. At the same time, Mansbridge introduced an empirical perspective, devoting a large part of her work to a detailed analysis of two participative experiences (supported by a rich series of theoretical foundations and categories from sociology, ethnography and anthropology, in addition to those coming from political science), namely, 'a town meeting government' in a village in Vermont and a 'participatory workplace' (that is, an enterprise characterised by co-operative, democratic and participative self-management).

Previous theorists of 'participatory democracy' idealised this micro-communitarian dimension, taking it as a basis on which to construct a different form of democracy that would take the first steps to becoming an educational process for active citizenship. Mansbridge's analysis, on the contrary, showed how participatory democracy had actually been experienced and, above all, noted the dilemmas, difficulties and conflicts it entailed in practice. She no longer sought to 'prove' the plausibility or feasibility of new participative institutions and practices, idealising them (often beyond their actual political relevance): rather, she concretely analysed the functioning of real participative social practices that had been inspired by this ideal, highlighting their virtues and potential, but also – and mercilessly – their limits and contradictions, as well as the reasons why they had often turned out to be 'fragile bubbles' (Mansbridge 1983: 22). She did so especially in relation to one of the pillars of a normative view of the democratic ideal: equality.

For theorists of democracy in the participatory mode, 'participation' meant, first of all, self-government, self-determination and the community's control over its own environment and life. But it was from this understanding that several problems arose: the aspiration to experience forms of equality, freedom and brotherhood clashed with other logics and dynamics. Mansbridge's use of the expression 'participatory democracy' is truly original and significant: hers is a *plural* use, which today is rather unusual. 'This book', the author wrote in the new Preface to her 1983 edition,

> ... deals with two great themes in American political thought: democracy and equality. I began work on it in the late 1960s, when I was a member of *several small 'participatory democracies'*. Sooner or later, internal struggles over equality left each of these groups in disarray. Most of my friends in these organizations attributed inequality and the pain it caused to the warped personalities of particular individuals and, ultimately, to the destructive effect of a capitalist society on the individual personality. I always felt that these explanations had some force. But I also believed – and still believe – that certain kinds of inequality would appear in any society, no matter what its ideology or social system, and that organizations with egalitarian ideals would have to find ways to deal with this fact (Mansbridge 1983: vii, my emphasis).

Mansbridge then retraced the stages of her research: sharing those egalitarian ideals, and trying to understand the deeper reasons for the difficulties encountered by these ideals in practice, she searched for the most successful 'participatory democracies'. Her belief was that there were two types: 'the government of a town and workplace, since [she] assumed that participants would be more passionately concerned about town and workplace decisions than about decisions made by other sorts of organizations' (*ibid.*: vii).

Using the theme of 'inequality' to frame her analysis of these small 'participatory democracies' led Mansbridge to an understanding of how and why, in their internal mechanisms, they reproduced dynamics that resulted in the creation of a dominant 'elite', or forms of delegation or 'representation' that sometimes gave rise to, or aimed for, the selection of the best, most capable, or 'strongest' people. In other words, the point was to understand whether the democratic ideal of equal power actually was (or could be) practised, under what conditions, and if and how this might or might not happen. And for those who saw these small communities as microcosms within which to experience democracy and make it thrive, the realisation of how much inequality and difference could undermine or contradict an ideal democratic politics was certainly disturbing.

Thus, in her quest for 'a town where, at least initially, "the people" seemed to govern', Mansbridge excluded town meetings in some large states such as Connecticut or Massachusetts because they were clearly dominated by economic and professional elites. She chose, instead, a small town in Vermont, with only 350 adult inhabitants.[9] As for workplaces – bypassing once again some 'participatory

---

9. Here, we find the issue of 'community control', which I discussed in the previous chapter: 'The late 1960s were the heyday of the "community control" movement, whose implicit model was the town meeting, an inspirational symbol of American democracy since before the Revolution' (Mansbridge 1983: vii–viii).

workplaces ... dominated by a readily identifiable élite' – the choice fell on an enterprise 'whose forty-one paid employees had deposed its founding elite and ran their organization on an extremely egalitarian basis' (*ibid.*: viii). However, it must be noted that this enterprise was not properly a private company but rather what today we'd call a 'social co-operative', a 'crisis centre', funded by religious and philanthropic organisations and the Federal Government but also selling some of its services on the market, offering support in situations of personal emergency.[10]

Basically, rather than a commercial enterprise, this was what Mansbridge herself more correctly described as 'a radical collective', a group that acted on the basis of strongly idealistic motives and that intended to engage in self-rule in accordance with strongly egalitarian and participative procedures. However, as the author noted, 'the most important function of the time-consuming democratic procedures ... was to meet the staff's ideal of the way their world should work'. Such 'idealism' made this group 'a dubious prototype for the worker-controlled organization of the future' (*ibid.*: 147). Yet, while these features may have made this organisation less suitable as a practical and easily reproducible example of economic democracy, it nevertheless could serve as an excellent case-study for 'the internal tensions of a democracy' (*ibid.*: 148).

Mansbridge acknowledges that these two cases were 'atypical' and 'deviant': namely, 'democracies that did not, at least at first glance, have an obvious elite' and that succeeded 'in promoting equal power among their members more than any other democracies' (*ibid.*: viii). However the anomalous nature of these experiences became methodologically useful in understanding how to practise democracy in other places that did not evidence this high level of democratic 'purity'.

Today, this *plural version* of the expression 'participatory democracy' may sound quite unusual but Mansbridge herself recalled its origins:

> ... in the late 1960s and early 1970s, the thousands of small collectives that sprang up across the Unites States called themselves 'participatory democracies'. They used the term not just as a slogan, but to define themselves as organizations that made decisions: 1) so that the members felt equal to one another; 2) by consensus rather than majority rule; and 3) in face-to-face assembly, not through referenda or representation (*ibid.*: 290).

---

10. An advertisement cited by Mansbridge (1983: 140) described its activities thus: 'counselling and referral information for people with emotional, legal, medical, drug, or life-support problems, plus access to ambulance services, emergency shelters, short- and long-term counselling, special programs for teenagers'. This company operated 'in a major American city, a city not necessarily at the forefront of the New Left but not far behind: the cosmopolitan, youth-oriented parts of this city and their adjoining interracial, ethnic, and working-class areas had spawned a variety of women's centers, underground papers, legal collectives, health clinics, food co-ops, free schools, and experimental universities, most of these attempting to govern themselves as radical "participatory" democracies'. This description conveys the climate of the time well. *See also* Mansbridge 1983: 146–7.

Following this line of research and reflection, the author reaches the core of her theoretical proposal: 'the model of democracy unconsciously adopted by the participatory democrats of the late 1960s and early 1970s, which I call "unitary" democracy, was in essence and in form directly opposed to the model of democracy that I, like most Americans, had grown up with, a model I call "adversary" democracy'.[11]

The author's starting point (why do inequalities arise even within small, cohesive and egalitarian democratic communities?) is examined in an original way. 'Every American schoolchild knows that when you set up a democracy you elect representatives', at every level, from school to Congress; also, every American knows that 'when you do not agree, you take a vote, and the majority rules'. Well, precisely 'because this conception of democracy assumes that citizens' interests are in constant conflict, I called it "adversary" democracy'. However, she added, 'every step in this adversary democracy violates another, older understanding of democracy', in which

> people who disagree do not vote: they reason together until they agree on the best answer. Nor do they elect representatives to reason for them. They come together with their friends, to find agreement. This democracy is consensual, based on common interest and equal respect. It is the democracy of face-to-face relations. Because it assumes that citizens have a single common interest, I have called it 'unitary' democracy (*ibid.*: 3).

Thus, there are two different models. The first is 'unitary' democracy, based on common interests and 'friendship' (that is, on the Aristotelian *philìa*, a common ground of solidarity, brotherhood and sharing of values).[12] The second is 'adversary' democracy, based on conflicting interests, to which it must grant equal protection. As the author herself specifies, 'interests' are not to be taken as 'narrowly conceived' self-interest but rather as a whole range of motivations, concerns and attention to ideals, values and principles:

---

11. Elsewhere in her book, Jane Mansbridge dwelled more extensively on that historical period: 'These were years in which millions of people felt that existing democratic institutions had somehow failed them. As early as 1956, C. Wright Mills had said of the mass of American citizens: "They feel they live in a time of big decisions; they know they are not making any" (Wright Mills 1956). A decade later, with the escalation of the Vietnam War, this sense of estrangement had more become far more intense' (Mansbridge 1983: 20–1).

12. The author tells how, in the course of her research and, especially, of her many interviews, she came to realise that the ultimate basis of participatory democracies was actually 'brotherhood', or what many people preferred to define as 'solidarity', 'community' or even 'sisterhood'. The search for this theme, Mansbridge added, induced her to capture a far and 'classical' root of present 'solidarity': 'I found a recurrent concept in Aristotle's *Ethics* increasingly relevant. Aristotle tells us that the Greeks saw a kind of solidarity, which they called "friendship" [*philìa*], as the necessary basis of the state' (Mansbridge 1983: viii–ix). On the topic of *philìa* as the foundation of 'unitary' democracy, see particularly *ibid.*: 6–8 and 13–14. Jane Mansbridge had more broadly dealt with this theme in a previous essay, 'The limits of friendship' (Pennock and Chapman 1975: 246–75).

I will therefore use the one word, 'interest', to cover all these different types of enlightened preferences. 'Self-regarding' or even 'selfish' interest will mean a purely personal good: 'other-regarding' and 'public-regarding' interest will denote making the good of another individual or group one's own: and 'ideal-regarding' interest will mean identifying one's own good with the realization of some principle (*ibid.*: 26).

In the unitary model, the commonality (or even identity) of interests makes it so that some people might possess more power than others without this seeming harmful to the principle of equality: in the adversary model, instead, precisely the fact that there are conflicting interests is a fundamental argument for equal power, as it is necessary to ensure that each of these interests have an equal right to be expressed, 'protected' and 'represented'. Therefore:

… we value equal power not as an end in itself, but as a means to the end of protecting interests equally. When interests do not conflict, equal power is not necessary for self-protection. If everyone has the same interests, the more powerful will protect the interests of the less powerful automatically. Equal power is also a means to two other ends – maintaining a community of equal respect and promoting personal growth. But these ends too are met by other means when respect does not derive from power and when everyone in a community has the opportunity to take political responsibility. Thus equal power is a conditional value, not an absolute one. Rather than opposing 'democracy' to 'elitism' as if equal power were an end in itself, members of a group should spend their scarce resources on making power more equal only when equal power is most needed – when interests most conflict, when equal respect cannot be generated from other sources, and when citizens are atrophying from not having enough power and responsibility. Understanding that even a radical democrat need not press for more equal power in every instance but only when these three ends cannot be achieved by other means is, in my view, the most practical lesson in this book (*ibid.*: ix).

Certainly, the two new categories presented by Mansbridge as 'ideal types' (*ibid.*: 27) were in striking opposition to the usual oppositions (participative *versus* representative; direct *versus* delegated) and enabled the earlier disputes to be overcome: 'my argument has very little in common with the "participatory" critique of democratic elitism that emerged during the 1960s' (*ibid.*: xi). Specifically, the author writes:

What I call adversary democracy is not synonymous with democratic elitism, since the ideal of adversary democracy is fully consistent with, and may well require, the active participation of all citizens to ensure that their interests are protected equally. Nor is what I call unitary democracy simply a matter of widespread participation. On the contrary, when interests coincide, participation is sometimes unnecessary and irrelevant (*ibid.*: xi).

Moreover, neither the unitary model (which assumes the presence of common interests) nor the adversary model (which assumes the pluralism of conflicting interests) 'banish[es] or exclude[s] conflict in the political process itself'. Unitary democracy is anything but conflict-free: rather, it is precisely this model that often causes and exacerbates forms of conflict. Since it is assumed that 'a political problem has an underlying correct solution', contestations and discussions may continue indefinitely, even aggressively, as all participants need to agree on and accept a conclusion. On the contrary,

> [i]f there is no solution that serves everyone's interest, more debate will not usually produce agreement, and it is often better to cut short a potentially bitter debate with a vote. A pure unitary democracy is likely to be passionate – full of love and hate – while a pure adversary democracy is designed to be emotion-free – an impersonal mechanism for handling disembodied conflicting interests (*ibid.*: xi).

Furthermore, there is no analogy between unitary and direct democracy, or between adversary and representative democracy. If it is true that face-to-face forms of direct democracy may favour the creation and maintaining of common interests, there are forms of direct democracy (such as referendums) that are not face to face and instead often 'discourage the development of common interests by encouraging people to register their personal preferences privately, without having to participate in public debate' (*ibid.*: 126–7).

Mansbridge is also critical of some classical views of direct democracy (*ibid.*: 275–6). Citing a famous text by Ralph Waldo Emerson praising the original formula of town meetings,[13] Mansbridge recalled that

> ... radical democracy in its classic form – opening the marketplace or town hall to the citizens to gather, to debate, and make their own laws – does not guarantee the realization of Emerson's vision that every individual [have] 'his fair weight in the government', that 'every opinion [have] an utterance' and that all 'the people truly feel that they are lords of the soil' (*ibid.*).

Since 'no political system can ever fully overcome the patterns of advantage and disadvantage generated by its social and economic systems', a 'voluntarist model of direct democracy' is even less likely to succeed. Rather, the 'open doors' model (which legitimates the right to decide of the attendants, presuming the indifference of those who are absent) is even more likely to reflect only the 'persistent patterns' of those systems, reproducing the inequality inherent in them.

The views argued for by Jane Mansbridge were not only the result of theoretical reflection: they were developed following extensive fieldwork, with an inquiry that highlighted the different ways of conceiving a democratic decision-process. The

---

13. Ralph Waldo Emerson's 1835 text is known as the 'Historical discourse at Concord' (cited in Mansbridge 1983: 126).

importance of this work lies precisely in its ability to take claims for participatory democracy away from the field of ideal constructions, grasping the actual dynamic of social and communitarian practices of self-rule. The broad and detailed analyses of the interactions that took place within a small community in Vermont during its town meetings, or the 'collective' self-management of that particular workplace, thus highlighted the insurmountable difficulties inherent in an idealised view of a direct democracy.

Above all, in this work by Jane Mansbridge, we find an outline of the distinctions that would later be conceptually systematised in the new paradigm of deliberative democracy. In particular, she pointed out the problematic character of 'interests' within a deliberative democratic procedure – an issue deliberative theorists would later deal with. Are interests a factor to be 'transcended' in the name of the 'common good' or should they be 'addressed' in deliberative and discursive terms? And, on a normative level, are interests something to be 'bracketed' or should they be fully included within the conceptual framework of theory? Even in this 1980s text, Mansbridge's position fully takes the pluralism of interests (broadly understood also as self-commitment to a value or an ideal principle) as a fact that has to be discussed and deliberated upon, not as a distortion to be overcome or to be 'isolated' and circumscribed.

'Reasoning together' until an agreement is reached; consensus and conflict; representative and face-to-face procedures; and then, the decisive alternative: a common and unitary interest to 'discover' through discussing and reasoning ('to the bitter end', even at cost of hostile oppositions and tiring debates)? Or, on the contrary, conflicting interests to choose from by majority vote (or by negotiation)? As we can see, all the elements of a complicated theoretical puzzle were already on the table.[14]

Many crucial elements of the deliberative paradigm were already present in Mansbridge's work: the scale and dimension of deliberation; the costs and benefits of participation (*ibid.*: 110–1); symmetries or asymmetries in participants' cognitive resources; the exclusion of the poorest and most marginal social groups (*ibid.*: 118–25); the quality of dialogical interactions; and polarised dynamics within a setting based on a face-to-face relations. Most of all, Mansbridge highlighted the distinction between the 'aggregative' and 'transformative' dimensions of a democratic decision-procedure, between 'counting' preferences and 'discussing' them to achieve consensus (*ibid.*: 4–5).

---

14. Consensus does not mean unanimity: Mansbridge theorises how, in unitary democracies, unanimity is not always required, and even less must it be explicitly expressed by a vote. In such discursive contexts, deciding by consensus means ascertaining that a solution appears to be generally agreed on, insofar as either nobody objects or, if doubts and objections are advanced, they are not such as to block a prevailing solution. So, the intensity of opposition may be variable but not be such as to prevent a decision (on this, see Mansbridge 1983: 163–4) On decision by 'apparent consensus'– a decision made without an explicit vote, only through the absence of explicit vetoes – which would not appeal to either the principle of majority or that of unanimity, see the most recent contributions by Philippe Urfalino (2007 and 2014).

Yet Mansbridge was firm in rejecting any opposition between these two models:

These two conceptions of democracy persist, side by side, in every modern democracy. The adversary ideal and the procedures derived from it have dominated Western democracies' thinking since the seventeenth century. But unitary ideals and procedures continue to influence the way legislative committees, elected representatives, major institutions like the Supreme Court, and local democracies actually act. In crises of legitimation, citizens often reverted to the unitary ideal, as young people did in the small participatory democracies that flourished in America in the 1960s and early 1970s (*ibid.*: 3).

Thus, the answers to the questions initially posed by the author are very clear: despite the drawbacks of the experiences of participatory democracy in those years, these relatively 'unitary' forms of democracy met demands and needs that 'adversarial' institutions were not able to satisfy. But the causes of their failures were also clear; often, such failures derived 'from their refusal either to recognize when interests conflict or to deal with those conflicts by adversary procedures' (*ibid.*: 4).

Mansbridge avoids a fruitless juxtaposition of opposing models of democracy: 'unitary' and 'adversary' are two adjectives denoting different, but still democratic, decision-procedures. The difference between them is the nature of the interests at stake and their conflicting and/or communal structure. Neither is 'superior' to the other. On the contrary, in the view proposed, even the ideals typical of an adversary democracy acquire a strong normative character. Precisely because there may be a radical, irreconcilable diversity of interests and values, this view of the democratic ideal requires that equal respect and protection be accorded to all interests at stake, despite inequalities in social and economic resources.[15]

3. Beyond participatory democracy: two different paths

Albeit in different ways, both Barber and Mansbridge were faced with the legacy of 'participatory democracy' as it appeared in the 1960s and 1970s. In Barber's work, as we have seen, the answer was sought in a view with strong 'republican' and communitarian traits, which considered democracy as a shared 'way of life'; as self-government and self-realisation of human potential; as self-determination; and as the formation of civic attitudes and responsibilities. Jane Mansbridge outlined instead a theoretical framework that aimed to determine two different conceptions of democratic decision-making and their corresponding conditions and assumptions, both views being fully justified from the point of view of a democratic ideal. Both Mansbridge and Barber tackled many of the topics that would later be central to the emerging deliberative paradigm. However,

---

15. In the following years, Jane Mansbridge would return to these issues: see, for example, Mansbridge 2007: 253, where she maintains a 'neo-pluralist approach' to deliberative democracy. Such an approach, 'while wanting to rehabilitate deliberation, virtue, and the common good in the face of atomizing and aggregative strands in democratic practice and theory, also believes that aggregative procedures and the negotiation of conflicting interests produce democratically legitimate results'.

the opposed adjectives 'thin–strong' and 'unitary–adversary' – although certainly evocative – were not really taken up by the theoretical research that followed. One of the possible reasons (I can only hypothesise) is that the new deliberative paradigm would turn out to be able to put together and, at the same time, better distinguish these pieces of the puzzle.

Nevertheless, it is worth noting that Jane Mansbridge's work marks the end of the season of 'participatory democracy', a much sharper break than is found in Barber's almost contemporary work. This emerges, in particular, from the new importance given to the dimension of conflict and pluralism: Barber (but also other supporters of 'participatory democracy' before him) adopted a sort of 'organicist' democratic ideal. This view did take the inequalities of the present as a starting point but, deep down, it assumed that a full realisation of the democratic ideal could and should entail the overcoming of conflict arising from inequalities, in a co-operative and communitarian dimension. In Pateman, Macpherson and Barber we can sense a teleological tension that entrusts human self-rule – developed through participation – with the ability to gradually overcome the self-interest typical of a liberal society.

In Mansbridge's text, on the contrary, the pluralism of interests and values appears as an unavoidable feature of any political community; the conflict deriving from it requires a democratic dimension based on the respect and equal protection of such interests and values. Adopting (or not) a specific democratic procedure of decision-making mostly depends on the nature of the interests at stake: if they seem to be shared, then consensual procedures can be adopted and differences in power roles can be authorised; if they are irreducibly plural, then it's preferable to choose a procedure that ensures their equal consideration.

The comparison between Barber's and Mansbridge's positions also shows something more: the two authors outline two different theoretical (and political) strategies – two different ways to go 'beyond' the participatory democracy of the 1960s and 1970s. Barber's strategy mainly takes on the traits of *a political-cultural project*: it assumes or constructs an idea of what democracy should be and seeks the best way to realise it – at least approximately. Mansbridge's strategy, on the other hand, mainly aims to construct *a theoretical model of democracy*: that is, to elaborate interpretative categories that can account for what democracy actually *is* and *how it works*. Such a theoretical model is also able to explain the transformations of democracy and to infer normative implications about possible and desirable changes to democracy.

As I mentioned, at the end of the 1970s, participatory democracy as it was conceived in the 1960s and early 1970s seemed to disappear over the theoretical and political horizon. The term would come back in the late 1990s, with a different connotation and in a profoundly different political context. Some of the original terms would be used again but the debate would revolve around a new idea: 'deliberative democracy'. The alternative approaches exemplified by Barber and Mansbridge would also be revisited, both in the debate on how to understand deliberative democracy and in the discussions that defined the relationship between deliberative democracy and the legacy of participatory democracy.

PART II

THE BUILDING PROCESS OF THE
THEORETICAL FIELD OF DELIBERATIVE
DEMOCRACY

At the Origins of 'Deliberative Democracy': Interpretations of the American Constitution

In the 1980s, the theoretical model of 'participatory' democracy undoubtedly underwent a period of decline: Carole Pateman herself, as early as 1982, observed that 'for many people in the 1980s 'participation' and 'participatory democracy' are merely echoes of a time past' (Pateman 1982: xiii). At this point in the present project, a question arises: is there some connection between the decline of the idea of *participatory* democracy and the emergence and affirmation of the idea of *deliberative* democracy? In this chapter and the following ones I will try to construct a possible theoretical genealogy of the new deliberative model, its conceptual links and its lines of influence and intersection with other models. However, I can already say that the answer to the question is *no*. Deliberative democracy was born in the 1980s, with its own original foundations. It was not in any way a *direct* response to the crisis of participatory democracy. There is no *logical* and/or *chronological* succession between participatory democracy and deliberative democracy: these terms are related to different times and contexts that lead to paths of research that would overlap only later (and then only partially). In the 1980s, while authors like Barber and Mansbridge were faced with the theoretical legacy of participatory democracy, a whole new story began: that of deliberative democracy.

1. Joseph M. Bessette: the American Constitution as a blueprint of deliberative democracy

The term 'deliberative democracy' is generally believed to have been first used by Joseph M. Bessette, a scholar of American democracy and institutions. The expression appears in an essay he published in 1980 as part of a collection.[1] As we shall see in the next section, however, it cannot be said that this article was

---

1.   At present, Bessette teaches Government and Ethics at Claremont McKenna College, in Claremont, California. His essay ('Deliberative democracy: the majority principle in republican government') was published in a book edited by R. Goldwin and W. Shambra, *How Democratic is the Constitution?*, published by the American Enterprise Institute for Public Policy Research in Washington. Bessette later developed his position in 1994's *The Mild Voice of Reason: Deliberative democracy and American national government*. The first chapter expanded his 1980 essay, while the rest of the volume was devoted to a cogent demonstration of the presence of 'deliberation' in the American Congress and Senate as well as in their relations with the president. This view went against all the interpretations that saw those political relations as solely ruled by bargaining and log-rolling. For the purposes of the present 'critical genealogy', it is important to mention a passage from Bessette's Preface, where he credits Jane Mansbridge for believing in his

the only source of the expression: in fact, some essays by Cass R. Sunstein were probably more influential in its diffusion. The works of another constitutionalist and philosopher of law, Frank I. Michelman, also played an important role in that period. What's certain – and should be noted – is that the idea of deliberative democracy was essentially born from reflection on American political institutions and within American constitutionalist thought (especially as part of a very heated debate on the interpretation of the American Constitution and the view of democracy it embodies). In other words, the context of deliberative democracy was as far from the 1960s 'radical collectives' and small participatory democracies as it could be!

Bessette's essay was published in a collection revolving around the title question: *how democratic is the constitution*? The book contained the answers given by historians and constitutionalists of different political orientations. In the Preface, the editors (R. A. Goldwin and W. A. Schambra) outline the issues discussed by the various contributors. One of these topics was the work of Charles A. Beard,[2] one of the main American historians of the first half of the twentieth century. In 1913, at the peak of the Progressive Era, he wrote a book that radically contested the democratic nature of the American Constitution. According to Beard, in the words of the editors, the Constitution was 'designed to protect the wealthy by frustrating popular majorities' (1980: i), as an instrument for containing and reacting to the democratic pressure of the revolutionary phase. This position echoed the Anti-Federalists' polemic against Madison while actualising its implications: if these were the social and political origins of the US Constitution, the project of 'democratising' the American democracy, restoring a link between the original

---

work after Bassette's ten-year break from the academic world, during which he played various roles as a 'civil servant' (among other things, at the Department of Justice in Washington): 'during the break in my academic career, Jane Mansbridge came across my earlier work on deliberation and strongly encouraged me to move ahead with the book-length project. Had it not been for her encouragement then, it is doubtful that this work would now be at its present stage' (Bessette 1994: xv). A search of Google Books in English reveals that the phrase "deliberative democracy" had been used earlier, in passing, by a few other authors including Alexander Bickel in 1962 and Arnold Kaufman in 1968, but none of these made the concept at all central to their investigations, as Bessette did.

2. Charles A. Beard, *An Economic Interpretation of the Constitution of the United States* (1986 [1913]). This text was widely influential but also received much criticism: on the history of this debate, see Forrest McDonald's Introduction to the new 1986 edition of Beard's book. Hannah Arendt, for example (1963: 94–5), was very critical of Beard's work. On the relevance of Beard's work in the American historiographical and constitutionalist debate, also as a polemical target, see another text that I shall mention often in what follows: the essay 'Discovering the Constitution' by Bruce Ackerman, (1984; on Beard, see esp. pp. 1015–18). A significant recovery of the historical tradition of Progressivism which sees the Jacksonian era (roughly, two decades following the election of Andrew Jackson as President in 1828) – and not that of the Founding Fathers – as the true birth of American democracy, can be found in Robert H. Wiebe's *Self-Rule: A cultural history of American democracy* (1995). The classic liberal reading of the American constitutional tradition is Hartz's *The Liberal Tradition in America* (1955). A lively comparative analysis of Hartz's liberal vision, Pocock's republican view and Sunstein and Michelman's liberal-republican perspective was proposed by Ackerman (1989: 480–6).

democratic ideals and the institutions that embodied them, would gain strength and credibility.

Bessette critically engaged with an interpretation of the Founding Fathers' project that mainly highlighted its 'elitist' inspiration: in that reading, the Fathers were mainly preoccupied with constructing an institutional order that would limit the danger of 'tyrannical' popular majorities, neutralising the threat of an uncontrolled supremacy of the people's immediate passions and interests. Of course, Bessette didn't deny that the Framers' original design had such a purpose. What he claimed was that emphasising only this aspect was to forget another, equally important side of their position: there was 'the need to restrain popular majorities, but also to effectuate majorities' rule' (*ibid.*: 104). But how could this happen? This is where we see the novelty of Bessette's interpretation: 'it is the thesis of this essay that the key to the reconciliation of these apparently contradictory intentions lies in the Framers' broad purpose to establish a "deliberative democracy"' (*ibid.*).

Bessette argues for this thesis starting from some famous texts by Madison. The Framers surely believed that the inadequacy of direct democracy was due to a much deeper reason than its simple 'impracticability' in a big modern republic: history shows that 'democracies were continually subject to tumult, disorder, and confusion; that citizens often sacrificed their independent judgement to the pleasing promises of artful orators; and that rights of minorities (whether economic, religious, or ethnic) were regularly violated by tyrannical majorities' (*ibid.*).

Hence, a representative government was the most suitable choice for a large-scale democracy. However, as Madison famously wrote, a representative government is mainly able to

> ... refine and enlarge the public views by passing them through the medium of a chosen body of citizens, whose wisdom may best discern the true interest of their country and whose patriotism and love of justice will be least likely to sacrifice it to temporary or partial considerations. Under such a regulation it may well happen that the public voice, pronounced by the representatives of the people, will be more consonant to the public good than if pronounced by the people themselves, convened for the purpose (*Federalist* 10).

Madison's seminal text is Bessette's cue to introduce the new concept: 'this quote', he writes, 'contains the germ of the notion of "deliberative democracy"' (Bessette 1980: 105). Here, Madison does more than identify the need to filter citizens' immediate preferences, which are volatile and emotive – there is more than a 'negative' and 'protective' view of representative institutions in this text. On the contrary, Madison states that the formation of choices made through representatives turns out to be a *public voice* that better responds to the common good than a direct statement of the people 'convened for the purpose'. But how to reach this positive outcome? Is such foresight just due to the wisdom and public-spiritedness of that 'chosen body of citizens'? Bessette rereads Madison's text, claiming: 'the essential point is that through the operation of the representative principle' *public views* are 'refined' and 'widened' without being 'simply displaced by the personal views of the representatives' (*ibid.*). But then what can be the meaning of this *public voice*?

A first answer is that it is reasonable to expect representatives to produce better laws than the people. Certainly, this is because elected individuals have greater and better knowledge and experience compared to their constituents; but also because 'they operate in an environment that fosters collective reasoning about common concerns', while voters 'usually lack the time, inclination, or setting to engage in a similar enterprise' (*ibid.*). Nevertheless, this does not imply 'any failing' on the part of citizens. There is no aristocratic prejudice in play here but only a realistic observation: it is true that 'it is wholly unrealistic to expect people who spend most of their time earning a living to match the effort devoted by the legislator to public issues'; but this statement does not 'necessarily lead to undemocratic results, that is, to laws that violate the will of the majority'. Here, Bessette proposes a 'hypothetical test', that is, a *counterfactual reasoning*:

> ... if the citizens possessed the same knowledge and experience as their representatives and if they devoted the same amount of time to reasoning about the relevant information and arguments presented in the legislative body, would they reach fundamentally similar conclusions on public policy issues as their representatives? If the answer is yes, then we must conclude that the result is basically democratic, even though the outcome may differ substantially from the citizens' *original* inclinations or desires (*ibid.*: 105–6, my emphasis).

Those who are familiar with later theoretical literature on deliberative democracy will easily perceive here, in a nutshell, some forms of argument and assumptions that would have widespread appeal in the years to come. First, there is the idea that a decisional and deliberative democratic process should require the *transformation* of citizens' immediate and original preferences; second, the idea that the formation of the collective will should not derive from the *direct* registration of individual wills or the mere sum of their interests but from a process of rational, argumentative and informed public deliberation. Above all, however, we find here the idea that such a process can only take place within an appropriate setting, in which those levels and forms of public reasoning can allow the consideration of all relevant information and arguments. The notion of empirical experimentation (though limited and circumscribed) to identify the conditions under which the counterfactual hypothesis will be shown to stand on solid ground derives precisely from this theoretical core; all the *ad hoc* deliberative settings proposed by deliberative theorists over the following decade would proceed from this assumption.[3]

---

3. See, for example, Fishkin 1991: 81: 'A deliberative opinion poll models what the electorate would think if, hypothetically, it could be immersed in intensive deliberative processes. The point of a deliberative opinion poll is prescriptive, not predictive. It has a recommending force, telling us that this is what the entire mass public *would* think about some policy issues or some candidates if it could be given an opportunity for extensive reflection and access to information'. I shall go back to Fishkin and the theoretical assumptions of his view in Section 3 of Chapter Seven. It should be noted that only Sunstein makes explicit reference to Bessette's essay.

In his text, Bessette expressed a fundamental intuition: the public voice cannot be immediately observed but is something produced *discursively*; elected representatives elaborate it not by virtue of any exclusive capability they possess but because they are able to grasp what Madison, in one of his speeches before the US Senate, defined as 'the cool and deliberate sense of the community' and what thereby emerges as the 'majority sentiment' (*ibid.*: 106).

There are, thus, 'two types of public voice':

> the one is more immediate or spontaneous, uninformed, and unreflective; the other is more deliberative, taking longer to develop and resting on a fuller consideration of information and arguments. It is the second type that the Framers sought to promote; this is what they meant when they talked about the rule of the majority. In the service of this end, the rule of the *deliberative majority*, political leaders were obliged to resist, at least for a time, unreflective popular sentiments that were unwise or unjust (*ibid.*).

As Madison stated in another famous passage cited by Bessette, those who are called 'to be the guardians' of citizens' interests must know how, and be able, 'to withstand the temporary delusion[s]' of citizens, 'to give them time and opportunity for more cool and sedate reflection' (*ibid.*).

Yet, despite this distinction, an important puzzle remained to be solved: *how* can this deliberative majority be shaped? How is it possible to ensure the prevalence of informed and reasoned judgements? How can we guarantee that key government decisions do not reflect only the personal viewpoint of those elected but express the deliberative sense of the community? How to ensure that representatives share 'the basic values and goals of their constituents' and that 'their own deliberations about public policy' are 'firmly rooted in popular interests and inclinations'? (*ibid.*: 107) According to Bessette, the Framers gave an *institutional* answer: 'when the Framers rejected direct popular participation in the governing process, they put their faith instead in political institutions. It was their hope that these institutions would in effect actualize the deliberative sense of community'(*ibid.*).

The main mechanism that can ensure 'periodic accountability' is that of election, which takes different forms for the House, the Senate and the presidency. For Bessette, the internal logic of the American constitutional order seems to be characterised by the typical mechanism of 'advanced reactions' added by Carl J. Friedrich (1963) to Schumpeter's original model. However, in that case, candidates' actions (whether as incumbents or challengers) brought about not only a utilitarian logic but also a capacity to interpret 'popular sentiments' through a deliberative logic. There were surely specific historical reasons for this institutional order, with its 'different degrees of accountability' (Bessette 1980: 107) and, in particular, the need to control 'the pronounced popular character of the early state legislatures' (*ibid.*). Nevertheless, there was also a deeper reason: the idea that those electoral mechanisms 'could (and did) function as a vehicle for the expression of popular sentiments': 'the reason why they were chosen reveals an important aspect of the Framers' plan for deliberation' (*ibid.*: 108). It is by virtue of these mechanisms, indeed, that the elected could manifest 'sensitivity' to the voters' 'interests' and 'concerns'. If this sensitivity, responsiveness and opening 'continued while they served, the results of their deliberations would broadly approximate what the people themselves would have decided had they engaged in a similar reasoning process' (*ibid.*). Note here, once again, the 'counterfactual' form of reasoning that we have examined above.

Of course, there is no guarantee that the individuals elected will 'continue faithful to the deepest desires of their constituents'; however, imperfect as it may be, 'the electoral connection discourages substantial deviations'. Indeed, as Bessette noted with reference to the political present, Massachusetts voters would surely not have re-elected Senator Edward Kennedy if he had followed a conservative line during his term of office; and South Carolina voters would certainly have voted out their conservative Republican senator, Strom Thurmond, 'if he became a born-again liberal' (*ibid.*: 109).

Still, the Framers clearly understood that 'too much accountability' could be 'dangerous to sound deliberation': the reason why different time-cycles were adopted for the elections of the House, Senate and president – as well as the reasons for other mechanisms like the presidential veto – are rooted in the aim of making the entire institutional order 'more truly deliberative without sacrificing the popular connection' and preventing a situation in which 'legislative deliberations would turn almost exclusively on short-range considerations, forcing from view the long-term consequences of national action' (*ibid.*).

In the final part of his essay, Bessette set his position within the contemporary theoretical debate: on one hand, 'while the theory of deliberative democracy outlined here [stood] in sharpest contrast to "aristocratic" or "elitist" interpretations of the Constitution', it significantly detached itself also 'from other basically democratic interpretations' – interpretations that we can link to the pluralistic school and to the Schumpeterian legacy.

As for the former, Bessette recognised its tendency 'to depreciate the role of deliberation within the governing institutions by interpreting the Framers' design as one in which the pursuit of personal interest by citizens and leaders alike will almost automatically work to foster the larger public good'. Bessette objected that an effective public policy, instead, 'demands more than the pursuit of private ambition. It requires also leaders of knowledge and experience who work in a setting that fosters collective deliberation about "the permanent and aggregate interests of the community"' [*Federalist* 10]. The contemporary pluralist school, he said, completely overlooked this because of the predominant and semi-exclusive role it attributes to log-rolling and compromises between different interest-groups (*ibid.*: 112).

On the other hand, Bessette noted, there was a trend (which could be defined as 'Schumpeterian') 'to reduce the democratic principle to little more than the people's right to select their leaders'. Some political theorists,[4]

---

4. Bessette quoted not Schumpeter but an essay by Willmoore Kendall (Kendall 1971). Kendall (1909–68), was born in Oklahoma, studied at Oxford and participated in the Spanish Civil War as a Trotskyist. He rejected communism in 1940 and, from 1947, taught political philosophy at Yale, and then Dallas, from an increasingly conservative position.

Bessette added, 'accord great importance to deliberation by wise and virtuous representatives, but the connection between that deliberation and community wishes seems tenuous at best'. How is it possible for governmental decisions to reflect 'the deliberate sense of the community', if the function of election is only that of selecting virtuous men and not 'to argue and debate policy issues'? According to this view, a democratic and constitutional system should be based only on the capacity 'to make sound judgements regarding the virtues of their neighbours, not on the ability of the people to deliberate on matters of policy' (*ibid*.: 113).

We can conclude that Bessette seeks to re-read and reinterpret the arrangements of the American Constitution and its system of government in the light of a new paradigm: that of deliberation, classically understood as a reflective and pondered judgment based on the reasons for and against a given choice, as opposed to the immediacy of passions and selfish interests. The importance of this essay lies in two elements: first, the sharpness with which it interprets – in a deliberative light – the logic and mechanisms of political representation; second, the consequent opposition to both any *direct* and any *narrowly elitist* view of democracy. Representation is not the selection of a 'chosen body' of virtuous and wise people but rather the choice of politicians able to draw on a public and collective deliberation that expresses the 'sentiments' of the majority.

Obviously, the idea that a representative assembly operates, or should operate, in deliberative terms, was not new: what is more original in the text, in my view, is the intuition that a legislative body could express a 'public voice', a 'public view' emerging from citizens' public debates. Nevertheless, *how* this could happen remained largely unexplained, or better, was entrusted essentially to mechanisms of electoral accountability, which would hopefully express a sort of *common sentiment*. Thus, deliberation was seen as a pondered and reflective decision-making process, consisting of argumentative exchange and rational dialogue, detached from the immediacy of self-interest and passion: this is the characteristic feature of Bessette's position. However, his text also laid the groundwork for the notion of a public and diffused deliberation through which a deliberative majority, 'the deliberative sense of the community', could be achieved and expressed.

Democracy is not – as argued by the pluralist school – merely the log-rolling and bargaining of private interests; nor can it be reduced to a procedure that merely aims to select political leaders on the basis of their personal virtues and abilities. A representative government requires the capacity to express widespread ideas, values and generally held views and it is predicated on the possibility that public discussion happens in a reflexive and far-reaching way. In this reading of the American democratic-constitutional order proposed by Bessette, we can find some elements – originally and independently elaborated in the context of American constitutionalist culture – which were soon to be rearticulated and employed to develop a deliberative theory of democracy that comprises, but also transcends, the classical sources of political representation and parliamentary system.

2. Cass R. Sunstein: deliberative democracy and republicanism

One of the first texts containing an exhaustive definition of the ideal and model of 'deliberative democracy' is an essay by Joshua Cohen entitled 'Deliberation and democratic legitimacy' (Cohen 1989).[5] This work is generally considered one of the foundational texts of the new theory. In a footnote, Cohen remarks how he came across the term 'deliberative democracy' in an essay by the constitutionalist Cass R. Sunstein, called 'Interest groups in American public law' (Sunstein 1985). Also, Cohen notes that Sunstein quoted, in turn, 'an article of Bessette, which I have not consulted' (Cohen 2009a: 16, note 1). In another footnote (*ibid.*: 17, note 2), Cohen says that he was also inspired by the 'recent discussion of the role of the republican conception of self-government in shaping the American constitutional tradition and contemporary public law', referring to two other essays by Sunstein – 'Naked preferences and the constitution' (1984); 'Legal interference with private preferences' (1986) – and to an essay by Bruce Ackerman called 'Discovering the Constitution' (1984) and one by Frank I. Michelman, 'The Supreme Court, 1985 Term. Foreword: traces of self-government' (1986).

In the light of this, it seems helpful to reread these works and, in particular, Sunstein's essay, for the 'genealogical' value Cohen grants them. Also, Sunstein's work can be considered one of the most important examples of an approach to the 'deliberative democracy' that arose in the context of American constitutional and legal thought and would involve, in those years, other important authors.[6] Such an approach received little consideration in the view of deliberative democracy that prevailed after the theory, and the experiments inspired by it, became much better known; and yet I believe it is essential in order to understand the roots of this conception of democracy. Sunstein's position (as well as those of Michelman and Ackerman) deserves to be fully considered as constitutive of what today we understand by 'deliberative democracy'.[7]

---

5. This essay was first published in Hamlin and Pettit (eds) (1989): 17–34 and later republished in Cohen 2009a: 16–37.

6. Cass R. Sunstein (born in 1954) has taught at the Chicago University Law School from 1981 to 2002 and now teaches at the Harvard Law School. Barack Obama's consultant, from 2009 to 2012 Sunstein directed the Office of Information and Regulatory Affairs of the White House. As for his scientific production related to the issues of interest here, he wrote many essays in this period, some of which I'll consider later (Sunstein 1984, 1985, 1986, 1988a, 1988b, 1991, 1993a). His view of constitutionalism and deliberative democracy would later be summed up in the volumes *The Partial Constitution* (1993b) and *Designing Democracy: What constitutions do* (2001).

7. Apart from the above-mentioned essay, in the late 1980s, Michelman wrote a number of other essays (Michelman 1988a, 1988b, 1989a, 1989b, 1989c) proposing a 'republican' and 'deliberative' view of American democracy and its Constitution. Habermas later frequently referred to such a view in *Between Facts and Norms* (1996, chapter 6; *see* Chapter Eight, Section 3 in this volume). For the conception of deliberative democracy that Michelman developed in the 1990s, see Ferrara 1999: 133–50. Bruce Ackerman worked with James Fishkin (*see* Chapter Seven, Section 3.2). A closely 'disciplinary' definition is quite inadequate for this group of scholars. As Habermas noted (1996: 267), 'in the United States, constitutional scholars argue about the legitimacy of constitutional adjudication more from the standpoint of political science than from that of legal methodology'; one could add that a properly philosophical dimension is also very much present.

Much like Bessette, Sunstein focused on an interpretation of American constitutional design in open contrast to that offered by the pluralistic school, the ultimate expression of which – according to Sunstein – is Dahl's *A Preface to Democratic Theory* (1956) (Sunstein 1985: 30, note 6).[8] Sunstein's reading of the American Constitution and the idea of democracy embodied by it centres on the theme of interest-groups and the related issue of the role that 'naked' and private preferences play, or could play, in the context of democratic politics.

It is not necessary to analyse Sunstein's work in detail here – it is largely devoted to specific issues of the American tradition of public law (and judicial review in particular). Nevertheless, for the purposes of this book, it is useful to recall the programmatic intentions that Sunstein assigned to his work: 'at the normative level', the aim was to 'help to revive aspects of an attractive conception of governance – we may call it republican – to point out its often neglected but nonetheless prominent place in the thought of the Framers'. For Sunstein, 'the central commitments of the republican conceptions are far from anachronistic'; in fact, 'in its belief in a deliberative conception of democracy, it provides a basis for evaluating administrative and legislative action that has both powerful historical and considerable contemporary appeal' (Sunstein 1985: 30–1). In the footnotes, Sunstein recalled how 'the republican understanding is in the midst of a general revival in various disciplines', quoting, in the field of historiography, J. G. A. Pocock's famous work *The Machiavellian Moment* (1975) and, in the field of political theory, the contribution of Alastair MacIntyre in *After Virtue: A study in moral theory* (1981). However, he added that 'for present purposes it is unnecessary to distinguish the various kinds of republican thought, though the differences are important and considerable' (Sunstein 1985: 30, notes 7 and 8).[9]

---

8. This critique of the 'pluralistic' view also appears in an essay of the previous year (Sunstein 1984).

9. The revival of the republican tradition was born in the field of historiography and the turning point is represented by the work of Pocock (1975), who radically challenged the Lockean matrix of the Founding Fathers' political thought and proposed an alternative line: republicanism as a 'form of political Aristotelianism' that, from Machiavelli and through Harrington, would fuel the political culture of the American revolutionaries. Other interpretations of the republican tradition would soon emerge. In particular, Quentin Skinner proposed a different genealogy, emphasising the juridical and rhetorical culture of early civil humanism, linked to Roman sources and particularly the works of Cicero, long before Aristotle was rediscovered (Skinner 1978, 2002). For an analysis of the theoretical and methodological positions of Pocock and Skinner, see Bevir 2011a: 14–19. Within a few years, the 'republican' paradigm migrated to the field of political philosophy (in the 'communitarianism' of authors like Michael Sandel and Charles Taylor, who used it in their criticisms of Rawls' liberalism; for this debate see Taylor 1989; Mulhall and Swift 1996; Dagger 2004; Rasmussen 1990. It is also relevant to note how this affected constitutionalist thought. In 1988, the *Yale Law Journal* 97(8) published a wide-ranging Symposium on the Republican Civic Tradition, opened by the essays by Michelman (1988a) and Sunstein (1988a). On Sunstein and Michelman's 'liberal republicanism' and their differences, see Ferrara 2008: 103–6. Later, other versions of republicanism would emerge, especially the 'neo-Roman' version proposed by Pettit (1997), centred on the concept of freedom as 'non-domination' or 'absence of dependence' (see Skinner 1998, 2002), while the former versions were centred on 'civic virtue' and political participation as self-government. For an overview of the latest developments of the 'republican revival', see Laborde 2013. On the republican tradition and its legacy, see Castiglione

The polemical target of the discussion was very clear, as was its political and theoretical relevance: it was the issue of *factions*, recurrent in American politics, and of the different ways of interpreting the solution proposed by Madison – who had made it 'the centerpiece of his defence of the proposed Constitution'. But, above all, this topicality was due to the contemporary translation that could be given to the latter in terms of 'interest-groups'. 'The bicentenary of the Constitution', writes Sunstein at the beginning of his essay (*ibid.*: 29),

> ... is approaching in a time of considerable dissatisfaction with the American scheme of governance. The dissatisfaction takes various forms, but many of the concerns have a common root in the problems produced by the existence of interest groups, or 'factions', and their influence over the political process. The scheme is challenged on the grounds that it allows powerful private organizations to block necessary government action;[10] that the lawmaking process has been transformed into a series of accommodations among competing elites; and that the rise of a large bureaucracy exercising broad discretionary power has undermined original constitutional goals by circumventing the safeguards of separation of power and electoral accountability.

In order to outline his 'republican' and 'deliberative' vision, Sunstein compared the 'two different conceptions of politics' that competed in the constitutive period of American democracy. The republican conception was animated by the principle of 'civic virtue' (*ibid.*: 31).

> [T]o the republicans, the prerequisite of sound government was the willingness of citizens to subordinate their private interests to the general good. Politics consisted of self-rule by the people; but it was not a scheme in which people impressed their private preferences on the government. It was instead a system in which the selection of preferences was the object of the governmental process. Preferences were not to be taken as exogenous, but to be developed and shaped through politics. To the republicans, the role of politics was above all deliberative. Dialogue and discussion among the citizenry were critical features in the governmental process. Political participation was not limited to voting or other simple statements of preference. The ideal model for governance was the town meeting, a metaphor that played an explicit role in the republican understanding of politics.[11]

2005 and Geuna 1998. The republican criticism of democracy, especially in reference to Pettit's theses, is analysed by Urbinati (2012).

10. Here, Sunstein cites Theodore Lowi and his fundamental *The End of Liberalism* (1979 [1969]), which was very important for American political science in those years.

11. In a previous work (Sunstein 1984: 1691), the author added: 'Civil republicanism embodies a conception of politics in which preferences are not viewed as private and exogenous. Their selection is the object of the governmental process. The model for this conception of government is the town meeting, where decisions are made during a process of collective self-determination'. As for the original model of the town meeting in New England, Sunstein recalled a classic text by Alexander Meiklejohn on the principles of the First Amendment and freedom of speech (Meiklejohn 1948).

Therefore politics has as its intrinsic function *transforming preferences*. It can be seen as co-operative research aimed at defining the *public good* (*ibid.*: 31–2).

[T]he republican conception carries with it a particular view of human nature; it assumes that through discussion people can, in their capacities as citizens, escape private interests and engage in pursuit of the public good. In this respect, political ordering is distinct from market ordering. Moreover, this conception reflects a belief that debate and discussion help to reveal that some values are superior to others. Denying that decisions about values are merely matters of taste, the republican view assumes that 'practical reason' can be used to settle social issues.

This view was set against the *pluralist* conception as expressed in the works of Dahl or Truman (1951). For the pluralist view, (Sunstein 1985: 32),

... politics mediates the struggle among self-interested groups for scarce social resources. Only nominally deliberative, politics is a process of conflict and compromise among social interests. Under the pluralist conception, people come to the political process with preselected interests that they seek to promote through political conflict and compromise. Preferences are not shaped through governance, but enter into the process as exogenous variables.

Also, quoting Schumpeter, Sunstein argued that pluralist theory considers instead 'the republican notion of a separate common good as incoherent, potentially totalitarian, or both'. The common good consists only of an 'aggregation of individual preferences'; indeed, 'the efforts to alter or shape preferences – through, for example, the education so highly prized in the republican tradition – may assume the status of tyranny' (*ibid.*: 32–3).

On this basis, Sunstein initially addressed feasible solutions to the problem of 'factions' and then thoroughly reconstructed the debates between Federalists and Anti-Federalists that characterised the constitutive phase of American constitution-making, focused on these diverse conceptions of politics and democracy. Sunstein's account of these debates is strongly anchored to the profound reasons that guided the Federalist vision and also features some rather polemical annotations.[12]

On the one hand, the Anti-Federalists were guided by a 'classical' republican view: as is well known, their hostility towards a national, strong and distant government was based on the conviction that only in a local and decentralised context could civic virtues be practised and citizens fully exercise the *self-rule* that is at the core of a republican conception of democracy. Only within this *communitarian* dimension is direct participation in government possible; only by this means can people develop education and public morality as the sole antidote to the poison of corruption and contending factions. Individuals may raise

---

12. 'In recent years, there has been a resurgence of enthusiasm for the arguments of the Anti-Federalists – opponents of the proposed Constitution who claimed that the document amounted to a betrayal of the principles underlying the Revolution' (Sunstein 1985: 35).

themselves from a selfish and narrow-minded vision of private interests only by directly experiencing the responsibilities of self-rule, without being overshadowed by a distant, invasive and threatening power.

On the other hand, Sunstein noted, the Madisonian view – especially that highlighted in the famous *Federalist* 10 – 'is sometimes thought to be a conventional pluralist document, and there are indeed traces of pluralism in the analysis' it proposed: more precisely, it is true that, for Madison, 'the primary problem of governance was the control of faction' (*ibid.*: 39). However, Madison's position cannot be *reduced* to this claim: rather, the crucial point was his conception of political representation and *deliberative democracy*, on the basis of which citizens' immediate interests, naked preferences and burning passions are not taken as given *as such* by the governmental process but are subjected to a process of examination and transformation and shaped by and through public debate and discussion.

In Madison's well known view, only a large republic is capable of limiting and neutralising the power of factions – an unavoidable evil, rooted in human nature, which can only be countered by appropriate institutional arrangements – and certainly not by merely relying on the virtues of civic education and participation. The means that could guarantee a far-sighted view of the common good, detached from the unreflective preferences of citizens and from their uncontrolled passions, are the mechanisms of representation and accountability.

So, according to Sunstein, the Federalists' conception 'reformulated the principles of republicanism in an attempt to synthesize elements of traditional republicanism and its emerging pluralist competition' (*ibid.*: 38–9). That is to say, it was an attempt to translate the classical ideal of civic self-rule into the conditions of a large-scale, modern democracy, marked by an irreducible pluralism of interests and values. The tasks of ensuring the democratic principle of self-rule and, at the same time, escaping the tyranny of the majority and the abuse of factions, are only achievable if the view of representative government adopted is characterised by a deliberative conception of democracy. In such a view, 'deliberation' is not only produced by wise and prudent people within legislative bodies but also in society, by citizens debating in order to shape a 'public view' of the common good and express a 'public voice'.

As Sunstein himself noted, the account he proposed of the two opposing conceptions did not claim to be original: what was original, rather, was his attempt to transpose these two models into the terms of contemporary theoretical debate and then to compare the original design to what actually happened in American political and constitutional history. 'It should hardly be controversial', Sunstein argued, 'to suggest that Madison's understanding of the role of the representatives has been only imperfectly realized. Few would contend that nationally selected representatives have been able to exercise the role Madison anticipated' (*ibid.*: 48). And there is no doubt, Sunstein added, that there is 'mounting evidence that the pluralist understanding captures a significant component of the legislative process and that, at the descriptive level, it is far superior to its competitors' (*ibid.*). Take, for example, the analyses that underscore the exclusive re-election-seeking logic of many members of Congress, or the relevance of interest-group 'pressures' to the legislative process.

Nevertheless, Sunstein did not adapt to the vision proposed by pluralistic theory in the name of descriptive realism: he did not accept its translation to the normative level but rather contested such a univocal view of the political processes characterising the American institutional order. Instead, according to Sunstein, what emerges is a sort of *continuum*: on the one hand, there are cases where interest-group pressures are predominant and the outcomes of decision-making processes are to be considered covenants or agreements among competing interests; on the other, there are cases 'where legislators engage in deliberation in which interest-group pressures, conventionally defined, pay little or no democratic role'. Democratic politics acts precisely between these two poles: 'at various points along this continuum a great range of legislative decisions exist where the outcomes are dependent on an amalgam of pressure, deliberation, and other factors' (*ibid.*: 48–9).

Thus, there is a constant tension between the normative and empirical spheres but there is no juxtaposition of a disillusioned acceptance of reality on the one hand, and a sterile proposition of ideals on the other. The tension between the deliberative dimension and the dimension of the interplay of competing interests – the tension, we might also say, between communicative and strategic rationality – is intrinsic to every actual decision-making process; we should evaluate case by case which factors are dominant and how they combine.[13]

Sunstein's essay, therefore, contains some of the theoretical building blocks of the new deliberative paradigm, that is, some aspects of the conceptual framework that would later be the focus of more fully articulated accounts of deliberative democracy. First, there is the definition of the democratic political process as a *preference-shaping process* through dialogue and discussion; then, the refusal to consider preferences as *mere data*, as something *exogenous* that needs only to be aggregated. Furthermore, there is the view of the 'common good' as something that does not derive from the aggregation of private preferences but from the collective capacity of deliberation and the search for shared solutions through public discussions.

In the Republican view – as Sunstein wrote in 'Beyond the republican revival', one of his most quoted essays of the time (1988a) – deliberation does not require

> … some standard entirely external to private beliefs and values (as if such a thing could be imagined). The republican position is, instead, that existing desires should be revisable in light of collective discussion and debate, bringing to bear alternative perspectives and additional information'(1988a: 1549).

---

13. I believe it is no coincidence that these passages of Sunstein's would be quoted and discussed by Habermas: *see* Chapter Nine, Section 5. Sunstein also extensively quotes Habermas (up to the very recent, back then, *Theory of Communicative Action*), especially in his essay on 'naked preferences'. There is a need, Sunstein wrote (1984: 1731), to create 'mechanisms to guarantee that the values to be served by legislation are genuinely public, in the sense that they are selected through processes designed to ensure that government decisions are the product not of pre-existing private interests but of broad and open-ended public deliberation'.

Elsewhere he wrote (1993a: 204–5): 'One goal of a democracy, in short, is to ensure autonomy not merely in the satisfaction of preferences, but also, and fundamentally, in the process of formation of preferences'; he also quoted Dewey's *Freedom in the Modern World* (1936): 'choice signifies a capacity for deliberately changing preferences.'

The questions Sunstein posed at the end of his 1985 essay triggered a huge debate:

> ... was Madison correct in his rejection of pluralist approaches to politics in favour of an understanding that relies on the existence of a common good distinct from the aggregation of private interests? Would it be more desirable to perfect the processes of pluralism than to adopt a deliberative model of politics? (1985: 81).

The answers given would be elaborated by the new deliberative paradigm in the years to follow (*ibid.*: 81–2):

> A pluralist approach to politics views private preferences as exogenous variables and will not subject them to critical scrutiny and review. Under a pure version of the pluralist understanding, the representative responds mechanically to constituent pressures. Those pressures are in turn a product of the existing distribution of wealth, the existing set of entitlements, and the existing structure of preferences. But all three may be objectionable to some degree or another; the task of political actors, either representatives or citizens, is to reflect critically on them, not necessarily to accept them.

It is in 'the process of deliberation and debate' that 'objectionable or distorted preferences might be revealed as such'. At this point, Sunstein quotes Jon Elster (a scholar who, as we will see, would soon afterwards make a decisive contribution to outlining the theoretical field of deliberative democracy), drawing on the latter's newly published work, *Sour Grapes* (Elster 1983) and, in particular, on the concept of 'adaptive preference':

> ... the preferences adapt to the available options; they are not autonomous. In these circumstances, politics properly has, as one of its central functions, the selection, the evaluation, and shaping of preferences, not simply their implementation. For this reason, the Madisonian ideal is likely to result in better laws than an approach that takes for granted the existing distribution of wealth, power, and entitlements as well as the existing set of preferences. There is, in short, something a like a 'common good' or 'public interest' that may be distinct from the aggregation of private preferences or utilities (Sunstein 1985: 82).[14]

---

14. Sunstein devoted much of a later essay (1986: 1146–58) to Elster's notion of 'adaptive preferences' and its delicate political and juridical implications (the potential to legally 'interfere' in 'private' preferences, while respecting – or indeed, strengthening – the individual's actual autonomy).

In short, the nature of politics is defined as '*transformative or deliberative*' (*ibid.*: 83): this view, while being aware of the actual tendencies that point in another direction, does not give up its own ideals and normative dimensions, rooted in the potential of the constitutional design imagined by Madison and the Founding Fathers. Thus, Sunstein concluded, it can certainly be said

... that the Madisonian conception of politics, and especially its republican roots, have themselves become anachronistic. The notion that representatives might engage in the deliberative task of which the *Federalist* spoke seems increasingly romantic, with the declining belief in civic virtue and with the mounting authority of powerful private groups over the processes of government. But as the bicentenary of the Constitution approaches, it is especially important to appreciate the grounds on which Madison and his peers stopped short of pluralist approaches, and sought a system in which private preferences are subjected to critical evaluation (*ibid.*).

Chapter Four

Jon Elster: 'Non-Orthodox' Versions of Rationality and Models of Political Theory

As I have already noted, in his essay 'Deliberation and democratic legitimacy' (1989), Joshua Cohen referred to the texts and authors that suggested to him the 'idea' of deliberative democracy. In the same footnote (2009a: 21, note 20), Cohen also described the theoretical framework of his work and, above all, acknowledged his debt to his teacher, John Rawls. He also signalled a convergence with other authors: since writing the first draft of that essay, recalls Cohen, he had read Jon Elster's essay 'The market and the forum: three varieties of political theory' (Elster 1986) and Bernard Manin's article 'On legitimacy and political deliberation' (Manin 1987), 'which both present', Cohen underscored, 'parallel conceptions' to his own; he noted, crucially, that 'the overlap is explained by the fact that Elster, Manin and I all draw on Jürgen Habermas'.[1]

Cohen's statement gives us an important track to follow: what's being outlined is a constellation of ideas and theoretical approaches that start *positively* marking the boundaries of deliberative democracy as a theoretical field. Bessette's and Sunstein's works, as we have seen, bring out the 'critical frontiers' against which the new deliberative model began to take shape; however, it would soon gather and be influenced by other positions coming from very diverse theoretical traditions. In this chapter and the two following ones, I will dwell on this crucial moment, reconstructing the contributions of three authors: John Elster, Bernard Manin and Joshua Cohen. The analysis of their work will also lead to a particularly complex topic, namely, that of the encounter between the theoretical work-in-progress of deliberative democracy on the one hand and two great figures of political philosophy in the second half of the twentieth century, Habermas and Rawls, on the other.

1. The forum and the market

As I have already highlighted in Chapter Three, in his 1985 essay, Sunstein quoted John Elster – in particular, the recently published book *Sour Grapes* (Elster 1983). This is an important clue: Elster is one of the authors whose work contains some

---

1. Cohen quotes *Theorie des kommunikativen Handelns*, translated into English in 1984 and 1987 by Thomas McCarthy as *Theory of Communicative Action*. The other works by Habermas cited by Cohen are *Legitimation Crisis* (1975), the translation of *Legitimationprobleme im Spätkapitalismus* (1973) and *Communication and the Evolution of Society* (1979), the translation of two essays drawn from *Zur Rekonstruktion des Historischen Materialismus* and of the essay 'Was heisst Sprachpragmatik?', in K. O. Apel (ed.) *Sprach-pragmatik und Philosophie* (1976). I took this information from Luca Corchia's most valuable *Jürgen Habermas: A bibliography – works and studies (1952–2010)* (2012).

crucial intersections of the present genealogic reconstruction. In fact, it is through Elster that social-choice theory – or better, *criticism* of the current and prevailing version of that theory – enters the arena of theoretical reflection on deliberative democracy.

In those years, Elster had begun his studies on what, in the subtitle of his book *Sour Grapes* (Elster 1983), he'd call 'the subversion' of the orthodox canons of rationality; he did not reject the standard model of rational utilitarianism but did limit and circumscribe it, as well as enriching and making more complex the possible models of rational behaviour. Elster's line of research had already produced the publication in 1979 of *Ulysses and the Sirens*: that work, as you can read in the Preface to *Sour Grapes* (*ibid.*: vi), recalled that 'men sometimes are free to choose their own constraints'. *Sour Grapes*, instead, revolved around the idea that 'the preferences underlying a choice may be shaped by constraints'. And, 'considered together', added Elster, 'these non-standard phenomena are sufficiently important to suggest that the orthodox theory is due for fundamental revision' (*ibid.*).

We can begin this analysis with the very pages that Sunstein quoted in support of his thesis. Here Elster claims that (*ibid.*: 35)

> ... the central concern of politics should be the *transformation of preferences* [my emphasis], rather than their aggregation. On this view, the core of the political process is the public and rational discussion about the common good, not the isolated act of voting according to private preferences. The goal of politics should be unanimous and rational consensus, not an optimal compromise between irreducibly opposed interests. The forum is not to be contaminated by the principles that regulate the market, nor should communication be confused with bargaining.

It is important to highlight that the pages of *Sour Grapes* quoted by Sunstein are the same that Elster would later transpose to his 1986 essay 'The market and the forum: three varieties of political theory'. This essay was first published in a collection edited by Elster himself and Aanund Hylland called *The Foundations of Social Choice Theory* (1986)[2] and later appeared in the first important anthology

---

2. The book also included contributions by Brian Barry, Donald Davidson, Allan Gibbard, Robert Goodin, John Roemer and a conclusion by Amartya Sen. In Elster and Hylland's Preface, it was noted that, in contemporary social science and especially in social-choice theory, 'from a means, formal modelling is becoming an end in itself' and 'formalism is gaining the upper hand'. For this reason, said the editors, the time had come to bring the discussion back to the 'foundational issues' of the theory (Elster and Hylland 1986: 2). Among the essays in this collection, Goodin's 'Laundering preferences' deserves to be mentioned. In this essay, the preferences to be 'laundered' are those so 'dirty' and 'nasty' that 'there must be something terribly wrong with any principle that requires us to respect' them (Goodin 1986: 77). Goodin proposed to overcome 'an impoverished conception of individual preferences', by aiming to go beyond the so-called 'utility information' of the canonical social-choice models, and to fully consider the 'non-utility information': information 'about why individuals want what they want, about the other things they also want, about the interconnections between and implications of their various desires, etc.'(*ibid.*: 76–7). In later years, Goodin would contribute to the debate around deliberative democracy, with his *Reflective Democracy* (2003) and with the essays collected in *Innovating Democracy: Democratic theory and practice after the deliberative turn* (2008).

on deliberative democracy (Bohman and Rehg (eds) 1997). Thanks to the latter, Elster's essay gained a great deal of notice, emerging as one of the texts regarded as 'foundational' of the new theoretical paradigm.[3]

Elster's open intent was to compare 'three views of politics generally, and of the democratic system more specifically'. On the one side, there was 'the economic theory of democracy', 'most outrageously stated by Schumpeter, but in essence also underlying social choice theory' (Elster 1997: 25). This theory is founded on the idea that 'the political process is *instrumental*, rather than an end in itself' and that 'the decisive political act is a private rather than a public action, *viz.* the individual and secret vote', so that 'the goal of politics is the optimal compromise between given, and irreducibly opposed, private interests' (Elster 1997: 3).

The other two views of politics, adds Elster, are on the opposite side and both arise when 'first, the private character of political behavior' and then also 'the instrumental nature of politics' are denied. However, these two models are profoundly different. For the former, Elster refers to Habermas's theory; for the latter, he recalls 'the theorists of participatory democracy, from John Stuart Mill to Carole Pateman' (*ibid.*: 3). The first model claims that 'the goal of politics should be rational agreement rather than compromise, and the decisive political act is that of engaging in public debate with a view to the emergence of a consensus'. As for 'participatory democracy', instead, 'the goal of politics is the transformation and education of the participants': 'politics, on this view, is an end in itself – indeed, many have argued that it represents the good life for man' (*ibid.*).

I believe it is essential to note two things. First, as we'll see, Elster's reference to Habermas appears rather cursory and would be a source of future misunderstanding. Second, there is a fact that, for the purposes of the theoretical genealogy I am reconstructing, seems particularly significant: in what will come to be considered as one of the 'seminal' texts of the deliberative paradigm, Elster takes an openly polemical position with regards to the view of politics proposed by theorists of participatory democracy.

When outlining these three views, Elster describes as 'central to [his] analysis' the distinction between '*politics as the aggregation of given preferences and politics as the transformation of preferences through rational discussion*' (*ibid.*: 4, my emphasis). In the first part of his essay, Elster tackles the assumption of the *given* character of preferences, analysing 'two sets of objections' to the approach of the political model inspired by social-choice theory (*ibid.*: 5–11).[4] When

---

3.   The quotations by Elster come from the version of his essay in Bohman and Rehg (eds) 1997. In this 1986 text, Elster quotes many passages from *Sour Grapes*, word for word, resetting them in a different context, within a more direct treatment of the possible models of political theory. In particular, pp. 5–19 and 19–25 of the Bohman and Rehg edition correspond, with some cuts and slight modifications, to pp. 33–42 and 91–100 respectively of *Sour Grapes*. On Elster's essay and its influence in the constituting phase of deliberative theory, see Bouvier 2007: 8–10 and Girard and Le Goff 2010: 22–3.

4.   It should be noted that Amartya Sen, in his final comments, (Sen 1986: 232–7), was quite critical of Elster's essay. In particular, in addition to reproaching him for a rather rough and impoverished view of the complex field of social-choice theory Sen objected particularly to the interpretation of the *given* character of preferences that Elster attributed to the theoretical models of social choice.

summing up his argument, Elster says that he will claim: 'first, that preferences people choose to express may not be a good guide to what they really prefer; and secondly, that what they really prefer may in any case be a fragile foundation for social choice' (*ibid.*: 6). From the first point of view, preferences are never *given* 'in the sense of being directly observable. If they are to serve as inputs to the social choice process, they must somehow be *expressed* by the individuals'; but it is far from obvious that an action expressing those preferences 'as they are' should be rational (*ibid.*: 6). From the latter point of view, there are two notable phenomena: that of *adaptive preferences* (described by the fable of the fox and the grapes) and that of *counter-adaptive preferences* ('the grass is always greener on the other side of the fence', 'the forbidden fruit is always sweeter'). Such phenomena, remarks Elster, are 'baffling' for a social-choice theorist (*ibid.*: 8).

Finally, Elster expresses the fundamental objection that can be made 'to the political view underlying social choice theory' (and to the 'economic' theories of democracy): such a view implies 'a confusion between the kind of behaviour that is appropriate in the marketplace and that which is appropriate in the forum' (*ibid.*: 10–11):

> The notion of the sovereignty of the consumer is acceptable because, and to the extent that, the consumer chooses between courses of action that differ only in the way they affect him or her. In political-choice situations, however, the citizen is asked to express preferences over states that also differ in the way in which they affect other people. ... A social choice mechanism is capable of resolving the market failures that would result from unbridled consumer sovereignty; but as a way of redistributing welfare it is hopelessly inadequate. ... [The] task of politics is not only to eliminate inefficiency, but also to create justice – a goal to which the aggregation of pre-political preferences is a quite incongruous means. ... This suggests that the principles of the forum must differ from those of the market. A long-standing tradition from the Greek polis onwards suggests that politics must be an open and public activity, as distinct from the isolated and private expression of preferences that occurs in buying and selling.

Faced with the possible reply of a social theorist for whom the only true alternative to the mechanisms of aggregation of preferences is *censorship* or a *paternalistic* attitude, Elster appeals to another viewpoint: that of 'a *transformation*

For Sen, the problems in Elster's essay arise 'from a misinterpretation of the contents of what he calls "given preferences". While it is true that social-welfare functions map "given" individual preferences to social choice, this only pinpoints a *functional relation* that holds between individual preferences and social choice. It does not, of course, require that preferences be "given" *over time*. If education or dialogue, or the political process, changes individual preferences, then the input into the social-choice mechanism must be seen as changing with the process in question'(*ibid.*: 235). This theme would be very much present in the rich critical discussion that would develop in the following years between deliberative democracy and social-choice theory, which eventually also included attempts at 'reconciliation' (see, e.g. Dryzek and List 2003). Among the contributors to this debate, see Miller 1992; Christiano 1993; Johnson 1993; Knight and Johnson 1994; van Mill 1996; Hardin 1993 and 2002; Heath 2001.

of preferences through public and rational discussion' (*ibid.*: 11). Elster notes that such an idea was then 'especially associated' with Habermas, to his 'discourse ethics' and his notion of an 'ideal speech situation'; but how does Elster justify this judgment? As the definition of 'ideal speech situation' is extremely relevant to the future development of deliberative democracy, I will now proceed to an analytical reconstruction of Elster's reading of it and to a comparison with Habermas's texts (the ones available *at that time*) to which Elster himself referred.

2. The 'ideal speech situation': a pragmatic presupposition of communicative action or a political ideal?

Elster is rather cautious about his presentation of Habermas: 'I shall present a somewhat stylized version of his views, although I hope they bear some resemblance to the original' (Elster 1997: 11). Indeed, it is safe to say that his exposition is not only quite schematic but also marked by serious misunderstandings that later affected the reception of Habermas's thought in the field of deliberative democracy. For Elster, the core of Habermas's view is that

> ... rather than aggregating or filtering preferences, the political system should be set up with a view to changing them by public debate and confrontation. The input to the social choice mechanism would then not be the raw, quite possibly selfish or irrational, preferences that operate in the market, but informed and other-regarding preferences. Or rather, there would not be any need for an aggregating mechanism, since a rational discussion would tend to produce unanimous preferences. When the private and idiosyncratic wants have been shaped and purged in public discussion about the public good, uniquely determined rational desires would emerge. Not optimal compromise, but unanimous agreement is the goal of politics in this view (*ibid.*: 11–12).

Elster wrote this in 1986 and it would be unfair to assess his interpretation of Habermas while relying on the comprehensive knowledge of Habermas's work we have *today*. However, it is important to look at the peculiar influence that this specific reading of Habermas had on the construction of the theoretical field of deliberative democracy.

From this point of view, it is worth noting that Elster actually only refers to one work by Habermas (*ibid.*: 11, note 21): a 1982 *mimeographed* text, *Diskursethik – notizen zu einem Begründingsprogram*, which later became (we don't know exactly how) the third chapter of Habermas's 1983 *Moralbewußtsein und kommunikatives Handels.*[5] Elster especially referred to this text in order to evoke 'the ideal speech situation' and draw from it the idea or model of a politics

---

5. This chapter was translated as 'Discourse ethics: notes on a program of philosophical justification' and published in English in 1990 (in *Moral Consciousness and Communicative Action*). The importance of the *mimeographic* diffusion of this chapter to the American debate is signalled in Bouvier 2007: 7.

able to produce 'unanimous preferences' or bring out 'uniquely determined rational desires' through rational discussion (*ibid.*: 12).

In so doing, however, Elster improperly transposed Habermas's notion of the 'ideal speech situation' into a 'model of political theory'. In fact, Habermas gave the 'ideal speech situation' a very different status and meaning, addressing it at a level of formal abstraction that made it ill suited to an *immediate* reading like Elster's. If we stick to those years and to Habermas's works of that period, Elster's 'stylized' version of his thought actually amounted to a drastic simplification, if not an outright distortion. It is surprising that Elster didn't take into account other texts – by Habermas himself or by scholars debating his thought – that were available at the time. For instance, there was an important and well known collection of essays (Thompson and Held 1982, which also included Habermas's 'Reply to my critics') offering an exhaustive critical overview of the theoretical path of the German philosopher; this book could surely have suggested greater interpretative caution. Because of the key role it would have in the future development of deliberative democracy, it is necessary to anlyse the idea of 'ideal speech situation'. Far from being readable as a *political-theoretical* category, this notion can be correctly understood only in the light of Habermas's research of those years: that is, the foundation of a 'universal pragmatics' as a 'reconstructive science' in the framework of what others would call the 'linguistic turn'.[6]

According to Habermas, the very *condition of possibility* of a communicative practice is that a subject (one who speaks, acts and acts through language) presupposes that his or her statements can claim some validity and that the latter will be inter-subjectively recognised. If an agent did not presume (at least intuitively or implicitly) that there could be an 'understanding' with the *other*, the conditions for a communicative interaction would not be met. The *consensus* Habermas talks about in his strategy of theoretical foundation is the one emerging from the co-operative search for a terrain of communicative understanding, even on the terms by which to define an agreement or a disagreement on something in the world, or a norm of shared social life involving interpersonal relations. Thus, *consensus* is the positive answer to the validity-claims of a speech act through which people construct a common definition of the situation and *co-ordinate* their actions. These validity-claims can always be contested, criticised and reviewed and, as they need intersubjective recognition, understanding may very well fail. The ideal speech situation is not a regulative principle in the Kantian sense but the *factual and counterfactual presupposition* of every communicative action: a 'social facticity' (Habermas 1982: 235) or an *anticipation* inherent in everyday communicative practice.

---

6. In the volume edited by Thompson and Held, the issue was addressed by John B. Thompson (1982: 116–133). For an introduction to Habermas's research in this phase, see Outhwaite 1994: 38–57 and Brunkhorst 2006: 24–45. One of the first texts in which Habermas states his aim to work on a 'universal pragmatics' was in the Introduction to the second edition of *Theorie und Praxis* (1971[first German edition 1963], translated as 'Introduction: some difficulties in the attempt to link theory and praxis' (Habermas 1973).

Habermas's most important early theoretical production, in which he defined the notion of the ideal speech situation, dates from 1973 (*Auszug aus 'Wahrheitstheorien'*).[7] In the chapter quoted by Elster, Habermas refers to this text, albeit explicitly underlining the 'elaboration, revision, and clarification that my earlier analysis requires' (Habermas, 1990: 88). In fact, you could say that Habermas rather struggled to define this notion, which, over the years, lost the relevance it had in the early 1970s. References to it became scarcer and the notion itself was reformulated, losing its early idealising traits.[8]

Wahrheitstheorien presents the most complete definition of the 'ideal speech situation' in this first phase of Habermas's thought: here it is presented as an 'inevitable presupposition' that agents are bound to make when they engage in communicative interaction:

> *If it is true* that we can ultimately distinguish rational consensus, achieved in a way that is argumentative and at the same time guarantees truth, from simply forced or misleading consensus, only by reference to an ideal speech situation; *if it is also true* that we can start from the fact that we always trust – and have to trust – that we are able to distinguish rational consensus from a misleading one, because otherwise we would sacrifice the rational character of speaking; *finally, if nevertheless*, one cannot uniquely determine in every empirical case whether there is an ideal speech situation or not, *then there is only the following explanation: the ideal speech situation is neither an empirical phenomenon nor a mere construction, but an inevitable presupposition reciprocally put forward in discourse.* This presupposition can (but doesn't necessarily have to) be counterfactual; but even if it becomes counterfactual, it is an operatively effective fiction in the communicative process. Therefore I would rather speak of anticipation of an ideal speech situation. Only this anticipation is a guarantee that we can connect the claim of rational consensus to actually achieved consensus; at the same time, it is a critical measure by which one can question any actually achieved consensus, and see if it is an adequate

---

7. This text by Habermas was never translated into English. The original German text was reprinted in Habermas 2009. An earlier and rather sketchy formulation of the ideal speech situation in English could be found in a 1970 essay ('Towards a theory of communicative competence: Patterns of communicative behaviour'), in which Habermas critically analyses Chomsky's approach and remarks his own affinity to J. L. Austin's *How To Do Things With Words* (Austin 1962) and especially John Searle, who had published *Speech Acts* in 1969. The issue was then taken up and amplified in a 1971 essay ('Vorbereitende Bemerkungen zu einer Theorie der kommunikativen Kompetenz' ['Introductory remarks for a theory of communicative competence'] that appeared in a book co-written with Niklas Luhmann, which was never translated into English either (Habermas 1971b).

8. Alessandro Ferrara (1987: 45) noted that the issue of how to understand the ideal speech situation had always been 'a considerable source of concern for Habermas': 'in 1971 he characterized the ideal speech situation as the prefiguration of a liberated form of life. The same formulation was used in his paper "Wahrheitstheorien" (1972). Most of Habermas's later remarks on the status of the ideal speech situation are devoted to retracting this infelicitous early formulation and to stressing an alternative conception, according to which the ideal speech situation is only an "unavoidable presupposition of argumentation"'.

indicator for justified consensus. One of the presuppositions of argumentation is that in performing speech acts we act counterfactually, as if the ideal speech situation were not purely fictitious, but real – this is exactly what I define as a presupposition. The normative basis of linguistic understanding is anticipated, but also active as an anticipated foundation … Consequently, the concept of ideal speech situation is not simply a regulative principle in the Kantian sense; for we must always already make this presupposition *de facto* upon the first act of linguistic comprehension (Habermas 2009: 265–7; my and translator's translation, my emphases).[9]

However, there were also some passages that could cause misunderstandings: in fact, the 'ideal speech situation', in addition to a *pragmatic presupposition*, seems to be taken as the *anticipation* of some *future state*: '… the formal anticipation of the idealized dialogue (as a form of life to be realized in the future …?)'. Here the interrogative form certainly betrays considerable uncertainty (2009: 267). Elsewhere (1971b: 139), Habermas emphasised formulations he would later abandon: 'the counterfactual conditions of the ideal speech situation are revealed as the conditions of an ideal form of life', as they designate 'what we, in the traditional way, try to understand with the ideas of truth, freedom and justice'.

In his 1980s works, however, this ambiguity seems to be overcome, and Habermas now clearly favours a definition of 'ideal speech situation' as a pragmatic presupposition of argumentation. So, in the text quoted by Elster, we read this passage:

In argumentative speech we see the structures of a speech situation immune to repression and inequality in a particular way: it presents itself as a form of communication that adequately approximates ideal conditions. *This is why I tried at one time to describe the presuppositions of argumentation as the defining characteristics of an ideal speech situation. I cannot here undertake the elaboration, revision, and clarification that my earlier analysis requires,* and accordingly, the present essay is rightly characterized as a sketch or a proposal. The intention of my earlier analysis still seems correct to me, namely the reconstruction of the general symmetry conditions that every competent speaker who believes he is engaging in an argumentation must presuppose are adequately fulfilled. The presupposition of something like an 'unrestricted communication community', an idea that Apel developed following Peirce and Mead, can be demonstrated through systematic analysis of performative

9. A little below, he added: 'On the other hand, the concept of ideal speech situation is not even a concept that exists in the Hegelian sense: in fact no historical society coincides with the form of life that we can characterize in principle by referring to the ideal speech situation'. And in a note Habermas specifies, on this last point, that no 'historical society' coincides with 'a communicative form of life characterized by the fact that the validity of all the norms of action full of political consequences can be made dependent on discursive processes of formation of the will' (Habermas 2009: 267).

contradictions. Participants in argumentation cannot avoid the presupposition that, owing to certain characteristics that require formal description, the structure of their communication rules out all external or internal coercion other than the force of the better argument and thereby also neutralizes all motives other than that of the cooperative search for truth (Habermas 1990: 88, my emphases).

In his 'Reply to my critics', Habermas had illustrated his strategy of pragmatic-transcendental foundation of communicative practice:

[D]iscourse ethics refers to those presuppositions of communication that each of us must intuitively make when we want to participate seriously in argumentation. My position is that those who understand themselves as taking part in argumentation *mutually suppose*, on the basis of the pre-theoretical knowledge of their communicative competence, that the actual speech situation fulfils certain, in fact quite demanding, preconditions. I shall leave aside [in this reply] the question of whether these presuppositions of communication can be adequately reconstructed in the form of the 'ideal speech situation' that I proposed. I shall also put aside the question of the extent to which the requirements that we have to set as participation in discourse are actually realised. We have been forced, only as it were, in a transcendental sense, to suppose that these requirements are, under the given empirical limitations, *sufficiently* realised; for so long as we do not consider external and internal constraints to be sufficiently neutralised to exclude in our eyes the danger of a pseudo-consensus based on deception or self-deception, we cannot *suppose* that we are taking part in argumentation (1982: 254–5).

Habermas finally comes to a radical redefinition and a further reduction of this notion in *Facts and Norms* (1996: 322–4) and, even more clearly, in his 'Reply' given to the conference on *Facts and Norms* that the Cardozo Law School held in September 1992 (1995–6: 1518). 'What I find more disturbing is the fact that the expression "ideal speech situation" which I introduced decades ago as a shorthand for the ensemble of universal presuppositions of argumentation, suggests an end state that must be strived for in the sense of a regulative ideal.'

In any case, it is evident that such a notion does not imply a properly or directly 'political' dimension: this is quite another level. And one does a disservice to Habermas – as does Elster in some sense – if the idea of a *successful communicative understanding* is translated into the idea of a *rational consensus* immediately transposed into a model of *political theory*, or even referred to the search for 'unanimous preferences'. Also because – it goes without saying – Habermas expressed these views in 1982 after writing *Theory of Communicative Action* (first published, in German, 1981), in which he outlined the complex architecture of a *theory of society* and *forms of rationality* based on the distinction, and the inescapable tensions, between understanding-oriented *communicative action* and success-oriented action (in the two forms: instrumental and strategic); between the logics of *social integration* and those of *systemic integration*; and between *systemic imperatives* and the *life-worlds*.[10]

Of course, it would be equally incorrect to miss the *potential implications* of this approach – with all the necessary mediations – for the analysis of a properly political dimension. For Habermas, the idea of a *communicative rationality* already incorporated in daily practice was the core of a *critical-emancipatory potential*. It both co-existed with and opposed other logics; it may be put under pressure by these logics but remains always open and normatively unyielding.[11]

In his 'Reply to my critics' (1982: 235), Habermas says that, using the 'model' of an ideal speech situation, he

> ... tried (very crudely) to clarify the formal-pragmatic presuppositions of argumentative speech. Discourses are islands in the sea of practice, that is, improbable forms of communication; the everyday appeal to validity-claims implicitly points, however, to their possibility. Only to this extent are idealisations *also* built into everyday practice.

In the conclusion of *Moral Consciousness* (1990: 106), Habermas recalls the image: 'like all argumentation, practical discourses resemble islands threatened with inundation in a sea of practice where the pattern of consensual conflict resolution is by no means the dominant one'.

If we refer specifically to the chapter of *Moral Consciousness* quoted by Elster, the theme is the 'pragmatic-transcendental' foundation of the *practical-moral discourse*, in which there are claims to *normative rightness*, not to *truth* or *truthfulness*:

> ... in cases where agreement is reached through explicit linguistic processes, the actors make three different claims to validity in their speech as they come to an agreement with one another about something. Those claims are claims to truth, claims to rightness, and claims to truthfulness, according to whether the speaker refers to something in the objective world (as the totality of existing states of affairs), to something in the shared social world (as the totality of the legitimately regulated interpersonal relationships of a social group), or to something in his subjective world (as the totality of experiences to which one has privileged access). Further, I distinguish between communicative and strategic action. Whereas in strategic action one actor seeks to *influence* the behaviour of another by means of the threat of sanctions or the prospect of gratification in order to *cause* the interaction to continue as the first actor desires, in communicative action one actor seeks *rationally* to *motivate* another

---

10. Habermas has illustrated these concepts in many places but a very clear and effective synthesis can be found in *Postmetaphysical Thinking* (1992a: 59–72).

11. For an example of how Habermas's link between communication and emancipation was seen in those years, see Wellmer 1974 and 1977.

by relying on the illocutionary binding/bonding (*Bindungseffekt*) of the offer contained in his speech act (Habermas 1990: 58).

In particular, claims to *normative* validity, for their very reference to a social world and their being founded on intersubjective recognition, are always subject to possible 'failure' and can be the object of potential conflict:

> ... while there is an unequivocal relation between existing states of affairs and true propositions about them, the 'existence' or social currency of norms says nothing about whether the norms are valid. We must distinguish between the social fact that a norm is intersubjectively recognized and its worthiness to be recognized. There may be good reasons to consider the validity claim raised in a socially accepted norm to be unjustified. Conversely, a norm whose claim to validity is in fact redeemable does not necessarily meet with actual recognition or approval ... [A] positivistic enactment of norms is not sufficient to secure their *lasting* social acceptance. Enduring acceptance of a norm *also* depends on whether, in a given context of tradition, reasons for obedience can be mobilized, reasons that suffice to make the corresponding validity claim at least appear justified in the eyes of those concerned. Applied to modern societies, this means that there is no mass loyalty without legitimacy (*ibid.*: 61–2).[12]

The political implications of Habermas's view can be seen only at this level, where other dimensions of social complexity come into play. As such, the ideal speech situation is the presupposition and foundation of a communicative action that can result both in a *mutual understanding* of something in a world or of a norm and in *criticism, dissent* or *disagreement* on 'validity-claims' (of normative rightness). Therefore, such a properly argumentative practice – one that puts forward 'good reasons' – *might* lead to a rational consensus (which is not at all guaranteed or assumed *a priori*), but can also turn out to produce radical conflict.[13] If this is the case, it seems wholly improper to interpret the ideal speech situation as a goal to be pursued – let alone as a political ideal that promises an ideal of rational society. The ideal speech situation is an *idealising anticipation* we cannot escape as soon as we enter the logic of argumentation; however, it also implicitly and pre-reflectively affects the forms of everyday communicative action.

---

12. In a footnote, Habermas refers to the final chapter ('Legitimation problems in the modern state') of his 1976 *Zur Rekonstruktion des Historischen Materialismus* (trans. in Habermas 1979: 178–205).

13. For an idea of the significant theoretical space that Habermas assigns to conflict and 'disrupted consensus', *see also* other passages of *Moral Consciousness* (1990: 67 and, in particular, 103–9): when comparing argumentatively different validity-claims, 'facts and norms that had previously gone unquestioned can now be true or false, valid or invalid' (*ibid.*: 107). Of course this theme would be central to *Facts and Norms*: 'The starting point is the problem of how social order is supposed to emerge from processes of consensus formation that are threatened by an explosive tension between facticity and validity' (1996: 21; on the tension between social validity and legitimacy, see *ibid.*: 28–34).

Finally, one must keep in mind those *against whom* Habermas was defending his project of a moral theory preserving and renewing a cognitivist approach – this project (as Habermas recalls, 1990: 43) was in line with a tradition inaugurated by Kant and later supported by many other authors, including Rawls. Habermas's theoretical opponents were precisely those communitarian positions – as described in MacIntyre 1981 – claiming 'that the Enlightenment's project of establishing a secularized morality free of metaphysical and religious assumptions has failed' (quoted in Habermas 1990: 43); other 'noncognitivist theories like emotivism and decisionism'; 'intuitionist value ethics'; or ethics marked by radical moral scepticism (*ibid.*: 44), differently inspired by Nietzsche and, more recently, by Foucault. All these views, for Habermas, are the expression of a 'stubborn tendency to narrow down to the cognitive-instrumental domain the domain of questions that can be decided on the basis of reasons'. For these positions, 'moral-practical questions of the form "What ought I do?" are considered not amenable to rational debate unless they can be answered in terms of purposive rationality' (*ibid.*: 45). On the contrary, Habermas states that 'moral phenomena can be elucidated in terms of a formal-pragmatic analysis of communicative action, a type of action in which the actors are oriented to validity claims' (*ibid.*: 44).[14]

Nevertheless, the point here is not to investigate how correct was Elster's reading of Habermas as such: the aim is rather to reconstruct the origins of the new model of deliberative democracy, which undoubtedly finds significant expression in Elster's text and which would very much affect its future development. From this point of view, it is certain that this work contributed considerably to imbuing the idea of deliberative democracy with a strong *consensualist* aspect: it validated the idea that this model of democracy aimed to achieve a *consensus on a rational basis* and, above all, that this was a plausible and feasible *political ideal*. However, in these terms, it also contributed to exposing this definition – and, as a consequence, Habermas himself – to an all-too-easy imputation of being 'unrealistic' or 'utopian' (or worse, of concealing the intrinsically and irreducibly conflictual nature of 'the political').[15] In his 1982 'Reply', Habermas reacted rather forcefully to the accusation of 'utopianism' (1982: 235):

... nothing makes me more nervous than the imputation – repeated in a number of different versions and in the most peculiar contexts – that because the theory of communicative action focuses attention on the social facticity of recognised

---

14. The texts in which Habermas goes back to the moral theory are gathered in *Erläuterungen zur Diskursethik* (1991; published in English as *Justification and Application*, Habermas 1993b). Here (see in particular 1993b: 54–7), he widely takes up the issues of the 'pragmatic presuppositions' of communicative action and argument as well as the 'ideal speech situation'; and yet, it should be noted that this expression is mentioned only once, cited in quotation marks and preceded by the description 'so-called' (1993b: 56). In this regard, a 1996 essay is particularly important: 'A genealogical analysis of the cognitive content of morality' (in Habermas 1998a: 3–46). For an evaluation of the different stages of development of Habermas's moral theory, see Ferrara 1999: 37–45.

15. See, for instance, Mouffe 2005.

validity-claims, it proposes, or at least suggests, a rationalistic utopian society. I do not regard the fully transparent society as an ideal, nor do I wish to suggest *any* other ideal.

On the other hand, though, one cannot help noting that the concept of the ideal speech situation and the political model derived from it – *if expressed* in the terms we have seen proposed by Elster – made such an imputation objectively plausible, as happened with Amartya Sen in his commentary on Elster's essay,[16] and as Elster himself would be forced to admit in a later passage of his essay. In fact, after outlining the model of political theory attributed to Habermas as mentioned above, Elster considered a number of possible objections that could be made to it, explaining that 'the goal of this criticism is not to demolish the theory, but to locate some points that need to be fortified'. 'I am, in fact, largely in sympathy with the fundamental tenets of the view, yet fear that it might be dismissed as Utopian' (Elster 1997: 13).

The objections and doubts that Elster analysed at this point would be the focus of many subsequent discussions on the new deliberative model. They concerned: the limitations and constraints of a decision-making process based on public discussion (such as time-shortages and unequal information and cognitive resources); the (questionable) *epistemic* or cognitive superiority of the 'many' compared to the 'single parts',[17] the mechanisms of *group-thinking* and conformist polarisation;[18] and the relationship between 'common good' and selfish goals. Two of these objections, in particular, would be crucial in future theoretical debate on deliberative democracy:

> ... even assuming unlimited time for discussion, unanimous and rational agreement might not necessarily ensue. Could there not be legitimate and unresolvable differences of opinions over the nature of the common good? Could there not even be a plurality of ultimate values? ... Since there are in fact always time constraints on discussions – often the stronger the more important the issues – unanimity will rarely emerge. For any constellations of preferences short of unanimity, however, one would need a social choice mechanism to aggregate them. One can discuss only for so long, and then one has to make a decision, even if strong differences of opinion should remain. This objection, then, goes to show that the transformation of preferences can never do more than supplement the aggregation of preferences, never replace it altogether (Elster 1997: 14).

---

16. 'I find this a rather utopian view, as does Elster himself, judging from what he says elsewhere (Elster 1997: 14) and it is not really easy to see how antagonistic interests, including class conflict, would all get submerged in "unanimous preferences" merely by "a rational discussion"' (Sen 1986: 234).

17. The objection concerns 'the implicit assumption that the body politic as a whole is better or wiser than the sum of its parts. Could it not rather be the case that people are made more, not less, selfish and irrational by interacting politically?'.

18. Sunstein would later intervene on this topic (2002).

Such objections were *well founded*, we might add, in the presence of such a grand and ambitious goal as is that to achieve 'unanimous preferences' through rational discussion. In the face of these objections, Elster's answer appears rather weak: in fact, he merely appeals to the *regulative value* of the notion of 'ideal speech situation'. Most supporters of the theory, admits Elster, would have, no doubt, to accommodate those objections but would respond that, 'even if the ideal speech situation can never be fully realized, it will nevertheless improve the outcome of the political process if one goes some way towards it' (*ibid.*: 14). These are eloquent words: a *pragmatic presupposition* of communicative action is taken as *something to be achieved*, or at least something that one can or should try to achieve.

This would be a future ground for discussion and differentiation within the theoretical field of deliberative democracy, also involving Habermas's notion of 'ideal speech situation'. In many texts that, in years to come, would allude to the normative definition of deliberative democracy, the reference to this notion often appeared rather generic, both when authors accepted its foundational value and when they addressed it polemically as the premise of a consensualist, hyper-rationalist and conflict-free idea of democracy. Faced with the impossibility of pursuing a rational and unanimous consensus, or with the unrealistic nature of the claim that such an agreement is feasible, a question arose: is it possible or sufficient, so to speak, to be contented with asserting such a demanding view of what a deliberative democracy should be while, at the same time, reducing it to a mere *regulative ideal* – something to strive for, knowing that it will never be fully realised? Does this not weaken the theoretical and normative scope of the model?

These are legitimate and well justified critical questions but I don't believe they should be addressed to the notion of the ideal speech situation, considering the role this notion actually played in Habermas's theory. In fact, Habermas's idea of a communicative rationality embodied in everyday practice (and identified as the core of a critical-emancipatory potential) goes in a very different direction: it can induce one to grasp a *deliberative dimension (a deliberative rationality) already present in the forms of democratic politics*, analytically distinguishing it from other logics of interactions with which it coexists and is confronted (as happens in some insights found in Sunstein's works, as we have seen).[19]

Discourse theory 'aims at the *conditions of possibility* of the emancipatory process, but not at its possible promotion, translation and practical activation' (Brunkhorst 2006: 19). The image of the 'deliberative ideal' that, instead, would be derived from Elster's (and others') reading of the ideal speech situation has often led to a rather reductive view and to a traditional juxtaposition between 'ideal' and 'real'. As a consequence, deliberative practices or institutions were seen as partial attempts at 'approximation' to a rather demanding and very abstract model of democracy that, as such, was very much exposed to criticism, in the name of 'realism'.

---

19. It is safe to say that, in Sunstein, this insight did not come out of a complete and conscious theoretical strategy but was primarily the result of an interpretation of democracy and the US Constitution that caught the 'deliberative' dimension actually incorporated in the institutions and political practices that have characterised their genesis and development.

3. The nature of politics and the aim of participation

Elster's essay is crucial because, in addition to the view of the deliberative ideal on which we have focused, it proposed other conceptual elements and theoretical schemes that would become part of the common heritage of the theoretical field of deliberative democracy. In particular, in this 1986 essay – drawing on claims he had previously made in *Sour Grapes* – Elster expressed his view both on the constraints that the *publicity of the deliberative procedure* impose on the possible expression of self-interested preferences and on the constraints of consistency that are produced by a speaker's *repeated public reference to the common good.*[20] These two elements are identified as the two fundamental premises of the idea of politics conceived as the process through which preferences change, in an *ideal* striving for a rational agreement (Elster 1997: 12–13):

> ... the first [premise] is that there are certain arguments that simply cannot be stated publicly. In a political debate it is pragmatically impossible to argue that a given solution should be chosen just because it is good for oneself. By the very act of engaging in a public debate – by arguing rather than bargaining – one has ruled out the possibility of invoking such reasons. To engage in discussion can in fact be seen as one kind of self-censorship, a pre-commitment to the idea of rational decision. ... An additional premise states that over time one will in fact come to be swayed by considerations about the common good. One cannot indefinitely praise the common good '*du bout des lèvres*' ['unwillingly'], for – as argued by Pascal in the context of the wager – one will end up having the preferences that initially one was faking.

It's not just an inner conviction that can be developed over time, or the 'psychological difficulty of expressing other-regarding preferences without ultimately coming to acquire them' (Elster 1997: 12) but a stronger external constraint. As Elster would write, in a text included in the collection he himself edited (1998a), 'a deliberative *setting* [my emphasis] can shape outcomes independently of the motives of the participants. Because there are powerful norms against naked appeal to interest or prejudice, speakers have to justify their proposal by the public interest'. Of course, proposals may also be instrumental or hypocritical but public discourse creates a bond of consistency: once you have publicly expressed a preference for a common vision, it is difficult go back without losing credibility and reputation (Elster 1998b: 104).

In the second part of his essay, Elster devoted himself to an intense critical discussion of the idea of politics proposed by participatory democracy in the 1960s and 1970s, and of the purposes that had been assigned to it. 'It is clear from Habermas's theory, I believe, that rational political discussion has an *object* in terms of which it makes sense. Politics is concerned with substantive decision-making,

---

20. On this basis, Elster then proposed the well known formula on the 'civilizing force of hypocrisy', discussed in particular in 'Arguing and bargaining in two constituent assemblies' (Elster 2000). On this essay by Elster, *see* Chapter Nine, Section 3, note 32.

and is to that extent instrumental.' It is true that this can be understood in a very limited sense (as if the political process were only one through which individuals pursue their own selfish interests), but this 'instrumental' nature of politics can and should be understood in a much broader sense: 'it implies only that political action is primarily a means to a nonpolitical end, only secondarily, if at all, an end in itself'. And the target of this critique is clear: the theorists who 'suggest a reversal of this priority and that find the main point of politics in the educative or otherwise beneficial effects on the participants' (Elster 1997: 19).

On this point, Elster proposes an argumentative model destined to be taken up and developed in subsequent literature. It marks a clear departure from previous versions of participatory democracy (but also from those versions of deliberative democracy that will tend to give it a predominant 'participatory' and 'educational' purpose). According to Elster, this view is 'internally incoherent':

> ... the benefits of participation are by-products of political activity. Moreover, they are essentially by-products, in the sense that any attempts to turn them into the main purpose of such activity would make them evaporate. It can indeed be highly satisfactory to engage in political work, but only on the condition that the work is defined by a serious purpose which goes beyond that of achieving the satisfaction. If that condition is not fulfilled, we get a narcissistic view of politics – corresponding to various consciousness-raising activities familiar from the last decade or so (*ibid.*: 19–20).

Elster's attack could not be more scathing and his detachment from the 'participatory democracy' of previous decades could not be more marked. Elster supports this polemical goal by evoking Tocqueville, John Stuart Mill and Hannah Arendt. In particular, quoting a famous passage from *Democracy in America*, Elster observes that, for Tocqueville, 'the advantages of democracy are mainly and essentially by-products' (*ibid.*: 22). But this argument is not a sufficient 'public justification' for democracy, as it is possible to formulate it only after enough time has passed and by placing oneself, as Tocqueville did, in the position of an outside observer: 'if the system has no inherent advantage in terms of justice or efficiency, one cannot coherently and publicly advocate its introduction because of the side effects that would follow in the wake. There must be a *point* in democracy as such' (*ibid.*: 22–3).[21]

The same goes for John Stuart Mill. Elster notes that 'in current discussion [... he] stands out both as an opponent of the purely instrumental view of politics,

---

21. In any case, Elster clarifies that Tocqueville 'did not argue that political activity is an end in itself. The justification of democracy is found in its effects, although not in the intended ones, as the strictly instrumental view would have it'. In this sense, Tocqueville's endorsement of the jury system is significant: 'I do not know whether a jury is useful to the litigants, but I am sure that it is very good for those who have to decide the case. I regard it as one of the most effective means of popular education at society's disposal' (1969: 275). Elster comments: 'this is still an instrumental view, but the gap between the means and the end is smaller. ... The justification of the jury system is found in the effect on the jurors themselves' but this effect would disappear 'if they believed that the impact on their own civic spirit was the main point of the proceedings' (Elster 1997: 23).

that of his father James Mill, and as a forerunner of the theory of participatory democracy' (and in the related footnote Elster quotes Pateman). 'In his theory', he adds, 'the gap between means and ends in politics is even narrower, since he saw political activity not only as a means to self-improvement, but also a source of satisfaction and thus a good in itself' (*ibid.*: 23). According to Elster, the more recent words of Albert O. Hirschman also go in the same direction: 'the benefit of collective action for an individual is not the difference between the hoped-for result and the effort furnished by him or her, but the *sum* of these two magnitudes' (Hirschman 1982: 82). But this way of setting out the problem, notes Elster, creates an insurmountable difficulty: do we really believe that participation can produce a beneficial effect even when the desired result is null? Is it not rather the case that the effort 'is itself a function of the hoped-for result, so that in the end the latter is the only independent variable?' (Elster 1997: 23–4).

Finally, Ester refers to Hannah Arendt, whose work is indispensable to 'a fully developed version of the noninstrumental theory of politics' (*ibid.*: 24). Arendt had an idealised view of the original American town meetings (people would participate 'neither exclusively because of duty nor, and even less, to serve their own interests but most of all because they enjoyed the discussion, the deliberation, and the making of decisions' (Arendt 1963: 119). Elster objected that, 'although discussion and deliberation in other contexts may be independent sources of enjoyment, the satisfaction one derives from *political* discussion is parasitic on decision-making. Political debate is about what to *do* – not about what ought to be the case. It is defined by this practical purpose, not by its subject matter' (Elster 1997: 24–5).

In short, one cannot have a *narcissistic* view of politics: 'a chess player who asserted that he played not to win, but for the sheer elegance of the game, would be in narcissistic bad faith – since there is no such thing as an elegant way of losing, only elegant and inelegant ways of winning' (*ibid.*: 25). Also, proving that the memory of recent participatory practices and conceptions was very much present in the background of these disputes, Elster's final 'shot' in his essay is reserved for the well known English historian and militant pacifist E. P. Thompson.[22]

In the conclusion, Elster defines his position in regard to the three models of political theory he outlined: on the one hand, there is 'the economic theory of democracy', which 'rests on the idea that the forum should be like the market, in its purpose as well as in its mode of functioning. The purpose is defined in economic terms, and the mode of functioning is that of aggregating individual decisions'

---

22. Elster writes that when they asked Thompson 'whether he really believed that a certain rally in Trafalgar Square had any impact at all, [he] answered: "That's not really the point, is it? The point is, it shows that democracy's alive ... A rally like that gives us self-respect. Chartism was terribly good for the Chartists, although they never got the Charter."' Of course, remarks Elster sarcastically, 'the Chartists, if asked whether they thought they would ever get the Charter, would not have answered: "That's not really the point, is it?". It was because they believed they might get the Charter that they engaged in the struggle for it with the seriousness of purpose that also brought them self-respect as a side-effect' (*ibid.*: 25). In *Sour Grapes*, Elster described this joke of Thompson's as 'the best statement of the self-defeating view of political behaviour that I have yet come across' (Elster 1983: 100).

(*ibid.*: 26). On the other hand, there is the idea that 'the forum should be completely divorced from the market, in purpose as well as in institutional arrangement'. The point here is that 'citizenship is a quality that can only be realized in public, i.e., in a collective joined for a common purpose. This purpose, moreover, is not to facilitate life in the material sense. The political process is an end in itself, a good or even the supreme good for those who participate in it' (*ibid.*).

Between these two extremes lies the view of politics that Elster wants to embrace: in it, the forum surely distinguishes itself from the market as to the way it works but it still has *substantive decisions* as its object:

> ... it is the concern with substantive decisions that lends the urgency to political debate. The ever-present constraint of *time* creates a need for focus and concentration that cannot be assimilated to the leisurely style of philosophical argument in which it may better to travel hopefully than to arrive. Yet within these constraints arguments form the core of the political process. If thus defined as public in nature and instrumental in purpose, politics assumes what I believe to be its proper place in society (*ibid.*).

Chapter Five

Bernard Manin: Public Deliberation and Democratic Legitimacy

1. Rousseau, the 'general will' and the deliberation 'of all'

I have mentioned how Joshua Cohen, in his 1989 essay, noticed that 'parallel conceptions' were emerging from his and John Elster's work and Bernard Manin's article 'On legitimacy and political deliberation' (1987). This remark of Cohen's, of course, has an intrinsic documentary value; however, there are some doubts about how 'parallel' the three authors actually are, especially as regards the nature of their alleged common Habermasian inspiration. In fact, as I shall show, Manin outlined a conception of *democratic deliberation* and its goals that was, at least on some crucial points, very far from what we have just seen in Elster. Where this critical distance emerges most clearly is in the idea of *rational consensus*, or even the instance of *unanimity* or *agreement of all*, which Elster (starting from his reading of Habermas) had placed at the centre of one of his three models of 'political theory'. This critical comparison is *indirect*, as there has been no direct dialogue between the two authors: Manin compared himself directly with Rawls and, to a lesser extent, with Habermas. It is the latter thinker, as we shall see, that would later identify important common ground with Manin's claims.

Manin's essay, which came out in France in 1985 without attracting much notice, received great attention from American academics, as the author himself recalled a few years later.[1] This work encountered the 'participatory current' that had characterised part of the American intellectual Left in the 1960s and 1970s and which was now looking for new theoretical perspectives. Manin's essay revolves around a reconstruction and interpretation of the concept of deliberation that, as we shall see, leads to a very clear thesis: the source of democratic legitimacy is not unanimous agreement as a direct expression of the will of all but a *deliberative* process of formation of opinion and will in which everyone should have the right to participate. Manin formulates this view by revisiting some classic democratic themes and authors – especially Rousseau – while locating this topic within the contemporary debate, with particular attention to Rawls's *Theory of Justice*.

---

1. See Manin 2002: 44 (co-written with Loïc Blondiaux). The original title was 'Volonté generale ou délibération? Esquisse d'une théorie de la délibération politique', (*Le débat* 1985, 33(1): 72–94). The text was later published in English as 'On legitimacy and political deliberation', in *Political Theory* 1987. It should be noted that the English translation was by Jane Mansbridge (with Elly Stein). Just as she had enhanced Bessette's contribution (*see* Chapter Three, note 1), Mansbridge also played an important role in 'weaving' the network of intellectual relationships that paved the way for the 'deliberative turn'.

Manin's central topic is that of the *universal agreement* that people can ideally pursue about the regulating principles of a just society, which 'follow necessarily from the rationality of individuals placed in the original position' (*ibid.*: 339). Rawls's aim, notes Manin, 'is to deduce a strictly universal conception of justice' or a 'conception of justice that will produce, at least in principle, a unanimous agreement among rational beings' (*ibid.*: 340). Manin stresses the fact that this requirement of legitimacy – *the unanimity* or *the agreement of all* – cannot be criticised or abandoned just because of its 'unrealistic' nature: it is necessary to discuss it because it is inextricably linked to the 'fundamental principles of modern individualism': that is, it arises from principles that affirm the freedom and equality of all.

In this search for the foundation of legitimacy there is a cogent logic: if 'there is no essential difference or natural hierarchy among individuals to justify the domination of some over others', it follows that 'political power and the rules it promulgates can have no other legitimate basis than the will of these equal individuals' (*ibid.*). And so, if this power is exercised over individuals and, to various degrees, binds them, the rules can only be considered legitimate if 'they arise from the will of all and represent the will of all' (*ibid.*). The search of this *universal* and *rational* foundation seems therefore hard to avoid; it is not enough to 'relax' these 'exorbitant demands of unanimity' (*ibid.*) – as Rawls also proposes – by affirming that this *unanimous agreement* can and should be sought only in the fundamental principles and not in every single decision. 'These distinctions and nuances', underlines Manin, 'in no way change the fundamental principle' – in other words, 'that unanimity alone is the basis of legitimacy'. And that is the reason why 'universalist theories of justice seek to show that principles do in fact exist that can form the basis for unanimous agreement' (*ibid*: 341).

This approach appears in liberal as well as modern democratic thought: 'how can we establish a political and social order based on the will of individuals?' is the starting question for both. Indeed – in spite of their differences – they reach the same conclusion: 'in the political sphere, it is unanimity that provides the principles of legitimacy' (*ibid.*). And if most democratic theories approach the topic of 'efficiency', the very *way* in which they do so – that is, by seeking 'a more realistic principle of decision making than that of unanimity, namely the majority principle' (*ibid.*) – implicitly presupposes the assumption of unanimity as a requirement of legitimacy. Indeed, such a requirement is typical of a political thought based on modern individualism.[2] Manin focused mostly on Rousseau's position: 'the only legitimate source of political obligation is the will of individuals. In obeying the

---

2. Manin first describes this claim by commenting on Sieyès's justification of the principle of majority rule: the nature of men is to be free; when they create an association, the relations among them can be only founded 'on the free act of will of each individual', and so 'laws can only rest upon the will of individuals'. 'In order for a society to exist and to act', summarises Manin, 'it must have a common will', but this common will can actually be derived only from, and founded on, the will of each individual. However, in a big political community unanimity is impossible to achieve and so it is necessary to have recourse to a 'convenient convention' – the principle of majority rule. So, as Sieyès wrote, 'with good reason, plurality becomes legitimately a substitute for unanimity' (cited in Manin 1987: 341–2). On Sieyès and his view of political representation, see Urbinati 2006: 138–61; for his concept of the role of discussion in representative assemblies in particular, see Manin 1997: 187–9.

common will, each person is in fact merely obeying himself. Therefore, the general will must equal unanimous will as a matter of principle' (*ibid*.: 343). 'Unanimity thus remains the true source of legitimacy' (*ibid*.: 342).

On this basis, we can also understand the famous distinction that Rousseau makes between the 'general will' and the 'will of all': 'if disagreements arise, and certain people do not agree with what has been decided, it is because those who disagree had in fact misunderstood the question put to them' (*ibid*.). And commenting on a famous passage of *The Social Contract*,[3] Manin highlights: 'A minority opinion is, therefore, nothing but a mistaken *opinion* about the general will. But we must then also acknowledge that people were not really asked what they *wanted*, but only what they *believed to be the general will*' (*ibid*.: 343). This argument, according to Manin, shows how difficult to comprehend and contradictory is the assumption that 'the sole source of legitimacy is to be found in the will of individuals' (*ibid*.: 343–4) and how difficult it is to reconcile it with a realistic decision-principle, such as the majority principle. But most of all, this analysis reveals the characteristics of the individual's *will*: positions like those of Sieyès and Rousseau

> … do not merely affirm that legitimate collective decision making must proceed from individuals; they also state more precisely that political obligation flows from individual wills, that is to say, from choices arrived at by individuals. Thus it is not only the free individual who makes legitimacy possible, it is his *already determined will* (*ibid*.: 344).

Here, different meanings of 'deliberation' come into play (*ibid*.:345):

> This appears with great clarity in Rousseau and becomes particularly apparent in the meaning he gives to the term deliberation. Following a usage that goes back to Aristotle, philosophic tradition generally takes deliberation to mean the process of the formation of the will, the particular moment that precedes choice, and in which the individual ponders different solutions before settling for one of them. Rousseau uses the term deliberation in a different sense, one that is accepted in common language, and uses it to mean 'decision'. We can see the difference that separates these two definitions: in the vocabulary of philosophy, deliberation describes the process that precedes decision; in Rousseau's writings, it signifies decision itself.[4]

---

3. Rousseau, Book IV, Ch. 2 (Rousseau 2012: 101–2), cited in Manin 1987: 343, but with a different translation.

4. As an example of this use of the term *deliberation* in Rousseau, Manin refers to a famous passage of *Social Contract* (Book II, Ch. 3 'Whether the general will can err'). 'It follows from the preceding that the general will is always right, and always tends toward the public good. But it does not follow that the people's deliberations have always the same righteousness [*rectitude*]. One always wishes for one's own good, but one cannot always see it. The people cannot be corrupted, but they are often deceived, and it is only then that they seem to wish for what is bad' (Rousseau 2012: 32, cited in Manin 1987: 345, but with a different translation).

To be sure, Rousseau sees individuals as free and equal; but these individuals are *isolated* and *silent*, as shown by a passage of the *Social Contract* that Manin cites as an example of Rousseau's identification of the terms *deliberation* and *decision*, and which marks his rejection of what 'normally constitute the mainstay of public discussion: the groups or parties who face each other in an exchange of argument' (*ibid.*). 'If citizens had no communication between each other while a sufficiently well-informed public deliberated', Rousseau wrote, 'the general will would always become apparent, in spite of a great number of small differences, and the deliberation would always be good'.[5]

This statement, Manin comments, is noteworthy because, with it, Rousseau identified 'decision' with 'deliberation' and, at the same time, rigorously excluded any form of communication among citizens (*ibid.*). Famously, Rousseau considered communication among citizens to be dangerous, because through it 'the rhetoric and the powers of persuasion' influence and distort citizens' opinions, thus becoming the instrument by which the interests of some corrupt the general will (*ibid.*: 346). Manin stresses one presupposition of this thesis: this rejection of 'the parties' did not derive from a 'pre-totalitarian point of view' that is often thought to characterise Rousseau's position, but from something deeper. 'Rousseau's individuals are already supposed to know what they want when they come to a public assembly to decide in common. They have already determined their will, so that any act of persuasion attempted by others could only taint their will and oppress it' (*ibid.*).[6] From Rousseau's point of view, the formation of the will is an individual act and it is truly free and autonomous because it escapes the potential influence that others can discursively exercise. The collective decision, therefore, is a mere *ratification* of what the will of each citizen, individually, feels as an expression of the 'general will'.

With this view, according to Manin, Rousseau distances himself from a classic – and, specifically Aristotelian – notion of deliberation: as one can read in a passage of *Rhetoric* (I, 1357a), quoted by Manin, 'the subjects of our deliberation are such as seem to present us with alternative possibilities; about things that could not have been and cannot now or in the future be other than they are, nobody who takes them to be of this nature wastes his time in deliberation.' But this concept of deliberating as pondering the different reasons that can be advanced in favour of possible alternatives is completely absent in Rousseau's work: 'the citizens of Rousseau's democracy do not deliberate, not even within themselves', Manin comments, 'because Rousseau considers politics to be essentially a simple matter. That is why the process of the formation of the will, individual as well as collective, does not concern him. He is thus able to identify deliberation with decision making and decision with self-evidence' (*ibid.*: 347).

The different moments of deliberation and decision are reduced to one, in the act of will. And the latter, in turn, is guided by intuitive knowledge and by the

---

5. Rousseau, *Social Contract*, Book II, Ch. 3 (Rousseau 2012: 32, but with a different translation).

6. On these topics in Rousseau, see Urbinati 2006: 60–100.

moral powers of citizens and their common sense of citizenship: there's no need for refined thinking or intense argumentation, because, as Rousseau wrote, 'peace, unity, and equality are the enemies of political subtleties'.[7] The roots of this idea, underlines Manin, lie in a well defined conception of *democratic legitimacy*. 'The basis for legitimacy lies not in the free individual capable of making up his mind by weighing reasons, but rather in the individual whose will is already entirely determined, one who has made his choice.' Hence the requirement of unanimity: 'the individualistic and democratic principle requires that collective decision emanate from all individuals' (*ibid.*: 347).

For present purposes, it is important to note that Manin's reading radically opposed the positive view of Rousseau held by the theoreticians of participatory democracy. In fact, Rousseau's profile as it emerges from Manin's pages is very similar to the view of one proposed by the early theorists of participatory democracy – but the sense of this interpretation is completely different. As we have seen, for Carol Pateman, for instance, Rousseau was the theorist of a 'direct' and non-mediated vision of democracy: the citizens 'participate' *as* they 'decide', and are free and equal as they all equally participate in a collective decision. The idea that this decision should imply a deliberative dimension was absent from, or at least less important to, the early theories of participatory democracy: what mattered was that the citizens could directly exercise an equal amount of power. For Manin, instead, Rousseau cannot be an acceptable reference precisely because his view lacks a decisive element: deliberation as a *process of formation* of opinions and will.

2. Debating with Rawls: deliberation, the original position and 'rational choice'

After proposing this reading of Rousseau, Manin moves on to the contemporary debate by referring to John Rawls and stressing the strong analogy between these two *contractualist* views:

> We find the three elements of Rousseau's conception (the requirement for unanimity, the absence of deliberation, the predetermined will of individuals) in the work of John Rawls. One cannot avoid being struck by the close resemblance between the situation of Rousseau's citizen and that of the individuals in the original position that we find in the work of Rawls (Manin 1987: 347–8).

---

7. Regarding this theme, Manin quotes another passage from the *Social Contract*, Book IV, Ch. 1: 'Whenever men who have gathered together, consider themselves as one single body, they will have only one will, dedicated to the preservation of the community, and the general well-being. Then all the actions of the state would be vigorous and simple, its maxims clear and luminous. There will be no tangled, contradictory interests, the public good would be evident everywhere, and would only need common sense to be apprehended. Peace, unity, and equality are the enemies of political subtleties' (Rousseau 2012: 99, but with a different translation).

Of course, notes Manin, Rawls does use the term *deliberation*: 'individuals behind the veil of ignorance are supposed to deliberate in order to know what principles of justice they are to adopt. But what does deliberation mean in this situation?' (*ibid.*).

Manin seeks the answer in an analysis of Rawls's texts (taken from the chapter about the original position in *Theory of Justice*)[8] that brings out the absence or exclusion of a dimension that can be traced back to some sort of idea of *deliberation*. Here, too, there is a cogent logical concatenation: since all individuals are equally rational and placed in the same conditions, 'each is convinced by the same arguments' (Rawls 1971: 139). 'There can be no arguments among individuals', Manin comments, 'because, by definition, they all have the same point of view' (Manin 1987: 348). There can't be *public* deliberation: coalitions are forbidden – (a point that, Manin underlines, 'cannot but recall Rousseau', *ibid.*); and there can't be *internal* deliberation either because the individual's rationality in the original position only aims at choosing 'those principles of justice, that most clearly advance his own interests. He is the classic *homo oeconomicus*' (*ibid.*). Ultimately,

> ... this means that what Rawls calls deliberation is nothing but the calculation of the classic economic agent: he is provided with a coherent set of preferences ... certain given constraints restrict his actions, and he chooses the optimal solution, taking these constraints into account. He is assumed to have criteria for evaluation that permit taking all possible solutions into account, and ranking them so that he selects the best one (*ibid.*: 348–9).

Rawls therefore adopts a model of rationality that is typical of the canonical models of rational-choice theory, as, after all, he clearly stated himself in *Theory of Justice* (and as he would repeat later, with profound self-criticism).[9] In this

---

8. Specifically, Manin focuses on this passage by Rawls: 'To begin with, it is clear that since differences among the parties [i.e., the individuals] are unknown to them, and everyone is equally rational and similarly situated, each is convinced by the same arguments. Therefore we can view the choice in the original position from the standpoint of one person selected at random' (Rawls 1971: 139).

9. Manin supported his analysis by quoting another text by Rawls: 'the concept of rationality invoked here, with the exception of one essential feature, is the standard one familiar in social theory. Thus in the usual way, a rational person is thought to have a coherent set of preferences between the options open to him. He ranks these options according to how well they further his purposes; he follows the plan which will satisfy more of his desires rather than less, and which has the greater chance of being successfully executed' (Rawls 1971: 143). Yet, the passages in Rawls's texts supporting Manin's opinion are many. For example, in the opening, when sketching the first features of the 'original position', Rawls writes that 'the concept of rationality must be interpreted as far as possible in the narrow sense, standard in economic theory, of taking the most effective means to given ends' (*ibid*: 14). Rawls would later openly correct his original thesis in this regard: in 1985, in the essay 'Justice as fairness: political not metaphysical' (1985; in Rawls 1999: 401, note 20), Rawls writes that 'it was an error in *Theory of Justice* (and a very misleading error) to describe the theory of justice as a part of the theory of rational choice' A similar observation can be found in *Political Liberalism* (2005: 53, note 7). For more on Rawls' early adhesion to the theoretical framework of 'rational choice', and for the subsequent review process, see Ferrara 1999: 16–18.

view, Manin adds, 'the procedure of forming the will loses its importance': given the criteria for evaluation and the set of solutions,

> ... the result is already contained in the premises and is only separated from them, one might say, by the time needed for calculation. Reflection and the calculations necessary for obtaining a solution teach the individual nothing new; in particular, he learns nothing about his own preferences. There is, therefore, no *deliberation*, in the full sense of the term, to be found here (*ibid*: 349).

The conclusion is clear: according to Rawls, 'as with Rousseau, the individual is already supposed to know exactly what he wants, or more precisely, he already possesses the criteria for evaluation that will permit him to appraise all possible alternatives' (*ibid*.).

Manin's subsequent arguments against Rawls reject the conditions and constraints that the latter ascribes to individuals in the original position and replace them with the real conditions of political decision-making and with a different theoretical model of rationality that now comes into play. Here, the crucial point is the insufficiency of *informational resources* (*ibid*.):

> In the real world, when individuals make a decision concerning society, they can never avail themselves of all necessary information. They certainly have *some* information but it is fragmentary and incomplete. Yet they must reach a decision within a limited time, there is generally an urgency pertaining to action ('life's actions brook no delay,' as Descartes put it) that acts against the search for complete information (*ibid*.)

'Political decision making' Manin concludes 'is by its nature a choice under uncertainty'. And this is the *space* of deliberation: *a dialogical process among individuals*, where the information resources – incomplete, partial and uncertain at first – become 'firmer without however becoming complete'. Through this exchange 'individuals discover information they did not previously have'; they learn that a specific choice has consequences and that if the latter contradict the original purpose, they may alter that purpose. 'It is not reasonable to suppose as Rousseau does that individuals deliberate when they are already sufficiently well-informed ... In reality, deliberation is in itself a procedure for becoming informed' (*ibid*.). Similarly, it is impossible to presume both that individuals have, from the very beginning, a well defined and complete set of preferences and that their preferences are correlated to all the arguments of a debate, to all the aspects of a decision or to all possible solutions. 'Even when they reach a decision at the close of the debate, their preferences are still not complete, their choices do not cover the entire ground of the debate, but they have become more focused' (*ibid*.: 350).

Manin also emphasises the topic of the *transformation* of preferences: 'in the course of collective deliberation, the individual may also discover that the opinion he held at the outset was nothing more than prejudice and he may decide to change it' (*ibid*.). And finally, 'it is unrealistic and unreasonable' to suppose that individuals would immediately have a complete and also *internally coherent* set of preferences: 'experience shows, on the contrary, that their initial desires are most frequently in conflict' and that only 'in the course of deliberation' can people become aware of this, changing their convictions and reformulating their goals, abandoning some and harmonising others with those of other people. Therefore,

> It is unreasonable to assume that this conflict is already settled at the outset, given that politics is by nature the arena where opposing demands must be weighed, where an attempt is made to reconcile these demands wherever possible, and where a decision is taken in favour of those whose position seems most justified. All this must also be done in a timely fashion. We can, therefore, state that during political deliberation, individuals acquire new perspectives not only with respect to possible solutions, but also with respect to their own preferences (*ibid.*).

In sum, Manin proposes an idea of *political deliberation* as a process through which to look for solutions, starting from a set of preferences that are *incomplete, incoherent* and *conflicting*, founded on partial and/or contradictory information and understanding. It is significant that, to support his thesis, Manin (*ibid.*: 349) even refers to Herbert Simon's well known notion of 'bounded rationality' (Simon 1983). Here, the claim of a *synoptic* view – founded on the completeness of the relevant information, on the perfect knowledge of every available alternative, and on a rational procedure of *maximising calculation* – is replaced by a *sequential* view of the decision-making process, on the basis of incomplete information, with the aim of defining a *satisfactory* solution.

Deliberation is a process of formation and transformation of preferences, of acquisition of information, of research into and evaluation of acceptable and shared solutions; but this doesn't assume in any way that that is always possible: on the contrary, a compromise or an agreement can be made 'wherever possible', but not always and not necessarily. Moreover, deliberation 'requires not only multiple but conflicting points of view because conflict of some sort is the essence of politics' (*ibid.*: 352): deliberation therefore implies an effort to *persuade* others – in other words, an *argumentation*, which Manin defines as 'a sequence of propositions aiming to produce or reinforce agreement in the listener' – that is, part of 'a discursive and rational process' (*ibid.*: 353). However, 'in contrast to logical proof, argumentation does not result in a necessary conclusion that the listener cannot reject'.

Manin's definition of deliberation is openly inspired by Aristotle (in particular, he refers to a passage of *Nicomachean Ethics*).[10]

---

10. *Nicomachean Ethics* (III, 3, 1112a; Eng. edn 2009, pp. 43–4): 'Do we deliberate about everything, and is everything a possible subject of deliberation, or is deliberation impossible about some things? ... Now about eternal things no one deliberates, e.g. about the material universe or the incommensurability of the diagonal and the side of a square ... But we do not deliberate even about all human affairs, for instance, no Spartan deliberates about the best constitution for the Scythians. For none of these things can be brought about by our own efforts. We deliberate about

It is, therefore, not said of a conclusion developed from arguments that it is either true or false, but that it simply generates more or less support depending on whether the argument was more or less convincing. Nor is an argument either true or false; it is stronger or weaker. Whatever the force of an argumentation, its conclusion is never strictly necessary (*ibid.*).[11]

Furthermore, in the political sphere, there is also pluralism and conflict of *values*:

> ... we must admit, with Weber, that no science can resolve this conflict in a rigorous and necessary manner. However, contrary to Weber's thesis, it does not follow that the choice of values remains ineluctably arbitrary. Some values are more likely than others to win the approval of an audience of reasonable people. It is impossible to demonstrate their soundness; they can only be justified ... The relative force of its justification can only be measured by the amplitude and the intensity of the approval it arouses in an audience of reasonable people (*ibid.*: 353–4).

On this basis, Manin offers his alternative view and draws his conclusions: in particular, he rejects the identification of and overlap between *deliberation* and *decision* that, in different forms, appears in both Rousseau and Rawls. The foundation of democratic legitimacy is not the *general will* but the *deliberation of all*. 'It is, therefore, necessary', concludes Manin,

> ... to alter radically the perspective common to both liberal theories and democratic thought: the source of legitimacy is not the predetermined will of individuals, but rather the process of its formation, that is, deliberation itself. An individual's liberty consists first of all in being able to arrive at a decision by a process of research and comparison among various solutions. As political decisions are characteristically imposed on all, it seems reasonable to seek, as an essential condition for legitimacy, the deliberation of all or, more precisely, the right of all to participate in deliberation. We must, therefore, challenge the

---

things that are in our power and can be done, and these are in fact what is left. For nature, necessity, and chance are thought to be causes, and also reasons and everything that depend on man. ... and in the cases of exact and self-contained sciences there is no deliberation ... but the things that are brought about by our own efforts, but not always in the same way, are the things about which we deliberate ... Deliberation is concerned with things that happen in a certain way for the most part, but in which the outcome is obscure, and with things in which it is indeterminate ...'. Manin notes that his concept of deliberation 'here is, therefore, in a sense, close to that of Aristotle', but without the ontological implications it had in Aristotle's thought. 'In the theory of deliberation outlined here, I make no assumptions about the order of the world. Individuals are assumed to be relatively uncertain, not because of the intrinsic nature of the subjects they deliberate, but because they lack complete information, and their preferences are not entirely determined' (Manin 1987: 366–7, note 33).

11. It should be noted that, in a footnote, 'with reference to the conception of argumentation sketched here', Manin recalls the classic work of Chaim Perelman and Lucie Olbrechts-Tyteca (1969 [1958]).

fundamental conclusion of Rousseau, Sieyès, and Rawls: a legitimate decision does not represent the will of all, but is one that results from the deliberation of all. It is the process by which everyone's will is formed that confers its legitimacy on the outcome, rather than the sum of already formed wills. ... We must affirm, at the risk of contradicting a long tradition, that legitimate law is the result of general deliberation, and not the expression of the general will (*ibid.*: 351–2).

3. The 'deliberation of all' as a source of democratic legitimacy

After defining his theory of political deliberation, in the second part of his essay Manin devoted himself to the *pluralist* model (Manin 1987: 355):

> ... a diversity of points of view and of arguments is an essential condition both for individual liberty (for individuals must have a choice among several parties)[12] and for the rationality of the process (for the exchange of arguments and criticisms creates information and permits comparing the reasons presented to justify each position).

This perspective and this idea of *pluralism* – he adds – are different from that of 'traditional pluralism'; as examples of the latter he cites Dahl's *Preface to Democratic Theory* (1956); Sartori's *Democratic Theory* (1962); 'and, especially, Anthony Downs' and his *Economic Theory of Democracy* (1957).

Here we find again the *market–forum* pairing. Manin proposes a critique of the *analogy* between the competitive logic of democracy and that of the marketplace. In particular, he notes how two aspects 'make it impossible to attribute the self-regulating virtues of the economic market to the political one' (Manin 1987: 356): the *temporal distance* of the effects produced by the choice of one particular politics and the *dispersion* of these same effects, albeit in a different manner, on the *whole* society – that is, not only and always on people, who, with their votes, contributed directly to determining that choice. These two factors explain why 'political persuasion' is necessary:

> ... citizens must be persuaded to adopt a policy because they cannot simply choose according to the immediate effects that they perceive themselves. In the *marketplace*, individuals feel the effects of their choice immediately and directly. This cannot be the case in the *forum* where they deliberate political decisions (*ibid.*).

On this basis, Manin explains his idea of what can be actually defined as a 'deliberative process'. Schumpeter is right to describe the function of democracy

---

12. Manin here uses the term *parties*, stating in a note that he uses it in two senses: *parties* involved in decision-making and *political parties* and their platforms.

as the process of selection of those who are elected to rule, and he is also right when he underlines the element of competition that this involves: 'yet we need not deem the programs these entrepreneurs represent and the points of view they advocate as being without importance, as Schumpeter does' (*ibid*.: 358). Politicians, notes Manin, offer two strictly related elements: their 'services in governmental functions' and also 'a particular point of view concerning the public good'. Therefore, 'even when voters decide primarily on the basis of a global, though often confused image they have of the candidates, this image is still related to voters' idea of his or her community good'.

For this reason, there is competition not only among the elites who are competing for power but also between different views of the common good. In the creation of this arena, there is 'a sort of competition for generality' (*ibid*.): that is, every party knows that they can only increase the consensus for their own position by 'showing that its point of view is more general that the others' (*ibid*.). In the final part of his essay, Manin thus exposes his solution to the issue of *agreement* or *rational consensus* as the goal of a deliberative process:

> Therefore, universalism also plays a part here, but it is not assumed at the start. It seems rather to be the ideal term of the process. In truth, no party will ever become an actually universal party; there will always remain opponents; this is the core of political pluralism. Nevertheless the structure of the deliberative system usually makes the protagonists strive to enlarge their points of view and propose more and more general positions. ... [U]niversality remains the unattainable end, but the system provides an incentive to generalization (*ibid*.: 359).

And it is on this basis that we can justify the principle of majority vote as the conclusion of the deliberative process: approval by the majority affirms the greater strength of a given set of topics over others but 'the process nevertheless institutionalizes the admission that there were also reasons not to desire the solution finally adopted. The minority (or minorities) also had reasons, but these reasons were less convincing'. Decisions thus made are legitimate because they are, 'in the last analysis, the outcome of the deliberative process taking place before the universal audience of all the citizens' (*ibid*.).[13]

This is how Manin understands the justification of the majority principle: 'the mere fact of being the will of the greatest number does not *by itself* confer any special privilege upon it' and 'there is no need to have recourse to the untenable fiction

---

13. Here, we cannot deal with the relationship between this essay by Manin and his later and well known work *Principles of Representative Government* (1997) – a theme which Manin himself would talk about in a dialogue with Blondiaux (Manin 2002). However, in the passages quoted, we should note a connection: the category of 'audience democracy' in Manin hasn't got a normative value nor can it only be regarded as a mere descriptive category of the 'metamorphosis' of democracy. Rather, it is an ideal-typical concept that, as such, leaves several questions entirely open: how 'a public' is formed; what are the deliberative qualities of the processes of opinion-formation and the conditions (of freedom, equality and pluralism) in which it happens; as well as to what extent an actual 'competition for generality' takes place.

that the majority will is in essence the will of all, or that it must be considered as the equivalent of unanimous will' (*ibid.*: 360). Rather, the outcome has democratic legitimacy only because it is reached at the conclusion of a deliberative process in which everybody was able to participate and all points of view – even those of the minority – were considered and freely compared.[14] In considering the majority will as a representation of the *general will*, the minority doesn't play any role or have any recognition: 'it is supposed that by submitting to the decision that was finally made, the minority merely obeys itself, or achieves what it really wanted or should have wanted'. Instead, assuming 'that the minority will is in no way included in the will of the majority, it becomes necessary to find the means that will allow the minority to express its opinions and interests between two elections', 'against the omnipotence of the majority' (*ibid.*: 361). And, therefore,

> ... institutions must be set up that will compel the majority to take the minority point of view into account, at least to a certain extent. This is the essential justification of social pluralism, of associations and interest-groups. Their power must force the majority to take into account in its actions the interest of those it does not represent. These counter-forces, checks, and balances are necessary because majority will is not the equivalent of the will of all (*ibid.*: 360).[15]

Finally, Manin formulates a thesis that would have a crucial importance for subsequent theoretical research on deliberative democracy but which would not be come to be shared or highly regarded by scholars in the theoretical field that developed around the new paradigm. 'The procedure preceding the decision is a condition for legitimacy, which is just as necessary as the majority principle. It is the conjunction of these elements that creates legitimacy' (*ibid.*). To go back to the initial topic, for Manin, 'the deliberative perspective allows us to drop the requirements of either strict universality of application or unanimity of approval' (*ibid.*: 359).

> ... the failure of unanimistic theories of justice or legitimacy leads us to note, once more, that the definition of what is just remains the subject of constant debate ... But a society cannot live and maintain itself solely on the basis of principles and institutions that reflect only an ultimately indeterminate

---

14. On the justification and nature of the majority principle, Manin's position could be compared to Kelsen's classical theses: for example, see Kelsen's words on the 'specifically dialectical process' of parliamentary democracy and about the mutual legitimation between majority and minority (2013 [1929]: 67–78). The majority vote, according to Kelsen, is 'a synthesis', 'a compromise, and not ... a "higher" absolute truth or an absolute value standing above group interest' (*ibid.*: 70).

15. On this basis, Manin judged 'inadequate' the claims of 'traditional pluralism'. For the latter, a variety of forces, interests and groups are able to spontaneously find a balance, similarly to what happens in a market economy (*ibid.*: 360–1). And it should be noted as well that Manin (as did Sunstein and others) here refers to Theodore Lowi, citing in particular Lowi's critique of the idea of an 'automatic society' (Lowi 1979: ch. 1).

justice. For a society to continue to exist, decisions must be made and conflicts resolved; power also must be exercised and in the last resort must be sufficient to restore some unity to the multiplicity of actions and desires that make up social life (*ibid*.: 362).

'We cannot content ourselves with the idea that pluralism and the irreconcilable conflict of social forces are a necessity', writes Manin, because 'if pushed to its extreme, such conflict and pluralism would mean the dissolution of society. On this point, Hobbes's argument has lost none of its force' (*ibid*.: 361). Thus, we have to 'try to uncover the procedures most likely to make those decisions reasonable'. Between a universal and rational agreement and the reign of arbitrariness, there is 'the domain of the *reasonable* and the *justifiable*' (*ibid*.: 363). This is the domain of a public discourse in which arguments are proposed that are not incontestable but that may be convincing for most citizens. And the theory of deliberation, indeed, 'offers only an imperfect method for making the decision process as reasonable as possible'.

On the other hand, Manin identifies the real weakness of universalist theories of justice: it is not only and not so much their 'unrealistic' character –because these theories are well aware of this limitation and are often consciously presented as only offering an evaluational standard, 'a goal that must be pursued with the knowledge that it can never be attained' (*ibid*.: 363) – but also and rather their indefinite teleological projection.

We want not only to know whether a society is more or less just, and what the ideal society should be like, but we also want concrete means to make real societies as reasonable as possible. The idea of setting standards that are explicitly unrealistic is unsatisfactory because it leaves totally open the question of the means necessary to approach this state.

Rawls is certainly central to these critical observations; the extent to which this criticism was also addressed to Habermas will be examined in the next section. For the moment, however, we can draw some conclusions about the significance of Manin's contribution to the 'constitutive' phase of the new theoretical model of deliberative democracy: Manin introduced a specific notion of *political deliberation* and its strong connection to the theme of *democratic legitimacy*:

As long as we accept the predetermined will of individuals as the unique basis for legitimacy, we must inevitably conclude that only the object of unanimous agreement is legitimate. The requirement for unanimity is justified in a pure theory of justice because a pure theory does not encompass the practical conditions for its realisation, nor the means necessary for attaining it. Yet unanimity is an unsuitable prerequisite for a theory of political decision-making; a theory of decision-making cannot, without falling into pure empiricism and relativism, avoid concerning itself with legitimacy (*ibid*.: 363).

Therefore, if 'it is unrealistic, and, more important, unjustified, to assume that individuals faced with the necessity of having to make a political decision already know exactly what they want', the foundation of democratic legitimacy cannot be the pre-determined will of individuals, 'but the process by which they determine their will': that is, 'the process of deliberation' (*ibid.*: 363–4).

In subsequent theoretical literature on deliberative democracy, there would be frequent disputes over the *purpose* of deliberation: a rational consensus; a *reasonable* understanding; shared pragmatic solutions; a compromise and so on. In this essay, Manin outlines an idea of *public* deliberation – the more inclusive, the more democratic – which plays an essential role in the legitimation of political decisions insofar as it is the process wherein the will and opinions of individuals are formed, by way of an exchange of reasons and ideas. In this sense, democratic deliberation *also* has an *epistemic* function: it allows for the creation and the enrichment of the *cognitive* and *informative* bases of the role of individuals as political agents. It allows to them make more 'solid' decisions – based on consideration of every point of view – and more 'legitimate' ones, too, because every point of view has contributed to them, to an extent. However, in his essay, Manin did not properly propose a *justification* of an *epistemic theory* of democracy as such. A democratic order is, rather, a *constitutive premise*, the *field* wherein the *epistemic functions of deliberation* can best be exercised and so strengthen the legitimacy of a decision. Democracy, as such, does not present itself as a procedure that proposes the best or wisest solutions: it is the *public deliberation* that can characterise, in various ways, the procedures of a democracy that can *therefore* potentially lead to better and wiser decisions (which are not, however, 'true' or 'more correct'). Public deliberation leads to these results insofar as it activates the whole social potential of knowledge, information and experiences that enrich and qualify a democratic decision.

Manin also proposed some ideas that subsequent mainstream versions of deliberative democracy would disregard: in Manin's text the 'deliberative' dimension is to be found in *all* methods and institutions of a democracy, starting from its constitutional bases. Moreover, to my knowledge, here Manin introduced the term 'deliberative system' for the first time, albeit just *en passant*.[16] In his analysis, Manin proposed some important cues on *political parties* – 'the existence of political parties is essential for deliberation' (*ibid.*: 357), which would later be recalled by James Johnson (2006) as some of the ideas that *could have* suggested greater attention to the theme of parties in the further investigations of

---

16. 'In truth, no party will ever become an actually universal party; there will always remain opponents; this is the core of political pluralism. Nevertheless the structure of the *deliberative system* usually makes the protagonists strive to enlarge their points of view and propose more and more general positions' (Manin 1987: 359, my emphasis). The concept of a 'deliberative system' would, in the years following, be very much related to the work of Jane Mansbridge (1999) and, more recently, that of a numerous group of deliberative theorists (see Parkinson and Mansbridge 2012 and Chapter Twelve).

the deliberative field. In fact, however, this wasn't the case and the role of parties has been until recently almost entirely ignored.[17]

Last but not least, Manin's work offered a view of deliberation that completely took on the dimension of pluralism and conflict: the development of deliberative democracy would foster many misunderstandings in this regard. Public, democratic and inclusive deliberation is a procedure that enables us to deal with the conflict and pluralism of interests and values via reason and discourse: it does not *negate* them but proposes to prevent conflict and pluralism from being entrusted to the uncontested supremacy of a 'strategic' and 'instrumental' reason; or to a mere (widespread and irreducible) *clash between powers* and *counter-powers*; or to a logic of residual resistance, thereby annihilating the fundamentals of any type of democratic 'order', legitimate and recognised as much as possible.

4. Debating with Habermas: the public sphere, 'consensus of all' and democratic deliberation

As I mentioned at the beginning of this chapter, there are some doubts about the Habermasian matrix Cohen claimed to share with Elster and Manin. Habermas is certainly very present in the reflection of these authors; but in very different ways. In the case of Manin, in particular, references to Habermas are not very frequent: one could even say, as I will now endeavour to show, that it was rather Habermas who found some important elements of consonance between his own theoretical reflection on deliberative politics and Manin's essay.

What relationship is there, then, between Manin's conception of deliberation and Habermas's? Here, we must pay attention to dates and bibliographical notes. Just as Manin refers to Rawls's first edition of *Theory of Justice* (1971) with regard to the 'original position', the text of Habermas's quoted by Manin also dates from the 1970s: *Legitimationsprobleme in Spätkapitalismus* (1973).[18] 'In the political sphere', writes Manin, 'deliberation does not permit us to arrive at necessary and universally admitted truths, but it also does not permit the absolute and incontestable refutation of a norm or a value' (Manin 1987: 354). And in a footnote to this passage, he observes: 'the conception defended here differs, therefore, from that of Habermas' (*ibid.*: 367, note 35). Manin shares Habermas's view that the validity of a norm is not 'susceptible of proof' but neither is it purely arbitrary or the result of a 'decisionist' act either; and therefore 'the recognition of the validity claim of a norm can be rationally motivated'. But Manin no longer agrees with

---

17. In Manin's view, the parties are essential as actors who select and structure topics of public discussion and facilitate citizens' resolution of them (Manin 1987: 356–7). Manin adds in a footnote, quoting Burke and John Stuart Mill: 'It is striking to note that the theoreticians who stress the role of deliberation (in contrast to the will) in politics are also those who justify the existence of parties (which, as we have seen, Rousseau opposes)' (*ibid.*: 368, note 39). The relationship between political parties and deliberative democracy has recently been receiving more attention: see Muirhead 2010, 2014; Floridia 2015; Wolkenstein 2016, White-Ypi 2011.

18. Published in English as *Legitimation Crisis* (1975); *see* Chapter Four, note 1.

Habermas when the latter seems to mean that this 'rationally motivated' consensus should, or could, have the *consensus of all*.

Quoting a passage from Habermas,[19] Manin noted how the German philosopher, 'maintains, in my view, the requirement for unanimous consensus, at least in principle'; however, in doing so, Habermas consequently

> ... fails to recognize that there are various degrees of agreement, which, if the appropriate rules for deliberation are respected, reflect in turn the respective strengths of the arguments put forward in the defence of the conflicting norms. ... the better argument is simply the one that generates more support and not the one that is able to convince all participants (*ibid.*: 367).

There are no further references to Habermas in Manin's 1987 essay. However, the dialogue between Manin and Habermas would acquire great significance a few years later. In 1990, in the new Preface to *Strukturwandel der Öffentlichkeit* (1999b), published in English as *The Structural Transformation of the Public Sphere* (1989), Habermas himself would extensively refer to the very passage of Manin's text that I have quoted above, about the *deliberation of all* as a source of democratic legitimacy, appearing to wholly endorse it.[20]

The context of that quotation is very important. In his new Preface, Habermas addressed criticisms made of his 1962 work over the nearly thirty years since its publication. In some cases, he acknowledged that the critique had merit and redirected the subsequent evolution of his research. However, while welcoming many objections, Habermas maintained that the theme concluding his old work was still crucial: 'the mass democracies constituted as social-welfare states, as far as their normative self-interpretation is concerned, can claim to continue the principles of the liberal constitutional state only as long as they seriously try to live up to the mandate of a public sphere that fulfils political functions' (Habermas 1992a: 441).

---

19. 'Since all those affected have, in principle, at least the chance to participate in the practical deliberation, the "rationality" of the discursively formed will consists in the fact that the reciprocal behavioural expectations raised to normative status afford validity to a common interest ... The interest is common because the constraint-free consensus permits only what all can want' (Habermas 1975: 108).

20. To understand the reception of Habermas in the theoretical debate, especially in the United States, aimed at defining the new paradigm of deliberative democracy, note that the English translation of *Strukturwandel der Öffentlichkeit* was published only in 1989, twenty-seven years later than the original. On that occasion, in September 1989, a major conference was held at the University of North Carolina at Chapel Hill, attended by Habermas himself: the texts of the wide and lively debate were published in an important, and much quoted, volume edited by Craig Calhoun (1992). Habermas also wrote a new Preface for the new German edition of *Strukturwandel der Öffentlichkeit* that appeared in 1990 and this Preface was then included in the book edited by Calhoun, under the title 'Further reflections on the public sphere' (Habermas 1992a). Because of the widespread influence that Calhoun's volume had in America, I'll mainly refer to this text. For the fiftieth anniversary of the publication of *Strukturwandel*, in 2012, a symposium of the journal *Political Theory* was held, published as 40(6), with contributions by A. Allen, R. Bernstein, M. Cooke, I. Katznelson, J. Mansbridge, A. Norval and W. Scheurmann.

Consequently – and here Habermas refers to a passage of *Structural Transformation of the Public Sphere* – it must be proved that it is possible, in our society, 'to set in motion a critical process of public communication' (*ibid.*). On this point, Habermas admits that his old work had some limits: 'this question drew me back, at the close of the book, to the problem on which I had touched but failed to address properly' (*ibid.*). Above all, the contribution of *Structural Transformation* to contemporary democratic theory – Habermas argued – should be considered a failed attempt, if one had to admit that an irreducible plurality of interests makes it impossible for some *general interest* to emerge, so that the public sphere can refer to it as a critical criterion. 'On the basis of the theoretical means available to me at the time', notes Habermas, 'I could not resolve this problem. Further advances were necessary to produce a theoretical framework within which I can now reformulate the questions and provide at least the outline of an answer' (*ibid.*).

There are three steps in this critical-theoretical evolution. The first is due to the final overcoming of an approach typical of the Marxist 'critique of ideology', which merely opposes the ideals of bourgeois humanism (assumed in their 'utopian potential') to a political and social reality that denies them. For this, writes Habermas,

> I suggested … that the normative foundations of the critical theory of society be laid at a deeper level. The theory of communicative action intends to bring into the open the rational potential intrinsic in everyday communicative practices. Therewith, it also prepares the way for a social science that proceeds reconstructively, [and] identifies the *entire spectrum* of cultural and societal rationalization processes (*ibid.*: 442).

The second step – also culminating in the theory of communicative action – is the overcoming of a (now unsustainable) 'holistic notion' of society, namely, the idea that 'the society and its self-organization are to be considered a totality' (*ibid.*: 443): 'the presumption that society as a whole can be conceived as an association writ large, directing itself via the media of law and political power, has become entirely implausible in view of the high level of complexity of functionally differentiated societies' (*ibid.*). I will come back to this point (*see* Chapter Nine, Section 2), because it is precisely on this subject that, in *Between Facts and Norms*, Habermas would raise some radical objections to the ideal of deliberative democracy proposed by Joshua Cohen – Habermas himself, in turn, would be the recipient of criticism from some deliberative democrats in this respect.

Finally, let's come to the third step, which brings us back to Manin (and to Rousseau). We can summarise this point as follows: on the one hand, Habermas expresses the unavoidability of the institutional mediation produced by a democratic rule-of-law state, despite the demands of *immediacy* supposedly originated by a socially integrative force rooted in the community and in the 'solidarity' it produces; on the other hand, he restates the necessity of a *political public sphere* as a place for the discursive formation of opinions and wills – as a place, we could now say, of *public and democratic deliberation*.

The social integrative power of communicative action is first of all located in those particularized forms of life and lifeworlds that are intertwined with concrete traditions and interest constellations in the 'ethical' sphere ('*Sittlichkeit*') to use Hegel's terms. But the solidarity-generating energies of these fabrics of life do not directly carry over into democratic procedures for the settling of competing interests and power claims on the political level. This is especially so in post-traditional societies in which a homogeneity of background convictions cannot be assumed and in which a presumptively shared class interest has given way to a confused pluralism of competing and equally legitimate forms of life. ... [T]he word 'solidarity' must not suggest the false model of a formation of will *à la* Rousseau that was intended to establish the conditions under which the empirical will of separate burghers could be transformed, *without any intermediary*, into the wills, open to reason and oriented toward the common good, of moral citizens of a state (*ibid.*: 444).

At this point, it is becoming clear why Habermas refers so extensively to Manin's text.[21]

In section 12 of *Structural Transformation* I criticized Rousseau's 'democracy of non-public opinion' because he conceives of the general will as a 'consensus of hearts rather than of arguments'. The morality with which Rousseau demands citizens be imbued and that he places in the individuals' motives and virtues must instead be anchored in the process of public communication itself. *The essential aspect here is pinpointed by B. Manin* [and here there are large quotations from the above-mentioned passage: Manin 1987: 351–352]. Therewith the burden of proof shifts from the morality of citizens to the conduciveness of specific processes of democratic formation of opinion and will, presumed to have the potential for generating rational outcomes, and of actually leading to such result (*ibid.* 445–6); my emphasis).

Habermas found in Manin's position (the 'deliberation of all', not the 'general will', as source of the democratic legitimacy) a substantial consonance with the idea of 'deliberative politics' he was elaborating and, shortly afterwards, presented in *Between Facts and Norms*. In Habermas's theoretical framework, the place of this deliberation (the more inclusive it is, the more legitimating) is the 'political public sphere'. Hence the centrality of this notion, defined as 'the quintessential concept [*Inbegriff*] denoting all those conditions of communication under which there can come into being a discursive formation of opinion and will on the part of a public composed of the citizens of a state' (*ibid.*: 446). This notion therefore plays a fundamental role in 'a theory of democracy whose intent is normative'.

---

21. In a footnote, however, Habermas stresses that the text to which Manin referred was *Legitimation Crisis* (1975). A reconstruction of the concept of 'legitimation', in the diverse phases of Habermas's thought, can be found in McCarthy 1995-6.

This text by Habermas is the first work in which he engages directly in dialogues with authors who had proposed their own idea of 'deliberative democracy': not only Manin but also Joshua Cohen.[22] Above all, here Habermas presents some themes central to his notions of deliberative politics and 'a discourse-centered' democracy. This concept of democracy, Habermas argues, 'places its faith in the political mobilization and utilization of the productive force of communication';[23] but is faced with a choice:

> ... consequently, it has be shown that social issues liable to generate conflicts are open to rational regulation, that is, regulation in the common interest of all parties involved. Additionally, it must be explained why engaging in public arguments and negotiations is the appropriate *medium* for this rational formation of will. *Otherwise, the premise of the liberal model would be justified, that the only way in which irreconcilably conflicting interests can be 'brought to terms' is through a strategically conducted struggle* (ibid.: 447, my emphasis)

In conclusion, it's one of the two: either we believe that politics has to be considered *only* as a field of *irreducible* conflicts, and that democracy is but a procedural stage for strategic actions aiming either at the prevalence of some interests over others or at possible compromises; or we have to presuppose the existence of *another* form of social action – a *communicative* one. In this sense, we'd have to assume that social and political conflicts can *also* be settled rationally, *handled deliberatively*, and that it would be possible to define a 'general interest' by means of a discursive procedure (but also by means of *fair forms of negotiation*, in which a discursive dimension operates)[24] to which all parties involved can, or should, contribute.

The *place* where this collective (and always provisional) definition of a 'general interest' takes shape and transforms itself is the 'political public sphere', where a *public discourse* is produced which can interact with, and thus influence, the institutional procedures of a democratic state. These will later be key issues in *Between Facts and Norms*: the political dimension relies upon an ineliminable tension between critical-communicative *deliberative* rationality, which *can* emerge in the public sphere, and *strategic* rationality, which expresses itself through a bare

---

22. 'In this sense' (that is, of 'a theory of democracy whose intent is normative'), adds Habermas, Joshua Cohen 'defines the concept of deliberative democracy as follows' (1992a: 446), then quoting a passage from Cohen's 1989 essay on which I shall dwell in the next chapter. This definition of deliberative democracy would be taken up and discussed in *Between Facts and Norms* (*see* Chapter Ten, Section 2). Note that there was a mistake in the text: Joshua Cohen was referred to as 'Jean'.

23. The English translation, here, refers to 'communicative force of production' but the equivalent German original reads 'Produktivekraft Kommunikation' (Habermas 1990b: 39): therefore I believe it is more correct to speak of a 'productive force of communication'.

24. The issue would subsequently be extensively taken up in *Between Facts and Norms* (*see* Chapter Eight, Section 4).

conflict of interests. Can we entrust only this strategic sphere of individual and social action – Habermas wonders skeptically – with the basis of a normative definition of democracy?

When writing this text, Habermas had already published *Theory of Communicative Action* and was about to publish *Between Facts and Norms*: it would really be misleading not to take into account the way in which Habermas, in these texts, proceeds to theoretically anchor the inescapable reasons for conflict within contemporary democracies and societies. This conflict stems from the tension between communicative and strategic forms of rationality and action; between 'systemic imperatives', which act impersonally and behind the individual's back, and the critical viewpoints and perspectives that can originate from 'lifeworlds', from individuals' forms of self-understanding and from their communicative interactions. Ultimately, at stake in this conflict is the very legitimation of collective choices and this can also appear as a *legitimation crisis*, in the clash among various normative validity claims, between solutions which seek 'reasons' and justifications and a 'consensus' which is only laboriously achievable. The pluralism of interests and values and the resulting conflicts are a *fact*; but if we consider them *irreducible*, or, in principle, *undiscussable* and *unmanageable* in discursive and procedural terms, *then* a solution can only be found in the area of purely strategic conflicts, of *power relationships* or even violence and coercion.

Therefore Habermas cannot be said to have a *conflict-free* idea of democracy and politics, or a 'utopian' and idealistic vision of a future society which governs itself through rational discourse. In response to societies and politics where 'a generalized particularism' (1992a: 451) prevails, and to a theory of democracy that only records this empirical fact, Habermas states the necessity of conceiving democracy and politics as an area where a conflict among radically different logics of social action is indeed unfolding; but in which these logics coexist and intertwine, too. Thus, Habermas maintains the necessity of a normative view of democracy, which is not, however, merely projected into the sphere of 'ought to be' but is deeply rooted in the very *factual* presuppositions of existing social and political processes. That is, his is a normative theory that can both understand the inner potential of *facts* and work as an analytical and critical paradigm, thus acting also as a guide for action. So, Habermas adds, 'the deciphering of the normative meaning of existing institutions within a discourse-centred theoretical approach additionally supplies a perspective on the introduction of *novel* institutional arrangements that might *counteract the trend toward the transmutation of citizens into clients*' (1992a: 450; my emphasis). That is, institutional arrangements able to counteract the dominance and intrusiveness of the self-ruling systemic logic, based on the medium of money and administrative power and acting 'behind' the individual's back, compared to critical-communicative rationality and its potential, of which individuals are still the expression and bearers.

This text is extremely important to the ends of the current book, both because of its direct dialogue with Manin and Cohen and because of its popularity in the field of the new concept of deliberative democracy. Here, we find a possible answer to the problems we have encountered so far. Habermas believes that if we want to oppose a convincing theoretical approach to the views of politics and democracy generally provided by the liberal tradition (or, on the other hand, by a Schmittian view of 'the Political'),[25] we need to assume that democratic politics can (at least *also*) be a sphere in which a discursive formation of opinions and wills is possible and in which *moral-practical* conflicts can be rationally dealt with. In this sphere, there is no 'general interest' – previously established, or rooted in popular *ethos* – to be understood intuitively, or on which to decide in a voluntaristic way. Rather, there are 'reasons' and 'arguments', that can act and engage discursively with one another, changing and therefore going beyond the immediacy of the context in which opinions and wills first develop. We could say that the conflict takes place over different and alternative ways to conceive a 'general interest', which must be politically *constructed*, not just *discovered*. The *normative* call to the *possibility* of a 'general interest' thus plays a crucial role with regard to validity claims that do not stand the test of an argumentative exchange, that is, the displaying of 'good reasons' which challenge their actual generalisability.

This *discourse-centred* theoretical approach, added Habermas, does not aim at affirming the possibility of deriving

> ... a general principle of morality from the normative content of the indispensable pragmatic preconditions of all rational debate. Rather, this principle itself refers to the discursive redemption of normative validity claims, for it anchors the validity of norms in the possibility of a rationally founded agreement on the part of all those who might be affected, insofar as they take on *the role of participants in a rational debate*. In this view, then, the settling of political questions, as far as their moral core is concerned, depends on the institutionalization of practices of rational public debate (1992a: 447–8).[26]

Of course, Habermas clarified, 'political controversies frequently concern empirical questions, the interpretation of state of affairs, explanations, prognoses, etc. ... The majority of conflicts have their sources in the collision of group interests and concern distributive problems that can be resolved only by means of compromises' (*ibid.*: 448). But even within this sphere, a strategic or instrumental logic never dominates exclusively. 'Empirical and evaluative questions are frequently inseparable and evidently cannot be dealt with without reliance on arguments.' It is also the case that 'negotiations must rely on the exchange of

---

25. 'If questions of justice cannot transcend the ethical self-understanding of competing forms of life and if existentially relevant value conflicts and oppositions must penetrate all controverted political questions, then in the final analysis we end up with something resembling Carl Schmitt's understanding of politics' (Habermas 1995–6: 1492–3).

26. We should keep in mind what has been said above: this is the field of practical-moral issues, where at stake are not truth-claims but claims of justice; and these can be the subject of a rational discourse. In a passage of his text (1992a: 447), Habermas says that this approach, though in various forms, was at the core of the theoretical projects of other authors (Rawls, Dworkin, Ackerman, Lorenzen and Apel).

arguments and whether they lead to compromises that are *fair* depends essentially on procedural conditions subject to moral judgment' (*ibid.*).

In this context, it should be noted that the call for 'participation', as such, seems absolutely ambiguous to Habermas:

> ... there may actually be circumstances under which a direct widening of the formal opportunities for participation and involvement in decision making only intensifies 'generalized particularism', that is, the privileged assertion of local and group-specific special interests that, from Burke to Weber, Schumpeter, and today's neoconservatives, had provided the arguments of a democratic elitism. This can be prevented by procedurally viewing the sovereignty of the people as comprising the essential conditions that enable processes of public communication to take the form of discourse (*ibid.*: 451).

In short, '*Diskurse herrschen nicht*': 'discourses do not govern'. Instead, '*[t]hey generate a communicative power that cannot take the place of administration but can only influence it. This influence is limited to the procurement and withdrawal of legitimation*' (*ibid.*: 452, my emphasis).

As Habermas had already written in 1988,[27] popular sovereignty is now 'subjectless and anonymous': 'intersubjectively dissolved'; it 'withdraws into democratic procedures and the demanding communicative presumptions of their implementation' (Habermas 1997b: 58–9). Therefore, the idea that 'the vacant seat of sovereignty' can be filled by a 'network of associations' (1997b: 58) – that is, by a body of 'physically present, participating, and jointly deciding members of a collectivity' (1992a: 451) – also turns out to be weak and 'too concrete'. The sovereignty of the people can now be only expressed in 'forms of subjectless communication that regulate the flow of the formation of political opinion and will so as to endow their fallible results with the presumption of practical rationality' (*ibid.*: 451–2).

This sovereignty 'comes to fore in the power of public discourses that uncover topics of relevance to all of society, interpret values, contribute to the resolution of problems, generate good reasons, and debunk bad ones. *Of course, these opinions must be given shape in the form of decisions by democratically constituted decision-making bodies*' (*ibid.*: 452, my emphasis), because a political decision still requires a clear institutional accountability and responsibility. And, indeed, discourses as such cannot govern; what they *can* do is make decisions legitimate or not, or influence them. And here is the space for *public and democratic deliberation* but also – we can say – for conflict between *different* validity claims *aspiring* to present themselves as 'universal' or 'general' but not necessarily proven as such after the test of public scrutiny and rational discourse.

---

27. In the essay 'Popular sovereignty as procedure'. First written in 1988, this essay was then included in the anthology on deliberative democracy edited by Bohman and Rehg (1997: 35–65), from which my quotations come.

Here, there is no need to proceed further in the reconstruction of Habermas's position. However, we can see in this text the outlines of a possible, indirect response to the objections that Manin sketched in his essay. Manin had argued that a universalistic foundation of democratic legitimacy entrusted to the immediate expression of the *will* was unsustainable. He also agreed with Habermas that practical and moral issues also could and should be addressed in terms of rational discourse. However, he noted that universalistic claims persisted even in Habermas' works (especially those of the 1970s, we might add), where he defined the terms of a potential *rational consensus*, *if* all the necessary conditions of symmetry and equality between *all* those participating in a discourse are in place.

The evolution of Habermas's position, already evident in this text of the early 1990s and then even more in *Between Facts and Norms*, includes a definite shift of emphasis. Habermas does not abandon a universalistic tension, especially when the issues at stake require a moral discourse, but his idea of democratic legitimacy is now based on a notion of 'deliberative politics' that includes the first elements proposed by authors such as Manin and Cohen. The 'generalisability' of ideas and interests aspires to be an essential critical prerequisite, not an objective datum to be conformed to. The universalistic tension arises as a prerequisite that we cannot give up without abandoning the notion of a normative theory of democracy and if we do not want to open the door to a purely 'strategic' vision of political rationality. So, we might conclude that there were much deeper reasons for Manin's disagreement with the 'first' Rawls (with Rousseau's shadow looming in the background) than for his divergence from Habermas; nevertheless, Manin's objections to Habermas's position raised issues and questions that would be central to the evolution of the latter's theoretical work in the 1990s, as we shall see in the forthcoming chapters.

Chapter Six

Joshua Cohen: An 'Ideal Deliberative Procedure'

1. 'Deliberative democracy' as an ideal

In the introduction to a recent collection of his essays, Cohen goes back to the previous decades, offering some 'semi-autobiographical remarks' (2009c: 1) and recalling how the mid 1970s turned out to be 'a period of great creativity in political philosophy', with the publication of the great works of Rawls and Nozick. Cohen notes that it was also

> ... a period of political rethinking for people who, like me, identified themselves as democratic and socialist and thought of their socialism as principally a matter of political values – egalitarian, participatory, and anti authoritarian – rather than more specifically institutional convictions about public ownership or a planned economy (*ibid.*: 5).[1]

For those who recognised themselves in this democratic and participatory view of socialism, Cohen adds, it was natural to find Rawls's positions 'deeply attractive'. However, he goes on, 'I also found it striking that Rawls (not to mention Nozick and others) had very little to say about democracy and was focused instead on individual rights and opportunities, and a fair distribution of income and wealth' (*ibid.*: 6). This was a mistaken assessment, notes Cohen: he later realised that 'Rawls's views were far more deeply shaped by a conception of democracy than I then understood'.[2] It is from this perception – that is, from a reflection on the implications of Rawls's political philosophy on democratic theory – that Cohen's theoretical project was born in the late 1980s. This project would find its principal expression in the essay 'Deliberation and democratic legitimacy', first published in 1989 (Cohen 2009a).[3]

If Elster had drawn mainly from Habermas, and Manin had openly distanced himself from Rawls, Cohen takes Rawls as his essential reference point: in fact,

---

1. Cohen, born in 1951, obtained his PhD at Harvard, under Rawls's supervision; at present, he is Professor of Ethics in Society at Stanford, after teaching at MIT, Yale and Harvard.

2. Cohen refers to his 'For a democratic society', published in the *Cambridge Companion to Rawls*, edited by Samuel Freeman (Cohen 2003).

3. The essay appeared first in the book edited by Alan Hamlin and Philip Pettit, *The Good Polity* (1989). In his introduction to the recent reissue of his essays (2009c: 8), Cohen points out that the drafting of this text dates back to 1986.

we could define Cohen's proposal as an attempt to transpose a typically Rawlsian theoretical strategy into the definition of an *ideal model of deliberative democracy*. The consequences of this move would turn out to be very significant for the development of the deliberative paradigm: while Elster still spoke of a *model of politics* inspired by the ideal of deliberation, and while Manin proposed his own *theory of political deliberation* as the foundation of democratic legitimacy, Cohen offered his own view of *deliberative democracy* as a *democratic ideal* and of an *ideal deliberative procedure* as the normative core of this ideal model. This shift had important implications: Cohen himself, as early as 1989 but also (or even more) in later years, drew the appropriate conclusions from this approach, taking the 'ideal deliberative procedure' as a model wherein social and political institutions can be 'mirrored' – that is, as a guide to building new institutional arrangements or designing specific institutions.

In particular, Cohen indicated three sources that led him to what he calls 'the ideal of a "deliberative democracy"': the first is the 'recent discussion of the role of republican conceptions of self-government in shaping the American constitutional tradition and contemporary public law';[4] the second lies in the 'radical democratic and socialist criticisms of the politics of advanced industrial societies'. The third source is the fundamental one, for Cohen: some 'central features' of the ideal of deliberative democracy 'are highlighted in Rawls's account of democratic politics in a just society, particularly in those parts of his account that seek to incorporate the "liberty of the ancients" and to respond to radical democrats and socialists who argue that the "basic liberties may prove to be merely formal"' (Cohen 2009a: 17).

Cohen's essay, very much imbued with Rawls's theoretical 'style', is divided into three parts. The first discusses Rawls's conception of democracy, expressing some doubts about it; the second offers 'a formal conception' of deliberative democracy and the definition of 'an ideal deliberative procedure'; while the third part considers four possible objections to such a definition. In subsequent theoretical literature, Cohen's essay would generally be mentioned and remembered for its definition of the 'ideal deliberative procedure'; but we cannot fully understand the character of this definition without analysing the theoretical assumptions contained in four dense pages that precede it, in which Cohen describes his relationship with Rawls.[5]

The key to understanding this position can be found, in a nutshell, in the introductory words of the essay (*ibid.*: 16):

---

4.   Quoting Sunstein and other authors we have mentioned, *see* Chapter 3, Section 2, notes 6 and 7.

5.   An essay by Samuel Freeman (2000, esp. pp. 389–93) contains a detailed analysis of Cohen's essay, with some important critical observations, made from a point of view that could be characterised as 'orthodox Rawlsian'. Cohen would reject an 'entirely procedural' conception of democracy in his essay 'Procedure and substance in deliberative democracy' (1996) and the subsequent 'Democracy and liberty' (1998b). 'I aim to show', wrote Cohen, 'that democracy, on the deliberative conception, is a substantive, not simply a procedural, ideal and that the substance comprises egalitarian and liberal political values' (2009a: 225). On the reasons for this evolution, *see* Chapter Eleven, Section 6, note 36.

In this essay I explore the ideal of a 'deliberative democracy'. By a deliberative democracy I shall mean, roughly, an association whose affairs are governed by the public deliberation of its members. I propose an account of the value of such an association that treats democracy itself as a fundamental political ideal and not simply as a derivative ideal that can be explained in terms of fairness or equality of respect.

Therefore: 'deliberative democracy' is, first of all, an *ideal*; secondly, it must be understood as an *association*; an ideal that aims to inform a certain kind of political association, one that is democratic and deliberative as it governs itself through the 'public deliberation' of its members. 'Deliberative democracy', moreover, takes democracy as a fundamental and primary political ideal and not as something that has to be *justified* or *founded* by other values, such as fairness or equality.

This last point is critical for understanding Cohen's theoretical move with regards to Rawls. As we have seen, in the first part of his essay, Cohen discusses Rawls's conception of 'democratic politics in a just society'.[6] There is no need to offer a detailed analysis of those pages here: it is enough to recall the way in which Samuel Freeman defined Cohen's position with regard to his teacher. The ideal deliberative procedure, writes Freeman (2000: 390–1),

> ... differs from Rawls's hypothetical social contract, which is not a model for institutions, but a 'thought experiment' (Rawls) that aims to provide principles of justice that are to apply to institutions. Cohen then does not aim to describe a hypothetical procedure that justifies substantive principles of justice and the common good to regulate the deliberations of a democracy. Rather, he describes an ideal procedure that democratic institutions are to emulate as a pattern for deliberating about justice and the common good. He seeks to set forth the conditions for the possibility of this ideal.

Thus, Cohen proposes a sort of reversal of the terms in which we should conceive of the relationship between the principles of justice and democratic principles, which has important consequences. On the basis of this observation, Freeman concludes that an implication of Cohen's argument is that 'while justice itself requires a deliberative democracy, still democratic decisions can be legitimate (so far as they accord with the deliberative ideal) without being always just' (*ibid.*: 393).

For Cohen, there are three central points in the definition of the 'deliberative democratic ideal' as it may be deduced from Rawls's theory (Cohen 2009a: 19):

---

6. In a footnote, Cohen quotes the texts by Rawls that he was most inspired by: §36, 37, 43 and 45 of *Theory of Justice* and a 1982 Tanner Lecture called, 'The basic liberties and their priority', which would later become Lecture VIII of *Political Liberalism* (Rawls 2005). The sections quoted belong to Part Two of *Theory of Justice*, 'Institutions' (Chapters IV–VII). In it, writes Rawls, his aim was 'to show that the principles of justice, which so far have been discussed in abstraction from institutional forms, define a workable political conception, and are a reasonable approximation to and extension of our considered judgments' (Rawls 1971: 195).

a. 'public deliberation is focused on the common good';[7]
b. this deliberation 'requires some form of manifest equality among citizens'; and,
c. it 'shapes the identity and interests of citizens in ways that contribute to the formation of a public conception of common good'.[8]

Well, Cohen wonders, are Rawls's principles of a 'just society' enough to found those three aspects of a *well ordered democracy*? For Cohen, Rawls's view is insufficient, as he trusts too much – so to speak – in the implications of 'the intuitive ideal of a fair system of cooperation': if we take this ideal, 'we should want our political institutions themselves to conform, insofar as is feasible, to the requirement that terms of association be worked out under fair conditions' (*ibid.*: 20). That is to say, there is an immediate transposition from the principles of justice to the idea that such principles may be *mirrored* by democratic political institutions, founding their legitimacy. In Rawls, for Cohen, 'the original position serves as an *abstract model* of what fair conditions are, and of what we should strive to mirror in our political institutions, rather than as an initial-choice situation in which regulative principles for those institutions are selected' (*ibid.*: 20). Rawls is right in positing those three conditions, but

> ... what I find less plausible is that the three conditions are natural consequences of the ideal of fairness. Taking the notion of fairness as fundamental, and aiming ... to model political arrangements on the original position, it is not clear why, for example, political debate ought to be focused on the common good, or why the manifest equality of citizens is an important feature of a democratic association. The pluralist conception of democratic politics as a system of bargaining with fair representation for all groups seems an equally good mirror of the ideal of fairness (*ibid.*).

We are now getting to the turning point that leads Cohen to propose 'deliberative democracy' as a *procedural ideal of democracy*. The 'fundamental', 'basic', aspect cannot be an ideal of fairness as such, taken as a model for political and institutional orders; rather – says Cohen at the end of the first part of his essay – the basic aspect

---

7. 'In a well-ordered democracy, political debate is organized around alternative conceptions of the public good.' Hence the inadequacy – for a 'just society' – of 'an ideal pluralist scheme, in which democratic politics consists of fair bargaining among groups each of which pursues its particular or sectional interest'. 'Citizens and parties operating in the political arena ought not to "take a narrow or group-interested standpoint"' (Cohen 2009a: 17–18, quoting from Rawls 1971: 360).

8. A democratic politics, writes Cohen, 'should be ordered in ways that provide a basis for self-respect, that encourage the development of a sense of political competence, and that contribute to the formation of a sense of justice' (and here Cohen refers to Rawls 1971: 473–4); 'it should fix "the foundation for civic friendship and [shape] the ethos of political culture"' (Rawls 1971: 234)'. Therefore, 'the importance of democratic order is not confined to its role in obstructing the class legislation that can be expected from systems in which groups are effectively excluded from the channels of political representation and bargaining. In addition, democratic politics should also shape the ways in which the members of the society understand themselves and their legitimate interests' (Cohen 2009a: 19).

is 'an independent and expressly political ideal that is focused in the first instance on the appropriate conduct of public affairs – on, that is, the appropriate ways of arriving at collective decisions' (*ibid.*: 21). And to understand this *political* ideal, 'we ought not to proceed by seeking to 'mirror' ideal fairness in the fairness of political arrangements, but instead to proceed by seeking to mirror a system of ideal deliberation in social and political institutions' (*ibid.*).

Here starts the second part of the essay, formally defining and analysing the ideal deliberative procedure. Before looking at it, though, we should dwell on Cohen's theoretical strategy and on its consequences for the future development of deliberative democracy. Recalling, twenty years later, the points made in the 1989 paper, after recounting several attempts he had made in the 1980s to define his vision of 'radical' democracy, Cohen presented his final departure point as follows (*ibid.*: 7–8):

> The angle of approach that I was eventually drawn to centered on the idea of deliberative democracy. The deliberative democrat emphasizes that democracy is not simply about treating people as equals in a process of collective decision-making, or about fair bargaining among groups, but also about reasoning together as equals on matters of common concern (or it could be described as treating people as equals by relying on our common reason as a basis for justification). Here, I was moved in part by Habermas's ideal of decision arrived at through a process that reflects no force other than the force of the better argument (though Habermas had not presented this ideal in connection with a conception of democracy). And I was working with the intuitive idea that democracy might be thought of not only as a fair process or as an instrument for achieving just ends but as a way to realize in actual political life an ideal of justification through public reason-giving.

In short, the values of freedom and equality, or the principles of fairness and justice, are not extrinsic and independent goals, but must be incorporated in *democratic procedures themselves*: these, thus, escape an *instrumentalist* justification (that is, motivated only by the outcomes they produce or by their purposes). Therefore we can consider Cohen's view of deliberative democracy as a *constructivist* vision, because it defines the democratic political process as the result of a choice procedure, governed solely by the same reasoning power of free and equal individuals, and not as a process that is guided or inspired by 'independent' or pre-existing values or truths.[9]

If a just society, for Rawls, is one in which there is a fair system of co-operation between free and equal citizens, for Cohen, it is mainly one in which the very *decision-making procedures* (instituting that 'fair system') are *deliberative* and *democratic*. Such procedures are *deliberative* as they are founded by mutual *reason-giving* – by the public exchange of reasons between free and equal citizens treating each other with respect and committed to justifying their judgments to

---

9.   On this topic, see Ottonelli 2012: 111.

others. They are *democratic* as they are fully inclusive and egalitarian: they allow all those free and equal individuals to agree, with equal dignity and on the basis of mutual recognition, to the making of decisions. Therefore, they are deliberative and democratic procedures that, *ipso facto*, produce *legitimate* decisions: not surprisingly, the key to Cohen's position lies in the strong link between deliberation and democratic legitimacy (as signalled by the title of the essay).

This theoretical foundation of 'deliberative democracy' would prove to be suggestive, encouraging a *strong idealising character* in some subsequent elaborations of the theoretical field of deliberative democracy. As we have seen, Cohen rejects a justification of democratic procedures and institutions centred on the possibility that they are able to immediately mirror the principles of a theory of justice. Nevertheless, he affirms and fully adopts this logic of 'mirroring'.

One of the places where this logic is expressed in *Theory of Justice* is the so-called 'four-stage sequence' (§31). Here, Rawls outlines the steps through which citizens, or parties, first establish an agreement on the principles of justice in the original position, and then, giving rise to a 'constitutional convention', translate them into a 'just' constitution. These principles must, in turn, be 'mirrored' in the legislation and, finally, in the 'application' of individual judgments.[10]

Cohen intervenes in the deductive structure of Rawls's model with a sort of *interposition*: he accepts the internal logic of this model but feels the need to articulate, in a democratic and deliberative decision-making procedure, all that Rawls (in *Theory of Justice*) 'squeezed' into the terms 'choice' or 'rational agreement'. Rawls constantly evoked the choices and rational decisions that the parties make in the transition from one stage to another but left undetermined the *procedures* of these choices and decisions. Cohen asserts that these can or should only take place through a properly deliberative procedure. One could also say that Cohen traces Rawls's 'original position' to a previous stage: before rationally agreeing on the principles of a just society, the participants must agree on the democratic procedure by which to discuss it.

Cohen fully welcomes Rawls's axiomatic and deductive construction but shifts its terms: a 'well-ordered' democracy should mirror, first of all, an ideal deliberative procedure, which, in turn, incorporates some *fundamental procedural values*. Thinking back to his essay, twenty years later, Cohen claimed (*ibid.*: 8) that his intent, then, had been to place

> ... deliberation – understood as a kind of mutual reason-giving – as central to the democratic ideal in its most attractive form. By making such reason-giving central, the deliberative conception of democracy also showed how democracy was connected, so I argue, with the idea of autonomy, equality, and the common good: democracy, understood deliberatively, was both a procedural and a substantive ideal. And also, I thought, a specifically political

---

10. We will see in Chapters Eleven and Twelve how Rawls revisits the 'four-stage sequence' in both *Political Liberalism* and in his 'Reply to Habermas' (Rawls 2005: 364), inserting it into the new theoretical framework outlined in this work.

ideal, not tied to an encompassing moral outlook. The idea was not that people ought to reason about everything, or guide their personal choices by reflective, autonomous judgment, or that the unexamined life is not worth living, but that the legitimacy that emerges from democratic collective choice reflects the role of reason-giving – a kind of mutual justification – in the process.

So, 'deliberative democracy' also takes on the traits of an *ideal model of democracy* that can and should inspire the design of specific institutional settings, being put into *practice* through the construction of specific deliberative institutions. As we will see, this would be one of the areas in which Cohen, in the following years, would try to develop his approach.

In sum, Cohen agrees with what Rawls affirms about the 'principle of participation' and the principles of a 'fair constitution': 'we are in the way of describing an ideal arrangement, comparison with which defines a standard for judging actual institutions, and indicates what must be maintained to justify departures from it' (Rawls 1971: 227). The theory of deliberative democracy that Cohen builds, therefore, is an 'ideal theory', in the same specific sense in which Rawls called his theory of justice 'ideal' – distinguishing it from a 'non-ideal theory' – and with all the problematic, and perhaps even unresolved, aspects that this distinction entails.[11]

2. The democratic ideal of a 'deliberative association'

The central part of Cohen's essay is devoted to the illustration of the 'ideal deliberative procedure' and, at the beginning, the author proposed a definition of the 'notion of deliberative democracy' which would become very well known and often cited as a 'canonical' formulation of it (Cohen 2009a.: 21–2):

> The notion of deliberative democracy is rooted in the intuitive ideal of a democratic association in which the justification of the terms and conditions of association proceeds through public argument and reasoning among equal citizens. Citizens in such an order share a commitment to the resolution of problems of collective choice through public reasoning and regard their basic institutions as legitimate insofar as they establish the framework for free public deliberation. To elaborate this ideal, I begin with a more explicit account of the ideal itself, presenting what I shall call the 'formal' conception

---

11. 'The intuitive idea is to split the theory of justice in two parts. The first or ideal part assumes strict compliance and works out the principles that characterize a well-ordered society under favourable circumstances. It develops the conception of a perfectly just basic structure and the corresponding duties and obligations of persons under the fixed constraints of human life. My main concern is with this part of the theory. Nonideal theory, the second part, is worked out after an ideal conception of justice has been chosen; only then do the parties ask which principles to adopt under less happy conditions' (Rawls 1971: 245–6). And in another passage he writes: 'the ranking of the principles of justice in ideal theory reflects back and guides the application of these principles to nonideal situations' (*ibid.*: 303).

of deliberative democracy. Proceeding from this formal conception, I pursue a more substantive account of deliberative democracy, by presenting an account of an *ideal deliberative procedure* that captures the notion of justification through public argument and reasoning among equal citizens and serves in turn as a model for deliberative institutions.

So, we can see a double move here: having posited the autonomy and independence of a deliberative democratic ideal, and having also established its 'primacy' compared to an ideal of justice, Cohen first describes its 'formal' traits and then defines the ideal procedure in which these traits are 'substantiated'.

There are five 'main features' of the 'formal conception' and they are all related to the characteristics of an association: indeed, deliberative democracy can be defined precisely as an association with these given features. Cohen sets out the first principles that allow us to define an 'association' as a 'deliberative democracy' (*ibid.*: 22–3):

a. permanence in time and independence ('a deliberative democracy is an ongoing and independent association, whose members expect it to continue into the indefinite future');
b. a shared and conscious commitment (a pre-commitment) to taking deliberation as the basis of the legitimacy of collective decisions;
c. pluralism and the acceptance thereof, the absence of preventive obligations and constraints that pre-determine the outcome of the deliberation;
d. publicity; and
e. the mutual recognition of every citizen's deliberative capacities.

Given the overtly 'formal' character of this first definition of the ideal of deliberative democracy, the next step will be 'to give substance' to it, 'by characterizing the conditions that should obtain if the social order is to be manifestly regulated by deliberative forms of collective choice' (*ibid.*: 23). And this 'substance' can be pursued if, from this ideal, we infer the content of an 'ideal deliberative procedure', through which 'to give an explicit statement of the conditions for deliberative decision-making that are suited to the formal conception' and therefore 'to highlight the properties that democratic institutions should embody, so far as possible' (*ibid.*). Thus, from Cohen's perspective, the ideal of deliberative democracy appears as a *regulative model* (*ibid.*: 23): 'I should emphasize that the ideal deliberative procedure is meant to provide a model for institutions to mirror – in the first instance for the institutions in which collective choices are made and social outcomes publicly justified'. Furthermore (*ibid.*: 29), 'the role of the ideal deliberative procedure is to provide an abstract characterization of the important properties of deliberative institutions'.

In general terms, deliberation has some fixed characteristics: it involves deciding on an agenda; proposing alternative solutions to problems; supporting these solutions on the basis of reasons and arguments; and concluding by opting for one of these alternatives. A democratic deliberation requires that additional requirements are met, 'in particular, outcomes are democratically legitimate if and only if they could be the object of a free and reasoned agreements among equals' (*ibid.*: 21). The ideal deliberative procedure is one that 'captures' this principle. Cohen articulates its definition in four points, in very dense passages that could be discussed at length. From my point of view, it is particularly important to highlight here the *implications* of this conceptual stylisation of the ideal conditions that must be met for a decision-making procedure to be considered democratic and deliberative.

An ideal deliberation is:

a. *Free from constraints or preliminary restrictions.* Decisions resulting from it, then, are legitimate as the exclusive result of deliberation itself (*ibid.*: 23–4).

b. *'Reasoned'.* A democratic procedure of choice or collective decision can be said to be deliberative if it comes from an exchange of reasons. Participants are asked for a pre-commitment to act only using arguments and reasons in favour or against proposals. The assumption is that all participants have a common and reasonable expectation that these reasons and the 'strength of the better argument' cause the acceptance or rejection of a proposal. It cannot be the 'power' (whatever it is) of a participant that determines the decision. The deliberative arena, from this point of view, must also be 'purified' of strategic or instrumental behaviour. On this point, Cohen 'meets' Habermas: but in a particular way which should be noted. First of all, Cohen still refers to *Legitimation Crisis*, which dates from 1975.[12] Second, like Elster, Cohen makes a shift: the 'strength of the best argument', which Habermas called a feature of the 'ideal speech situation' and of the latter acting as an 'inevitable presupposition' of argumentation, is now taken as a principle of an ideal conception of democracy.[13]

But this second point of the definition shares even more conceptual elements with the work of other authors that was giving shape to the new deliberative paradigm. For instance, there is the theme of the nature and role of 'preferences', which appeared in Sunstein, Elster and Manin. A deliberative conception of democracy, argues Cohen, offers a vision of the decision-making process that produces 'collective choice' in a deliberative way, and therein lies the source of their legitimacy – and

---

12. 'Deliberation is reasoned in that the parties to it are required to state their reasons for advancing proposals, supporting them, or criticizing them. They give reasons with the expectation that those reasons (and not, for example, their power) will settle the fate of their proposal. In ideal deliberation, as Habermas put it, "no force except that of the better argument is exercised"' (*ibid.*: 24). Here, the reference is Habermas 1975: 108.

13. In a passage of his Introduction (2009a: 7–8), Cohen shows he is aware of the problem that Habermas 'had not presented this ideal in connection with a conception of democracy'. Habermas's influence was later critically noted by Freeman (2000: 393), who underlined the 'proceduralist' flavour of this first essay by Cohen, which was corrected in subsequent works by a more balanced view of the 'substantive' nature of the democratic deliberative ideal.

not in the fact that these choices correspond immediately to citizens' preferences. 'The deliberative conception', writes Cohen (*ibid.*: 24), 'emphasizes that collective decisions should be made in a deliberative way, and not only that those choices should have a desirable fit with the preferences of citizens'.

An ideal deliberative procedure, then, is also:

c. *Characterised by equality between the participants.* In ideal deliberation, parties are both formally and substantively equal. They are formally equal in that the rules regulating the procedure do not single out individuals. Everyone with the deliberative capacity has equal standing at each stage of the deliberative process. Each can put issues on the agenda, propose solutions, and offer reasons in support of or in criticism of proposals. And each has an equal voice in the decision. The participants are substantively equal in that the existing distribution of power and resources does not shape their chance to contribute to deliberation, nor does that distribution play an authoritative role in the deliberation (*ibid.*: 24).

In an ideal deliberative procedure, therefore, there is not only a formal condition of equality (everyone has an equal 'say') but also a kind of neutralisation of the inequality (of resources and power) between individuals. These inequalities do not affect individual deliberative capacity.

This, of course, is a rather problematic point. Cohen makes it clear that the ideal deliberative procedure provides a model that can be mirrored by institutions but the ideal character of this procedure should not be confused with a hypothetical-choice situation (like Rawls's original position),[14] that abstracts from the information, resources and life-conditions of single individuals. The ideal deliberative procedure does not aim 'to characterize an initial situation in which the terms of association themselves are chosen' (*ibid.*: 22): rather, it outlines the necessary conditions for making collective decisions in a deliberative way and for them to be considered democratically legitimate. So, the citizens involved may and do have a different endowment of resources and power but enter into the ideal deliberative process only as free and equal.

Programmatically, Cohen works at a high level of abstraction. He proceeds through a chain of axiomatic stipulations ('I have *stipulated* that the members of the association are committed to resolving their differences through deliberation'; *ibid.*: 26, my emphasis). And yet, as we have seen, it is Cohen himself who ultimately authorises a regulative transposition of the ideal conditions of a deliberative procedure ('deduced' logically from a definition of democracy as political ideal). Many problems for deliberative democracy, in its later empirical turn, arose precisely when

---

14. Elsewhere in the essay, Cohen writes: 'the role of the ideal deliberative procedure is thus different from the role of an ideal social contract. ... It is not a choice situation in which institutional principles are selected.' (*ibid.*: 29).

such a transposition was proposed in immediately operational terms, through the design and testing of *ad hoc* devices or methods for trying to reproduce the conditions defined at a theoretical level artificially.

Finally, an ideal deliberative procedure is:

d. *Aimed at reaching a rationally motivated consensus.* So we come to the last point, which will also be a harbinger of countless misunderstandings and controversies: an ideal deliberation, writes Cohen,

> ... aims to arrive at a rationally motivated consensus – to find reasons that are persuasive to all who are committed to acting on the results of a free and reasoned assessment of alternatives among equals. Even under ideal conditions there is no promise that consensual reasons will be forthcoming. If they are not, then deliberation concludes with voting, subject to some form of majority rule.[15] The fact that it may so conclude does not, however, eliminate the distinction between deliberative forms of collective choice and forms that aggregate non-deliberative preferences. The institutional consequences are likely to be different in the two cases, and the result of voting among those who are committed to finding reasons that are persuasive to all are likely to differ from the results of an aggregation that proceeds in an absence of this commitment (*ibid.*: 25).

The purpose of an ideal deliberative procedure, therefore, is to achieve a rationally motivated consensus. The idea that such consensus *can* be actually achieved is a logical implication of the above conditions: in particular, it follows from the assumption that deliberation must only be based on mutual (and exclusive, 'pure') *reason-giving. But such an outcome is not obvious*, in the presence of that 'pluralism' which – remember – was even listed as one of the constitutive conditions of an ideal association of individuals that make up a deliberative democracy. It is not obvious, but it cannot be ruled out *a priori* either: these pages of Cohen's show the difficulty of a theoretical approach based on using regulative principles as practical guidelines. This perspective surely rebuts the accusation of 'unrealism' but opens a dangerous gap between the ideally demanding character of the model and its potential practical operation. Rational consensus remains an ideal, a guideline to follow, but the gap between 'ideal' and 'real' risks becoming unbridgeable.

3. From the ideal deliberative procedure to institutions

In the last part of his essay, Cohen wishes to say something 'more substantive about a deliberative democracy' (*ibid.*: 25). In this sense, he gives special attention to the issue of the 'common good': there is no 'common good' defined *a priori* or

---

15. Here, Cohen cited Manin 1987: 359–61 'for criticism of the reliance on an assumption of unanimity in deliberative views'.

placed in some way as an end outside of deliberation. Indeed, in Cohen we find clearly visible traces of the 'republican' conception we have seen in Sunstein (who is recalled by Cohen), or the idea of a deliberative civic practice *constructing* the common good (*ibid.*: 27):

> Deliberation, then, focuses debate on the common good. And the relevant conceptions of the common good are not comprised simply of interests and preferences that are antecedent to deliberation. Instead, the interests, the aims, and ideals that constitute the common good are those that survive deliberation, interests that, on public reflection, we think it legitimate to appeal to in making claims on social resources.[16]

Cohen comes to this statement on the basis of the postulates of the initial definition of ideal deliberation: *given* that 'the aim of ideal deliberation is to secure agreement among all who are committed to free deliberation among equals', and *given* the ineliminable condition of *pluralism*,

> ... the focus of deliberation is on ways of advancing the aims of each party to it. While no one is indifferent to his/her own good, everyone also seeks to arrive at decisions that are acceptable to all who share the commitment to deliberation ... Thus the characterization of an ideal deliberative procedure links the formal notion of deliberative democracy with the more substantive ideal of a democratic association in which public debate is focused on the common good of the members (*ibid.*: 25).

But of course, to 'talk about the common good is one thing; sincere efforts to advance it are another'. What saves us from the fact that even an ideal deliberation could actually harbour an attempt 'to disguise personal or class advantage as the common advantage?' (*ibid.*: 25–6).

The answer to this question is significant. Of course, says Cohen, one could resort to a formal definition and to those postulates that tell us how to distinguish a democratic deliberation proper – excluding, *by definition*, the cases in which the idea of a common good is but a fiction. Admittedly, this answer is insufficient. Cohen's line of argument that follows draws extensively on John Elster's *Sour Grapes* (1983) and Habermas,[17] in addition to Rawls: for the latter, Cohen quotes his 1987 essay on the idea of an 'overlapping consensus'.[18] Cohen here claims that the *public and communicative* dimensions of a deliberative process affect the

---

16. Cohen (1986a) had previously defended, *contra* Riker (1982), an 'epistemic' conception of democracy: theories that are based on the 'general will' assume that the 'common good' is something to construct, not an existing datum.

17. Cohen quotes the above-mentioned passage of *Legitimation Crisis* (in particular, the discussion of 'needs that can be communicatively shared') and refers to the entire chapter of *Communication and the Evolution of Society* (1979) entitled 'Moral development and ego identity', which originally appeared in *Zur Rekonstruktion der Historischen Materialismus* (1974).

18. *See* Chapter Eleven of this volume. Rawls's essay first appeared in the *Oxford Journal of Legal Studies* 1987, 7(1): 1–25, and then became Lecture IV of *Political Liberalism*.

motivations of the participants and therefore create *restraints* that tend to limit or even annihilate the role of personal or partial interests:

> A consequence of reasonableness of the deliberative procedure together with the conditions of pluralism is that the mere fact of having a preference, a conviction, or an ideal does not by itself provide a reason in support of a proposal. While I may take my preferences as a sufficient reason for advancing a proposal, deliberation under conditions of pluralism requires that I find reasons that make the proposal acceptable to others who cannot be expected to regard my preferences as sufficient reason for agreeing (*ibid.*: 26).

A *public* deliberative procedure implies a *pre-commitment* 'to the deliberative resolution of political questions'; this very fact increases the 'likelihood of a sincere representation of preferences and convictions', while reducing the probability of their 'strategic misrepresentation'; most of all, it entails a *transformation* of the contents of initial preferences and convictions:

> Assuming a commitment to deliberative justification, the discovery that I can offer no persuasive reason on behalf of a proposal of mine may transform the preferences that motivate the proposal. Aims that I recognize to be inconsistent with the requirements of deliberative agreement may tend to lose their force ... Consider, for example, the desire to be wealthier come what may. I cannot appeal to this desire itself in defending policies (*ibid.*: 26–7).

Hence a motivation 'to find an independent justification that does not appeal to this desire and will tend to shape into, for example, a desire to have a level of wealth that is consistent with a level that others (i.e., equal citizens) find acceptable'.

Autonomy also appears as a substantive value embodied in a deliberative procedure: in general – notes Cohen, openly recalling Elster's analysis – an individual's autonomy of action and choice can be threatened when their preferences are determined by external factors out of their control, or when the absence of real alternatives limits the exercise of their deliberative abilities. Hence the phenomenon of 'adaptive' or 'accommodationist preferences': 'psychological adjustments to conditions of subordination in which individuals are not recognized as having the capacity for self-government' and in which they have no real alternatives – such as when 'Stoic slaves' seek to 'minimiz[e] frustration' and therefore deliberately choose to 'cultivate desires to be slaves', without this making their choice autonomous (*ibid.*: 27–8). These 'dimensions of autonomy' ('conditions that permit and encourage the deliberative formation of preferences'; 'favorable conditions for the exercise of the deliberative capacities') are both foreseen and assumed in the definition of an ideal deliberative procedure (*ibid.*: 28).

One cannot help noticing a classic *petitio principii* here. Cohen 'deduces' from his initial definition the logical demonstration that a *substantive* ideal of autonomy is also *implied* by the original tenets of an ideal deliberative procedure. And yet, this is obviously an *ought-to-be*: the burden of proof then shifts to the possibility of translating this ideal on to a practical and empirical level, especially in institutions able to embody it. 'Beginning, then, from the formal ideal of a deliberative democracy', Cohen sums up his theoretical path at the end of the second section of his essay:

> ... we arrive at the more substantive ideal of an association that is regulated by deliberation aimed at the common good and that respects the autonomy of the members. And so, in seeking to embody the ideal deliberative procedure in institutions, we seek, *inter alia*, to design institutions that focus on political debates on the common good, that shape the identity and interests of citizens in ways that contribute to an attachment to the common good, and that provide the favourable conditions for the exercise of deliberative powers that are required for autonomy (*ibid.*: 28).

This idealising projection stands out in the final part of the essay, where Cohen underlines that a crucial aim of deliberative democracy is to specify the institutional preconditions for deliberative *decision-making*: 'the ideal deliberative procedure provide a model for institutions, a model that they should mirror, so far as possible'. The crucial point, Cohen says, is that institutions 'should *make deliberation possible*', and must therefore offer 'the *framework* for the formation of the will; they determine whether there is equality, whether deliberation is free and reasoned, whether there is autonomy' (*ibid.*: 28, my emphasis).

Finally, in the last part of his work, Cohen discusses four possible objections to the deliberative ideal.

a. *The accusation of sectarianism*, that is, of being an ideal relying 'on a particular view of the good life – an ideal of active citizenship'. However, for Cohen, a conception of democracy cannot be considered a view of the good, as 'it is organized around a view of political justification – that *justification proceeds through free deliberation among equal citizens – and not around a conception* of the proper conduct of life' (*ibid.*: 30).

b. *The accusation of incoherence*, which comes from 'an important tradition of argument' starting with Schumpeter and culminating in William Riker's (then) recent work (Riker 1982) on social choice and democracy. Riker's thesis – that any claim that 'popular self-government', is the outcome of a procedure aggregating single wills bound to external institutional boundaries and rules is incoherent and unstable, as shown by Arrow's theorem – does not hold for the deliberative conception. Indeed, the latter denies the possibility of considering 'preferences and convictions that are relevant to collective decisions apart from the institutions through which they are formed and expressed' (Cohen 2009a: 31).

c. *The accusation of injustice*, that is, that considering democracy a 'basic ideal' would jeopardise the individual's 'basic liberties', making them 'dependent on judgments of majorities', thereby acknowledging 'the democratic legitimacy of decisions that restrict the basic liberties of individuals'. Cohen rejects this objection with a long discussion of the issue of freedom of expression, concluding that 'the liberties are not simply among the topics for deliberation; they help to provide the framework that makes it possible' (*ibid.*: 32--4).

However, for the purposes of this present work, what matters most is Cohen's answer to the fourth objection, that:

d. '*the notion of public deliberation is irrelevant to modern political conditions*' (*ibid.*: 34), referring to Carl Schmitt 'for an especially sharp statement of the irrelevance objection' (*ibid.*; note 37). This accusation rests on an assumption rejected by Cohen, namely, that 'a direct democracy with citizens gathering in legislative assemblies is the only way to institutionalize a deliberative procedure' (*ibid.*). In these pages, Cohen's strategy of institutionalising deliberative procedure stands out very clearly. This objection gives Cohen a chance to distance himself from any undue identification between deliberative democracy and direct democracy: 'the impossibility [today] of direct democracy is plainly correct. But I see no merit in the claim that direct democracy is the uniquely suitable way to institutionalize the ideal procedure' (*ibid.*). Moreover: 'there is no reason to be confident that a direct democracy would subject political questions to deliberative resolution, even if a direct democracy were a genuine institutional possibility.' And, in a footnote – as a further sign of the importance of the debate on the origins and the foundations of American constitutional democracy – Cohen recalls the dialogue between Madison and Jefferson (*ibid.*: 35, note 39).

At this point, Rousseau comes back into play: 'we cannot simply assume that large gatherings with open-ended agendas will yield any deliberation at all' (*ibid.*: 35). Cohen notes how this vision 'is sometimes associated with Rousseau, who is said to have conflated the notion of democratic legitimacy with the institutional expression of that ideal in a direct democracy' (*ibid.*: 34, note 38). For Cohen, this is not the case and, 'for criticism of this interpretation', he refers the reader to his essay 'Autonomy and democracy: reflections on Rousseau' (Cohen 1996b).[19] Rousseau's social contract answers the question 'what kind of association would be rationally agreed to by socially interdependent individuals who are moved by self-love and, above all, by an interest in securing their freedom?' (*ibid.*: 277). Cohen's analysis of the institutional implications of Rousseau's thought rejects an interpretation of it as supporting direct democracy with no mediations or articulations. What Rousseau proposed, writes Cohen, is rather an 'institutional ideal that realizes autonomy under conditions of interdependence' among individuals. That's why, concluded Cohen, despite the criticism one might make today, 'Rousseau's work as a theorist of institutions remains a paradigm of, and reasonable point of departure for, egalitarian political criticism' (*ibid.*: 297).

---

19. At the end of this essay, Cohen especially thanked John Rawls and, indeed, Rousseau's profile in this text seems to be very much inspired by Rawls's interpretation. Cohen also devoted one of his later works to Rousseau (Cohen 2010b).

Once any undue identification between deliberative and direct democracy has been rejected, space opens up for an adequate institutionalisation of deliberative procedures, to which Cohen would devote much attention in his subsequent works.[20] The institutional projection of the deliberative ideal goes as far as to propose a justification of the costs of this strategy, which entails (Cohen 2009a: 35)

> ... the existence of arenas in which citizens can propose issues for the political agenda and participate in debate about those issues. The existence of such arenas is a public good and ought to be supported with public money. This is not because public support is the only way, or even the most efficient way, of ensuring the provision of such arenas. Instead, public provision expresses the basic commitment of a democratic order to the resolution of political questions through free deliberation among equals. The problem is to figure out how arenas might be organized to encourage such deliberation.

One can say that, with these last words, Cohen gave a significant input to the 'work programme' of many deliberative theorists and deliberative practitioners over the next years.[21] But this strategy of institutionalisation would face several problems, some of which were noted by Cohen himself. First of all, there was the problem of preventing material inequalities from translating into political ones. There was also the risk that deliberative arenas 'organized on local, sectional, or issue-specific lines' would fail to produce deliberation that was truly 'open-ended' enough to justify its institutionalisation. Here, Cohen introduces the topic of political parties, in very similar terms to Manin's: parties 'can provide the more open-ended arenas needed to form and articulate the conception of the common good that provide the focus of political debate in a deliberative democracy' (*ibid.*: 36), helping reduce the inequalities that undermine the possibility of a truly fair and free deliberative procedure.[22]

Cohen's essay, together with Elster's and Manin's, decisively marks the beginning of the first, constitutive phase of the new field of deliberative democracy. These three contributions converged on the idea of public deliberation as the

---

20. Particularly in the essay, 'Directly deliberative polyarchy', which he co-wrote with Charles Sabel in 1997 and is now in Cohen 2009a. *See* Chapter Ten; *see also* Cohen and Rogers 1993.

21. For a critical observation on Cohen's influence in this sense, see Heath 2011; also *cf.* Chapter Thirteen, note 6).

22. Cohen derives from this an explicit statement in favour of the public funding of parties: 'political parties supported by public funds play an important role in making a deliberative democracy possible' (Cohen 1989: 36). Cohen also refers to a debate that was then going on within political science: 'the idea that parties are required to organize political choice and to provide a focus for public deliberation is one strand of arguments about "responsible parties" in American political science literature' and, in particular ('on the implication of party decline for democratic politics'), he quotes a famous scholar of the political system and of American electoral history, Walter D. Burnham, in *The Current Crisis in American Politics* (1982). The reference to the issue of 'responsible' parties probably gestures towards a well known report of the American Political Science Association (APSA) Committee on Political Parties, *Toward A More Responsible Two Party System* (APSA 1950).

foundation of democratic legitimacy but also had significant differences from one another that are perhaps easier to notice today, in the light of later developments. The critical point of Cohen's proposal is basically his theoretical approach, which implies a decisive choice: his is not a *theory* of democracy but *an ideal model* of democracy. That is: *not* a theory with both an analytical-interpretative dimension and a normative one (that is, one telling us through what theoretical categories to understand the 'fact of democracy' as well as its normative implications). Instead, Cohen had a different focus, deliberative democracy as an *ideal model* that could and should be mirrored by democratic institutions. This shift has important consequences: in the next years, it would be reflected in the prevailing image of deliberative democracy as an *ideal to strive for* but, also, ultimately, as a *political proposal* aiming to cure the ill health of our democracies – including indicating a series of methodological prescriptions through which to design new democratic institutions, thus showing its plausibility and practicability.

As we have seen, this image of deliberative democracy as an *ideal* was not the only one possible. At the origins of it, there was another line of development: that of a deliberative *theory* of democracy, mainly based on the critical understanding of the deliberative dimension inherent in a democracy, which historically developed with the emergence of modern democracy. According to this view, a deliberative dimension can characterise a democratic order in various ways and to various degrees and it is only starting from here that we can grasp the normative potential of such an order. In the background of these two options, of course, we can glimpse the thought of Rawls and Habermas, to whom, as we have seen, many authors referred in different ways in the constitutive phase of this new theoretical field. We shall see later how Habermas and Rawls came into play directly in this debate. But first, to complete this picture of the framework of the theoretical field of deliberative democracy in the early 1990s, we must look at the intersections, overlaps and new developments that constituted the full theoretical development of the field.

Chapter Seven

Intersections, Convergences and New Developments: Expanding the Theoretical Field of Deliberative Democracy

In previous chapters, I have reconstructed the steps by which, during the 1980s, the idea of a 'deliberative democracy' was first formulated. We have seen that this early development took place in theoretical works belonging to specific disciplinary areas. However, the field of deliberative democracy as it would be consolidated over the next decade was a product of the *convergence* of several currents of thought, and the *entry*, so to speak, of other theoretical traditions. In this chapter, I will present some of these new developments, without which it would be impossible to understand what, today, we call 'deliberative democracy'. There are two crucial aspects to this process in the early 1990s: the emergence of a theoretical and empirical interest on part of the tradition of political theory and some first forms of encounter with the theoretical and practical legacy of participatory democracy.

On the one hand, the encounter between deliberative democracy and political theory owes a lot to James Fishkin and his relation to Robert Dahl's work. On the other hand, the recovery of some of the traditional themes (especially American ones) of participatory democracy took place in more 'underground' but clearly identifiable forms – especially through theories and practices of *planning*, the public-policy field that, since the 1960s, had sought to guide and regulate urban and regional development and to create and test new models of territorial governance. This tradition of study and practice came to intersect with Habermas's work.

1. John Forester: communicative interaction, policy analysis and planning practices

During its development, the field of deliberative democracy was influenced from many directions but Habermas's categories and concepts (as well as some misunderstandings resulting therefrom) had influence well beyond authors directly engaged on the philosophical side. As Brunkhorst recalls (2006: 18–19), 'in the course of the Seventies, concepts such as *communication* and *discourse*, which Habermas initially used in a strictly theoretical sense, were widely spread' and, even though 'Habermas felt mostly misunderstood', such concepts inevitably

> … did not lack a diagnostic and allusive value. The concept of *Diskurs*, for example, ended up secretly matching – regardless of the diversity of contexts – the concept of *discours* advanced by French post-structuralism: a concept that,

in Paris, was immediately politicized and instrumentalized in a voluntarist way (for example, in Michel Foucault's work). Although Habermas always rejected post-structuralist voluntarism, the concept of *discourse* – for him no less than for Foucault – served to envisage the complex, diverse and modern '*knowledge-based society*' [*Wissengesellschaft*] within the framework of a critique of power and domination (*ibid.*).

And thus, 'Habermas's idea of discourse ended up having an immediately political, albeit reformist, value'. It is true that Habermas, on several occasions, stressed 'the need to institutionalize practical discourses',[1] in contrast to the ideological theorising of 'political spontaneity' common in those years. But this warning was not sufficient to prevent the use of these notions in a distorted way. As Brunkhorst also pointed out (*ibid.*: 19):

> In the early Seventies, concepts such as 'discourse' or 'domination-free communication' were immediately taken up, spread and understood too concretely. In his theory of communication, Habermas had identified the ideal *presuppositions* (truth, normative rightness, sincerity, logical consistency) that people *always* postulate as implied in any 'speech act' ... Instead, in the secondary literature referring to Habermas and his concept of discourse, all this was misunderstood as a sort of programme *to be put into practice*.

In the following years, as we shall see, this 'practical' projection acquired greater critical awareness and the immediately political 'uses' of Habermas's categories gradually disappeared. However, we have also seen the shift, full of theoretical and political implications (the 'ideal speech situation' that turns from 'presupposition' into an 'ideal model'), that accompanied the development of the idea of deliberative democracy and influenced projects to verify its plausibility 'practically'.

Among the many intersections that occurred in those years, I want to highlight one that seems, from my perspective, particularly significant. We have seen how the models of participatory democracy constructed in the 1960s and the first half of the 1970s, especially in the United States, owed a lot to the political culture that accompanied the generational uprising of that time. And we have also seen how these models (Sherry Arnstein's work is a good example: *see* Chapter One, Section 4) were very closely connected to the political climate of the Great Society and federal programmes for urban renewal and fighting poverty, and thus also connected to the ideas of *community planning* and *community control*. In this context, of course, the main points at issue were the role and features that citizens' participation could and should have.

Any attempt, even if cursory, to reconstruct this story would lead me away from my topic. Nevertheless, I wish to highlight this 'border area' that would

---

1. See the Introduction to the 1971 edition of *Theorie und Praxis* (for English translation, see Habermas 1973).

soon be created between 'participatory democracy' and the developing field of deliberative democracy; I also want to identify, even if only by way of example, some texts and authors more directly related to the 'genealogical' itinerary that we have followed so far.

In 1985, John Forester – an American community planner[2] who later made an important contribution to the theory and practice of deliberative democracy with his successful *The Deliberative Practitioner* (1999)[3] – edited a collection of essays, *Critical Theory and Public Life*, all openly inspired by Habermas and, in particular, by his notions of 'systematically distorted communication' (Forester 1985: xiii) and 'ideal speech situation', which were taken as critical-evaluative parameters.

Forester's essay collection was not an isolated product: it belonged to a current of criticism that sought to radically rethink models of planning practices that were based on a purely technical-instrumental conception of rationality. Research on the operational effects of traditional planning practices (especially in the field of urban policies) brought planning scholars very quickly, particularly in the United States and Great Britain, to discover an *interactive* dimension characterising territorial governance processes – that is, there being arenas in which a plurality of actors form and transform their identities and define their own interests through a co-operative and confrontational 'game', involving a constitutive dimension of dialogue and communication. Thus, the search for a new paradigm was outlined: a 'communicative planning theory' (Healey 1997: 28–30), that drew from Habermas's discourse ethics and from a concept of communicative rationality intended as a normative principle by which to evaluate and design interactive planning practices.[4]

In the Introduction to the volume (which also included Habermas's short essay on 'Modern and post-modern architecture'),[5] Forester wrote that the essays in the collection aimed to 'examine the research implication and the empirical

---

2. Born in 1948, at present he is Professor of Urban and Regional Planning at Cornell University.

3. Other works by Forester worth mentioning are: *Planning in the Face of Power* (1989); *Critical Theory, Public Policy, and Planning Practice* (1993); and the collection co-edited with Frank Fischer *The Argumentative Turn in Policy Analysis and Planning* (1996).

4. On this evolution of the theoretical paradigms of urban and regional planning, see Healey 1997 (especially chapter 1). Healey's work allows us to reconstruct the theoretical debate in those years, the intertwining of policy analysis, planning and participation. It also allows us to situate Arnstein's 'ladder' in its original context (*ibid.*: 22–7). 'Planning systems and practice', Healey writes (*ibid.*: 3–4), 'have their power and justification in the role they play in helping the political communities of places work out how to manage their collective concerns about the qualities of shared spaces and the local environment'. Hence (*ibid.*: 40, my emphasis), the proposal of 'a *communicative* approach to the design of governance systems and practice, focusing on ways of fostering collaborative, consensus-building practices'. It 'takes as a normative position an ethical commitment to enabling all stakeholders to have a voice. It offers a way of mobilising for change through collective efforts in transforming ways of thinking. It thus presents a way forward in realising the practical meaning of participatory democracy in pluralist societies.' On these subjects, *see also* Perrone 2010 and 2011.

5. It was the text of a lecture given in Munich and published for the first time in *Süddeutsche Zeitung* on December 5–6 (Habermas 1985).

applicability of Habermas's theory' in the field of public policies and planning practices and 'to explore issues of public life', such as 'the vulnerabilities and the contingencies of the everyday life and social action in workplaces, in schools, in planning processes, and in broader social, political, and cultural settings' (Forester 1985: ix). These essays were 'concerned with social research efforts that will enable practical analysis of – and political responses to – operative, systemic distortions of everyday communicative interactions' (*ibid.*: xvi). Such texts were also full of references to the experiences of *community planning* in progress at that time and to forms of citizen involvement that, especially in the United States and Great Britain, already had a solid background.[6]

An essay written by Forester himself, entitled 'Critical theory and planning practice' (1985: 202–30) offered the theoretical framework of this new approach to the construction of public policies with a participatory dimension. Relying on 'eighteen months of regular observation' of a metropolitan city-planning department dedicated to environmental review, Forester affirmed that 'critical theory gives us a new way of understanding action, or what a planner does'. The planner's course of action can be defined as 'attention-shaping', or moulding public discourse, and therefore as a 'communicative action, rather than more narrowly as a means to a particular end (instrumental action)' (*ibid.*: 203). But these intentions were not only 'critical': 'if planners do not recognize how their ordinary actions may have subtle communicative effects, the planners may be well-meaning but counterproductive nonetheless'; thus, 'by recognizing the practical, communicative character of planning actions, we can suggest strategies to avoid these problems and improve practice as well' (*ibid.*).

Later, this approach tended to overlap with (or return to) the field of deliberative democracy and to recall other specific intellectual and disciplinary traditions therein.[7] In fact, many specific models and practices of deliberative democracy went in this direction, aiming to 'improve the practices' by which participatory and deliberative processes of policy-making or community planning were constructed. However, for the purposes of this book, it is interesting to notice the role that Habermas's thought played in this process: it is a good example of how theoretical reflection, usually regarded as very 'abstract', can be 'translated' to serve the purposes of a discipline with strong 'practical' implications, such as

---

6. For example, Ray Kemp's essay on the increasing use in Britain of 'public hearings' and 'public inquiries' in the field of energy policies argued that their primary function was 'to legitimize the actions and interests of dominant groups. ... Following Jürgen Habermas, I contend that a primary mechanism through which this is achieved is the systematic distortion of the communication process that takes place at public inquiries' (Kemp 1985: 177).

7. This disciplinary tradition would also be enriched by its intersection with 'consensus building' models (Susskind, McKearnan and Thomas-Larmer 1999; Susskind-Cruikshank 1987), an approach developed in the early eighties, particularly at Harvard and MIT, and which has its roots in the traditions (very deep in the United States) of non-political and extra-judicial consensual resolution of local environmental conflicts. This approach would also develop through specific methodological proposals (e.g., the so-called 'alternative dispute resolution' method).

that of territorial planning. In Forester's text, but not only there,[8] the reference to Habermas is still closely connected to the legacy of the critical theory of the Frankfurt School, though emphasising Habermas's detachment from the 'desperate' conclusions reached by Adorno, Horkheimer and Marcuse. Therefore, important spaces opened up for political action that could be called both *critical-radical* and *reformist*. The theoretical presuppositions of the new theory of communicative action that Habermas had developed in those years were therefore being read in this context. According to Forester, the point was to deal with a '*linguistic phenomenology* as phenomenology of performative speech' (*ibid.*: xi). In fact, for Forester, Habermas's objectives would be much better clarified if, instead of talking of a 'linguistic turn', the terms 'performative turn' or 'turn to social action' were employed (*ibid.*: xii).

The already controversial topic of the 'ideal speech situation' was, of course, crucial. 'This discussion allows us to dissolve a recurrent misunderstanding' of this notion, Forester wrote. It is not 'a matter of political strategy'; interestingly, 'none of the essays [included in the volume] present the ideal speech situation as a goal to be realized concretely. Nevertheless, deviations from the formal idealization might still be usefully identified and assessed'. Obviously 'an ideal speech situation is never practically realized' because 'communication is always imperfect', but this does not imply that the concept isn't important from a practical standpoint (*ibid.*: xv). Forester derives this interpretation from Thomas McCarthy's introduction to *Legitimation Crisis* (McCarthy 1975), citing a passage that, I believe, is a good example of how Habermas was read in the English-speaking world in those years:

The very act of participating in a discourse, or attempting discursively to come to an agreement about the truth of a problematic statement or the correctness of a problematic norm, carries with it the supposition that a genuine agreement is possible. If we did not suppose that a justified consensus was possible and could in some way be distinguished from a false consensus, then the very meaning of discourse, indeed of speech, would be called into question (McCarthy 1975: xvi).

In his work, Forester refers to Habermas's theoretical categories, being well aware of their *linguistic* and *communicative* dimensions. In Forester's view, to transpose and valorise those categories in a specific context such as that of policy analysis and planning practices, it was necessary to introduce conceptual

---

8. According to Healey (1997: 265–6), 'Habermas' communicative ethics' was one of the premises of the new models of 'communicative planning': it 'performs a vital role, in providing a vocabulary to critique dialogical practices and to highlight communicative "distortions"'. The principles of communicative ethics, Healey added, are derived from Habermas, specifically 'from a notion of ideal speech situation ... Habermas of course does not imagine that such a situation could exist. ... These criteria do not describe a dialogical state to be reached. Rather, they represent the evaluative criteria that inhere within the process of communication itself' (Healey 1997: 266–7). Of course, in this disciplinary field too, Habermas's reception has always been controversial and many critics of the 'theory of communicative planning' held it responsible for overlooking the dimension of 'power'.

mediations. Forester intended to draw on both Habermas's theoretical suggestions and operational models. As Forester wrote a few years later (1989: 226, note 23):

> Habermas's notion of systematically distorted communication may be developed concretely, in organizationally and politically practical ways, by locating its effects within the basic communicative processes of the reproduction of social relations that constitute any real social organization. Habermas's analysis of the structure of ordinary communicative action and speech, his so-called universal pragmatics, suggests the dimensions of that reproduction (relations of knowledge, consent, trust, and comprehension).[9]

Thus, the 'ideal speech situation' is not taken as an ideal goal or an immediately political objective but as a *critical-evaluative criterion* by which to orient analyses and practices of policy-making. So, the attention shifted mainly to the *communicative forms* that shaped, or could shape, not only general daily practices but also the specific practices of political planning, with a strong emphasis on the responsibility and critical awareness of mediation figures (analysts, experts, 'facilitators', practitioners); such figures would acquired great importance in the subsequent development of participatory methodologies with a deliberative inspiration. Participation thus acquires a significant *communicative substance*: one participates, first of all, *because* one discusses (with all that this entails: acquisition of knowledge and information; clarification of one's interests and purpose; argumentative exchange; experience-based learning and so on). And the discussion, in turn, cannot be only informal and spontaneous. It must be organised and structured through appropriate procedures:

> ... simply to say that analysts provide information is correct, but not terribly helpful. *How* do they provide information, and what practical, political, and ethical differences can they make? The analysts' talk matters. When they speak, the analysts act: they notify, inform, alert, point out, designate, ask, warn, and so on. In asking for citizens' responses to proposals, analysts also shift responsibility to others and shape their participation, thus organizing (or disorganizing) attention both to project alternatives and to possibilities of action. So analysts are not apolitical problem-solvers or social engineers. Instead, they are actually pragmatic critics who must make selective arguments and therefore influence what other people learn about, not by technically calculating means to ends or error signals, but by *organizing attention* carefully to project possibilities, organizing for practical political purposes and organizational ends. ... Planning analysts transmit facts, but they also shape relationships, political ties, and others' attention, thus shaping not only others' thinking but their concerns, and participation, too (*ibid.*: 18–19).

---

9.   Here, Forester recalls two of Habermas' works: 'Reply to my critics' (1982) and the first chapter of *Communication and the Evolution of Society* (1979; *see also* Chapter 4, Section 1, note 1).

These words show how Habermas's theory of communicative action had also become a powerful *working theory*, able to inspire even in an 'operational' setting such as that of planning. And it did so – at least in the case of Forester, who can be judged one of the most attentive readers of Habermas – not in *idealising* terms, but with *reconstructive* intent. This definition of planning practices helps us to understand what planners do in their daily work, both when they are at the service of specific and organised interests and when they work to protect a wider and more disorganised public. In the latter case, planners can help voices that would otherwise remain unheard to have their say.

> ... by broadening the content of alternatives presented to affected citizens in community, labor, and environmental organizations, planners may work to expand citizens' vision, to clarify real policy and productive possibilities, and to focus public attention on actions that directly address the needs of the poor, the underserved, and the powerless (*ibid.*: 20).

In these texts published during the 1980s, Forester does not yet talk of 'deliberation': he would only pick up the term a few years later. Nevertheless, the importance of this theoretical and practical path, which would lead to 'deliberative democracy' proper, cannot be underestimated. Thanks to this, a new model of policy-making (participatory *and* deliberative) would intersect with the 'linguistic turn' that was being affirmed in philosophy. The idea of the dialogic and deliberative construction of public policies would acquire, in this way, full 'citizenship' within what today is called 'deliberative democracy'; conversely, a deliberative approach would enter the field of policy analysis.[10] However, as a result of this theoretical cross-fertilisation, the theoretical current of the idea of participation would also become a *movement*: a real *political proposal* to innovatively reactivate the idea of a 'participatory democracy' with particular attention to the *discursive* dimension and practices of public dialogue.

This significant intersection also caused many misunderstandings about the meaning of *empowerment* in these practices (as we shall see in Chapter Eight). In general, it is possible to say that, in this phase, in addition to the theoretical elaboration of the model, the *design* and *experimental* dimensions that could be derived from it became more and more relevant. This trend would also be hospitable to an overlap with the tradition of 'participatory democracy'. But these intersections and overlaps have not only led to different theoretical orientations or suggested possible practical projections: they have also generated different ways of understanding their possible political implications.

---

10. One of the first examples of the intersection between policy analysis and deliberative democracy can be found in Majone 1990. For a comprehensive overview of 'deliberative policy analysis', *see* Hajer and Wagenaar 2003.

2. John S. Dryzek's 'discursive democracy'

In one of his latest works, John Dryzek[11] (2010: 6, note 1), claims to be the author of the widely used expression '*deliberative turn*' in contemporary democratic theory. The appearance of this term dates from work published ten years earlier, entitled *Deliberative Democracy and Beyond: Liberals, critics, contestations* (Dryzek 2000). By this time, it was possible to make an initial assessment of the situation of deliberative theory (think of James Bohman's oft-cited 1998 review article, 'The coming of age of deliberative democracy').

Dryzek's 2000 analysis is important because he identified a dividing line in the development of deliberative democracy, distinguishing between a first phase in which deliberative democracy was characterised by its *critical* nature and a second phase in which it seemed to have lost this attitude, reaching an '*accommodation*' (Dryzek 2000: v) with the liberal state and the power structures of modern society. Rawls and, above all, Habermas, were taken to be principally responsible for this setback. In fact, Habermas's appears to be a genuine 'defection' (*ibid.*: 27) from his previous orientation. In contrast, Dryzek affirmed,

> ... unlike many of those who now sail under the deliberative banner, I will argue that a defensible theory of deliberative democracy must be critical in its orientation to established power structures, including those that operate beneath the constitutional surface of the liberal state, and so insurgent in relation to established institutions (*ibid.*: 2).

This 'assimilation of deliberative democracy to liberal constitutionalism', Dryzek argues, had been strengthened by the 'defection' of Habermas and 'Habermasians' such as Bohman (see Bohman 1996) but it was neither inevitable nor irreversible. Rather, Dryzek proposed his own theoretical 'genealogy', identifying a sort of first *critical* phase of deliberative democracy marked by authors such as Benjamin Barber (1984), Seyla Benhabib (1996b), David Miller (1992), Nancy Fraser (1992) and 'Habermas, *in his earlier work*' (Dryzek 2000: 27, my emphasis). In his 2000 book, Dryzek added himself and his *Discursive Democracy* (1990) to that list. 'In particular', he added, all of these authors 'have criticized the limited, aggregative account of democracy that appears in much liberal theory and practice (what Barber would call "thin democracy")' and 'have sought either radical reform of the liberal state, to make it more authentically deliberative, or the specification of alternative venues where deliberation might be sought' (Dryzek 2000: 27).

Dryzek's account – and his opposition to the claims in Bohman's review (*ibid.*: 27–8) – is important because it highlights how, in the late 1990s – after a decade of significant expansion – the 'boundaries' of the deliberative theoretical field were anything but unambiguous. In fact, significant differences of direction were

---

11. Born in Britain in 1953, Dryzek is Professor of Political Theory and Social Theory at the Australian National University at the time of writing. Previously, he was Head of the Department of Political Science at the Universities of Oregon and Melbourne.

already obvious. From this point of view, Dryzek's 1990 work can be considered the forerunner of a *critical-radical* approach to deliberative democracy that would become very relevant in the next two decades. His was a vision of democracy as a '*discursive contestation*', presented as a 'stronger and critical version of deliberative democracy' (*ibid.*: 30).

Dryzek's 1990 contribution introduced many elements that would be taken up in subsequent theoretical literature. However, his contribution is also notable for its well informed and very heated debate with the tradition of policy analysis.[12] In his stated intentions and in the design of his volume, Dryzek merged several trains of thought[13] but also openly highlighted his connection with previous models of participatory democracy, expressing particular affinity with Barber's position (Dryzek 1990: 124), while avoiding Barber's more openly 'communitarian' tone. This bringing together of participative and deliberative theory was made possible by a proposed model of democracy (based on communicative and discursive rationality) as a *political-cultural project* capable of facing the evils of liberal democracy. This new political-cultural orientation found its most consistent 'political form' in 'a more participatory democracy – "strong democracy" – in Barber's (1984) terms' (Dryzek 1990: 13).

Dryzek acknowledged that 'there is no simple dichotomy between liberal and participatory democracy' but he reiterated their radically different characters:

> As one moves toward the participatory pole ... politics becomes increasingly discursive, educational, oriented to truly public interests, and needful of active citizenship. In contrast, the liberal pole is dominated by voting, strategy, private interest, bargaining, exchange, spectacle, and limited involvement (Dryzek 1990: 13).

But above all, as is inevitable when trying to define a political-cultural *programme*, Dryzek also tried to identify the *subjects* of this radical transformation of democracy and noted significant 'signs of renewal in a variety of political movements, be they Green, feminist, peace oriented, or communitarian, and, I shall argue, in a variety of *institutional experiments*' (*ibid.*, my emphasis). This last statement (albeit already highlighted in a previous essay: Dryzek 1987) is where the novelty lies: in putting forward a critical and radical version of deliberative democracy while also trying to identify the social or political subjects to whom this project would be addressed, Dryzek also introduced the possible expression of deliberative democracy in terms of *institutional experimentation*. Hence the proposal of '*discursive designs*', as they are called, as an 'institutional

---

12. On the 'policy sciences of democracy', see also Dryzek's article of the same name (Dryzek 1989).

13. When he set out his intentions in the 1990 work, 'discursive democracy' was defined, rather ambitiously, as 'a coherent, integrative, and attractive program for politics, public policy, and political science', gathering contributions from various sources, such as 'a classical (Aristotelian) model of politics, participatory democracy, communicative action, practical reason, and critical theory' (Dryzek 1990: ix).

manifestation of discursive democracy, offering an alternative to the more familiar liberal institutions of the open society' (*ibid.*: 22).

Dryzek proposed his own (and somewhat questionable) theoretical genealogy:

I shall stress the Aristotelian and not the Kantian or Rousseauean aspects of communicative rationality. The more well-known contemporary heirs to the Aristotelian themes of *phronesis* and *praxis* include Arendt (1958), Gadamer (1975), MacIntyre (1981), and Habermas (1984–1987). Despite major differences, especially concerning the extent to which talk and action must and should be constrained by tradition, the common aim of these philosophers is to resurrect authentic and reasonable public discourse (*ibid*: 14).

But it is still (and above all) Habermas, with *Theory of Communicative Action*, who provides the theoretical background, acting as a sort of palimpsest, over which Dryzek draws the outlines of this ideal of discursive democracy.

[C]ommunicative rationality clearly obtains to the degree social interaction is free from domination (the exercise of power), strategizing by the actors involved, and (self-)deception. Further, all actors should be equally and fully capable of making and questioning arguments (communicatively competent). There should be no restrictions on the participation of these competent actors. Under such conditions, the only remaining authority is that of a good argument, which can be advanced on behalf of the veracity of empirical description, explanation, and understanding and, equally important, the validity of normative judgments (*ibid*: 15).

Dryzek is a careful reader of Habermas's works and, most of all, he takes account of Habermas's 'Reply to my critics' of 1982 (*see* Chapter Five, Section 2), in which he responded to utopian-idealising interpretations of the 'ideal speech situation'.

… the ideal speech situation does not exist, and clearly cannot exist in this world of variety in opinions and traditions. Its canons are always and unavoidably violated in the real world. But as Habermas postulates, the ideal speech situation is anticipated in every act of communication between individuals (see, e.g., Habermas 1970)[14] such that it is not just an invention of the philosopher or political theorist. Any individual communication, collective decision, or social practice that *could only* be justified by diverging from the precepts of the ideal speech situation is indefensible. The ideal speech situation and its hypothetical consensus can be used both within traditions and across the traditions to criticize real world practices. Like any utopia … its primary practical value is critical. It … is not supposed to be a blueprint (any more than

14. Dryzek recalls here one of the first essays in which Habermas started to deal with linguistic pragmatics, 'Toward a theory of communicative competence' (1970). *See* Chapter Four, note 7.

Rawls's, 1971, original position is intended to be a place to which rational actors can retreat). Critical purity might at most allow comparative evaluation (Dryzek 1990: 36–7).

Therefore, the ideal speech situation is not only a kind of regulative ideal or an evaluative paradigm; essentially, for Dryzek, it is 'a critical theory's counterfactual ideal' (*ibid.*: 36) and *insufficient* as such to *positively* delineate the contents of an alternative project. Dryzek would base his further theoretical programme on exactly the goal of showing how a discursive and communicative rationality can be translated and embodied in the discursive designs of new, real-world, social and institutional practices – an institutional design itself constructed by the protagonists in a discursive way and with a strongly 'participatory' and egalitarian dimension (*ibid.*: 40–56). It is also interesting to notice how Dryzek categorises as among the 'incipient' examples of 'discursive designs' – despite all their limitations – models of *alternative dispute resolution*, the examples of *regulatory negotiation* and various practices of *conflict-mediation* (especially in environmental matters), with numerous references to a literature that had already studied and analysed these early experiences in the 1980s (*ibid.*: 48).

However, the 'new social movements' were the ground for a more advanced and promising possibility of affirming, in '"real-world" approximations', the 'precepts of discursive democracy' (*ibid.*: 49–50). Thus, Dryzek's approach allowed him to recover the tradition of participatory democracy, with a strong emphasis on collective problem-solving as the goal of 'a model of politics that is discursive, democratic, and participatory' (*ibid.*: 147–8). Such an approach was needed to leverage the contradictions of contemporary capitalism, in order to bring about radical reforming action, with all the risks that entails. Once a classic 'revolutionary' route is ruled out, a 'reformist approach' is the only option left, even though it still carries risks of 'co-optation' and 'manipulation' (*ibid*: 80–4).[15]

For Dryzek, too, the ideal discursive (or communicative) situation is a key notion assumed as a kind of *critical* and *operational* criterion in the search for the difficult reconciliation between the ideal and the real. 'The fact that an ideal is unattainable does not preclude its use for evaluative purposes; ... the precepts of communicative rationality can be used as critical standard to distinguish degrees of departure from the ideal' (*ibid.*: 87). In Dryzek, however, this programme tends to take on politically radical traits. To go beyond a mere 'critical theory', an 'authentically open public sphere' is needed (*ibid.*: 38); the public sphere should not only be able to resist the 'colonization' of lifeworlds, or to obstruct and contrast the logic of 'instrumental rationality' that dominates the economic and political systems, but also be able to 'conduct a counteroffensive' aimed at the core of these systems (*ibid.*: 20). And Dryzek's criticism of Habermas, with a degree of political disappointment, is very significant (*ibid.*: 19).

---

15. Dryzek particularly recalls (1990: 77 ff.) Claus Offe's analysis of contemporary capitalism (Offe 1984).

By now it is a standard criticism of Habermas's work (though no less true for repeated telling) that he fails to develop anything that meets the specifications he himself has laid out for a critical theory. That is, he has formulated no theory addressed to a specific audience and designed to liberate them from their sufferings.

In a word, Habermas was ultimately blamed for being ... Habermas, or rather for not having done something that, in his project, he openly stated he did *not* wish to pursue: that is, to propose some sort of 'philosophy of history' that identifies some kind of *subject* endowed with a theory, who would be the conscious protagonist of a global process of social transformation.[16]

As already noted, it is not my primary task to verify if those authors who were building the new theoretical deliberative paradigm read Habermas in a correct or in a misleading way. Habermas, after all, can be considered a 'classic' author and, as such, must suffer the same fate as all classics: readers will draw from his writings what seems most consonant to their intent. However, there are two important elements to note in the story that I am reconstructing here. Firstly, with his 'cumbersome' presence, so to speak, Habermas was still a *contemporary* 'classic'; second (and most importantly), from the point at which he began to be referred to as an inspirer of 'deliberative democracy', Habermas himself felt the need to express his own opinions, causing great bewilderment (in Dryzek, as we have already discovered, and in others as well, as we shall see). This gives rise to the questions of in what sense is Habermas *really* a theorist of or even an inspiration for deliberative democracy? And, if not, how should this widespread view of him be understood? In the next few chapters, I will try to answer these questions but, first, we need to complete the general picture as it appeared in the early 1990s.

3. James Fishkin: deliberative democracy and political theory

In addition to the plurality of approaches and disciplinary traditions that we have recalled, James Fishkin brought *political science* and *political theory* to the table, which would be essential for the subsequent development of deliberative democracy. In this section, I will first reconstruct the theoretical background of Fishkin's views and positions and then highlight its deep connection to the work of Robert Dahl, one of the leading figures of contemporary political science and theory. We will also see that Fishkin's work sounds somewhat familiar after our analysis of authors like Bessette and Sunstein: in particular we will see, once again, the importance of the interpretation of American constitutional design to the construction of the deliberative 'model'. We will also see that, to understand Fishkin's position, we must consider the theses of another protagonist of this debate: Bruce Ackerman.

---

16. This position was already evident in the first phase of Habermas's intellectual career (*see* e.g., Habermas 1973) and then constantly restated.

Fishkin and Dahl: minipopulus and 'enlightened understanding'

Fishkin's first major work – *Tyranny and Legitimacy: A critique of political theories* – (1979),[17] addressed one of the greatest themes of American politics but it is especially thanks to *Democracy and Deliberation: New directions for democratic reform* (1991) that Fishkin became one of the protagonists of what would later become 'deliberative democracy'. This monograph, in which the proposal of 'Deliberative Polling®' was presented for the first time, was based on a diagnosis of the worrying state of contemporary American democracy, which Fishkin attributed to the prevalence of forms of 'direct-majoritarian' democracy. At the theoretical level, Fishkin emphasised how difficult it was to 'hold together' the three fundamental principles of a normative vision of democracy: political equality; non-tyranny; and deliberation. How to find the balance between these three dimensions was precisely the goal of Fishkin's Deliberative Polling® proposal. This was perhaps the first example (and certainly the first with a strong influence) of the *operational translation* and *application* of a theoretical model of democratic deliberation through the creation of a specific institutional setting.[18]

The Deliberative Polling model is very well known and there is no need here to dwell on its characteristics and methodology.[19] I am instead interested in pointing

---

17. Later, Fishkin published a work on social justice (Fishkin 1983) as a contribution to the great debate started by Rawls and Nozick. Several other theorists participated in this debate, including Bruce Ackerman (*see* Ackerman 1980), a scholar to whom Fishkin has always been very close.

18. In *Democracy and Deliberation* (1991), Fishkin did not mention Bessette, nor Elster and Cohen, and referred to only one of Sunstein's essays ('Beyond the republican revival', Elster 1988a), confirming that the first steps of the new theoretical field were linked to the work of different and independent theoretical and disciplinary approaches that only later (and then only partially) began to converse with each other. Instead, the separation from the 'participatory' tradition was clear: in his notes, Fishkin quoted Barber's book, judging it as a 'thoughtful defence' of a 'small-scale direct democracy' (Fishkin 1991:110) but also considering it an expression of the 'chimerical goals of a great deal of recent reforms' (*ibid.*: 50). Fishkin also cited Jane Mansbridge (1983), with reference to the limits of a *face-to-face* democracy. The only other author cited by Fishkin, among those mentioned by other theorists of deliberative democracy, as we shall see, was Bruce Ackerman and his essay 'Discovering the Constitution' (1984). Briefly, in Deliberative Polling one to two hundred relatively randomly selected citizens are first surveyed on their opinions on one or more policy issues, then brought together to discuss these issues in facilitated structure designed to produce inclusive and thoughtful deliberation, and finally surveyed after the deliberation to determine their now 'considered' preferences. Fishkin procured a registered trademark for the words "Deliberative Polling" (Deliberative Polling®) in order to prevent the use of the term for designs that did not have the specific features required for this model.

19. Fishkin returned to this theme in *The Voice of the People* (1995). He then provided a summary of his experience as an active experimenter with his model in *When the People Speak* (2009) and, more recently, in another essay (Fishkin 2014). *See also* the website of the Center for Deliberative Democracy at Stanford University (http://cdd.stanford.edu (accessed 15 November 2016)). In the 1991 book, Fishkin announced the upcoming trial of Deliberative Polling that was to take place in Texas in 1992. However, as he wrote (Fishkin 1995: 163), the project was cancelled due to the start of the first Gulf War and the withdrawal of financing. The first DP took place in Britain in 1994 (on the theme: 'Crimes are on the rise: what can be done?') and was co-produced and then broadcast by a national television channel. On this DP, other than Fishkin 2003: 137, *see also* Luskin, Fishkin and Jowell 2002 and Parkinson 2006. Another DP was held in Britain in 1998, on

out some theoretical assumptions of Fishkin's position that directly refer to the work of one of the 'fathers' of modern political science and political theory, namely, Robert A. Dahl.[20] Although Dahl's work, especially *Preface to Democratic Theory* (1956), was a target of polemic for the first theorists of participatory democracy, his idea of 'polyarchy' and the pluralistic model of democracy (and the attention he paid to developing a *normative* vision of democracy) actually contained many theoretical openings for the exploration of the roles of participation and deliberation. Dahl's discussion, in the *Preface*, of the *intensity* of the preferences characterising citizens' active engagement or apathy was particularly important (*ibid.*: chapter 4). In the years to come, Dahl would polemically emphasise the condition of 'real democracies', especially with works such as *Dilemmas of Pluralist Democracy* (1982) and *Controlling Nuclear Weapons: Democracy versus guardianship* (1985), whose core was the tension between democracy and technocracy. Later on, all these themes found full expression in *Democracy and its Critics* (1989a), which received considerable attention from Habermas, as we shall see.

Fishkin's purpose was to explore how to 'reconcile democracy and deliberation' and this rationale was introduced right from the opening pages: the proposal of Deliberative Polling, which is described as 'a new kind of democratic event', shows 'what the public *would think*, if it had a more adequate chance to think about the questions at issue'. This proposal sought to bring 'some of the favourable characteristics of small-group, face-to-face democracy to the large-scale nation-state' (Fishkin 1991: 1). In Fishkin's diagnosis of the state of American democracy,[21] the three aspects of a normative definition of democracy (equality, non-tyranny, deliberation) were not in a good balance today. 'We seem to face a forced choice between politically equal but relatively incompetent masses and politically unequal but relatively more competent elites.' Pollings® should solve this dilemma as 'they embody political equality because everyone has an equal chance of being represented in the national sample of participants. But they also embody deliberation because they immerse a selected group of citizens in intensive, face-to-face debate' (*ibid.*: 2). Here, we find the first formulation of the model of what Archon Fung (2003) would call mini-publics, that is deliberative arenas in which randomly selected citizens

---

the new strategic guidelines for the National Health Service (*see* Parkinson 2006: 12–13). A DP was also held in China in 2005 and others have followed (on these experiences of deliberation in an 'authoritarian' institutional context *see* He and Warren 2011, Fishkin *et al* 2010, and He 2014). In his 2009 book, Fishkin analyses thirty-three Pollings that took place between 1994 and 2008 (2009: 137).

20. In the Acknowledgements of one of his recent works, Fishkin recalls how much he owes to Robert Dahl: 'on the normative side I want to thank some key teachers and colleagues. Robert Dahl first inspired me to think about democratic theory' (2009: ix).

21. I'll leave out of my reconstruction Fishkin's very critical analysis of US presidential campaigns. But note how, among the factors that have 'largely emptied the process of deliberation', Fishkin also cites the 'proliferation of mass primaries' (1991: 1). The 'open' primary system pioneered in 1968, Fishkin writes, presents us with 'a false dilemma': either we accept the classic smoke-filled rooms 'or we end up choosing our candidates more or less as we choose detergents' (*ibid.*: 3–7).

hypothetically and counterfactually become a representative microcosm of what *every* citizen *would think* if they could deliberate 'isolated' from the distortions induced by ordinary political communication and if they had sufficient cognitive skills and informative material about the issues to be discussed (*ibid.*: 4).[22] Mini-publics have become very important in the subsequent development of the theory and practice of deliberative democracy.[23]

Subsequent theoretical reflection has focused on the nature of the 'representativeness' of the mini-public, raising many doubts about it, particularly in the versions that are considerably smaller than Fishkin's 100-200 person Deliberative Pollings. Fishkin was well aware of the problem: in his model, in fact, the results of a Deliberative Polling are 'prescriptive, not predictive': in other words, they only have 'recommendation force' (*ibid.*: 81). In order for a mini-public's recommendation to have such 'force', for Fishkin, it is essential that *media coverage* of deliberation disseminates the results of the deliberations of 'representative' citizens to a wider audience. The idea of a Deliberation Day later proposed by Fishkin and Ackerman (2004) would be inspired by the same goal, that is, to try to find a connection between micro- and macro-level deliberation.[24]

---

22. See one of Fishkin's texts we have already mentioned (Fishkin 1991: 81; *see* Chapter Three, note 3), which examines, in an exemplary way, this counterfactual logic and its required 'insulation conditions'.

23. As in the case of the smaller and earlier citizens juries that Fishkin explicitly recalls (*ibid.*: 9), focusing on the experiments promoted by Ned Crosby and the Jefferson Center (*ibid.* 96–7; *see also* Chapter 8, Section 2, note 12) In the early 1970s, both Ned Crosby and Peter Dienel had already, independently, developed this use of randomly chosen deliberating citizens. Dienel referred to this idea as 'Plannunszellen' (Dienel 2002). On citizens' juries, *see* Smith and Wales 2000. On juries in Italy, *see* the special issue of *Rivista italiana di politiche pubbliche* 2007 (1). Generally, on deliberative methods based on choosing participants by random sampling, *see* Carson and Martin 1999. On mini-publics, *see* Grönlund, Bächtiger and Setälä 2014; Elstub 2014; Smith 2009: 7–110; Felicetti, Niemeyer and Curato 2016. Parkinson (2006: 74–84) critically examines the many theoretical tensions in conceptions of the 'representativeness' of mini-publics. In the literature on deliberative democracy, the use of the expression 'citizen panel' is also frequent. This expression refers to institutions or settings (e.g. the consensus conference) based on the random sampling of a number of citizens (*see* Brown, M. B. 2006). For a review of the different types and conceptions of mini-public, *see* Fung 2003. In this work, Fung introduces a distinction, widely evoked and developed later on (*see*, e.g., Bobbio 2010a), between 'hot' forms of deliberation (in which the participants' direct interests come into play) and 'cold' forms (in which it is assumed that citizens are detached and impartial). On Fung's proposal and Fishkin's position, *see* Ryan and Smith 2014.

24. Deliberation Day would be considered a national holiday, occuring in proximity to the elections. During this day, several deliberative arenas (scattered across the whole country and connected to appropriate media coverage) would allow citizens to develop better informed opinions about all the great topics of national politics, the candidates' profiles and their platforms. There has never been a Deliberation Day experiment but some important examples of deliberative 'mini-publics' have addressed issues of great political significance on a political and national scale. One of the most important was the British Columbia Citizen Assembly, in Canada, which dealt with the theme of a new electoral system (on which, see Warren and Pearse 2008 and Fournier *et al.* 2010). We should also remember the case of the Australian Citizens' Parliament (Carson *et al.* 2013). Recently, Iceland has offered an important example of deliberative procedure applied to constitutional reforms: *see* Reuchamps-Suiter [2016] and Landemore [2015].

From where does the Deliberative Polling model draw its inspiration? And what are its underlying theoretical assumptions? At the end of his Introduction (Fishkin 1991: 12–13), Fishkin expresses a note of caution: his proposal is not 'a panacea', but 'only one step', an example of the kind of institutional 'spirit of innovation' showed by the Founders that the current generation should aspire to replicate. Fishkin draws on the history of American democracy to illustrate the terms of the difficult coexistence between those three different principles (equality; deliberation; non-tyranny). What emerges here is Fishkin's connection to Dahl and his concept of 'Madisonian democracy'.

In his discussion of the problem of the scale or 'size' of democracy,[25] Fishkin emphasises the contrast between the Anti-Federalists' direct-majoritarian vision ('champions of small-scale democracy') and Madison's view, which is alert to the dangers of tyranny and focused on the value of deliberation (*ibid.*: 17–19). Fishkin believes that the *direct-majoritarian* vision 'lost the initial battle over the Constitution' but 'has largely won the war in the long march of history': many changes 'have taken us closer and closer to a direct-majoritarian version of democracy' and 'a plebiscitary model of leadership ... is coming to displace the more complex vision of democracy that animated the Founders', with 'millions of atomistic citizens who bounce back unreflective preferences from the mass media', up to the point where those political leaders who 'go against popular preferences reported in opinion polls' are considered 'antidemocratic' (*ibid.*: 17–18).[26] And thus, against 'a direct-majoritarian vision reminiscent of the Anti-Federalists' (*ibid.*: 20) and against 'the lure of direct democracy' (*ibid.*: 21–5), it is necessary 'to supply a theoretical framework' and elaborate institutional proposals that can reverse whatever 'has led us to empty the system of effective deliberation' (*ibid.*: 20).

Fishkin dedicates the central part of his book to the theoretical framework of the three 'democratic dimensions' of political equality, non-tyranny and deliberation, creating a scheme that allows him to classify democratic systems based on the tensions and trade-offs created between those different conditions (*ibid.*: 42–3). The scheme is constituted by two axes: the first axis places a system on a 'Madisonian' *versus* 'majoritarian' scale, measuring the degree of 'impediment' placed on majority rule; the second on a 'direct' *versus* 'representative' democracy scale; then each of these four possible dimensions can combine with a transversal dimension expressing the possible range from wholly 'deliberative' to wholly 'non-deliberative', giving eight possible combinations (*see* Figure 7.1). In the quadrant combining direct democracy and majoritarian democracy (*ibid.*: 50–3),

---

25. *Ibid.*: 14–25. Here, there is a reference to Dahl and Tufte 1973 and, 'for an attempt to systematize' (*ibid.*: 107, note 11) Madison's arguments, to Dahl's *Preface* (1956). Obviously, *Federalist 10*, which we have already encountered in our analysis of Bessette (*see* Chapter Three, Section 1) is crucial to this topic.

26. Fishkin extensively referred also to one of Sartori's articles (1989) and also recalled one of Dahl's Tanner Lectures (Dahl 1989b), in which Dahl reported an ongoing tendency towards 'pseudodemocratization'.

Figure 7.1: Fishkin's three democratic dimensions scheme

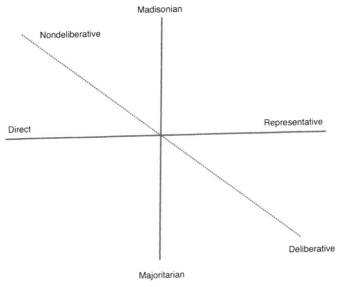

Source: Fishkin 1991: 43

Fishkin places the forms of *face-to-face* democracy, emphasising the risks of 'tyranny' involved in them and the frequent absence of deliberation. In this context, participation (whose educational function, citing Pateman, is valued more than anything else) is an 'instrumental' value, not an end in itself: it is valuable only insofar as it guarantees political equality and contributes to effective deliberation. And Fishkin also adds a polemical note against the idea, which had 'some currency in the United States in the sixties', that local rallies and demonstrations could be seen as a form of 'direct democracy' (*ibid.*: 77).

It is necessary to notice here that the very definition of these conditions is built around a specific theme: the degree of citizens' freedom, autonomy and equality *in shaping and expressing their preferences*. 'By political equality', Fishkin writes, 'I mean the institutionalization of a system which grants equal consideration to everyone's preferences and which grants everyone appropriately equal opportunities to formulate preferences on the issue under consideration' (*ibid.*: 30–1). In order for this to happen, some particular 'insulation conditions' of the political process must be protected from external factors: 'the political sphere must be protected from being determined by spillover effects from social or economic inequalities in the society' (*ibid*).

In these pages, it is possible to see Dahl's distinctive influence explicitly. Starting from Madison's and Hamilton's famous statements in *Federalist* 10, Fishkin writes that 'the distinction between the inclination of the moment and public opinions that are refined by "sedate reflection" is an essential part of any adequate theory of democracy'. Political equality would be meaningless without deliberation, 'for it amounts to nothing more than power without the opportunity to think about how that power ought to be exercised' (*ibid.*: 36). Therefore, citizens must achieve what Dahl called an 'enlightened understanding' of their own preferences, a normative 'criterion' of democracy that Dahl had defined as follows:

> *Each citizen ought to have adequate and equal opportunities for discovering and validating (within the time permitted by the need for a decision) the choice on the matter to be decided that would best serve the citizen's interests.*

This criterion implies, then, that alternative procedures for making decisions ought to be evaluated according the opportunities they furnish citizens for acquiring an understanding of means and ends, of one's interests and the expected consequences of policies for interests, not only for oneself but for all other relevant persons as well. Insofar as a citizen's good or interests requires attention to a public good or general interest, then citizens ought to have the opportunity to acquire an understanding of these matters. Ambiguous as the criterion may be, it provides guidance for determining the shape that institutions should take. Thus the criterion makes it hard to justify procedures that would cut off or suppress information which, were it available, might well cause citizens to arrive at a different decision; or that would give some citizens much easier access than others to information of crucial importance; or that would present citizens with an agenda of decisions that had be decided without discussion, though time was available; and so on. To be sure, these may seem like easy cases, but a great many political systems – perhaps most – operate according to the worse not the better procedures (Dahl 1989a: 112).

Fishkin recalls Dahl's notion and finds in it 'an ideal of deliberation which ... could be pushed further' (Fishkin 1991: 36). And it's really striking, at this point, that Fishkin, too, feels the need to bring up Habermas: this ideal of deliberation leads us 'ultimately to something like the "ideal speech situation" of Jürgen Habermas – a situation of free and equal discussion, unlimited in its duration, constrained only by the consensus which would be arrived at by the "force of the better argument"' (*ibid.*). Given the fame and spread of Fishkin's work, it is possible to find here another instance of scholars in the field of deliberative democracy using a rather simplistic understanding of Habermas's categories. Fishkin, like others, cannot help asserting that 'the requirements of the ideal speech situation are, of course, purely hypothetical and, in that sense, utterly utopian' (*ibid.*).[27]

However, this 'ideal' of deliberation can inspire people to imagine a *continuum* between non-deliberation and 'pure' deliberation: it is 'a matter of degree' and, therefore, Fishkin declares, 'I will sometimes speak of an institutional innovation

---

27. Fishkin mentioned, among other Habermas works, 'Reply to my critics' (1982). For anything else, as 'a good summary, with some criticisms', he refers the reader to Geuss's text on 'critical theory' (Geuss 1981) (*ibid.*:109, note 14). The same argumentation and the same reference to Habermas is found in Fishkin 1995: 40–1.

serving deliberation when it falls far short of the ideal but nevertheless represents a significant improvement over the lack of deliberation that we routinely encounter at present' (*ibid.*: 38). Such an innovative strategy lies within one of the quadrants described above: reshaping representative institutions in order to ensure political equality and deliberation (*ibid.*: 67).

A second essential connection to Dahl is the very idea of 'a statistical microcosm of society' (*ibid.*: 93). Fishkin understands Deliberative Polling as a form of representation different from those of 'conventional' representative institutions (*ibid.*: 81), which sacrifice both equality (because, at best, deliberation takes place only among elites) *and* deliberation (because bargaining and log-rolling prevail in elite deliberation). The origins of Deliberative Polling, and of all the other forms of mini-public based on a random sample of potential participants, can be found in Dahl's idea of a 'minipopulus'. Dahl had originated this notion in the previous decade (Dahl 1985) and then revisited it in *Democracy and its Critics*, in the concluding chapter titled 'Sketches for an advanced democratic country' (1989a: 322–41.)[28]

If Dahl's book was permeated throughout by the tension between the normative criteria of the democratic ideal and their (always partial) translation into 'real democracies', in his conclusion he looks forward, in an openly 'utopian' way, to the possible future of democracy. 'If we could design a society that, within feasible human limits, would facilitate the maximal achievement of democracy and its values – that is, an advanced democratic society – what would it look like?' (Dahl 1989a: 322).

Dahl's answer to his own question was to set out this general principle:

> … an advanced democratic country would actively seek to reduce great inequalities in the capacities and opportunities for citizens to participate effectively in political life that are caused to an important degree by the distribution of economic resources, positions, and opportunities and by the distribution of knowledge, information, and cognitive skills (*ibid.*: 324).

The reference to economic inequalities recalls, in Dahl's view, the 'discord between democracy and capitalism' and the ways in which it can be regulated (*ibid.*: 326–32) but it is participatory inequalities that we should look at here. According to Dahl, however serious the dangers arising from economic and social inequalities might be, the threat to democracy 'from special knowledge' and from the modern forms of Platonic 'guardianship' are far more serious (*ibid.*: 504).

---

28. Among the early discussions on the idea of deliberative democracy, it is worth mentioning a rather polemical debate between Joshua Cohen and Robert Dahl, starting from Cohen's short review of *Democracy and its Critics* (Cohen 1991). In his reply, Dahl recalled the connection between 'enlightened understanding', 'minipopulus' and deliberative democracy. To Cohen, who blamed him for having an aggregative vision of democracy, Dahl responded that: '(a) my conception is not aggregative in the way I understand him to mean the term; (b) my Criterion of Enlightened Understanding incorporates his notion of deliberation and yet goes beyond it; and (c) while he does not explain how deliberation is to take place, my proposed minipopulus would enhance deliberation and enlightened understanding' (Dahl 1991: 229).

Such dangers are not posed by 'intellectuals' in general but by a 'particular subset' of them: that is, 'those who are particularly concerned with public policy and actively engaged in influencing governmental decisions, not only directly but also indirectly through their influence on public and elite opinion' (*ibid.*: 334). This is a 'policy elite' that operates in a variety of locations, from state bureaucracies to universities, from mass media to lobbies. Dahl goes on to say that its role would not be so disturbing were it not for the 'increasing complexity of public policies' that 'threatens to cut the policy elites loose from effective control by the demos' (*ibid.*: 335). In the conditions of a 'classic' representative democracy in a nation-state, it was still possible to think of a 'process of successive approximation' (*ibid.*: 336) that, from citizens' electoral decisions, would lead (in mediated but clearly recognisable forms) to 'the clerk who finally carried out the activity'. The democratic process could no longer be carried out 'in the simple and direct way of assembly democracy' but its requirements could, nevertheless, be considered fulfilled. 'But what if important decisions are now so complex that ordinary citizens no longer understand what will best serve their interests?' In other words, how can we prevent guardianship from replacing democracy 'not in symbols or even beliefs, perhaps, but in practice' (*ibid.*: 336–7)?

Before answering these questions, Dahl explains why, from a democratic point of view, some sort of modern version of guardianship would be unacceptable: all policy areas involve decisions that 'require (implicitly or explicitly) judgments both moral and instrumental'. They do not concern only goals and means and therefore, 'no intellectually defensible claim can be made that policy elites (actual or putative) possess superior moral knowledge or more specifically superior knowledge of what constitutes the public good'; and trust in expert knowledge ought not to be unlimited, because it 'provides too narrow a base for the instrumental knowledge that an intelligent policy would require' (*ibid.*: 337). In addition, political decisions 'are virtually always made behind a thick veil of uncertainty'; they demand evaluations 'about the acceptability of risks' and 'judgments about trade-offs among values or policy goals'. All these arguments confirm that citizens have 'scant reason for trusting themselves to policy elites' (*ibid.*: 337–8).

But how to prevent 'the drift toward government by *de facto* quasi guardians'? We must focus on the 'weakest link' of the 'chain of successive approximation' that makes up a democratic process; in other words, intervening in how citizens' judgments are formed. '[T]he gap between the knowledge of the policy elites and the knowledge of ordinary citizens' must be tackled to prevent the drift toward guardianship. This is likely to be taken as a utopian goal but, Dahl adds, 'I think important possibilities are yet to be explored'. The different phases of the history of democracy (the different forms of 'polyarchy') have always involved the 'creation' or 'the addition of new institutions' that responded to new conditions (*ibid.*: 338). At this point, Dahl indicates some general objectives: to intervene in the forms and sources of information, 'to create easily available and universally accessible opportunities to all citizens', making it possible for them 'to participate in a relevant way in political discussion'.

Dahl trusted a lot in the possibilities of technological innovation in the field of communication and glimpsed some of the problems that such developments would involve (*ibid.*: 339). What I wish to emphasise here is the outcome of this approach. The reconstruction of that 'process of successive approximation' today cannot depend on it being a necessity 'that every citizen should be informed and active on every major issue'. Instead, what is necessary is 'a critical mass of well-informed citizens large enough and active enough to anchor the process, an "attentive public", as Gabriel Almond put it many years ago' (*ibid.*: 339).[29] Certainly, Dahl observes, 'advocates of participatory democracy will fault my solution as inadequate' but, as hopeful as one can be about a *demos* being an 'attentive public', this is clearly an unachievable goal. And perhaps such an objective is not even desirable: 'after all, political life is not the whole of life, and all of us ought not to be obliged to devote all of our daily lives to becoming extraordinarily well-informed and active citizens' (Dahl 1985: 87). These words are taken from a previous work in which Dahl talked about participation, the 'usual panacea' that many see as the antidote to citizens' incompetence: 'lying behind the hope for political participation as an educative force there is sometimes, I suspect, a conception of a process of *discussion* in a highly idealized town meeting or Athenian assembly. But discussion with other equally uninformed citizens will not solve the problem we confront' (Dahl 1998a: 340).[30]

The question then becomes how to make sure that an 'attentive public', informed and thoughtful, is also 'representative of the broader public'. 'The idea', Dahl admits (Dahl 1989: 514), 'seems self-contradictory' but is not necessarily so.

[S]uppose an advanced democratic country were to create a 'minipopulus' consisting of perhaps a thousand citizens randomly selected out of the entire demos. Its task would be to deliberate, for a year perhaps, on an issue and then to announce its choices. The members of a minipopulus could 'meet' by telecommunication. ... A minipopulus could exist at any level of government – national, state, or local. It could be attended ... by an advisory committee of scholars and specialists and by an administrative staff. It could hold hearings, commission research, and engage in debate and discussion.[31]

---

29. Dahl refers to *The American People and Foreign Policy* (Almond 1950).

30. In one of his notes (1985: 100–1, note 2), Dahl recalls Barber's *Strong Democracy* (*see* Chapter Two of this volume), published while Dahl was editing his book. 'Sympathetic as I am with his wish to strengthen "democratic talk"', Dahl notes, 'his analysis and proposals do not seem to me to be adequate for the problem posed here. The nine functions of strong democratic talk he describes all appear to presuppose that citizens possess whatever latent knowledge is necessary to make wise decisions in their own or the general interest ... To focus on discussion to the exclusion of learning by means other than, and in addition to, discussion seems to me overestimate the contributions of "talk"'. However, it is important to highlight Dahl's idea that some of Barber's specific proposals 'are very similar to what I suggest'.

31. The idea of a 'minipopulus' had already been proposed in several conferences that Dahl held in 1984 at Syracuse University and that were later published in Dahl 1985. In particular, *see* chapter 5, 'Vision of a possible future'. In this text Dahl proposed 'small scale experiments' (*ibid.*: 89).

Here, we quite clearly find the starting point for the ideas of Deliberative Polling, Deliberation Day and all subsequent experimentation with deliberative mini-publics.[32] But we also find the ambiguous *status* of these institutions: 'the institution of the *minipopulus* in the Polyarchy III',[33] Dahl writes (*ibid.*), should be considered 'not as a substitute for legislative bodies but as a complement. It would supplement, not replace' the previous institutions. But, then, 'what weight, it might be asked, would the judgments of a minipopulus have?' In the answer to this question lies, once again, a hypothetical and counterfactual argument: the 'judgments of a minipopulus 'would "represent" the judgments of the demos'. Note that Dahl does *not* say that they *are* those judgments. Dahl clearly must have been aware of the problematic nature of these statements, since he put the verb 'represent' in inverted commas: 'its verdict *would be* the verdict of the demos itself, if the demos were able to take advantage of the best available knowledge to decide what policies were most likely to achieve the ends it sought. The judgments of the minipopulus *would thus derive* their authority from the legitimacy of democracy' (*ibid.*: 340, my emphasis).

Obviously, Dahl proposes this idea at the end of his book as an example of institutional innovations (among other innovative institutions that the citizens of 'an advanced democratic country' could discover) by which to 'adapt' democracy 'to a world that little resembles the world in which democratic ideas and practices first came to life' (*ibid.*: 340). This projection into the future – this exercise of creative imagination – is inspired by the belief that, of course, there will be many changes but that, nevertheless, 'the vision of people governing themselves as political equals, and possessing all the resources and institutions necessary to do so, will, I believe, remain a compelling if always demanding guide' (*ibid.*). In short, Dahl's slightly utopian enthusiasm is encouraged by his faith in democracy's potential for self-transformation.

The idea of a *minipopulus*, however, would continue to develop beyond Dahl's conception, especially after Fishkin's reformulation. It would inspire a series of models whose goal was to create the conditions in which a 'common' citizen could acquire that 'enlightened understanding' Dahl identified as one of the normative criteria of the democratic ideal. But in Dahl's work we can already see a number of unsolved problems that will continue to trouble subsequent experiments with this model. First, what is the relationship between these selective points of informed deliberation and two different 'external' levels: that of the broader public sphere and that of representative institutions? (The continuing existence of such institutions is generally not questioned but they are no longer considered a place in which 'real' deliberation occurs or at least they are taken as places in which other logics dominate.)

---

32. Dahl's role as primogenitor of the idea was highlighted by Robert Goodin and John Dryzek in an essay of 2006, reprinted in Goodin 2008. In a recent essay, Ian O'Flynn and Gaurav Sood ask 'What would Dahl say? An appraisal of the democratic credentials of Deliberative Polls' (2014). Dahl himself, however, even without evoking his own idea of a minipopulus, paid attention to both the citizens' juries proposed by the Jefferson Center and to Fishkin's proposal in his 1992 essay 'The problem of civic competence' (Dahl 1992).

33. Dahl describes as 'Polyarchy III' a hypothetical new developmental stage of democracy, after Polyarchy 'I' and 'II', which we have already seen.

The problematic nature (not only in 'practical' but also theoretical and political terms) of the inspiring principle of mini-publics would be at the heart of much subsequent discussion. What grounds the transition from a single arena (however 'representative' it may be from a statistical and sociological point of view) to a wider public sphere? How can it be achieved? What can guarantee – many wonder – that the 'new' informed preferences of those citizens who were lucky enough to deliberate in tranquillity for a whole weekend will radiate and persuade, or even just influence, millions of fellow citizens who, in the meantime, have been exposed to other sources of information?[34]

Fishkin was well aware of this problem and in fact – as already mentioned – the design of Deliberative Polling specifies adequate media coverage of the event as a requirement (see, for example, Fishkin 1991: 9). However, the more local the scale on which the mini-public experiment takes place, the harder this 'transition' from the 'micro' to the 'macro' level will be or appear to be.[35] Frequently taking place within concrete policy-making processes, and often submerged in conflicts developing in many other more or less 'deliberative' places, these experiments raise a critical question about the democratic legitimacy of the locations of the discussion and the sources of the decision.

These questions lead to the heart of an issue that affects the entire debate on deliberative democracy. We have seen how Fishkin started from a very critical analysis of dominant trends in contemporary democracy: hence, recovering a space for 'deliberation' was an essential task, in order to counter the (today prevalent) *direct-majoritarian* and plebiscitary distortion of democracy. Fishkin and Dahl were greatly concerned about the deep weakening of the basic conditions of possibility of a good democracy: the presence of citizens who were as informed, careful, critically aware of their interests and open to the consideration of the general interest as possible. It was no longer the lack of 'participation', as such, that was cause for concern but the absence of participation sustained by strong 'civicness' and citizens' effective capacity to form autonomous and reflective

---

34. 'Of course, it is an open question', Goodin and Dryzek wrote, commenting on Dahl's passage, 'whether decision-makers will prefer this kind of public opinion to the raw and uninformed public opinion (or lack of opinion) that the mass of ordinary voters will still exhibit' (Goodin 2008: 22). Of course, in some cases, influence on subsequent decisions is produced. On several occasions, Fishkin valorised the result of a DP in Texas on energy policies and Goodin and Dryzek recalled an Australian DP on GMOs that convinced a big corporation to modify its strategy (Goodin 2008: 23–6). In these cases, such influence was able to act, in mediated and indirect forms, on a wider public and communicative sphere (but, of course, the interventions of other causal variables cannot be excluded).

35. On the legitimacy of deliberative principles and practices and on the deliberation 'scale', *see* Parkinson 2006: 3–8 and chapter 2). Parkinson, analysing in particular the case of a citizen jury in Leicester, UK, notes how this type of arena lacks 'the legitimating bonds of authorization and accountability between participants and non-participants' (*ibid.*: 33). For some Italian cases, in this same sense, *see* Floridia 2012: 175–8 and 190–6). On the connection between micro-deliberative spaces and the macro 'discursive context', *see* Hendriks 2006. On the different, and perhaps greater 'legitimacy' of the forums characterised by the presence of partisan citizens, compared to those with non-partisan citizens, *see* Hendriks, Dryzek and Hunold 2007.

opinions. This prerequisite of democracy seemed to have vanished and it was a democratic concern, aimed at reviving it, that drove these authors. But not without paradoxical effects and unresolved problems, whose first traces can be seen in Dahl's distinction between an 'attentive public' and 'the broader public'.[36]

In the years to come – when the idea of mini-publics developed wide appeal – the lack of fit between a severely critical diagnosis of the evils of our democracies and the incompleteness, or weakness, of an answer ultimately relying on the progressive extension of isolated experiments would often seem discordant. Scholars in the deliberative field had many different reactions to this, as we shall see in Chapter Thirteen. The notion of entrusting the destiny of democracy to the existence (or 'creation') of a citizenry that has adequate information and understanding lead many to emphasise the 'educational' traits of the mission of participation and deliberation. Above all, it produced (not always consciously) certain theoretical assumptions whose implications were anything but 'neutral'. These include what we can characterise as the *myth of the common* (or 'ordinary') *citizen*: the bearer (under the right cognitive preconditions) of a capacity for 'impartial' judgement.

Fishkin, Ackerman and the 'dualist conception' of democratic politics

Fishkin's work, as we have seen, is marked by a long collaboration with Bruce Ackerman, one of the protagonists of the great debate on the American Constitution in the 1980s. In *Discovering the Constitution* (1984), in particular, Ackerman – based on a strong critique of the historiographical interpretations proposed during the Progressive Era – laid the foundations of his monumental work (*We, the People: Foundations* (1991) and *We, the People: Transformations* (1998). This was a comprehensive evaluation of American constitutionalism, which Ackerman saw as marked by three great 'moments', each marking a break with 'legal' continuity (that is, 'foundational' and 're-foundational' moments of constitutional legitimacy). Each moment was characterised by lively popular participation and widespread deliberative practices.[37]

---

36. Of course, it is impossible not to recall that 'civic culture' was one of the central themes in post-war political science, from Almond's and Verba's eponymous 1963 work to Putnam's influential contributions (Putnam 1993 and 2000). A critical point of connection with Putnam was signalled by Ackerman and Fishkin (2004: 177); their idea of a Deliberation Day, and other similar institutions, might help build 'a reasonably healthy civil society'. They describe Putnam's theory of civicness as 'neo-Tocquevillean'. New deliberative institutions, according to Fishkin and Ackerman, are means to produce not only 'social capital' (of which Putman takes care) but also 'political' capital. It is no longer possible to rely only on the spontaneity of associative networks in civil society, and 'quite simply, many traditional contexts for citizenship are dead or dying (*ibid.*: 178). 'Television, when combined with the spread of such democratic reforms as the direct primary, killed the political party as a popular institution. The citizen jury barely survives on the periphery of ordinary life. The only significant institution that still invites involvement by ordinary citizens is the public school, and it too is under attack' (*ibid.*).

37. These three historical moments were: the War of Independence and the foundation of the United States of America; Reconstruction after the Civil War; and the New Deal. In his latest work (2014), Ackerman adds a fourth: the 'Civil Rights revolution'.

In the final pages of his 1991 book, Fishkin refers to Ackerman's essay: the analysis of the positions expressed in this text allows us to better grasp some of the basic theoretical premises underlying Fishkin's proposal. Starting from a reading of the *Federalist Papers*, Ackerman identifies in these texts 'a dualistic conception of political life' (Ackerman 1984: 1022).[38] The former, 'one form of political action – I shall call it *constitutional politics*', Ackerman writes (*ibid.*: 1022–3),

> is characterized by Publian[39] appeals to the common good, ratified by a mobilized mass of American citizens expressing their assent through extraordinary institutional forms. Although constitutional politics is the highest kind of politics, it should be permitted to dominate the nation's life only during rare periods of heightened political consciousness. During the long periods between these constitutional moments, a second form of activity – I shall call it *normal politics* – prevails. Here, factions try to manipulate the constitutional forms of political life to pursue their own narrow interests. Normal politics must be tolerated in the name of individual liberty; it is, however, democratically *inferior* to the intermittent and irregular politics of public virtue associated with moments of constitutional creation.

Faced with this dualism, the authors of the *Federalist* had two options: one was 'fatalism', considering this cyclical nature as inevitable and intended to reproduce itself 'endlessly to the end of human history'; the other was what Ackerman defined as 'constitutional activism', which was pursued by the Founders:

> Although there is no way to prevent the rise of normal politics, perhaps the Revolutionary generation can take steps that will palliate the most pathological aspects of the normal condition. The aim here is to use the resources of constitutional law to channel the ebb and flow of normal politics in ways consistent with Revolutionary principle (*ibid.*: 1024).

The Founders were not inspired by an optimistic view. In fact, their view was based on the belief 'that constant appeals to public virtue could not be expected to sustain the normal politics of the American people' (*ibid.*: 1025).

Hence, the rise of the 'peculiarly modern' institution of political representation. 'It was this invention of modern political science, not any increase in the quantity of human virtue, which permitted the rational hope that Americans might succeed where both ancients and moderns had failed before them' (*ibid.*: 1025). And hence also 'the supreme importance of constitutional law. By manipulating the forms of constitutional representation, Publius hopes to drive normal politics into directions

---

38. A wider formulation of this 'dualist constitutionalism' was explained by Ackerman, particularly in the first chapter of *We, the People* (1991: 3–33). For a criticism of Ackerman's ideas *see* Sunstein 1988a.

39. 'Publius' was the pseudonym used by Madison, Hamilton and Jay in their essays in the *Federalist*.

that do not endanger the principles of the American Revolution' (*ibid.*). How to do so was precisely the object of constitutional design but

> ... only one thing is clear: disappointment awaits all those who fail to understand the distinctive character of representative institutions and who strive instead to create a national government that resembles, as much as possible, the face-to-face democracy of ancient Greece (*ibid.*: 1026).

However, Madison also rejects an idea of representation as *synecdoche*, that is, the figure of speech that 'represents' and replaces the whole with one of its parts (such as, Congress as 'the People Assembled'), since this would only lead to an elective despotism. In the institutions of 'normal politics', as Madison wrote, there is the 'total exclusion of the people in their collective capacity' from *direct* participation in public affairs (*Federalist* 63; Ackerman 1984: 1027). And yet, Ackerman highlights, Madison reaffirmed how the totality of the new institutions, 'in some other way' still 'do "represent" the People'. This could happen because the idea of representation acting in these institutions is not 'mimetic' but 'semiotic' (*ibid.*: 1028) – as happens when, in front of a portrait, we recognise that 'it is impossible to interpret the picture's meaning without self-consciously understanding that the picture is only a symbol, and not the thing which the symbol symbolizes'. The Constitution thus states that 'Congress is merely a "representation" of the People, not the thing itself' (*ibid.*: 1028).[40]

The possible malfunctions of 'normal politics' are then fixed 'by proliferating the modes of representation'. '[T]he separation of powers operates as a complex machine which encourages each official to question the extent to which other constitutional officials are successfully representing the People's true political wishes.' The separation of powers 'deconstructs all such naive synecdoches' and 'the result of the rhetorical interchange will be precisely the opposite of each partisan's hopes' (*ibid.*: 1028–9).

And here the dualistic nature of the Constitution comes into play:

> So long as normal politicians are revealed as mere 'stand-ins' for the People, the Constitution also allows them to 'stand for' the People in a more straightforward way – by making its principal officials responsible, directly or indirectly, to popular election. There is no inclination to deny the fundamental importance of recurring popular elections, only an effort to establish that the pushings-and-shovings of normal politics are not the highest form of political expression (*ibid.*: 1029).

---

40. On the concept of representation, Hanna Pitkin's work (1967) remains essential. The conflict between different conceptions of representation was intense, particularly in the debates on the ratification of the Constitution that took place in the different states: Antifederalists supported a 'descriptive' conception of representation as similarity between elected and voters, and thus defended the idea of a wider legislative assembly. On this debate, *see* Manin 1997:102–31. On Madison and the Federalists' reply, based on institutional mechanisms of electoral accountability and on the reasons to choose large congressional districts, *see* Manin 1997: 115–21 and Manin 1994.

Of course, the *Federalist* tried to reassure us that, in this way, 'even during normal times', it was possible to select representatives who could 'rise above the parochialism of special interest'; but, Madison himself admitted, 'it is in vain to say that enlightened statesmen will be able to adjust these clashing interests and render them all subservient to the public good. *Enlightened statesmen will not always be at the helm*' (*Federalist* 10, my emphasis). Subsequent history, Ackerman adds, actually confirms that, 'in the absence of a mobilized mass of virtuous citizens, there can be no guarantee that the constitutional machine will invariably produce tolerable results'.[41]

Therefore, the entire constitutional mechanism presupposes this tension between the (few) moments of a constituent 'high politics' and the (many) moments of 'low' and 'ordinary' politics. In this sense, 'the *Federalist* proposes a democratic constitution *that tries to economize on virtue*' (*ibid.*: 1031, my emphasis). Not being able to count on a community constantly thinking of the common good (that is, a virtuous community with an 'enlightened understanding' of it), the entire constitutional mechanism seeks to limit the worst effects of normal 'politics' and economise, indeed, on its scarce civic virtues, 'investing them' for the best return. Citizens, 'normally', are not 'private *citizens*', but are mostly only '*private* citizens', according to the solution (made evident in typographic terms, by shifting the italicisation) adopted by Ackerman (*ibid.*: 1042).[42] Since people are neither entirely 'angels' nor entirely 'demons', the only solution is to find institutional arrangements that adapt to human nature. As Hamilton wrote, 'the supposition of universal venality in human nature is little less an error in political reasoning than the supposition of universal rectitude. The institution of delegated power implies that there is a portion of virtue and honor among mankind, which may be a reasonable foundation of confidence' (*Federalist* 76, cited in Ackerman 1984: 1031). The Constitution is the living memory of the 'heroic' moment of a democratic political community; however, people will be able to create moments like this only in exceptional circumstances, when a 'heightened political consciousness' comes into play (*ibid.*: 1022).[43]

---

41. In Ackerman's analysis, judicial review is one of the 'filters' that characterised the historical evolution of American constitutional design. Ackerman dedicated the final and predominant part of his text to it: according his interpretation of Madison, 'when normal representatives respond to special interests in ways that jeopardize the fundamental principles for which the Revolutionaries fought and died, the judge's duty is to expose them for what they are: merely "stand-ins" for the People themselves' (Ackerman 1984:1030). It is important to remember that judicial review (the authority of the Supreme Court to nullify those legislative acts that are in conflict with the Constitution) was not initially provided by the Constitution itself; but it was progressively affirmed, starting from – and in particular – an 1803 Court judgment with Chief Justice John Marshall presiding (he was leader of the Court from 1801 to 1835).

42. On this distinction, *see also* Ackerman 1991: 230 ff. and Ackerman and Fishkin 2004: 173 ff.

43. Ackerman and Fishkin (2004: 159), recalled elsewhere how, among the Founding Fathers, Jefferson supported another line of thought: recalling Arendt (*see* Chapter Four, Section 3), the authors note how Jefferson's works 'contain ingenious proposals for integrating a dense network of face-to-face deliberative assemblies into the Founding scheme'. A century later, during the Progressive Era, Jefferson's spirit emerged again: the Progressives 'carved out new spaces for

At this point, Ackerman shifts to contemporary politics. In fact, what dominates is still the 'civic privatism' that the Founders had so presciently taken into consideration. And in today's scenario, that 'economy of virtue' is even more important: 'if politics is not the preeminent path to virtue, it is all the more important for the Constitution to make the most of what little public virtue we can expect' (*ibid.*: 1032–3). Thus, 'the dilemmas of private citizenship' are delineated. If we exclude the (many) individuals who are 'perfect privatist' (*ibid.*: 1040) and those who, on the contrary, are 'perfectly public citizens' (*ibid.*: 1043) (those who dedicate themselves 'body and soul' to a cause), under normal circumstances a 'private citizen', even if preoccupied with his own affairs, is able to respond to an issue that affects the political community. At the very moment in which he intervenes as a 'private *citizen*', he must 'at least *say*' he supports something more than just his simple, personal interest. Otherwise, he loses his nature of 'private *citizen*' and appears to his fellows as only driven by selfish intentions. And yet, Ackerman notes (*ibid.*: 1033–4),

> … while most Americans answer to the name of private citizen, they have learned not to take their protestations of civic virtue too seriously. Indeed, even gaining a rudimentary empirical understanding of a national problem often requires a lot of work. While we may occasionally make this effort, an ongoing commitment to informed citizenship may unduly deflect our energies from the innumerable struggles of everyday life.[44]

Thus, a political community has three major problems: *apathy*; *ignorance*; and *selfishness*. How can they be tackled? Excluding a 'coercive democracy' that would try to eradicate these evils, Ackerman considers what he calls *levelling democracy*: a vision that he attributes to the section of American constitutional thought that was most directly influenced by the Anti-Federalist tradition and then revived in the Progressive Era. Here, a '*single-track* democracy' seems to be the answer: the political will of the American people is embodied by Congress and, 'if the Congress enacts a law, the People have spoken; if not, not. It's that simple, and no talk about the problematics of representation should be allowed to obscure this fundamental reality' (*ibid.*: 1035). For *levellers*, this immediate expression of the will is the only thing that matters. '[I]f, in a formally free and fair contest, every voter chooses between the candidates on the basis of the winsomeness of their

---

public deliberation. In contrast to the Founders, they sought to make these new procedures available to citizens all the time and did not reserve them for specially mobilized conditions of constitutional politics' (ibid.), issuing 'a frontal challenge to Madisonian premises' (*ibid.*: 160). Ackerman and Fishkin retrace the historical reasons that profoundly changed the role Madison gave to political representation (rather than 'to refine', representatives often tend only to 'gratify' in every possible way the elector's preferences) but they also highlight how certain institutions of direct democracy, such as 'citizen initiatives', did not favour the production of an effective deliberation at all.

44. Notice here how Ackerman basically accepted the assumptions of 'rational ignorance' (Downs 1956), as well as Dahl's important analysis of 'decisional costs' (1956).

respective smiles, the leveller would treat this result no differently from another election in which every voter chose between the candidates on the basis of their position on black slavery' (*ibid.*: 1036).[45]

The American 'dualist Constitution' offers a different solution, indicating two different systems of *law-making*: a 'higher' and a 'lower' one (*ibid.*: 1042–3).

> By providing a higher lawmaking system, the American Constitution succeeds in constituting something more than a government in Washington, D.C. It constitutes a system of political meanings that enable all Americans to indicate the rare occasions when they mean to present themselves to one another as private *citizens*, and mark them off from the countless ordinary occasions when they are content to understand themselves as merely *private* citizens – for whom political life is but one of many diversions in the ongoing pursuit of happiness. Not that every effort at establishing our claim to private *citizenship* is fated to meet with Publian success. Instead, we must expect that most of our fellow citizens will look upon most political efforts at national renewal with the apathy, ignorance, and selfishness characteristic of normal life in a liberal democracy. And yet, from time to time, some would-be Publians begin to strike a resonant chord; their strong appeals to the public good are no longer treated as if they were the ravings of fringe elements in American society. Instead of encountering ignorance or contempt, the new movement is taken seriously by more and more Americans – even when they find its message deeply repugnant. In turn, the movement's success in penetrating political consciousness provokes a general effort to assess its ultimate significance: Is it a passing fad or something of genuine public significance? Slowly the half-remembered rituals of higher lawmaking begin to take on a deeper meaning, for it is through these rituals that we may test the seriousness of our fellow Americans' effort at national renewal and redefinition. Needless to say, most movements will fail to generate the kind of widespread support for their Publian pretensions that is required before they can constitutionally speak, once more, in the special accents of We, the People of the United States.

This transformation occurred historically in several instances, according to Ackerman. Based on this theoretical framework, Ackerman gives, for example, his interpretation of the sharp conflict between Roosevelt and the Supreme Court in

---

45. It is important to notice that Ackerman considers Schumpeter's 'the classic work in levelling political philosophy', bearer of 'a hard-boiled view of modern citizenship' (Ackerman 1984: 1036, note 52). This approach, Ackerman adds, presents itself in two forms: a liberal and a democratic one. The liberal one has some credibility, especially since it understood 'the transparent dangers involved in forcing people to be good citizens' so that 'nobody is obliged to spend time tediously discussing the fate of the Republic when he would rather be doing something else'. The democratic one, instead, emphasises the symbolic value of popular participation in elections and enhances the possibility of expelling bad rulers by voting (*ibid.*: 1037). Ackerman highlights the inadequacy of both: 'what the private citizen finds wanting in levelling democracy is adequate insurance against a political landslide engineered by well-organized special-interest groups speaking with the full authority of the People' (*ibid.*: 1038).

the first phase of the New Deal. The 'old' Court, resisting Roosevelt's offensive for a long time, indeed played its constitutional role of checking the depth and strength of the innovations that the New Deal legislation would introduce. Thanks to this 'resistance', which cannot be interpreted as purely conservative, the 'solution of continuity' of the New Deal later gained stronger democratic and constitutional legitimacy (*ibid.*: 1053–6).

At this point, I can go back to Fishkin. In the final pages of his book, he recalls Ackerman's dualistic theory. According to Fishkin, Ackerman's theses are important because the initial 'dilemma' – the gap between 'the nondeliberative (formal) political equality of the masses and the deliberative political *in*equality of the elites' – 'is based on the presumption that the masses will not be sufficiently engaged or aroused to be deliberative on national issues in the large-scale nation-state' (Fishkin 1991: 101). It is impossible to avoid this presumption but Ackerman comes to our aid by showing 'one further possibility': 'the masses may become engaged *episodically*' (*ibid.*, my emphasis). As we have seen, for Ackerman this happens only in a few 'moments of crisis when everyone is open to continuing, deliberative mass discussion'. But Fishkin adds – noting, of course, the very different scope of the two questions – that there is some sort of parallel between the notion of a 'constitutional moment' and the idea of Deliberative Polling. Although we can only expect significant mass deliberation in the 'special moments' of 'constitutional politics', we can, nevertheless, create institutional conditions which, even in a period of 'normal politics', allow deliberation that may not involve the mass but which is still 'representative'. Deliberative Polling is a tool with which a '*private* citizen' can, *episodically*, become 'a private *citizen*' urged to come out of his 'civic privatism' to play the role of Publius, or at least that of a citizen who strives to gain an 'enlightened understanding' of the general issues affecting his country.

Ackerman's theory offers Fishkin a background against which to deal with the sense of 'representativeness' of a minipopulus: the objections, which we mentioned above, to the lack of or doubtful connection between the 'virtuous' deliberations of a sample of citizens and the 'coarse' opinions of a wider audience are thus eliminated completely. Properly speaking, a problem of 'representation' does not even arise, since the 'general public' is, constitutively and inherently, a public of *private* citizens who either have no views or have such thoughtless and random opinions that they cannot be taken seriously as the basis of political decisions. Note that there is no aristocratic prejudice here: it is the 'normal' condition of a liberal democracy that guarantees this 'civic privatism'. *All* citizens, potentially, could live up to Publius; but, in normal times, there is no need for this republican heroism (and, anyway, if they so wish, citizens are free to fight for their ideas, vote, acquire information and so on). Deliberative Polling merely offers *one more* possibility, in the face of routine and apathy: 'it is merely a process', Fishkin says, 'that would make our system better satisfy all of our proposed conditions of deliberation, political equality, and non-tyranny' (*ibid.*: 103). In a certain sense, therefore, the *recommendation force* of the outcome of a Deliberative Polling acquires importance because such outcomes are *not* 'representative' of what the 'general public' ordinarily thinks. Rather, they are the 'experimental' creation of a moment of 'high politics' and indicate what the people *would think* if they could (or wanted to) devote time, energy and resources to the acquisition of a higher and more virtuous knowledge of common problems.

Ackerman emphasised the difference between moments in which a solution to the 'legal' continuity of a constitutional settlement is produced and moments in which politics runs ordinarily. In the former, there is mass deliberation (pervasive deliberation, resulting from a 'status of exception'). In this deliberation, *everything is questioned* and all citizens are involved in redefining and creating the terms of their political co-existence. In the latter, deliberation is a scarce resource. Against this background, Fishkin considers the possibility of deliberative spaces and places in which we could, at least *episodically*, revive the charm of a high and noble politics. A possibility for some private citizens to play once more the role of Publius … at least for a while.

Chapter Eight

The 'Constitutive Phase' of Deliberative Democracy: An Assessment

1. The five 'critical frontiers' of deliberative democracy

In Part II of this work (Chapters Three to Seven), I have traced the first phase of development of the theoretical field of deliberative democracy, pointing out important signs of its emergence in Chapter Two, especially in Jane Mansbridge's work. At this point, we can draw some preliminary conclusions: during the early 1980s, a 'theory' or 'conception' of deliberative democracy started to become the subject of a debate mostly involving scholars of American constitutional thought and history. Faced with the emergence of a vision, inspired by the Anti-Federalist tradition, which tended to read the American Constitution as a project to contain the original radical democratic aspirations of the revolutionary phase and another that traced it back to and closely related it to the theoretical framework of contemporary pluralist theories, some scholars now began to reinterpret Madison's original design.

This reinterpretation started from a discussion of alternative views on the classic problem of *factions* and whatever this issue entailed, in light of the transformations of contemporary democracy. What is the role of interests and interest-groups? How to conceive the political process? How to prevent these private interests from overshadowing the 'general interest'? Is there such a thing as a general interest? Is there a 'common good'? And how is it to be defined: as a mere aggregation of private, exogenous preferences rooted in citizens' natural pre-political rights; or, reviving the republican tradition, as arising from the political practice of citizens' self-determination – a good defined and constructed by and through a democratic and deliberative process?

These questions involved different possible interpretations of the Founding Fathers' original design (a 'protective' vision of democracy *versus* a vision that aimed for civic self-determination). However, they became part of the contemporary theoretical debate on models and conceptions of democracy and on the way American democracy, in particular, had changed (the supremacy of big interest-groups and the exhaustion or even failure of the classic liberal model). As we have noted, it is no coincidence that a work like Lowi's (1979 [1969]), about 'the end of liberalism', was often and openly evoked in these discussions.

The alternative that would later be crucial in defining a new theoretical paradigm, that of deliberative democracy, had already been outlined in different forms by various authors. To an idea of democracy based on the *aggregation* of *given, exogenous* preferences, 'privately' defined on the basis of individual interests, was opposed an idea of democracy based on the *transformation* of these preferences, defined and formed as reflectively as possible through public debate. Such a process was considered the most important prerequisite, if the fundamental principle of democracy in line with the tradition of republicanism, that is, citizens' *autonomy* as the foundation of their freedom, was to be guaranteed.

Thus, the borders of the theoretical field of deliberative democracy started to be defined by the identification of a series of contemporary democratic paradigms against which the new theoretical vision was contrasted. In this way, we can also grasp deliberative theory's growing distance from previous theories of 'participatory democracy'. In particular, it is possible to identify *five critical frontiers* along which the new deliberative theory was developing:

a) *A critique of the pluralist paradigm* of contemporary political science (seeing interest-group pluralism as the key balancing mechanism by which the risk of the tyranny of the majority was averted). On the basis of this critique, a revised conception of the republican ideal of a 'common good', to be defined and constructed in a deliberative way, by a civic practice of self-determination, was proposed.

b) *A critique of Schumpeter's and Downs's competitive-elitist vision of democracy.* As we have seen in Chapter One, from the 1960s on, critical arguments against this conception had been developed by advocates of a participatory vision of democracy. However, these were now transposed into a different context and new forms of them were being developed. It was no longer (or not only) a matter of contrasting those democratic conceptions variously definable as Schumpeterian with one based on the *direct empowerment* of citizens. Rather, it was the mounting of a radical challenge to this 'minimalist' vision of democratic procedures as merely the competitive selection of ruling elites. What was offered instead was a different conception of *democratic legitimacy* itself: this legitimacy was not only a result of fair electoral procedures but was also *discursively* constructed, in a *public* dimension, by *deliberation* that would be more democratic the more *inclusive* and *egalitarian* it became.

c) *Criticism of the utilitarian paradigm of contemporary social sciences.* What fully comes into play here is the critical confrontation that developed *within*, and *about*, the theories of *rational choice* and *social choice*. As we have seen in Chapter Four, Elster played a key role in defining certain crucial points in this area. In fact, it was through his work that radical criticism of the prevalent version of social-choice theory came to be included in theoretical reflection on deliberative democracy. This criticism, the proposal of a more complex and nuanced image of the individual (*versus* the idea of the merely self-interested agent), and reflection on how preferences are formed and their varied nature, became essential theoretical elements of a new conception of what makes decision-making procedures *democratic*. It is John Rawls who played the largest and most important role in this respect, however. As James Bohman and William Rehg recall (1997: xxviii, note 99), Rawls's criticism of the utilitarian model and the 'non-aggregative conception of the common good' that emerged in *Theory of Justice* certainly deeply influenced the general democratic culture and theory of those years. However, more specifically, Rawls's work paved the way for the emergence of the deliberative conception of democracy, as the discussion of Joshua Cohen's work and contribution in Chapter Six demonstrates.[1]

d) *A critique of the idea, rooted in Rousseau, that equated deliberation and decision and saw participation as direct expression of citizen power.* Theorists of participatory democracy had often made Rousseau their model. Here, Bernard Manin's contribution seems decisive, in pointing out that Rousseau did not advocate citizen deliberation. By re-proposing an Aristotelian notion of deliberation, Manin arrived at a new conception of the *legitimacy* of democratic procedures as based on citizens' *inclusion* in the deliberative process, rather than seeing legitimacy as a direct and immediate expression of citizens' will.[2]

e) *New directions in interpretation of the design of the US Constitution.* As we have seen in my analysis of Bessette's and Sunstein's works, interpretation of the fundamentals of the Constitution turned against *both* the 'pluralist' understanding of the Madisonian topic of 'factions' *and* the view typical the Anti-Federalist tradition, based on community self-government and face-to-face decision-making procedures; direct exercise of citizens' civic virtue; and education for active citizenship. Instead, a new conception of the American constitutional project (as well as an analysis of the present American political system), based on the idea of 'deliberative democracy', was offered. This did not reduce democracy to a matter of bargaining or the selection of ruling elites; nor did it trust in the virtues of a community of *self-ruling* citizens; nor in the immediate translation of the citizens' opinions and interests into political and institutional choices. In different ways, Bessette's, Sunstein's and Michelman's works (but also Ackerman's) propose an interpretation based on a deliberative dimension already *embodied* in the history of democracy and the American Constitution, as well as an interpretation of its institutions and government as mechanisms designed to facilitate and encourage properly deliberative practice.[3] The importance of this 'critical frontier' cannot be underestimated: as we have seen, James Fishkin's work also began from a critical diagnosis of the health of contemporary democracy, which had been rather deformed by 'direct-majoritarianism', distancing it from Madison's original design, which gave deliberation a major role.

In Chapter Seven, we began to see how the deliberative field has quickly expanded, overlapping and intersecting with some aspects of the tradition of participatory democracy. In the following chapters, we will look at other aspects

---

1. On Rawls and his approach to deliberative democracy, *see* Chapter Eleven.

2. As we have seen, Rousseau comes into play – in a very different way – in Cohen's position as well (*see* Chapter Six, Section 3, note 20): a 'Rawlsian' Rousseau, so to speak. However, also in this case, this Rousseau is very different from the one assumed as a theorist of direct democracy by the first exponents of participatory democracy.

3. Obviously, here it's possible to find the roots of President Obama's view, which I quoted in the Introduction to this work. As is well known, the President was formerly Professor of Constitutional Law at the Law School of the University of Chicago and started his political career as a lawyer in poor neighbourhoods of the city.

of this process. If we look at this 'constitutive' phase of the theoretical deliberative model, and if we consider these five 'critical frontiers' as a whole, however, the most important points to grasp are the decisive elements that mark a break with – or maybe even an estrangement from – the 'participatory' models of the previous two decades, along with some elements of partial *contiguity* with it.

Critics of the pluralist and elitist schools of democracy (as we saw in Chapter One) also tried to elaborate a participatory model of democracy. However, that line of thought would prove to be weak, particularly in regard to theorising the institutional structures needed to support such a model. Criticism of the utilitarian rationality of mainstream contemporary social and political science had (often) been only in the background or even absent; only later did it receive adequate attention, from Barber. Nevertheless, it was a critical ground compatible with a 'participatory' model of democracy. However, on other critical 'fronts', there was a marked discontinuity with previous conceptions of participatory democracy (entailing a radical rethinking of some crucial theoretical tenets).

Previous conceptions had – to varying degrees and in different forms – some common elements: a strong focus on a local and communitarian dimension; a vision of participation as *direct empowerment* and *community control*; a rejection of, or at least a strong distrust of, political representation; the adoption or idealisation of consensual decision-making procedures, attributing little importance to the deliberative dimension while giving a central role to some form of direct and egalitarian exercise of power. Well, these pieces *did not fit*, in any way, into the early view of 'deliberative democracy'. In fact, these elements were – partly – rooted precisely in the Anti-Federalist tradition that was one of the polemical objectives of authors such as Bessette and Sunstein.

Thus, the new theoretical field of deliberative democracy was constructed through the work of several independent theoretical and disciplinary approaches that only later entered into dialogue with each other. In the first phase, there were philosophical approaches (Cohen, Manin); legal-constitutionalist approaches (Bessette, Sunstein, Michelman); and approaches typical of *social-choice theory* (Elster); afterwards, there were approaches related to *political theory* and *political science* (Dryzek, Fishkin). Of course, the borders between the different approaches are not always easy to define: the works of authors such as Sunstein and Michelman, as well as Elster, for example, have a strong and openly 'philosophical' element; Bessette's approach (especially in his 1994 book) also has a strong 'empirical' element, linked to the analysis of the institutional mechanisms of American politics.

At this point, a question arises: what role do Rawls and Habermas play in this context? As we have seen in relation to all the authors analysed so far, Rawls's and Habermas's work – in different ways and to varying degrees – supplied some terms of reference, categories, concepts and the theoretical core on which different authors constructed the first framework of deliberative democracy. But, at this early stage, their work only acted *in the background*.[4] Moreover, it was only their

---

4.   Of course, Cohen is an exception. As we have seen, his connection with Rawls's work is quite strong.

1970s (and some 1980s) works whose ideas were taken up by new theorists of deliberation. It's almost as if Rawls and Habermas, so often referred to as the 'inspirers' of this new conception of democracy, thought it was time to intervene personally, by developing their own wider theoretical and philosophical projects. The idea of deliberative democracy (or politics) would thus acquire a significant and increasing importance *within* their own thinking. Their great works of the early 1990s (*Between Facts and Norms* and *Political Liberalism)* would, each in its own way, contribute directly to strengthening the foundations of the new theoretical perspective.

In the following four chapters, I will extensively analyse how Habermas and Rawls performed this task. But, first, I need to complete the analysis of the relationship between the participatory tradition and the new field of deliberative democracy.

2. 'Participatory' and 'deliberative': continuity, contiguity or break?

It must be said that my claim of a clear discontinuity between the 'participatory democracy of the 1960s and 1970s and the new field of deliberative democracy of the 1980s is neither self-evident nor universally shared. In this regard, the first major anthology of essays dedicated to deliberative democracy (Bohman and Rehg 1997)[5] can be a reference point. In this collection, only four contributions are considered to be the 'major statements' of the new theory: Elster's 'The market and the forum' (1986); Cohen's 'Deliberation and democratic legitimacy' (1989); Habermas's 'Popular sovereignty as procedure' (1997b) and Rawls's 'The idea of public reason' (1993). In their Introduction, the editors identified the contemporary theoretical paradigms against which the new theory was being critically defined: 'the *elitist theory* of democracy propounded by Joseph Schumpeter and his disciples' and the *economic theory of democracy*, which tended 'to model the competitive political process on rational-choice assumptions' (Bohman and Rehg 1997: x). According to Bohman and Rehg, these were 'the two main sources for liberal democratic theory up to 1970'; in such a context 'the *pluralist model of democracy* proposed by Robert Dahl and others provided an influential framework for interpreting Madisonian democracy'; and, 'although Dahl's decentralized, "polyarchal" version of pluralism shed much of Schumpeter's elitism, it retained the emphasis on competition, interests, and voting' (*ibid.*: xii).

Bohman and Rehg noted that 'this climate was a rather inhospitable one for conceptions of public deliberation about a common good' (*ibid.*). Indeed, those theories strongly focused on demonstrating either the scant plausibility of the very idea of a 'common good' or on its logical inconsistency, as well as on the 'tyrannical' or paternalistic outcomes that it could entail. According to Bohman and Rehg, however relevant was the presence of intellectuals such as John Dewey

---

5.   We have also seen (Chapter Seven, Section 2) how Dryzek built his own 'genealogy' of deliberative democracy including writers such as Barber who, in my opinion, are properly part of the tradition of participatory democracy.

and Hannah Arendt during the post-war period, 'the competitive-pluralist trend began to reverse itself' only 'in the late 1960s'. The Vietnam War (which produced an 'increasing perception that decision making in government was bureaucratic and beyond the control of citizens') and, more generally, the spread of a critical evaluation of the liberal model of government created opportunity for opinion-movements and ideas that challenged elitist–pluralist theories and identified 'participatory democracy' as an alternative vision.

Although Bohman's and Rehg's account seems to converge, so far, with what we have seen in previous chapters,[6] their next stage appears less convincing. They recall that 'it was only in the 1980s that a concept of deliberative democracy began to take definite shape' and note how the same term 'seems to have been first coined by Joseph Bessette', in his polemic 'against an elitist (or "aristocratic") interpretation of the Constitution'. Yet they seem to suggest continuity, or a substantial admixture between the two theoretical perspectives: 'Bessette's challenge joined the chorus of voices calling for a participatory view of democratic politics' (as we have seen, however, this was not the *focus* of Bessette's work). These voices questioned the underlying assumptions of the 'economic' and 'pluralist' models of democracy and, at the same time, drew on a combination of the experiences of

> ... direct democracy, town-hall meetings and small organizations, workplace democracy, mediated forms of public reason among citizens with diverse moral doctrines, voluntary associations, and deliberative constitutional and judicial practices regulating society as a whole, to name just a few (*ibid.*: xiii).

This list clearly shows the context from which the deliberative approach emerged. However, it also conflates somewhat disparate phenomena and therefore is not helpful in grasping the true theoretical distinction from participatory democracy that defines deliberative democracy.

My thesis is that this distinction is the result of different ways of tackling the issue entailed in the connection between *participation, deliberation* and *political decision*. For the participatory understanding of democracy, the dimensions of *direct empowerment* and *equal power* are the essential features. The close connection between participation, power and decision is the heart of this model. In this context, Carol Pateman's vision is particularly emblematic – 'in the participatory theory, "participation" refers to (equal) participation in the making of decisions, and political equality refers to equality of power of determining the outcome of decisions ...' (Pateman 1970: 43)[7] – as is Sherry R. Arnstein's 'ladder

---

6. But not on this point: 'the theoretical critique of liberal democracy and revival of participatory politics gradually' – the authors affirm – 'developed through the 1970s' (Bohman and Rehg 1997: xii). However, as we have seen, it is more correct to date the origins of participatory democracy to the 1960s; the social and political movements of that decade brought participatory democracy on to the political and cultural scene.

7. Carole Pateman (2012: 8), in one of her most recent speeches, highlighted her view about the differences between participatory and deliberative democracy: 'Participatory democracy, I argue, is different from deliberative democracy. Deliberation, discussion, and debate are central to any form of democracy, including participatory democracy, but if deliberation is necessary for

of participation' – 'there is a critical difference between going through the empty ritual of participation and having the real power needed to affect the outcome of the process' (Arnstein 1969: 216). Equality of power directly exercised by individuals in the making of a decision is the key to this vision of participation and democracy. What comes primarily into play is neither public discussion nor argumentative exchange: what matters is to take part in a *decision-making process* and to do so equally, allowing everyone to exercise an equal share of power and to assert their will immediately in determining a decision. It is from *this* vision of participation that the idea of deliberative democracy sharply distances itself.

Jane Mansbridge's critical reflection on the experiences of *small participatory democracies* had already introduced some fundamental theoretical distinctions. It emphasised the conditions that could allow forms of democratic self-government based on consensus-oriented procedures, on a radical egalitarianism and on practices of *face-to-face* interaction; but it also showed those conditions that demanded instead *equal protection* and *respect* for *different* and *conflicting* interests, through democratic procedures requiring negotiations and/or aggregation-mechanisms based on the majoritarian principle.

Moreover, throughout the 1980s, deliberative theorists would focus on themes that are entirely absent from the first 'participatory' theorists – namely, the themes informing the five 'critical frontiers' along which the new paradigm was being defined. As my analysis indicates, criticism of the competitive-elitist and 'pluralist' conceptions of democracy was certainly common to both perspectives.[8] However, the idea of the *direct* exercise of some form of power was alien to the first theoretical elaborations of a deliberative conception of democracy. I believe that this is an essential distinction. The source of Bohman's and Rehg's 'continuity' vision is, I believe, their choice to adopt a definition of deliberative democracy as an *ideal* from which to derive a *political* and *cultural* proposal, with a strong emphasis on 'civic self-governance' and 'participatory politics' but raising the consequent questions about the practical *feasibility* of this ideal as well (Bohman and Rehg 1997: ix):

> ... broadly defined, *deliberative democracy* refers to the idea that legitimate lawmaking issues from the public deliberation of citizens. As a normative account of legitimacy, deliberative democracy evokes ideals of rational legislation, participatory politics, and civic self-governance. In short, it presents an ideal of political autonomy based on the practical reasoning of citizens. But is this ideal feasible or even desirable? What exactly is public deliberation? Given the complex issues that confront contemporary societies, is an intelligent, broad-based participation possible? In societies as culturally

---

democracy it is not sufficient. Some of the more enthusiastic advocates of deliberative democracy tend to present deliberation as if it were synonymous with democracy itself.'

8. It is important to stress that the two perspectives (elitism and pluralism) are not the same, although some theorists of participatory democracy, in the sixties, used to conflate them (*see* Chapter One, Section 2). Furthermore, as we have seen in Fishkin, Dahl's version of pluralism became part of what would later become one of the most influential elaborations of deliberative democracy.

diverse as our own, is it reasonable to expect deliberating citizens to converge on rational solutions to political problems? Does deliberation actually overcome or only exacerbate the more undesirable features of majority rule?

During the following years, up until very recent times, much of the theoretical literature and experimental planning of the deliberative field tried to answer these questions. However, this approach blurs the distinction between the perspective that emerged in the 1980s as deliberative democracy and what the participatory democrats of the 1960s and 1970s had proposed. In fact, it is no coincidence that Bohman and Rehg, in their bibliographic notes, quoted in the same way and without making any particular distinction from Pateman's, Barber's and Mansbridge's works, as well as Rawls's *Theory of Justice* (*ibid.*: xxviii).

Two other key terms that, if not properly understood, could lead us to underestimate the distance between the two models are *consensus* and *common good*. Reconstructing the climate from which these approaches emerged, Bohman and Rehg recall that 'leftist political activism, with its emphasis on participatory democracy, sparked a renewed interest in the possibilities for consensual forms of self-government' (*ibid.*: xii). Participatory democracy, indeed, made *consensus* the goal of democratic decision and emphasised the *consensual procedures* (the agreement of all or, at least, the absence of any openly expressed disagreement) necessary to reach a decision. For some authors (Barber, for example), the idea of civic participation oriented towards the 'common good' and the construction of consensual choices, against any narrowly self-interested logic, was strongly linked to a *community* dimension within which to exercise direct forms of *self-ruling*. However, as Mansbridge emphasised, this could only happen (and not without problems) in 'small organizations', which, on the other hand, often had a strongly conflictual vision of their outward-oriented political practice. Therefore, there could be other, just as democratic, decision-making procedures, in conflict situations, with other prerequisites: conditions of equal respect for all the interests and values at stake, as well as fair mediation or aggregation procedures.

The conceptions of *common good* and *consensus* emerging (in very different terms) from the texts of the first theorists of deliberative democracy were another matter. For Bessette and Sunstein, but also for Michelman, a vision of the common good as the sum, aggregation or balance of private and individual interests had to be rejected. Proposed instead was an idea (of republican origin) in which the common good was constructed by a widespread deliberative process, by the practice of civic self-determination and by the public view thus formed on the basis of a reflective transformation of individuals' *immediate* preferences. For Elster, criticism of the theory of *expressed* or *revealed preferences* typical of canonical rational choice models was crucial. Furthermore, his reflection on the *conditions* and *mechanisms*, *constraints* and *opportunities* by which these preferences are formed and transformed was also central. For Manin, the idea of democratic legitimacy produced as a result of the *deliberation of all*, and not as an expression of the *unanimous will of all*, was a fundamental theme.

Among the topics used in early delineations of the new deliberative model, those of empowerment and of participation as the *direct exercise of an equal share of power* in decision-making were completely absent; there was not even any opposition to the principles and forms of political representation. On the contrary, the idea was that the fundamental legitimacy of processes and mechanisms of representation (as well as the majority principle) came from a widespread and inclusive deliberative process. And there was more: the idea of a 'deliberative' democracy was essentially supported by a clear perception of the dangers coming from an immediate identification between 'will' and 'decision' that considered neither those *communicative conditions* necessary to produce what Habermas later called 'the processes of opinion and will formation' nor those *institutional procedures* by which special interests must be 'filtered' and immediate opinions 'transcended' and made reflective.

I therefore consider it appropriate to emphasise the profound differences and points of disconnection that separate the participatory democracy of the 1960s and 1970s from deliberative democracy as it was defined in the course of the 1980s. In my reconstruction, however, I have also identified connections that helped to bridge the gap between them, or even produced a degree of overlap between them. I believe that the theoretical premise of these processes should be located in an element that we have seen in Cohen's position but that later became widespread: the conceptualisation of deliberative democracy as a normative model or as an 'ideal' of democracy, to aspire to, to 'mirror' in institutions or to experience through new participatory models. Thus, the idea that political participation could and should take on the characteristics of public and democratic deliberation was born and developed. And, at the same time, the idea that democratic deliberation, in order to be considered a source of legitimacy for political decisions, had to take on (or at least, also include) the requirement of extensive and widespread participation was developed as well.

This understanding of deliberative democracy as a *political ideal* would not be limited to theoretical or philosophical reflection and would soon come to be seen as a veritable *political and cultural programme*. In fact, it would be on this assumption that relevant sectors of the deliberative field would theorise participatory models and experiment with participatory practices of deliberative inspiration, which would take on either more 'gradualist' political traits; or more 'radical' ones, as we have seen in John Dryzek; or characteristics that are relatively 'internal' or 'alternative' to a liberal-democratic political vision. This opened the way to what is commonly called the '*empirical turn*' in deliberative democracy; the presuppositions for this 'turn', though, had already been set at a theoretical level (I will deal with this topic in detail in Chapter Thirteen).

Of course, this encounter and intersection would occur in different forms and the connections between deliberative theory and the tradition of participatory democracy would be varied and vary in strength. In John Forester, and in the 'communicative turn' characterising the theories and practices of planning, we find one of the most important examples of a true *confluence* of the theoretical field of deliberative democracy as it was developing and a tradition whose roots are in the culture of participatory democracy of the 1960s (or, in some respects and even further back in time, in the ideas and experiences of the Progressive Era). In this case, the encounter takes place in relation to the themes of *community control* and *empowerment* but it is enriched by a more critical awareness of the communicative and discursive dimensions characterising the very construction of public policies. A partial overlap between participatory democracy and deliberative democracy would be created through this path as well.

This intersection, especially in the US, would be further powered by the recovery of typical and never-really-forgotten traditions of American political culture and it would accentuate the features of deliberative democracy understood as a social and political 'movement' that aimed to revive *civic culture*. The progressive, but slow and inevitably partial spread of deliberative experiments is thus read as a strategy of 'transplanting' 'healthy cells' (that is, innovative democratic practices) into the 'dying bodies' of our democracies in the hope that they would spread and regenerate a tired representative democracy devoid of legitimacy. Mark Button and David M. Ryfe, for example, write (2005: 30, my emphasis):

> What are the intrinsic values of democratic deliberation, and why do they matter? What sorts of evaluative standards or benchmarks would we propose in accordance with which we could judge the relative success of deliberative practices? From our point of view, deliberative democracy gives individuals the chance to live (*however briefly*) and to experience (*however artificially*) the essential meaning of democracy: free and equal opportunity to participate in a shared public life and to shape decisions that affect their lives. A more fully deliberative form of politics is a more fully democratic kind because it enlists the skills and virtues that make it possible for individuals to see themselves as interdependent, equal, and sovereign members of a political association. In this respect, then, deliberative democratic forums are a powerful political and cultural resource for combating the dual forces of privatism and demobilization, individual withdrawal, and institutional marginalization or exclusion that are taking place in our social and political lives today.[9]

The theoretical starting point of this approach is, of course, attributable to Dewey and the tradition of American pragmatism. The quoted extract is taken from one of the most influential books of the past decade in the field, the *Deliberative Democracy Handbook* (Gastil and Levine 2005), whose subtitle, *Strategies for*

---

9. It is impossible not to notice a deep consonance with Barber's view (*see* Chapter Two, Section 1) of democracy as 'shared public life': a definition whose extraordinary 'noble fathers' are precisely evoked by Button and Ryfe. Jefferson, Tocqueville, John Stuart Mill and Hannah Arendt are thinkers who 'have helped us to appreciate' how 'part of the intrinsic value of democracy is that it allows citizens to see things from different points of view and that it enables individuals to come to see themselves as equal, capable, and responsible members in a shared political life'. Thus, 'the call for more deliberative forums within the dispersed, plural, and overlapping domains of civil society is at once a call for restoration of the conditions that make a civic culture and civic actors possible' (Button and Ryfe 2005: 30).

effective civic engagement in the 21st century, is extremely indicative.[10] This book is one of the best examples of an approach offering a large number of more-or-less original methodologies (and consequent analysis of their empirical application). Such methodologies were often derived from the world of *practitioners*[11] who took up, in a more or less direct way, certain aspects of the original participatory democracy model, especially with regard to the *educational* purposes entrusted to participation. *To form a public* is the primary objective of the participatory-deliberative devices that are inspired by such a vision.

At the same time, this development of deliberative democracy could easily incorporate a tradition that never completely disappeared from American political culture, that is, the practices and experiences of *public talk*, community self-government and local civic culture. As evidence of such continuity, note that Ned Crosby founded the Jefferson Center for New Democratic Processes – the centre that was most important in developing and spreading the deliberative model of citizens' juries – as early as 1974.[12]

Generally, such approaches did not give particularly 'subversive' or radical roles to the new practices: they were mostly intended as opportunities and tools for reinvigorating the conventional institutions of representative democracy. In some respects, however, the distinction between more 'gradualist' and more 'radical' approaches is not always easy to identify; some positions assume that the new institutions might also be designed to *replace* the old ones. In these cases, the borderline between participatory and deliberative theories tends to be less well defined and, although several authors self-identify as belonging to the deliberative field, other formulas are often used as well.[13]

However, what does make it possible to distinguish a gradualist approach from a more 'radical' one is a definite shift of tone. If, for the former, it is a matter of the spread and experience of forms of democratic life counteracting the exhaustion of traditional civic virtues, for the deliberative 'radical' theorists, on the contrary, the progressive spread of these deliberative practices could and should be a 'counter-power' tending to replace existing institutions, or at least to show that another form of democracy is possible. As we have seen in John Dryzek's position, the 'established power structures', including those that operate beneath the 'constitutional surface' of the liberal state, can and must undergo a critical and participatory transformation, inspired by the deliberative democratic ideal and an

---

10. In the *Handbook*, *see also* the concluding essay (Gastil, Fung and Levine 2005).

11. This would happen, for example, in the 21st Century Town Meeting model, openly inspired by the traditions of New England; *see* Lukensmeyer, Goldman and Brigham 2005.

12. Crosby, Kelly and Shafer 1986; Crosby and Nethercut 2005; *see also* the website www.jefferson-center.org. The Jeffersonian inspiration is not a coincidence. To know more about the history of public deliberation in the history of the American democracy, *see* Gastil and Keith 2005; Mattson 1998 and 2011; and Keith 2011. On the concept of the public forum in the American constitutional tradition, *see* Post 1987.

13. As we will see in Joshua Cohen's case (*see* Chapter Ten); *see also* Fung and Wright 2003: chapter 13.

'*insurgent*' mobilisation of civil society (Dryzek 2000: 2). Civil society, and the movements and associations operating within it, are the focus of this vision. The goal of deliberative policy, here, is stimulating the creation of 'oppositional public spheres', capable of obstructing and combating the mechanisms of the economic and political domain.

Overall, we can say that these ramifications of deliberative democracy have certainly contributed to the development of a theory and practice of public and democratic deliberation. In their best expressions, they have also helped to spread and nurture a creative and experimental spirit, bringing to life the idea of a democracy that can change and find new ways to express and manifest itself. However, these approaches have often proved to be weak on other grounds. In particular, they have left important questions unanswered. Is deliberative democracy a *theory* that can cope with the *full range* of issues that face the democracy of our time? Is it an *idea of democracy* able to credibly challenge the usual and consolidated understandings (and practices) of democracy as we know it today? And is it only an *ideal* to aspire to or is it also, or perhaps especially, a *theoretical and interpretative model* that we can use to understand the ways in which our democracies actually work?

PART III

HABERMAS AND RAWLS: THE THEORETICAL
FOUNDATIONS OF DELIBERATIVE
DEMOCRACY

Chapter Nine

Habermas and 'Deliberative Politics'

1. *Between Facts and Norms*: a 'defection' from the field of deliberative democracy?

We have seen how Habermas's work offered essential reference points in the infancy of deliberative democracy as a theoretical field: this happened in different ways but his influence was mostly through reading of his 1970s works and only partly (and later) by that of *Theorie des kommunicakativen Handelns* (1981) and *Moralbewußtsein und kommunikatives Handelns* (1985). We have also seen how Habermas himself started to engage directly with some of the authors working on the idea of deliberative democracy.[1]

From the standpoint of the present reconstruction, this presents some paradoxical aspects: some of Habermas's categories and concepts, elaborated in the first half of the 1970s, made their way into the emerging theoretical field precisely when Habermas was critically revising them and was about to propose his own, more comprehensive, theory of politics and democracy. From this perspective, we can see why a work like *Between Facts and Norms*, which first appeared (in German)

---

1. Over the 1980s and 1990s, Habermas's production was particularly rich and followed a recognisable internal logic. Published in 1981, *Theorie des kommunicakativen Handelns* (trans. and ed. by T. McCarthy as *The Theory of Communicative Action*, 1984–7) is not only the culmination of Habermas's work of the two previous decades but also the centre of his entire theoretical framework. After this book, he went on to develop his theory in terms of *discourse ethics* – in *Moralbewußtsein und kommunikatives Handelns* (1983) (trans. as *Moral Consciousness and Communicative Action*, Habermas 1990) – and *moral theory*, in 1991's *Erläuterungen zur Diskursethik* (trans. as *Justification and Application: Remarks on discourse ethics*, Habermas 1993b). Later, in 1992, with *Faktizität und Geltung* (trans. as *Between Facts and Norms*, Habermas 1996), he came to a *discursive theory of right and democracy*. In the same period, with the great philosophical works *Der philosophische Diskurs der Moderne* (1985) (trans. as *The Philosophical Discourse of Modernity*, Habermas 1987) and *Nachmetaphysisches Denken* (1988) (trans. as *Postmetaphysical Thinking*, Habermas 1992b), Habermas established his position in the landscape of contemporary philosophical thought, proposing his own understanding of the detachment from all 'philosophy of the subject'. In his 1999 Introduction to a collection of essays he wrote between 1996 and 1998 – *Wahrheit und Rechtfertigung* (trans. as *Truth and Justification*, Habermas 2003a) – and dedicated to 'issues in theoretical philosophy', taking up 'a line of thought that I had set aside since *Erkenntnis und Interesse*' (Habermas 1968, trans. as *Knowledge and Human Interests*, Habermas 1971a), Habermas reconstructs his philosophical journey: 'The linguistic turn did not acquire its significance for me in connection with these traditional [philosophical] problems. Rather, the pragmatic approach to language [*Sprachpragmatik*] helped me to develop a theory of communicative action and of rationality. It was the foundation for a critical theory of society and paved the way for a discourse-theoretic conception of morality, law, and democracy' (Habermas 2003a: 1).

in 1992, baffled many previous supporters of Habermas – especially those who, generally favouring a participatory view of democracy, had counted on a directly political reading of his theory of communicative action and discourse ethics.

In 1999, for instance, William E. Scheuerman (1999: 155) described Habermas's as 'a *defensive* model of deliberative democracy in which democratic institutions exercise at best an attenuated check on market and administrative processes', highlighting the 'profound weakness' of the theory of democracy exposed in *Between Facts and Norms* by

> … its failure to give adequate expression to legitimate unease and anxiety about the fate of representative democracy at the end of the twentieth century. Despite rapidly growing evidence of widespread dissatisfaction with the operations of contemporary capitalist democracy, Habermas's work at times offers a surprisingly moderate and even conciliatory picture of 'really-existing' democracy (Scheuerman 1999: 156).

In 2000, John Dryzek went even further. Habermas's was 'no longer a true critical theory of democracy' (2000: 27); rather, his 'model of law and democracy' represented '*an accommodation* with key tenets of liberal constitutionalism, especially as interpreted by the liberal American deliberative democrats' (*ibid.*: 26, my emphasis). Furthermore, this model could be considered 'old-fashioned' by many political scientists and jurists. 'Setting aside the public sphere, Habermas's normative theory of the state is virtually identical to that proposed long ago by Theodore Lowi (1969) under the rubric of "juridical democracy"' (*ibid.*: 26). But what was the reason for such a harsh judgment? Under attack was Habermas's idea that the 'communicative power' expressed in the 'informal' public sphere can only *influence* the 'administrative power' and the law-making processes and it cannot do so without the *institutional and procedural mediations* typical of a democratic rule-of-law state. For Dryzek, Habermas turned elections into 'the main channel of influence from the public sphere to the state'; but then, 'what are we to make of the multiple channels of influence that for better or worse do not involve elections – such as protests, demonstrations, boycotts, information campaigns, media events, lobbying, financial inducements, economic threats, and so forth?' (*ibid.*).

Beyond what, to me, is a substantial misunderstanding of Habermas's position (on the topic of the forms and sources of *democratic legitimation*, on which I shall dwell later), Dryzek's judgment significantly testifies to how hard it was for a work like *Between Facts and Norms* to be seen as consistent with Habermas's ideas and categories as they had been understood and used while the new deliberative model was being constituted. In a review of the book, James Bohman wrote that

> … many faithful readers of Habermas may find his approach to legal and political legitimacy in *Faktizität und Geltung* somewhat surprising. Rather than defending participatory democracy directly, he instead embeds these radical democratic principles in a complex account of the political and legal institutions of constitutional democracies (Bohman 1994: 897).

Bohman himself (1996: 186) openly wondered how Habermas could still call his theory of democracy 'deliberative', since

> ... 'will formation' is entirely given over to institutional actors who are only 'influenced' by the public or 'open to' reasons it puts forward. It also makes it difficult to see why Habermas continues to call his democratic theory deliberative, since the public is given only an opinion forming (and thus an advisory and a merely critical) capacity.[2]

Another passage by Bohman can give us further insight (and perhaps validate my interpretation). For Bohman, what induced the German philosopher to review his work (1996: 173) was the new relevance attributed to 'social complexity', along with the idea that democracy 'cannot organize society as a whole' (*ibid.*: 172). For Habermas, Bohman noted,

> ... at the normative level, the strong analogies between the justification of moral norms and democratic decision making that were so prominent in *Legitimation Crisis*, have to be abandoned. Exploring moral justification served the epistemological purpose of pointing the way beyond Weber, but it proves a misleading and undercomplex model for democratic deliberation. Besides leading to the subordination of law and politics to morality, the idealizations and abstractness of moral discourse set the standard of agreement too high for democratic theory. This shift set the stage for Habermas's more modest approach ... (*ibid.*: 173).

Bohman here grasped a fundamental point and yet didn't seem to understand its full implications: as Habermas himself would say in *Between Facts and Norms*,

> [a]n *unmediated* application of discourse ethics (or of an unclarified concept of discourse) to the democratic process leads to muddled analyses; these then offer skeptics pretexts for discrediting the project of a discourse theory of law and politics at its inception. Hence, differentiations are necessary (1996: 158).

---

2. 'In his recent writings on democracy', Bohman had stated a little earlier, 'Habermas abandons his demand in *Legitimation Crisis* [1975: 36] for some participatory and "substantive" form of democracy characterized by the "genuine participation of citizens in political will formation" to replace the merely "formal" one typical of welfare-state capitalism. This stronger and substantive notion of a democratic will formed by citizens' participation was to continue the critical theorists search for a wider notion of rationality with which to ground a richer and more demanding form of democratic politics. In *Between Facts and Norms*, Habermas rejects even this task for a critical theory of democracy. Democracy, he argues, cannot organize society as a whole, since it is embedded in contexts of social complexity that it can neither regulate nor control' (Bohman 1996: 172–3). I'll come back to this point, as it constitutes the core of Habermas's discussion of Cohen's 'ideal deliberative procedure' in *Between Facts and Norms*.

To fully understand this statement it would be necessary to address Habermas's theoretical project in depth.[3] Here, however, I'll have to limit myself to a smaller task: I'll focus my analysis on the pages of *Between Facts and Norms* in which Habermas dialogues with the authors we have encountered so far, who had sought to define the concept or model of deliberative democracy. It is through this critical dialogue that Habermas defined his notion of *deliberative politics*.[4]

2. A procedural conception of democracy and the tension between 'facticity' and 'validity'

In the first section of chapter 4 of *Between Facts and Norms* (*BFN*: 133–7) Habermas analyses 'the internal relation between law and politics': 'the law receives its full normative sense neither through its legal *form* per se, nor through an a priori moral *content*, but through a procedure of lawmaking that begets legitimacy' (*BFN*: 154). Against the tradition of legal positivism; voluntaristic and 'decisionist' conceptions *à la* Carl Schmitt; and strategies of moral or ethical foundation of the law, Habermas proposes 'a discursive process of opinion- and will-formation' as the one procedural dimension that can give *legitimacy* to the law and to the exercise of political power (*ibid.*):

> It is not the legal form as such that legitimates the exercise of governmental power but only the bond with *legitimately enacted* law. At the post traditional level of justification, as we would say today, the only law that counts as legitimate is one that could be rationally accepted by all citizens in a discursive process of opinion- and will-formation (*ibid.*:135).

One problem immediately arises, that is, *how* such a 'discursive process of opinion- and will-formation' is or could be produced. It doesn't merely unfold in the 'horizontal association of consociates who reciprocally accord rights to one another' but also in 'the vertical organization of citizens within the state' (*ibid.*). What Habermas here calls '*the practice of self-determination*' of citizens [*die Selbst-bestimmungspraxis der Bürger* (*FG*: 170)] – namely, the public formation process of the people's opinion and will – 'is institutionalized in a number of ways': 'it appears as informal opinion-formation in the political public sphere, as participation inside and outside political parties, as participation in general elections, as deliberation and decision making in parliamentary bodies, and so on' (*BFN*: 135). Thus, 'popular sovereignty … is interlaced … with governmental

---

3. Of course, there is wide literature on *Between Facts and Norms*: a first series of essays and commentaries appeared in a voluminous issue of the *Cardozo Law Review* (vol. 17, 1995–6), which gathered the proceedings of a 1992 conference and Habermas's own reply. For an introduction to *Between Facts and Norms*, see Rehg 1996; Baynes 1995; Rosenfeld and Arato 1998; and Von Schomberg and Baynes 2002, Baynes 2015.

4. I'll refer to the 1996 English translation of *Faktizität und Geltung* [*Between Facts and Norms*] by William Rehg, hereafter, as *BFN*. When necessary, I'll refer to the original German, quoting from the reprint dated 1998 (hereafter, *FG*).

power' but the classical principle that 'all governmental authority derives from the people' can now only be realised 'through the communicative presuppositions and procedures of an institutionally differentiated opinion and will-formation' (*ibid.*).

Once again, we find the theme – which I have already addressed (see Chapter Five, Section 3) – of a 'popular sovereignty' that it is now impossible to conceive of in 'physical' or 'personal' terms:

> … according to the discourse-theoretic conception of government by law, popular sovereignty is no longer embodied in a visibly identifiable gathering of autonomous citizens. It pulls back into the, as it were, 'subjectless' forms of communication circulating through forums and legislative bodies (*BFN*: 135–6).

Of course, the *forums* [*Foren*] mentioned here are to be broadly understood. 'Forums' are all the places and moments in which citizens *debate*, or even *argue* about, politics or specific policies, forming opinions and judgments that then translate into their 'wills': 'only in this anonymous form can [the] communicatively fluid power [of popular sovereignty] bind the administrative power of the state apparatus to the will of the citizens. As we will see, in the democratic rule-of-law state [*Rechtstaat*], political power is differentiated into communicative power and administrative power' (*BFN*: 136).[5] There might not be any *direct* connection linking the sovereignty of the people to the decision but only a complex process of *procedural mediation*, which is, itself, legitimately justified and generated. 'Popular sovereignty no longer concentrates in a collectivity, or in the physically tangible presence of the united citizens or their assembled representatives, but only takes effect in the circulation of reasonably [*vernünftig*] structured deliberations and decisions' (*ibid.*).

In these pages, Habermas doesn't talk at all about 'deliberative democracy' but about the normative foundations of a democratic *Rechtstaat*; his aim is to elaborate a theory in which popular sovereignty – now only considered possible 'in this anonymous form' (*ibid.*), escaping any attempt to capture it concretely and *immediately* in some 'physically tangible presence' – still should not be deprived 'of its radical-democratic content' (*ibid.*). It is only at the end of his theoretical and conceptual journey (at the end of chapter 6 and then in chapter 7), that Habermas uses the adjective 'deliberative', albeit referring to *politics* and not *democracy*. At the same time, he warned his readers against a potential misunderstanding: 'this investigation is not concerned with the gap between norm and reality, and thus does not yet approach power as a *social* facticity able to make ideas look foolish' (*ibid.*). At that stage, in the first part of *Between Facts and Norms*, the point was to investigate 'the tension between facticity and validity *inside* the law' – a tension 'found in political power *per se* inasmuch as the latter is internally connected with law, in relation to which it must legitimize itself' (*BFN*: 137). Only after clarifying

---

5.   On the dichotomy between 'communicative power' and 'administrative power', and the problems it poses, *see* Chapter 10, Section 4.

this 'conceptual relation', states Habermas, referring to chapter 8, can one grasp the *empirical* forms of this 'opposition between norm and reality' in contemporary democracies (*ibid.*).

The latter statement is important, because it shows how Habermas totally rejects any theoretical attitude that first sets up an 'ideal' and then tries to adapt it to reality. Habermas *reconstructs* the 'self-understanding' of modern law and power and the first thinkers mentioned in the next paragraph, in fact, are Machiavelli and Hobbes (*BFN*: 137–9): that is, a historical process that itself thrives on the tension between facticity and validity, whose various 'empirical' manifestations can then be reconstructed and interpreted. 'The gap between norm and reality' (*BFN*: 136) would be incomprehensible if one didn't grasp the *social facticity of the norms* and the *normative dimension of facts*. Even when speaking of a theory of law and democracy, Habermas takes on the position of someone who, giving up any 'philosophy of the subject', mainly wants to construct a *social theory*, identifying the conceptual categories for *reconstructing* what actually happened and what still happens today. Indeed, it is a critical theory and not an ideal model of law and democracy.

The 'viewpoint' chosen by Habermas (regardless of the plausibility of the single outcomes of his reconstruction) is mainly that of a *theoretician of society* and its historical evolution, making full use of all the contributions of the humanities and the social sciences. In this context, the tension between facticity and validity is not between the actual reality and the ideals or norms that some subject (or even a philosopher) proposes, but a constitutive feature of the very social and historical reality that we are trying to understand; at the same time, it is a cornerstone of the conceptual reconstruction that we can make of it. In order to understand it adequately we have to construct *abstract conceptual models* able to account for historical-empirical variability and therefore able to acquire *concrete* determinations over time. In other words, Habermas wants abstraction to be *full of meaning and content*, not empty theoretical notions resulting from a progressive 'liberation' from empirical determination or from inductive generalisation of empirical data. Precisely for this logical character, Habermas's theoretical categories allow us *to rise from the abstract to the concrete*, because they remain (hypothetically and potentially, if they stand the test) valid and operative even as they acquire historical-concrete and empirical determinations. The processes and the connections that the 'abstract model' identifies do not lose, so to speak, their *factual operationality* when they live and reproduce within specific historical conditions.[6]

3. Models and concepts of 'deliberative politics': constitutional legitimacy and republicanism

'Deliberative politics' enters the argumentative fabric of *Between Facts and Norms* in chapter 6, devoted to the 'role' and the 'legitimacy of constitutional

---

6. To mention one example of Habermas's 'reconstructive method', see the pages devoted to 'the genesis of law and politics' and their connection (*BFN*: 138–9).

adjudication'. 'The constitutional court's decision making', with the heated controversy it arouses, offers Habermas the opportunity to introduce an intense discussion on the 'dissolution of the liberal paradigm of law', especially in the American debate on the Supreme Court, and on a critical analysis of the forms of 'methodological self-understanding' of the German Federal Court. The underlying theoretical question guiding this discussion concerns the type of *discourse* and the nature of the *judgments* that a constitutional court expresses, as well as the *source* on which it bases the *legitimacy* of its decision-making practice (with the different possible interpretations of it).

For the purposes of the present book, this chapter of Habermas's work is particularly interesting. In fact, among the many authors Habermas engages with, there are some we have already encountered in the previous chapter: Cass Sunstein; Frank I. Michelman; and Bruce Ackerman. What's more, Habermas discusses the very same texts by these authors (generally dating back to the second half of the 1980s) that had been debated during the constitutive phase of deliberative democracy.[7]

The main interlocutor, albeit not the only one, is Michelman: as Habermas puts it in his 'Reply' to the conference of the Cardozo Law School:

> It is no accident that Frank Michelman is one of the three or four contemporary authors whom I have cited most frequently. Michelman's works have taught me the most about deliberative politics, and through reading them I have been encouraged to apply the discourse principle to law and lawmaking, or 'jurisgenesis,' as he calls it (1995–6: 1485).

Therefore, before illustrating the discussion that takes place in *Between Facts and Norms*, it might be useful to recall how Habermas, in a later essay, would present Michelman's theses:

> In the United States, a debate has been going on for some time over the legitimacy of the highest-level judicial review exercised by the Supreme Court. Again and again, civic republicans who are convinced that 'all government is by the people' bristle at the elite power of legal experts to void the decisions of a democratically elected legislature, although these experts themselves are not legitimated by a democratic majority but can only call on their technical competence in constitutional interpretation (Habermas 2001: 768–9).

---

7. Habermas quotes from and analyses Sunstein's essay of 1985, which I have dwelt on in Chapter Three, Section 2, but also Michelman's 1986 essay, quoted by Joshua Cohen as one of his sources of inspiration. Habermas also refers to other texts by the same authors: Sunstein 1990; Michelman 1988a, 1988b, 1989a, 1989b, 1989c; and Ackerman 1984. In particular, Habermas's dialogue with Michelman on the themes I'll tackle in this chapter will continue to preoccupy him in the years to come: *see* the essay 'Constitutional democracy – a paradoxical union of contradictory principles?' (Habermas 2001) and Habermas 2003b. Michelman's contribution to the Cardozo Law Review Symposium was titled, significantly, 'Family quarrel' (Michelman 1995–6) On the dialogue between Habermas and Michelman, *see* Ferrara 2001.

The solution offered by Michelman (especially in his 1999 book *Brennan and Democracy*)[8] rests on a sort of *democratic and discursive legitimation* of court decisions:

> Michelman uses Brennan to exemplify the role of a 'responsive judge' who qualifies as *democratically above suspicion* when it comes to interpreting the Constitution. Brennan qualifies for this trust because he renders his decisions as best he knows how and according to his conscience and only after he has listened as patiently as possible – with an inquisitive hermeneutic sensitivity and a desire to learn – to the tangle of views in the relevant discourses conducted in civil society and the political public sphere. Interaction with the larger public, before which legal experts are held responsible, is supposed to contribute to the democratic legitimation of the decisions of a constitutional judge who has not been democratically legitimated or at least not sufficiently legitimated ... Michelman is apparently guided by the intuition that the discursive besiegement of the Court by a mobilized society gives rise to an interaction that has favorable consequences for both sides (*ibid.*).[9]

The focus of the discussion in *Between Facts and Norms* is a reading of American constitutional design inspired by the 'republican' conception. According to Michelman, Habermas says, 'the task posed by abstract judicial review' must ultimately be based on 'a derivative authority coming from the people's right to self-determination'(*BFN*: 267). Constitutional jurisprudence, no longer able to confine itself to applying a general norm to particular cases, and – for the same reason – also able to enlarge and modify the existing legal framework, 'should be allowed to resort only to arguments that, within the framework of a procedural understanding of the Constitution, justify an appeal to popular sovereignty as the origin of all authority for making law' (*ibid.*). Its judgments, its discourses and the reasons that justify them root their legitimacy in a *shared ethos*, in a 'background consensus' that is expressed in the practice of self-determination of citizens. The recovery of a particular version of 'republicanism' shows how far this is from a classic 'liberal paradigm' (*BFN*: 268):

> In the modern period, concepts of Roman law were used to define the *negative liberties* of citizens in order to secure the property and commercial trade of private persons against the interventions of a political authority from whose exercise those persons were excluded. By contrast, the language of ethics and rhetoric preserves the image of a political practice in which the *positive liberties* of equally entitled, participating citizens are realized. The republican

---

8. William J. Brennan was a judge of the Supreme Court from 1956 to 1990; he was known for his progressive positions and an 'activist' interpretation of the role of the Court.

9. Habermas doesn't think that this solution is sufficient: 'For our main issue, I find the way Michelman arrives at his model of the "responsive" judge more interesting than the proposal itself' (2001: 770).

concept of 'politics' refers not to rights of life, liberty, and property that are possessed by private citizens and guaranteed by the state, but pre-eminently to the practice of self-determination on the part of enfranchised citizens who are oriented to the common good and understand themselves as free and equal members of a cooperative, self-governing community. Law and legal statute are secondary in comparison to the *ethical* life context of a *polis* in which the virtue of active participation in public affairs can develop and stabilize. Only in this civic practice can human beings realize the *telos* of their species [*Gattung*].[10]

In his 1986 essay, Michelman highlighted traces of this republican vision in the debates between the Founding Fathers and in the text of the Constitution, identifying 'two traditions of constitutional interpretation but also two competing trends in the constitutional reality'; mostly, from all this he developed 'a normative concept of the political process and its procedural conditions' (*BFN*: 268). According to the liberal view,[11] politics 'has the function of clustering together and pushing through private interests against an administration specialized in the employment of political power for collective goals' (*BFN*: 269). From the republican viewpoint, on the other hand,

> [p]olitics involves more than just this mediating function; it should be constitutive for the social process as a whole. 'Politics' is conceived as the reflexive form of substantial ethical life – as the medium in which the members of more or less naturally emergent solidary communities become aware of their dependence on one another and, acting with full deliberation, further shape and develop existing relations of reciprocal recognition into an association of free and equal citizens (*ibid.*).

Next to 'the hierarchical requirements of the state and the decentralized requirements of the market', there is (and here Habermas starts to 'translate' the texts he analyses into his own jargon) also the '*solidarity* and the orientation to the

---

10. 'Michelman', writes Habermas (*BFN*: 267–8), 'relies on the tradition of Aristotelian "politics" that, having come down through Roman philosophy and the political thought of the Italian Renaissance, was framed in modern natural-law terms by Rousseau. Entering the American constitutional discussion via Hobbes's opponent, James Harrington, this tradition presented an attractive alternative to Lockean liberalism and partly inspired the Founding Fathers' understanding of democracy. J. G. A. Pocock stylizes this strand of republican thought as a form of civic humanism that, unlike modern natural law, does not draw on a legal vocabulary but on the language of classical ethics and politics'. (Here, he refers to Pocock 1981.) Some authors accuse Habermas of simply adopting Pocock's view of republicanism and ignoring different articulations of this tradition (*see* Chapter Three, note 9). On different readings of political republicanism, *see* Ferrara 2008: 99–120.

11. At this point, Habermas introduces a note about the meaning of 'liberal': 'here I use the shorthand accepted in the American discussion' (*BFN*: 268). In a later footnote he clarifies: 'as in the previous chapter, when I refer to "liberal" conceptions of the state, I use the term in the narrow sense of the tradition going back to Locke. "Liberals" like Dworkin or Rawls cannot be confined to this tradition' (*BFN*: 549, note 10).

common good appear as a *third source* of social integration' (*ibid.*). Therefore, to go back to the 'sources' of legitimacy of the law and its supreme 'instance' (that is, constitutional jurisprudence) 'this horizontal political will-formation aimed at mutual understanding or communicatively achieved consensus is even supposed to enjoy priority, both in a genetic and a normative sense' (*ibid.*).

The two 'competing' conceptions – liberal and republican – are reflected in a different conception of *citizenship* (*BFN*: 269–71); in a different conception of the *law* itself (*BFN*: 270–2); in a different vision of the *political process* (*BFN*: 272–3); and, finally, in a different conception of *procedural conditions*, which 'confer legitimating force on institutionalized opinion- and will-formation' (*BFN*: 273–4). If politics is modelled upon the market, as in the liberal paradigm, the 'contest of power is determined by the rational choice of optimal strategies' and – consequently – assuming 'an indissoluble pluralism of prepolitical values and interests that are at best *aggregated* with equal weight in the political process, politics loses all reference to the normative core of a public use of practical reason' (*BFN*: 274).[12] So, 'the republican confidence in the force of political discourses stands in contrast to this liberal skepticism about reason'. Discursive processes 'that encourage each to adopt the perspectives of the other members or even of all other persons', allow for a 'rationally motivated' *transformation* of the initial positions of every citizen. This is the nature of *deliberation*, as it emerges from a passage by Michelman that Habermas quotes at this point:

> Deliberation ... refers to a certain *attitude* toward social cooperation, namely, that of openness to persuasion by reasons referring to the claims of others as well as one's own. The deliberative medium is a good faith exchange of views – including participants' reports of their own understandings of their respective vital interests – in which all participants remain open to the possibility of persuasion by others and in which a vote, if any vote is taken, represents a pooling of judgments (Michelman 1989b: 293).

So, 'as participants in such a discursive process of opinion- and will-formation', comments Habermas, 'citizens exercise their right to political self-legislation': however, such a process must develop through procedures able to *legitimate* the institutional processes of legislative production (*BFN*: 273–4).[13]

---

12. In the original, Habermas writes: ' ... *verliert* [loses] *die Politik den Bezug* [reference] *zum ethischen und moralischen Gebrauch der Vernunft*' (*FG*: 333).

13. Here Habermas quotes another passage by Michelman (1988a: 1526), which is a significant statement of the latter's deliberative and republican view: 'Given plurality, a political process can validate a societal norm as self-given law only if (i) participation in the process results in some shift or adjustment in relevant understandings on the part of some (or all) participants, and (ii) there exists a set of prescriptive social and procedural conditions such that one's undergoing, under those conditions, such a dialogic modulation of one's understandings is not considered or experienced as coercive, or invasive, or otherwise a violation of one's identity or freedom, and (iii) those conditions actually prevailed in the process supposed to be jurisgenerative.'

During this long digression, Habermas objects that both conceptions blur 'intersubjective meaning' (*BFN*: 271), on which his discursive theory, instead, constructs a 'system of rights that citizens mutually accord one another' (this is the topic of chapter 3 of *Between Facts and Norms*). Nevertheless, with a significant shift, Habermas adds that 'republicanism at least comes close to this concept of law', considering 'the integrity of the individual and his liberties on a par with the integrity of the community in which individuals are first able to mutually recognize one another both as individuals and as members'. Thanks to this balance, and thanks to the bond between 'the legitimacy of laws' and 'the democratic procedure governing their genesis', the Republican view manages to keep 'the internal connection between the people's practice of self-determination and the impersonal rule of law' (*BFN*: 271).[14]

But the reader should not be deceived by the manifestly 'supportive' attitude with which Habermas presents Michelman's republican theses. Habermas does not share the republican view as such, but thinks it allows us to analyse constitutional jurisprudence with a 'heightened "republican" sense for the deliberative components of the legislative process' (*BFN*: 274). Here, he introduces the expression '*Deliberative Komponente*' (*FG*: 333). I believe this shows that, for Habermas, the legislative process (that is, the process by which one makes political decisions that are legally binding for all) cannot be considered (in itself and only) deliberative, that is, entirely entrusted to the discursive formation of opinions and the public exchange of arguments by which citizens exercise their ability to civic self-determination. The *deliberative component* comes into play for its 'legitimating power' but it must penetrate the *procedures* by which legitimate political and legislative decisions are made. And a 'component', by definition, is not the whole.

One example of this is, indeed, constitutional jurisprudence. The 'judgment' of a constitutional court always appears – to an extent, and, especially in the most difficult and controversial cases – as the outcome of a *constructive interpretation* that cannot disregard the 'discursive formation of opinion and will' that takes place in a *political public sphere*. And the latter is to be understood as the place where citizens' ideas are produced and transformed, along with their understanding and perception of collective problems, their judgment on the emergence of *new* problems (that could not be 'foreseen' when a given constitutional norm was established) and so forth. It should noted that all these issues have been raised and widely discussed in American political and constitutional literature in relation to some crucial historical moments: the issue of slavery; the conflict between

14. Here, Habermas quotes from another essay by Michelman (1989: 446): 'In a republican view, a community's objective, common good substantially consists in the success of its political endeavor to define, establish, effectuate, and sustain the set of rights (less tendentiously, laws) best suited to the conditions and *mores* of that community. Whereas in a contrasting liberal view, the higher-law rights provide the transactional structures and the curbs on power required so that pluralistic pursuit of diverse and conflicting interests may proceed as satisfactorily as possible.'

Roosevelt and the Supreme Court in the first phase of the New Deal; and the civil rights movement in the 1950s and 1960s.

However, a problem arises: what 'hierarchy of sources' can provide the 'ultimate' foundation of a judgment of constitutional legitimacy? Can one rely only on a kind of intuition that is able to identify what is expressed as the 'will of the people'? And who will be the 'authentic' and 'authorized' interpreter? Habermas's answer relies on a radically *procedural* conception of the democratic process. Therefore he distances himself both from those answers of 'republican' origin that have too much faith in *substantial ethicality*, and from those answers that rely on some foundational principle of a moral or ethical nature. Thus, it is true that a constitutional court finds itself exposed to the processes of formation of opinion and to the deliberative practice of citizens, but this *influence* can only be exercised through a procedural mediation and can only be founded on the respect of given rules and procedural conditions. 'If the Supreme Court is supposed to oversee adherence to the Constitution,' comments Habermas, referring to John Hart Ely's position,

> ... then it must in the first place look after the procedures and organizational norms on which the legitimating effect of the democratic process depends. The Court must ensure that the 'channels' for the inclusive opinion- and will-formation processes through which a democratic legal community organizes itself remain intact: 'unblocking stoppages in the democratic process is what judicial review ought preeminently to be about' (Ely 1980: 117, quoted in *BFN*: 264).[15]

These are the very pages in which we find for the first time a reference to *deliberative politics* (*BFN*: 274–5):

> The constitutional court must work within the limits of its authority to ensure that the process of lawmaking takes place under the legitimating conditions *of deliberative politics*. The latter is in turn bound to the demanding communicative presuppositions of political arenas that do not coincide with institutionalized will-formation in parliamentary bodies, but rather include the political public sphere as well as its cultural context and social basis. A deliberative practice of self-legislation can develop only in the interplay between, on the one hand, parliamentary will-formation institutionalized in legal procedures and programmed to reach decisions and, on the other, political opinion-formation

---

15. Habermas, in particular, aims to further specify John Hart Ely's 'proceduralist proposal' (*BFN*: 274), and quotes one of Ely's most important works, *Democracy and Distrust: A theory of judicial review* (1980: 100). Earlier in chapter 5, Habermas sums up Ely's views thus: 'His approach is admittedly intended to relieve adjudication of any orientation to legal principles with moral or ethical origins. Ely proceeds on the assumption that the United States Constitution primarily regulates organizational and procedural problems and is not designed to single out and implement basic values. In his view, it is not substantive but formal regulations (like equal protection or due process) that make up the substance of the Constitution' (*BFN*: 264–5).

along informal channels of political communication. Relevant initiatives, issues and contributions, problems and proposals come more from the *margins* than from the established center of the spectrum of opinions.

In this context, the Constitutional Court plays a crucial *constructive role*: as Michelman writes – in a passage that Habermas cites showing, this time, his full acceptance of it – 'the suggestion is that the pursuit of political freedom through law depends on "our" [the Supreme Court's] constant reach for inclusion of the other, of the hitherto excluded – which in practice means bringing to legal-doctrinal presence the hitherto absent voices of emergently self-conscious social groups' (Michelman 1988a: 1529).

Habermas's analysis of the 'decisional practice' of constitutional courts thus goes beyond the specific sphere of a very high juridical function: rather, precisely because of this, his investigation becomes paradigmatic of a whole way of understanding the meaning of a 'deliberative politics'. The discussion does not start from what a court *should aim to do*, or what the *ideal* function of a court should be. Rather, it seeks to answer these questions: *what does a court actually do* when it emits a judgment of constitutionality? What kind of discourse does it engage in ('moral', 'ethical', 'pragmatic', merely 'applicative' and so on)? What kind of justifications does it put forward? The most crucial question, however, is this: how is all this related to the idea (and procedures) of popular sovereignty? Once again, the fundamental example is that of the Civil Rights Movement in the US, as emerges from a long quote from Michelman that Habermas cites in full. This text, at this point, can be taken to be exemplary not so much of an *ideal model of deliberative democracy* but rather of a *theoretical model of democracy* that is able to understand the real processes of democratic politics and to identify the *deliberative components* that represent an essential dimension of it:

The full lesson of the civil rights movement will escape whoever focuses too sharply on the country's most visible, formal legislative assemblies – Congress, state legislatures, the councils of major cities – as exclusive, or even primary, arenas of jurisgenerative politics and political freedom. I do not mean that those arenas are dispensable or unimportant. Rather I mean the obvious points that much of the country's normatively consequential dialogue occurs outside the major, formal channels of electoral and legislative politics, and that, in modern society, those formal channels cannot possibly provide for most citizens much direct experience of self-revisionary, dialogic engagement. Much, perhaps most, of that experience must occur in various arenas of what we know as public life in the broad sense, some nominally political and some not: in the encounters and conflicts, interactions and debates that arise in and around town meetings and local government agencies; civic and voluntary organizations; social and recreational clubs; schools public and private; managements, directorates and leadership groups of organizations of all kinds; workplaces and shop floors; public events and street life; and so on. Those are all arenas of potentially transformative dialogue. Understandings of the social world that are contested and shaped in the daily encounters and transactions of civil society at large are, of course, conveyed to our representative arenas. ... Those encounters and transactions are, then, to be counted among the sources and channels of republican self-government and jurisgenerative politics. (Michelman 1988a: 1531, quoted in *BFN*: 275).

4. Deliberative politics: ethical self-understanding or an ordinary trait of a democracy?

With Michelman, we have seen the importance of the republican tradition and of the idea of 'deliberative politics' re-read in the light of this model. However, in Habermas's work, we also re-encountered the works of Cass R. Sunstein and Bruce Ackerman, whose relevance for the early phase of deliberative democracy I have already emphasised.

In his discussion, Habermas always keeps in mind the other *logics* that co-exist and come into conflict with those typical of deliberative politics – that is, the tension between the different models of political rationality acting within our democracies. For Habermas, too, interpretations of the American constitutional design and its history are an essential point of reference: in the United States, he writes,

> ... the influence of interest groups that implement their private aims through the government apparatus at the cost of the general interest is considered the real problem, at least since the famous discussion between the Federalists and the Anti-Federalists. In this classical stance against the tyranny of societal powers that violate the principle of the separation of state and society, rejuvenated republicanism, too, conceives the role of the constitutional court as that of a custodian of deliberative democracy (*BFN*: 275).[16]

Thus, Habermas meets Sunstein's interpretation of the practice of the Supreme Court – in particular those 'review proceedings in which the Supreme Court rejected statutes for their "discriminating classifications" on the grounds that the legislature omitted a "reasonable analysis" of the material in need of regulation' (*BFN*: 275–6). Sunstein's criterion ('a *reasoned analysis requirement*') refers to the presence or lack of discursive and inclusive modalities in the process of law-making. In other words, the point is to check 'whether the legislative decision turned on reasons that can be publicly advocated or on private interests that cannot be declared in the framework of parliamentary negotiations' (*BFN*: 276). At this point, comments Habermas, the Supreme Court, 'which does not have control over the justifying political reasons, does not have to refer to hypothetically ascribed reasons but can rely on the reasons that were actually brought forth' (*ibid.*).

---

16. On the constitutional debate between Anti-Federalists and Federalists, *see* Manin 1994

'[T]he Court', he then says, 'may not arrogate to itself the role of an ideology critic *vis-à-vis* the political legislature' (*ibid.*).

One possible objection to this argument is that we can always find *ex post* justification for decisions that were, in fact, taken under the pressure of illegitimate interests. Sunstein answered with an argument that Habermas judged 'convincing': 'for the citizens themselves, it makes a difference, in normative terms, whether the legitimate policies and goals that may require them to accept disadvantages are the outcome of a legitimating, deliberative process or whether, on the contrary, they merely emerge as side effects of programs and processes motivated by other, private concerns unfit for the purposes of public justification' (*ibid.*). That is to say, the latter phenomenon can always take place but this is the very reason for the *tension between legality and discursive legitimation* that constitutes the focus of a deliberative politics in a democratic rule-of-law state.

However, despite showing some fondness for republicanism, Habermas still distances himself from it. The vision inspiring republican constitutionalism ultimately rests upon a juxtaposition between ideal and real: the activism of constitutional judgments has 'to compensate for the gap separating the republican ideal from constitutional reality' (*ibid.*). More generally, 'as long as deliberative politics is rejuvenated in the spirit of Aristotelian politics, this idea will depend on the virtues of citizens oriented to the common good. And this expectation of virtue pushes the democratic process, as it actually proceeds in welfare-state mass democracies, into the pallid light of an instrumentally distorted politics, a "fallen" politics' (*ibid.*).

This 'external tension between facticity and validity' cannot be solved by the dualistic view proposed by Bruce Ackerman (1984), either.[17] In fact, he ultimately gives constitutional jurisprudence the task of acting as 'a mediator between the ideal and the real' (*BFN*: 277): thus, as Michelman (1988a: 1522–3) noted, Ackerman's solution is analogous to the model of scientific development proposed by Kuhn (1962).[18] Habermas regards Ackerman's theses as a 'vitalistic reading of democratic self-determination' (*BFN*: 277), giving the Supreme Court a '*vicarious*' function with regards to a popular will that is 'usually slumbering through long latency periods' (*ibid.*). Indeed, the popular will is only active in exceptional situations, if there are the conditions and the need for a break with the continuity of a pre-existing paradigm of legitimacy. Therefore, in this perspective,

---

17. *See* Chapter Seven, Section 3.

18. Ackerman, writes Habermas, proposes to 'conceive the ups and downs of political innovation along the lines of Thomas Kuhn's model of scientific development. Just as the "normal" business of science is interrupted only in rare moments by "revolutions" that bring new paradigms on the scene, so also is politics normally the business of managers and bureaucrats whose behavior matches the liberal description of strategic market competition steered by personal interests. Only when history overheats, in "moments of constitutional excitement", do "the People" step forth from their normal civil privatism, appropriate the politics that has been bureaucratically estranged from them, and temporarily supply an unanticipated legitimacy to far-reaching innovations (as happened, for example, in the New Deal era)' (*BFN*: 277). For a comprehensive evaluation of Ackerman's work, *see* Ferrara 1999: 87–132.

'the constitutional court thus assumes the role of republican guardian of positive liberties that the citizens themselves, as nominal bearers of these liberties, fail to exercise', as clearly emerged from the words with which Michelman himself – quoted by Habermas – commented on Ackerman's position: in Ackerman, 'the Court at the last appears not as *representative* of the People's declared will but as *representation* and trace of the People's absent self-government' (Michelman 1986: 65).[19]

For Habermas, at the basis of this search for a 'pedagogical guardian or regent' there is an '*exceptionalistic* description of political practice' and of how 'it really ought to be': thus, the 'regency' is exercised

> … only as long as the sovereign prefers to keep to the private realm rather than occupy the place he has inherited, the political public sphere, and appropriately fulfill its duties. The exceptionalist image of what politics should be is suggested by a republican tradition that binds the citizens' political practice to the ethos of an already integrated community. Only virtuous citizens can do politics in the right way (*BFN*: 278).

Here Rousseau comes back into the picture: 'this *expectation of virtue* already led Rousseau to split off the citizen, who is oriented to the common good, from the private man, who would be overburdened by such ethical-political demands' (*BFN*: 312). In a footnote, Habermas recalls the pages he had devoted to Rousseau in *Strukturwandel* and in his new Preface (1990b):[20] 'The unanimity of the political legislature was supposed to be secured in advance by a substantial consensus not so much of minds as of hearts'. He also quotes Manin's essay: 'for Rousseau', Manin wrote, 'the basis of legitimacy lies not in the free individual capable of making up his mind by weighing reasons, but rather in the individual whose will is already entirely determined, one who has made his choice' (Manin 1987: 347).

Deliberative politics, as a practice of civic self-determination, cannot be seen as a special time with *exceptionally* 'virtuous' citizens, nor can it be founded on the substrate of a shared *ethos*, or a 'background consensus' transmitted by the traditions of a community: it must be seen as an *ordinary* time and component of the democratic political process and its procedures. And so, writes Habermas, proposing his own interpretation, discourse theory

> … insists on the fact that democratic will-formation does not draw its legitimating force from the prior convergence of settled ethical convictions. Rather, the source of legitimacy includes, on the one hand, the communicative presuppositions that allow the better arguments to come into play in various

---

19. Thus, added Habermas, the court 'slips back, however, into just the paternalistic role that Ely strives to resist with his proceduralist understanding of the Constitution' (*BFN*: 278). However, for Habermas, albeit in trying to avoid the paternalism of the constitutionalist court, Michelman also 'bridges the gap between ideal and real in a similar way' (*ibid.*).

20. *See* Chapter 5, Section 3. The new Preface was published in English as 'Further reflections on the public sphere' (Habermas 1992a).

forms of deliberation and, on the other, procedures that secure fair bargaining conditions. Discourse theory breaks with an ethical conception of civic autonomy, and thus it does not have to reserve the mode of deliberative politics to exceptional conditions (*BFN*: 278).[21]

Michelman, 'like other "communitarians"' (*BFN*: 279),[22] conceives of *citizenship* 'not primarily in *legal* but in *ethical terms*': 'persuasive arguments and discussions', wrote Michelman,

> … seem inconceivable without conscious reference by those involved to their mutual and reciprocal awareness of being co-participants not just of this one debate, but in a more encompassing common life, bearing the imprint of a common past, within and from which the arguments and claims arise and draw their meaning (Michelman 1988a: 1513).

Nevertheless, Habermas radically objects that this substantial ethicality, 'characteristic of an unproblematic background consensus, does not sit well with the conditions of cultural and societal pluralism that distinguish modern societies' (*BFN*: 279). The communitarian versions of republicanism produce 'an *ethical constriction of political discourses* that is often but by no means necessarily linked with the concept of deliberative politics' (*BFN*: 280). Political deliberation and ethical self-understanding cannot be put on the same level: in the

---

21. To conclude the discussion of constitutional jurisprudence, hence also Habermas's reply, close to Ely's theses: 'a constitutional court guided by a proceduralist understanding of the constitution does not have to overdraw on its legitimation credit. It can stay within its authority to apply the law – an authority clearly defined in terms of the logic of argumentation – provided that the democratic process over which it is supposed to keep watch is not described as a state of exception' (*BFN*: 279). However, 'we cannot carry on the discussion of the Supreme Court's activism or self-restraint *in abstracto*'. In determinate situations, an 'activist' jurisprudence could also turn out to be necessary: 'to be sure, we have to free the concept of deliberative politics from overly strenuous connotations that would put the constitutional court under permanent pressure to act. The court may not assume the role of a regent who takes the place of an underage successor to the throne. Under the critical gaze of a robust legal public sphere – a citizenry that has grown to become a "community of constitutional interpreters" – the constitutional court can at best play the role of a tutor' (*BFN*: 280–1).

22. Here Habermas attributes to Michelman a 'communitarian' view but it is interesting to note what Michelman himself said some years later, in the Introduction to the Italian edition of *Brennan* (Michelman 2004): 'In the late '80s, I published several papers in which I investigated the possibility to recover and rebuild, for liberal purposes, the trend of civic republicanism that historically manifested in American constitutional thought. I tried to see if this trend could provide answers to the question as to how, in the modern conditions of an ethical pluralism, popular self-government can, through constitutionalism, be conceived as an exercise of the political freedom of each individual. Due to this incursion … into civic republicanism, many readers [and here he refers to Habermas] have classified me among the "communitarians" and, therefore, among those who oppose the Liberals on the fundamental principles of political morality and constitutionalist ideals. As natural and correct as these classifications of my work, which dates back to the late 80s, may have seemed – given the historical context, and my lack of clarity – I never burned my liberal-individualistic card and have no intention to do so', even if, he added, 'this is not to say that my meeting with republicanism has left no trace in my reflection'.

present conditions of modernity, deliberative politics can rest on nothing but the communicative and procedural 'presuppositions' that can orientate 'democratic will-formation' (*BFN*: 278).

Habermas does not at all deny that,

> ... discourses aimed at achieving self-understanding are also an important component of politics. In such discourses, the participants want to get a clear understanding of themselves as members of a specific nation, as members of a local community, as inhabitants of a region, and so on; they want to determine which traditions they will continue; they strive to determine how they will treat one another and how they will treat minorities and marginal groups; in short, participants in such discourses (or in identity politics) hope to become clear about the kind of society in which they want to live (*BFN*: 282).

However, in legislative politics – that is, in the making of legitimate decisions binding for all – these ethical discourses are never exclusive, nor can they be considered dominant. But then, what discourses make up deliberative politics and what discourses allow us to define it as an ordinary moment of democratic politics?

5. Deliberative politics: pragmatic discourses, ethical discourses and moral discourses

After critically analysing a conception of deliberative politics marked by an 'ethical constriction of political discourses', as well as what is defined a 'communitarian reading of the republican tradition' (*BFN*: 285), Habermas also discusses precisely those same pages of Sunstein that I have analysed earlier (*see* Chapter Three, Section 2). Here, as we have seen, Sunstein attributes to Anti-Federalists a classic republican view; on the other hand, he claims that Madison's position cannot be considered merely 'liberal' or related to the modern pluralist school; rather, it is a view in which deliberative components combine in various ways with the political forms of pluralist competition of interests and values characterising a modern society.

Habermas here engages directly with Sunstein's view of the concrete process of *legislative decision-making* in contemporary American democracy. Sunstein's idea of a *continuum* (*see* Chapter Three, Section 2) is insufficient according to Habermas, because it 'sketches a realistic but somewhat flat picture of legislative politics'. In fact, it is possible to try to 'break up and structure the empirical continuum' between the two poles of 'pure' bargaining and 'pure' deliberation. And discourse theory offers the 'conceptual tools that allow us both to analyze the observable communication flows according to the different issues and to reconstruct them in terms of the corresponding forms of communication'. It is not always easy to 'make out the different depth grammars that distinguish the pragmatic, ethical, and moral uses of reason' but that doesn't mean that 'the forms of politics that Michelman opposes as ideal types are in fact *indistinguishably* fused' (*BFN*: 285). Also, 'the rational reconstruction of a given sequence of communication with discourse-theoretic means allows one to identify deviations that have their source in effects of social and administrative power that cannot be publicly advocated' (*BFN*: 319).

In these words of Habermas we can grasp the theoretical foundation of an important line of research that, in the following years, characterised some significant sectors of deliberative democracy theory: the analysis of deliberative processes conducted through the deconstruction of the 'communication flows' that occur within them and the evaluation of the various kinds of 'speech acts' that distinguish them.[23]

For a better understanding of what Habermas means by 'different depth grammars', we need to refer to the fundamental distinction, previously introduced (*BFN*: 157–68), between the various forms of discourse, based on the issues that need to be tackled: that is, *pragmatic*; *ethical-political*; and *moral* issues.

> In deliberations over policies and laws, the basic question 'What ought we to do?' is differentiated according to the kind of material in need of regulation. The meaning of 'ought' remains unspecified as long as the relevant problem and the aspect under which it can be solved are undetermined … The standpoints of expediency [*des zweckmässigen*], goodness [*des Guten*], and justice [*des Gerechten*] each define a different use of practical reason. These correspond to different types of discourse, which I can only outline in broad strokes here (*BFN*: 159).[24]

Therefore, deliberative politics is articulated in a plurality of levels and dimensions that obviously, on the empirical level, can intertwine and combine in

---

23. *See*, in particular, the theoretical and empirical research by Jürg Steiner and his collaborators, analysing first a series of parliamentary debates (Steiner *et al.* 2003 and 2004) and then also other places or moments of deliberation (Steiner *et al.* 2017). Steiner has come up with a Discourse Quality Index (DQI), which allows the user 'to operationalize the essentials of the Habermasian logic of communicative action', measuring the quality of deliberation through a series of indexes. 'The objective of the DQI is to tap an underlying continuum of deliberation that ranges from the complete violation of Habermas's discourse ethics to ideal speech acts' (Bächtiger *et al.* 2010: 38). Habermas himself explicitly expressed his approval of the DQI – 'I admire the inventive introduction of a Discourse Quality Index for capturing essential features of proper deliberation' (Habermas 2005: 389) – while commenting on some empirical analyses of deliberative settings and processes, as happened in a seminar arranged by Jurg Steiner and held at the European University Institute of Florence in 2004. (*See Acta Politica* 2005, vols 40(2) and 40(3).) Habermas here underlines 'the reconstructive character of any empirical research that is guided by discourse theory as I understand it'. And adds that one could think 'that "rational discourse" is a kind of philosophical "ideal" belonging to what Rawls calls "ideal theory". This is not how I understand the term. The conception of rational discourse results from the reconstruction of an actual practice and captures just those pragmatic features of a communicative setting that anybody tacitly presupposes once he seriously enters an argumentation in order to check a problematic validity claim by either supporting or denying the truth or rightness of some statement, with reasons pro and con' (Habermas 2005: 385).

24. For more on this topic, Habermas refers the reader to his essay, originally written in 1988 and translated as 'On the pragmatic, the ethical, and the moral employments of practical reason' (Habermas 1993a: 1–18).

various ways. '*Pragmatic questions*' are those related to the search for the best means to realise 'goals and preferences that are already given' (*ibid.*). However, these very goals can turn out to be problematic; so it is no longer a matter of discussing the most rational means for the goal but rather of assessing the goals in the light of chosen values. In this phase, the *cognitive* or *epistemic* dimension of deliberation is therefore particularly relevant:

> The value-oriented weighing of goals and the purposive-rational choice of means lead to hypothetical recommendations that interrelate perceived causes and effects according to value preferences and chosen ends. These directives have the semantic form of conditional imperatives. Ultimately, they borrow their validity from the empirical knowledge they take in. They are justified in pragmatic discourses. In these, the outcome turns on arguments that relate empirical knowledge to given preferences and ends and that assess the (usually uncertain) consequences of alternative choices according to previously accepted maxims or decision rules (*BFN*: 159–60).

'In this first stage of opinion- and will-formation' (*BFN*: 164), 'a certain expert knowledge is requisite, which is naturally fallible and rarely value-neutral, that is, uncontested.' However, *values* can also be problematic and controversial in the articulation of a discourse; at this point, the horizon of a purposive rationality is insufficient. So, pragmatic questions can take two different paths. In the first, 'sometimes conflicting preferences express oppositions between interests that cannot be defused at the level of discourse' (*BFN*: 160) and therefore the conflict can only be faced in instrumental, strategic or merely 'aggregative' terms. Nevertheless, it can also happen that this conflict refers to an unsolved problematic collective self-understanding: in other words, 'the contested interest positions and value orientations are so interwoven with a community's intersubjectively shared form of life that serious decisions about values touch on an unclarified collective self-understanding' (*ibid.*).

Thus we enter the field of '*ethical-political questions*'. Here, 'the 'existential' questions of 'who I am and would like to be', and of what is my own model of a good life, is formulated in the first person plural: 'who we are and would like to be as Citizens'.[25] The answer takes the form of an *ethical discourse* and 'clinical advice'[26] on a good and self-aware form of life: 'the imperative sense of this advice can be understood as an "ought" that does not depend on subjective ends

---

25. Habermas here underlines how 'the identity of a group refers to the situations in which the members can utter an emphatic "we" ... [but] it is not an ego identity writ large but rather supplements the individual's identity'. In other words, it is still individuals who critically and selectively relate to the legacy of traditions and life-forms (*BFN*: 160).

26. Habermas defines 'clinical' as advice emerging from an ethical discourse. Here he uses a term drawn from psychoanalysis to connote such pieces of advice as 'recommendations' that aspire to 'cure' the discontent of a subjectivity (in this case, collective) and to reconstruct a higher and more mature 'self-understanding' and a more conscious awareness of the self and its own history.

or preferences but states which value orientations and practices are in the long run and on the whole "good for us"' (*BFN*: 161).

Thus far, the 'processes of rational [*vernünftigen*] political will-formation' – the 'deliberative processes' [*die Beratungen*] – have been considered for their possible *pragmatic and ethical-political* nature: 'an adequate justification of policies and laws must, however, consider yet a further aspect, that of justice' (*ibid.*). Thus, the structures and the argumentative rules typical of *moral* discourse come into play: 'whether we should want and accept a program also depends on whether the corresponding practice is *equally* good for all. This shifts the meaning of the question "What ought we to do?" yet again'. Moral discourse is founded upon a principle of universalisation: the question 'what ought we to do?' here has a different meaning, and requires an answer that takes 'the normative point of view from which we examine how we can regulate our common life in the equal interest of all'. 'A norm is just', writes Habermas, 'only if all can will that it be obeyed by each in comparable situations', that is, when it can be *universalised* and when the argumentation is ideally addressed to an 'unlimited communication community', forcing each individual to see things from the other's perspective. '[M]oral precepts have the semantic form of categorical or unconditional imperatives', 'an "ought" that depends neither on subjective ends and preferences nor on the (for us) absolute goal of a good, or not misspent, way of life' (*BFN*: 161–2).

However, moral discourses always revolve around 'contested norms in view of *foreseeably typical cases*, in order to determine whether the norms could meet with the considered agreement of all those affected'. Therefore, a 'universalization test' is not enough: moral rules cannot only be exposed 'in a general, decontextualized form', but must also translate into *discourses of application*. 'Discourses of justification cannot take into consideration *ex ante* all the possible constellations of future cases', so, every time, 'the application of norms calls for an argumentative clarification in its own right', based on a 'principle of appropriateness' (*ibid.*).

For the purposes of a *concrete* definition of the forms of a *deliberative* politics, this separation of discourses into *pragmatic*, *ethical* and *moral* (but also *applicative*) forms is decisive. It is through these different forms of discourse that deliberative politics, in fact, constructs a public and democratic *discursive legitimation* of the processes of decision-making through institutional procedures that are constitutionally 'entitled' to make decisions.

In a political public sphere, a 'communicative power' is produced, intertwining a series of discourses that may have a purely 'pragmatic' dimension but, at the same time, may also have *ethical-political* or *moral* implications. The controversial political problems that constitute the object of a deliberative process can require discussions related to the best *means* for reaching a shared goal. However, they can also consider the different relevance attributed to different goals; this, in turn, can entail an *ethical-political* discussion of the *collective goals* of a community and the correspondence between means and/or goals and what *seems* like a 'common good'. This can also open the way to a critical and problematic revision of what tradition has thus far regarded as a 'common good' but that no longer seems such, at least to some of the participants.

And finally, when the nature of the problem requires it, there can also be a *moral* dimension to the argument, when there are questions about how 'right' it is to adopt a certain solution, or whether a given solution is 'more just' compared to another. In this case, the 'demanding communicative presuppositions' typical of moral argumentation come into play: that is, the ability to take the other's viewpoint; the ability to wonder what *all* could accept; to *practise* the 'ideal role taking' which George H. Mead, the American pragmatist philosopher and social theorist, had spoken of.[27]

Of course, it is possible that the same problem could raise both pragmatic and ethical-political or moral issues. In his 1994 Postscriptum (*BFN*: 506), Habermas clarified that this distinction of discourses is an *analytic* dimension, as 'political questions are normally so complex that they require the simultaneous treatment of pragmatic, ethical, and moral aspects' (*BFN*: 565, note 3).[28] And it is also possible (or even very likely) that there should be what – in his Reply to the Cardozo Law School conference (1995–6: 1534) – he described as a '*collision of discourses*'. This happens

> ... when the participants cannot agree about whether an issue involves, for example, a conflict of compromisable interests or irreconcilable values; or whether it involves an ethical or moral question; or whether it at all concerns something that must be addressed politically and can be regulated legally.

And it is before these 'collisions' that 'legally institutionalized procedures' are required, in the absence of some 'metadiscourse' able to solve them (*ibid.*). In short – and I think this is a crucial point – Habermas does not describe an ideal model of politics to be pursued but draws a theoretical model ('a highly abstract process model') that allows us to grasp the internal logic characterising the connection between the discursive legitimacy produced by 'communicative power' and the process of law-making:

> In the discursively structured opinion- and will-formation of a legislature, lawmaking is interwoven with the formation of communicative power. We

---

27. *See* e.g. Mead 1934. As is well known, Habermas gave much space to Mead in *Theory of Communicative Action* (1984–7, in particular, chapter 5). On Habermas's relationship with the tradition of American philosophical pragmatism, *see* Bernstein 2010 and the essays gathered in Aboulafia, Bookman and Kemp 2002. This collection features a text in which Habermas himself describes his relationship with pragmatism as well as his review of Dewey's *Quest for Certainty* (Habermas 2002).

28. In this Postscriptum, Habermas judges 'misleading' his 'attempt in *BFN* chapter 4 (pp. 164 ff.) to exemplify different types of discourses by ordering concrete questions in a linear fashion' (*ibid.*: 565, note 3), which is illustrated in the section of *Between Facts and Norms* that I am analysing here. In my view, this is excessive self-criticism: the analytical nature of the distinction between the various types of discourse and their possible articulation is made quite clear by the very fact that Habermas speaks of an 'abstract process model'. Habermas also deals with this point in his Reply to the Cardozo Law School conference (1995–6: 1534): the 'interdiscursive relations' (the 'crossing points' from a type of discourse to another) are not pre-determined, but 'emerge from the logic of questioning within a given discourse'.

can clarify this connection with the help of a highly abstract process model that starts with pragmatic issues, advances along the branches of compromise formation and ethical discourse to the clarification of moral questions, and ends with a judicial review of norms (*BFN*: 162–3).

In the examples that follow, Habermas shows the actual operation of these different argumentative logics. Habermas here takes a parliamentary discussion and decision as his starting point but the description of the different stages of this 'process of discursive formation of political will' can very well be thought of – at least in my opinion – as typical of a deliberative process that might take place elsewhere, according to specific procedures:

> For the sake of simplicity, let us assume that in a parliament political questions initially arise in the pragmatic form of a purposive-rational choice of collective goals and strategies according to established value preferences. Our process model starts with the pragmatic justification [*Begründung*] of general programs that must be further explicated and implemented by the executive branch. Such justification depends primarily on a correct interpretation of the situation and the appropriate description of the problem at stake, as well as on the flow of relevant and reliable information, on the efficient (and, if necessary, theoretically guided) processing of this information, and so on (*BFN*: 185–7).

In this first ('pragmatic') phase, therefore, one sees the specific cognitive and epistemic components of a deliberative process (for instance, knowing and sharing the data of a problem, if only to define and circumscribe the terms of a conflict). However, soon a dimension of *value* might also come into play, as fully emerges in the second stage of this process. At this point,

> … the problematic value orientations themselves are up for discussion, which necessitates a change in the level of discourse … In the ideal case, which we assume in our model, a procedural decision is first made about the level at which the controversy should be continued with arguments. How this is decided depends on the aspect under which the matter in need of regulation permits further clarification (*BFN*: 164–5).

Now there are 'three alternatives' but *neither of the first two* – adds Habermas – seems feasible in our 'complex societies', not even 'under ideal conditions' (*BFN*: 165).

a) 'It may be that a morally relevant issue is immediately at stake'.[29] '[S]uch moral issues call for discourses that submit the contested interests and

---

29. Habermas offers the following examples: 'questions of social policy, of tax law, or of the organization of educational and health-care systems, where the distribution of social wealth, life opportunities, and chances for survival in general are at stake' (*BFN*: 165). The English translation is partial: in the original German, Habermas also mentions 'legal issues such as abortion, the proscription of certain crimes, the prohibition of certain methods in obtaining evidence' (*FG*: 204).

value orientations to a universalization test within the framework set by the system of rights as it has been constitutionally interpreted and elaborated' (*ibid.*).

b) 'In other cases, it may be that an ethically relevant issue is at stake.'[30] '[S]uch questions call for discourses that push beyond contested interests and values and engage the participants in a process of self-understanding by which they become reflectively aware of the deeper consonances [*Übereinstimmungen*] in a common form of life' (*ibid.*).

But *neither* alternative is truly feasible because, in our complex and pluralistic societies, very often 'it turns out that all the proposed regulations touch on the diverse interests in respectively different ways without any generalizable interest or clear priority of some one value being able to vindicate itself'. *That is to say, neither moral discourses nor ethical discourses, as such, can claim to found the legitimacy of a norm, making it appear as the translation of a 'generalizable' interest or as the expression of a univocal and prevailing 'value'.*

c) So what is left is the third option, which Habermas calls *Verhandlungen*, or *negotiations*. Sometimes, '*conflicting preferences express oppositions between interests that cannot be defused at the level of discourse*' (*BFN*: 160, my emphasis). In these cases, the solution of the conflict can only be left to power relations, through aggregative procedures or on a purely antagonistic basis – and, in extreme cases, in a coercive manner, through the use (or threat) of violence. However, even though they are very much present at the external borders of his theoretical frame, so to speak, here Habermas leaves those cases in the background. A possible failure of discourse is always looming and leaves the door open to the pure manifestation of claims to power – those 'wills to power' that are able to establish themselves as socially and factually *valid*, without being *legitimate*.

The solution to the conflict can be also sought in terms that are both *strategic* and *co-operative*: the *negotiations* require that the parts, while being 'success-oriented', are still 'willing to cooperate'.[31] In these pages Habermas distinguishes two kinds of negotiation or bargaining: he calls the first form '*naturwüchsige oder nicht-regulierte*', 'spontaneous or non-regulated'; the second, on the contrary, is '*verfahrenregulierte*', that is, '*procedurally regulated*'.[32]

Spontaneous or non-regulated negotiations can aim 'at compromises the participants find acceptable under three conditions': a) the outcomes must be positive-sum (that is, a new situation has to arise that is more advantageous for everyone); b) there must not be free-riders exploiting co-operation to their benefit; c) there must be an acceptable balance between the 'give' and 'take' of each

---

30. 'Consider, for example, ecological questions concerning the protection of the environment and animals, questions of traffic control and city planning; or consider questions of immigration policy, the protection of cultural and ethnic minorities, or any question touching on the political culture' (*BFN*: 204).

31. In a note, Habermas quotes a passage from *The Cement of Society* by Jon Elster (1989: 50): 'Bargaining occurs when there are several cooperative arrangements and the parties have conflicting preferences over them'.

32. Here, the English translation (*BFN*: 165–6) neglects the adjectives '*naturwüchsige oder nicht-regulierte*' and simply speaks of bargaining.

part, that is, there must be no coercion forcing some 'to contribute more to the cooperative effort than they gain from it' (*BFN*: 166). If these conditions are met, there is 'a negotiated agreement [*Vereinbarung*] that balances conflicting interests', 'whereas a rationally motivated consensus [*Einverständnis*] rests on reasons that convince all the parties *in the same way*, a compromise can be accepted by the different parties each for its own *different* reasons' (*ibid.*). However, even in those cases – albeit in a mediated and indirect form – there is still a discursive and argumentative dimension: 'the discursive chain of a rational will-formation would snap at such points of compromise if the discourse principle could not be brought to bear at least indirectly on bargaining processes' (*ibid.*). Therefore, in this case, one might add, the conflict would only be expressed in 'non-negotiable' forms, where there is no ground for co-operation and agreement.

But this is only *one* of the possible forms of negotiation: indeed, a spontaneous and non-regulated form. Next to it, in Habermas's theoretical frame, there is a second one: that of the 'procedurally regulated negotiation' (*BFN*: 167–8). Unlike the first, here, the discursive dimension – albeit indirect – appears in more self-aware and structured forms. In fact, the point is to activate

> ... procedures that provide all the interested parties with an equal opportunity for pressure, that is, an equal opportunity to influence one another during the actual bargaining, so that all the affected interests can come into play and have equal chances of prevailing. To the extent that these conditions are met, there are grounds for presuming that negotiated agreements are fair' (*BFN*: 166–7).

Once again, this is an analytical and 'reconstructive' distinction because, in fact, one form can turn into the other.

In the spontaneous forms of negotiation, a discursive dimension can only operate indirectly and informally, as the crucial factor is the *bargaining power* of the parties through the use of threats and promises. And here we meet Jon Elster again. Habermas quotes at length a passage from one of Elster's best-known and most important essays, 'Arguing and bargaining in two constituent assemblies':

> ... to bargain is to engage in communication for the purpose of *forcing* or *inducing* the opponent to accept one's claim. To achieve this end, bargainers rely on threats and promises that will have to be executed outside the assembly itself. Bargaining power does not derive from the 'power of the better argument,' but from material resources, manpower and the like. Statements asserted in a process of bargaining are made with a claim to being credible, in the sense that bargainers must try to make their opponents *believe* that the threats and promises would actually be carried out (Elster 2000, quoted in *BFN*: 166).[33]

---

33. The essay was originally a Storrs Lecture, given at Yale in 1991; it was later published by the *Revue française de science politique* (1994) and, finally, in a modified version, in the *University of Pennsylvania Journal of Constitutional Law*. In fact, Habermas only quotes the manuscripts

And yet it can also happen that, despite the impossibility of completely neutralising the unequal bargaining power of the parties, there are the conditions for *fair bargaining* (which can therefore be described as 'procedurally regulated'). Here, the *moral dimension of discourses* appears more clearly: in order to institute such bargaining, it is necessary that 'the procedural conditions under which actual compromises enjoy the presumption of fairness' must be themselves 'justified in moral discourses'. Such moral discourses are not only evaluated on the basis of the correctness or impartiality of the procedures that regulate a negotiation but are also a *presupposition* of bargaining itself, because one must first of all verify that there are no truly generalisable interests in play (*BFN*: 167).[34]

The final picture that emerges from the 'process model' that Habermas has outlined is that of '*a network of discourses and negotiations*' that can be linked up to one another '*via multiple pathways*' (*BFN*: 167, my emphasis). Deliberative politics, that is, the potential form of the process of 'rational political will-formation', is substantiated in a web of *discursive interactions*, of which Habermas only illustrates the simplest case (*see* Figure 9.1). These interactions start from a pragmatic question, from a condition of pluralism of interests and values and from conflict (open or potential) about the possible alternative solutions. Then they *can* articulate themselves in pragmatic, ethical-political or moral discourses, just as they *can* lead to deliberative negotiations (that is, negotiations with a discursive dimension). Such negotiations, in turn, can take place in more or less 'spontaneous' or 'procedurally regulated' forms. Here the discursive dimension is expressed through the 'reasons' that turn out to be the most publicly convincing or

---

(the passage quoted by Habermas does not appear in the text published in 2000 but only in the 1991 paper; but the arguments, of course, are the same). This text by Elster offers a fascinating reading of the intertwining of arguing and bargaining in two founding moments of the history of contemporary democracy: the Convention of Philadelphia (1787) and the French Constituent Assembly (1789–91). This text is often quoted in the literature on deliberative democracy because it is where Elster elaborates his famous formula on the 'civilizing force of hypocrisy' (2000: 349); however, it deserves to be mentioned mostly because it presents a cogent analysis of the connection between argumentative logics and strategic logics, introducing a distinctive analytical category – the strategic use of argumentation – which proved to be very fruitful in the analysis of actual cases of deliberative policy-making. Not surprisingly, Habermas referred to this text for the first time in the pages of *Between Facts and Norms* that I am analysing here, but later devoted to it an entire section of chapter 8, with some critical comments (*BFN*: 377–84); conversely, in the introduction to his text, Elster says that, 'to understand constitutional proceedings, we can benefit from Jürgen Habermas no less than from Thomas Schelling [1960]' (Elster 2000: 347). The border between argumentation and negotiation is also linked to the dilemma between the publicity of the argument and the secrecy that is sometimes required by a negotiating situation: the 'civilizing force of hypocrisy', in fact, can only act because, in public, one can be 'forced or induced to substitute the language of impartial argument for the language of self-interest' (Elster 2000: 349); the secrecy, instead, can promote flexibility in the search for a solution and prevent people from being entrenched in their positions (as is the case when one is led to a bond of coherence to what one publicly proclaimed). On the issues of secrecy and publicity in deliberation and negotiation, see Warren-Mansbridge 2016, Chambers 2004 and O'Flynn 2006: 98–119.

34. A common trait of current participatory and deliberative practices is controversy about the very modalities of discussions, or on the rules to apply to the process. For instance, we often find statements like 'it is (more) just to proceed this way'.

persuasive (also through *strategic uses* of argumentation); mostly, however, it is expressed through *moral* discourses on the *fairness* of the very procedures that the participants try to agree upon and share.

Despite the persisting image of Habermas as a philosopher dwelling in the rarefied world of pure abstraction and proposing completely unrealistic idealised models, it is easy to see that his definition of deliberative politics has many potential empirical and interpretative projections. In other words, it is able both to reconstruct the discursive logic that permeates everyday politics and policies *and* to consider the looming presence, outside this field, of purely strategic or coercive logics.

As emerges from Habermas's scheme (Figure 9.1), finally, this dialogic and discursive network 'terminates in resolutions about policies and legal programs that must be formulated *in the language of law*' (*BFN*: 167, my emphasis). Of course, as we know, Habermas describes the political public sphere as an informal sphere, in which 'the network of discourses and negotiations' can also merely signal the emergence of new problems and new normative horizons that can disrupt the legitimacy of the dominant paradigms. However – within the conditions of a democratic rule-of-law state – the formation of political opinions and wills, which takes place in the public sphere, translates (in mediated forms) into institutional decisions that take the juridical forms of norms that are binding for all. Once again, Habermas's theoretical framework shows its analytic and critical-interpretative potential: this institutional 'outcome'– which 'reconciles' discursive legitimacy and legal legitimacy – is not granted. The tension between the two levels might remain unresolved and a crisis of democratic legitimacy may arise: actually, such a condition can always potentially arise and constitutes the dynamic character of democracy, which should always be thought of as an 'unfinished project'.[35]

Therefore, deliberative politics is articulated through a *plurality of discourses*, with the related logics and argumentative rules, and through a multiplicity of *negotiations*. However, of course, it does not exhaust the entire horizon of politics and power. Not everything can be argued for or discussed with the various forms of 'practical reason': pragmatic controversies can also manifest themselves in forms that cannot be addressed discursively, when the logics of strategic action and of pure power relations prevail. The same can happen with controversies of an ethical or moral nature, if one presumes or claims that ethical or moral arguments can be immediately translated into the legal domain.

---

35. 'First of all, I am seeking a reconstructive analysis' said Habermas in conversation in 1995 (1997b: 132–3), 'in order to prove what we always tacitly assume, if we participate in the democratic and constitutional practices that have fortunately taken hold in our countries. A consciousness that has become completely cynical is incompatible with such practices – unless the practices were altered beyond recognition. ... Secondly, I try to show that this normative self-understanding of our established practices is not from the start illusory. I see these democratic constitutions as so many projects on which legislators, along with the legal and administrative system, work each and every day – and whose continuation is constantly being implicitly fought for in the public sphere.'

Figure 9.1: A process model of rational political will-formation[36]

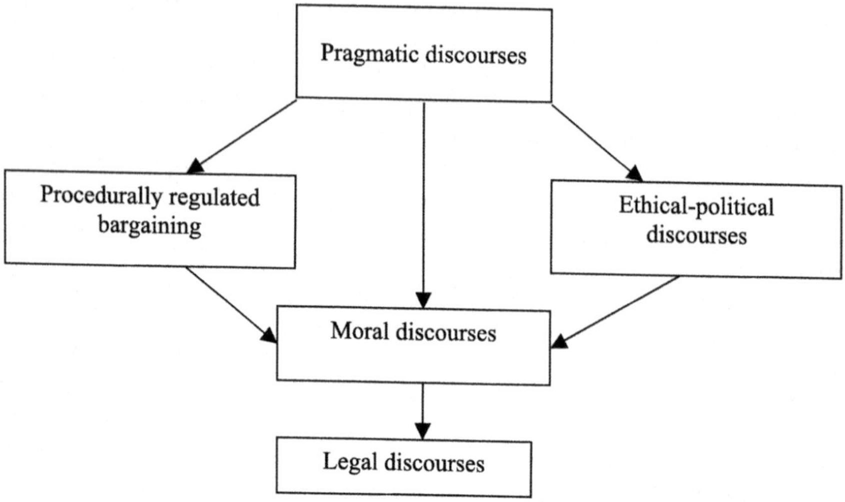

If we look at 'the democratic genesis of law', writes Habermas at the end of chapter 6 (*BFN*: 284):

> ... one can again see the various aspects under which the syndrome of deliberative politics can be resolved, clarified, and differentiated. In legislative politics, the supply of information and purposive-rational choice of means are interwoven with the balance of interests and compromise formation; with the achievement of ethical self-understanding and preference formation; and with moral justification and tests of legal coherence. In this way, the two types of politics Michelman had opposed in a polarizing fashion rationally *interpenetrate one another*. Unlike Michelman, therefore, Sunstein draws on the origins of the American constitutional tradition to reconstruct not two different strands that display an opposition between the republican and the liberal models but an integrated concept that he calls 'Madisonian Republicanism'.

Finally, this passage brings out the *exclusively procedural* nature of the conception of democracy that Habermas regards as sustainable today: the space of deliberative politics can no longer be that of 'an ethical discourse writ large', nor that of 'substantial ethical life holding the citizens together as they engage in their debates'(*BFN*: 285). In our day and age, when politics is trapped between a pervasive proliferating of conflicting interests and a highly problematic universalisation of values, 'democratic procedure can no longer draw its legitimating force from any prior agreement provided by the political ethos of a particular community. The

---

36. '*Ein Prozeßmodell der vernünftigen politischen Willensbildung*'.

democratic procedure must instead look for *an independent justification*' (*BFN*: 285, my emphasis).

6. Habermas and the 'democratic question': against 'normative defeatism'

Habermas intended chapters 7 and 8 of *Between Facts and Norms* to discuss 'how this procedural concept [of democracy], so freighted with idealizations, can link up with empirical investigations that conceive politics primarily as an arena of power processes' and analyse 'the political sphere in terms of strategic interactions governed by interests or in terms of systemic functioning' (*BFN*: 287). Nevertheless, Habermas restates his view that 'this question does not imply an *opposition [Gegenüberstellung]* between the ideal and the real'. Habermas's point of view is now the idea of 'a reconstructive sociology of democracy' (*ibid.*).

Therefore, the point is not to offer an *ideal model* of democracy, which would inevitably be contradicted by empirical facts or turn out to be a mere ought-to-be as opposed to reality; the point is to present a *theory of democracy* which can identify its ways of being and operating, and so 'can identify particles and fragments of an "existing reason" already incorporated in political practices, however distorted these may be' (*BFN*: 322). It is necessary to start from democracy as a *political practice* in order to grasp its inner tension between *facticity* and *validity*. Habermas had previously analysed this 'tension' *within* the law itself; now, it is considered from another point of view: as the tension 'between the normative self-understanding of the constitutional state, as explained in discourse-theoretic terms, and the social facticity of the political processes' (*BFN*: 288).

Chapter 7 of *Between Facts and Norms* is divided into three big sections: the first part analyses and criticises an empirically impoverished version of democracy, a 'reductionist concept of democracy that eliminates the element of democratic legitimacy from power and law' (*ibid.*). In the second part, after resuming the comparison between liberal and republican normative models, Habermas illustrates his own 'procedural concept of democratic process' (*ibid.*). Finally, in the third part he seeks to clarify 'what it means to 'confront' the idea of the self-organization of freely associated citizens with the reality of highly complex societies' (*ibid.*) by analysing how Robert Dahl attempted 'a sociological translation and empirical testing of the procedural understanding of democracy'. My analysis will focus on precisely this point. Habermas is looking for an answer to a specific question: in what way, where and how democratic procedures 'can find a place in the life of a complex society' (*BFN*: 353). His interlocutors here are Norberto Bobbio and, above all, Robert Dahl (*BFN*: 315).[37]

---

37. Habermas mainly deals with *Democracy and its Critics* (Dahl 1989a). It must be noted how Habermas still stays true to his peculiar critical and selective method of discussing with other authors, enhancing what could be included in his theoretical model. However, it is not an incorrect and improper use of other thinkers' contributions: the constant dialogue with all the other specialised fields of human and social sciences must be attributed to the logic of a *reconstructive* knowledge proper. This happens in *Between Facts and Norms*, with juridical knowledge in particular, and, by taking Dahl as an interlocutor, also with political theory and political science.

Habermas maintains that 'Robert Dahl chooses indicators that more fully capture the normative content of democratic procedures than does Norberto Bobbio's proposed operationalization' (*BFN*: 302). Habermas had previously discussed *The Future of Democracy* (1987), and described the Italian philosopher's approach as 'deflationary': a very cautious strategy based on 'skeptical diagnoses' that perfectly understood the 'procedural *minimum*' of a normative definition of democracy, in response to the social transformations that 'contradict the promise of classical conceptions'; on the other hand, though, this approach could not exhaust all the 'normative content' that can be attributed to democracy (*BFN*: 302–3).

In order to define this content, Habermas recalls one of Dewey's most famous passages[38] and observes:

> Deliberative politics acquires its legitimating force from the discursive structure of an opinion- and will-formation that can fulfill its socially integrative function only because citizens expect its results to have a reasonable *quality*. Hence the *discursive level* of public debates constitutes the most important variable (*BFN*: 304).

The *quality* of a democracy is measured not only by how it respects certain essential procedural conditions but also by the quality of the *public discourses* that accompany institutional decisions and *can*, to *various* degrees, give them a basis of legitimacy. For this reason, Dahl's proposal – that is, his attempt to establish 'five postulates that specify a procedure for reaching binding decisions that lie in the equal interest of all', a set of *indices* to evaluate and measure such a democratic quality – is particularly interesting in Habermas's view: inclusion; truly equal opportunities; equal voting rights; also 'an equal right to choose topics and, more generally, to control the agenda'; and finally, the ultimate 'procedural condition', which was crucial from the viewpoint of a discursive theory of democracy, 'a situation that allows all the participants to develop, in the light of sufficient information and good reasons, an articulate understanding of the contested interests and matter in need of regulation' (*BFN*: 315). In Dahl's terms, the point is to allow citizens to have an 'enlightened understanding' of the terms of political decisions,[39] or, following Dewey, of the 'methods and conditions' *with which a public is formed.*

Of course, if we compare the normative content of democracy and what existing democracies actually are, we quickly see that the requirements are only *partially* met: 'to date, the five criteria mentioned above have not been *sufficiently* satisfied by any actual political order' (*ibid.*). Moreover, social transformations impose

---

38. 'Majority rule, just as majority rule, is as foolish as its critics charge it with being. But it never is *merely* majority rule ... The means by which a majority comes to be a majority is the more important thing: antecedent debates, modification of views to meet the opinions of minorities ... The essential need, in other words, is the improvement of the methods and conditions of debate, discussion and persuasion. That is *the* problem of the public' (Dewey 1984[1927]: 365).

39 Habermas (*BFN*: 354) quotes the same passage by Dahl that we quoted above while discussing Fishkin (*see* Chapter Seven, Section 3).

procedures to reduce both juridical and administrative complexity, modifying the conditions on which those requirements can today be met. However, 'the existing pluralist democracies' can still be seen 'as systems in which democratic procedures do not just have the *nominal* form of *rights* of political participation and communication, but have *actually* been implemented in the form of practices, even if only selectively' (*BFN*: 316).

So, Habermas does not indulge in an easy condemnation of the *gap* between the ideal and modern 'real democracies': we must still understand the normative dimension embedded in the *facticity* of a society in which a democratic rule-of-law state could, historically, be established. Therefore, an area of tension is created: on the one hand there are the *premises* and *promises* of democracy (as Norberto Bobbio would define them), which can become *widespread* in political culture and so become themselves bearers of a communicative power (to use Habermas's terms: forms of 'normative self-understanding' of the citizens and their communicative praxis); and on the other hand there is the strength of economic, bureaucratic and technocratic *social powers*, which obstruct democratisation processes and which a democratic rule-of-law state, in turn, seeks, or should be able, to 'tame'.

From this perspective, we can understand how Habermas can use an approach such as Dahl's, which sought to positively identify the '*favorable social conditions*' that facilitate the establishment and stabilisation of democratic procedures. 'Dahl wanted to show that the idea and procedure of deliberative politics do not have to be externally imposed on the reality of developed societies, because this type of politics has had a secure hold on the institutions of such societies for a long time' (*BFN*: 317). At the same time, however, Dahl also sought to understand the conditions and factors that limit the full development of this idea and this procedure – or even totally frustrate them. Among these factors, Habermas stresses the importance that Dahl gives to the growing 'specialization of the technical steering knowledge used in policymaking and administration' (*BFN*: 317): 'the chief danger consists in the technocratic variant of a paternalism grounded in the monopolization of knowledge' (*ibid.*).[40]

Dahl, however, offers only *weak* solutions to this risk: on the one hand, he places 'his hopes on the technical possibilities of telecommunications'; on the other hand, with his idea of a *minipopulus*, he seems to have faith in creating specialised and decentralised places to enable the development of citizens' 'enlightened understanding' that appears to be impossible or endangered elsewhere. But, as Habermas critically observes, 'the abstract and somewhat utopian tenor of this recommendation oddly contrasts with the intention and structure of the investigation' (*ibid.*): searching for, inventing and designing *ad hoc* experimental or almost laboratory solutions will not give any responses to the dangers that threaten democratic procedures. This judgment reveals that Habermas takes a different approach from the one that would later characterise relevant areas in the deliberative field (as we have seen in Fishkin).

---

40   'Privileged access to the sources of relevant knowledge makes possible an inconspicuous domination over the colonized public of citizens cut off from these sources and placated with symbolic politics' (*BFN*: 317).

According to Habermas, the limit of Dahl's analysis lies in the type of sociological analysis he adopts: by only looking at the social structure through statistical indexes, he cannot wholly understand those 'indicators of rational potentials already at work in society itself, potentials that can be taken up and developed by the political system'. To do this, one must look at the 'deeper processes of social reproduction' (*BFN*: 318) and also have a language and a theoretical approach to understand them.[41]

So Habermas goes back to the premises of his discursive theory, in order to find a possible answer to the same issue that Dahl had addressed: 'the conditions for a more extensive democratization of the existing political system' (*BFN*: 321). But the very fact that he raises this issue implies that he was taking a stand: any answer, in fact, becomes pointless if one assumes that the tendencies to the autonomisation of 'systemic integration' mechanisms, which regulate the government of complex societies, are irreversible and insuperable and so are going to escape any democratic procedure and democratically legitimated legal regulation.

Habermas points out that, if that were the case, it would be incomprehensible why 'in changing constellations, the "*democratic question*" in one version or another has continually returned to the agenda' (*BFN*: 320). The origin of this reviving 'issue' is in the critical tension between '*functional gaps* opened when other mechanisms of social integration are overburdened' (*BFN*: 318), (functional gaps, *Funktionslücken*, *FG*: 386, are the 'voids', the 'failures' of functional and systemic integration) and the space and role of deliberative politics. In general,

> … where other regulators – for example, the coordination patterns operating through settled values, norms, and routines for reaching understanding – fail, politics and law raise these quasi-natural problem-solving processes above the threshold of consciousness, as it were. In filling in for social processes whose problem-solving capacities are overtaxed, the political process solves *the same kind* of problems as the processes it replaces (*BFN*: 318).

But now, in complex societies, because of the growing 'need for functional coordination', 'the simple model of a division of labor between experts and laypersons no longer suffices' (*BFN*: 320), and this need for 'integration' requires administrative systems to exert their control and management functions. This factor could (and often does) lead people to consider the idea of 'deliberative politics' unrealistic and inadequate, since it is overshadowed by an ineliminable '*cognitive overburdening*': that is, to think such politics 'lacks the complexity to take in and digest the *operatively necessary* knowledge' required by control and government (*ibid.*).

---

41 The meaning that Habermas ascribes to 'rationalization' is not the common one (which generally evokes some process that makes a choice or a social/institutional process more 'rational' or 'effective'). Rather, in Habermas's lexicon, 'rationalization' means a process through which a social phenomenon is subject to a rational, dialogic and deliberative dimension, one that makes it consciously understood and directed by those who are involved in it. Thus, the 'rational potentials already at work in society itself' are those elements that can activate processes of 'rational' self-awareness on part of the social actors or participants involved.

Habermas admits that these data are manifest and indisputable but thinks they 'should not lead one to forget the other fact': that the various impoverishments of the characteristic features of democratic politics ('the uncoupling of administrative action from parliamentary control' and also 'the displacement of pertinent topics from public arenas') 'did not take place without resistance'. Otherwise, we could not understand why a '*demokratische Frage*' (*FG*: 389), 'a question of democracy', is still on the agenda, or why a diffuse need to rethink the reasons and forms of democracy (*BFN*: 320) keeps arising. These are not, however, residual phenomena or niches of opposition to the intrusiveness of anonymous systems of economic and technocratic domination:

> ... that these countertendencies should arise is by no means accidental, if one assumes that the very medium of law, to which political power is internally linked, requires the supposition that law has a democratic genesis – and that this partly counterfactual supposition also has empirical effects. On this premise, the deployment of political power, even for cognitively quite demanding steering processes, is still subject to constraints that result directly from the juridical form of collectively binding decisions. In a political system under the pressure of societal complexity, these constraints manifest themselves in a growing cognitive dissonance between the validity suppositions of constitutional democracy and the way things actually happen in the political process (*BFN*: 320–1).

These words may be seen as evidence of Habermas's rooted (or almost 'incorrigible', some might say) 'rationalistic' approach: today, the conflict expresses itself through a *cognitive dissonance*. But I believe that this objection does not grasp all the implications (also of a political nature) originating from Habermas's position. 'Cognitive dissonance' *expresses* an irreducible tension between control and 'systemic' regulation and the logic of a deliberative politics that seeks to connect the solution to unavoidable *social integration* problems to a democratic procedure of forming opinions and wills.

This general statement is able to grasp the several various real conflicts typical of complex societies: each and every one of such problems originates from a social *problem* that needs to be solved and creates a problem of *democratic legitimacy*. But this raises the question of the forms, places and procedures through which such a solution is sought and acquires legitimacy:

> ... the centerpiece of deliberative politics consists in a network of discourses and bargaining processes that is supposed to facilitate the rational solution of pragmatic, moral, and ethical questions – the very problems that accumulate with the failure of the functional, moral, or ethical integration of society elsewhere (*BFN*: 320).

The range of possible empirical situations is, of course, extremely broad; sticking to Habermas's theoretical system, however, it is possible to distinguish two main kinds. At one end, there are all those forms of expressions of a *social power* that asserts its will *against* or *outside* any democratic and publicly discursive procedure (that is, all those systemic economic, bureaucratic and technocratic logics that assert their 'imperatives' *from above* citizens or *behind their backs*). At the other end, there are all the forms of *communicative power* that express deliberative politics (based on a strong bond between democratic institutional procedures generating legitimate decisions and the processes, places and practices of public deliberation and discursive formation of political opinions and judgments).

'The future of democracy' is at stake within this tension: but its fate cannot be entrusted to some collective 'subject' endowed with a critical, all-inclusive conscience – let alone to some 'ideal' set against an unruly reality. If one takes 'the participant's point of view' and not that of an 'external observer' (this is an essential distinction of Habermas's entire theoretical and philosophical approach), that is, if one puts oneself in the position of those who *experience* this tension, then the *first* form of critical self-understanding is precisely *cognitive dissonance*: a *gap* arises between the claims of validity embedded in the code of a democratic rule-of-law state (which are 'redeemable' in the forms of deliberative politics) and the logics regulating systemic integration mechanisms. This *dissonance* can foster an individual and collective capabilities of learning, *primum movens* of social reproduction and transformation: 'the normative fault line that appears with this ability to say no' (*BFN*: 324). '*Normative fault line*' is an effective translation of the term Habermas uses '*Soll-bruchstelle*' (*FG*: 394), literally, a 'point of rupture' or a 'breaking point', evoking the sense of 'ought-to-be', of what *could be otherwise*.

In response to complex and highly differentiated societies, in which a 'generalised particularism' (Habermas 1992a: 451) tends to rule, Habermas wants to avoid any form of 'normative defeatism' (*BFN*: 330) that draws unwarranted conclusions from the disenchantment produced by reality. In our complex societies, a threatening gap is taking shape, one that may sweep democracy away. On the one hand, we find the conflagration of micro-particularisms and endemic micro-conflicts, susceptible to solutions entrusted solely to the prevalence of *power relationships*, to strategic and instrumental acting, to the collision and unstable balance among countless powers and micro-powers; on the other hand (but actually in a complementary manner), there is the domination of systemic logics that escape every democratic regulation procedure and the prevalence of technocratic politics.

Faced with such a scenario, the *normative anchorage* to the principles of a democratic rule-of-law state, the call to democratic procedures (starting from the perception of a *dissonance*) can acquire the strength of a *fact*, introducing logics of individual and collective communicative action that contrast, interact, intertwine and combine with other logics of action and with the 'systems of action' in which they are concentrated. Therefore, any appeal to 'democracy' that aims at *bypassing*, or that casually underestimates, the power of *juridical and institutional mediation*, not only proves to be weak or ineffective but also ends up contributing to emptying the fundamental *procedural* dimension that characterises democracy.

In this context, unlike at other historical periods, the task of *theory* certainly cannot be to offer 'from the outside' some kind of conscience to a collective subject (or maybe, nowadays, to 'civil society' as such) which – as happens, for example, in the classic Marxist view – is considered and considers itself *inscribed* in the objective movement of history. The task of theory can *only* be to rebuild the conditions in which mechanisms and forms of 'social reproduction' develop today and the way in which the inescapable problems of 'social integration' come up, understanding all their tensions but also all their *possible* normative implications. In a 1995 conversation, Habermas recalls how some opposed to his view certain 'unchallengeable facts', such as the public sphere being distorted by the media, or the diffusion of forms of 'regressive' mass awareness. His reply was clear:

> But to what do they represent an objection? For it cannot be to the philosopher who – in the name of his normative theory and with the gesture of impotent Ought – furthers a postconventional consciousness, thus sinning against a human nature that pessimistic anthropology has always led into battle against the intellectuals' dream dances. *All we do is reconstruct the Ought that has immigrated into praxis itself*, and we only need to observe that in positive law and the democratic constitutional state – that is, in the existing practices themselves – principles are embodied that depend on a postconventional grounding, and to that extent are tailored to the public consciousness of a liberal political culture. This normative self-understanding introduces into our relationships, which are not what they ought to be, a certain dynamic: *we see the constitution as a project we can continue working on – or abandon in discouragement* (1997b: 145, my emphasis).

Chapter Ten

Deliberative Politics: the State, the Public Sphere and Civil Society

Part Two of this book has been devoted to reconstructing the genealogy of the theoretical field of deliberative democracy and identifying the progressive emergence of its central conceptual elements and its internal articulations. To complete this framework and to better understand what *today* is defined (in various ways) as deliberative democracy, two more steps are necessary: first, to look at the role played by John Rawls, which I will do in the next chapter; second, to dwell on a few other points of the 1990s debate, especially the critical dialogue between Joshua Cohen and Jürgen Habermas. In this way, I will also be able to complete the analysis of Habermas's notion of 'deliberative politics' and add an important element to my reconstruction of the intense discussion that has accompanied the development of the deliberative field.

1. Habermas, the 'two-track model' and 'sluices'

In chapter 7 of *Between Facts and Norms*, after criticising 'empiricist models of democracy', Habermas takes up the two classic liberal and republican 'normative models', develops some further implications of them and defines his own *procedural* conception of democracy in opposition to them. In particular, Habermas underlines that his 'procedural concept of democratic process' appears as a break 'with a holistic model of society centered in the state' and 'claims to be neutral with respect to competing worldviews and forms of life' (Habermas 1996: 288). In different and opposite forms, both the republican and the liberal conceptions are defined *in relation to the state*. According to the former,

> ... the citizens' opinion- and will-formation forms the medium through which society constitutes itself as a political whole. Society is, from the very start, political society – *societas civilis* – for in the citizens' practice of political self-determination the community becomes conscious of itself, as it were, and acts upon itself through the citizens' collective will. Hence democracy becomes equivalent to the political self-organization of society as a whole. This leads to an offensive *understanding of politics directed against the state apparatus* (*ibid.*: 297).

Democracy thus – from the 'republican' perspective – appears as 'self–organization of society': this idea also characterised the origins of participatory democracy and is rooted in a political culture that was very much present at the foundation of American democracy. I am referring in particular to Jefferson, who was deeply suspicious of any state not welcoming the practice of civic self-government: it is not by chance that, just after the passage quoted, Habermas evokes Hannah Arendt: 'in Hannah Arendt's political writings, one can see where republican argumentation directs its salvos' (*ibid.*). The way Habermas summarises this position cannot but recall the traits of a 'participatory' democracy conceived as essentially *communitarian* and as the expression of a truly active citizenship. From this perspective,

> ... in opposition to the civil privatism of a depoliticized population and in opposition to the production of mass loyalty through parties that have become arms of the state, the political public sphere should be revitalized to the point where a regenerated citizenry can, in the forms of a decentralized self-governance, (once again) appropriate bureaucratically alienated state power. In this way society would finally develop into a political totality (*ibid.*).[1]

The liberal model is also suspicious of the state but judges its presence inevitable and merely tries to limit its power (*ibid.*: 297). According to this view,

> ... the democratic will-formation of self-interested citizens has comparatively weak normative connotations, and it forms only one element in a complex constitution. The constitution is supposed to curb the administration through normative provisions (such as basic rights, separation of powers, and statutory controls) ... This state-centered understanding of politics can forego the unrealistic assumption of a citizenry capable of collective action.

In a way that might seem paradoxical, Habermas defines this view of politics as also 'state-centered', because the liberal model sees the state as the *only* space of politics: while the republican vision aims to *re-absorb* the separation of the democratic state into the self-rule of civil society, the liberal view *confines* the space of politics to the protective functions of the state (*ibid.*: 298):

> Liberal argumentation aims its salvos against the potential for disruption posed by an administrative power that hinders the spontaneous social commerce of private persons. The liberal model hinges not on the democratic self-determination of deliberating citizens [*deliberierender Bürger*] but on the constitutional framework for an economic society that is supposed to guarantee

---

1.   As we have seen in Chapter One, the Anti-Federalist tradition – especially Jefferson – is the fundamental matrix of the visions and practices of participation in American political culture. And the thought of Hannah Arendt represents a fundamental point of reference: a work like *On Revolution* (1963) proposed a deeply sympathetic reading of Jefferson's ideas. *See*, in particular, the pages dedicated to the idea of 'elementary republics', that is, townships in New England (Arendt 1963: 252–9). On Jefferson's influence during the Progressive Era, *see* Mattson 1998: 79–82.

an essentially nonpolitical common good by satisfying personal life plans and private expectations of happiness.

As opposed to these two ideal-typical models, Habermas proposes his own view, based on discourse theory: 'it takes elements from both sides and puts them together in a new way'. From the republican conception, it takes the importance of 'the process of political opinion- and will-formation, but without understanding the constitution as something secondary'. In fact, it considers constitutional principles as 'a consistent answer' to the need for institutionalised forms of communication through which opinions and wills can be formed democratically, in a process grounded 'on the interplay of institutionalized deliberative processes with informally developed public opinions' (*ibid.*).

The concept of democracy that comes from the theory of discourse, therefore, 'no longer has to operate with the notion of a social whole centered in the state and imagined as a goal-oriented subject writ large', nor does it have to conceive institutional norms as a system of rules only guaranteeing 'the balance of power and interests in accordance with a market model' (*ibid.*: 298). The novelty of the discursive approach to democracy lies in the fact that, with it, there are no longer 'all those motifs employed by *the philosophy of consciousness*'. The latter created a dilemma: either one thought of 'the citizens' practice of self-determination' as the practice of 'a macrosocial subject', 'a collective actor that reflects the whole and acts for it'; or one traced back the whole of society to the anonymous coexistence of 'individual subjects', through 'processes that operate blindly because beyond individual choice there can be at most aggregated, but not consciously formed and executed, collective decisions' (*ibid.*: 298–9).

Faced with this alternative (*macrosocial* subject *versus individual* subjects), discourse theory relies on a constitutive *intersubjective* dimension, which is expressed in the network of *discursive interactions* that take place both in the *public spheres* and in *democratic procedures*.[2] In these pages, Habermas outlines his 'two-track model' and also introduces the image of 'sluices': between the public spheres (and the 'civil society' that is their 'social basis') and the institutional sphere producing political decisions, there are 'subjectless' communication flows creating 'arenas in which a more or less rational opinion- and will-formation can take place for political matters, that is, matters relevant to the entire society and in need of regulation' (*ibid.*: 299). This discursive pattern takes place between different elements: the 'public opinion-formation', the 'institutionalized elections' and the 'legislative decisions': in this way, 'the influence and communicative power' are turned 'into administrative power'. More precisely, Habermas here distinguishes between '*die kommunikativ erzeugte Macht*', that is, *power produced communicatively*, and '*der publizistisch erzeugte Einfluß*', that is, influence produced through the media and the press (*FG*: 362–3): in other words,

---

2. 'Discourse theory reckons with the higher-level intersubjectivity of processes of reaching understanding that take place through democratic procedures or in the communicative network of public spheres' (*ibid.*: 299).

a wider and stronger 'power' [*Macht*] produced through a variety of forms of communication and a more specific 'influence' [*Einfluß*] exercised through the various media [*publizistisch*].

The border between state and civil society is not erased at all, as Habermas clarifies: rather, it is made open and permeable (far from the dualism typical of liberalism and republicanism) while being redefined and articulated. 'The civil society [*Zivilgesellschaft*], as the social basis of autonomous public spheres', is differentiated 'from both the economic system and public administration' (*BFN*: 299). This conception, adds Habermas, 'has implications for how one understands legitimation and popular sovereignty' and has evident 'normative implications' (*ibid.*). Modern societies can rely on 'three resources' to 'satisfy their needs for integration and steering': money (the systemic integration produced by economic mechanisms); administrative power (the systemic integration produced by political and bureaucratic power); and 'solidarity'[3] (the *social and intersubjective* integration that comes from communicative action). Within this theoretical framework, it is possible to understand, from a historical and empirical point of view, what can be defined as the *relative weight* of each of these three 'resources' and the *balance* between them. However, 'from a normative standpoint' (*ibid.*), we also face the issue of 'a realignment in the relative importance' or a 'shift of weight' [*Gewichtsverschiebung*] between those elements. In our complex societies,

> ... the socially integrating force of solidarity, which can no longer be drawn solely from sources of communicative action, must develop through widely diversified and more or less autonomous public spheres, as well as through procedures of democratic opinion- and will-formation institutionalized within a constitutional framework. In addition, it should be able to hold its own against the two other mechanisms of social integration, money and administrative power (*ibid.*: 299).

This is the 'force-field' defining the space of democracy: a constant tension between different mechanisms of integration and social regulation and conflict on the 'relative weight' with which they are combined and the 'relative importance' that each of them acquires. The point is to understand if, and to what extent, *widespread deliberative practices* – discursive and public formation of opinions and wills that are also democratically institutionalised – would be able to compete, counter, and interact with other powerful logics that both 'hold together' and, today, constitute, the social order.

For Habermas, this conception of democracy deeply affects the conception of *democratic legitimation* and *popular sovereignty*. According to the liberal paradigm, 'democratic will-formation has the exclusive function of *legitimating* the exercise of political power', *authorizing it* through vote and electoral competition. From the republican viewpoint, on the contrary, 'democratic will-formation has

---

3.   In a footnote, Habermas clarifies: 'As in the first two chapters, I am using "solidarity" here not as a normative but as a sociological concept' (*BFN*: 549, note 11).

the significantly stronger function of constituting society as a political community and keeping the memory of this founding act alive with each election' (*BFN*: 299–300): the logic of a 'predominantly free mandate' typical of liberal democracy is here replaced by the idea that political power and government are merely an 'executive committee', closely linked to the programmatic instructions given by citizens. Faced with these alternatives (*BFN*: 300),

> ... once again, discourse theory brings another idea into play: the procedures and communicative presuppositions of democratic opinion- and will-formation function as the most important sluices for the discursive rationalization of the decisions of an administration bound by law and statute.

'Discursive rationalization of the decisions' is neither the claim – as some have misinterpreted – that political decisions *are* or *should be* 'rational' or correspond to some external standard of 'rationality', nor the thesis that this always happens or ideally should happen. Rather, it is the idea that the processes of democratic formation of opinion and will allow for a *possible deliberative construction* (which, therefore, is 'rational') of political decisions; the latter, in turn, are always subject to a potential *discursive*, *public* and *communicative examination*. This process can be represented as a 'sluice', through which opinion and will must pass in order to be filtered. This is necessary precisely because the expression of opinion and will can never be *immediately* transposed into a binding and legally legitimate political decision. On the one hand, these 'sluices' can make the citizens' political judgments more reflective and aware (as well as epistemically more grounded); on the other hand, they can allow such judgments to act within the institutional procedures that legitimate political decisions that are binding on all.

Thus, once again, there is a potential field of empirical variability that Habermas's theoretical frame aims to address. On one side, the processes of formation of opinions and wills can 'just monitor the exercise of political power *ex post facto*' (*ibid.*): that is, in the presence of a weak or residual public and deliberative dimension, the citizens' opinions and wills can be expressed *only* through the mechanisms of reward and sanction typical of an accountability conceived in exclusively electoral terms. On the other side, such processes can also acquire the strength of a communicative power that, 'more or less', manages to orientate and 'programme' political power (*BFN*: 300): that is, to exert an *influence* that manages to be translated into institutional decisions. In this way, such decisions are *discursively legitimated*: using the 'sluice' metaphor, we could also say that as the opinions and will formed within the public sphere are filtered by the 'sluice', their *hydraulic energy* is converted to *legitimacy*. Of course, communicative power can also act in the opposite direction, *subtracting* legitimacy from decisions that are not the outcome of an adequate procedure of discussion and democratic inclusion. In between these two poles, to various degrees, democratic politics can be a deliberative politics: one in which the formation of opinions and wills is produced through argumentative exchange, critical reflection and public discourse on everything that is or can be on the public agenda.

'Nevertheless', Habermas soon clarifies, 'only the political system can "act"': in other words, once again 'discourses do not govern'. The political system

> ... is a subsystem specialized for collectively binding decisions, whereas the communicative structures of the public sphere constitute a far-flung network of sensors that react to the pressure of society-wide problems and stimulate influential opinions. The public opinion that is worked up via democratic procedures into communicative power cannot 'rule' [*herrschen*] of itself but can only point the use of administrative power in specific directions (*ibid.*).

The boundary that separates the political system from the public sphere is thus permeable and porous, but steady and identifiable. And in any case, the influence that a public sphere can exercise cannot presume to get around, so to speak, the institutional channels of democratic legitimacy: as Habermas says in chapter 8 of *Between Facts and Norms* (371–2):

> ... the influence of a public opinion generated more or less discursively in open controversies is certainly an empirical variable that can make a difference. But public influence [*publizistisch-politische Einfluß*] is transformed into communicative power only after it passes through the filters of the institutionalized *procedures* of democratic opinion- and will-formation ... The popular sovereignty set communicatively aflow cannot make itself felt *solely* in the influence of informal public discourses – not even when these discourses arise from autonomous public spheres. To generate political power, their influence must have an effect on the democratically regulated deliberations of democratically elected assemblies and assume an authorized form in formal decisions.

Even the idea of 'popular sovereignty', therefore, is profoundly reformulated. Once we have abandoned both the republican idea that it may be 'bound to the notion of embodiment in the (at first even physically present) people' and the view *à la* Rousseau that such a sovereignty 'in principle cannot be delegated' (*BFN*: 300–1), the liberal model certainly appears 'more realistic', entrusting the representation of popular sovereignty to electoral processes and the constitutional structure based on the separation of powers (*BFN*: 301). However, both paradigms still mistakenly consider 'state and society in terms of the whole and its parts, where the whole is constituted either by a sovereign citizenry or by a constitution' (*ibid.*). On the contrary, the 'discourse theory of democracy' proposes 'the image of a *decentered society*' (*ibid.*).

> Once one gives up the philosophy of the subject, one needs neither to concentrate sovereignty concretely in the people nor to banish it in anonymous constitutional structures and powers. The 'self' of the self-organizing legal community disappears in the subjectless forms of communication that

regulate the flow of discursive opinion- and will-formation in such a way that their fallible results enjoy the presumption of being reasonable. This is not to denounce the intuition connected with the idea of popular sovereignty but to interpret it inter-subjectively. Popular sovereignty, even if it becomes anonymous, retreats into democratic procedures and the legal implementation of their demanding communicative presuppositions only in order to make itself felt as communicatively generated power. Strictly speaking, this power springs from the interactions among legally institutionalized will-formation and culturally mobilized publics.

'A decentered society' is a society that cannot be thought of as a 'macro-subject': it is based on this underlying theoretical assumption that Habermas outlines his theory of democracy and his idea of 'deliberative politics'. There are precise consequences deriving from this: the political system is only a 'subsystem' and, in any case, deliberative politics (which *can* characterise it and, *in fact*, *does* characterise it in partial and various degrees) cannot be considered a pervasive dimension able to rule and govern 'society as a whole'. 'The normative self-understanding of deliberative politics' (that is, the normative or ideal implications we can draw from the notion and practice of deliberative politics) might lead one to generalise the idea of 'a discursive mode of sociation for the legal community'. However, notes Habermas (*BFN*: 301–2),

> … this mode does not extend to the whole of the society in which the constitutionally organized political system is embedded. Even on its own self-understanding, deliberative politics remains part of a complex society, which, as a whole, resists the normative approach practiced in legal theory.

This is the core of the dialogue with Cohen and his idea of an 'ideal deliberative procedure' in which, in the following pages, Habermas engages.

2. Habermas *versus* Cohen: can deliberative politics 'shape' the whole of society?

Before analysing Habermas's dialogue with Cohen, we should reflect on this point: it might be objected that Habermas's idea of deliberation ends up being so broad and comprehensive that it loses all specificity. In fact, 'deliberation' could be identified with all the forms of communication that characterise the practice of civic self-determination and the processes by which the opinions and will of the people is formed. However, it is here that one sees the particularity of Habermas's approach: deliberation – strictly defined as an argumentative exchange during which people offer and receive *good reasons* in favour of, or against, a claim or a solution and validity claims are reflectively redeemed – is not a discursive modality that can appear in its *pure form* within a wider communicative practice. We need to think of it as a *component* acting within that practice and characterising it in different ways.

However, this does not mean that we cannot grasp its character at a theoretical and reconstructive level, conceptually and analytically isolating its constitutive profile. Habermas's *reconstructive* approach aims at finding the dimensions and deliberative components that are *factually present and active* in the political and institutional social practices of a democracy or a constitutional state. It also outlines the tensions that this *deliberative factuality* produces with regard both to the forms of 'normative self-understanding' that such practices accompany and to other social facts depending on other logics. Nevertheless, this very work of 'reconstruction' on the one hand gives a solid foundation to the possible critical and normative projections (*an anchor to real processes*) and, on the other hand, allows theoretical development, with relative autonomy, even on a normative level.

Thus it is easy to understand why, for Habermas, the 'development of an ideal deliberative procedure', *in itself*, is not a pointless or unfounded theoretical exercise: the decisive point, however, is the role given to it and the way in which this exercise is designed. It is starting from this matter that very different perspectives can, and actually do, arise: in fact, it's one thing to believe that the 'ideal deliberative procedure' can and should be taken as a *model* to discuss or embody in social, political and institutional practice, or even as an ideal that society as a whole should strive for; it is another thing to believe that this elaboration (so demanding from the normative standpoint) can be used as an analytical and reconstructive criterion with regards to *real* processes.

I believe this is the decisive theoretical line that also allows us to understand the gap between Habermas's *theoretical* model of deliberative politics and Cohen's *ideal* model of deliberative procedure; in the background lies the critical debate between Habermas and Rawls and the difference between their positions.

Thus, we can see why, in the pages I am analysing here, Habermas often critically attributes to his interlocutors an approach typical of a 'philosophy of the subject'. This is an *idealising* approach, confined to the sphere of the *ought-to-be*: it constructs an ideal of what we *think* a deliberative democracy should or could be (and, as we have seen in Cohen, we then draw out of it all the possible implications in terms of actual *institutional design*). The approach emerging from Habermas's work, in contrast, constructs a *theory* of deliberative politics. The discussion of constitutional law, for example, can only be understood starting with an initial theoretical move, namely, the question of what are the sources and forms of legitimacy of the *practice* of constitutional courts, trying to identify possible explanatory theoretical models and the role played in courts' practice by deliberative politics. Following this approach, deliberative politics is *set within* a theoretical model involving the differentiated set of logics and 'systems of action' that characterise modern social complexity.

I believe this is the necessary premise for understanding Habermas's dialogue with Joshua Cohen. In the pages of *BFN* that he devotes to Cohen (304–8), Habermas *seems* to agree with Cohen's definition of 'ideal deliberative procedure'; however, he makes some decisive critical notes both before and after it, thereby significantly changing the extent of his endorsement. Habermas recalls Cohen's central definition (deliberative democracy as an 'intuitive ideal' of a 'democratic association' making its decisions in deliberative terms; *see* Chapter Six, Section 2). With this definition, writes Habermas,

> Joshua Cohen has elucidated the concept of deliberative politics in terms of an 'ideal procedure' of deliberation and decision making that should be 'mirrored' in social institutions as much as possible. It seems Cohen has still not completely shaken off the idea of a society that is deliberatively steered *as a whole* and is thus politically constituted (*BFN*.: 304–5).

In a way, Habermas appropriates the definition of the ideal deliberative procedure proposed by Cohen but he radically redefines its scope: this procedure can be taken as 'the core structure [*Kernstruktur*] in a separate, constitutionally organized political system' but 'not as a model for all social institutions (and not even for all government institutions)' (*BFN*: 305). 'If deliberative politics', adds Habermas (*ibid.*),

> … is supposed to be inflated into a structure shaping the totality of society, then the discursive mode of sociation expected in the *legal system* would have to expand into a self-organization of *society* and penetrate the latter's complexity as a whole. This is impossible, for the simple reason that democratic procedure must be embedded in contexts it cannot itself regulate.[4]

This passage will be taken by some deliberative theorists as a kind of confession: the emblem of Habermas's 'defeatist' theoretical strategy, or the sign of his abandonment of the 'radical' and participatory ideal of democracy. For example, according to Bohman, Habermas supported the idea that democracy 'cannot organize society as a whole, since it is embedded in contexts of social complexity that it can neither regulate nor control. These contexts are constituted by a non-intentional social order of differentiated and systemically related parts' (Bohman, 1996: 172–3). For Bohman, this statement signals a change of mind from the model of a 'critical theory of democracy' Habermas previously supported, leading to his acceptance of the impossibility of a full 'democracy' in the presence of a high level of functional differentiation of society and its sub-systems. '[I]t means', adds Bohman, 'that both direct forms of self-rule and the application of democratic control to all areas of social life are impossible to achieve'. Now, it is certainly true that, for Habermas, 'direct forms of self-rule' are impossible. However, Bohman seems not to grasp that here Habermas is not referring to democracy but to *deliberative politics*: it is the latter that cannot be ideally extended to 'society as a whole'. But the assumption that all the democratic

---

4. This passage by Habermas deserves to be carefully evaluated in its original version: in Rehg's translation there is an expression ['must be embedded'] that was not present in Habermas's text. The latter reads as follows: '*Das ist schon deshalb nicht möglich, weil das demokratische Verfahren auf Einbettungskontexte, die es selbst nicht regeln kann, angewiesen ist*' (*FG*: 370). That is: 'this is not possible, because the democratic procedure is dependent [or embedded into] contexts that it cannot itself regulate'. Notice: 'it *is* embedded', not 'it *must be* embedded'.

procedures and institutions of the rule-of-law state *can* and *should* aim to regulate and control the logics of the 'systems' of money and power, or even try to counter their intrusiveness, is of course strongly present throughout the theoretical model proposed by Habermas.

'Deliberative politics', according to Habermas, cannot be thought of as the process by which an entire society politically constitutes itself. A society as diverse and complex as a 'post-traditional' one can be cannot be thought of as a macro-association that is self-governed through deliberative procedures. 'Deliberative politics' is defined as a *possible* mode of functioning (which is already in place to a degree and which can surely be wished for at a normative level) of the interactions between democratic institutions, civil society and the public sphere. But the claim that it stands as a possible mode of 'self-organisation' of all social complexity, presenting itself as another *form* of democracy, cannot be sustained. As Habermas says later in the chapter, 'we must not look on civil society as a focal point where the lines of societal self-organization as a whole would converge' (*BFN*: 371): civil society can never 'occupy *the position* of a macrosubject supposed to bring society as a whole under control and simultaneously act for it' (*BFN*: 372).

These are the assumptions on which Habermas bases his dialogue with Cohen. After recalling the various 'postulates' (*BFN*: 305–6) of Cohen's definition of an 'ideal deliberative procedure', Habermas comments: '[e]very association that institutionalizes such a procedure for the purposes of democratically regulating the conditions of its common life thereby constitutes itself as a body of citizens [*Bürgerschaft*]' (*BFN*: 306). However, not only does this idea of deliberative politics annihilate any universalist foundation of the idea of citizenship,[5] it also fails to clarify 'the relation between decision-oriented deliberations, which are regulated by democratic procedures, and the informal processes of opinion-formation in the public sphere' (*BFN*: 307); moreover, it neglects the 'internal differentiations' Habermas describes in chapter 4 of *BFN* (that is, the articulation between pragmatic, ethic and moral discourses).

Now we can see why, introducing the section devoted to Cohen, Habermas stated that he wanted 'to develop the concept of a two-track deliberative politics' (*BFN.*: 304) at exactly this point of his work. Deliberative politics finds its 'reference point' (*ibid.*: 307) in parliamentary procedures (if they are not restricted to mere *ratification*, that is, if they 'do not simply organize the voting that follows informal opinion-formation') and in the 'decision-making powers (and assigned political responsibilities)' typical of parliamentary procedures (*ibid.*). However, this point connects to other levels that make a decisive contribution to the process of formation of opinions and will. Here Habermas, in a rather elliptical way, seems to locate two other distinct moments in which deliberative politics is articulated: the first is constituted by various 'socially bounded and temporally limited publics'

---

5. This *Bürgerschaft* 'forms a particular legal community, delimited in space and time, with specific forms of life and traditions. But this distinctive cultural identity does not designate it *as* a political community of citizens. For the democratic process is governed by *universal* principles of justice that are equally constitutive for every body of citizens' (*BFN*: 306).

(*ibid.*) and the places where 'negotiations' are 'structured through argument';[6] the second is 'a procedurally unregulated public sphere that is borne by the general public of citizens' (*ibid.*).

But the decisive point is that of the 'uncoupling' of this public sphere from any *decisional* responsibility or dimension: recalling Nancy Fraser's definition of 'weak publics',[7] Habermas says:

> ... this 'weak' public is the vehicle of 'public opinion'. The opinion-formation uncoupled from decisions is effected in an open and inclusive network of overlapping, subcultural publics having fluid temporal, social, and substantive boundaries. Within a framework guaranteed by constitutional rights, the structures of such a pluralistic public sphere develop more or less spontaneously. The currents of public communication are channelled by mass media and flow through different publics [*Öffentlichkeiten*], that develop informally inside associations. Taken together, they form a 'wild' complex that resists organization as a whole (*ibid.*).[8]

Of course, given this 'anarchic structure', the general public sphere is always 'vulnerable to the repressive and exclusionary effects of unequally distributed social power, structural violence, and systematically distorted communication' (*BFN*: 307–8); and yet it always has a great 'advantage', that of being 'a medium of unrestricted [*uneingeschränkter*] communication', expressing the potentialities of communicative action related to the world of life.

> Here new problem situations can be perceived more sensitively, discourses aimed at achieving self-understanding can be conducted more widely and expressively, collective identities and need interpretations can be articulated with fewer compulsions than is the case in procedurally regulated public spheres. Democratically constituted opinion- and will-formation depends on

---

6.   The German text (*FG*: 373) talks about '*sozial abgegrenzte und zeitlich limitierte Öffentlichkeiten*' and '*Verhandlungen*' ('negotiations': the English translation uses the more generic term 'deliberations'). Here we can generally understand it as *public spaces and times* offering ideas and opinions to the decision-making process, as well as actual negotiation arenas where bargaining takes place in argumentative forms. Soon after, Habermas adds that '[d]emocratic procedures in such "arranged" publics structure opinion- and will-formation processes with a view to the cooperative solution of practical questions, including the negotiation of fair compromises' (*BFN*: 343).

7.   Nancy Fraser made one of the contributions at the conference for the English publication of *Strukturwandel* (*see* Chapter Five, Section 4, note 21), later published in Calhoun 1992. Fraser gave this definition: 'I shall call weak publics, publics whose deliberative practice consists exclusively in opinion formation and does not also encompass decision making' (Fraser 1992: 134).

8.   The translation introduces a sentence here ('The currents of public communication are channeled by mass media') that does not appear in the original: Habermas only speaks of 'publics' in the plural [*Öffentlichkeiten*]. They are internally organised ('*vereinsintern veranstalteten*') and then become 'elements' [*Bestandteile*] of an '*allgemeine Öffentlichkeit*' (*FG*: 373–4), a wider public sphere.

the supply of informal public opinions that, ideally, develop in structures of an unsubverted [*nicht-vermachtete*] political public sphere (*BFN*: 308).

Therefore, it is impossible that a deliberative procedure should be proposed, as does Cohen, as the foundation of an *integral* form of the democratic self-organisation of society; also, the very widespread forms of communicative and deliberative practice that can be and are developed in public spheres cannot be thought of as places of decision-making. What is more, *it is good that it is so.* The processes of formation and transformation of opinion developed in the public sphere are the more efficacious, creative and productive the more they are *untied* from ('relieved' of) some task or decision-making function.

This 'open' and non-decisional nature of the public sphere guides Habermas's criticism of those positions (within the liberal matrix) that would set limits or (self-) restrictions to the public debate, to prevent 'private' ethical beliefs or worldviews from becoming the subject of 'intractable' conflicts.[9] *Nothing* can be excluded from public discourse *a priori*. However, obviously,

> ... making something that so far has been considered a private matter a topic for public discussion does not yet imply any *infringement* of individual rights. Again, we must draw the distinction between public and private matters in two respects: accessibility and *thematization*, on the one hand, and the *regulation of powers* and responsibilities, on the other ... [E]very affair in need of political regulation should be publicly discussed, though not every legitimate object of public discussion will in fact be politically regulated (*BFN*: 313).

The very distinction between 'public' and 'private' cannot be taken as given once and for all and is itself the object of public discussion (*BFN*: 312–3). A 'non-restricted' public sphere thus becomes the best-suited place 'for the "struggle over needs" and their interpretation', concludes Habermas, quoting Nancy Fraser again (Fraser 1991).

'Processes of opinion-formation', Habermas says later,

> ... especially when they have to do with political questions, certainly cannot be separated from the transformation of the participants' preferences and attitudes, but they can be separated from putting these dispositions into action. To this extent, the communication structures of the public sphere *relieve* the public of *the burden of decision making*; the postponed decisions are reserved for the institutionalized political process (*BFN*: 361–2).

By their very nature, *public discourses* cannot be conceived as spaces or phases that *immediately* (that is, without filters or 'sluices' or some selective

---

9. In particular, Habermas discusses Ackerman's position on 'conversational constraints' (Ackerman 1980). Although he doesn't make any direct references to them, it is also reasonable to think of the 'gag rules' theorised by Holmes (1998a) or of the 'strategy of avoidance' proposed by Rawls (2005: 138–42) in this context.

mechanism) produce legitimate political decisions. The deliberative practice of the public sphere produces *communicative power* that can influence the decision-making processes of institutions and, thus, *gives* (or *takes away*) legitimacy; but it cannot be conceived as the making of legitimate decisions; these can only 'pass' through institutional democratic procedures. The meaning of the 'double track', therefore, is not an (obvious) distinction between public sphere and institutional sphere: what matters is the form that this *communicative circularity* between the opinion and decision can take. Nevertheless, in this way, the role of discourses and opinions is not at all belittled or depreciated: quite the opposite. What's at stake is fundamental: the degree of *democratic and discursive legitimation* that can (or *cannot*) accompany institutional decisions.

3. Cohen and Sabel's 'democratic experimentalism': a model of deliberative governance

In collaboration with Charles F. Sabel,[10] Cohen published an essay entitled 'Directly deliberative polyarchy' (Cohen and Sabel 1997; this essay is now in Cohen 2009a, from which my page references are taken); Cohen later took up the ideas proposed in this text in an essay devoted to Habermas, in which he rather harshly criticises the conclusions drawn in *Between Facts and Norms* (Cohen 1999). Cohen and Sabel's essay appears in many ways as a coherent development of the premises of Cohen's early works, where he indicated the ideal deliberative procedure as a possible model to follow in the project of new institutions. Here, this plan is made concrete in the proposal of an organic model of deliberative policy-making, or of deliberative governance, able to fully valorise the participatory dimension of democracy and exalt the potentialities of a *direct* and, at the same time, *deliberative* exercise of power within decisional processes. It was a proposal of 'democratic experimentalism', as Sabel and Michael Dorf defined it in a long and complex contemporary text, 'A constitution of democratic experimentalism' (1998), which Cohen and Sabel referred to as 'a companion' to their essay. Sabel and Dorf's text is also important because it fully encompasses the proposal of a 'directly deliberative polyarchy' within the very historiographical, political and constitutional debate we have come across many times throughout the present analysis. That debate revolves around a precise question: how to respond to the increasing distance between the 'administrative state' born with the New Deal and the form of government affirmed in American politics and the original design of

---

10. The case of Charles Sabel is another significant example of the great 'expansive' transdisciplinarity of the deliberative paradigm. A long-time lecturer at MIT in Boston, Sabel is currently Professor of Law and Social Science at Columbia University and is especially known for his studies on the 'post-Fordist' model, related to the field of political economy, conducted since the 1980s (*see* Piore and Sabel 1984; Sabel and Zeitlin 1997). A number of his works focus on the possible forms of deliberative governance, especially in a global and supra-national context (including Cohen and Sabel 2005; Sabel and Zeitlin 2010, 2012a and 2012b; Sabel *et al.* 2013). But also note an essay on 'Dewey, democracy and democratic experimentalism' (Sabel 2012).

the Constitution, with its view of the separation of powers.[11] 'To reinvigorate our Madisonian heritage', write the authors, 'we need a new model of institutionalized democratic deliberation that responds to the conditions of modern life' (Dorf and Sabel 1998: 283). However, they add,

> ... we offer the model of democratic experimentalism not as an alternative to the American constitutional tradition but as an interpretation of it. ... It reinterprets democratic deliberation to advance the Madisonian project of using the institutions of government itself to foster practical cooperation despite the human propensity for opportunism, including especially the abuse of public power for private ends (*ibid.*: 289).

Cohen and Sabel define a *directly deliberative polyarchy*[12] both as 'a form of democracy' (Cohen 2009a: 181) and as 'a novel form of public governance'. The authors write that it is 'an attractive kind of radical, participatory democracy with problem-solving capacities useful under current conditions and unavailable to representative systems'. 'In directly deliberative polyarchy', they write,

> ... collective decisions are made through public deliberation in arenas open to citizens who use public services or who are otherwise regulated by public decisions. But in deciding, those citizens must examine their own choices in the light of the relevant deliberation and experiences of others facing similar problems in comparable jurisdictions or subdivisions of government. Ideally, then, directly deliberative polyarchy combines the advantages of local learning and self-government with the advantages (and discipline) of wider social learning and heightened political accountability that result when the outcomes of many concurrent experiments are pooled to permit public scrutiny of the effectiveness of strategies and leaders (Dorf and Sabel 1998: 181).

The starting point of this proposal is 'a commonplace of contemporary political debate', that is, the widespread belief that, in all the important areas of public policies, 'current economic, and political institutions are not solving problems they are supposed to solve' (Cohen 2009a: 181). A second premise is given by the 'intrinsic appeal of collective decision-making that proceeds through direct participation by and reason-giving between and among free and equal citizens' (*ibid.*: 181–2). The aim and hope is to offer 'a consoling prospect for democrats in hard times' (*ibid.*: 182) but Cohen and Sabel are aware of how hard the task is: 'gestures of radical democracy' are usually exposed to many 'skeptical observations' that cast doubt on the problem-solving ability of a 'participatory self-government in vast, heterogeneous societies', or focus on the 'dark side' of localism. The first

---

11. *See*, in particular, Dorf and Sabel 1998: 270–83.

12. The term 'polyarchy' is accompanied by an explicit reference to the meaning given to it by Dahl, while stressing the insufficiency of Dahl's view with regard to a 'full democracy' (Cohen 2009a: 187–8).

part of the essay, then, is devoted to the analysis of 'conventional interpretations' of the crisis of contemporary democratic governance and its regulatory models: both those that focus only on the 'failures' of state regulation; those that emphasise market failures; and also those that trust in the recovery of a communitarian and pre-political dimension (*ibid.*: 182–6).

An alternative answer is sought through the proposal (of which they supply a few examples)[13] of regulatory models or arrangements that 'are not conventionally public because, in solving problems, they operate autonomously from the dictates of legislatures or public agencies' but which are not 'conventionally private' either, 'in that they do exercise problem-solving powers and their governance works through discussion among citizens rather than assignment of ownership right' (*ibid.*: 185). At the same time, Cohen and Sabel distance themselves from a vision of 'associative democracy': the new models of deliberative governance do not require a 'densely organized, trust-inspiring network of associations'; rather, they often emerge because the associative fabric is in a condition of 'distress' (*ibid.*).

Precisely because they are aware of the scepticism surrounding the idea of a 'radical democracy', the authors engage in a detailed proposal of their model of deliberative governance and its institutional architecture: they want to show 'the new form of state that would result from the generalization of deliberative problem-solving arrangements and foster their successful operation' (*ibid.*: 186). Note that the theoretical matrix of this new model seeks a fusion between the idea of direct participation and the idea of deliberative participation. In fact, the definition of the 'virtues' of the democratic ideal inspiring this proposal (*ibid.*: 188–90) encompass both the most recent developments on deliberative democracy but also the more distant roots of participatory democracy.

On the one hand, Cohen and Sabel take up a definition of the 'concrete benefits' of deliberation that, at the time, was already widespread in the deliberative field: deliberation increases cognitive and informative resources, allowing 'a more complete revelation of private information'; a deliberative setting induces an other-regarding attitude oriented towards (more) general interests; deliberation pushes the participants 'to be more reflective in their definition of problems and proposed strategies for solution' and originates 'a more complete definition and imaginative exploration of problems and solutions'; finally, 'if things work', it produces mutual trust and 'fosters future cooperation' (*ibid.*: 210–1).

On the other hand, they recall the roots of participatory democracy and, in particular, the culture of American pragmatism (politics as collective problem-solving and social learning). In a long footnote, Dorf and Sabel (1998: 415–8,

---

13. 'Our approach is conjectural. We are guided by political values, a view of current failures, and some hunches about promising developments ... [W]e take the very existence of these arrangements as a sign of the insufficiency of theories that explain what democracy can do and try to imagine what democracy could be from the vantage point of the possibilities suggested by their presence' (Cohen and Sabel 1997: 186). Among the experiences they recall are those conducted in Chicago on security and public order, reported by Archon Fung (2004) and in Fung and Wright 2003.

note 468) refer to 'the kinship between our proposal for directly deliberative democracy and certain strands of participatory democracy within the skein of Progressive thought in the early decades of this century'. Furthermore, also quoting Mattson's work (1998, *see* chapter 1, note 33), they mention various instances of participatory self-rule during those years and the role played by Mary Parker Follett and another eminent intellectual of the Progressive Era: Herbert Croly, the editor of the journal *New Republic*. Of course, they conclude, presenting 'these more or less distant antecedents to our own project' has one goal:

> ... the history matters because it attests to the perennity [sic] of the problem of reconciling democratic participation with the exercise of technical expertise. The (likewise perennial) hope of democratic experimentalism is to politicize the technocracy and transform the meaning of politics through practical collaboration (*ibid.*: 418, note 468).

Overall, Cohen insists on the value of a classic conception of 'radical democracy'. Such a conception

> ... emphasized the deficiencies of centralized power, the virtue of decentralization, the expressive and instrumental values of participation, and the values of citizen discussion both as an intrinsically attractive form of politics and as a good method of problem-solving (Cohen 2009a: 185).

From this perspective, democracy has *instrumental* finalities but also implies relevant 'educative aspects': 'by participating, citizens acquire political ideas in the light of which democracy itself is justified', that is, the sense of their freedom and equality as citizens. However, democracy also has an *epistemic* function: 'democracy provides a way to pool dispersed information relevant to problem-solving and to explore the range of possible solutions to practical problems: in short, a framework for collective learning' (*ibid.*: 190).

In particular, the philosophically pragmatist premises of this position are openly expressed in Dorf and Sabel's essay (1998: 284–6):

> The backdrop of our design is the pragmatist account of thought and action as problem solving in a world, familiar to our time, that is bereft of first principles and beset by unintended consequences, ambiguity, and difference. Thus, a central theme of the pragmatism of Peirce, Dewey, and Mead is the reciprocal determination of means and ends. Pragmatists argue that in science, no less than in industry and the collective choices of politics, the objectives presumed in the guiding understandings of theories, strategies, or ideals of justice are transformed in the light of the experience of their pursuit, and these transformations in turn redefine what counts as a means to a guiding end. ... Pragmatism thus takes the pervasiveness of unintended consequences, understood most generally as the impossibility of defining first principles that survive the effort to realize them, as a constitutive feature of thought and action, and not as an unfortunate incident of modern political life.

Referring to Dewey's *The Public and its Problems*, the authors conclude that democracy is indeed 'a method for identifying and correcting through public debate and action the unintended consequences of coordination among private actors' (*ibid.*: 286). For Cohen and Sabel, however, relying on the 'classical institutions of direct, assembly democracy' (Cohen 2009a: 186) or on more recent ones, like 'workers' councils' (*ibid.*: 194) is not the solution. Rather, it is possible to look forward to a new, 'modern set of arrangements of collective decision-making' inspired by the principles of *directness* and *deliberativeness* (*ibid.*).

This proposal follows a precise diagnosis of why traditional institutions fail at problem-solving: generally, they produce 'uniform solutions' which are rigid and come 'from above'. The more problems require 'locally specific' solutions, and the more the very environment is 'volatile' and complex, the less efficient and stable such top-down solutions prove. The paralysis and inefficiency of traditional policy-making can also be interpreted, 'in the game-theoretic sense', as a problem of '*failed coordination*' (*ibid.*: 194–5, my emphasis). However, it is expressed in various ways: the imbalance between centralised regulation (even if appropriate) and the control costs (such as safety in the workplace, because there may be 'too many workplaces for a central inspectorate to review' (*ibid.*: 207); the gap between goals and means in different situations and the variability of this relation; the need for continuous adjustment in the light of new information; and, most of all, 'the complexity of problems and solutions'. When 'problems are substantially the product of multiple causes and connected with other problems, crossing conventional policy domains and processes', such as 'urban poverty, local economic development, and effective social service delivery' (*ibid.*), for example, an appropriate co-ordination strategy is needed between the various areas. 'No surprise, then', add Cohen and Sabel, 'that the new problem-solving institutions have begun to emerge just in those areas – public safety, public education, economic restructuring – where established institutions have most broken down' (*ibid.*: 195).[14]

This '*mismatch* between solutions and available structures of decision-making' (*ibid.*: 208) cannot be overcome by a traditional 'strategy of federalist decentralization' (*ibid.*: 198) proposing a rigid division between central powers and local competences: this way of understanding federalism creates as such many other difficulties, 'because it does not require the units of decision-making to communicate and pool their information'. Therefore, it is not enough to say that 'uniform solutions are not optimal': local units, if operating in isolation, also 'lack the capacity to explore the full range of possible solutions' (*ibid.*: 198).[15]

---

14. For a wider analysis of these topics – government 'under diverse and volatile conditions' – *see* Dorf and Sabel 1998: 315 ff.

15. Cohen and Sabel signalled 'a familiar and inconclusive tug of war' very much present in American politics, especially when it comes to criticising federal agencies ('created precisely to adapt law to particular circumstances'). When specific problems arise, the trend is to 'stretch' the boundaries of a uniform state regulation; on the other hand, it is feared that 'the rule of law' might be threatened by pervasive particularism, so then the opposite direction is followed (Cohen and Sabel 1997: 197). The essay by Dorf and Sabel (1998: 277–9) dwells at length on these topics.

The proposal emerging from this diagnosis is that of an *institutionalised network of deliberative cooperation*: 'optimal problem-solving requires a scheme with local problem-solvers who, through institutionalized discussion, learn from the success and the failure of problem-solving efforts in locales like their own' (*ibid.*). But how to conceive of this network? For Cohen and Sabel, we must think of institutions that 'are friendly to local experimentation and are able to pool the results of those experiments in ways that permit outsiders to monitor and learn from those efforts' (*ibid.*: 199). Hence, a model of governance free from the localism typical of a communitarian participatory conception and yet able to preserve a form of participation that is both *direct* and *deliberative*:

> *direct participation* helps because participants can be assumed to have relevant information about the local contours of the problem and can relatively easily detect both deception by others and unintended consequences of past decision. *Deliberative participation* helps because it encourages the expression of differences in outlook and the provision of information more generally (*ibid.*: 199–200, my emphasis).

This is a polyarchic system of 'deliberative coordination' (*ibid.*: 200): a set of interrelated organisations and institutions corresponding to the conditions of *directness* and *deliberativeness*, but also very varied, 'from networks of private firms to public institutions working alongside associations' (*ibid.*). It is a network of deliberative arenas open to all those who, in one way or another, are touched by a problem and its possible solutions. Therefore, the architecture of this system involves a first level in which there are deliberative processes both *within* and *between* different deliberative units. However, it also implies the action of higher institutional levels that perform functions of control, co-ordination, monitoring and assessment but *do not rule* directly: in other words, they make sure that the single decisional units '*act deliberatively*' but they avoid replacing them 'so far as possible' (*ibid.*: 205–6).

A 'directly deliberative polyarchy', thus outlined, involves all the typical institutions as well as a *constitutional* framework (legislative assemblies, courts, executive and administrative agencies) and does not call into question the functions and roles of democratic electoral procedures. However, as Cohen and Sabel note, with this focus on problem-solving, the role of these institutions 'change[s] markedly'. Take, for instance, the function of legislative assemblies. Rejecting 'the Neo-Liberal Constitutionalist idea that problems are essentially recalcitrant to collective address', as well as 'the modern Civic Republican idea' that facing these issues 'requires only a more vigilant exclusion of private interests from national policy-making (and a correspondingly more acute intervention by technically adept guardians of the common good' (*ibid.*: 211), direct-deliberative democracy gives legislative assemblies a new role: 'to empower and to facilitate problem-solving through directly deliberative arenas operating in closer proximity than the legislature to the problems' (*ibid.*: 210–1). Concretely, this means that legislative assemblies can (*ibid.*: 212)

... declare areas of policy (education, community safety, environmental health) as open to directly deliberative polyarchal action; state general goals for policy in the area; assist potential deliberative arenas in organizing to achieve those goals; make resources available to deliberative problem-solving bodies that meet basic requirements on membership and benchmarking; and review at regular intervals the assignments of resources and responsibility.[16]

In parallel, the role of administrative agencies also changes: they must 'provide the infrastructure for information exchange between and among units'; and 'instead of seeking to solve problems', their task is to reduce 'the costs of information faced by different problem-solvers' (*ibid.*).[17]

There is no need here to delve deeper into the answers the authors gave to potential objections. What matters is to note that this model of deliberative governance should be considered quite unlike the many other methodological proposals that had already been, and would later be, made in the deliberative field. In fact, the latter often focused on specific *arenas* in which good deliberation could take place, whereas the present idea is different and more ambitious. The underlying basis of this model was the knowledge that a traditional emphasis on the 'participation' of citizens proves fragile and insufficient in the face of policy-making in complex societies. The supporters of 'radical democracy' could not escape a substantial burden of proof: to demonstrate the possibility of a comprehensive model of governance that was both 'participative' and 'deliberative' and that did not circumvent the crux of the democratic legitimacy of the procedures so defined. That's the reason why I believe that Cohen and Sabel's proposal, despite raising many problems, is a deeply ambitious approach to deliberative democracy: it aims to provide an innovative model to construct public policies and collective choices, giving widespread participation a deliberative function, oriented to problem-solving.

---

16. This role 'does not, of course, preclude national solutions through legislative enactment when uniform solutions are preferable ... or when externalities overwhelm local problem-solving' (Cohen and Sabel 1998: 212). A wider and more detailed analysis of the national institutional context can be found in Dorf and Sabel 1998: 339 and ff. Note what Jane Mansbridge wrote in her contribution to the volume edited by Fung and Wright on *Empowered Participatory Governance* (Mansbridge 2003a: 176–8): 'the original theory of participatory democracy simply devolved power to the lowest possible level'. This model has not worked and the new reflection on participatory democracy must today be based on a 'recombination', on a different articulation between local levels and central levels endowed with essential functions of control, evaluation and monitoring, as well as power of sanction.

17. The essay by Dorf and Sabel dwelt longer on the 'architecture' of this new institutional design (1998: 283 and ff.), underlining that it wasn't an 'abstract' project but something that was already inscribed in the potential of American democracy: 'We claim that many of the elements of this structure have already been established in the practices of state and local governments, Congress, administrative agencies, and the Supreme Court, and that its adoption might be accomplished piecemeal by drawing on the available precursors' (*ibid.*: 284).

4. Cohen *versus* Habermas: the 'public sphere' – informal or structured?

I have dwelt extensively on the essays by Cohen and Sabel and Dorf and Sabel because they can be considered among the most significant examples of a phenomenon to which we have already referred: that is, the overlap between the theoretical developments of 'deliberative democracy' and the return of the idea of 'participatory democracy'. In many ways – with their emphasis on *directness* – these authors propose a view that is a veritable theoretical synthesis between the two perspectives. However, their proposal tries to escape the risks of 'participatory elitism' found in those approaches to deliberative democracy that saw the *mini-public* as a potential answer to the critical condition of contemporary democracies. In fact, Cohen, in a later essay written with Archon Fung, distanced himself decisively from the logic of mini-publics (Cohen and Fung 2004). Acknowledging that there is, undoubtedly, tension between participation and deliberation, and claiming that it is nevertheless possible to achieve a 'participatory deliberation' (*ibid.*: 28), they disagree with two ideas: first, that a 'mass' participatory deliberation might only take place in the informal public sphere, with no direct exercise of power; and, second, that the solutions should be entrusted to a 'randomly selected small groups of citizens'. The latter, note the authors, only work as '*advisory bodies*', 'whose impact – to the extent that they have impact – comes from their ability to alter public opinion or change the minds of public officials (*ibid.*: 29–30). On the other hand, the proposal of '*directly deliberative polyarchy*', or the similar one of 'empowered participatory governance', could open the way to wider participation. '[W]hereas political juries recruit impartial and disinterested citizens by randomly selecting them, participatory-deliberative arrangements recruit participants with strong interests in the problems under deliberation' (*ibid.*: 30).

Cohen and Sabel did not just 'come up with' their new model: apart from the experiments with new models of participatory governance it could refer to, this proposal was rooted in a precise diagnosis of the 'evils' of contemporary policy-making, as well as in a reading of the social transformations of the 'post-Fordist' age (where you can see a more specific contribution by Sabel). Rigid, uniform and centralised models of social regulation have turned out to be increasingly inefficient, with a growing tension between 'contextual knowledge' and 'formal knowledge'; between claims of rule 'from above' and instances of control 'from below'. However, we can also interpret this as an attempt to answer Habermas's criticism of the early formulations of the ideal deliberative procedure proposed by Cohen; after all, Cohen himself, in his 1997 essay and even more so in his 1999 work, presented these theses as a critical response to Habermas and his 'two-track' model.

A very widespread reading of Habermas's view of the relation between public sphere and institutional sphere had heavily underlined some aspects of this theoretical model: in particular, the idea that the former is an *informal* sphere, one in which an 'anarchic', 'peripheral' and 'subject-less' network of discourses can only *influence* – at most, 'besiege' – the central sphere of the state and its legitimate decisional procedures. There is no way it could go further than that

('*Diskurse herrschen nicht*' ...). Many, including Cohen, considered this view insufficient and rather reductive: most of all, this view appeared resigned, devoid of critical edge or ambition. Habermas, writes Cohen (1999: 385), 'is a radical democrat', as he keeps referring to the 'ideal of 'a self-organizing community of free and equal citizens [Habermas, 1996: 7] coordinating their collective affairs through their common reason' (Cohen 1999: 385). And yet, just like many others, his view has now become

> ... defensive, self-consciously chastened, typically directed more to limiting (at times by novel means) the erosion of the institutions of nineteenth-century parliamentary democracy than to transforming and extending them. In part, these limited ambitions are a prudent response to the temper of the times, hostile since the fall of the planned economies to any hint of collective control over life choices of individuals, and skeptical, more broadly, about the very idea of public action (Cohen 2009a: 217).

Cohen quotes a passage from the Preface to *Between Facts and Norms* (Habermas 1996: xiii–xiv):

> I have no illusions about the problems that our situation poses and the moods it evokes. But moods – and philosophies in a melancholic 'mood' – do not justify the defeatist surrender of the radical content of democratic ideals. I will propose a new reading of this content, one appropriate to the circumstances of a complex society.

'We agree', commented Cohen, 'with the observation about moods and their unfortunate consequences, but – as will emerge – think that Habermas has surrendered too much' (Cohen 2009a: 217, note 34).

The main focus of criticism is therefore Habermas's 'dispiriting meltdown of popular sovereignty', as Michelman describes it in an article quoted by Cohen (Cohen 1999: 409): popular sovereignty can now only be expressed dispersedly, finding new themes to submit to the public agenda and perhaps influencing legislation and administration; it cannot take the form of actual *self-ruling*. On the contrary, Cohen writes that 'the "old-fashioned", radical-democratic ideal of a self-governing association of free and equal citizens – authors of laws, not merely their addressees – still can connect to modern politics' (*ibid.*: 410). As you can see, this is the same view of democracy as a 'macro-association', self-governed through deliberative procedures, that Habermas had already polemically addressed – only, in the light of the new developments of his theory, Cohen thinks he can now provide a more articulated and 'concrete' view of it (*ibid.*: 410–11):

> Habermas thinks it suffices to make the case for autonomous influence flowing from the periphery, under conditions of crisis. But once that the case is on hand, we can ask whether there are other forms of citizen participation that would more fully achieve the radical-democratic promise. Those forms would need

to meet three conditions: they must permit and encourage inputs that reflect experiences and concerns that may not occupy the current agenda (sensors, rooted in local experiences and information); they must provide disciplined assessments of proposals through deliberation that encompasses fundamental political values; and (here we go beyond Habermas's emphasis on social movements in periods of crisis) they must also provide more institutionalized, regularized occasions for citizen participation in collective decision-making (and, perhaps, by so doing, improve the quality of discourse in the 'informal public sphere'). In brief, they must be autonomous, deliberative, and institutional.

For Cohen, this view offers a different, more critical and '*redemptive*' (*ibid.*: 414) approach than Habermas's. First of all, 'the public arena' is conceived as '*organizationally dispersed*', not focused on the impact that it can have on a national legislative assembly but on the multiplicity of decision-centres that act in a democracy; yet capable (based on the criteria defined above) of creating a network of deliberative co-operation. Second (and most importantly), public deliberation thus conceived 'cuts across the distinction between reflection on political purposes and efforts to address problems in light of those purposes' (*ibid.*). 'This marriage of principles and problem-solving' allows for 'an effectiveness to public engagement that is absent from Habermas's account' (*ibid.*). For Habermas, instead, 'the problem-solving institutions remain fixed in design and conception' and citizens can only discuss 'and not solve problems' (*ibid.*). Ultimately, Cohen concludes, Habermas's idea cannot tell us anything about how 'to redirect the ensemble of institutions to ensure a controlling role for the communicative power of free and equal citizens. I see no compelling reason for that self-limitation' (*ibid.*: 415).

This criticism does grasp some gaps or weaknesses of Habermas's theoretical model; however, it does not take into account many other aspects of this model that, in my view, are fully compatible with Cohen and Sabel's idea of deliberative governance. More generally, I'd say that Habermas's model is compatible with a vision of *democratic procedures* that manages to understand fully the space of *new participatory and deliberative institutions* and the role of a new institutional articulation of decision-making endowed with *democratic legitimacy*. In fact, there is no doubt that the dichotomy on which Habermas constructs his 'two-track' model is rigid and fails to understand the complexity of contemporary policy-making. However, the dichotomy that should be critically analysed is not that between public sphere and institutional sphere but rather that between *communicative* power and *administrative* power.

Habermas has no intention of giving up a classical view of the separation of powers – and he has very good reasons not to. Nevertheless, his approach collapses the functions of executive power into administrative ones and tends to conceive of the latter as merely technical and bureaucratic. He is too busy reaffirming the bonds of democratic *legality* and *legitimacy* that administrative apparatuses must respect, curbing their tendency to become autonomous: the heart of political decision, thus, can only be entrusted to the legislative dimension and the rule of law.[18] It is a fact of daily experience, however, that there is a relevant space for forms of governance that cannot be reduced to mere 'administration' (execution and application of laws) but are fully political and *can* – this is the decisive point – be based on democratic and deliberative processes, just as they can, in the opposite sense, be the victims of technocratic or oligarchic 'closure' (which is what happens fairly often nowadays). The networks of governance that today govern many spheres of public policy *can* be open and deliberative, endowed with their own democratic legitimacy, or they can be *closed* and ruled (mainly or exclusively) by logics of bureaucratic rule and/or negotiation between constituted interests. This is the theoretical and political space within which to conceive the *possible* development of new forms of deliberative governance: in this sense, approaches like Cohen and Sabel's democratic experimentalism certainly offer important insights and suggestions, not least because the two authors are careful not to forget the *constitutional frame* of their direct-deliberative model.

Nevertheless, I believe that imagining these (or similar) institutional innovations does not at all imply abandoning Habermas's theoretical basis. The distinction between a public political sphere – where deliberative practice takes place, expressing its own communicative power – and an institutional sphere – guaranteed by a constitutional framework and therefore endowed with its own *democratic legitimacy* – is still valid. Furthermore, *at the same time*, the idea that the communicative power produced in the public sphere is what ignites another source of democratic legitimacy – the discursive and deliberative one – should not be abandoned either. The risk of adopting Cohen's idea while giving up Habermas' theoretical framework is that we will still have *too concrete* a view of popular sovereignty (as Habermas defined it): that it can only exist if *directly* exercised – as it is generally taken for granted that if citizens *only discuss* and 'do not solve problems', this, as such, implies a devaluation of the role and special 'power' of deliberative participation.

The real potential weakness of Habermas's model is a view of the public sphere that sees *only* its *informal* traits – and there is no doubt that many passages by Habermas support this idea. Nevertheless, at many crucial points in *Between Facts and Norms*, we find that the *network of discourses* that makes up deliberative politics is, or can be, an *institutionalised network* (and we can reproach Habermas for lack of clarification and sufficient explanation here). In other words, this network can only result in legitimate decisions that must have a legal and juridical form but it unfolds in a multiplicity of separate places and moments. Such a network (*see* Chapter Eight, Section 4) is articulated through pragmatic, ethical and moral, but also *applicative* discourses; the discursive dimension also enters fully within

---

18. Habermas remains faithful to a classic vision of 'executive' power; nor does he provide any specific definition of governance. On this, see Ferrara 1999: 56–8. I have dealt with some aspects of this topic elsewhere (Floridia 2012: 54–60). Today, the literature on governance is wide and increasing: for a general overview, *see* Rhodes 1997; Bevir 2009, 2010, 2011b and 2013; and Palumbo 2015.

the 'institutionally regulated negotiations' and the 'spontaneous' ones where the parties negotiate a fair compromise. Also, in Habermas's view, the public sphere is not only anonymous or atomised but also involves collective and/or organised agents: both those that strategically enforce their *social power* (a *distorting* power) and those who keep its critical and open nature alive (movements, associations and so on). Finally, the public sphere is articulated at *three levels* (Habermas 1996: 360–1): that of informal communications and daily interactions; the 'abstract' and virtual level created by mass communications; and, at an intermediate level, also that of 'public spheres [that] still cling to the concrete locales where an audience is physically gathered', which can usually rely on 'architectural metaphors' ('forums, stages, arenas, and the like').

This theoretical scheme, in my view, is fully consistent with the idea that the public sphere can also involve the action of deliberative 'institutionalised' arenas producing a more structured *public discourse*; focused on specific 'problems to solve' and located indeed at this intermediate level identified by Habermas.[19] The German philosopher surely failed to see some possible implications of his own approach but the characteristics of his 'reconstructive' theoretical model invite us to verify its validity in the presence of *new* phenomena yet to be critically understood. And these processes can indeed be those of a new *institutional articulation* of the places and moments through which, in different circumstances, opinions are formed or political decisions and collective choices are made.

Of course, if we adopt the idea of deliberative politics and the 'two-track' model proposed by Habermas, decisions necessarily take on a *juridical* form or framework that is certainly new and different from the past, but that still has such a form: their legitimacy must ultimately rest on a basis of constitutional legitimacy. But, upon closer inspection, what is it that Cohen and Sabel (rightly) have in mind when they imagine a *superior* institutional level, co-ordinating and supporting the network of local deliberative units? What are they thinking of when they hypothesise a type of *legislative* production, albeit different from the past (rigid, general and abstract) one? What can give democratic *legitimacy* to the network of de-centred and co-ordinated deliberative arenas, if not a *procedural framework* that institutionalises the discourses produced and the choices made there?

Naturally, the *informal, open, anarchic* public sphere – which produces and communicates opinions, finds new problems, produces new ideas – remains ineliminable from the background. However, we might very well think that the

---

19. Habermas later (2005: 388) gave some important insights on this: here he also recalls his idea of 'the functional differentiation of discourses, depending on the place deliberation and decision-making in each case occupy within the larger context of the political system as a whole. With this "systemic view" in mind, we can develop more specific hypotheses on what kind of results discourse and negotiation are expected to yield in different settings and in view of different conflicts. Political deliberation can serve many purposes, for example, the formation of relevant, instructive and influential opinions in the public sphere, or the generation of informed votes on competing platforms among citizens … or reasonable decisions on legal programs in parliament, or the rational choice and effective implementation of policies within the administration, or legitimate solutions for legal conflicts in court, etc.'.

electoral and parliamentary procedures of a representative democracy, though these remain fundamental and unavoidable, are, nevertheless, not the only 'sluice' filtering the communicative power of public discourses (channelling the deliberative practice and structuring political opinions and judgments). There can be other 'sluices' at a preliminary level, 'upstream', so to speak, *before* the flow reaches the democratic institutions whose task it is to produce legitimate decisions. These 'sluices' organise and institutionalise public discourses and fair negotiations, institutions and practices that can enrich the deliberative quality of a democracy. After all, as Nadia Urbinati put it (2014: 12–13),

> ... through its long and honourable history, democracy has shown great imaginative ability to devise institutions and procedures that are capable of solving problems that democracy's political process of decision prompts. ... [D]emocracy survived in difficult times and circumstances thanks to its uniquely fertile institutional and normative imagination and capacity of innovation.

The times in which we now live force us to exercise such a capacity.

Chapter Eleven

Rawls: The Idea of 'Public Reason' and Deliberative Democracy

1. Introduction

In the previous chapters, we have seen how relevant Rawls was to the constitutive phase of the theoretical field of deliberative democracy. Nevertheless, his influence was controversial: if Manin questioned the lack of a proper deliberative dimension in the original theoretical framework of *Theory of Justice*, Cohen had based his 'deduction' of an ideal of deliberative democracy precisely on Rawls's theory. As we have seen, Cohen had introduced a 'deliberative' element into Rawls's theoretical structure: the mutual reason-giving between free and equal citizens as the key of the democratic legitimacy of a decisional procedure. This move, I think, might have influenced Rawls himself.

Rawls's impact, though, surely cannot be reduced to specific dialogue with his various interlocutors: we can agree with Bohman and Rehg when, as we have recalled, they identify the 'non-aggregative conception of the common good' proposed in *Theory of Justice* as Rawls's contribution to the creation of a new horizon of democratic thought in the 1970s (1997: xii and xxviii, note 9). But Rawls's input appears to have been important mainly with regard to one particular point, at that stage: his radical criticism of the utilitarian paradigm that dominated political philosophy at the time and the construction of new theoretical tools able to attack the mainstream of democratic theory, then based on Schumpeter's and Downs's models (even though participatory democracy had already criticised that paradigm). Rawls's proposition of an updated contractualist approach to political philosophy, bringing back figures like Kant and Rousseau, had great critical potential with regard to the then-dominant models. The idea of a just society based on the freedom, equality and the moral/political autonomy of citizens – as well as the idea of citizens as *constructors* of social co-operation and not merely individual *agents* trying to maximise their wellbeing and protect their private freedom – opened up very different perspectives from those that had prevailed until then.

The importance of Rawls's position to the landscape of contemporary political philosophy and, in particular, the power and scope of his project to redefine an idea of political liberalism, are unquestionable. However, what is not obvious is what role Rawls's played in the 'deliberative turn' characterising contemporary democratic thought between the 1980s and the 1990s.[1]

This discussion has mainly centred on the interpretation of a key notion of *Political Liberalism*: the idea of 'public reason'. This idea – along with the ways in which Rawls presented it in 1993, supplemented in the 1995 Introduction to the paperback edition of *PL* and 'revisited' in 1997 – is not immediately and intuitively understandable. The notion of public reason raises many questions: is public reason a form of deliberative rationality? What status can we attribute to it? Why does Rawls sometimes speak of the 'idea' of public reason while at other times, perhaps more often, he presents it as an 'ideal'? Is it an interpretative and descriptive category or, on the contrary, a normative and prescriptive one? That is, does it indicate a way of being of the public and collective rationality at work in our constitutional democracies or is it some regulative ideal, an *ought-to-be* that is essential for a well ordered democracy?[2]

In this chapter, I present and analyse the concept of public reason, asking how, through this notion, Rawls contributed to the definition and consolidation of the theoretical foundations of deliberative democracy, as well as how this contribution affected the way in which the theoretical deliberative field was articulated. In the next chapter, I will look at the dialogue between Rawls and Habermas that took place in 1995; for now, I can anticipate this far: the ideal of democracy proposed by Rawls is that of a democracy that can be called *deliberative* if and insofar as the principle of legitimacy underlying it is a *principle of discursive reciprocity*. In other words, a society can be well ordered and democratic if its citizens, free and equal bearers of (sometimes radically) different worldviews, are still able to find potential agreement on the *constitutional essentials* and the *matters of basic justice*, doing so based on a mutual and public process of *reason-giving*. During such a process, every citizen publicly *justifies*, proposes and supports freestanding political values that other citizens can reasonably be expected to accept. Therefore, we can read a key notion like that of public reason as Rawls's particular answer to an issue that, as we have seen, was crucial to all those trying to elaborate a deliberative conception of democracy: a notion of *public deliberation* as a *source of democratic legitimacy*.[3]

1. Charles Girard and Alice Le Goff (2010: 32), argue that both Habermas and Rawls, with their works of the 1990s, 'fully participate in the development of deliberative democracy'; however, 'even though he presents his concept of public reason as an essential element of all deliberative democracy, Rawls is not always considered as belonging to this current'. For an illustration of this thesis, *see also* Girard 2009. Dryzek (2010: 29) claims that 'Rawls is a deliberative theorist, but not a deliberative democrat, his own self-description notwithstanding'.

2. Henceforth, I will abbreviate *Political Liberalism* as *PL*; the essay 'The idea of public reason' as IPR; and the later essay 'The idea of public reason revisited' as IPRR. When I refer to an '*Introduction*' I mean the new introduction to the 1995 paperback edition of *PL*; the page numbers all refer to the *expanded edition* of *Political Liberalism* published in 2005.

3. In his work on Rawls, Freeman writes that 'the two main questions' that *PL* tries to answer are: 'one regarding the practical *possibility* of a well-ordered liberal society, and the other the conditions of the *legitimacy* of the exercise of power in a liberal society' (Freeman 2007a: 324).

2. The idea of public reason

The text in which, for the first time, Rawls speaks of deliberative democracy is 'The idea of public reason', published in 1993 as Lecture VI of *Political Liberalism*.[4] However, he only mentioned 'deliberative democracy' in a footnote, referring to Joshua Cohen's essay 'Deliberation and democratic legitimacy' 'for a valuable discussion of the idea of deliberative democracy' (IPR: 214).[5] Of course, the sense of Rawls's contribution to the idea (and the ideal) of deliberative democracy lies, as we shall see, in the overall theoretical proposal Rawls makes in this work. Nevertheless, the fact that the expression 'deliberative democracy' appears so marginally (this is already 1993) surely raises some questions. Rawls openly comes to a notion of deliberative democracy only at the end of his theoretical journey – even though, obviously, when interpreting his thought, one could rightly claim that the presuppositions for it were already present. 'Deliberative democracy' appears more extensively in his next essay, 'The idea of public reason revisited', even though again in reference to Cohen.[6]

So, in his 1993 essay, Rawls doesn't yet speak of deliberative democracy. What the philosopher speaks of, instead, is the idea of *public reason*. As an authoritative interpreter of Rawls has put it, this idea is 'easily misunderstood' but also objectively 'complicated' (Freeman 2007a: 383).[7] To understand this notion, we have to start from the fundamental problem Rawls tackles in *Political Liberalism*: 'how is it possible that there can be a stable and just society whose free and equal citizens are deeply divided by conflicting and even incommensurable religious, philosophical, and moral doctrines?' (*PL*: 133).[8] In other words, the issue is that

---

4. As often happens with Rawls, preliminary versions of this text had already been the subject of lectures and conferences (held, in this case, in 1990 at the University of California). However, unlike the other essays in *Political Liberalism*, 'The idea of public reason' was published for the first time in the first edition of the book (1993).

5. I should point out that this note was devoted to 'some recent views that are roughly speaking liberal though different', quoting, among others, Charles Larmore in *Patterns of Moral Complexity* (1987) and the essay 'Political liberalism' (1990) and Ronald Dworkin in *A Matter of Principle* (1985).

6. 'The idea of public reason revisited' was first published in the *Chicago Law Review*, in the summer issue of 1997 and is one of the last things Rawls wrote before he fell ill (he died in 2002). Rawls wanted to include this essay in a new edition of *Political Liberalism* because, as he wrote to his editor at Columbia University Press, he thought it was 'by far the best statement I have written on ideas of public reason and political liberalism' (IPRR: 438).

7. For a general introduction to Rawls, *see* Freeman 2007a and Maffettone 2010. *See also* the two *Companions* dedicated to Rawls: one edited by Freeman (2003a) and a more recent one edited by Jon Mandle and David A. Reidy (2013). A chapter devoted to Rawls and the evolution of his thought can be found in Ferrara 1999: 13–36. In general, on Rawls's liberalism, *see* Nagel 2003 and Dreben 2003. On *Political Liberalism*, *see also* a recent collection of essays, edited by Thom Brooks and Martha C. Nussbaum (2015). More specifically, on the notion of public reason, *see* Larmore 2003; Freeman 2007a: 342–415, 2007b: 215–58; Maffettone 2010: 260–92; and Ferrara 2008: 63–79).

8. The same question, with slightly different formulations, will reoccur in *PL* on p. 4, at the opening of Lecture IV, dedicated to the idea of *overlapping consensus* (*PL*: 133) and in the 1995 Introduction (xxxvii).

of the possible ways in which to reconcile 'justice', 'stability' and 'pluralism'. In order to avoid possible misunderstandings, I should clarify that in Rawls's jargon 'stability' does not refer to the instrumental problem of a political and social order that must receive 'consensus' or that should be protected or immunised from conflict or change. Rather, 'stability' evokes the classical and radical questions asked by Hobbes or Rousseau: how is social order possible? What grounds the possibility that a society can exist and reproduce itself over time, without falling into chaos or regressing to the 'state of nature'? What are the bases of social unity?

The idea of public reason, though, is not logically deduced based on the internal need for development of a theoretical model (as was the case for many concepts present in *Theory of Justice*); it emerges from a specific question regarding *our* constitutional democracies, the historical process of how they were constituted and the problems they are facing *today*. The idea of public reason appears as an answer to a constitutive and irreversible datum of contemporary democracies: 'the fact of reasonable pluralism'. 'The diversity of reasonable comprehensive religious, philosophical, and moral doctrines found in modern democratic societies is not a mere historical condition that may soon pass away; it is a permanent feature of the public culture of democracy (*PL*: 36).[9]

Many other questions revolve around this issue: how to guarantee that the radical pluralism of our societies can be democratically governed? How to avoid liberalism collapsing into scepticism and relativism or tolerance becoming merely the expression of a mutually indifferent co-existence or of a fragile *modus vivendi*? And, most of all, how to affirm, in these conditions, a new conception of democratic legitimacy? Rawls answers these questions with his view of a renewed political liberalism and using the entire complex conceptual apparatus that he had developed during his theoretical journey from *Theory of Justice* to *Political Liberalism*: his conception of the two *moral powers* of the person – their 'sense of justice' and ability to have and review their own idea of the common good (*PL*: 19); the distinction between 'conceptions' and 'political values' on the one hand and 'comprehensive doctrines' on the other; the distinction between 'rational' and 'reasonable';[10] the idea of *overlapping consensus*.

In this process, the idea of public reason plays a fundamental role. As we have seen in the authors analysed thus far, including Habermas, deliberative 'democracy' or 'politics' appears as a possible answer to the issues of a renewed and appropriate conception of democratic legitimacy or of the ways in which processes of democratic legitimation take place. We can say that the notion of *public reason*, in Rawls, plays a similar role: public reason is an *ideal* (or a

---

9.   Note that Rawls speaks more precisely of a pluralism of 'reasonable comprehensive doctrines'. I'll go back to the terms comprehensive and reasonable later in this chapter but, for now, I want to note that the threat to stability does not come from 'unreasonable' doctrines (fundamentalist, closed to dialogue, impermeable to any possibility of revision) - Rawls acknowledges their existence, but he thinks they are not strong enough to endanger the stability of a democratic order. Rather, the threat is the very fact that there is a radical pluralism of *reasonable* comprehensive doctrines. On this point, *see* Freeman 2007a: 340–1 and Dreben 2003: 318–9.

10. Rawls introduces and deals with this distinction in *PL* (Lecture II, § 1).

paradigm, as we shall see) to follow so as to give stable and legitimate bases to our constitutional democracies. And perhaps we can also understand Rawls's terminological oscillation: public reason is an *ideal* but also an *idea*, something that can be seen *at work*, so to speak, in the history and reality of *our* constitutional democracies.

At the beginning of his essay, Rawls offers a few preliminary definitions:

> A political society ... has a way of formulating its plans, of putting its ends in an order of priority and of making its decisions accordingly. The way a political society does this is its reason; its ability to do these things is also its reason, though in a different sense: it is an intellectual and moral power, rooted in the capacities of its human members (IPR: 212–13)

Every political society – just as any individual and any other associated body – lives by the use of reason: it formulates plans, defines priorities and makes decisions accordingly. However, 'not all reasons are public reasons' and not all *uses* of reason are public: rather, the reasons given by individuals *as citizens* (not as private individuals or as members of an association) are public and they are such because their object is the *public good*. The reasons whose object is 'the political conception of justice' relating to 'society's basic structure of institutions' are public, with the consequent implications this has in relation to the ends and goals of the citizens (IPR: 213).

The adjective 'public' referred to reason, adds Rawls, has a triple value: reason is public 'as the reason of citizens as such' ('the reason of the public': that is, what emerges from the exercise of the collective rationality and reasonableness of the citizens); it is public as 'its subject is the good of the public and matters of fundamental justice'; and it is public as it is publicly exercised. So, reason is 'public' insofar as it is *publicly* expressed by *citizens* and deals with the ideals and contents of a political conception of justice of a society and its basic institutions (*PL*: 213). Elaborating on a Kantian distinction[11] and, as McCarthy (1994: 50) noted, distinguishing 'public from non public uses of reason in a somewhat unusual way', Rawls clarified that the adjective 'public' is not set against 'private' but rather against *non-public*:

---

11. In a footnote (IPR: 213, note 2) Rawls recalls Kant's 'What is enlightenment?' and the German philosopher's distinction between public and private reason. For 'a valuable account' of Kant's theses, Rawls refers the reader to chapter 2 of Onora O'Neill's *Constructions of Reason* (1989). Apart from this reference, O'Neill's text is important because it clearly shows the Kantian matrix of the notion of 'public reason': for instance, in the interpretation of Kantian *sensus communis* (O'Neill, 1989: 25–6), that is, the capacity to have the 'sense' of what is or can be in common with others, expressing judgments from the point of view of other people. However, another decisive source of the notion of public reason is certainly Rousseau, especially some passages of his 'Discourse on political economy' of 1755, in which Rousseau distinguishes between an individual's 'own reason' and the 'public reasons' which the same individual must answer to as a citizen (*see* Freeman 2007b: 20).

... first of all, there are many nonpublic reasons and but one public reason. Among the nonpublic reasons are those of associations of all kinds: churches and universities, scientific societies and professional groups. As we have said, to act reasonably and responsibly, corporate bodies, as well individuals, need a way of reasoning about what is to be done. This way of reasoning is public with respect to their members, but nonpublic with respect to political society and to citizens generally. Nonpublic reasons comprise the many reasons of civil society and belong to what I have called the 'background culture', in contrast with the public political culture. These reasons are social, and certainly not private (IPR: 220).

Based on these first definitions, Rawls tackles the issue of the problems and content of public reason as well as the 'forums' and places in which citizens exercise their *public reasoning*: that is, the use of their reason that is specifically referred to the *public* dimension of their social life (unlike 'private' or 'social' but non-public uses). The 'public reason' is not the set of discourses (and, we could also say, of deliberations) that citizens produce while generally facing political problems and public issues: the exercise of public reason mainly revolves around the discussion of the 'constitutional essentials' and 'the questions of basic justice'. In other words, it mainly revolves around the discussion of the very principles of constitutional legitimacy. 'In a democratic society public reason is the reason of equal citizens who, as a collective body, exercise final political and coercive power over one another in enacting laws and in amending their constitution' (IPR: 214). As Charles Larmore (2003: 383) put it, 'the terms of political association must form part of a public consensus because of their essentially coercive character'. Only if there is consensus on the constitutional essentials can people accept the unavoidable coercion related to the application of ordinary legislation – the outcome of a changing and contingent application of the majority principle.

At this point, and in what follows, the reader might feel rather disoriented by Rawls's recurrent reference to the *limits* of public reason, which seems like a sort of worry about an unwarranted extension of the areas where public reason applies. 'The first point is that the limits imposed by public reason do not apply to all political questions but only to those involving what we may call "constitutional essentials" and questions of basic justice' (IPR: 214). Rawls gives examples of such issues ('special subjects of public reason') soon after: 'who has the right to vote, or what religions are to be tolerated, or who is to be assured fair equality of opportunity, or to hold property' (*ibid.*). These issues must only be solved by invoking '*political values*', that is, drawing *not* on the reasons rooted in the comprehensive doctrines of each citizen (their 'worldviews', be they religious or philosophical) but only on *political* (public) reasons that should be acceptable to other citizens, too. That is why public reason imposes limits: when it comes to issues of constitutional relevance or basic justice, its exercise is bound to the search for *political* justifications, abstracting them and separating them from moral, religious or philosophical ones, which are expressed in the 'background culture' of a society.

These 'limits', adds Rawls,

> ... do not apply to our personal deliberations and reflections about political questions, or to the reasoning about them by members of associations such as churches and universities, all of which is a vital part of the background culture. Plainly, religious, philosophical, and moral considerations of many kinds may here properly play a role. *But the ideal of public reason does hold for citizens when they engage in political advocacy in the public forum* ... (IPR: 215, my emphasis).

And at this point, Rawls makes a series of precise identifications and restrictions, which seem to *reserve* the use of public reason to specific agents and places or moments: this limitation seems to contradict his statement that the ideal of public reason holds for all citizens who enter a public forum. However, Rawls actually identifies a series of *figures* that, by their nature, have to respect the ideal of public reason more than others, as well as *moments* in which this duty must especially be respected or in which public reason can be expressed exemplarily: still, public reason is an idea or an ideal that concerns *all* citizens *as* citizens. This 'ideal', writes Rawls, thus holds 'for members of political parties' and 'for candidates in their campaigns'; 'it holds equally for how citizens are to vote in elections when constitutional essentials and matters of basic justice are at stake' (*ibid.*). And as for citizen-voters, Rawls refers the reader to § 2.4, where he critically discusses the idea that voting is 'a private and even personal matter', based on the view either that citizens vote according to their preferences and personal interests, or that they vote following 'what they see as right and true as their comprehensive convictions direct without taking into account public reasons'. However, neither view 'recognizes the duty of civility' nor does either respect 'the limits of public reason in voting on matters of constitutional essentials and questions of basic justice': 'the first view is guided by our preferences and interests, the second view by what we see as the whole truth' (IPR: 219). The *ideal* of public reason, instead, expresses 'a view about voting on fundamental questions in some ways reminiscent of Rousseau's *Social Contract*', in which voting was considered 'as *ideally* expressing our opinion as to which of the alternatives best advances the common good' (IPR: 219–20, my emphasis).

This reference to Rousseau offers a key for interpreting the logic of Rawls's argumentation; more precisely, here we find the distinction between *homme* and *citoyen* (which takes on the value of an ideal and normative projection). Public reason is something one can find in the reality of our democratic societies (and therefore is *an idea* that allows us to understand how they work) but it is also defined as an *ideal*: 'an ideal conception of citizenship for a constitutional democratic regime' (IPR: 213). When there are fundamental political issues at stake *we should think and act* in accordance with the idea of public reason: that is, we should each *reason by thinking of ourselves as citizens* and be *public-spirited*, so to speak. These passages of Rawls's argumentation were well clarified in the later IPRR, when the sense of the first restrictions became explicit (which leads us to exclude any interpretation seeing public reason as something only concerning representatives, judges, parties and candidates, or citizens *only as voters*):

> ... how, though, is the ideal of public reason realized by citizens who are not government officials? ... To answer this question, we say that ideally citizens are to think themselves *as if they were legislators* and ask themselves what statutes, supported by what reasons satisfying the criterion of reciprocity, they would think it most reasonable to enact (IPRR: 444–5).

Therefore, the ideal of public reason produces an approach to fundamental political issues that looks like a counterfactual reasoning and a regulative ideal orientating our judgments. Thus, going back to IPR, we can understand why Rawls introduces the theme of the Supreme Court as 'exemplar' of public reason (which he later dwelt on in § 6): the model of justification of one's interpretations and decisions, which is or should be a constitutional court, appears *paradigmatic* because it *should* express at the highest level, in its purest and most authentic way, an exercise of reasonableness applied to political issues which is inspired by the ideal of public reason. 'To check whether we are following public reason', says Rawls at the end of his essay, 'we might ask: how would our argument strike us presented in the form of a supreme court opinion? Reasonable? Outrageous?' (IPR: 254).

3. Public reason and the dilemmas of 'reasonable pluralism'

In the light of what we have said so far, the meaning of the *idea* and *ideal* of public reason becomes clearer and we can better appreciate the role public reason plays in Rawls's search for a solution to the dilemmas of 'reasonable pluralism' that characterise and threaten contemporary democratic societies. From this point of view, I believe that a key to understanding Rawls's position is his substantial adhesion to a *dualistic* view of democracy and the constitutional rule-of-law state. Here we can see the specific influence of Bruce Ackerman, whose works are referred to by Rawls in the paragraph devoted to the Supreme Court.[12] The first instance of dualism (*à la* Ackerman) is the distinction between an 'ordinary' and a 'constitutional' politics: the former is open and subject to the 'non-public reasons' emerging from civil societies and acting on procedures of ordinary legislation; the latter is open and subject to the limits and commitments of a 'public reason' that is addressing itself to the foundations of a constitutional democracy and matters of basic justice and their possible revision. A second instance of dualism can be found in the very conception of citizenship: each individual lives (or should

---

12. In particular, Rawls quotes an essay by Ackerman titled 'Constitutional politics/constitutional law' (1989) and the first volume of *We, the People* (1991). The former essay, in turn, referred to the article 'Discovering the Constitution' (Ackerman 1984) for a more extensive discussion of the dualist approach. Rawls also quoted Ackerman in his 'Reply to Habermas' (*PL*: 405, note 40), clarifying that he shares the latter's 'dualist' perspective and his vision of the few, great 'foundational' moments of American constitutional history but does not accept all the implications that Ackerman draws from this.

be able to live) in *dual* dimensions. One is *private* and *social*, where she exists as a member of society, immersed in a 'background culture' and endowed with her own 'comprehensive' view (religious, philosophical or moral). The other is *public*, where the individual is a *citizen* committed to the use of public reason when discussing the constitutional essentials with other equal citizens – that is, when she tries to identify *political* values (not philosophical or religious ones) that other citizens might reasonably accept.

As Rawls wrote in his 1995 Introduction, when moving from a comprehensive doctrine to a political conception, 'the idea of a person as having moral personality with the full capacity of moral agency is transformed into that of the citizen' (2005: xliii). In political liberalism, adds Rawls, 'the person is seen ... as a free and equal citizen, the *political person of a modern democracy* with the political rights and duties of citizenship, and standing in a political relation with other citizens' (*ibid.*, my emphasis). I believe this usage of the word *person* (evoking the original Latin meaning of *persona* as 'mask' or 'role') is not coincidental. The *homme* is *transfigured* into a *citoyen*: that's how a 'political conception' of the person emerges.[13] Some critics have seen this as an unsustainable *inner scission;*[14] others as a burden that falls entirely on individuals and their *moral power*: having a sense of justice and a conception of what is good that, if necessary, can be revised. Individuals must be able to *abstract* from the deepest bases of their convictions to be able to have some *political* relation with their equals, from citizen to citizen. *'The same human being is a person in the background culture and a citizen in the public forum'* (Dreben 2003: 325, my emphasis). That's why their *duty of civility* is fundamental: it is a 'duty of civil behaviour', or perhaps also simply a 'civil duty', that is, 'an ideal of democratic citizenship' imposing on citizens

> ... a moral, not a legal, duty – the duty of civility – to be able to explain to one another on those fundamental questions how the principles and policies they advocate and vote for can be supported by the political values of public reason.

13. In IPRR, Rawls would come back to this point, with a much more complete and effective formulation: 'in public reason, ideas of truth or right based on comprehensive doctrines are replaced by an idea of the politically reasonable addressed to citizens as citizens. This step is necessary to establish a basis of political reasoning that all can share as free and equal citizens. Since we are seeking public justifications for political and social institutions ... we think of persons as citizens. This assigns to each person the same basic political position. In giving reasons to all citizens we don't view persons as socially situated or otherwise rooted ... Rather, we think of persons as reasonable and rational, as free and equal citizens, with the two moral powers and having, at any given moment, a determinate conception of the good, which may change over time' (IPRR: 481).

14. *See* Cooke 2000: 960 on citizens as 'divided selves'. As is known, the critique of Rawls from the communitarian perspective is also very important (Sandel 1982; MacIntyre 1981; Taylor 1989). Raz's criticism (1990) of the 'epistemic abstinence' is based on a more traditional liberal point of view, taken as an autonomous moral doctrine. I'll come back to Habermas's position later. Critical considerations concerning IPR specifically can also be found in McCarthy 1994: 52: 'the weight of the art of separation falls on individuals. We have to monitor and restrain ourselves, to know when we are speaking in what Rawls calls the "public forum" and when not'. On the 'political conception of the person', *see PL* 28–34; *cf.* Freeman 2007a: 333–6.

This duty also involves a willingness to listen to others and a fairmindedness in deciding when accommodations to their views should reasonably be made (IPR: 217).[15]

This position is obviously related to other cornerstones of Rawls's position, which here I can only briefly recall, in particular, the distinction between 'rational' and 'reasonable' grounding of the principle of 'overlapping consensus'. In Rawls's definition, an individual's 'rationality' is expressed through the search for the best means to achieve one's end. 'Reasonableness', instead, is the willingness to change and adapt one's beliefs or behaviour; to engage in the construction of 'fair terms of cooperation'; and to morally commit to respect them, starting from the assumption of a *criterion of reciprocity*. 'Our exercise of political power is proper', as Rawls put it in the 1995 Introduction, 'only when we sincerely believe that the reason we offer for our political action may reasonably be accepted by other citizens as a justification of those actions' (2005: xliv).

A 'reasonable' person, acknowledging the 'burdens of judgment' weighing on a public discussion – which make it hard to presume that all may think the same way or easily reach an agreement – fully accepts that others might rightly and legitimately disagree with her, or rather, that this is often the case. '*Burdens of judgment*' is another key concept (*see*, in particular, *PL*: 50–5), one that is particularly important to the construction of a notion of *public deliberation* in Rawls's theory: the 'burdens of judgment' are born from a *fallibilist* awareness of one's own deepest convictions and from a sense of the finiteness of human skills of judgment. In any discussion, our capacity and ability to justify a position is always limited and *dissent* and *disagreement* are more than likely, if only for a few matters of fact: our ability to reason is imperfect and incomplete; we can all assign different weights to different topics; our information is partial; our experiences are all different; and so on. There is, therefore, an essential *epistemic* dimension that limits the claim to definitively overcome the *reasonable disagreements* that characterise public discussion.[16]

---

15. On this point, in a footnote Rawls refers to an article by Amy Gutmann and Dennis Thompson, ('Moral conflict and political consensus', 1990), in which they first presented the positions they later developed in their 1996 book. Gutmann and Thompson could only quote Rawls's 'Justice as fairness' and based their considerations on dissatisfaction with the classical liberal principle of 'exclusion', based on the notion that political conflicts that imply a moral conflict must be 'excluded' from political decision-making, 'avoided', brought back to the private sphere of citizens. Instead, they proposed a principle of accommodation that allows us to treat moral disagreement publicly.

16. On this point, the epistemic dimension of 'reasonableness', *see* Samuel Freeman (2007a: 346): 'the suggestion seems to be that Rawls uses "reasonable person" epistemically, in the sense of a person who reasons correctly, assesses all the available reasons and evidence and assigns them the appropriate weight ... There is an element in Rawls's account of "reasonable person" that relies on some degree on these epistemic elements ... But the main sense of Rawls's many uses of the concept of reasonableness is moral'. As Rawls himself puts it, 'being reasonable is not an epistemological idea (though it has epistemological elements). Rather, it is part of a political ideal of democratic citizenship that includes the idea of public reason'. (*PL*: 62).

However, a reasonable person – albeit aware of the 'burdens' weighing on her judgment – is not simply *tolerant*: she fully accepts a *criterion of reciprocity* in her relation with other people. For this very reason, 'the reasonable is public in a way the rational is not' (*PL*: 53). Therefore, public reason – that is, the citizens' *public reasoning* on *constitutional essentials* and *matters of basic justice* – should be guided and inspired by the idea that we have to produce arguments that are publicly and mutually acceptable, potentially shared by all reasonable citizens. For this reason – as we'll see better later on – we can also start from our comprehensive doctrines, finding in them reasons to identify with a political conception of justice; but no one can appeal *directly* to these doctrines. In publicly discussing a basic question, I cannot put in place my claim to possess the 'whole truth': I can only hope for a convergence with my fellow-citizens views about what seems reasonably and relatively '(more) just', finding areas of 'intersection' or 'overlap' on reasonably desirable contents and goals.

This convergence, though, cannot be reduced to a mere *modus vivendi* or a merely tolerant (albeit indifferent) co-existence between different ideas. There has to be a partial but true and, so to speak, 'convinced' area of consensus on a political conception of justice – even if this can happen *based on different reasons* rooted in different religious, philosophical or moral views. And only a *deliberative politics* – one might add – can lead to such an outcome: it is the more necessary the more the comprehensive doctrines in play are different or openly conflicting.[17] When we discuss publicly, in short, we must try to produce a public justification, whatever the deepest beliefs that motivate it in our view. And even if the 'whole truth' (if the point is to reach decisions binding for all) cannot be brought into the public forum (but on this point, as we shall see, Rawls's position would change significantly in IPRR), there is still space for a 'reasonable' discussion. Citizens can search for a reasonable agreement that would be acceptable to all or – in any case – if they ascertain a permanent reasonable dissent they can find an agreement on institutional procedures that can lead to a decision perceived as legitimate.[18]

In the texts I am analysing here, Rawls tackles more than once the difficulties and objections that might be raised regarding his idea of public reason. One of them is enunciated in the very first pages of IPR and is returned to many times throughout the book, as a central topic of Rawls's reflection:

---

17. 'The idea of overlapping consensus is based in the conjecture that reasonable citizens in a well-ordered society still can affirm the freestanding political conception for reasons peculiar to their comprehensive views. Different comprehensive views should be able to accept the political conception since it can be justified according to reason already affirmed within each comprehensive view' (Freeman 2003b: 36). What is left to clarify is the nature of this convergence: in the end, doesn't it still presuppose a 'moral' choice, that is, the belief that it is morally right and not just pragmatically convenient to trust only a political conception? On this point, *see* Ferrara 1999: 154–5.

18. Rawls focuses on the outcomes of a discussion when it reaches a 'stand-off' – that is, when it is verified that an area of consensus cannot be reached – in the final pages of IPRR (476–9). In these cases, the use of a voting procedure based on the majority principle is the only possible solution but, at the end of a deliberative process, that principle itself acquires greater legitimacy in the eyes of the participants.

… why should citizens in discussing and voting on the most fundamental political questions honor the limits of public reason? How can it be either reasonable or rational, when basic matters are at stake, for citizens to appeal only to a public conception of justice and not to the whole truth as they see it? (IPR: 216).

Rawls replies by referring to the 'the liberal principle of legitimacy' (*ibid.*: 217). The latter tells us that

… our exercise of political power is proper and hence justifiable only when it is exercised in accordance with a constitution the essentials of which all citizens may reasonably be expected to endorse in the light of principles and ideals acceptable to them as reasonable and rational (IPR: 217).

In short, citizens must 'honor' and accept the limits of public reason, as this is intrinsically related to the constitution of a democracy:

… as reasonable and rational, and knowing that they affirm a diversity of reasonable religious and philosophical doctrines, [citizens] should be ready to explain the basis of their action to one another in terms each could reasonably expect that others might endorse as consistent with their freedom and equality. Trying to meet this condition is one of the tasks that this ideal of democratic politics asks of us. Understanding how to conduct oneself as a democratic citizen includes understanding an ideal of public reason (IPR: 218).

Therefore, citizens are called to a difficult exercise of self-restraint: they must make a constant effort to listen and understand the reasons of others and they must be able to justify, before the forum of public reason, their ideas (on key issues) such that these can be accepted or at least 'not rejected' by other citizens – keeping in mind that the latter, as Rawls says many times, are inspired by *different* and *varied* worldviews and conceptions of the good (comprehensive reasonable doctrines), which are often in conflict with each other. For this reason, the ground on which we can hope to finally find an 'overlapping consensus' is *political*, and exclusively political: it is around a political conception of what is 'just' or relatively 'more just' that one can build a stable and legitimate democratic and constitutional order.

This search is also open to conflict and its outcomes are far from guaranteed. 'It is inevitable and often desirable' – concludes Rawls – 'that citizens have different views as to the most appropriate political conception; for the public political culture is bound to contain different fundamental ideas that can be developed in different ways. An orderly contest between them over time is a reliable way to find which one, *if any*, is most reasonable' (IPR: 227, my emphasis). In that 'if any', we can detect a tone that might come across as *sceptical* but mainly denotes a constitutive feature of Rawls's thought: he displays a certain *disenchantment* in the face of the radical plurality of comprehensive visions of the world and their truth-claims.

At this point we can begin to grasp the properly deliberative dimension of a democracy thus conceived, even though Rawls, in his text dated 1993, does not use this expression yet. The laborious exercise of constructing this area where the elements of consensus and political convergence overlap is a practice of mutual reason-giving, argumentative exchange, dialogue, listening and mutual persuasion. The citizens' *public reasoning* is the only thing that can produce this area of consensus. Their reasoning is *public* in a dual sense: as a way of reasoning that arises 'from the point of view' of a public dimension and as a universe of discourses that manifest themselves openly and publicly. As Charles Larmore put it (2003: 377):

> [I]n a well-ordered society, citizens do not determine basic matters of justice by announcing to one another the conclusions they each have derived from their own first principles and then resorting to some further mechanism, such as bargaining or majority voting ... they reason from what they understand to be a common point of view; their aim is to adjudicate disagreements by argument.[19]

We can also better grasp the dualistic perspective guiding Rawls's model: one cannot presume that this deliberative quest of an area of political consensus, inspired by an idea of public reason, can concern *all political issues*; it mainly regards fundamental issues related to the constitutional essentials and the matters of basic justice. It is on this ground that moments of 'high' politics can take place: those extraordinary historical moments in which popular participation is more intense and creative. And a dualistic conception of democracy can account for such moments.

4. Public reason as a deliberative paradigm

Rawls's position lends itself to a double evaluation and to objections that would later be considered by Rawls himself in 'The idea of public reason revisited'. On the one hand, is it right, or even 'realistic', to think that the discussion on public issues or political controversies should *presume* that citizens would not bring forward their ideal, moral or religious views, or that they wouldn't try to affirm their own 'truth'? As we shall see, Rawls replies to this objection in the final part of IPR, first by distinguishing between an 'inclusive thesis' and an 'exclusive thesis' in the understanding of public reason and then with his idea of a *proviso*, (that is, a 'conditional clause'). On the other hand, there seems to be a matter of 'realism' in favour of Rawls's position: can we really think that citizens could or should

---

19. Note that, in Larmore's view, citizens start from shared premises, from 'a common point of view'. As we will see later while analysing the concept of 'wide reflective equilibrium', Rawls also seems to presuppose a common basis from which to start. But even if this is so, one might add, the 'shared premises' are by no means a foregone conclusion, as they themselves must be patiently elaborated and defined by the citizens' deliberative practice. On these issues, *see* Ferrara 2008: 61–72.

be committed to an intense, constant deliberative practice on *all* political issues of a democracy? Wouldn't it be wiser or more credible to think that this can only happen when what's at stake are fundamental issues, while the rest is addressed by ordinary politics with its rules, rituals and – if you will – its mediocrity? After all, doesn't Ackerman's historical reconstruction tell us precisely this when he claims that, in two centuries of American democracy, there have only been three great *foundational* and *re-foundational moments of the constitutional essentials*, involving intense popular participation and widespread deliberative practice?[20]

As is known, Rawls's position is expressed even more clearly in § 5 of IPR, where he elucidates the contents of the 'essential constitutional elements' that may be subject to public reason, reaching the conclusion that they concern the 'fundamental principles that specify the general structure of government and the political process' (the form of government and the power relations) and the 'basic rights of citizenship'. They do *not* regard issues related to *distributive justice* (IPR: 227–8): that is, issues related to economic and social inequalities, as we are less likely, and it is much harder, to reach an agreement on these matters. It follows that those matters should be entrusted to ordinary politics and the varying circumstances in which it can regulate them, even though they, too, 'are to be discussed in terms of political values' (*ibid.*: 229). In short, not all political values can be considered as 'essential constitutional elements' and therefore the public debate on them cannot always display the traits that would be dictated by an ideal of public reason.[21]

However, it is in § 6, dedicated to the 'Supreme Court as exemplar of public reason', that we find the most explicit manifestation of Rawls's dualist approach. '[I]n a constitutional regime with judicial review, public reason is the reason of its supreme court' (IPR: 231). Rawls recalls the five fundamental principles of constitutionalism (IPR: 212):

a. The Lockean distinction between 'constituent power' and 'ordinary power'.

b. The distinction 'between higher and ordinary law'.

c. The idea that 'a democratic constitution is a principled expression in higher law of the political ideal of a people to govern itself in a certain way. The aim of public reason is to articulate this ideal'.

d. 'By a democratically ratified constitution with a bill of rights, the citizen body fixes once and for all certain constitutional essentials, for example, the equal basic political rights and liberties…'.

e. 'In constitutional government the ultimate power cannot be left to the legislature or even to a supreme court, which is only the highest judicial interpreter of the constitution. *Ultimate power is held by the three branches*

---

20. Ackerman's latest book (2014) identifies a fourth moment: the era of Civil Rights (1954–74).

21. On Rawls's view of constitutionalism and on his classification of the constitutional essentials, *see* Michelman 2003. More generally, *see also* Freeman 1994.

in a duly specified relation with one another with each responsible to the people (IPR: 231–2, my emphasis).[22]

Rawls identifies the role of the supreme court within a 'dualist constitutional democracy' as 'one of the institutional devices to protect the higher law'. 'By applying public reason, the court is to prevent that law from being eroded by the legislation of transient majorities, or more likely, by organized and well-situated narrow interests skilled at getting their way' (IPR: 233). Given this role, we can safely say that the supreme court is 'antimajoritarian with respect to ordinary law'; however, Rawls concludes, in open reference to Ackerman, it cannot be described as antidemocratic. The essential point is that 'the political values of public reason' are what grounds the interpretations expressed by the Supreme Court: 'a political conception of justice covers the fundamental questions addressed by higher law and sets out the political values in terms of which they can be decided' (IPR: 234).[23]

Therefore, the sense of the 'exemplary', paradigmatic value of the Supreme Court as an eminent place for the 'application' of public reason appears clear. Hence, the criticism sometimes directed at Rawls (for example, Dryzek 2010: 6), according to which he saw deliberation reductively, identifying the Court as the sole place of its exercise, does not appear correct. First of all, public reason is no synonym of public deliberation: public reason is *a form* of deliberative rationality, constructed through the deliberative practice of citizens. This practice, though, evidently manifests itself in many other forms and places. Rather, public reason is an *ideal model of deliberation* – the deliberation that is realised when citizens face the fundamental issues of their democracy and mainly when they do so by playing their public role of citizens. In such a scenario, the crucial question is: can my ideas reasonably be accepted by others? Also, as one cannot presume that one's 'truth' can ground the bases of social co-operation, the path to be pursued is that of seeking that foundation for co-operation in a potential agreement about *political* values and *political* conceptions that are able to justify themselves autonomously. In his Introduction, Rawls writes: 'a political conception of justice is what I call freestanding when it is not presented as derived from, or as part of, any comprehensive doctrine. Such a conception of justice in order to be a moral

---

22. In a footnote, Rawls clarifies that 'there is nothing at all novel in my account' (IPR: 231, note 13) and quotes various authors, including Stephen Holmes (1988a and 1988b) and some pages from Jon Elster's *Ulysses and the Sirens* (1979: 81–86, 88–103).

23. Here, Rawls recalls an essay by Samuel Freeman (1992). This text is important mainly because Rawls himself confesses he is 'indebted to his [Freeman's] discussion' (IPR: 239, note 29); but it also allows us to better grasp some premises and theoretical implications of Rawls's idea of public reason. In fact, Freeman offered an answer to the so-called 'originalist' thesis (according to which, the task of the Court should be to interpret the original meaning of the Constitution) and goes back to an idea of popular sovereignty inspired by Kant and Rousseau (Freeman 1992: 20). Furthermore, Freeman proposed (*ibid.*: 22–8) a discussion of the term 'public reasons' (in the plural), which may be regarded as largely in tune with Rawls's positions to come; moreover, it has the merit of bringing to light the contractualist roots of the notion.

conception must contain its own intrinsic normative and moral ideal' (2005: xliv). On this topic, Thomas M. Scanlon comments that

> The idea is that a society should be organized around *some* reasonable political conception of justice (justice as fairness being only one example, albeit Rawls's own preferred choice) and that this conception, rather than any particular comprehensive view, should serve as the basis for settling questions about its basic institutions. Such a political conception will specify particular political values and principles of justice, will order them in a distinctive way, and will specify more fully the standards of political justification. Since he is allowing for the possibility that different reasonable political conceptions will do this in different ways, Rawls does not, *in discussing public reason*, specify a set of political values. As he says, 'Political liberalism does not, then, try to fix public reason once and for all in the form of one favoured political conception of justice' (IPRR: 451, quoted in Scanlon 2003: 162).

Thus we can understand better in what sense the 'model' of discussion, interpretation and justification attributed by a constitutional order to a supreme court has a wider paradigmatic value. In fact, the court's judges are expected to formulate judgments that are not only (of course) prescinded from their personal views or from specific moral, religious or philosophical perspectives but are also expressed as *reasons* that can be reasonably accepted by citizens with different worldviews. In short, if there is a place where public reason can find its exemplary expression, this place is in the deliberations of a constitutional court, when the court is called to express judgments and take decisions about the consistency of an ordinary piece of legislation with the basic principles of a political community.

But of course this does not always happen. 'It must be said', added Rawls in a note, 'that historically the court has often failed badly in this role' (IPR: 233, note 18).[24] This observation (that is, the possibility of a gap between ideal and real) further clarifies the *paradigmatic* and *regulative* nature of the ideal of public reason. At the same time, though, for Rawls, public reason is also an *idea* at work in the historical reality of constitutional democracies; an idea that has had many instances of 'realization'. Ackerman's theses on the history of American constitutional democracy prove that there are indeed some historical moments in which public reason, through the intensive political and deliberative participation of citizens, has manifested itself.[25]

---

24. He recalled the reception of the Alien and Sedition Act, in 1798; or, in 1857, the distortion of the Reconstruction amendments (interpreted 'as a charter of capitalist liberty rather than of the liberty of the freed slaves') or, in the same direction, the pronouncements of the '*Lochner* era' Court, which struck down many early pieces of New Deal legislation.

25. 'Suppose we agree that the three most innovative periods of our constitutional history are the founding, Reconstruction, and the New Deal ['here I follow Ackerman's account', note 19]. Here it is important that all three seem to rely on, and only on, the political values of public reason' (IPR: 234).

Of course, for the role it plays

> ... in the midst of any great constitutional change, legitimate or otherwise, the Court is bound to be a center of controversy. Often its role forces political discussion to take a principled form so as to address the constitutional questions in line with the political values of justice and public reason. Public discussion becomes more than a contest for power and position. This educates citizens to the use of public reason and its value of political justice by focusing their attention on basic constitutional matters (IPR: 239–40).

As Rawls would say later, we must surely expect that citizens, or some of them, 'will think that nonpolitical and transcendent values are the true ground of political values' (IPR: 241); but in order for a principle of democratic legitimacy to be realised, it is necessary that political values are expressed as such, independently from non-political ones:

> ... it is only in this way, and by accepting that politics in a democratic society can never be guided by what we see as the whole truth, that we can realize the ideal expressed by the principle of legitimacy: to live politically with others in the light of reasons all might reasonably be expected to endorse (IPR: 243).

As we have noted, Rawls is well aware that the main challenge to his idea of public reason and the paradigmatic value he attributes to it would come from 'realist' objections, referring to the difficulty or impossibility of finding in real life such a sharp distinction between public and non-public reasons. Rawls apparently lays himself open to this criticism in many passages, by adopting a language that seems to emphasise public reason as an ideal *offered* to imaginary listeners or *recommended* by an outside party. For instance, he often uses a sort of *hortatory* appeal: citizens 'should honor' public reason; 'they must vote' following public reason and so on; in one passage, there is even talk of an 'injunction' to the use of public reason (IPRR: 462). But all this raises an immediate objection: why on earth *should* citizens do so? Who decided this? In the name of what are these claims being made? Indeed, citizens do not really always 'honor' public reason and, in fact, it remains to be seen for what reasons it would be good if they did so.

Rawls seems to acknowledge the potential weakness of his way of conceptualising the ideal of public reason and, in the final pages of IPRR, he'd go back to this issue, as we shall see. For now, in IPR, Rawls is tackling the difficult topic of the possible (or impossible) distinction between public and non-public reason; to do so, he introduces two different ways to understand public reason: an 'exclusive' and an 'inclusive view'. The former says, rigidly, that 'on fundamental matters, reasons given explicitly in terms of comprehensive doctrines are never to be introduced into public reason. The public reasons such a doctrine supports may, of course, be given but not the supporting doctrine itself' (IPR: 247). The 'inclusive' thesis instead allows citizens 'to present what they regard as the basis of political values rooted in their comprehensive doctrine, provided they do this in ways that strengthen the ideal of public reason itself'.

As soon as we ask 'which view best encourages citizens to honor the ideal of public reason', 'the inclusive view seems the correct one'. Rawls hypothesises three typical situations. The first, 'the ideal case', is that of a well ordered society, which is 'not stirred by any deep disputes' and in which there is 'a firm overlapping consensus'. In this case, there is no need to resort to 'other considerations' than those of 'ordinary politics' and 'public reason in this well-ordered society may appear to follow the exclusive view' (IPR: 248). The second situation is intermediate: that of a society in which there is 'a serious dispute ... in applying one of its principles of justice' (Rawls gives the example of a conflict about 'the principle of fair equality of opportunity as it applies to education for all' and, in particular, about the 'rightness' of public funding for religious schools). Here, we can presume that, when different positions are discussed in the public forum, some discussants will resort to arguments referring to their comprehensive doctrines. In this case, the best way to strengthen the ideal of public reason 'may be to explain in the public forum how one's comprehensive doctrine affirms the political values' (IPR: 248–9), so as to clarify what is affirmed on its bases and what is deduced from it, expressing it in political terms.

Finally, the third case is that of an open conflict, 'when a society is not well ordered and there is a profound division about constitutional essentials'. This is the historical case of the abolition of slavery: before the Civil War, abolitionists supported their position by openly referring to religious arguments. How to judge this situation? Here 'the nonpublic reason of certain Christian churches supported the clear conclusions of public reason' (IPR: 249–50). And the same can be said of some famous public speeches made by Lincoln (IPR: 254) and by Martin Luther King and other leaders of the Civil Rights movement – in the last case, this was especially evident, because the religious dimension of those speeches often referred to the values expressed by the Constitution. Therefore, these are examples of the validity of an 'inclusive' conception of public reason, also based on considerations that one might call 'strategic' or prudential, related to historical and social circumstance: for abolitionists, 'the comprehensive reasons they appealed' were also indispensable 'to give sufficient strength to the political conception to be subsequently realized' (IPR: 251). Of course, we might observe how Rawls's argument raises quite a few problems here: it is *we, today*, who say that abolitionists were guided by public reason but at the time they were actually guided by a *religious* conception of the person – this was their form of consciousness and it was only through their struggle that those values were later affirmed as *political*.

Rawls would often come back to these themes, which shows that he felt that these aspects of the definition of public reason were crucial (and, perhaps, at least partly unsolved). In his 1995 Introduction, Rawls devotes a few pages to public reason and its ideal, explicitly stating his wish to 'supplement' what he had written in the first essay. The direction of this discussion is a further 'stretching' of the terms within which to conceive the relation between public reason and comprehensive doctrines. 'When engaged in public reasoning', Rawls wonders, 'may we also include reasons of our comprehensive doctrines?' (2005: xlix). The answer to this question is related to an explicit correction of his previous thesis, which makes the framework of conditions of the inclusive thesis more permissive:

> I now believe, and hereby I revise VI: 8, that reasonable such doctrines may be introduced in public reason *at any time*, provided that *in due course* public reasons, given by a reasonable political conception, are presented sufficient to support whatever the comprehensive doctrines are introduced to support. I refer to this as the proviso and it specifies what I now call the wide view of public reason (*ibid.*: xlix–l, my emphasis).

This 'conditional clause', this *proviso*, indicates the ways in which certain public reasons can find support in a comprehensive doctrine. Rawls now appears to reject altogether the 'exclusive thesis' presented in IPR and 'admits', so to speak, that the public reasons supported by a comprehensive doctrine can enter as such in the public debate, *at any time*, without thereby requiring a improbable translation and abstraction: the only condition is that the 'conclusions' are expressed in terms of public reason. Showing openly the deep roots of our adherence to a political conception – how they are rooted in our comprehensive doctrines – can also strengthen the basis of a reasonable overlapping consensus, fostering mutual trust between the parties.

However, even the notion of *proviso* does not seem to be decisive: in the subsequent IPRR, Rawls would return to this notion in the context of new reflection on what is called 'the wide view of public political culture'. On the one hand, he reaffirms its content and offers a clearer definition of it:

> … reasonable comprehensive doctrines, religious or nonreligious, may be introduced in public political discussions at any time, provided that in due course proper political reasons – and not reasons given solely by comprehensive doctrines – are presented that are sufficient to support whatever the comprehensive doctrines introduced are said to support. This injunction to present proper political reason I refer to as the *proviso*, and it specifies public political culture as distinct from the background culture (IPRR: 462).

On the other hand, he clarifies that the many questions aroused by the issue (who decides, and when, that the proviso is met?) cannot be solved in advance, based on some rule that predetermines the judgment of it, but can be only answered in the concrete cases in which the presence of comprehensive doctrines manifests itself in the public debate. Rawls's answer might seem elusive but it actually reveals some deep traits of his way of understanding philosophical research, at least in the final stage of his thinking.[26]

---

26. 'This is Rawls at his best', comments Dreben (2003: 343), 'and many people might say at his least philosophical. For me it is at his most philosophical. You cannot do moral philosophy, at any

Besides, Rawls seems to accentuate the positive role that reasonable comprehensive doctrines, when their intervention is properly mediated, can play in strengthening the foundations of a constitutional democracy and the 'public political culture' that supports it. In fact, Rawls goes so far as to claim that the very 'roots of democratic citizens' allegiance to their political conceptions lie in their respective comprehensive doctrines, both religious and nonreligious': the citizens' mutual and public recognition of this fact contributes to giving 'enduring strength and vigor' to the 'social basis' that a constitutional democracy can count on (IPRR: 463).

Perhaps we could say that Rawls's best presentation of the issue is in the long part of IPRR (pp. 466–73), in which he deals with the 'family as part of the basic structure' of a society. Rawls's declared goal is to show 'the ample space for debate and argument comprehended by public reason as a whole' (IPRR: 467); that is – we might say – to show how, despite the limits, restrictions and conditional clauses, there are no univocal conclusions dictated by public reason, as public reason contemplates a wide set of possible solutions and positions. Rawls chooses the family as an example precisely because it is one of the most delicate issues in which the border between political conceptions and comprehensive doctrines can be discussed and evaluated. It's also an issue within which we can easily see whether comprehensive doctrines, which public reason has the task of limiting and bringing within the field of the 'political', are 'trespassing'.

Rawls affirms a general principle: 'the principles defining the equal basic liberties and opportunities of citizens always hold in and through all so-called domains' (IPRR: 471): this means, of course, that the principles of justice cannot dictate the rules of a church but public law mustn't consider apostasy and heresy to be crimes. And, in the same way, 'since wives are equally citizens with their husbands, they have all the same basic rights, liberties, and opportunities as their husbands' (IPRR: 469). The judgments inspired by an idea of public reason intervene, in all these cases, to define the areas in which it is right and proper that a public dimension prevails over non-public reasons (social or communitarian) and private ones. But the definition of this boundary is itself a possible subject for a discussion, an argument and a *public* justification.

Of course, Rawls seems to claim now, it is inevitable that in such a discussion the arguments based on 'comprehensive doctrines' forcefully enter the public debate: the point is to see if those who advocate them are then able to present

---

serious level, and certainly you cannot do serious political philosophy, by trying to lay out rules in advance. You have to work out what it is implicitly accepted. That is what Hegel saw. He messed it up with his lousy dialectical metaphysics, but at least he saw that you have to be *in mediis rebus* and work through. You cannot do substantial political or moral philosophy in any Cartesian-framed manner or shape of mind whatsoever. That is what Rawls has always seen. That was at the heart of *A Theory of Justice*. That is the content of what he calls "reflective equilibrium"' (Dreben 2003: 343). Thus we can see why, at the beginning of his text, Dreben stated: 'some might think there is no connection between Frege and Wittgenstein, on the one hand, and Rawls, on the other. For me there is a very close connection, and I hope to bring it out implicitly if not explicitly' (*ibid.*: 316).

their beliefs (at least, *also*) in terms that can be themselves *discussed* (that is, terms formulated and justified by the standpoint of a public reason) and possibly accepted by other people. For instance, I can argue against the right to abortion, and I can draw this belief from my philosophical or religious view, but I cannot do so by appealing to, say, the *sacred* value of life; or rather, I can *declare* or *testify* to this belief[27] but I cannot assume that such testimony could be accepted among the public justifications of a political and institutional decision on the issue. Or else, to refer to another example made by Rawls, let's 'consider the familiar story of the Good Samaritan' (IPRR: 456): from *our* perspective, we can give the story a philosophical or religious value but as soon as the story falls within the *public* discourse we must 'give a public justification for this parable's conclusion in terms of political values' (IPRR: 465).

At this point, the complex (and rather difficult, for Rawls himself) construction of the meaning of public reason as a *deliberative paradigm* seems clearly outlined: it doesn't make sense to wonder if it is too 'restrictive' (or, on the contrary, too vague), as many critical analyses have done (Rawls himself mentions it in his Introduction (2005: li–lii) and in IPRR (478)). As such, public reason sets itself on a level that cannot help being formal or abstract: 'it does not, as such, determine or settle particular questions of law or policy. Rather, it specifies the public reasons in terms of which such questions are to be politically decided' (2005: li). 'The idea of public reason is not a view about specific political institutions or policies, but *a view about how they are to be argued for and justified*' (2005: lii, note 29, my emphasis). Public reason is a *mode* of argumentation and justification, 'a way of reasoning about political values shared by free and equal citizens' (IPRR: 490).[28]

5. Public reason and deliberative democracy

In the 1995 Introduction to the paperback edition of *PL*, the main theme is that of the relationship and differences between *Theory of Justice* and *Political Liberalism*, with an emphasis on the new ideas that the latter introduces and its different point of view. *Theory* is seen as the presentation and explanation of a *comprehensive conception of justice*, whereas the problem that *Political Liberalism* was intended to solve stands on quite another level: how can free and equal citizens, in a liberal

---

27. Rawls distinguishes (IPRR: 465–6) between *public reasoning* and other forms of discourse constituting the 'background culture': *witnessing*; *declaration* (an affirmation of our comprehensive conception that, from the beginning, 'we do not expect others to share' IPRR: 465); and *conjecture* (that is, 'when we argue from the comprehensive doctrine that we attribute to other people in order to show them that they do have reasons for endorsing the political conception under discussion' (Ferrara 2008: 64).

28. 'Rawls emphasizes that public reason is not to be thought of as an effective decision procedure, guaranteed to produce agreement, but rather as a special kind of disagreement, argument, and counterargument, which tries to use mutually recognized methods of evaluation and evidence, whether these produce consensus or not. ... [T]he concept of public reason is not put forward by Rawls as a mechanical test for the admissibility of arguments but rather as a characterization of what we should looking for in an admissible ground for the design of basic institutions' (Nagel 2003: 76).

and democratic society, produce fair forms of social co-operation, starting from comprehensive, religious, philosophical or moral visions that differ radically? Basically, *Theory* presented one of the possible answers: the one Rawls (along with those who share his view) offers to the philosophical (and public) debate on the core issues of a political community. But the theory of justice as fairness remained, as such, a 'comprehensive doctrine', since it is based on Kant's conception of the individual's moral autonomy – a philosophical conception on whose content and assumptions other comprehensive visions may or may not converge. Therefore, how this vision and many others – expressing a 'reasonable pluralism' – could contribute to the construction of a stable and just liberal and democratic society remained an open question.[29]

For this reason, Rawls writes, 'two ideas that are not found in *Theory* are needed to meet the fact of reasonable pluralism, namely, the ideas of a reasonable overlapping consensus and of public reason' (2005: xlv). Furthermore, the concept of 'reasonable pluralism' had to be clarified as well. In these pages, Rawls strengthens the sense of *possibility*, and *possibility only*, that such an ideal of 'public reason' might be an appropriate response. The idea of public reason '*presents how things might be*, taking people as a just and well-ordered society would encourage them to be. It describes what is possible and can be, yet may never be, though no less fundamental for that' (IPR: 213, my emphasis). Actually, Rawls's words seem to show an intention to convey a sense of the *precariousness* of these ideals and the knowledge that 'reasonable pluralism' represents a major challenge, which can only be approached based on a political (and autonomous) conception of justice. 'For rather than confronting religious and nonliberal doctrines with a comprehensive liberal doctrine, the thought is to formulate a liberal political conception that those nonliberal doctrines might be able to endorse' (2005: xlv). A public debate shaped as a *direct challenge* among comprehensive visions does not lead to positive results, nor does it create 'stability for the right reasons'. On the contrary, it risks being, one could say, highly *destabilizing*. For this reason, 'the aim of striking a balance or average' among these visions is not enough:

> … rather, we formulate a freestanding political conception having its own intrinsic (moral) political ideal expressed by the criterion of reciprocity. *We hope in this way that reasonable comprehensive doctrines can endorse for the*

---

29. 'Thus, a main aim of PL is to show that the idea of a well-ordered society in *Theory* may be reformulated so as to take account of the fact of reasonable pluralism' (2005: xl). Rawls deals with this topic in the first introduction to *PL*, too, stating explicitly that the solution to the problem of 'stability' in the third part of *TJ* 'is not consistent' with the 'fact of reasonable pluralism' (2005: xxxix–xl). This makes 'unrealistic' (*ibid.*: xvii) 'the idea of a well-ordered society' expressed in *TJ*, creating a 'serious problem'. 'A modern democratic society is characterized not simply by a pluralism of comprehensive religious, philosophical, and moral doctrines but by a pluralism of incompatible yet reasonable comprehensive doctrines. No one of these doctrines is affirmed by citizens generally. Nor should one expect that in the foreseeable future one of them, or some other reasonable doctrine, will ever be affirmed by all, or nearly all, citizens' (*ibid.*: xvi).

right reasons that political conception and hence be viewed as belonging to a reasonable overlapping consensus (ibid., my emphasis).

But *Political Liberalism,* Rawls adds, did not aim 'to prove, or to show' that such consensus is always produced: 'the most it does is to present a freestanding liberal political conception that does not oppose comprehensive doctrines on their own ground and does not *preclude the possibility* of an overlapping consensus for the right reasons' (2005: xlvi, my emphasis). Being guided and inspired by the ideal of public reason, in many issues (such as the right to abortion: *ibid:* liv), does 'not often lead to general agreement of views, nor should it' (*ibid.*: lv); and yet, even in these cases, it could result in positive consequences: 'citizens learn and profit from conflict and argument, and when their arguments follow public reason, they instruct and deepen society's public culture' (*ibid.*). There are 'limits' to the possibility of 'reconciliation by public reason' and Rawls distinguishes three types of conflict: conflict among comprehensive doctrines as such, which can only be 'mitigated' by political liberalism but never 'eliminated'; conflict among citizens arising 'from their different status, class position, and occupation, or from their ethnicity, gender, and race', which can be tackled and 'reconciled' through 'principles of justice of a reasonably just constitutional regime'; and, finally, conflict 'resulting from the burdens of judgment' and which are intended instead to be always present and 'limit the extent of possible agreement' (*ibid.*: lviii).

As is well known, the search for this 'reconciliation' is only possible if the pluralism of reasonable comprehensive doctrines finds an area of *overlap* in a political and independent conception of justice. In Rawls's 1995 Introduction there is a clear expression of the *deliberative rationality* through which one can (*perhaps*) reach such 'consensus':

Citizens are reasonable when, viewing one another as free and equal in a system of social cooperation over generations, they are prepared to offer one another fair terms of social cooperation (defined by principles and ideals) and they agree to act on those terms, even at the cost of their own interests in particular situations, provided that others also accept those terms. For these terms to be fair terms, citizens offering them must reasonably think that those citizens to whom such terms are offered might also reasonably accept them (*ibid.*: xlii).

As Rawls will say in IPRR, public reason is a mode and a paradigm of the argumentation through which we, as citizens, publicly justify the conclusions we have reached 'about what we think are the most reasonable political institutions and policies' (IPRR: 465). It is no longer a *rational choice* among given alternatives, one might say, but rather the *reasonable construction* of a solution that other citizens can find convincing and consider acceptable: 'public justification is not simply valid reasoning, but argument addressed to others; it proceeds correctly from premises we accept and think others could reasonably accept to conclusions we think they could also reasonably accept' (*ibid.*).

At this point, the question that must be answered concerns the connection between the idea of public reason and an idea of 'deliberative democracy', and the way in which Rawls, first in the Introduction of 1995 and then in IPRR, faces this theme. In the Introduction, Rawls proposes a list of 'institutions' (2005: lvi–lvii) through which it is possible to ensure the right balance between freedom and equality – a balance that is part of a liberal conception and that can guarantee 'stability for the right reasons'. '[T]he ideal of public reason contains a form of public political deliberation', Rawls writes, and these institutions 'are necessary for this deliberation to be possible and fruitful' and 'to support and encourage it' (2005: lvii).

Through a conceptual move that we have already found in Cohen's essays (from principles and ideals to 'institutions'), Rawls identifies three main institutional prerequisites, three characteristics of the 'basic structure' of a society that can allow for the full unfolding of citizens' public deliberation: a) 'public financing of elections and ways of assuring the availability of public information on matters of policy';[30] b) 'a certain fair equality of opportunity, especially in education and training'; c) 'a decent distribution of income and wealth meeting the third condition of liberalism: all citizens must be assured the all-purpose necessary means for them to take intelligent and effective advantage of their basic liberties' (2005: lvi–lvii).

However, one has the impression that, in these passages of the Introduction, there is still something unresolved or a lack of conceptual connection: Rawls states that the ideal of public reason 'contains' a form of 'political public deliberation' but he does not yet affirm that a 'well ordered' democracy can be defined *as a deliberative democracy*. Rawls will finally take this step in IPRR, in which he talks more openly and directly of 'deliberative democracy'. The passage in which Rawls defines the essential aspects of a deliberative democracy is not very long, nor does it contain particularly innovative elements compared to the definitions of deliberative democracy given thus far, starting with those developed by Joshua Cohen. Rather, the characteristic of these pages is the connection between Rawls's *own* idea of public reason and what by then was more generally meant by 'deliberative democracy'. In short, it seems possible to say that Rawls first of all pursued his own theoretical and philosophical path, motivated by the primary purpose of developing and supporting a renewed vision of political liberalism. Then, in the course of this theoretical strategy, when the notion of 'public reason' turned out to be essential for this model, he acknowledged how this notion could intersect and combine with the idea of deliberative democracy that, in the meantime (it is now 1997), had become well known in the theoretical debate. And in IPRR, Joshua Cohen is the only author through whose work Rawls related to deliberative democracy.

Rawls now introduced this term for the first time, saying that a 'well-ordered' constitutional democracy can be defined or 'understood *also* as a deliberative

---

30. These measures have a clear purpose: to take politics away from the conditioning of 'particular social and economic interests' and to make sure to provide 'the knowledge and information upon which policies can be formed and intelligently assessed by citizens using public reason' (IPR: lvi).

democracy' (IPRR: 447–8, my emphasis). And the definition of a deliberative democracy originates from the idea of deliberation:

> … when citizens deliberate, they exchange views and debate their supporting reasons concerning public political questions. They suppose that their political opinions may be revised by discussion with other citizens; and therefore these opinions are not simply a fixed outcome of their existing private or non-political interests. *It is at this point that public reason is crucial, for it characterizes such citizens' reasoning concerning constitutional essentials and matters of basic justice* (IPRR: 448, my emphasis).

We can now try to give some definitions:

a.   Deliberation is the citizens' way of reasoning about political issues, based on argumentative exchange and the possibility to change and revise their beliefs.

b.   Public reason is a deliberative reasoning that citizens choose, or may choose, when issues of particular importance – constitutional essentials and matters of basic justice – are discussed. This way of thinking requires the assumption of a criterion of reciprocity and reasonableness and the adoption of a public 'point of view', that is, the ability to offer reasons that can be publicly justified.

Rawls adds that he could not dwell exhaustively on 'the nature of deliberative democracy' but he could only focus on 'a few key points'. This, though, allowed him 'to indicate the wider place and role of public reason' (*PL*: 448). However, the following discussion does not seem very organic and is actually rather elliptical and allusive, at times tautological or circular. The 'three essential elements' are identified as follows: the first is that very 'public reason'; the second is the 'framework of constitutional democratic institutions that specifies the setting for deliberative legislative bodies'; and the third – the most problematic element, at least as Rawls presents it here – is 'the knowledge and desire on the part of citizens generally to follow public reason and to realize its ideal in their political conduct' (*ibid.*). What does Rawls mean here? That the citizens' 'desire' to be inspired by public reason is a presupposition (a kind of *precondition*) of deliberative democracy? That a deliberative democracy can exist only if citizens *want* to be inspired by public reason and prove their desire to do so? The way Rawls presents this idea emphasises its 'subjective' and 'voluntaristic' features. Perhaps, though, the author here intends to evoke a possible prerequisite of any democracy that can be called deliberative: that is, that there must be a political culture inspired by a criterion of 'public reason' (something similar to what we commonly allude to when the precondition of a solid democracy is identified as an adequate 'civic spirit' or as a widespread 'democratic culture').

However, Rawls does not analyse these points. Rather, he devotes the last page of this section to 'the immediate implications of these essentials', going back to the themes already treated in the 1995 Introduction: the institutional prerequisites of public deliberation that allow one to define a democracy as deliberative. These prerequisites are the public funding of elections (to free democracy 'from the curse of money')[31] and what can be defined as the *infrastructures* of public deliberation: 'the providing for public occasions of orderly and serious discussion of fundamental questions and issues of public polity' (IPRR: 448–9). The consistency between these considerations and Cohen's seems rather obvious here. In addition, there is the issue of education and information, which is an essential prerequisite for public deliberation: the opportunity for citizens to receive adequate information and thus to develop their deliberative capabilities.[32]

At this point, Rawls reverts to a very disenchanted tone. The more he tries to *urge* citizens to follow the dictates of his ideal of public reason and the more frequently he encourages us *to hope* that this could happen, the more Rawls comes across as resigned to recognising that, 'as things are', 'the great game of politics' – *politics as usual*, we could say – takes place on quite another level, making it difficult for serious discussion of even those 'sensible proposals' which could otherwise be taken into consideration to take place. 'Even should farsighted political leaders wish to make sound changes and reforms', Rawls writes, 'they cannot convince a misinformed and cynical public to accept and follow them' (IPRR: 449).[33] Rawls thus shows a dual attitude: the passionate, almost sorrowful proposal of a political ideal and, at the same time, the disillusioned view of a reality that seems to go in a completely different direction. What should one make of this?

This discrepancy implies a question of great theoretical import: what conception of normativity can we detect in Rawls's theoretical and philosophical approach? We have already seen how, in the definition of public reason first as an *idea* and then as an *ideal*, we can capture the tension between an *idea* graspable in the historical reality of our constitutional democracies (*implicit* and *active* in the public political culture of these democracies, so that the theoretical researcher or philosopher has to uncover and reconstruct it) and an *ideal*, a normative projection that – starting from this uncovering and reconstruction – it is possible to envisage in the political and cultural debate. We have also seen how Rawls's anxiety (particularly evident in the pages dedicated to public reason) arises from his awareness of this tension: is it 'realistic' to think that we can really make the distinction – required by both the idea and the ideal of public reason – between 'public reasons' and 'non-public reasons'? As Dreben (2003: 323) observes: 'For Rawls, the task of

---

31. In the note, Rawls recalls one of Dworkin's articles that appeared in the *New York Review of Books*. This article harshly criticised the Supreme Court verdict in the Buckley *vs* Valeo case (1976) abolishing some limits on electoral campaign spending. '[M]oney' Dworkin wrote, 'is the biggest threat to the democratic process'.

32. 'Deliberative democracy also recognizes that without widespread education in the basic aspects of constitutional democratic government for all citizens and without a public informed about pressing problems, crucial political and social decisions simply cannot be made' (IPRR: 449).

33. On the role that 'ordinary' politics, the 'big game of politics', plays in Rawls's theory, *see* Muirhead and Rosenblum 2006.

political philosophy is to work out from this "fund of implicitly shared ideas and principles" an explicit (and hopefully coherent) liberal conception. This fund, this "tradition of democratic thought" is the starting point. You do not argue for it. You do not ground it. You see what it leads to'.

On the one hand, as stated in the first pages of *Political Liberalism*, one of the aspects of a 'political conception of justice'

> ... is that its content is expressed in terms of certain fundamental ideas seen as implicit in the public political culture of a democratic society ... In a democratic society there is a tradition of democratic thought, the content of which is at least familiar and intelligible to the educated common sense of citizens generally. Society's main institutions, and their accepted forms of interpretation, are seen as a fund of implicitly shared ideas and principles (*PL*: 13–14).

On the other, Rawls's entire theoretical framework is based on a constant normative projection driven by a dual ambition: to be able to show, theoretically, that the ideas of a just society and of 'public reason' could consistently be justified and, at the same time, 'to hope' that such an idea could be convincing for and adopted by an ideal interlocutor (or by the public culture of a democratic society).

It is not up to me here to judge the validity of such an approach; nor can I discuss whether and to what extent Rawls was aware of this tension, if he managed to resolve it, or if this very unresolved tension was instead particularly fruitful. Recall, however, the wider background against which this tension must be read. As we have seen, when Rawls speaks of 'public reason', he is very well aware of the difficulties this concept encounters. Yet in his view, however serious these difficulties may be and however widespread cynicism and scepticism (which Habermas called 'normative defeatism') may be, there are no real alternatives to an idea of democratic and constitutional politics based on *reasonableness* and the difficult, deliberative construction of areas of consensus that can govern the radical pluralism of our time and make it productive. Or rather, there is an alternative, and Rawls too – in the opening passage of IPRR which recalls a similar intervention by Habermas (see Chapter Five, note 25) – evokes a political vision *à la* Carl Schmitt:

> ... those who reject constitutional democracy with its criterion of reciprocity will of course reject the very idea of public reason. For them the political relation may be that of friend or foe, to those of a particular religious or secular community or those who are not; or it may be a relentless struggle to win the world for the whole truth. Political liberalism does not engage those who think this way. The zeal to embody the whole truth in politics is incompatible with an idea of public reason that belongs with democratic citizenship (IPRR: 442).

Perhaps Rawls's final statement in the 1995 Introduction (in which the great tragedies of the twentieth century are evoked with dramatic emphasis) can help us to a better understanding of his conception of the relationship between *philosophy*, *public political culture* and *political processes* and between *ideas* and *real processes*. Rawls tells us that, in his works, he has tried 'to say how a reasonably just and well-ordered democratic society might be possible', proposing his own 'political conception', justice as fairness, which could find a place among the political conceptions of our time. Of course, he wrote, there will always be someone radically objecting to this proposal, arguing that 'a just and well-ordered democratic society is not possible' and even considering it 'obvious' that this should be so (2005: lviii). In the face of such a cynical attitude, political philosophy, has a modest – but perhaps indispensable – task: 'it may study political questions at many different levels of generality and abstractness, all valuable and significant'. It may wonder about a number of issues, for example, 'whether a just and well-ordered constitutional democracy is possible and what makes it so' (2005: lix). The answer to this question is not just a philosophical matter: it 'affects our background thoughts and attitudes about the world as a whole. And it affects these thoughts and attitudes before we come to actual politics, and limits or inspires how we take part in it'. Of course, general philosophical debates, as such, could never be 'the daily stuff of politics' but, nonetheless, they will not be meaningless or without effect since 'what we think their answers are will shape the underlying attitudes of the public culture and the conduct of politics' (*ibid.*).[34]

Therefore, developing ideas that show the *possibility* of a democratic and just society is anything but a useless or trivial task. To assume the opposite – or not to oppose ideas that affirm its impossibility – has real effects, both in public culture and in the historical making of politics. 'A cause of the fall of Weimar's constitutional regime was that none of the traditional elites of Germany supported its constitution or were willing to cooperate to make it work. They no longer believed a decent liberal parliamentary regime was possible' (*ibid.*). Everyone knows very well what happened afterwards.

Thus it is possible to understand Rawls's frequent choice to adopt what might be called an *optative* approach, expressing both *possibility* and *desirability*: it is a way, perhaps, to express good reasons for hoping. In *Theory of Justice* and in *Political Liberalism* (as we can read in the last part of the 1995 Introduction) Rawls presented 'a candidate', a theory that aspired to be considered a reasonable response to a radical and 'existential' question for our societies: whether 'a reasonably just political society is possible' (2005: lx). Of course, it is a 'candidate' that, first and foremost, takes part in a competition between ideas, theories and doctrines that philosophy must clarify and resolve; but it is also a 'candidate' that, by implication, already lives and works on a daily basis in the public political culture: it is from here that it moves to philosophy. Philosophy, in turn, can help to make this political culture richer and more aware.

According to Rawls, 'a reasonably just political society' is a constitutional democracy that, at its best, is a *deliberative democracy*. In other words, it is a

---

34. It is impossible not to notice the consistency between Rawls's words and a passage of Dewey's that I recalled in the Introduction to this book (Dewey 1984 [1927]: 240–1). In the first pages of *Justice as Fairness: A reformulation* (2001), Rawls would give a concise and meaningful account of the duties and role of political philosophy 'as part of the public political culture of a society'.

democracy in which citizens offer reasons that can be considered acceptable by others whenever they must define the constitutional basis of their coexistence and the principles of justice that can regulate their social cooperation. Such a view may be regarded with scepticism or cynicism but one must also be aware of the alternative already proposed by history: 'the wars of this century', Rawls reminds us, 'with their extreme violence and increasing destructiveness, culminating in the manic evil of the Holocaust, raise in an acute way the question whether political relations must be governed by power and coercion alone' (*ibid.*); or whether a form of *political* and *deliberative reasonableness* is, in fact, possible.

6. The Rawlsian approach to deliberative democracy

So far, I have reconstructed Rawls's theoretical journey, at the end of which he defined 'a well-ordered constitutional democracy' also as 'a deliberative democracy' (IPRR: 447–8). Rawls could no longer contribute to developing and clarifying this definition. Nonetheless, with the few final pages of his work, he sent a strong message and opened the way for a possible, subsequent theoretical work of great importance for all those who have worked and want to work on an ideal of and/or a theoretical model of deliberative democracy: he showed how the idea of deliberative democracy might find a strong foundation in the assumptions and theoretical/ philosophical content of his idea of political liberalism and constitutional democracy. It is perhaps at this level that we can see Rawls's most significant contribution to the theoretical consolidation of a deliberative conception of democracy: his theoretical categories (the distinction between 'comprehensive doctrines' and 'political views'; the distinction between *rationality* and *reasonableness*; the 'burdens of judgment'; the notion of *overlapping consensus*; the idea of *public reason* as a deliberative paradigm) that an ideal and/or a theoretical model of deliberative democracy can hardly avoid facing up to.

The authors who had already been inspired in their research by Rawls's idea of deliberative democracy soon began to develop the suggestions coming from Rawls's notion of public reason. Joshua Cohen, in particular, in essays subsequent to his 1989 text on which we have already dwelt extensively, developed his theories (and, according to Freeman, revised them considerably)[35] precisely on the basis of the notions of public reason and of reasonable pluralism.[36] Amy Gutmann and Dennis Thompson did the same in their work on reasonable disagreement

---

35. Freeman 2000: 393. Here he noted a different balance between 'process' and 'substance' in Cohen's writings after 1989. According to Freeman, in the first essay, the model of democratic decision did not seem to incorporate any 'hypothetical standard or other means that determines the validity of actual deliberated decisions'.

36. 'Procedure and substance in deliberative democracy', which originally appeared in 1997, and 'Democracy and liberty' (1998), the latter also quoted by Rawls in *PL*. In his 1997 essay, Cohen explains how he 'modified the conception of deliberative democracy to take account of the fact of reasonable pluralism' (2009a: 8–9), also because of Rawls's growing attention to this topic since the mid-1980s. *See also* Cohen 1993 and 1994.

(1996) one of the most important texts on deliberative democracy of the 1990s, which is positioned within the theoretical co-ordinates set by Rawls. This text has differences from Rawls's but it would not have been possible without his work. Soon, many other authors adopted Rawls's categories as essential terms of reference: for example, Cass Sunstein, with his concept of *incompletely theorized agreements*[37] and, more critically, John Dryzek and Simon Niemeyer, with their concept of *meta-consensus* (Dryzek and Niemeyer 2006).

An essay by Samuel Freeman (Rawls's close associate and then editor of his works) has been strongly influential in surveying and developing the implications contained in Rawls's texts and in systematising a Rawlsian approach to deliberative democracy. 'Deliberative democracy: a sympathetic comment', published in 2000 in *Philosophy & Public Affairs*, was widely referenced and quoted in subsequent critical literature and also in the premises of much 'empirical' literature. These references, however, often contained a degree of ambiguity. In many cases, Freeman's essay is introduced as a presentation of deliberative democracy *tout court*, without informing the reader of the Rawlsian roots of the positions expressed.

Freeman tries to explain and develop indications from Rawls's texts. The idea of public reason, Freeman says, 'is a complicated idea, but it is essential to understanding what may be called "the political liberal ideal of deliberative democracy" endorsed by Rawls, Cohen and others' (Freeman 2000: 397). At the end of his essay, Freeman recognises that 'one of the more pressing problems confronting Rawlsian deliberative theorists is to respond to doubts about the fruitfulness of the concepts of reasonableness and public reason' (*ibid.*: 417).[38] It is not possible – or necessary – here to discuss how Freeman presented Rawls's idea of public reason. What is more important, because of the wide circulation of this essay, is to note how Rawls's difficult balance between the *idea* and the *ideal* of public reason, between the *constructive* and *reconstructive* sides of his concept, tends to be lost here. This loss had significant consequences for the understanding of deliberative democracy: 'the idea of deliberative democracy' – Freeman wrote – '*serves more as political ideal than as an explanatory concept. For political scientists, this may be reason enough to disregard the idea. For political philosophers, the question remains of the feasibility of this ideal and*

---

37. The idea of 'incompletely theorized agreements' and the idea of 'overlapping consensus' are clearly correlated. Sunstein states: 'both ideas attempt to bring about stability and social agreements in the face of diverse "comprehensive" doctrines. But the two ideas are far from the same. I am most interested in the problem of producing agreements on particular outcomes and low-level principles to justify them, with the thought that people who disagree on general principles can often agree on individual cases. Rawls in a related but different possibility – that people who disagree on comprehensive doctrines can agree on certain political abstractions and use that agreement for political purposes. Of course this is also true.' (Sunstein 1995: 1735, note 8; *see also* Sunstein 1999).

38. Freeman distinguishes between different 'arguments' supporting deliberative democracy: the epistemic ones (among which he includes Habermas, mistakenly, I think); the ones that see deliberative democracy as 'a fundamental moral ideal' (Cohen); and, lastly, those based on the idea of public reason (Freeman 2000: 393–6).

whether it can ever play a role in explaining political conduct' (*ibid.*: 373, my emphasis).

Here, the emphasis has definitely shifted to deliberative democracy as an *ideal*, its 'practicability' and the conditions that make its realisation possible. The risk associated with this is of a subjective-voluntarist approach obscuring Rawls's effort to think about a normative dimension *immanent* to the historical reality of our constitutional democracies, as well as his effort to look at the way in which an idea of public reason had acted, acts and would act in the historical reality of our constitutional democracies. Habermas faced the relationship between factuality and normativity in a different way, as we have seen. This variety of approaches can be found in subsequent developments in the theoretical field of deliberative democracy, mirroring different ways of understanding and practising it, as I will show in Chapter Thirteen of this work.

In any case, it would soon become possible to speak properly of a 'Rawlsian' approach to deliberative democracy: this approach would affect many authors but, of course, would also be set next to – and against – other approaches and other ideas of how to conceive deliberative democracy and what theoretical basis for it is more convincing or more solid. As we have seen, in the same years and from within his own theoretical perspective, Habermas also encountered the idea of deliberative democracy. Rawls and Habermas, with their works of the early 1990s, both played (in different ways) decisive roles in establishing the theoretical foundations of deliberative democracy. It is possible to say that this 'encounter' casts a retrospective light on each philosophers' entire theoretical approach.

Hence, perhaps, the risk of an optical illusion, so to speak: *in retrospect*, it is possible and entirely licit to trace the theoretical and conceptual elements that can now be considered basic elements of a theory of deliberative democracy back to Rawls and Habermas.[39] But it would be a mistake to confine Rawls and Habermas within this perspective: both of them follow a strategy of research of their own, starting from certain philosophical and theoretical presuppositions and producing major works (such as *Theory of Justice* and *Theory of Communicative Action*) without the theme of 'deliberative democracy', as such, being either directly or immediately present. Yet, in the end, both of them speak of deliberative democracy

---

39. Larmore (2003: 369–73), for example, sets out the preconditions of subsequent 'public reason' in the same way in which Rawls, in *Theory of Justice*, formulates the principle of *publicity*. Another example can be found in Cohen (2003: 101–2), who revisits some passages of *Theory of Justice*: 'although Rawls says little about democratic process, he seems there to endorse some variant of a deliberative conception. In justice as fairness, the justice of law is defined by reference to an idealized legislative process in which representatives aim to enact just laws. Rawls does not explain precisely how this idealized legislative process, which is part of the theory of justice, is connected to an actual legislative process in a just society. But it is clear that actual political process will not adopt just laws, as defined by the ideal process, unless citizens, representatives, and officials aim to enact just laws, and, as in the ideal process, jointly explore how best to achieve that aim ... In *Theory of Justice* Rawls assumes this view of democratic politics as an arena of argument rather than a tamed competition for power, fair aggregation of interests, or expression of shared cultural commitments'.

and find, each one with their own tools and theoretical assumptions, the reasons to do so consistently with their previous path.

Because of their later influence, trying to grasp similarities and differences, agreements and disagreements, between what are now commonly called 'Rawlsian' and Habermasian' approaches to deliberative democracy – that is, trying to understand in what different ways Rawls and Habermas have contributed to the subsequent developments of the theoretical field of deliberative democracy – is a theoretical task of great importance that I will tackle in the concluding chapter of this work. Here I want to forewarn the reader that the entire theory of deliberative democracy cannot be attributed to a dichotomy between Habermas's and Rawls's matrixes. Indeed, many authors would note the limits and contradictions of the two great scholars' positions and would search for new theories and approaches, even on specifically philosophical grounds. Future reference (polemical or not) to Habermas and Rawls will, however, be unavoidable. Precisely for this reason, and to complete the present analysis, I will now consider the *direct dialogue* between Rawls and Habermas that took place in 1995: a debate that is generally considered one of the most important episodes in the philosophy of the end of the twentieth century.

Chapter Twelve

The Dialogue between Habermas and Rawls: Just a 'Family Quarrel'?

1. Introduction

The direct dialogue between Habermas and Rawls in 1995 has implications for the larger theoretical positions of both thinkers. Analysing this debate is complex, not only because of its many implications but also because of the complicated timeline of when and to which texts, interventions, and responses were made.[1]

At the beginning of his first essay, in 1995, Habermas describes Rawls's philosophical project as the proposal of 'an intersubjectivist version of Kant's principle of autonomy'. 'We act autonomously when we obey those laws which could be accepted by all concerned on the basis of a public use of their reason.' Habermas writes: 'In *Political Liberalism*, in which Rawls has concluded a twenty-year process of extension and revision of his theory of justice', Rawls 'exploits this moral concept of autonomy as the key to explaining the political autonomy of citizens of a democratic society'. Habermas then goes on to say, 'because I admire this project, share its intentions, and regard its essential results as correct, the dissent I express here will remain within the bounds of a family quarrel' (*ibid.*: 50).

How to understand this famous reference to a 'family quarrel'? Was Habermas's remark a courtesy, a deliberate *understatement* or the result of true conviction? And is Habermas's 'dissent' truly limited to relatively marginal aspects of a shared view? The debate between Habermas and Rawls has been, and still is, the object of great interest and it is surely not possible to address it here in its entirety. In

---

1. Habermas's first statement on Rawls, 'Reconciliation through the public use of reason: remarks on John Rawls' *Political Liberalism*', originally responded to an invitation extended by the *Journal of Philosophy* 92(3), March 1995, and was later included in the collection *Die Einbeziehung des Anderen* (1996), published in English as *The Inclusion of the Other* (1998a). Rawls's reply ('Political liberalism: reply to Habermas') was published in the same issue of *JoP*. A later essay by Habermas ('"Reasonable" versus "true", or the morality of worldviews') also appeared in 1996, in the collection *Die Einbeziehung des Anderen*. Habermas could not have taken into account Rawls's later 'The idea of public reason revisited', and Rawls could not have read, at that stage, '"Reasonable" versus "true"'. These asymmetries make it difficult to analyse the dialogue and must be kept in mind. Habermas himself, in his 'Reply to my critics', which appeared in Finlayson and Freyenhagen (eds) 2011a, speaks of this 'asymmetry' (Habermas 2011: 283). Henceforth, I'll refer to Habermas's 'Reconciliation through the public use of reason' as REC, quoting from *The Inclusion of the Other* (1998a); to Rawls's reply as RH, quoting from the 2005 edition of *Political Liberalism*; and Habermas's '"Reasonable" versus "true"' as RvT, quoting once again from *The Inclusion of the Other* (1998a).

particular, there have been many interpretations of the actual differences and similarities between Rawls's and Habermas's perspectives.

Rainer Forst, for instance, believes that there is 'considerable common ground'. Their approach, 'standing in the Kantian tradition, seeks to forgo metaphysical foundations and instead relies on an intersubjective and procedural interpretation of moral autonomy and of the public use of reason as the basis for justifying principles of justice' (Forst 2012: 79–80).[2] 'Practical reason', which, in Kant, is founded on a transcendental constitution of the subject, becomes, in Rawls, an *intersubjective construction* of ideas and principles and, in Habermas, a *communicative rationality*, with its various discursive logics. However, within this framework (in which the common enemies are ethical realism, intuitionism, and scepticism about values and contextualism) there can be very different ways to understand the forms and processes with which the 'public uses of reason' are *socially and politically* constructed and expressed. So, despite the 'common ground', I think we shouldn't underestimate the (sometimes deep) differences between the two theoretical perspectives. Family quarrels can be very heated.

The dialogue between Habermas and Rawls concerns, more or less directly, all the crucial themes of their respective theoretical positions. I do not have the space to analyse all of its implications here[3] but I will note how this debate involves some of the issues that were crucial in the 'constitutive' process of the theoretical field of deliberative democracy. In particular:

a. The issue of the 'original position' and the 'ideal speech situation': do these two concepts play a similar role, or have a similar status?

b. The 'overlapping consensus' and the idea of 'reasonableness': what is the space for deliberative civic practices and what is the role of public deliberation as a source of democratic legitimacy?

c. The relationship between philosophy and public political culture, between the 'philosophers' and the 'citizens': how to conceive of the role of political philosophy and what follows from this for our understanding of deliberative democracy?

---

2. The debate between Habermas and Rawls is the subject of a collection of essays edited by James G. Finlayson and Fabian Freyenhagen (2011a, *see also* 2011b). For other texts specifically devoted to it *see* Rainer Forst (2012: chapter 4) and Charles Larmore (1999), although both start from their own theoretical viewpoints. Maffettone (2010:177–88) and Ferrara (1999: 26–9) also make direct reference to this debate. The literature on the general relationship between Habermas and Rawls is much wider: an important work by Kenneth Baynes (1992) addressed it before *Political Liberalism* and *Facts and Norms* came out, while an essay by McCarthy (1994) proposed a comparison between their 'Kantian constructivism and reconstructivism'.

3. Habermas, in his opening remarks, focuses mainly on three issues: a) the 'original position' (the way Rawls builds it, its implications); b) the question of 'reasonableness' and 'overlapping consensus' and the distinction between 'rational acceptability' and 'acceptance'; and c) the question of the relationship between private and public autonomy, including the 'liberties of the moderns', and 'liberties of the ancients' (or in Habermas, the issue of the 'co-originality' between individual freedoms and the forms of popular sovereignty).

2. 'Original position' and 'ideal speech situation'

In his 'Reply to Habermas', Rawls analyses the difference between what he describes as *'two devices of representation'*: his 'original position' and the 'ideal speech situation' proposed by Habermas. He acknowledges that these two notions have 'different aims and roles, as well as distinctive features serving different purposes' (RH: 373); and yet, as we shall see, he finds significant parallels between them.

The original position is 'an analytical device used to formulate a conjecture' (RH: 381) and to answer a question about the principles of political justice on which citizens – considered free and equal, rational and reasonable – can find agreement, given certain binding conditions (the 'veil of ignorance'). In this Reply Rawls underlines, more than elsewhere, the *open and conjectural* character of the conclusions reached by citizens. Their character is conjectural, because 'we must check it against the fixed points of our considered judgments at different levels of generality' (using the method of 'reflective equilibrium', a theme to which we shall come back) and 'we also must examine how well these principles can be applied to democratic institutions and what their results would be and hence ascertain how well they fit in practice with our considered judgments on due reflection' (*ibid.*). Therefore, 'in either direction, we may be led to revise our judgments' (*ibid.*). This is Rawls's response to Habermas's objection that Rawls's model is fundamentally *monological*, as 'each of us considers privately what all could will' (REC: 57) and the conclusions are implied 'from the beginning' (*ibid.*: 58), given the conditions imposed by the philosopher on the original position.[4]

Habermas also noted that, despite abandoning the initial purpose of conceiving the choice in the original position in terms of the theory of 'rational choice', Rawls continues to exclude a 'moral standpoint' from the parties' logics of choice: the parties 'need not regard matters from the moral point of view which would require them to take account of what is in the equal interest of all, for this impartiality is exacted by a situation that throws a veil of ignorance over the mutually disinterested, though free and equal parties' (REC: 51). For Habermas, Rawls is not consistent: *de facto*, he *introduces* and *presupposes* 'normative content' in the original position ('above all those ideas he associates with the concept of the moral person: the sense of fairness and the capacity for one's own conception of

---

4. Habermas writes (REC: 58) that, in Rawls's model, 'the veil of ignorance constrains from the beginning the field of vision of parties in the original position to the basic principles on which presumptively free and equal citizens would agree, notwithstanding their divergent understandings of self and world .... Following the justification of the principles of justice, the veil of ignorance is gradually raised at the successive steps of framing the constitution, of legislation, and of applying law. Since the new information that thereby flows in must harmonize with the basic principles already selected under conditions of informational constraint, unpleasant surprises must be avoided. If we are to ensure that no discrepancies arise, we must construct the original position already with knowledge, and even foresight, of all the normative contents that could potentially nourish the shared self-understanding of free and equal citizens in the future. In other words, the theoretician himself would have to shoulder the burden of anticipating at least parts of the information of which he previously relieved the parties in the original position!'.

the good; and then "the concept of the fair cooperation of politically autonomous citizens'" [REC: 59]). Finally, the adoption of a 'distributive' paradigm of justice (which, in the first instance, leads us to consider the same basic rights as 'primary goods') leads Rawls to blur the distinction between norms and values, between ethically-oriented acting and teleological acting (REC: 53–6).

To this objection to the supposed 'monological' character of his original position, Rawls replies by proposing a *public* process of discussion and verification of the principles of justice: 'all discussions are from the point of view of citizens in the culture of civil society, which Habermas calls the *public sphere*. There, we as citizens discuss how justice as fairness is to be formulated, and whether this or that aspect of it seems acceptable' (RH: 349). Rawls thus tends to reinterpret in a 'deliberative' and 'public' key (and not only as a mere 'mirroring' of the initial principles) the four-stage sequence leading from the original position to juridical applications.[5]

It is not my aim here to assess Habermas's objections and Rawls's reply as respectively more or less well grounded or satisfactory. Rather, I'm interested in the surprising way in which Rawls considers Habermas's 'ideal speech situation'. After describing it as 'an account of the truth and validity of judgments of both theoretical and practical reason', he takes it as a 'comprehensive doctrine' that, just like other conceptions present in a society's 'background culture', can enter public discussion. 'The claims of the *ideal of discourse* and of its procedural conception of democratic institutions' (RH: 382–3, my emphasis) can be considered '*in the same way*' as the principles of justice are discussed in the public sphere (RH: 383, my emphasis).

I believe this is a manifest misunderstanding of the actual status that Habermas had given the concept of an 'ideal speech situation'. Besides, as we have seen, this notion had always been easily misinterpreted, to the point that Habermas himself used it less and less, even though it always remained 'stuck' to him, so to speak. In any case, Habermas had never set the 'ideal speech situation' as a principle for citizens to adopt as a basis of their social co-operation: if anything, the 'ideal speech situation' is rather an idealising presupposition acting within the discursive and argumentative practices in which citizens discuss validity claims emerging from their communicative interaction. In short, the 'ideal speech situation' is a *presupposition* of public discussion – certainly not its *object*. This theoretical status – a normative dimension necessarily implied by discursive practices – is openly recalled also in Habermas's discussion with Rawls.[6]

Rawls, instead, relies on what he describes as a 'general and wide reflective equilibrium', setting it against Habermas's 'test of moral truth or validity',

---

5. *See* Chapter Six, Section 1 for the issue of the four-stage sequence as it was presented in *Theory of Justice* and as Cohen reformulated it. Rawls illustrated it again in his 'Reply to Habermas' (RH: 397–9).

6. *See* REC 57–8. In the final footnote of this passage, Habermas quotes William Rehg's *Insight and Solidarity: The discourse ethics of Jürgen Habermas* (1994), one of the most important texts related to the reception of Habermas in the US.

founded on 'rational acceptance in the ideal discourse situation' (RH: 384–5). This 'general and wide reflective equilibrium' (unlike the 'restricted' one, which every individual can seek in themselves with regard to their judgments) indicates, we could say, an ever-open process of 'adjustment', verification and collective revision. It amounts to the citizens going 'back and forth' between judgments and principles with regard to the principles of justice and their application. A 'wide and general' reflective equilibrium indicates the formation of judgments outside the individual dimension (in which to seek coherence between one's *own* judgments and principles) and involves a dialogue and a *public* confrontation with *other* principles and judgments, and their 'good reasons'. Only in this sense, Rawls adds, does it 'resemble' Habermas's 'test': 'it is a point at infinity we can never reach, though we may get closer to it in the sense that through discussion, our ideals, principles, and judgments seem more reasonable to us and we regard them as better founded than they were before' (RH: 385). Once again, therefore, the 'ideal speech situation' is read as a *regulative ideal*.

Simplifying somewhat, we could say that the 'original position' is a thought-experiment that allows us to construct, in idealised conditions, the principles of justice on which free, equal, rational and reasonable citizens *must* (rationally) agree (in the original version of *Theory of Justice*) or *might* (reasonably) agree (in the 'deliberative' vision of *Political Liberalism*).[7] These principles may be taken, in non-ideal conditions (and Rawls 'hopes' that this will happen), as a model for the construction of constitutional essentials or for the definition of fair forms of social co-operation. On the other hand, the 'ideal speech situation' – leaving aside Habermas's early 'idealising' formulations, which he later abandoned – is a necessary presupposition, constantly active and operating in every form of the communicative and discursive practice directed at reaching an understanding. In a way, it is an 'ideal' but it isn't projected 'forward', so to speak: it is already implied by practice, being its *condition of possibility*. It is one of the ways to build communicative action; it indicates a normative tension immanent to the forms of communicative acting.[8]

This debate is interesting from many standpoints. However, what particularly interests me here is how these two central notions of Rawls's and Habermas's theoretical models influenced – often implicitly – the general understanding of deliberative democracy (as a democratic ideal) and deliberative politics (as a reconstructive and normative category).

---

7. Of course, the formulation that we have adopted here does not address an issue that, among scholars of Rawls, constitutes one of the central and most contentious problems: namely, the interpretation of the transition from *TJ* to *PL*, the sense of discontinuity between these two works but also the individual theoretical aspects that mark their differences from each other.

8. 'Rawls imposes a common perspective on the parties in the original position through informational constraints and thereby neutralizes the multiplicity of particular interpretive perspectives from the outset. Discourse ethics, by contrast, views the moral point of view as embodied in an intersubjective praxis of argumentation which enjoins those involved to an idealizing enlargement of their interpretive perspectives' (REC: 57).

3. 'Reasonableness' and 'consensus'; 'justification' and 'legitimation': the forms and ways of deliberative practice

The discussion of 'reasonableness' and 'truth' and of the foundations of the idea of 'overlapping consensus' – a central theme of the dialogue between Habermas and Rawls – has significant implications from the specific viewpoint of the present book. At stake, directly or indirectly, is one precise question: what is the nature, the appropriate space and the characteristics of public deliberation as a possible foundation of democratic legitimacy? The question can be posed in other terms: *how* to achieve 'overlapping consensus'? What kinds of discourses are produced in the course of this construction? What argumentative logics come into play in this process (ethical, moral or purely pragmatic discourses)? It is not easy to grasp all the nuances of this dialogue, not least because this issue was the most affected by the abovementioned temporal 'asymmetry': Habermas's extensive critical analysis of the notion of overlapping consensus and on the distinction between public reason and metaphysical doctrines is much better argued in '"Reasonable" versus "True"' (1996, English trans., 1998) than in his first essay (1995) and yet it couldn't take into account Rawls's 'revisiting' of the idea of public reason (1997), nor could Rawls discuss it directly in his "Reply to Habermas" (1995).

Habermas versus Rawls

In 'Reconciliation' (1995), Habermas critically examines Rawls's concept of 'overlapping consensus', trying to bring out the weakness of some of its theoretical assumptions. He raises two interrelated questions: a) whether 'the overlapping consensus, on which the theory of justice depends, plays a cognitive or merely instrumental role' (REC: 60); and b) what character Rawls attributes to the 'reasonable': if he uses it 'as a predicate for the validity of moral judgments or for the reflective attitude of enlightened tolerance' (*ibid.*). For Habermas, both issues raise several questions. Consider the process that leads to a defined overlapping consensus about a political conception, by citizens who maintain their own comprehensive views: is it based on some 'cognitive content' (that is, on ideas or norms provisionally certified as 'valid' after public discussion)? Or is that consensus simply based on pragmatic and 'instrumental' motivations (so that the parties only agree due to a common interest in maintaining some social order)? What differentiates overlapping consensus from a mere *modus vivendi*? Relatedly, can 'reasonableness' be regarded as a way to express a *moral* stance, or does it simply indicate the propensity to collaborate (a prerequisite of *any* form of co-existence)?

The key to understanding Rawls, Habermas notes, is his method of 'reflective equilibrium': the fundamental concepts of his theory ('moral person', 'fair cooperation', 'well-ordered society') are obtained through 'a rational reconstruction of proven intuitions, that is, intuitions actually *found* in the practices and traditions of a democratic society' (REC: 60). A reflective equilibrium can only be reached when it is certified that those institutions, reconstructed by the philosopher, are 'reasonably' accepted by the citizens of that society, or at least are not 'rejectable' based on good reasons.[9]

But this is only the first step: at this point, the principles of justice so defined must be subjected to another test, to check whether they are acceptable in the context of a pluralistic society. So, although derived from the political culture of a democratic society, those principles aspire to a normative validity that goes beyond the specific context from which they were derived.[10] It is necessary to show that 'the central concept of the person, on which the theory ultimately rests, must be sufficiently neutral to be acceptable from the interpretive perspectives of different worldviews' (REC: 61). Herein lies Habermas's fundamental objection: this second 'test of acceptability' of a conception of justice 'is problematic because the test cannot be undertaken in an immanent manner in the case of acceptability; it is no longer a *move within the theory*' (REC: 61, my emphasis). How to understand this objection? If we seriously take on the burden of 'placing' those principles in a pluralistic society, Habermas here seems to claim, we cannot adopt the same method that we applied at the 'first stage' (that of the theoretical construction of the original position):

> The principles justified at the first stage must be exposed to public discussion at the second stage. Only when the theoretical design is completed can the fact of pluralism be brought into play and the abstractions of the original position revoked. The theory as a whole must be subjected to criticism by citizens in the forum of public reason. But this now refers not to the fictional citizens of a just society about whom statements are made within the theory but to real citizens of flesh and blood. The theory, therefore, must leave the outcome of such a test of acceptability undetermined (REC: 61).

To be sure, Rawls 'has in mind real discourses whose outcome is open'; but Habermas finds Rawls's solution unsatisfactory and a little simplistic. He asked, 'What if it turns out that the principles of justice as fairness cannot gain the support of reasonable doctrines, so that the case for stability fails? ... We should have to see whether acceptable changes in the principles of justice would achieve stability' (*PL*: 65–6). Habermas notices a serious limitation here: after all, it is the

---

9.   For Rawls, according to Freeman, 'a political conception of justice is worked up from certain "fundamental intuitive ideas" that are implicit in the public culture of a democratic society. Rawls regards these fundamental ideas … as the building blocks and argumentative means of support for the political conception of justice. Fundamental intuitive ideas are themselves fixed considered convictions, in the sense that Rawls presumes that they are presupposed by public debate and deliberation in a democratic society, as a part of common-sense public reasoning' (Freeman 2007a: 332).

10. 'Of course, Rawls does not wish to limit himself solely to the fundamental normative convictions of a particular political culture: even the present-day Rawls, *pace* Richard Rorty, has not become a contextualist' (REC: 60). According to Alessandro Ferrara (1999: 29), the notion of overlapping consensus evokes problems due to 'an unsolved tension, underlying Rawls's intellectual trajectory, between a constructivist inspiration and a contextualist sensibility that underlie two different understandings of normative validity'.

philosopher who seeks 'to anticipate in reflection the direction of real discourses as they would probably unfold under conditions of a pluralistic society' (REC: 62). Who is the 'we' – the subject mentioned by Rawls – that should see what 'acceptable changes' of the justice principles are needed, if the public discussion brings out reluctance or refusal to accept them?

In any case, 'such a more or less realistic simulation of real discourses', which the philosopher can anticipate, 'cannot be incorporated into the theory in the same way as the derivation of possibilities of self-stabilization from the underlying premises of a just society. For now the citizens themselves debate about the premises developed by the parties in the original position' (*ibid.*). Ultimately, we could formulate Habermas's criticism as follows: in Rawls, the transition from the principles of justice elaborated in the conditions of theoretical 'purity' operative in the original position to the verification of their sustainability in the 'real discourses' of a pluralistic society lacks an essential connection, that is, a *theoretical vision* of how citizens *can discuss*, and *do actually discuss*, the principles of justice that should regulate their social life. Most of all, the theory does not *truly* leave the outcome of discussion open: it cannot be theory itself, as it was initially constructed, that accounts for this 'real' moment.

This point leads to Habermas's second objection: how is an overlapping consensus actually constructed? This notion only ends up expressing 'the functional contribution that the theory of justice can make to the peaceful institutionalization of social cooperation; but in this the intrinsic value of a *justified* theory must already be presupposed' (REC: 62). For Habermas, Rawls radically weakens the theoretical premises of this concept at the very moment when he seems to exclude the possibility that there might be 'some *epistemic* relation between the validity of his theory and the prospect of its neutrality toward competing worldviews being confirmed in public discourses' (REC: 63). In any case, from Habermas's point of view, if you accept the way Rawls conceives the distinction between 'political' and 'metaphysical', an overlapping consensus can only be produced on the basis of functional reasons.

Rawls's concept of 'moral person' is marked by reasonableness but, Habermas argues, 'the concept of a person itself already presupposes the concept of practical reason' (REC: 64) and therefore evokes the necessity that such a person be committed to producing *moral discourses*. However, Rawls, according to Habermas, tends to exclude the possibility that the construction of overlapping consensus could take place on this ground: the 'moral point of view' – with its claims of normative validity, its specific cognitive content and its specific rules of argumentation testing the possible universalisation of a norm – does not come into play for him. Rather, he believes that the moral point of view belongs to the domain of 'comprehensive doctrines' and these cannot be part of a shared consensus about an autonomous political conception. Rawls's sharp separation between the political domain and the metaphysical one of comprehensive doctrines (remembering that this features in Rawls's theory at the stage *before* IPRR) relates the creation of consensus to a neutralisation of the moral point of view, which is confined to the ethical dimension proper of worldviews.

Those who find an agreement on such exclusively political terms, thus, do not really discuss what is (more) 'just' and do not question the validity claims of *their* norms; from the perspective of public reason, they merely *acknowledge* that their idea of what is just, rooted in their comprehensive idea of what is 'good', is *compatible* with other ideas of what is just based on other ideas of 'good'. So, a certain political conception is *accepted* but its *rational acceptability* is not really discussed. For Rawls, instead, public discourse cannot address issues of normative validity but can only ascertain the possible existence of a common ground, which is entirely and solely political. Therefore, what matters is mainly reasonableness, as the outcome of fallibilist awareness and of a sense of *civility*, implying the propensity to tolerance and co-operation, with an accurate strategy of avoidance of all those issues whose discussion would inevitably involve truth claims.[11]

The plausibility of Habermas's criticisms is debatable and certainly it is not my task to assess it here. What matters for the purpose of this book is to note an important implication: for Habermas, moral discourses, with their claims of normative validity and their specific cognitive dimension, *cannot* be excluded from the public use of reason or from public discussion regarding politics. The deliberative practice of the citizens of a democratic society cannot pursue some common base of consensus while bracketing the moral point of view: if it doesn't address those issues of normative validity, such consensus risks being not too different from the mere *modus vivendi* that Rawls, too, wishes to avoid.

Thus far I have presented Habermas's criticism of Rawls; and many objections could be raised in this regard. For instance, we could note that in Rawls's view – at least the one shown in the 1995 Introduction and in IPRR – if citizens converge on an autonomous political conception, this happens insofar as, from *their* point of view, they consider their comprehensive vision true or just, believing that it allows them to recognise themselves in that political conception. Thus, for Rawls also, the moral point of view is fully part of the public discussion. From Rawls's perspective, the problem was rather to understand how *different* and *controversial* moral discourses could coexist in the political sphere – and how they can keep claiming their own truth when they enter such a sphere – in which no discourse could ever claim to have the whole or only truth. Instead, as we shall see shortly, Habermas believes that a moral discourse, to be such, has to imply a universalising tension: reaching an understanding on a claim of moral validity, *if and when such a thing is possible*, can only happen starting from 'the same reasons' (RvT: 86).

Rawls versus Habermas

In his extensive Reply, Rawls restates his theses and then significantly develops some of his points: 'the central idea is that political liberalism moves within the category of the political and leaves philosophy as it is'; it proceeds apart from all 'religious, metaphysical and moral' doctrines and 'abstains from assertions

---

11. On this point, *see* Habermas's reply (REC: 124).

about the domain of comprehensive views except as necessary when these views are unreasonable and reject all variations of the basic essentials of a democratic regime' (RH: 375). 'Habermas's position, on the other hand, is a comprehensive doctrine that covers many things far beyond political philosophy' (RH: 376). I shall tackle the implications of this statement (what is the task of philosophy and, in particular, political philosophy) in the next section. For now, I wish to go back to the main topic of discussion so far: how does Rawls reply to the objections on reasonableness and overlapping consensus?

On this point, Rawls's reply introduces significant new developments, which many scholars regard as new and original elements of his theoretical model. One of them is the theory of the 'three different kinds of justification'. We could say that here Rawls is deliberately taking the viewpoint of the participant, looking at the processes by which citizens, through deliberation, *justify* the overlapping consensus they reach about a political conception of justice.

The first level is what Rawls calls '*pro tanto* justification':

> ... in public reason the justification of the political conception takes into account only political values ... That is, the political values specified by it can be suitably ordered, or balanced, so that those values alone give a reasonable answer by public reason to all or nearly all questions concerning constitutional essentials and basic justice. This is the meaning of *pro tanto* justification. By examining a wide range of political questions to see whether a political conception can always provide a reasonable answer, we can check to see if it seems to be complete. But since political justification is *pro tanto* it may be overridden by citizens' comprehensive doctrines once all values are tallied up (RH: 386).

The '*pro tanto* justification' is a *partial* level of justification, proportioned to the rigid respect of public reason and its solely political motivations. Its 'partiality' (or *precariousness*, we could say) is also because it can always be *overridden* by comprehensive doctrines: the latter can 'take over' the solely political domain of such a justification, which calls into question the boundaries between political justifications and those rooted in comprehensive doctrines.

The second level of justification is 'full justification': it is the justification given by every citizen 'as a member of civil society': 'in this case, the citizen accepts a political conception and fills out its justification by embedding it in some way into the citizen's comprehensive doctrine as either true or reasonable, depending on what that doctrine allows' (RH: 386). Rawls underlines that the modes and terms of this embedding can vary greatly:

> ... it is left to each citizen, individually or in association with others, to say how the claims of political justice are to be ordered, or weighed, against nonpolitical values. The political conception gives no guidance in such questions, since it does not say how nonpolitical values are to be counted. This guidance belongs to citizens' comprehensive doctrines (RH: 386–7).

As freestanding as it may be, a political conception can always 'be embedded in various ways – or mapped, or inserted as a module – into the different doctrines citizens affirm' (RH: 387). Taking the standpoint of the single citizen, the latter can assess the relative weight of political and non-political values in several ways, as well as joining them together differently. But this is still a phase in which justification takes place in the 'inner forum' of each citizen individually: it is here that the citizen's evaluations take place, seeking a personal 'reflective equilibrium'.

In order to reach real overlapping consensus, therefore, a *third* level of justification is needed: the properly *public* one, involving an intersubjective, dialogical and deliberative dimension of reciprocity:

> ... public justification happens when all the reasonable members of political society carry out a justification of the shared political conception by embedding it in their several reasonable comprehensive views. In this case, reasonable citizens take one another into account as having reasonable comprehensive doctrines that endorse that political conception, and this mutual accounting shapes the moral quality of the public culture of political society (RH: 387).

There is one point on which Rawls seems to reject Habermas's objections fully: 'the express content' of comprehensive doctrines has

> ... no normative role in public justification: citizens do not look into the content of others' doctrines, and so remain within the bounds of the political. Rather, they take into account and give some weight only to the fact – the existence – of the reasonable overlapping consensus itself (RH: 387).

In short, the act by which citizens 'take one another into account' faces an insurmountable limit: all that we can do is discuss the *political implications* deriving from the reflective equilibrium of each citizen. As for all the rest, public reason can do nothing but abstain. This does not mean that one should not speak about all the rest: in the public sphere, or within a background culture, everyone can think or say whatever they wish. However, they surely cannot do so passing those discourses off as the outcome of public reason. At the level of *public* justification, there is a 'general and wide reflective equilibrium' that is different from the personal one of the previous level:

> ... the shared political conception is the common ground and all reasonable citizens taken collectively (but not acting as a corporate body) are held in general and wide reflective equilibrium in affirming the political conception on the basis of their several reasonable comprehensive doctrines (RH: 388).

Overlapping consensus is only produced through this process of reflective, wide and general verification. However, at this point, Rawls's argument risks appearing tautological: is the overlapping consensus *produced* at the end of this public justification, or is it (at least somewhat) *presupposed* by it?

> Only when there is a reasonable overlapping consensus can political society's political conception of justice be publicly – though never finally – justified. … There is, then, no public justification for political society without a reasonable overlapping consensus, and such justification also connects with the ideas of stability for the right reasons as well as of legitimacy (RH: 388–9).

Here, Rawls probably relies on a *necessary* circularity, a process that is necessarily recursive: to construct public justification one must rely on some basis of consensus (which is *already present* in the public culture of a democratic society) and, in turn, public justification can change, strengthen or widen it. In this sense, we could say, the method of reflective equilibrium is intrinsically 'deliberative' and the specific task of political philosophy is to bring up this shared foundation.

In any case, Rawls then distinguishes the consensus of 'everyday politics' – based on the different majorities that take shape every time in relation to a given political choice – from the 'reasonable overlapping consensus' related to an autonomous conception of justice. The latter form of consensus

> … tries to put no obstacles in the path of all reasonable doctrines endorsing a political conception by eliminating from this conception any idea which goes beyond the political, and which not all reasonable doctrines could reasonably be expected to endorse (to do that violates the idea of reciprocity) (RH: 389).

Such a form of consensus produces 'stability *for the right reasons*' (RH: 390–2), which is such because it represents the best form of 'social unity' that could reasonably be expected and 'the deepest' possible (RH: 391–2). It is a form of social unity comprising, on the one hand, agreement on the 'fundamental ideas of the political conception' and, on the other, these same ideas as 'endorsed' by the citizens' various comprehensive doctrines, expressing 'their deepest convictions – religious, philosophical, and moral' (RH: 392). The alternative is a simple *modus vivendi* in which every citizen produces their 'full' (second-level) justification, drawing from it their political conception, but there is no autonomous and truly shared political conception, able to ground social unity (so it is a form of stability but not for 'the right reasons'). Furthermore, a *modus vivendi* rests on the agents' instrumental motivations and, for this very reason, it is fragile and exposed to the constant risk that one of these agents might find it strategically useful to 'exit'.

As Rawls noted, a 'grave question' could potentially be raised at this point: 'if political justification is always *pro tanto*, how can public justification of the political conception of justice be carried out?' (RH: 392). Once again, here we find the idea that overlapping consensus (or better, a first 'basis' for it) is somehow already presupposed. 'The answer, of course', writes Rawls,

… is given by the existence and public knowledge of a reasonable overlapping consensus. In this case, citizens embed their shared political conception in their reasonable comprehensive doctrines. Then *we hope* that citizens will judge (by their comprehensive views) that political values either outweigh or are normally (though not always) ordered prior to whatever non-political values may conflict with them (RH: 392, my emphasis).

This hope is not 'unrealistic' for two reasons. First, it can be reasonably expected that citizens themselves understand (rationally and strategically) that they have a higher interest in ensuring the terms of equitable political co-operation (RH: 392–3). Second, there is 'the idea of legitimacy': citizens know they cannot expect or demand unanimity and that therefore a democratic constitution should include procedures based on the principle of majority. Then we can 'hope' that citizens will give priority to the 'political values' because they already have (as part of the basic intuitions of the public culture of a democratic society) an idea of the legitimacy and the principle of reciprocity on which it is based:

… the exercise of political power is legitimate only when it is exercised in fundamental cases in accordance with a constitution, the essentials of which all reasonable citizens as free and equal might reasonably be expected to endorse. Thus, citizens recognize the familiar distinction between accepting as (sufficiently) just and legitimate a constitution with its procedure for fair elections and legislative majorities, and accepting as legitimate (even when not just) a particular statute or a decision in a particular matter of policy (RH: 393).[12]

It is worth dwelling longer on Rawls's idea of legitimacy in order to highlight further contrasts in his view compared to Habermas's. As we have seen, Rawls has his own idea of the principle of liberal legitimacy; on the other hand, though, it should be noted that his notion of legitimacy seems rather weak in his discussion of Habermas's theses. Perhaps this is simply a misunderstanding of Habermas's position, as shown by the way Rawls almost seems surprised by Habermas's 'regular use' of 'the idea of legitimacy rather than justice' (RH: 427). A very obvious example is the issue of legality *versus* legitimation or, in Habermasian terms, social or factual validity *versus* discursive legitimation. In some pages of Rawls's Reply, (RH: 427–8), the idea of 'legitimacy' that emerges seems flattened to a mere notion of the 'legality' of political power and, indeed, according to Maffettone (2010: 226), here, 'Rawls employs legitimacy in a formal, Weberian

---

12. Immediately after these statements, Rawls exemplifies his argument by reference to the Quakers and their pacifist culture. The lesson is that, starting from a religious culture, we can derive many commitments and a wide variety of political attitudes. The different political and non-political values can be weighed and combined in many ways. Then, finally, the 'allegiance to a just and enduring constitutional government' may acquire a primary significance (RH: 393–4).

sense'. 'Just' and 'legitimate' are not the same thing, Rawls says, but we can sense that he understands legally or socially valid decisions as legitimate:

> ... democratic decisions and laws are legitimate, not because they are just but because they are legitimately enacted in accordance with an accepted legitimate democratic procedure. It is of great importance that the constitution specifying the procedure be sufficiently just, even though not perfectly just, as no human institution can be that. But it may not be just and still be legitimate. ... At some point, the injustice of the outcomes of a legitimate democratic procedure corrupts its legitimacy, and so will the injustice of the political constitution itself. But before this point is reached, the outcomes of a legitimate democratic procedure are legitimate whatever they are. This gives us purely procedural democratic legitimacy and distinguishes it from justice ... Legitimacy allows an undetermined range of injustice that justice might not permit (RH: 428).

This passage seems to show explicitly a substantive criterion of justice as a source of legitimation ('we always depend on our substantive judgments of justice': RH: 429), on which it should be necessary to dwell at length. As I do not have the space to do so, I'll merely note that Rawls's presentation of Habermas's thought entirely lacks a decisive Habermasian concept: the notion of 'communicative power' as the key to discursive legitimation of political decisions (or as criticism and contestation of a 'legal' or 'socially valid' norm that, nonetheless, is not legitimate).

In any case, in the end, Rawls believes he has answered Habermas's first objection: overlapping consensus is not a 'functional' or 'instrumental' idea of social stability. The answer, he concludes, 'is given by the third idea of justification – that of public justification – and by how it connects with the three further ideas of a reasonable overlapping consensus, stability for the right reasons, and legitimacy' (RH: 394).

As for the second objection – does the idea of 'reasonable' express the validity or truth of a moral judgment or does it merely indicate a tolerant attitude? – Rawls merely restates his convictions: 'political liberalism does not use the concept of moral truth applied to its own political (always moral) judgments. Here it says that political judgments are reasonable or unreasonable; and it lays out political ideals, principles, and standards as criteria of the reasonable' (RH: 394). For its purposes, political liberalism considers 'as sufficient' this idea of 'reasonable', founded on the two criteria we have already mentioned: the willingness of free and equal citizens to co-operate on a reciprocal basis and awareness of the 'burdens of judgment'. It is a 'minimal' idea, Rawls seems to say, but it is more than enough: there is no need to overload it with cognitive and epistemic meanings (RH: 395).

Implications for deliberative democracy

At this point, it is not up to me to propose judgments or evaluations that might appear as my taking the side of either Rawls or Habermas. I also cannot tackle the other great theme of the 1995 dialogue (the relationship between the 'liberties of the moderns' and 'liberties of the ancients', that is, whether private and public autonomy originated together or one before the other). I must limit myself to summing up my analysis in relation to my central question: does this debate have implications for our understanding of deliberative democracy and deliberative politics?

I believe that the fundamental dividing line between Habermas and Rawls concerns the way in which their positions conceive of the space and the role of citizens' deliberative practice as a constitutive moment of the legitimation of a democratic system: that is, the type and nature of public discourses that are involved in the process of construction (or criticism) of the legitimacy of such a system. Habermas does not think it is possible to place preliminary boundaries either on what can be publicly discussed or on the argumentative logics or types of discourse that are formed, coexist, and compete in the public sphere and in the procedures that link the formation of opinions and will to the institutional sphere of a democratic rule-of-law state. One of Habermas's main objections to the overlapping-consensus model is that the moral point of view, with its claims of normative validity, cannot be left out of the *political* construction of the possible grounds of agreement and co-operation. No deliberative politics could prescind from discussing 'what is (more) just to do', and doing so referring to the moral point of view.

These criticisms will be expressed even more sharply in '"Reasonable" *versus* "True"' (see especially RvT: 84–5). The impossibility of this exclusion – in Habermas's view – comes from a theoretical reconstruction of the discursive logics immanent to communicative action. In particular, Habermas believes that the *universalistic* dimension of the moral discourse cannot be left out of the political sphere. A deliberative politics cannot fail to include the moral point of view:

> that a public conception of justice should ultimately derive its moral authority from nonpublic reasons is counterintuitive. Anything valid should also be capable of public justification. Valid statements deserve the acceptance of everyone for the same reasons. The expression 'agreement' is ambiguous in this respect. Whereas parties who negotiate a compromise might accept the result for different reasons, participants in argumentation must reach a rationally motivated agreement, if at all, for the same reasons. Such practices of justification depend on a *jointly and public reached consensus* (RvT: 86).[13]

---

13. 'What Rawls calls the "public use of reason" presupposes the shared platform of an already achieved political consensus on fundamentals. The citizens can avail themselves of this platform only *post festum* [after the fact], that is, as a consequence of the emerging "overlap" of their different background convictions. ... This ingenious division of the burdens of justification relieves political philosophy of the troubling task of providing a substitute for the metaphysical justification of moral truths. Though struck from the public agenda, the metaphysical nevertheless remains the ultimate ground of the validity of what is morally right and ethically good. The political sphere, by contrast, is deprived of any source of validity of its own. The innovative

More precisely, therefore, what cannot be given up, for Habermas, is the peculiar *universalistic tension* proper to moral discourses: moral discourses presuppose that one should look for a 'rationally motivated understanding'. The problem is that it is not assured a priori that such understanding can be reached, yet this presupposition is inevitable if there are political issues requiring a moral discourse.

Rawls is much more parsimonious. From his perspective, to ensure a decent basis of 'social unity' and for our democratic societies – marked by radical ideological and religious pluralism – to 'hold together' reasonably, the political sphere must be as impartial as possible. It should be a shared ground that cannot but leave comprehensive doctrines, with their truth claims, in the background. However, as we have seen, in IPRR, Rawls comes to recognise – under certain conditions – the role of the public presence of non-public reasons. This role may also be positive, as those reasons can strengthen the motivations producing overlapping consensus; however, the paradigm of public reason offers a decisive *criterion of judgment* in this regard, allowing us to find, every time, the dividing line between shared or shareable political reasons and non-public reasons that are only 'true' from the viewpoint of a comprehensive doctrine. For Rawls, too, the 'political' implies a discussion of the fundamental principles of justice that can inspire fair social co-operation but such a discussion cannot involve the moral point of view rooted in the comprehensive view of each citizen. The public discussion concerns a *political* conception of justice: the properly *moral* premises or implications of this conception are up to every citizen to tackle or evaluate.

Rawls' final position on public reason seems to signal, however, a possible partial rapprochement with Habermas: for Habermas, the anarchic, subject-less dimension of the public sphere produces a network of discourses (pragmatic, moral, ethical and applicative) that cannot be regulated. We can *reconstruct* the type of discourses that take place within it but we cannot claim to define them *a priori* as political or non-political. In the public sphere deliberative politics produces communicative power, an *open* arena possibly producing consensus but also conflict and contestation, exercising a communicative power able to influence the process of formation of political will. In the later Rawls, as we have seen, there is no longer any claim to be able to define *a priori* the limits of public reason: it is a collective judgment formed through public deliberation that can establish, in specific cases, what can be truly considered public and political and what instead falls within the comprehensive view of the participants.

However, as we know, in Habermas's reconstructive model, there is more: if this were the case, the bases of social integration (or stability, in Rawls' jargon) would be radically undermined. Here comes into play the juridical *medium*, the

---

idea of an "overlapping consensus" preserves an internal connection between political justice and the moral components of worldviews, though with the proviso that this relation can only be grasped by the morality of worldviews and hence remains publicly inaccessible: "it is up to each comprehensive doctrine to say how its idea of reasonable connects with its concept of truth" [PL: 94]' (RvT: 84–5).

institutional mediation, the other 'track' that produces legitimacy. Discourses must be *filtered* by democratic and institutional procedures that produce legitimate and binding decisions. Such procedures, in turn, are founded on the principles of a constitutional and democratic rule-of-law state, as well as on a constitution that citizens see as an 'unfinished project', subject to constant public and collective action of legitimation, re-legitimation, interpretation and development.

This topic (the foundations of constitutional legitimacy) is one of the most important points of discussion between Habermas and Rawls. Habermas criticises Rawls's model because

> ... from the perspective of the theory of justice, the act of founding the democratic constitution cannot be repeated under the institutional conditions of an already constituted just society, and the process of realizing the system of basic rights cannot be assured on an ongoing basis. It is not possible for the citizens to experience this process as open and incomplete, as the shifting historical circumstances nonetheless demand. They cannot reignite the radical democratic embers of the original position in the civic life of their society, for from their perspective all of the *essential* discourses of legitimation have already taken place within the theory; and they find the results of the theory already sedimented in the constitution (REC: 69–70).

Rawls replied sharply to these claims:

> Why not? For we have seen above in considering the four-stage sequence that citizens continually discuss questions of political principles and social policy. Moreover, we may assume that any actual society is more or less unjust – usually gravely so – and such debates are all the more necessary ... The ideal of a just constitution is always something to be worked toward (RH: 400–1).[14]

In Habermas, social integration – which alone wouldn't be enough, as powerful factors of systemic integration (such as money and administrative and political power) are at work in our complex and post-conventional societies – cannot be produced only by a consensus created in the public political culture. The *procedural* dimension of democracy alone can ground the possibility that a society 'holds together', despite its irreversible pluralism of values and ideologies and its particularism and fragmentation at the level of material interests. And it is through this *juridical and institutional mediation* that *all* discourses must pass.

---

14. Of course, adds Rawls, 'not every generation is called upon to carry through to a reasonable conclusion all the essential discourses of legitimation and then successfully to give itself a new and just constitution. ... [T]hat the Founders of 1787–91 could be the Founders was not determined solely by them but by the course of history up until that time. In this sense, those already living in a just constitutional regime cannot found a just constitution, but they can fully reflect on it, endorse it, and so freely execute it in all ways necessary' (RH: 400–2). About this discussion, note that Habermas does not fully grasp the implications of the 'dualist' approach proposed by Ackerman and basically shared by Rawls.

Instead, Rawls thinks that 'stability for the right reasons' can only be produced by consensus on the *political values* of the public culture of a democratic society: a common ground underlying the constitutional fundamentals and the basic principles of justice. However, of course, we cannot presume that such a common ground is wide and comprehensive: indeed, to be solid enough, it *cannot* be too wide – that would be impossible as well as unrealistic. This common ground can only be *political*, and about *political* values, as well as *autonomous* as independent of comprehensive doctrines (even though the latter can offer, even publicly, reasons and motivations).

For Habermas, therefore, deliberative politics is a *reconstructive* and *normative* category, indicating how and to what extent arguments and discourses (of *all* kinds) act, or *can act*, in *constructing* the bases of democratic legitimation or in *criticising* norms that are socially valid and legal but not necessarily legitimate. As McCarthy noted (1994: 61), the conception of public justification proposed by Habermas is *participant-centred*, entrusting the participants with the task not only of finding common bases but also of '*creating, expanding, contracting, shifting, challenging and deconstructing*' such bases (my emphasis).[15]

In Rawls, deliberative democracy is both an *ideal model* and a *paradigm*. On the one hand, it is an *ideal model* of a constitutional democracy, describable as deliberative because its citizens (free and equal) are able to give one another good reasons to converge on some common constitutional foundations and on some fundamental principles of justice. On the other hand, it is a *paradigm*, because it allows us to express and orientate our judgments and to evaluate (also critically) what actually happens, inspiring our concrete pursuit of satisfactory political and institutional solutions. And yet, both as an *ideal model* and as a *paradigm*, deliberative democracy is founded on an *idea*: that of *public reason*, which is not a mere philosophical construction but an idea that has become historically sedimented in the public political culture of constitutional democracies. It is based on this history that we can grasp it, elaborate it and propose it as a normative horizon for the future of those democracies, facing the given irreversible and radical pluralism able to undermine every form of reasonable coexistence. But Rawls's vision isn't naïve or superficially optimistic: there are several passages in which the *precariousness* of the grounds of democracies emerges powerfully. For instance, in the final pages of IPRR, Rawls wrote that 'harmony and concord' between different doctrines 'are unhappily not a permanent condition of social life. Rather, harmony and concord depend on the vitality of the public political culture and on citizens' being devoted to and realizing the ideal of public reason. Citizens could easily fall into bitterness and resentment …' (IPRR: 485). Rawls's vision

---

15. More recently, Habermas wrote, (2011: 291): 'I use the term "reconstructive" to describe theories that seek to explain the implicitly assumed normative contents of empirically established practices – e.g., everyday communication – from the participant perspective, i.e., in a performative attitude. Thus a reconstructive theory of the constitutional state ... begins with the constitution-making praxis. Its aim is to exhume, as it were, the normative meaning of a democratic constitution out of the differentiated network of the corresponding institutionalised practices (general elections, parliamentary deliberations, judicial procedures, etc.).'

entrusts political philosophy with the task of showing that something different and better is simply *possible*. Habermas certainly does not disagree on this point but adds a peculiar theoretical and critical awareness to this: as we can read in a passage of *Between Facts and Norms*:

> ... an ethical theory does not lie at the level where it could make up for the weakness of Rawls' attempt to bridge the chasm between ideal theoretical demands and social facts. The resistant reality with which critical reason wants to keep in touch is not just, and not even primarily, made up of the pluralism of conflicting life ideals and value orientations, of competing comprehensive doctrines, but of the harder material of institutions and action systems (*BFN*: 64).

4. Philosophers and citizens

In his final remarks in IPRR, Rawls defines the meaning of his political liberalism: the proposal of a political (and *only* political) conception that is able to show how a reasonably just democratic society is *possible* in the radical pluralism of our time. This conception presented itself as a 'candidate' to *transfuse* into the public political culture and therefore act as an *idea* able to guide political conduct (through the thousand, unpredictable channels that a 'philosophy' uses to draw from public culture and its fundamental insights, interacting with it and modifying it).[16] Habermas, by contrast, rejects any approach that might contain or suggest a *voluntaristic* attitude and sees precisely this risk in Rawls's position. According to Habermas, the normative dimension must emerge from the logics of social action and from within 'real discourses': it cannot be a perspective given from the outside but must be reconstructed starting from the participant's point of view – not from that of an external observer (or a philosopher).

These terms of comparison had characterised Habermas's opinion about Rawls for some time. In *Moral Consciousness*, Habermas clearly distinguished a *philosophical foundation* of *moral principles* from a '*transcendental-pragmatic foundation*' of the *rules of argumentation of the moral discourse* (my emphases), which can only start from 'real discourses':

> ... the moral theorist may take part in them as one of those concerned, perhaps even as an expert, but he cannot conduct such discourses by *himself alone.*

---

16. It is interesting to notice how Joshua Cohen, in a recent introduction to a collection of his essays (2009a: 3), openly recalls Antonio Gramsci and his conception of the relationship between 'philosophy' and 'common sense' (Gramsci 1971: 323). '[Gramsci] says, "Everyone is a philosopher". That is because a "specific conception of the world" underlies our intellectual activity. That conception, Gramsci says, is typically implicit, often adapted from the "external environment", passively internalized rather than worked out "consciously and critically'. ... Gramsci's invocation of philosophy suggests continuity between endorsing the conception of the world that shapes our conduct – what he calls a spontaneous philosophy – and pursuing the activity that we call political philosophy.'

298 From Participation to Deliberation

To the extent in which a moral theory touches a substantive area – as Rawls' theory of justice does, for example – it must be understood as a contribution to a discourse among citizens (Habermas 1990a: 94).

It is possible to say that, in the transition from *Theory of Justice* to *Political Liberalism*, Rawls has substantially accepted this objection. *Justice as fairness* becomes a liberal political conception (within a broader family of liberal political conceptions), which can be the subject of public discussion and *may* thus contribute to the construction of overlapping consensus. Rawls, however, continues to be and to feel like a *political philosopher*: one with a more 'modest' role but a role nonetheless. On this point, a singular dispute – 'a competition over modesty' as Rainer Forst called it (2012: 88) – developed within this dialogue between the two philosophers.

Habermas criticises Rawls' theory as too modest on the one hand but too ambitious on the other. It is 'modest' because 'he wants to extend the *method of avoidance* – which is intended to lead to overlapping consensus on questions of political justice – to philosophical questions themselves': in this way, 'he hopes to develop political philosophy into a sharply focused discipline and thereby to avoid most of the controversial questions of a more general nature' (REC: 72–3). But it is also 'immodest' because he expects too much of political philosophy, asking it to elaborate an idea of a 'just society'. But holding together these two perspectives is impossible:

> This avoidance strategy can lead to an impressively self-contained theory, as we can see from the wonderful example before us [Rawls's theory itself]. But even Rawls cannot develop his theory in as freestanding a fashion as he would like. As we have seen, his 'political constructivism' draws him willy-nilly into the dispute concerning concepts of rationality and truth. His concept of the person also oversteps the boundaries of political philosophy (REC: 73).

Thus, according to Rawls's conception, philosophy 'claims to elaborate the idea of a just society, while the citizens then use this idea as a platform from which to judge existing arrangements and policies' (*ibid*).

Habermas goes on to say that his own theory, too, is simultaneously modest and immodest, albeit in a completely different way. '[I]t is more modest because it focuses exclusively on the procedural aspects of the public use of reason and derives the system of rights from the idea of its legal institutionalization.' It can leave many questions open and indeterminate 'because it entrusts more to the *process* of rational opinion and will formation' (*ibid.*). Philosophy, in short, can only limit itself

> … to the clarification of the moral point of view and the procedure of democratic legitimation, to the analysis of the conditions of rational discourses and negotiations. In this more modest role, philosophy need not proceed in a constructive, but only in a *reconstructive* fashion. It leaves substantial

questions that must be answered here and now to the more or less enlightened engagement of participants, which does not mean that philosophers may not also participate in the public debate, though in the role of intellectuals, not of experts (*ibid.*).

However, even Habermas's conception of the tasks of philosophy has its own ambition and thus its 'less modest' features: Rawls, Habermas argues, does not really succeed in 'leaving philosophy out', since the 'preliminary theoretical decisions' that he makes inevitably involve him in 'many long-running and still unresolved debates' (REC: 73) that have always characterised the work of philosophers. Thus, philosophy must shoulder its responsibilities and come into play at this stage. It must not design an 'ideal theory'[17] of a 'just society' but perform its own 'unavoidable and at times even fruitful' role, which consists of a 'presumptuous encroachment on neighboring fields' (*ibid.*), moving between different forms of knowledge and sciences. Thus, philosophy does exercise its critical and reconstructive action on the assumptions and conditions that make 'real discourses' possible.

Rawls, in his reply, starts with a very clear (and also questionable) judgment: in his view, Habermas's is a *comprehensive doctrine*, a philosophical doctrine that – as such – joins the philosophical disputes *against* other metaphysical and 'comprehensive' doctrines: it is not a 'non-metaphysical' doctrine in the sense that Rawls gives to these terms.[18] In addition,

> Habermas's own doctrine, I believe, is one of logic in the broad Hegelian sense: a philosophical analysis of the presuppositions of rational discourse (of theoretical and practical reason) which includes within itself all the allegedly substantial elements of religious and metaphysical doctrines. His logic is metaphysical in the following sense: it presents an account of what there is – human beings engaged in communicative action in their life-world (RH: 378–9).

Now, on the one hand, it is certainly possible to accept the presence of Hegel in Habermas's thought[19] – Habermas himself has certainly acknowledged it, for example, in the latest Preface that he wrote for the new Italian edition of *Faktizität und Geltung* (2013):

> The discourse theory of law and of the democratic rule-of-law state does not at all want to compete with political science in describing the political

---

17. On 'ideal theory' in Rawls, *see* Chapter Six, note 12.

18. Many years later, Habermas, thinking about this dispute, observed: 'At the time I did not defend myself more energetically against the charge of developing a "comprehensive" theory in Rawls's sense because I regarded it as a misunderstanding' (Habermas 2011: 264). On this subject, *see also*: Heath 2011. Cohen (1999: 386–7) recalls Rawls's criticism of Habermas on this matter.

19. Furthermore, according to Burton Dreben, Hegel's lesson is present in Rawls's philosophy as well (*see* Chapter Eleven, note 26).

process, nor does it want to be a normative theory committed to designing, in the manner of Aristotle's *Politics*, the ideal framework of a 'well-ordered society'.[20] Rather, it wants to rationally reconstruct (*in Hegelian terms: reduce to the concept*) the normative substance *already present* in the constitutions of existing democracies (Habermas 2013: ix, first emphasis mine).

On the other hand, I do not believe that Habermas's 'doctrine' can be called 'metaphysical' in the sense that Rawls gives to this expression: that is, it is not an overall picture of life and the world.[21] Habermas, throughout his entire theoretical journey, always remained loyal to the idea and the goal of building a *critical theory of society*. The normative foundations, 'factually' operating, which are able to establish a *critical* knowledge and practice, can only emerge from such a critical theory. A work like *Theory of Communicative Action*, which must be regarded as the core of Habermas's entire theoretical corpus, is completely constructed through a direct dialogue with the classics of social theory (Weber, first of all, and then Marx, Durkheim, Parsons, Mead and others) and with the developments of contemporary human and social sciences (anthropology and evolutionary psychology; linguistics; systems theory and so forth). Habermas fully embraces the 'linguistic turn' and 'post-metaphysical' condition of contemporary thought; he looks to philosophy 'as stand-in and interpreter', which is a 'modest' but irreplaceable role. And only in this 'less modest' or 'less presumptuous' role, within the framework of knowledge and contemporary sciences, is philosophy also able to do the 'unavoidable and at times even fruitful' work of critical reconstruction along the boundaries between 'neighboring fields'. In short, 'the self-understanding of political philosophy ... under conditions of postmetaphysical thought, should be modest, but not in the wrong way' (REC: 51).[22]

---

20. Notice here the polemical use of the typical Rawlsian expression 'a well-ordered society'.

21. As Forst notices, from Rawls's point of view, Habermas's 'philosophy' appears 'metaphysical' because it faces 'questions that are contested among metaphysical doctrines; it 'takes a position that a "political" conception of justice can and must avoid' (Forst 2012: 92). More generally, it appears possible to agree with Heath's observation (2011: 123) that many commentators, including Rawls, don't understand the 'weak transcendentalism' of Habermas's discourse ethics, deeming it therefore definable as 'metaphysics'. Heath highlights Cohen's influence in spreading some determined ideas (see also Chapter Thirteen, Section 2 and note 6) and he adds: 'In the same way that people continue to confuse Karl-Otto Apel's views on Discourse Ethics with Habermas's, there is still a very strong tendency to conflate Cohen's view [about Habermas and about "what people had expected" Habermas to support] with Habermas's. Some of the things Rawls says suggest that he fell prey to the same tendency.' About Cohen's influence on Rawls's final position, see the entry on Cohen in *The Cambridge Rawls Lexicon*. 'Much of Cohen's work is inspired by Rawls and his own writing significantly influenced the development of Rawls's mature thought' (Mandle and Reidy 2015: 115).

22. In 'Philosophy as stand-in and interpreter', the opening essay of *Moral Consciousness*, Habermas writes: 'It makes sense to suggest that philosophy, instead of just dropping the usher role [*Platzanweiser*] and being left with nothing, ought to exchange it for the part of stand-in [*Platzhalter*]. Whose seat would philosophy be keeping; what would it be standing in for? Empirical theories with strong universalistic claims. ... [T]here have surfaced and will continue to surface in nonphilosophical disciplines, fertile minds who will give such theories a try. The

This dispute over the role and tasks of philosophy may seem to have very little to do with our problem (that is, to consider whether, from the direct dialogue between Habermas and Rawls, we can discover implications about their understanding of deliberative democracy) but it is indeed related to it. The direct consequences of this different way of understanding the work of philosophers are to be found in the position assigned to theory and/or philosophy. In Rawls's philosophy, deliberative democracy is part of his definition of the *ideal* of a reasonably just and stable democratic political society. As we have seen, this *ideal* is elaborated starting from *ideas* or *fundamental insights* that are already present in the public culture of a society in which a constitutional liberal democracy has already been established. Nonetheless, it is still an *ideal offered* to the public debate and a 'candidate' in a difficult competition, in which the possibility of establishing and consolidating a 'well-ordered' and democratic society is at stake. And Rawls repeatedly expresses the 'hope' that his ideas might become part of the 'political public culture' and influence public debate. However, in his response to Habermas's critical solicitations, Rawls articulates his point of view further, recalling once again the method of 'general and wide reflective equilibrium': a method that – we might say – takes away (or tries to take away) the risk that the proposal of an 'ideal theory' will remain as merely a philosopher's 'monologue':

> ... citizens in civil society do not simply use the idea of justice as fairness 'as a platform [handed to them by the philosopher as expert] from which to judge existing arrangements and policies' [Habermas]. In justice as fairness there are no philosophical experts. Heaven forbid! But citizens must, after all, have some ideas of right and justice in their thought and some basis for their reasoning. And students of philosophy take part in formulating these ideas but always as citizens among others (RH: 426–7).

There is no need here to analyse Habermas's subsequent discussion in '"Reasonable" *versus* "true"'.[23] What is important for our purposes is to notice

---

chance for their emergence is greatest in the reconstructive sciences. ... Telling examples of a successful cooperative integration of philosophy and science can be seen in the development of a theory of rationality. This is an area where philosophers work as suppliers of ideas without raising foundationalist or absolutist claims *à la* Kant or Hegel. Fallibilistic in orientation, they reject the dubious faith in philosophy's ability to do things single-handedly, hoping instead that the success that has for so long eluded it might come from an auspicious matching of different theoretical fragments' (Habermas 1990a: 15–16).

23. On the one hand, Habermas restates his criticisms. Rawls's understanding of the philosopher's role in the construction of a political conception of justice puts the philosopher in a condition that is not 'fully compatible with the egalitarian status of the philosopher as one citizen among others' (RvT: 97). He 'sometimes seems to suggest that his professionally worked-out proposal should have a structuring influence on the citizens' worldviews' (RvT: 96–7). On the other hand, Habermas finds in 'wide reflective equilibrium' the sign of a different position for the philosopher ('a more modest role', in the right way): such method, indeed, seems to refer 'to the intersubjectively shared background knowledge of a liberal political culture. Of course, this knowledge can only serve as a control on the choice of basic theoretical concepts if it has already been shaped by the perspective of an impartial judgment of questions of political justice. Otherwise the philosopher

how, in Rawls's position, as well as in these words I have just quoted, Rawls's idea of his own 'mission' or vocation emerges: the mission of someone who *elaborates* ('works out', is a recurring phrase) a *philosophical proposal* and a *political* conception that speaks to a wider public culture but that, at the same time, draws from that culture essential content as well as elements of potential development.

In this case, one could say, what Rawls 'hoped' for has actually happened: his ideas (as well as having, of course, an enormous impact in many other areas) have also entered into the process of constructing an *idea* or an *ideal* of deliberative democracy. This idea, in fact, has quickly gone beyond the circle of professional philosophers, in order to become a benchmark for a broader intellectual community and a source of inspiration for many social practices. Of course, such a process cannot occur without mediation (and also without the inevitable distortions or over-simplifications that it entails). Here, it seems inevitable to acknowledge how, in Rawlsian approaches to deliberative democracy – we have seen an example of them in Freeman's essay (2000) – the balance (or tension) between the *constructive* and *reconstructive* aspects has decisively shifted to the *philosophical proposal* of an *ideal*, which becomes the focal point of a *political and cultural proposal* embraced by citizens (both 'ordinary' and 'philosophers') who try to 'apply', verify and achieve it in an always approximate but concrete way.

Habermas, as we have seen, spoke of 'deliberative politics' and not of 'deliberative democracy', starting from a theoretical project of his own, within his *reconstruction* of the normative foundations of constitutional democracies and modern law. 'Deliberative politics' is inscribed in the history of these democracies; it is a theoretical category that offers a key to understanding an immanent normative dimension but it is *never* defined as an *ideal*. Of course, the point here is not to 'take sides' or give judgements regarding which of these two different theoretical strategies might or should be considered more convincing; the point is not even to see whether, at a deeper level, they may even be compatible and, if so, to what extent. It is important, however, to notice the different results that derive from them, or the implications they have, for how to understand deliberative democracy. This will be one of the topics of the next chapter of this work.

---

could learn nothing from the citizens and their convictions. If the method of reflective equilibrium is to get off the ground, philosophy must "find" its own perspective already operating in civil society' (RvT: 97). Naturally, philosophy cannot 'unreservedly' trust in this 'basic consensus'; in this case, one would validate – Habermas notes – the 'contextual' interpretation of Rawls's theory proposed by Rorty: (RvT: 97, note 19). Philosophy cannot lose its 'critical force'; 'it must avoid equally the uncritical affirmation of the status quo and the assumption of a paternalistic role. It should neither simply accept established tradition nor construct a detailed design for a well-ordered society' (*ibid.*).

Part IV

THE THEORETICAL FIELD OF DELIBERATIVE DEMOCRACY TODAY

Chapter Thirteen

The Deliberative Field: A Possible 'Map'

1. Introduction

My reconstruction of the foundation and consolidation of the theory of deliberative democracy has now ventured up until the beginning of the new century. Of course, many other things happened before then that cannot be discussed here. Chronologically, the last work I have considered (Joshua Cohen's *Reflections on Habermas*) dates from 1999 but many other works had been published in previous years, including the first, and very influential, collections of essays on deliberative democracy, edited by Bohman and Rehg (1997) and by Elster (1998a).[1]

Since the mid 1990s, the deliberative 'field' has become much better articulated and has been expanded across many other disciplines and fields of empirical research; the practices inspired by deliberative democracy have also become increasingly widespread. Generally, we can refer to this period as an *empirical turn* in deliberative democracy. However, it is difficult, if not impossible, to provide precise terms for this 'turn'. Speaking of an *empirical turn* can give us a useful analytical distinction but only as long as we do not forget that, since the beginning, the 'practical projection' of an ideal model has always been very much present in theoretical reflection on deliberative democracy: indeed, it was often openly emphasised and wished for. Neither should we forget that, even after this 'turn', the theoretical elaboration of deliberative democracy has continued. It would be misleading to think of deliberative democracy as a thoroughly established and still less a concluded theoretical *corpus*, which now only needs to be subjected to empirical 'verification'. In fact, the very definition of deliberative democracy has always been subject to a variety of interpretations: this still holds true and can be seen as a sign of the vitality of the idea. Deliberative democracy is a 'field' that has not been 'stabilised' in some doctrinal formula.[2]

---

1. Later, Macedo's anthology (1999), dedicated in particular to Guttman and Thompson's 1996 *Democracy and Disagreement* was published, as well as Fishkin and Laslett 2003 and many other collections of essays (e.g. Besson and Marti 2006). On the different phases of development of deliberative democracy and on the different interpretations of it, *see* Mansbridge *et al.* 2012: 25–6); Pellizzoni 2009; Bohman and Rehg 1997; Bohman 1998; Chambers 2003; Girard and Le Goff 2010; Dryzek 2010; Elstub 2010, 2015 and some of my considerations in Floridia 2012: 23–8).

2. A complete framework of the development of deliberative democracy, and of the relationship between 'empirical research and normative implications' is given by Jürg Steiner (2012). An overall framework of the present state of deliberative democracy is offered by a recent *Oxford Handbook of Deliberative Democracy* (2017), edited by A. Bächtiger, J. Dryzek, J. Mansbridge,

Throughout this work, we have seen the diversity and fluidity of the ongoing interpretations. Is deliberative democracy an *ideal of democracy*? Or is it a *theoretical model* of democracy? In what sense can one speak of a deliberative *paradigm*? Again: are the practical projections 'realisations' (always partial, by definition) of an ideal model, something like approximations to a *regulative ideal*? Or, on the contrary (in neo-positivist terms), are they actual experimental tests that are able to 'falsify' or 'prove' the theoretical assumptions? And can we accept the idea of a deliberative *paradigm* in the same, specific meaning that Kuhn (1962) attributed to this term (that is, a theoretical *framework* that *re-interprets* the phenomenon, allowing us to grasp aspects hitherto hidden and to discover new ones)? Or can we say that deliberative democracy is, *at the same time*, an ideal, a theoretical model and a paradigm? Finally – I will talk about this in the Conclusion – what kind of relationship can we see between the emergence of this theoretical field and actual, current transformations – or deformations – of those political systems we call democracies?

I did not (and do not) claim to offer a comprehensive answer to all these questions. Throughout this work, however, I have reconstructed the story of this idea of democracy, highlighting for each stage its core conceptual propositions, the theoretical elements that were added and recomposed and the critical dialogue that accompanied and constructed this process. I intended this reconstruction to bring out the different theoretical strategies and the different ways of understanding deliberative democracy within a framework that, nonetheless, draws on common elements and shared principles.

To offer an overview of the *present* composition and structure of whatever goes by the name of deliberative democracy was not the objective of this work (nor could it have been). However, in this final chapter, I will try to construct a provisional 'map' to help us find our way through the complex landscape of the deliberative field. I will consider the reasons why deliberative democracy, today, is a 'working theory', (Section 2); the fundamental legacy of Rawls and Habermas, which nonetheless cannot be considered univocal or exclusive (Section 3); and the proposed distinction between two large 'families' of deliberative democracy (Section 4). Later, (Section 5) I will analyse the meaning of the *empirical turn* in deliberative democracy and finally (Section 6) the recent proposal of taking a 'systemic approach' to deliberative democracy – an approach that, in my opinion, is perhaps the most promising ground for the further development of theoretical and empirical research on deliberative democracy.

---

and M. Warren. Furthermore, throughout the years, many interventions have commented on the theoretical development of deliberative democracy and its research programme. Besides the texts quoted in the previous note, I would refer in particular to Freeman 2000; Bächtiger *et al* 2010; Sintomer and Talpin 2011; and Elstub and McLaverty 2014; Della Porta 2013. Other scholars have proposed a classification of the various internal approaches within the deliberative field: Forst (2001) proposed 'three models' of deliberative democracy ('liberal', 'communitarian' and a third model 'based on a theory of moral and political justification'). According to Talisse (2012: 210), it is possible to identify, although not in an exclusive way, 'three styles of deliberative democracy: liberalism, civic republicanism and radical democracy'.

2. A 'working theory'

As we have said, the field of deliberative democracy quickly became complex: Dryzek (2010: 3–10) has proposed a classification of the areas in which the *deliberative turn* has had a significant influence. However, in 2003, Simone Chambers (2003: 307) had already considered a first (non-exhaustive) series of 'research areas' in which deliberative theory acted as a 'working theory', that is, as a real *paradigm*, changing the conceptual *framework* of a discipline.[3]

According to Dryzek, deliberative democracy – no longer confined within the limits of *political theory* – is today 'a central topic for inquiry' in a diverse range of fields: communications, planning, ecological economics, science and technology studies, philosophy, policy-analysis, game theory, constitutional law, criminal justice, conflict-resolution, journalism, international relations, development studies and social psychology (Dryzek 2010: 3). This disparate list risks submitting the concept of 'deliberation' to a 'conceptual stretching' that could undermine the root of its real meaning.[4] Dryzek does not merely point out the areas in which deliberative democracy is being researched, however: he also defines it as 'a program of empirical research', in those areas as well as others, and as 'an international movement for political reform' that aims to intervene in existing institutions and create new ones. This movement may involve the risky phenomenon of 'commercialization' linked to 'an emerging profession of forum design and facilitation' (*ibid.*). Finally, quoting President Obama, Dryzek says that deliberative democracy is now also 'a way to interpret the point of the whole political system' (*ibid.*: 3–4). However, he also notes, 'there is still plenty of work to be done on the foundations of the theory' (although it is no longer the time for those 'comprehensive integrated statements of the essence of deliberative democracy' that characterised its first phase). This work should go in two directions: it should expand this theory towards new frontiers (*global governance* and those forms of '*networked governance*' that may provide an answer to the nation-state crisis) and it should respond to the many criticisms that deliberative democracy has received and still receives (which is, itself, a sign of the importance that the theory has acquired).

---

3. Chambers analysed only certain fields: 'public law, international relations, policy studies, empirical research and identity politics'. Many other disciplines could be included (e.g. social psychology). The deliberative paradigm would be evaluated, for example, within policy studies and studies of the logic of institutional change (*see*, e.g., the work on 'discursive institutionalism' particularly supported by Vivien Schmidt (2008; 2011). The paradigm has affected other fields as well, e.g., economic development (Heller and Rao 2015). Within public law, Carlos Santiago Nino (1996) made one of the first contributions. The great debate on the possibility of a form of global democracy or of (more) democratic global governance has been taken up by many scholars inspired by deliberative democracy: among them Bohman (2007); Benhabib (2006); Cohen and Sabel (2005); and Dryzek (2000, 2010, 2011). Deliberative democracy has made particularly important contributions to the reflection on 'divided societies' that experience deep ethnic and cultural conflicts (O'Flynn 2006; Steiner *et al.* 2017).

4. Several scholars had stressed the risk of such 'conceptual stretching': see Steiner 2008 and Bächtiger *et al.* 2010.

Recalling the terms mentioned above, then, deliberative democracy is a mixture of all these things: a political ideal that inspires a political and cultural movement for democratic reform; also a theoretical model and a paradigm for empirical research. Is this too much? Probably not, because, today, those who refer to deliberative democracy actually *do* at least one of these things. Of course, the risk of falling into indeterminacy is very strong. For this reason, it seems appropriate to try to shed light not on the 'essence' of deliberative democracy but on the *status* attributed to it: is it a political ideal, a political philosophy, an empirically verifiable theory, or something else? Empirical research and cultural-political proposals cannot be placed at the same level as *theory* and theory does not have to be understood as (or only as) *political theory*. Also, *philosophy* cannot be considered a discipline like any other (as Dryzek seems to do); rather, it should be seen as a perspective that helps to define the boundaries and the nature of the cognitive and practical undertaking called deliberative democracy. The ways of understanding empirical research, or defining the nature and purpose of a political-cultural movement, depend on the understanding of deliberative democracy and its underlying philosophical premises.

3. The legacy of Habermas and Rawls ... but not only

In order to outline a 'map' of the present field of deliberative democracy, we must first of all go back to Habermas and Rawls, emphasising, nevertheless, that their legacies are not the only ones that played a significant role in the formation of deliberative democracy.

Some important differences can be grasped not only in the content but also in the ways in which Habermas and Rawls affected the creation and developments of the deliberative theoretical field. Rawls's influence, in a sense, is more linear: he played a decisive role, thanks first to Cohen's mediation and then, more directly, to *Political Liberalism*. Habermas's presence and legacy is more complicated: he has always been fully immersed in (and also, so to speak, variously *forced* into) this process, because many theoretical categories – or even just a few suggestions – already present in his 1970s works had been widely referred to, reworked, or even used (more or less correctly) by the authors who later helped define and consolidate the 'deliberative turn' of the early 1990s. We have seen, for example, how the notion of an 'ideal speech situation' has been read and interpreted (and often misunderstood) in different ways. The 'theory of communicative action' or the idea of 'discourse ethics' offered theoretical schemes that could be *adopted* and *adapted* in many disciplines. We saw a particularly relevant example in the new epistemological paradigms inspiring the theories and practices of urban and regional planning in Chapter Seven. However, there has also been a more 'political' use of Habermas's theories. In general, Habermas, as a heir of the 'critical theory' of the Frankfurt School, inspired all those who, wanting to propose ideas and practices of 'radical democracy', emphasised the new role of civil society and social movements and thus, in some cases, renewed a relationship with the theoretical tradition of 'participatory democracy'.[5]

We have seen and can now better understand why the idea of 'deliberative politics' that Habermas proposed in *Between Facts and Norms* was so shocking to all those who shared a 'critical-radical' or 'participatory' perspective. Habermas's strategy totally rejected any proposal of an ideal model that would serve as guidance or inspiration for a political movement, or even just for a political culture seeking to expand or find new followers, in the light of a traditional conception of the relationship between theory and practice. There is a paradox here, for which Habermas himself is partly responsible. On the one hand, this vision of the deliberative model, in many cases, spread through an 'idealised' vision of some of the categories of the *early* Habermas (it is not important here to determine if this was supported by the texts or the author's original intentions) – an interpretation that was also strongly affected by the diffusion (sometimes belated or partial) in the English-speaking world of Habermas's various works in translation. On the other hand, this trajectory of diffusion, interpretations, and adaptation took place at the same time that the German scholar was developing his theoretical and philosophical itinerary. Habermas's itinerary has its own internal coherence but it also has significant discontinuities, precisely with regard to the relationship between discourse ethics and the 'discourse theory of law and democracy' (as the subtitle of *BFN* has it). Therefore, a complex work such as *Between Facts and Norms*, for many, seemed unrelated to the mainstream of 'deliberative democracy' and its reception would prove slow and difficult.[6]

Of course, Habermas's influence – like Rawls's – goes far beyond the narrow scope we are considering here, that is, their impact on the deliberative constellations. As happens with those thinkers who can be considered 'classic' or who, at least, seem to stand for an entire phase of our intellectual history, their influence must be measured in the long run. Historical events often shed a new light, one is more relevant to the present, on those views and conceptions that, when they first appeared, might have seemed outdated or even eccentric. This, we might well say, is the case for Rawls and his worry about the possible forms of a reasonable political coexistence between radically different cultures and visions of the world: a theme that has since acquired dramatic importance. However, it is also

---

5. In this context, Jean L. Cohen's and Andrew Arato's work *Civil Society and Political Theory* (1992) is important. In chapter 8 of *Between Facts and Norms*, Habermas called this work 'the most comprehensive study on this topic' (1996: 367).

6. As Joseph Heath wrote (2011: 122), 'Cohen articulated the view that everyone *expected* Habermas to have, prior to the publication of *Between Facts and Norms*. When the latter came out, some of the claims were so strongly at variance with what people had expected that Habermas's actual views were simply ignored'. Habermas's *Between Facts and Norms* 'explicitly rejects the idea – popularized by Joshua Cohen among others [1989] – that democratic institutions could be justified by virtue of the way that they help citizens more closely approximate the conditions of "ideal discourse". Such a view would entail a straightforward conflation of legal validity and moral rightness' [*ibid.*].

the case for Habermas and his reflections – for example – on the conditions that are necessary for political decisions to acquire democratic, public and discursive legitimacy; and his worry about the 'systemic' dynamics that crush any form of democratic construction of opinions and wills. Habermas's theoretical approach to deliberative politics is probably fully showing its effects only now – in 'the long run', so to speak.[7]

Rawls's and Habermas's legacies to the deliberative theoretical field are multi-faceted and decisive, but it would be a mistake to think that the entire theoretical field of deliberative democracy, in the mid 1990s (and even more today), was derived solely from the work of these two thinkers. It would also be misleading to consider Habermas's and Rawls's influence over other thinkers in the narrow terms of a 'school' that passively reproduces the teachers' lessons. Many authors – primarily Joshua Cohen but also others such as Amy Guttman and Dennis Thompson (1996, 2004) – work within the theoretical framework offered by Rawls; however, they propose changes to it and develop it in original ways. The same can be said of the authors who engaged in a critical dialogue with Habermas, such as Seyla Benhabib (1996b) and Simone Chambers (1996).

Other works openly positioned themselves as critical of, or at least autonomous from, views drawn from Habermas and Rawls, proposing instead a vision of deliberative democracy inspired by other philosophical traditions or based on original philosophical assumptions. It is not possible here to dwell extensively on these developments. However, at least two authors must be mentioned as an expression of two major theoretical, or even specifically philosophical approaches that, today, are very present within the deliberative theoretical field: James Bohman and David Estlund.

In his 1996 work *Public Deliberation: Pluralism, complexity and democracy*, James Bohman relates to the philosophical tradition of American pragmatism. Public deliberation, Bohman writes, can be defined as 'a dialogical process of exchanging reasons for the purpose of resolving problematic situations that cannot

---

7. See, for example, Robert C. Post's 2013 Tanner Lectures (published as *Citizens Divided*, 2014, with comments by P. S. Karlan, L. Lessig, F. Michelman and N. Urbinati). This work is dedicated to the problematic question of the financing systems of American politics and the last, controversial verdicts of the Supreme Court on this subject, in the light of the possible interpretations of the First Amendment on freedom of speech. Robert Post (professor at Yale Law School), in the first part of his lecture, offers a masterful 'Short history of representation and discursive democracy' in the American constitution and politics, starting from the assumption that 'from its inception, the government of the United States has been built on the premise of self-government. We were founded upon a belief in the value of self-determination. In American history this value has taken two distinct forms: republican representation and democratic deliberation' (*ibid.*: 5). Post reads the tension between these two forms, and their transformations, through an essentially Habermasian theoretical lens (*see*, in particular, 31–41, 53–4, 59–61), especially with regard to the impossibility of considering public opinion as a non-mediated source of political decisions. This work addresses a central issue of contemporary democracy, that is, the way in which public discourse is formed, articulated and then traduced in the forms of representative government (as well as the way in which a 'communicative rights' can be guaranteed and regulated today).

be settled without interpersonal coordination and cooperation' (Bohman 1996: 27).[8] The conditions for successful deliberation, therefore, lie neither in correspondence to more or less demanding discursive standards nor in mere procedural fairness. Such conditions are to be found in a public process of dialogue that is based, first of all, on ensuring that all participants can contribute to and possibly influence decisions, as well as on the participants' motivation to co-operate in order to produce a 'convincing' result (Bohman 1996: 33–4). These theories are clearly detached from visions that take as a deliberative ideal the creation of conditions that isolate or neutralise the participants' *interests*. As Bohman critically noted (1996: 255, note 15), 'the very stuff of deliberation are the needs and interests of citizens, some of which can be made into publicly convincing reasons'. A deliberative democracy is thus based on a '*dialogical construction of deliberative contexts*' (1996: 222), which are not reducible to the creation of specific *settings* but are developed within and throughout the entire public sphere and civil society.

Especially with his *Democratic Authority* (2008), which recalls and develops twenty years of reflection (see also Estlund 1993 and 1997), David Estlund offers a dense and sophisticated philosophical elaboration that he calls 'epistemic proceduralism'. His approach can be considered one of the most significant examples of an 'epistemic' conception of deliberative democracy. 'Democracy can seem to empower the masses', Estlund writes (2008: 1), 'without regard for the quality of the political decisions that will result. Concern for the quality of decisions can seem to lead in an antidemocratic direction, toward identifying and empowering those who know best'. According to Estlund, however, any defence of democracy that does not address this issue is weak: we can and must show that a democratic system is better able to produce 'good decisions'. Thus, 'procedure-independent standards' are necessary to help measure the quality of decisions, without, however, falling into some form of *epistocracy*, leaving the task of ruling to the wisest or most experienced people. The *fairness* of a procedure is not enough: in order to produce legitimate decisions, an epistemic dimension able to express itself during the procedure is necessary; and the epistemic value of the decisions must be publicly recognised and acknowledgeable. For this reason the role of deliberation is crucial.[9]

These are just two of the many authors who should be included in any attempt to give a complete picture of the current configuration of the deliberative field. My task here is more limited: when we construct a 'map', by definition, we omit many details and overlook many aspects. Thus, we have to go back to the – certainly

---

8. On the pragmatic and Deweyan origins of his conception of deliberative democracy 'as a mode of inquiry', *see also* Bohman 2004.

9. J. L. Martí (2006) can be connected to an epistemic vision of deliberative democracy as well. Reflection on the epistemic dimension of democracy has recently been the object of contributions such as *Collective Wisdom*, the collection of essays edited by Hélène Landemore and Jon Elster (2012); Hélène Landemore's *Democratic Reason: Politics, collective intelligence, and the rule of the many* (2013); and Josiah Ober's *Democracy and Knowledge: Innovation and learning in classical Athens* (2008). For a critical evaluation of the epistemic conception of democracy, *see* Urbinati 2014. On Estlund's thesis, *see also* Palumbo 2012.

schematic but fundamental – thread that we have followed throughout this work: is deliberative democracy an *ideal model* or a *theoretical model* of democracy?

4. An ideal model or a theoretical model of democracy?

The main thread that has run and still runs through the deliberative theoretical field can be expressed by the answers to a series of questions: is deliberative democracy a *political ideal* to promote, support and try to achieve? Or is it a theoretical, analytical and interpretive model to use in order to understand our democracies and their inner tensions? These two alternative ways of understanding deliberative democracy are reflected in alternative ways of conceiving the relationship with 'practice' or 'reality'. From the former derives the belief that the ideal model could provide useful directions for the building-process of social practices and institutions seeking to approximate or 'mirror' that model; from the latter derives the idea of a *normative paradigm*, which is constructed starting from 'real' social and discursive practices and is able to show the points of fracture and tension in social, political and institutional practices which social practices, in their autonomy and with their forms of self-understanding, can rely on to promote and govern the processes of change.

Further ramifications also appear within this framework. Two large 'families' of ideas, concepts and practices are connected to the first approach (deliberative democracy as an ideal).

a) Fishkin's work - which inspired and continues to inspire many deliberative theorists and deliberative practitioners - exemplifies the first 'family'. It is founded on a theoretical definition as well as an institutional design (and a designation of conditions for experimentation with that design) that aims to create conditions for deliberation that approach an ideal model as closely as is practically possible. This approach generated a widespread image of deliberative democracy, both as an ideal and an experimental model that aims to offer innovative solutions to the inadequacies and flaws of traditional democratic institutions, integrating them (or, depending on the case, replacing them) with institutions and systems able to revive a civic participation that has been in decline. Such an approach relies on the (possibly ever more pervasive) *diffusion* of such institutions and practices. This view, however, is often linked to the conception of a deliberation that occurs, each time, at a single place and time and, very often, on a small scale. As we have seen in various authors, those who take this position also see deliberative democracy as a *political* and *cultural movement* that aims to renew our democracies, introduce new institutions or revitalise the old ones, or else build a vibrant and lively civil society.

b) A second perspective, which we have seen in Cohen's thesis, also considers deliberative democracy as an ideal (and has the ambition to do so with absolute rigor, starting from the robust philosophical foundation of an 'ideal deliberative procedure'). However, it holds that deliberative democracy can and should act as a model for rethinking the *entire institutional structure*. For this reason – considering deliberative democracy to be a way to express in the most coherent possible form the classic democratic ideal of *self-ruling* – this approach sees as a limitation the idea of *mini-publics* (or rather, the idea of single spaces or moments in which a representative microcosm of citizens can act out an authentically democratic politics). From this perspective, a deliberative democracy must embody the ideals of *widespread participation* and of *popular commitment* experienced as democratic self-determination. Thus, a deliberative democracy is *also* essentially a participatory democracy. This vision implies the construction of devices requiring the citizens' *direct protagonism* as well as their commitment to co-operatively solving their common problems and conflicts that result from their coexistence. Hence Cohen's and Sabel's (and others') idea of a *deliberative policy-making* model, along with the idea of *participatory-deliberative arrangements*, primarily designed as places for *collective problem-solving* and as the source of a *social learning* process. In the light of this vision, the gap between the 'ideal deliberative procedure' and its partial approximations, in reality is not considered a deficiency or a 'falsification' of the ideal model. Such a gap is inevitable, conceived according to the schema of a *regulative ideal*. This formulation avoids every 'realistic' or 'empiricist' objection. We are, once again, faced with a *political-ideal proposal* relying on the potential consent of its interlocutors.

Despite their differences, these two branches are united by a fundamental common presumption: 'deliberative democracy' is an *ideal model* whose realisation is aspired to and sought in different ways.

The second approach, based on a theoretical model, can be contrasted with both of these two ideal model 'families'. It was first formulated in Manin's definition of public and democratic deliberation and later articulated in various definitions, from other theoretical approaches. Finally, it found its most complete expression in the idea of a 'deliberative system' (which I discuss later). We could also classify Habermas's idea of 'deliberative politics' as conforming to this line of thought.

This second model is a deliberative *theory* of democracy. That is to say, it is an *interpretative and reconstructive model of what a democracy is* and it offers a *particular theoretical view* of how democracy works, focusing on its fundamental *discursive* and *communicative* dimensions. Such a theoretical model suggests that a democracy can be better understood (and evaluated) by looking at citizens' communicative and deliberative *practice*, at the forms and processes by which political opinions and will are formed, and at the conditions by which these processes do or may take place. Above all, such a theoretical model does not view this discursive dimension in *isolation* but sets it within the context and connects it to an understanding of the principles, logics and mechanisms that generally guide the reproduction and transformation of society.

In short, rather than proposing an ideal of 'deliberative democracy', this approach looks primarily to the 'deliberative politics' that is produced within the social and institutional order historically defined as 'democracy'. From this assumption, this approach looks for possible *normative implications* of, and the *immanent tension* between, assumptions rooted in what democracy thinks of itself (its 'normative self-understanding') and the 'facts' that deny or contradict them, entirely or in part. The *condition of possibility* of democratic reform or transformation is not that some subject should take on the heavy burden of translating the ideal into reality; it lies in the *potentialities* that are intrinsic to the tension between 'factuality' and 'validity'. As Seyla Benhabib wrote (1996: 84), 'the deliberative theory of democracy is not a theory in search of practice; rather it is a theory that claims to elucidate some aspects of the logic of existing democracies better than others'. This definition can be contrasted to the first approach, as proposed by Freeman: 'the idea of deliberative democracy serves more as political ideal than as an explanatory concept' (2000: 373).

This second approach to deliberative democracy is not very interested (in the 'first person', so to speak) in the invention of and experimentation with specific participatory or deliberative institutions or systems, even though it does not deny their importance. The emphasis here is mainly on the *reconstructive analysis* of these new phenomena characterising contemporary democracies. Deliberative 'systems' and processes *are already present and active*; they are produced every day in a democracy and the point is to understand if and how they combine or coexist with other logics and systems of action, or if they are overcome by those other logics and systems. Of course, if *new* participatory and deliberative institutions arise and spread (as is happening, at least in part), this is also a 'fact'; but the real protagonists of these innovations are the actors (citizens and institutions) who give them life with their practices, their experiences and their learning processes. The theory only has to understand why and how this happens, providing interpretive and evaluative paradigms through which these actors can better understand their own practices and, if necessary, plan others. This is an *analytical-interpretative* or *critical-evaluative* approach, one that mainly looks at *deliberative practices* as they unfold in real life or at the *deliberative quality* of such practices.[10]

Such an approach distrusts those attitudes that are, in various ways, suspected of 'voluntarism' (excessive reliance on the subject's voluntary action). It avoids any form of 'exhortation' of citizens (as sometimes happens in each of the two 'families' within the 'ideal theory' approach described above). Also, it does not give up a *political* point of view: normatively speaking, leveraging those potentialities and immanent tensions, the point is to assess how to balance, realign or shift, the 'relative weights' between different 'rationalities' in the social processes of our time. This approach has a dual purpose: it wants to avoid the mere *ought-to-be*, seeing it as a weak teleological projection always destined to clash with the hardness of the facts; but, at the same time, it does not give in to a disillusioned view of democracy that fails to grasp either its inherent tension or its openness

---

10. Steiner and his colleagues nicely exemplify the critical-interpretative approach (*see* Chapter Nine, note 22). To such an approach, we can also connect all those contributions that, on the basis of Austin and Searle's theories as well, look at the 'speech acts' produced within, or around, a deliberative arena and that study their different nature or 'logic' (e.g., Holzinger 2004). A similar approach, devoted to the evaluation of the 'quality of deliberation', can be found in some of the contributions in the collection edited by Luigi Bobbio (2013). Claudia Landwehr (2009) uses 'the methods of speech-act analysis and argumentation analysis' to study the debate that took place in different locations in Germany on the question of 'embryonic stem cells' (*ibid*: 7).

to conflicts and potentialities. This undoubtedly difficult position is, perhaps, the most promising of those that make up the deliberative field today.

5. An 'empirical' or a 'policy-oriented' turn?

At the beginning of this chapter, I discussed the meaning and limitations by which it is right and possible to speak of an 'empirical turn' in deliberative democracy. The interpretation of this 'turn' understands it simply as a process of realisation and verification of the normative, theoretical premises and as a practical approximation to a democratic ideal. However, it is appropriate to distinguish between different ways of understanding this 'practical' translation of deliberative democracy.

A first meaning of the term *empirical turn* emphasises that deliberative democracy has increasingly become *a field of empirical research*. Starting from a multiplicity of approaches (political science, sociology, psychology and so on), much research has been devoted to the analysis and evaluation of 'real' deliberative processes, trying to verify to what extent and in what way these processes can be interpreted in the light of the theoretical categories or normative assumptions of deliberative democracy. Here, we can distinguish two different sub-sets of empirical research: a) analyses that look at the deliberative dimension of *existing* social, political and institutional practices; and b) analyses that study, instead, the *deliberative experiments* that have been made *ad hoc*, drawing inspiration from the normative principles and ideals of the theory and its methodological implications.

These two sub-sets are not always sufficiently distinguished from one another. We can see, for instance, how parliaments or institutions produce decisions using deliberative procedures,[11] or the way in which a social movement or association *adopts* deliberative practices.[12] Or we can study how a specific deliberative device has actually worked, whether the theoretical premises by which it had been designed have been efficacious and its results have been as expected and so on. This last ground has produced a vast field of empirical research on deliberative democracy, critically reviewed in many essays.[13]

A second meaning of the 'empirical turn' focuses, instead, on a more specific phenomenon (which could also be called a '*policy-oriented turn*' in deliberative democracy).[14] Some forms of 'practical translation' of the principles of deliberative

---

11. Bessette 1994; Steiner *et al.* 2004; Uhr 1998.

12. *See*, for example, Della Porta 2005.

13. In particular, *see* Delli Carpini *et al.* 2004; Ryfe 2005; Rowe and Frewer 2000; Smith 2009. Many studies have focused specific national experiences: e.g., for Brazil, Avritzer, 2009; for France, Bacqué, Rey and Sintomer 2005 and Blondiaux and Forniau 2011; for Italy, Bobbio 2004, 2008; for Germany, Geissel 2009; for the Netherlands, Akkerman and Hajer-Grin 2004. On Britain's experience during Blair's government, *see* Lowndes, Pratchett and Stoker 2001a and 2001b and Parkinson 2006. Particularly relevant is the French *Dèbat Public* on great infrastructural works, on which *see* Revel *et al.* 2007.

14. Warren (2009) defines the new participatory and deliberative forms as expression of a 'governance-driven democratization', highlighting its potentialities and ambiguities.

democracy are increasingly being incorporated into a real process of *policy-making* and presented as *a phase* of a political-institutional process of decision-making.

An important part of the *empirical* and *policy-oriented* turn of deliberative democracy took place when a) the new theoretical model inspired new *political-institutional practices*; and b) symmetrically, *new practices of policy-making arising from autonomous foundations and motivations* (or even *antecedent* practices) were interpreted in a 'deliberative key' and their justification, along with their 'theory' and 'language', was sought in a deliberative conception of democracy. Because both meanings intertwined in practice, a linear interpretation of the 'empirical turn' (according to which, at a certain point, from theory we pass naturally to practice) does not seem convincing.

Looking at both meanings allows us to capture an important area of *overlap* (but also of possible uncertainty and confusion) between the tradition of participatory democracy and the theoretical deliberative model. In fact, the new political-institutional practices of citizens' more or less 'deliberative' involvement in policy-making processes have often been defined, or have defined themselves, as an expression of '*participatory* democracy'. This term has, since the late nineties, come back into more frequent use thanks to the reputation of some innovative experiments, in particular, the Porto Alegre Participatory Budgeting process.[15]

These references to 'participatory democracy' were produced in connection with the process of globalisation and the criticisms of it, in a context quite different from the past, and they raised the new issue of the possibility of some form of *global democracy*. However some aspects of the original idea of participation, in particular a view of democracy as something that must be built and lived starting from the *places* of collective life, were also revived. Against the logic of the '*pensée unique*' of globalised capitalism, it was necessary to activate social protagonism starting 'from the bottom'. In this sense, participatory democracy became the instrument by which a new social, critical and antagonistic subjectivity could be built. Thus, what has come back in new forms is the idea of participation as the *empowerment* of local societies, directed today against the processes of homogenisation induced by globalisation; and the same can be said of the idea that local communities can and should self-govern, thus regaining control of their own destiny.[16]

---

15. On the Porto Alegre 'participatory budgeting' project, *see* Sintomer, Herzberg and Allegretti 2010; Baiocchi 2003, 2005; Gret and Sintomer 2005; Santos 1998. On the (problematic) spread of PB in Europe, *see* Sintomer, Herzberg and Röcke 2008. Baiocchi and Ganuza (2015) propose a critical evaluation and 'tell the story of the curious case of participatory budgeting and its global take-up': 'it emerged out of the cauldron of leftist experimentalism in Brazil in the early 1990s as a particularly successful instrument and diffused to neighboring countries before being awarded a prize as a "best practice" by the UN Development Programme in 1997, and featuring prominently in the Human Development Report in 2001. But at the same time it was heavily discussed and promoted at the first World Social Forum in Brazil (starting in 2001) and made headway in Europe through the institutional Left and through networks of alter-globalization activists' (*ibid.*: 188). See also the 2012 special issue of the *Journal of Public Deliberation* 8(2) (http://www.publicdeliberation.net).

16. Alberto Magnaghi's work (2005) better summarises this theoretical perspective.

This particular vision of participatory democracy reveals a fundamental difference from deliberative democracy. As other scholars (such as Bobbio and Pomatto 2007) have pointed out, participatory democracy often takes a dualistic and 'vertical' dimension: the 'lower level' against the 'upper level', or the 'ruled' against the 'rulers'. Moreover, it is primarily based on the idea of exerting pressure in order to change public decisions and therefore aims at the possibility of a change in power-relations between the actors, through behaviour mainly dictated by a strategic rationality. Deliberative democracy, instead, takes a pluralistic and 'horizontal' position that sees conflict mainly *between citizens* who have different interests and opinions, rather than only between citizens and 'power': through public deliberation, such a conflict can be better defined and (*perhaps*) overcome.

However, 'participatory democracy' is a very broad term. Indeed, in addition to the critical and antagonistic versions, this term has been also used to define very disparate social and political practices, including participatory processes directly promoted by political institutions (endowed with their own legitimate decision-making power) to give some active role to citizens in the processes of policy-making; or even, more simply, devices or processes which have merely adopted specific *techniques or methodologies* inspired by the deliberative model. A varied, sometimes chaotic universe of theories and practices, with indistinct borders and very diverse labels and definitions, has thus come into being.[17] Is it possible to find, today, some criterion to distinguish these approaches? I believe that one of the keys lies in the way we understand the link between participation, deliberation and *political decision*.

As soon as participatory and deliberative models and institutions become part of a real policy-making process (not limited, for example, to empirically detecting the transformation of the opinions of citizens who are involved in an experimental deliberative setting), the terms of the theoretical discussion change considerably as well. Then a subject such as the *decision-making power* of these participatory institutions is inevitably back in the spotlight. The numerous critical reviews that, over the years, have attempted to analyse and evaluate such experiences often start with this question: 'how much actual power' do such practices have? What impact do they have on *policy outcomes*? What kind of empowerment do they get from the representative institutions, or governance networks, that are often the promoters of these participatory practices? Or, again, as the title of an important review on this issue asks: 'are innovative, participatory and deliberative procedures in policy-making democratic and effective?' (Papadopolous and Warin 2007).

In answering these questions, some deliberative theorists and practitioners would draw on the theoretical tradition of participatory democracy, and Sherry Arnstein's 'ladder' will also make a comeback: the link-up will be constituted precisely by a certain idea of *empowerment* attributed (or to be attributed) to the participating and/or deliberating citizen. Such a citizen is often called 'lay' or

---

17. Loic Blondiaux's work (2008a) better introduces elements of clarity. A strict definition of 'participatory democracy', from a juridical and constitutionalist point of view, is given by Umberto Allegretti (2011, 2015).

'nonpartisan'. The presence of this figure (or rather, the call for the presence of such a figure) is the hallmark of many new participatory practices.[18]

This idea that deliberative processes can or should have decision-making power is shared by very different approaches. Paradoxically (but only *prima facie*), the ideas of participation as *empowerment* and of deliberation as a *decision-making process* will often be implicit assumptions in the discourses of both the critics and the most fervent defenders of deliberative democracy. Scholars who criticise deliberative democracy for allegedly embodying a strategy of depoliticisation and neutralisation of conflict often start from a syllogism: a 'real' deliberative democracy *should* have decision-making powers; however, this *does not* happen; *ergo*, deliberative democracy is not really democratic, and its claims to be so are only a mystification. On the contrary, those who support deliberative democracy and present it (sometimes naively) as a way to strengthen the feeble foundations of our democracies, are driven by a different syllogism: a 'real' deliberative democracy *must* have decision-making powers; this *can* happen and *is* happening; *ergo*, we are facing a new form of democracy on which to bet in the future.

In either case, an equation (participation and deliberation *as a place* for democratic *decision*) is assumed. Such an equation implies, in my opinion, some serious theoretical misunderstandings. The fundamental question is similar, in many ways, to the one of the first and most ambitious formulations of 'participatory democracy' (which highlighted their radical weakness): can these participatory models imagine, or postulate, a complete and different institutional setting? And what is the source of the democratic legitimacy of a participatory and/or deliberative decision-making process that aspires to exercise some form of *power* and produce policy outcomes able to act as binding political decisions for everyone?

The theme of the relationship between participation, deliberation and political decision, and the tension between the different models of 'participatory democracy' and 'deliberative democracy', is once again very much present in the contemporary debate. Furthermore, any immediate identification between 'participation' and 'democratisation' presents, today, many problematic aspects as well.[19] In the light of what we have seen so far, we can try to conceptually arrange all the elements of the disputes that regularly arise on this subject.

On the one hand, we have all the forms of *participation* that – in a formal or informal, spontaneous or organised way – are produced independently within

---

18. 'Organized groups and their representatives play a significant role in democratic polities, but we are interested here in whether institutions can be designed to directly engage what have been termed "lay" or "non-partisan" citizens, as opposed to experts and partisan campaigners' (Smith 2009: 2).

19. 'While in the 1960s participation was offered up as a solution to hierarchy and alienation, participation today is widespread and complicated enough that any equation of participation with democratization cannot be sustained without some ambiguity' (Lee, McQuarrie and Walker 2015: 8). On the connection and tension between participatory democracy and deliberative democracy, *see* Cohen and Fung 2004; Cohen 2009b: 341–2; Mutz 2008a; Sintomer 2011a and 2011b; and Rosenberg 2007.

civil society and the public sphere and that can also manifest themselves through deliberative practices. These forms of participation may have or exercise their own 'power'; but that power does not consist in making binding and legitimate decisions. These forms of participation can exercise only *communicative power* and thus only *indirectly influence* the outcome of a decision-making process. On the other hand, we have methods of *policy-building* promoted by institutions and inspired by a logic of public deliberation. Such policy-making policy-making processes include or envisage phases, spaces and moments of public discussion and reason-giving in a *preliminary* stage of the decision-making process, where several options are still possible.

What are the motivations underlying this second phenomenon? I believe that some institutions promote inclusive processes of public deliberation (or processes that aspire to be such) because of the shared *strategic uncertainty* and/or the *cognitive and informational deficit* that, today, affects policy-making processes. If a policy-maker experiences such uncertainty in relation to a given decision to be taken, or she feels the need to deepen its *legitimacy*, or even if she perceives that a paralysing conflict could be produced by the need for decisions, she might want to activate specific participatory and deliberative processes. The purpose of these processes and institutions is to include a wider set of interlocutors in the process of considering the opinions, judgments and interests involved in and/or stirred up by the policy under discussion, and thus to obtain a decision that is more 'legitimate' and/or 'fairer', or more shared, or even 'better' because it is based on more solid cognitive and informative ground. Of course, these attempts can succeed or fail, wholly or partially: the empirical analysis must evaluate, each time, their features, asking specific questions such as why would a policy-maker promote a certain participatory process inspired by a given deliberative model? How can we distinguish the processes that merely use, or just evoke, deliberative techniques from those processes in which 'deliberation' is properly produced?[20]

At this point, the normative paradigm that defines the features of a deliberative procedure can and must intervene in critical-analytical terms. Precisely for this reason, the frequent opposition between 'abstract' and 'realistic' versions of deliberative democracy appears confusing. Making this theoretical paradigm 'work' – with no need to relax its demanding normative assumptions – can help us see things that, perhaps, looking through another 'lens', we would fail to grasp. Quite simply, if a decision has already been taken, it is not possible to describe any subsequent 'participatory' processes as public and democratic deliberation procedures. Rather, they should be defined as tools that have other purposes (informative, consultative, 'communicative'; or, perhaps as *'market-testing'* procedures, for example, evaluating the degree of client-user satisfaction). The suspicion, or accusation, of *manipulation* – common in some empirical analyses of participatory and deliberative processes – thereby loses its special force. If

---

20. On the difference between properly deliberative procedures and techniques of (more or less) deliberative inspiration, Parkinson 2004, 2006: 65): I think this difference is fundamental and I do not agree with Pellizzoni (2013: 14–15), who considers it a *'subtilité linguistique'*.

anything – when some form of manipulation is really found – it's necessary to analyse the often-counterproductive logics that lead a policy-maker to act in this way. As Blondiaux noted,

> ... within the ordinary practices of participatory systems, it is clear that it is not always possible, for the organizers of the discussion, to instrumentalise participation. Indeed, it is less widespread than what is generally believed: ... the contemporary systems of participation and deliberation are always the source of a tension between the search for consensus and the expression of criticism (Blondiaux 2008a: 146).

The theoretical paradigm of deliberative democracy is thus revealed as a *theoretical, critical* and *normative paradigm* that could intervene in the analysis of three distinct levels:

    a. the deliberative dimension independently produced in the public sphere and in participatory practices that, formally and informally (and in varying degrees), operate in this space;

    b. the deliberative practices and procedures that may characterise, in varying degrees, the policy-making of institutions and forms of *governance*;

    c. the *specific* institutions or deliberative processes that, promoted by institutions or other subjects, aim to *connect* institutional processes of decision-making to the formation of opinions and political judgments produced in the public sphere.

Finally, we can also identify some fundamentally different approaches within the research on deliberative democracy, depending upon the initial 'point of view' adopted in studying a process or system.

On the one hand, there are those who can be described as '*confident*' deliberativists. They believe that the analysis of a participatory-deliberative process should show to what extent it approximates to the ideal model, with regard to the process, the resulting decisions and the effects of the process. For '*confident and optimistic*' deliberativists, it is a matter of 'proving' the practicality of the model, realistically analysing even the partial results that can be measured in real life, while enhancing its plausibility and indicating how it was actually concretised in the analysed experiences. Such an approach can have a variety of characters: schematising, it can be more or less 'reformist' or 'gradualist' (or, on the contrary, 'critical-radical'), depending on whether its positive impact on existing institutions or, on the contrary, its critical and antagonistic impact, is emphasised.

On the other hand, we have '*sceptical*' and '*dismissive*' critics. They, too, assume the deliberative ideal as an ambitious ideal model but seek to overturn its assumptions and show its impracticability or even its failure. Within this typology, we can distinguish two variants: the *empirical* one and the *antagonistic* one. In the former case, there is a neo-positivist 'short-circuit' between the normative and theoretical levels: it is claimed that the ideal model can and should be verified or 'proven' (in the strict sense). Often this critical approach assumes a simplified and impoverished version of the deliberative theoretical model. This approach mainly derives from some sectors of the empirical political sciences. Dennis F. Thompson (2008: 498–9) has understood their approach well:

> ... some researchers have assumed that they can dispose of deliberative theory by showing that political discussion often does not produce the benefits that theorists are presumed to claim for it. They extract from isolated passages in various theoretical writings a simplified statement about one or more benefits of deliberative democracy, compress it into a testable hypothesis, find or (more often) artificially create a site in which people talk about politics, and conclude that deliberation does not produce the benefits the theory promised and may even be counterproductive.[21]

Thus, the analysis of the deliberative processes becomes an 'experimental' opportunity to try, above all, to *empirically* demonstrate how the effects expected from the 'application' of a particular system (or from the deliberative 'ideal') have not been realised. As a conclusion, deliberative democracy is considered illusory, as 'ideal', and, as 'theory', it is 'falsified' by the facts.

The second variant can be defined as truly *antagonistic*. Here, the starting point of enquiry is not any assumption made in the deliberative model of which the researcher seeks to evaluate the relevance or applicability; the research goal is rather the pursuit of the *objective function* that participatory-deliberative processes have, or may have, within the processes characterising contemporary capitalist societies and their systems of governance. Such a function is considered to be active and working independently of the good intentions of the protagonists. The premise of this vision is often the adoption of a *holistic* theoretical and political scheme (a pervasive hegemony of neo-liberalism that includes and absorbs everything) that allows one to place the specific phenomenon (that is, the spread of participatory practices promoted by traditional institutions) within a global process. These analyses, in particular, owe a lot to Foucault's notion of *gouvernementalité* (Pellizzoni 2013 and 2015; Bevir 2006 and 2011b; W. Brown 2006) and leave little hope for the (possible) agency of the critical subjectivity of actors (or believe that these actors can only carve out some individual space of resistance or some collective moments of vitalistic insurgence). If Power and its Discourse dominate and pervade all, only the naive can think that 'deliberation' might damage that logic. Today's participatory revival is thus seen as instances of manipulation, condemned to irrelevance or read as an expression of the hegemonic strategy of elites (see, e.g., Gourgues-Rui-Topçu 2013; Clark 2010).

Some other critical approaches do not package everything under the aspect of neo-liberal hegemony but empirically evaluate different possible uses of participation and its 'rhetoric' within the hegemonic strategies of particular

---

21. One of the worst examples of this strategy given by Thompson is Hibbing and Theiss-Morse 2002. On these subjects, *see also* Diane C. Mutz's essay 'Is deliberative democracy a falsifiable theory?' (2008b) and Thompson's reply (2008: 505). *See also* Neblo (2015: 39–49).

subjects and institutions, even supranational ones. Despite being described as 'elite-driven forms of participation', these uses may also have unexpected effects or may open up significant spaces for a genuine process of democratisation.[22]

These critical schemes can be enthusiastic or sceptical, gradualist or radical, empiricist or antagonistic. However much they may differ in these respects, the major question that this literature seeks to answer is that of the *decisional* nature of a particular participatory process. Whether a process is deemed 'real' or 'fake' is only determined by the decision-making power given (or not given) to it. The theory underlying this approach is very similar to that of 'classic' participatory democracy: have the citizen-participants practised a real form of democratic *empowerment*? Did they live a 'real' democratic experience? Have the conclusions emerging from the participatory process been translated into 'real' political decisions formally taken by the institutions? Or have they *replaced* them? Or, on the contrary, has nothing of the sort happened?

Because of these differences in approach, it is crucial how to understand the link between participation, deliberation and political decision – specifically, the issue of the forms and sources of democratic legitimacy, as well as of the role and influence that participatory and deliberative processes can play in the construction of public decisions. I believe that some recent theoretical developments, in particular what has been defined as 'a systemic approach' to deliberative democracy, can provide important answers in this regard.

6. The 'systemic approach' to deliberative democracy

A 'deliberative system': definition and functions

The empirical turn in deliberative democracy was important and consequential. However, it soon brought about criticism and dissatisfaction. What emerged were positions of increasing distrust for any idea of 'deliberative democracy' that restricts its effort and scope, entrusting its destiny to the creation and experimentation of deliberative 'niches' – ones often lacking a significant political meaning. As Simone Chambers critically observed (2009: 323–4):

> The pathologies of the democratic public sphere, first articulated by Plato in his attack on rhetoric, have pushed much of deliberative theory out of the mass public and into the study and design of small-scale deliberative venues. The problem that Plato's discussion of rhetoric points to is this: while it is possible to enhance and promote deliberative encounters throughout civil society (i.e., Socratic dialogues), it is not at all clear that the broad informal public sphere can be deliberative. It cannot be deliberative because it cannot be dialogical. It would appear that a great deal of deliberative democracy literature has come to

---

22. *Cf.* Lee, McQuarrie and Walker (2015: 18): 'the contributions of this book seek to avoid both the valorization of participation and an (equally problematic) argument that the participatory practices are merely ideological cover for inequality'.

the same conclusion. The mass public is abandoned in favor of mini-publics, that is, designed settings that can achieve and maintain standards of critical dialogue or that can be modeled to do so. The move away from the mass public can be seen in a growing split in deliberative theory between theories of *democratic deliberation* (on the ascendancy), which focus on discrete deliberative initiatives within democracies, and theories of *deliberative democracy* (on the decline), which attempt to tackle the large questions of how the public, or civil society in general, relates to the state.

Much discussion involved the theoretical and normative premises on which some deliberative models are based, most notably, those requiring a somewhat mythical figure, that is, the 'ordinary citizen' as the bearer of an 'impartial' judgment. Such premises were later highlighted by interpreters such as Philip Pettit, who tend to openly proclaim the 'unpolitical' nature of deliberative democracy.[23] Pettit's position deserves to be considered carefully, both for its importance and because his image of deliberative democracy is sometimes taken, *tout court*, by critics committed to a 'agonistic' vision of democracy as the position that most properly interprets (or 'betrays') the true theoretical substance of this conception of democracy. Pettit claimed, in the title of an influential article, that 'deliberation requires depoliticization' (Pettit 2004: 52). Indeed, as happens within the 'neo-roman' tradition of republicanism recalled by Pettit (Pettit 1997), the core of a normative vision of politics is not 'democracy' (the realm of passions, factions and demagogy, always ready to fall into tyranny: to put it in Polybius's words, 'a ship without a helmsman') but the primacy of the *rule of law* and of *freedom* based on the principle of 'non-arbitrary interference'.

'Electoral interests', Pettit writes, 'can indirectly jeopardise the ideal of deliberative democracy' (2004: 57). Pettit's vision of electoral and representative democracy is disconsolate: electoral interests *prevent* the development of deliberation inspired by the search for the 'common good' or, more simply, they prevent rationality and wisdom from prevailing in the solution of collective problems. The scene as he conceives it, is dominated by politicians who are only interested in re-election, unable (note: *even if they so wanted*) to think of and act for a 'common good':

> ... even if elected officials have the interests of the community as a whole at heart they are still bound to be responsive to their own interest, or their party's interest, in being re-elected. If electoral interests of this kind are engaged in some of the policy-making decisions over which representatives have political control, then they cannot be reliably expected to decide those issues by reference just to considerations of the common good. *Nemo judex in sua causa.* No one to be judge in his or her own cause. The principle applies as much to those in politically elective office as it does to those in judicial and related areas (*ibid.*: 52–3).

---

23. On 'unpolitical democracy', *see* Urbinati 2010.

Hence the need to 'depoliticise' many collective decisions, entrusting them to entities able to avoid partisanship and reducing the power of representative authorities elected by citizens. Hence, expert committees, deliberative arenas or *citizen panels* (Pettit also references Fishkin's Deliberative Polling), under the control of but 'at arm's length from parliament and government', are promoted, in the hope of defeating the 'overblown rhetoric' that often dominates the public scene, minimising the impact of self-interest and encouraging a search for rational solutions. This trend is already present in 'a number of areas of decision-making', Pettit notices, and should be strengthened and extended; he cites as a positive example institutions for setting monetary policy.[24] In this context, what really characterises a democracy is the citizens' ability to exercise a constant function of *contestation*, control and criticism, rather than a role of 'participation' in the decision-making process: this is what Pettit, in another text (2003: 153), calls the '*contestability argument*' in support of deliberative democracy.[25]

A reaction to this understanding of deliberative democracy as a model for the 'neutralisation' of conflict and interests (even without embracing Pettit's extreme position), soon arose. We can see this in a 2010 essay, co-authored by a large group of scholars led by Jane Mansbridge, dedicated precisely to the role of 'self-interest' and 'power' in deliberative theory (Mansbridge *et al.* 2010).[26] But above all, this line of critical reflection has recently led a significant group of deliberative theorists to propose what has been called 'a systemic approach' to deliberative democracy. This expression in itself might lead to misunderstanding, insofar as it recalls some version of 'systemic theory' or a sociological, functionalist approach; in fact, this approach is fully internal to the history of deliberative democracy as it has been developing since the beginning.

The concept of 'deliberative system' lies at the core of this approach. This notion had previously been proposed by Jane Mansbridge in a 1999 essay (Mansbridge 1999) but, as we have seen, the same expression had already been used, albeit *en passant*, by Bernard Manin in 1987 (*see* Chapter Five, Section 3, page 112,

---

24. 'There are a number of areas of decision-making where democracies have depoliticized decisions, for fear of allowing electoral interests to dictate what government does; the outstanding example is interest-rate policy and exchange-rate policy, where relatively autonomous central banks are routinely given charge' (Pettit 2004: 53). This essay dates from 2004. Much more could now be said in this regard, in the light of the financial crisis that started in 2008 and what happened in the financial markets afterwards. Have decisions really been 'depoliticised' or have they been distanced from any sort of democratic legitimacy?

25. For a critical analysis of Pettit, *see* Urbinati 2014: 116–22) and Ottonelli 2012. Rosanvallon's position, his idea of 'counter-democracy' (2008), is somewhat similar to Pettit's ideas but it cannot be assimilated to them: according to Rosanvallon, democracy today has its foundation in the functions of obstacle, surveillance and sanction that citizens must carry out against the power of the rulers.

26. Beside Jane Mansbridge, the essay was also signed by J. Bohman, S. Chambers, D. Estlund, A. Føllesdal, A. Fung, C. Lafonte, B. Manin and J. L. Marti. Jane Mansbridge had dedicated previous important works to the theme of self-interest, in particular her introductory essay to a collected volume she edited entitled *Beyond Self-Interest* (1990).

note 19). As Jane Mansbridge, John Parkinson *et al.* note in a collective text that is somewhat of a *theoretical manifesto*,[27] the notion of 'deliberative system' has been elaborated, with different formulas, by numerous other authors and is also compatible with the Habermasian 'two-track' model (Mansbridge *et al.* 2012: 2). Although the authors particularly highlight a significant difference between their theses and those attributed to Habermas (see note 31), in my opinion it is not just a matter of 'compatibility': the notion of 'deliberative system' can find its most complete theoretical foundation precisely in Habermas's concept of 'deliberative politics'. However, this possible reference is neither decisive nor exclusive: as the authors point out, the notion of 'deliberative system' may constitute a common and shared point of reference among definitions of deliberation that proceed from different assumptions:

> Like any useful paradigm, deliberative democracy theory contains many theoretical variations, competing articulations, and contested definitions. Our aim is to articulate an overarching approach to deliberation that could signal a new and, we think, exciting direction for deliberative theory, but which is not itself a free-standing theory of deliberative democracy (*ibid.*: 4).[28]

A 'deliberative system' can be defined as the *network of discourses* that intertwine and mingle within the public sphere and between the public sphere and institutions, in relation to a political or public issue: it is the set of *discursive interactions* by which the citizens' opinions and political judgments are formed and modified. It is a *deliberative* system insofar as, through this network of public discourses, information and knowledge are exchanged; collective learning processes are introduced; arguments and counter-arguments to the discussion are offered; interests, values and individual and collective purposes are clarified. And it is a *system* because it is produced in a variety of places and moments that can be more or less related

---

27. Mansbridge *et al.* 2012. The volume also contains texts by T. Christiano, S. Chambers, J. Bohman, M. Mackenzie and M. Warren, Y. Papadopoulos and J. Parkinson. It was presented as a paper at an ECPR meeting in 2012 and then published as chapter 1 of *Deliberative Systems: Deliberative democracy at the large scale* (Parkinson and Mansbridge (eds) 2012).

28. Mansbridge *et al.* (2012: 2) signal the works and authors that contributed to the definition of this 'systemic' vision, or those that converge with it: Goodin 2008 (a 'distributed deliberation'); Parkinson 2006 ('legitimacy across multiple deliberative moments and the wider deliberative system'); Hendriks 2006 (an 'integrated deliberative system'); Bohman 2007 (an 'institutional differentiation', with a set of 'multiple and intersecting processes of public deliberation'). Although she is not quoted by the authors, Seyla Benhabib could be added to the list (1996: 73–4): 'a deliberative and proceduralist model of democracy ... privileges a plurality of modes of association in which all affected can have the right to articulate their point of view ... It is through the interlocking net of these multiple forms of associations, networks, and organizations that an anonymous "public conversation" results. It is central to the model of deliberative democracy that it privileges such a public sphere of mutually interlocking and overlapping networks and associations of deliberation, contestation, and argumentation'. John Dryzek, too (2010: 10–14), adopts a systemic perspective, proposing his own definition. Steiner (2014) discusses some aspects of the concept of 'deliberative system'. Owen and Smith (2015) give a critical analysis of the 'systemic approach'.

and interdependent, and that can also be *designed* in order to build this deliberative connection.[29] This network produces *deliberative systemic effects*, or rather, the consolidation and definition of cognitive and normative *frames* (orientations, beliefs, values, 'preferences') that produce particular *societal decisions*. *Societal decisions* are the ones marking, in an 'incremental' way ('*by accretion*'), the emergence and formation of new norms and social practices. In the face of a *framework* of public discourse 'locked' within rigid schemes that make a set of beliefs interpreting social reality seem 'given' or unchangeable ('*indisputable*', in fact), it is always possible for public discussion to reveal new points of view that can open up and disclose a new vision of things, change the agenda of the public sphere, redefine problems and affirm new cognitive and normative schemes that are socially widespread.[30]

These widespread deliberative processes of the discursive formation of opinion, which may be spontaneous or structured, interact with the institutional procedures of political decision-making, and can do so in a more or less mediated – but always indirect – way (that is, without being vested, as such, with decision-making power). The Civil Rights movement of the United States of America could be an example of this (Bohman 1996: 224): it was a social movement but also a widespread deliberative practice, which first managed to change the collective perception of racial segregation along with the 'public culture' it expressed and was then able to affect the judgments of the Supreme Court and the interpretation of constitutional principles of equality that had been used until that point.[31]

---

29. This approach, Parkinson writes (2006: 17), 'helps us to move away from a reliance on small, micro-deliberative forums towards a more discursive, macro conception of democracy in which a variety of institutions at various points of the public sphere are connected together in a deliberative system'. Such a deliberative system can also 'fail' when a 'deliberative decoupling' between its different places or moments is produced (Mansbridge *et al.* 2012: 23). Carolyn Hendriks (2015) has recently proposed the concept of 'designed coupling', that is, the 'institutional' design of a connection between different moments of a 'deliberative system'. Such a system is thus given not only by the spontaneous and informal production of a deliberative practice within the public sphere but also by the possible institutional construction of a (more or less 'loose' or 'tight') link between different deliberative moments. Such is the Australian case analysed by Hendriks, in which a citizens' jury intervened in the deliberative process of a Parliamentary commission and influenced its conclusions, particularly modifying and enhancing the cognitive and informative bases on which the commission based its conclusions.

30. 'When the majority of a society or a subgroup', Mansbridge *et al.* write, 'changes its norms and practices, bringing to bear social sanctions on those who deviate from the new norms and practices, it seems fair to say that in a general way that majority has taken a decision, especially when the change has been accompanied by extensive discussion of the pros and cons of such a change'. However, the authors admit that such decisions 'are binding only in a loose social sense' and they notice how these decisions are produced 'by accretion', so that there is 'no clear-cut point at which an observer can say that a decision has been taken' (Mansbridge *et al.* 2012: 8).

31. Michelman's text, which I quoted previously (Chapter Nine, Section 3) may be an example of a 'systemic' vision of deliberation. However, he obviously did not define it in these terms. Mansbridge *et al.* (2012: 9) identify, within the question of societal decisions, some distance between their 'deliberative system' model and Habermas's, emphasising how Habermas assumed a 'spatial metaphor of centre/periphery' and identified the 'core' within legislative assemblies. Contrarily, the authors write: 'our understanding of deliberative systems includes both informal decisions by accretion and binding decisions that take place outside the state ... We take the

Within a deliberative system, the *pure* deliberative quality of a single moment and segment of the network, or of a single arena, is not the essential matter – not all individual moments can fully express all the functions of deliberation (an epistemic function, an ethical function and a democratic function, according to Mansbridge *et al.* 2012: 10–13): what really counts is the *overall* discursive quality that emerges from the interactions.

The introduction of this notion of 'deliberative system' presumes a distinction between *two levels* of theoretical elaboration within the deliberative model: the first can be described as *a theory of democratic deliberation*; the second (which is wider and *includes* the first) is *a deliberative theory of democracy*. The former level specifies the preconditions and characteristics of a procedure that can properly be called both democratic and deliberative; the latter level focuses, instead, on a deliberative and democratic *dimension* that contributes, in varying degree and intensity, to defining the essence of an entire *polity* (even if counterfactually, allowing us to evaluate the partial or total absence of a deliberative dimension). In this *systemic* dimension, deliberative procedures and practices are combined. They coexist with other (democratic and non-deliberative) decision-making procedures and forms and, obviously, conflict with non-democratic ones. Furthermore, a deliberative dimension may also characterise, under certain conditions, different forms of *negotiation*: convergences; 'incompletely theorized agreements' (Sunstein 1995); and integrative negotiations and distributive negotiations (Mansbridge *et al.* 2010: 69–72; Warren-Mansbridge *et al.* 2015).

Recalling the pattern that has guided us in the previous chapters, it is clear that this category of 'deliberative system' is, first of all, a *theoretical* category playing a *reconstructive* and *analytical* role. From this category, which can also have *normative* implications, we can draw *critical-evaluative* criteria. However, it is not, nor can it be, properly speaking, an *ideal model* that we should aspire to achieve.

There is no need to dwell here on the meaning of this theoretical model and its relevant analytical potential.[32] However, I want to show to what extent this model can help solve some of the dilemmas that the theoretical field of deliberative democracy faced and still faces, in particular with regard to a) the relationship between 'deliberation' and other forms of participation in democratic politics; b) the relationship between 'participation', 'deliberation' and 'conflict'; and c) the 'epistemic' dimension of deliberation, that is, the answer to the question of when and in what sense we can speak of a 'good' or 'better' decision.

---

state and its legislature as the ultimate decision-makers in a polity, but not as a centre to which everything is aimed in the polity's deliberative system'.

32. The cases studied by Parkinson (2006) are excellent examples of the heuristic and interpretative capacities of the concept of 'deliberative system'. For a more detailed discussion of Mansbridge *et al.*'s essay, and of some of its problems (in particular, the question of societal decisions), but also for some Italian cases showing the analytical potential of this theoretical category, *see* Floridia 2012. Maia 2012 shows how a systemic approach can be used for the analysis of the relationship between 'deliberation, the media and political talk'.

Deliberation, participation and the forms of democratic politics

The 'systemic' approach to deliberative democracy allows us to consider the relationship between participation and deliberation in new way, thereby overcoming some classic objections to deliberative democracy. Some critics of deliberative democracy (even very authoritative ones) have contested the idea that democratic politics can be seen, in such a reductive and certainly unrealistic way, as a mere exchange of arguments or, as Iris Young wrote (2001: 675), that 'power can be bracketed by the soft tones of the seminar room'. Michael Walzer,[33] for example, controversially proposed 'a list of all the non deliberative activities that democratic politics legitimately, and perhaps even necessarily, involves' (1999: 58): political education; organisation; mobilisation; demonstration; statement; debate (in the sense of *oratory*, addressed to the *persuasion* of an audience); bargaining; lobbying; campaigning; voting; fundraising.[34] 'I have not made deliberation synonymous with thinking', Walzer explained: 'mine is not a list of thoughtless activities' (*ibid.*). As it is defined by deliberative theorists, Walzer added, deliberation can be described as 'a particular way of thinking: quiet, reflective, open to a wide range of evidence, respectful of different views' and as 'a rational process of weighing the available data, considering alternative possibilities, arguing about relevance and worthiness, and then choosing the best policy or person'. However, if deliberation is all this, we cannot help but ask: 'what else do we do? What is going on in the political world besides deliberation?' (*ibid.*). We cannot ignore the fact that 'a democratic political process' is 'pervasively non deliberative' (*ibid.*: 59).

Walzer could oppose all those activities to 'deliberation', or he could indiscriminately consider them as 'non deliberative', only because he transposed an *idealised* image of deliberation on to the various *practices* of democratic politics. In Walzer's list we find very different forms of political action. However, besides an *instrumental* and *strategic* component, all of these forms evidently have, in varying degrees, a decisive *communicative* and *discursive* component as well: that is, they are forms of political activity that contribute to the formation of opinions and political judgments in a public dimension.

From a systemic point of view, it is quite clear that many forms of political participation do not have a truly 'deliberative' dimension, or have it only in a partial or dependent way. Furthermore, it is equally clear that they can still contribute to a 'deliberative politics': that is, they form and transform opinions, transmit knowledge and information and provide 'good reasons'. All these moments build a *deliberative sequence* and also fuel the circulation of ideas both *within* the public

---

33. 'Deliberation, and what else?' (Walzer 1999). This intervention originally appeared among the essays collected in Macedo 1999, a volume dedicated to Gutmann and Thompson's 1996 book.

34. Walzer also considered some other 'non deliberative' activities, such as corruption ('my only negative example': 1999: 64). He also added the 'scut work': 'boring and repetitive' work that, as such, does not have any political feature but 'someone has to do it', and which is crucial for the success of a political activity, such as 'stuffing envelopes, setting up chairs, preparing placards, handing out leaflets, making phone calls ... none of this requires much thought, though it often takes a lot of thought, and even some ingenuity, to motivate one self to do it' (*ibid.*: 65).

sphere and *between* the public sphere and institutions. Walzer's objections are correct in relation to a particular concept that deliberation, due to its rational and 'impartial' nature, should be treated as a verdict issued by a citizen-judge: 'very few political decisions are "verdicts" in the literal sense of that term' (*ibid.*: 66). Such objections may be plausible against some particularly 'naïve' and idealising versions of deliberative democracy. However, I believe that they cannot be related to a notion of 'deliberative politics' that is intended, primarily, as a *reconstructive* model of real political practices. In fact, all the participative forms listed by Walzer can be reconsidered in the light of this paradigm: for example, debate in front of an audience – a place in which to exercise the classical arts of oratory and persuasion and a *dispute* in which someone wins and convinces, while others 'succumb' – can take very different forms.

Following a distinction proposed by Simone Chambers (2009), a public debate can be experienced and practised (and analysed) as a place in which to express a *plebiscitary rhetoric* or, on the contrary, a *deliberative rhetoric*.[35] The 'plebiscitary' rhetoric is a *non-dialogic* one and is based on the asymmetry between speaker and listener, as well as on the audience's passivity. On the contrary, the 'deliberative' rhetoric has to be understand in an Aristotelian sense, as an 'art of persuasion' that acts simultaneously through three dimensions: emotions (*pathos*), the 'speaker's character' (*ethos*) and the coherence of the argument (*logos*). 'If rhetoric in general', Chambers writes (2009: 335),

> ... is the study of how speech affects an audience then deliberative rhetoric must be about the way speech induces deliberation in the sense of inducing *considered* reflection about a future action. Deliberative rhetoric makes people think, it makes people see things in new ways, it conveys information and knowledge, and it makes people more reflective.

On the contrary, Walzer (1999: 61–2) describes a 'debate' somewhat differently:

> ... debaters do have to listen to one another, but listening in this case does not produce anything like a deliberative process: their object is not to reach an agreement among themselves but to win the debate ... A debate is a contest between verbal athletes, and the aim is victory. The means are the exercise of rhetorical skills, the mustering of favourable evidence (and the suppression of unfavourable evidence), the discrediting of the other debaters, the appeal to authority or celebrity, and so on. ... The others are rivals, not fellow participants; they are already committed, not persuadable.

Of course, Waltzer's description may well reflect many situations accurately (consider the many political talk-shows available on television today); however,

---

35. For a kind of rehabilitation of rhetoric within deliberative theory and political theory, *see*, in particular, Young 2000; Dryzek 2010: 66–84; Garsten 2006 and 2011. On the '*priorité du débat contradictoire sur la discussion*', *see* Manin 2011. For a criticism of the 'introduction of nonrational elements' within the concept of deliberation, *cf.* Talisse 2012: 215.

why should it be presented as *the* ordinary form of a debate? If anything, it perfectly adapts to a classical *demagogic* practice – the use of arguments *ad hominem*, discrediting the opponent. Thus, the problem is not to set 'debate' against 'deliberation' but to have a criterion of judgment to define the *deliberative quality of a debate* (and the rhetoric used) and to adopt a theoretical approach to interpreting and distinguishing the different forms of rationality and the different dialogic forms that are *implicit* and *co-present* within social and individual practices, as well as within the various forms of participation. Such an approach may also allow us to draw out some normative-level, and operational- and political-level indicators of what we can do – to stick to our example – in order to have a 'public debate' not dominated by *bad* rhetoric.

As this example shows, it is possible to employ the concept of 'deliberative system' to capture the different functions that different practices may assume within a politics. Therefore, attacks – like that of Lynn Sanders (1997), which is among the most often cited[36] – that might make sense if directed towards a simplified and idealised deliberative view (which, as we have seen, none of the major deliberative theorists has, in fact, adopted) are totally off-target when aimed at a notion of deliberative democracy that mainly functions as a critical and reconstructive paradigm.

The link between participation, deliberation and conflict

The relationship between deliberation and the more openly and consciously conflicting forms of participation is closely related to the previous point. Given 'the fact of pluralism' and the conflicts that it fuels, various options are possible from the participants' point of view. On the one hand, social groups and individuals may consider their own interest and their own values 'non-negotiable' and thus they may choose the path of antagonistic participation: the path of a *strategic* plan that relies on pure *power relations* to solve conflict. On the other hand, it is possible to choose a *communicative* and *argumentative* practice and a co-operative attitude that relies on the possibility of an agreement. Thus, it is possible to consider (even if only strategically) a more productive *management* of the conflict, one that takes the form of negotiation and mediation. In the public sphere – according to the 'systemic' perspective – even the most bitterly conflictual behaviour can produce 'deliberative effects': this happens when a strongly partisan action introduces a new point of view into the public sphere; such a point of view *may* then enter into a broader circuit of discursive interactions, enriching the deliberative substance of the public discussion. The opposite happens when a strongly partisan action leads people to become entrenched in their positions, or when the polarisation of the debate fails to produce any real communicative interaction. In these cases, there

---

36. Another example is found in those arguments that Iris M. Young attributes to 'an activist', in order to justify his diffidence towards deliberative democracy (2001). Young did not identify herself *in toto* with these arguments; however she considered them a 'challenge' that needed to be taken on. For a reply, *see* Fung 2005.

is – or may be – 'participation' but this participation is limited to the circle of *like-minded* individuals, including only people who 'think the same way' and do not encounter, nor want to have, opportunities to compare their views with those of others; or, at the very best, they tend only to *declare* or *testify to* their own ideas. Mansbridge *et al*. (2012: 19), identify such a case in the US Tea Party movement: although it 'brought new voices into public debate', overall, it created 'a toxic atmosphere' that did not help to strengthen the quality of the deliberative system.[37]

In cases in which participation takes the form of an 'intractable' conflict, things are dominated by the *power relationships* and the *strategic evaluations* of the various actors. In these cases, there is often *much* 'participation', while 'deliberation' can be entirely absent, or may be only *indirectly* present, as some kind of *by-product*: that is, only *if* and *when* what emerges from the conflict are transformations of ideas and opinions that may have an influence on the construction of political decisions. A 'systemic' approach allows the empirical analysis to show, each time, the development of this relationship between (mainly) *conflicting* participation, *informal* deliberation emerging independently in the public sphere and institutional *policy-making*.

The *deliberative policy-making* that a political decision-maker may choose to adopt is a completely different matter. In this context, it is necessary to understand how and to what extent this process succeeds in, or fails to, include all relevant voices and 'points of view'; the 'interests' and the 'values' at stake; the 'weak' subjects and the 'strong' powers; the formal and specialised forms of knowledge as well as the contextual ones; forms of knowledge and skills deriving from social practices and citizens' experiences, and so on. And even in this case, it is up to the empirical analysis to show how, each time, this relationship between (mainly) deliberative participation, *formal* deliberation in specific arenas and institutional policy-making is produced.

Finally, this understanding of the relationship between participation, deliberation and conflict also allows us to clarify some argumentative paradigms that characterise current discourses on participatory and/or deliberative democracy. It happens, for example, that 'institutionalised' participatory processes are accused of being 'closed' to the requests of the most active groups of citizens and of having the sole purpose of neutralising conflict. However, such a claim only leads to confusion between completely different kinds of situations: there can be, of course, groups of citizens who choose to place their action, within the *continuum* of participation, along a line that privileges conflicting and antagonistic attitudes. When one chooses this approach, there are only two options: either this action proves to be strong and influential and breaks down the oppositions of the established power; or, on the contrary, it does not and, thus, this action may

---

37. This problem is also related to the issue, widely debated nowadays, of the uses of the internet and social media: yet even for this field of communication, we can talk of an analytic criterion that distinguishes between deliberative and non-deliberative, or plebiscitary, uses. Sunstein (2003b) highlights that new information technologies may produce 'echo-chambers', in which 'like-minded' citizens talk only to each other.

continue to manifest itself as the more or less vital sign of *part* of the public sphere raising critical issues, attempting to gain visibility and consensus. Anyhow, the idea, or accusation, that 'institutional' forms of participation nullify or weaken conflict misses the point: conflicts are present, *regardless* – and there may also be many types of conflict. Thus, it is necessary to understand how they are tackled and managed, and maybe wonder, from a more general point of view, if the quality of our democracy has anything to gain from a proliferation of 'intractable' macro- or micro-conflicts.[38]

What makes a decision 'good' or 'correct'? The epistemic functions of deliberation

The systemic approach to deliberative democracy does not simply distinguish between the places and moments through which we can develop public deliberation. In fact, these places or moments can also be distinguished in terms of the different weight of the various *functions* or *dimensions* of deliberation. Mansbridge *et al.* (2012: 11) identify three of them: the epistemic function, the ethical function and the democratic function. From an *ethical* point of view, a primary function of deliberation is 'to promote mutual respect among citizens'. There may be different ideas as to what 'mutual respect' means, but – the authors note – it is possible to say that it is an *intrinsic* element of deliberation: 'to deliberate with another is to understand the other as a self-authoring source of reason and claims' (*ibid.*). The *democratic* function of deliberation is 'to promote an inclusive political process on terms of equality' (*ibid.*: 12): 'the inclusion of multiple and plural voices, concerns, and claims on the basis of feasible equality is not simply an ethic added to democratic deliberation; it is the central element of what makes deliberative democratic processes democratic'.

However, I would like to focus here mainly on the third function, the *epistemic* one, because it is the crux of many theoretical problems. In addition, there are many

---

38. On the 'paradoxical relationships between participation and conflict', and for a convincing critical analysis of the undifferentiated idea of 'conflict' that characterises some polemical approaches to deliberative or participatory democracy, *see* Bobbio and Melé 2015. According to some critics, conflict, as such, seems to be a value: however, as Bobbio and Melé note, conflicts have different natures and they cannot always be considered positively. Many concrete cases show how the creation of an 'institutionalised' deliberative space did not 'weaken' the conflict at all but rather and very often 'ignited' it. In other cases, however, a potentially paralysing conflict was prevented and participants' energies turned towards the search for shared solutions. Is it such a deplorable idea that conflict may also be, if not resolved, at least treated in a productive way? Many cases show how 'activists' have often found a place favourable to their claims in deliberative arenas. Polletta (2015: 240) criticises 'the notion that deliberation and activism are at odds': 'activism and deliberation are not only compatible; sometimes they may be necessary to each other'. In general, on the theme of '*démocratie délibérative vs. démocratie agonistique*?', *see also* Blondiaux 2008b. The relationship between deliberation, participation and conflict is multifaceted: for some examples, see the conflict on the issue of city hospitals in Leicester, analysed by Parkinson (2006) and many Italian cases (Bobbio 2010a; Pomatto 2011, 2013 and 2015; Ravazzi and Pomatto 2014; Floridia 2012 and 2013; Morisi and Perrone 2013).

misunderstandings in this regard within the present conceptions of deliberative democracy. Mansbridge *et al.* write (*ibid.*: 11):

> ... the *epistemic* function of a deliberative system is to produce preferences, opinions, and decisions that are appropriately informed by facts and logic and are the outcome of substantive and meaningful consideration of relevant reasons. A healthy deliberative system is one in which relevant considerations are brought forth from all corners, aired, discussed, and appropriately weighed.

Of course, these words deserve further consideration (how to decide which ones are the '*relevant reasons*', for instance?). Here, we can tackle the issue by starting, once again, from current discourses. In short, what does it mean to make a 'good' decision? How can public deliberation help to make a 'better' decision?

I believe that a crucial point is to be found in the distinction between an *epistemic* conception of *democracy* and the recognition of an essential, and more specific, *cognitive* and *epistemic* role for deliberation *within a deliberative system*. As I mentioned in reference to Estlund's position, an epistemic conception of democracy focuses on the need for a *justification* of democracy by some external standard of validity: a democratic procedure *must* be able to reach outcomes that are, in some way, 'correct'. An epistemic conception of *deliberative* democracy adds a decisive element: that is, the public and democratic dimension characterising a deliberative process. The 'many', free and equal individuals (rather than the assembly of few wise people) are the protagonists of this deliberative search for a 'right' solution to a problem that is of concern to a political community. And, of course, the entire problematic nature of this vision lurks right in this passage: what kind of *rightness* can be assumed as a result of a deliberative process? What 'epistemic authority' could set the standard of 'correctness' for a decision? These questions are leveraged by those who do not believe that a procedural conception of democracy, and of the principles of liberty and equality that are *immanent* in the same procedures, could or should lightly be abandoned. In short, although a vision of democracy based only on the legitimacy of its procedures may seem a little 'heroic', there is no way, according to such a proceduralist view, to find a more compelling alternative.

> Democracy does not need to advance toward some truth to be legitimate. ... Both in the case that we get good outcomes and in the case that we get disappointing results, procedures are legitimately democratic because they deliver what they are made for: to protect the freedom of its members to produce 'wrong' decisions (Urbinati 2014: 98).

Moreover, *uncertainty*, in this view, is the constitutive feature of democracy; and a *love of uncertainty* is perhaps the most central virtue necessary to democracy: that is, the habit of avoiding a search for final and absolute truths; openness to change and revision, 'by an open process of public-opinion formation (open to discussion and new information that questions consolidated beliefs)' (*ibid.*). This is the 'spirit' that characterises the *ethos* of democracy: 'a public propensity or passion for "openness". This term captures an attitude of receptiveness to novelty, of exploration of new possibilities for a life form, for a historical horizon, for a social configuration' (Ferrara 2014: 14). Democracy, in this view, can be considered nothing but an open field of conflicts and reversible decisions: the risks and tensions that this entails must be taken into account and cannot be eliminated – but they are not too high a price to pay. No absolute defence against undesirable outcomes is possible; the principles of freedom and equality would be thereby jeopardised.

This debate does not rest only on its intrinsic theoretical interest but also on a more widespread concern, whose evidence can be found in many of the authors we have encountered. That is, how to react to the profound weakening, which we are now witnessing, of a basic condition of democracy, that is, the existence of well informed and critically inclined citizens, capable of distinguishing facts from their demagogic deformation? Above all, how is it possible to rely on a purely procedural view of democracy, if the procedure, *per se*, can guarantee nothing regarding possible 'tyrannical' outcomes, degeneration into authoritarianism or the domination of a 'mass democracy' open to the most dangerous adventures? The attitude underlying the various epistemic visions of democracy seems to be that democracy can defend itself if, and only if, it is proved to be capable of producing 'better' decisions. Epistemic theorists argue that we cannot be content with a purely procedural democracy, since this provides only an impoverished vision, vulnerable to devastating criticism from a variety of opponents. That 'thin' vision runs from renewed technocratic versions of 'guardianship' to the many different versions of populism, for which all that matters is that the 'will of the people' (whatever its form or channel of expression) finds a way to establish itself; up to the resurgent proposals for direct democracy based on the random selection of 'ordinary' and 'impartial' citizens who, in principle, have a higher probability of producing 'better' decisions, compared to a professional class of politicians selected by an electoral process that is subject to a thousand distortions.

However, a procedural *and* deliberative concept of democracy has many valid reasons with which to oppose the various epistemic visions of democracy, without resorting to some – rather unlikely – standards external to the procedure itself. The notion of the *epistemic functions* of deliberation can play an important role in this regard. Democracy without deliberation can provide only an additive greater probability of being correct if each participant has more than a 50 percent likelihood of being correct (see Landemore 2012 on Condorcet). However, public *deliberation* within a democratic system can perform an even more important, even essential, epistemic function. In short, the quality of democracy is linked to the deliberative quality of the processes that occur both in the public sphere and within the institutional procedures designed to produce legitimate decisions. Deliberative quality *also* (but not only) implies an epistemic dimension. A good public discussion requires people to discuss not only general political values or purposes (the ground on which *partisanship* exerts beneficial effects) but also (as much as possible) relevant *facts* and *issues*, and *problems* and their possible *solutions*. Participants need to discursively and publicly agree on the identification and definition of these facts and issues, critically scrutinising unsound and groundless ideas; exposing prejudices; rejecting the most stubborn commonplaces; challenging or 'defeating' all those arguments that have no factual support or insufficient logical consistency; and proceeding on the basis of *reliable* and *verified* information (as opposed to fanciful imaginings); or even on the basis of knowledge (relatively and sufficiently) shared with them by the scientific community.

Thus, public and democratic deliberation can, in fact, aspire to produce a (relatively) 'better' decision, rather than *the* 'correct' solution. What makes it better is its being understood by the *participants in the discourses* as '(more) fair', '(more) shared', '(more) reasonable', but also (why not?) more epistemically 'solid', by virtue of the informative and cognitive bases that have been incorporated in it. Therefore, it is a '(more) *legitimate*' decision, thanks to the 'good reasons' that deliberation was able to introduce and which are – through argumentative exchange – publicly shared and acceptable; but also thanks to the enhancement of both social and contextual knowledge and formal and specialised knowledge, which it has been able to include in its formative public process.

Finally, this discussion allows us to outline another boundary on our map of the deliberative field: this boundary distinguishes between the *epistemic purposes* that are attributed to a deliberative practice and the *epistemic functions* that a deliberation can have within a deliberative system.

Some participatory models that follow the principles of deliberative democracy have, more or less consciously, an *exclusively epistemic* purpose: namely, those devices or arrangements that can be thought of as places for a 'non-political judgment', in which 'ordinary citizens', or *citizen-representatives* (Urbinati and Warren 2008), express an *impartial* view that is able to escape the biases of partisan politics. This is a conception of 'citizen-judges', or 'citizen-spectators', who issue 'verdicts' – as opposed to citizens who present themselves as *political actors*, capable of defending their own vision of things and the reasons they find convincing in dialogue with others. These models could be considered an expression of a 'depoliticised' conception of democracy, since they presuppose that a collective decision cannot be entrusted to such a conflict and mediation, in a public dimension of dialogue between different interests and values carried by the citizens (and their forms of representation). Rather, these models presume that, through deliberation and involving 'ordinary' citizens *as such*, the 'correct' solution can be found. However, as some case studies show (Floridia 2012), the idea that random selection can itself ensure the involvement of 'common' or 'ordinary' citizens, and that these citizens, by virtue of such selection, will be *impartial*, proves highly problematic. *All* citizens *always* have a political culture of their own, social and associative links of their own and a vision of their own interests as well as those of others: it never happens that a citizen can deliberate as if his opinions were being formed on a *blank slate*. Of course, in a systemic vision, *mini-publics* or deliberative *settings* composed of small groups of randomly selected citizens can play a significant role: but only as sources for *information-gathering*, appropriately placed in a *deliberative sequence* and as 'part of a wider deliberative decision-making process that involves the people more generally' (Parkinson 2006: 34).[39]

Other participatory models of deliberative inspiration are designed, instead, to enhance the epistemic and cognitive *functions* of deliberation, but not to reach decisions or solutions that are, *per se*, epistemically legitimised or grounded. These models, these open and inclusive arenas, are conceived as *phases* of a deliberative process of policy-making and also as processes of *social learning* and *public inquiry*: such processes are intended to *include* and *enhance*, within policy-making, common skills and social knowledge that cannot be enclosed within the limited circle of political decision-makers and their technical-bureaucratic apparatus, or within the *policy-elites* mentioned by Robert Dahl. Such processes can achieve a 'better' decision but not because of that decision's 'truth' or correctness: they can do so only if they are able to incorporate into the deliberative process a social patrimony of knowledge and experience, and if they prove to be good places in which *social intelligence* can be exercised and produced.

These two approaches (that is, in short, (citizens as *judges* versus citizens as political and social *actors*)) are very different and underestimating this difference may become the source of conceptual and political ambiguity. Models or devices with an epistemic *purpose* can be understood and interpreted as processes that replace the institutional forms of political representation (now considered prey of a *partisan* politics). Models or devices with epistemic *function* (along with other political dimensions) can be understood and interpreted as forms of *public discourse-enrichment*, bringing in knowledge and experiences that had previously been ignored or marginalised and thus contributing to building the *agenda* of the public sphere and of the institutional sphere of decision-making.

Political decisions always involve choice and/or mediation between alternative and conflicting options. A deliberative system unfolds through the (pragmatic, ethical or moral) discourses that can justify a given choice: decisions are made based on discussions regarding values and interests, and expressing the potential compromises that can be reached through public dialogue. However, within this process, 'good' arguments (arguments that can turn out to be acceptable) will also be those with an improved ability to appeal to shared 'facts', based on (relatively and provisionally) solid knowledge and on an interpretation of the participants' common experiences – something that can appear congruent with their reality as they see it and convincing in their eyes, by offering a satisfactory solution to the problems they are facing.

---

39. On the concept of 'deliberative sequence', *see* Goodin 2008: 86–202 and Steiner *et al.* 2010: 34–5.

Conclusion: In Praise of Mediation

In my Introduction, I laid out the principles guiding this research. Retracing the 'history' of the deliberative idea of democracy and the stages by which it was formed and structured means more than simply mapping out the dialogue and critical debate around that evolution. It also means understanding the reasons why a given set of ideas about politics and democracy emerges in a particular historical situation from the forms of self-understanding that actors in that context have formed from that experience and used to interpret the events in their lives. The political ideas that we find in the different theoretical models – even the more abstract ones – are, in more or less mediated or spurious forms, the same ideas that individuals used to *act* in that historical situation. They are the proffered *answers* to the problems caused by the events and politics of a given moment; *forms of action* pointing out possible paths of change and transformation; *interpretative models* of actual social, political, and institutional practices; and forms of *comprehension* and *definition* of the conflicts arising in that moment.

As for participatory democracy in the 1960s and 1970s, we have seen a strong circular relationship between determinate political and social practices, the forms of self-understanding of the actors, and the associated democratic theories. I have dwelt at length on the *reasons* why those who elaborated the idea of participatory democracy aimed to understand and inspire the social, cultural and political movements of that decade; but also on the *weaknesses* that caused the decline of the participatory idea. Its proponents tried to upend the conceptions and archetypes of democracy that prevailed not only in the upper ranks of academia and politics but also in public political culture, in common language and in the ordinary practices of institutions and political actors. This conflict took place not only in the 'realm of forms' and in political discourses: what was really at stake was the future direction of the governing of contemporary societies as well as the solutions to the problems that historical development was posing to the political agenda.[1]

Is it possible to outline a similar interpretative framework for the deliberative democracy model, which began to develop during the 1980s? Why did talk of deliberative democracy begin at that moment? And why, despite all its limitations and weaknesses, hasn't this model been just a fleeting, fashionable way of thinking, but rather continues to grow and develop, showing no decrease in its suggestive power? Deliberative ideas, although born within a restricted intellectual circle, have spread much more widely, gained broader influence and become recognised as offering a valid theoretical framework and an effective language through which

---

1. This was the explicitly pursued aim, judging by what we might describe as the 'theoretical manifesto' of the neo-liberal and conservative revolution taking place during the 1980s: the Trilateral Commission Report promoted by the Rockfeller Foundation, edited by M. Crozier, S. P. Huntington and J. Watanuki (1975). On this, *see* Mastropaolo's considerations (2012: 88–95).

to think and express what one believes to be right in a search for solutions to all the problems that democracies face today. Why is this? What reasons can we find to explain deliberative theory's success?

One of the most authoritative answers, I believe (and as we saw in Bohman and Rehg 1997), is correct but not sufficient. Put briefly, the idea of 'deliberative democracy', in substantial continuity with the idea of participatory democracy that preceded it, may be taken as the reaction of the most advanced democratic thought to the dominant point of view in philosophy and political science. Yet this answer risks limiting the issue to a merely intellectual one. In my opinion, the reasons for the growth and strengthening of *deliberative ideals* and *deliberative theoretical models* for over thirty years in contemporary political democratic culture must rather be sought in the fact that they turned out to be capable of offering a credible and coherent alternative to current practices to those concerned about the nature of contemporary democracy and deeply worried about its future. The deliberative theoretical perspective has provided an interpretative, critical and normative 'idea' and 'point of view' capable of effectively contesting a whole *spectrum* of other conceptions, ideas and practices that today permeate not only the field of theoretical reflection but also the institutional framework and political culture of contemporary societies as well as the 'common sense' about how we should conceive politics and democracy.

A deliberative conception of democracy thus opposes the dominant current practices and views (such as neo-liberalism and its political and institutional practices). It also contrasts with several disparate and varied rivals. These include all the models that, in different ways, re-propose some updated version of *direct* democracy, taking advantage, or *presuming* we can do so, of the great potential of new information and communication technologies; government models or political 'styles' characterised by more or less 'populist' traits and plebiscitary bents; views that focus on democratic politics as a merely *negative* form of control over power; views that theorise the overcoming of politics as partisanship;[2] views that entrust the fate of democracy to a widespread and 'vitalistic' diffusion of 'micro-conflicts'; and views that assume that, ultimately, the word 'democracy' itself has lost its meaning, becoming an empty label. Deliberative democracy offers an alternative perspective to all of these: its *theoretical lexicon* seems to provide both an effective way to understand contemporary democracies and their transformation and a means by which democracies can develop better self-understanding. The idea of deliberative democracy, so to speak, fights *on several fronts*.

There is no shortage of studies or analyses dealing with the transformation and the 'quality' level of democracy in the current theoretical and philosophical debate. I cannot offer here a complete review and critical analysis of all contributions. Instead, I am interested in the different diagnoses of and possible solutions to the so-called 'crisis of democracy'. I believe that this 'crisis' is far from univocal,

---

2.   On this, *see* Muirhead 2014 and Rosenblum 2008.

presenting many different and, I think, worrying possible outcomes. The word 'crisis' itself, though, appears inappropriate, because its use presumes a condition of 'normality' which never existed and never will exist: democracy is always in unstable balance, being a political order characterised by a constant propensity to change and transformation.

On the one hand, against the birth and growth of intangible entities who rule the destiny of entire communities (the 'markets'), and economic lobbies, technostructures and the like, which escape any form of democratic accountability, depriving democratic institutions of sovereignty, some see the only possible solution as going 'back to the people'. This conception of democracy appeals to the restoration of a directly decisive and immediate role for citizens and seeks to reclaim a 'popular sovereignty' that today has been 'stolen'. On the other hand, against an interpretation of the 'crisis' as a crisis of 'governability' – understood as the powerlessness of democratic institutions to provide 'fast' and 'efficient' answers to the issues troubling our new and complex societies – others see the best solution as deriving from a centralisation of powers, bypassing and devaluing traditional rules and procedures, with a sort of 'decisionism' that aims to interrupt, *de facto*, all the 'wearying' and 'slow' traditional forms of representative democracy.

These two tendencies can turn out to be complementary. Plebiscitary forms of government together with populist narratives are easy to combine with modern expressions of repurposed *guardianship* and the *technocracy* characterising contemporary decision-making. No matter how far from each other these two different reactions might seem, they share a common trait – *the rejection of mediation*. In this work, I have tried to focus, to the contrary, on *the virtues of mediation*. This approach entails accepting not just the necessity of compromise and negotiation in the daily governance of our complex societies but also the explicit rejection of the idea of direct and unmediated 'empowerment', without deliberation, of: a) personal opinion and individual preferences; b) group-interests and private interests; and c) religious beliefs and 'comprehensive' worldviews. The effort to channel such preferences, interests, and views, through direct procedures into immediate legitimate and binding political decisions *cannot* lay the foundations of a good democracy.

The idea of deliberative democracy tries to break the grip that plebiscitarism and technocracy have begun to have on our democracies. Deliberative democracy also opposes the visions of the future of our complex societies that envisage either a permanent and irreducible conflict between interests, values or identities unable to communicate with each other, or their extremely fragile coexistence (what Rawls called a mere *modus vivendi*), with a constant risk of degeneration into violence. The idea of deliberative democracy has emerged and gained credibility during the last decades because, in the midst of the tensions that current social and political processes produce on a daily basis, it suggests possible alternative paths of political action. The new deliberative paradigm tries not just to give a purely *defensive* response to the dangers to which democratic principles are exposed today but also to indicate possible innovative strategies while holding on to an essential dimension: that is, the *procedural* dimension of democracy and the normativity it embodies.

Deliberative democracy offers a vision of democracy and its procedures in which the democratic legitimacy of public decisions (whatever their 'scale') is not entrusted to the mere logic of *strategic* rationality and relations of strength and power. Rather, it is entrusted to *communicative* rationality and the conditions that such communication necessarily implies: that is, the very *possibility of a rational dialogue*, of a *mutual recognition* between different people. What matters *is not* the certainty that such a dialogue can always produce agreement or consensus but rather the knowledge that to live without it, or to abandon it in principle, might lead to a politics solely based on the destructive dichotomy of an irreducible antagonism between 'friends' and 'foes'. Without such *a positive tension*, typical of a deliberative politics, it does not seem that conflicts can be 'governed', understood in their very nature, treated in a productive way, or brought to a mediation that is acceptable by all as legitimate. In a time that doubts the very idea of *common human reason*, a deliberative conception of democracy appears as a radical and ambitious challenge, based on the idea that the 'public use of reason' is possible and that we can and should count on that public use of reason to regulate conflicts and disagreements.

What allows us to say that deliberative democracy is *not* just an ideal but rather an interpretation of facts and real processes that highlights their possible normative implications and their potential? On what 'facts' can this idea and this ideal of democracy be grounded? Our political and institutional realities encompass *different and alternative ideas of democracy*, which result in or are implicit in political and institutional practices. One of these – perhaps the one most widely accepted and practised today – is based on a 'decisionist' ideology. Such an idea implicitly assumes that we cannot rely on citizens' participation for collective problem-solving because citizens' opinions are volatile, contradictory, and based on immediate or local interests, thus easily falling prey to the ruling demagogy. Decisionism also relies on another cliché: problems are complex and require high levels of expertise, so how is it possible to think that it might be useful or productive to discuss them with citizens? One focus in this theory takes up what Habermas called the 'cognitive overburdening' produced by modern social complexity, from which we deduce the impracticability and the unsustainability of a vision of democracy as a *discursive and institutional process* of the formation of opinions and decisions, over time and according to rules. Another focus stresses the *unrealistic* and fanciful nature of a *reasonable* (to use Rawls's term) search for shared political and constitutional bases that can generate a productive and positive management of the unavoidable conflicts arising from the social complexity and the cultural pluralism of our time.

Of course, there are several variations of the decisionist position, including 'populist' and plebiscitary versions and 'technocratic' ones. If, by now, there is no space for the *participation by citizens*, for their *deliberative civic practices*, for a *public speech* that is rich and well argued, then greater space is opened up for one-way *communication to citizens*, through variously modulated forms of *direct* and *immediate* relationships between the leader and the people.[3] If there is no more room for the public discussion of problems, then power and space must be given to 'specialists' or more 'reliable' people: we must no longer argue about which among several alternatives is more 'just', or find the most widely accepted solution, but rather find *technically* 'bound' answers, or select political leaders who seem more 'suitable' to applying substantially univocal solutions.

This decisionist ideology and the consensus to which it appeals *are not illusory*: such an ideology may well be plausible as a concrete guide to action, within the current practices of governments and the 'political culture' in the consciousness of many actors.[4] The decisionist solution, however, raises many problems and its practical effectiveness clashes with other (and not marginal) counter-trends, on both the normative and the 'factual' levels. First, it is simply unacceptable from a democratic point of view. It inevitably clashes with intuitive ideas and with a more reflective normative awareness, of what is 'just' and what is 'democratic'. An elementary question can always rise in the individual and collective consciousness: 'Is all of this inevitable, or indisputable? Should I not have the chance to say something about those choices that, ultimately, affect me directly?' Our discussion of Habermas revealed that the 'dissonances' between 'systemic' mechanisms of domination and individuals' normative forms of self-understanding always open up a space of tension and conflict; these dissonances can lead to social-learning processes and consolidate into a different, more complex form of political culture, therefore producing new 'facts', supported by a different normative structure.

Forms of public deliberation, as a co-operative search for solutions to collective problems, can always disclose a different view of things and of what is *possible*. The tension between *social validity* and *legitimacy*, between *legality* and *discursive legitimation*, cannot be solved easily and once and for all. Despite everything, the idea of what is 'democratic', as well as the criticism of whatever is not or does not seem democratic, can still strongly affect individual and collective action, and then *can* help determine the course of things.

---

3. Some also theorise, as does Jeffrey E. Green (2010), that today the real 'organ' of democracy is the 'citizens' eyes' rather than their 'speech': that is, the empowerment of the citizen-audience proceeds only through the exercise of inspection, observation, and surveillance over the conduct of political leaders. On Green, *see* Urbinati 2014: 171–227) and Ragazzoni 2013.

4. *See* Roberto Cartocci's definition of 'political culture': 'Political culture consists of a relatively coherent repertoire of cognitive and evaluative models that enable members of a political community to give a sense to their role as political actors, to other political actors, to the community they belong to and to the institutional structure in which they live. Thanks to this framework, they can decide which objectives to pursue, and shape their actions and behaviours accordingly' (Cartocci 2011: 1949). Michael Freeden (2004: 6) similarly defines ideologies as 'clusters of ideas, beliefs, opinions, values, and attitudes usually held by identifiable groups, that provide directives, even plans of action, for public policy-making, in an endeavour to uphold, justify, change or criticize the social and political arrangements of a state or other political community'. Furthermore, 'ideologies – in discharging the above functions – compete deliberately or unintentionally over the control of political language, by means of which they attempt to wield the political power necessary to realize their functions' (*ibid.*).

However, if this were the only problem, one might think that the pervasive mechanisms of power and the forces of the *status quo* would be able in most cases to incorporate, neutralise or marginalise potential critical practices emerging from everyday life.

The point is that 'decisionist' ideologies, mechanisms of governance escaping every democratic legitimation, and systemic logics that are left un-regulated are showing a very dubious ability to solve problems or simply to control what happens. The 'sorcerer's apprentice' syndrome is obvious to everyone: suffice it to look at the economic crisis that began in 2008, or at the backlashes of the financial globalisation; or even at the disastrous effects, after 9/11, of a blind use of military force in response to the geo-political contradictions of the international scene. Thus, not only do these ideologies and these governance mechanisms turn out to be 'unjust' - or mostly 'un-' or 'non-democratic' - *in principle*, as well as being experienced as such by more or less extensive groups of people in different parts of the world. What's more, they often produce *practically* unworkable conditions and appear unsuccessful in resolving conflict or even reducing tensions. [5]

Critics of deliberative democracy sometimes adduce 'social complexity' as a reason why collective decisions produced in a discursive and public way must fail. But, in fact, this very complexity today exposes as illusory and unrealistic the presumptions of the neo-oligarchic and technocratic governance of social and political processes, from the biggest decisions of *global governance* to the smallest administrative decisions. The conditions for a 'solitary' practice of the governmental functions are no longer present and the idea that, to govern our complex societies, anyone can 'control' and command the daily making of policies and the evaluation of their effects 'from above' is no longer sustainable.

An effective *governance of complexity* does not follow from a *dirigiste* and technocratic reduction of complexity itself but rather from the construction of democratic and inclusive decision-making procedures that are able to 'hold together' all the actors involved and all the terms of the problem to be solved. This is a difficult task, no doubt, but what are the other options? What other form of governing and deciding appears possible and desirable, if we want to respect the premises and promises of democracy and remain within the conceptual boundaries of a normative definition of democracy itself? Actually, even those issues that can be traced back to ordinary *problem-solving*, on a small scale, imply awareness of the radical *pluralism* of the values and interests at stake, as well as the awareness of the radical *uncertainty* that pluralism and complexity involve. Anyone who imagines that a particular decision will be able to simply 'cut through' this

---

5. According to Wolfgang Streeck in *Buying Time: The delayed crisis of democratic capitalism* (2014), all the strategies used by capitalism since the second half of the 1970s on can be read as means to 'buy some time' in which to try to neutralise a potentially destabilising crisis of integration and legitimacy, even though a new balance between capitalism and democracy has not been reached or even outlined.

complexity, without dealing with this uncertainty, would find that such a decision would turn out to be ineffectual (and produce 'unjust' outcomes).[6]

The idea of deliberative democracy emphasises that, to face the problems of our age, it is necessary to create a twofold ground of public dialogue and mediation. First, we must mobilise all the cognitive resources able to contribute to a possible (and always partial and fallible) control of the outcomes and effects of decisions. Second and consequently, we must act so that all the different 'points of view' (an expression of not only interests but also ethical and moral visions) can be connected to a reasonable exchange and a discursive procedure. In this prospect, a deliberative conception of democracy can rely on some decisive strengths.

a) In the context of local and national democracies, and as part of what might be called *ordinary* policy-making, a deliberative conception of democracy neither *devalues* nor impoverishes the traditional procedures of representative democracy. Rather, it points out how the democratic legitimacy of the resulting decisions can and should be acquired and strengthened, thanks to their *discursive* legitimacy; or, more precisely, a legitimacy that comes from a public and inclusive process of forming opinions and political judgments. Here, *deliberation* comes into play as an argumentative and reflective process that *precedes* and *accompanies* a decision. The political institutions of democracy can no longer be considered a sort of 'black box' into which many different inputs from society are confusedly and arbitrarily placed. It is no longer possible to think that decision-making can happen *without mediation*, that is without the *filter* of a process of collective reflection that elaborates preferences, interests, values, beliefs and opinions.

b) As for the possibility of a *global or cosmopolitan democracy*, a deliberative conception of democracy emphasises the impracticability and limitations of merely transposing democratic procedures designed for the nation-state – starting with the principle of majority – to the supranational and transnational level. This open frontier of research is now only beginning to be explored. However, even here, the basic question concerns the democratic legitimacy of decisions and the possible democratic forms of *global governance*. How should this new dimension of democracy be understood, if not in the form of an *international* and *transnational* deliberative system that connects different places and moments of the formation of choices and orientations to produce decisions taken as legitimate, accepted (or acceptable, even when not shared) by all the actors involved?

c) Lastly, deliberative democracy points to a possible way to proceed in the face of the dramatic importance assumed, today, by the conflict between different worldviews or comprehensive doctrines, systems of ideas and values that are often declared 'non-negotiable' by their adherents or that are presumed to express some 'truth' entitled to be upheld by the coercive force of political power. Rawls's and Habermas's answers, as different as they may be, can be debated; however, they are not easy to bypass if we are not to surrender to a desperate *Realpolitik*. Habermas's and Rawls's ways of tackling the issue of

---

6. *See* Amartya Sen on the importance of 'public reflection' as a key element of a democratic politics (e.g., Sen 2009).

the radical, ethical and moral pluralism of our time are internally connected to their conceptions of 'deliberative' democracy. Rawls's deliberative search for an *overlapping consensus* and his idea of *public reason*, and Habermas's definition of *deliberative politics* (as an articulation of the *pragmatic, ethical* and *moral discourses* in a public sphere and of their relationship with the procedural dimension of a ruled-by-law state) represent a theoretical framework that, in my opinion, cannot be overlooked when facing the 'fact of pluralism' and the ethical and moral conflicts of our time.

This vision of democracy as relying on public and inclusive deliberation, working as a process for the democratic legitimisation of decisions, cannot be seen only as an *ideal* to impose on an unruly reality. This *normative* dimension is not a mere subjective construction; nor does it derive from an arbitrary juxtaposition between the ideal and the real. Rather, it is rooted in real experiences and in the succession of 'trials and errors' that these experiences involve.

Among the 'facts' that may explain the credibility of this model, we should consider one discussed in the last chapter: that is, the spread of different policy-making modes or models that appeal to citizens' participation and their deliberative capacity. This spread of ideas and models is a symptom of a phenomenon now starting to be widely perceived, namely that several current modes of decision-making and governance do not produce decisions perceived as legitimate, and thus turn out to be neither democratically justifiable nor effective in their outcomes. We cannot assume that the spread of new participatory and deliberative institutions is simply the result of theories seeking to be tested and applied. As we have seen throughout this work, the experimental projection of theory into practice has become a significant part of the deliberative field. The *practices* that have spread (at least to some extent) have arisen from scholars', researchers' and practitioners' testing of theories and methodologies developed initially in strictly academic or professional fields. However, we cannot think that this is the *primary reason* for their (still relatively limited) diffusion. Even when such practices can be defined as essentially *expert-driven* or *governance-driven*, they respond to a real demand – that is, they were designed as a possible answer to the emergence of real problems. The emergence and spread of new participatory institutions of deliberative inspiration must therefore be interpreted as the manifestation of a real trend, the search for alternative solutions to the exhaustion or even failure of the usual decision-making models.

These mechanisms, procedures and institutions are not limited to the involvement of established *stakeholders*. Rather, most of them try to include a wider circle of interests and opinions, along with more widespread forms of knowledge, contextual skills and social intelligence. It is no longer (or not only) a matter of relying on the participation of a figure that, in the course of this work, I have described as mythical and ambiguous in its *status*, namely, the 'ordinary citizen'. Rather, it is a matter of seriously facing a phenomenon that, stubbornly, refuses to disappear from our democracies: a *public sphere* in which – as manipulated, distorted or influenced it may be – unavoidable critical tensions continue to be expressed. In this public sphere, *deliberative systems* are created and *discursive networks* produced. And this public sphere is the place in which the *discursive legitimacy* of the decisions of a democracy is produced or lost.

The field of deliberative democracy, with its various articulations and significant internal differences, has offered and continues to offer a theoretical and interpretative framework, as well as a language, for addressing this set of phenomena and these real processes. Its potential and actual validity and expansion are linked to the plausibility of the answers that it can give, as well as the explicative effectiveness – the real 'purchase' – of its conceptual tools.

Finally, it is impossible not to discuss a recurring theme in the disputes concerning deliberative democracy: how should its relationship to 'representative democracy' be understood? Current discourses often include rather summary statements: for example, that deliberative democracy constitutes some form of 'integration' to direct and representative democracy, or a model that can aspire to 'replace', 'consolidate' or 'revitalise' representative democracy. All these formulas presuppose a kind of conceptual co-extension of the two terms, as well as the implicit assumption that, within a sort of 'menu' of possible 'democracies', we can choose, each time, what we like or what seems better. These discussions very often end up engaging in some purely verbal solution, ranging from the idea of a 'coexistence' or 'complementarity' to the idea of an opposition between different 'forms' of democracy. However, the most useful conceptual pair of opposites to which reference should be made is not that between 'deliberation' and 'representation' but, first, that between what is *democratic* and *deliberative* and what is *democratic* and *non-deliberative*; and second, on a different scale, between what is *democratic* (deliberative or not) and what is *non-democratic.*

An approach that merely lists, opposes or juxtaposes different 'models' of democracy does not therefore seem very useful. A democracy can be characterised by different qualities and forms that include both participation and deliberation and, more specifically, by the more or less *democratic* and more or less *deliberative* quality of its participatory elements. The notion that some sort of choice between forms or models of democracy is required, or that looks to the (more or less) linear succession of one model by another, is incorrect. Democracy (without adjectives), as it has historically developed over the past two centuries, can be seen as the stage of an ever-open and unstable conflict, one that has constantly defined and redefined the boundaries, nature, extent and quality of democracy itself. Our field today is still that of modern *representative* democracies and their many *variants* (expressions or 'distortions'). The deliberative idea of democracy acts as a theoretical, critical and normative paradigm *within this field.*

Thus, in principle, a representative democracy is *inherently* deliberative; and a democracy *is* appropriately representative insofar as the construction of its political and institutional representation is based on two pillars: fair and correct democratic procedures of electoral choice, within a framework of constitutional guarantees, and a widespread deliberative and discursive practice both *within* the public sphere and the institutions, and *between* the public sphere and the institutions. Of course, within the real processes of our democracies, much depends on what conception of political representation is accepted and practised. A 'minimalist' conception would understand political representation as a single *act* of authorisation (voting to select those who are to decide and govern) or as a merely functional delegation. Or, on the contrary, one can understand representation as a *process* (relatively complex or structured) through which a *relationship* and a *communicative interplay* are built between the represented and their representatives.[7] This relationship can take on the traits of a public and democratic deliberation – but, of course, it can also be impoverished or distorted. Instead of being democratic and deliberative, political decision-making processes can take the form of plebiscitary practices or can occur within *closed* procedures that have been 'captured' by more or less powerful actors and consolidated interest-groups. It is thus possible to *evaluate* the deliberative quality (or its lack) of a representative democracy and the forms of participation that occur within it.

A worrying aspect of the state of contemporary democracy is the increasing gap between the search for political consensus 'in the short term' and the need to implement inevitably slow and complicated strategies that can produce visible effects only in the medium or long term. This temporal gap contributes to the *de-legitimisation* of democratic institutions themselves. Additionally, the processes and forms assumed by globalisation, and the modes of operation of large supra-national institutions, create obscure and unaccountable decision-centres that nevertheless profoundly affect the life of entire communities. This opacity undermines not just the credibility of these entities but also the capacity of representative institutions to govern and control them. Thus, the popular hopes and expectations of 'salvation' that leadership often attracts are destined to be systematically disappointed, introducing potentially destructive cycles of enthusiasm and resentment.

Can anything other than improved deliberation help us handle these problems? I do not believe that, among democratic processes, there are many valid alternatives to aiming at improving our collective capability for public deliberation. We will always need patient, hard, but essential *public reasoning* about the different purposes that can be considered right and can be pursued, about positive and creative ways to deal with conflicts and possible mediations, about the best means to adopt to pursue our desired ends, about the foreseeable effects of these means, and about the ways by which to publicly evaluate and readjust what we are trying to achieve along the way.

In short, strong 'reasons' and 'good arguments' are at the core of the idea of deliberative democracy. But, above all, these reasons and arguments are fully inscribed in the contradictory processes happening in our time and our societies. Therefore, these strong reasons and good arguments can be plausible in the eyes of those who seek alternative answers and courses of action to prevailing social and political practices and ideologies. These 'good' reasons include those that are set against a 'hopeless' (or euphoric and aestheticising) vision of conflict and its forms

---

7. On these themes, *see* Urbinati 2006, 2011, 2014. On the new forms of self-authorising representation in the public sphere, *see* Urbinati and Warren 2008 and Montanaro *et al.* 2012. On so-called 'anticipatory', or 'surrogate' forms of representation, *see* Mansbridge 2003b.

of expression. A deliberative view of democracy presupposes an idea of politics as a patient search – co-operative and conflicting at the same time – for solutions to the problems of our social orders.

The idea of deliberative democracy recalls a classic democratic principle: *governing by discussion*.[8] Yet, it seeks to develop this idea in the conditions of modernity, or even 'post-modernity'. The key to the concept of governing by discussion – as I have tried to show throughout this work – lies in a notion of *democratic legitimacy* that is constructed not only through the procedures of a democratic state ruled-by-law but also, and no less, through *discursive* and *deliberative* procedures and practices — the process of 'formation of opinions and will' developed *within* both the public sphere *and* institutions, and *between* the public sphere and the institutions.

In our age, there are many 'inhospitable conditions' for democracy (Michelman 1997: 154; Ferrara 2014: 6–12). The conditions may seem even worse for deliberative democracy. Our time seems little inclined towards characteristics of deliberation as thoughtful reflection on the reasons for a choice, argumentative exchange, moments of collective learning and the co-operative search for a 'better solution' ('better', it should always be remembered, can mean different things in a democratic deliberative context but it can never mean 'true' or 'correct'). Contemporary political culture seems to vacillate. On the one hand, some lean towards a vision of democracy that emphasises the 'speed' of decision-making and the vertical integration and concentration of power and knowledge, evincing a drastic distrust in people's agency. On the other hand (but, as we said, these two perspectives are often complementary), others lean towards an 'immediate' and 'direct' vision of democracy, with a plebiscitary vision of how consensus is sought and reproduced; or a *staging* of popular passions, rather than the *political representation* of ideas, values and interests.

A deliberative conception of democracy opposes to these two tendencies the idea of a democracy in which the making of political decisions is based on, and accompanied by, a complex and reasoned public discussion, and in which even the search for compromise and negotiations between the plurality of interests and values at stake are entrusted to a public capacity for mediation and dialogue.[9] This

---

8. 'Deliberation' was a central theme of classic conceptions of representative government, from Burke and John Stuart Mill to Hans Kelsen. It was also important within the discussion between Kelsen and Schmitt of parliamentarianism and its crisis, a crucial confrontation in the history of the theory of democracy of the twentieth century. For Kelsen's thesis on the role of deliberation, *see* his famous books (*The Essence and Value of Democracy* (English edn 2013 [German 1929]). For Schmitt, *see Die geistesgeschichtliche Lage des heutigen Parlamentarismus* (English edn, *The Crisis of Parliamentary Democracy* 1988 [German]1923), where Schmitt theorised the 'end of deliberation', as well as its anachronistic character in the conditions of a mass democracy.

9. On this subject, Alfio Mastropaolo writes: 're-proposing the principle of "government through discussion" which is the basis of modern parliamentarism, deliberative procedures officially rediscover a principle recently undervalued by the post-democratic paradigm and by the new practice it inspired of majoritarian democracy, but historically rich in merits. This is compromise in dealing with conflicts. At the same time, deliberative democracy pays public homage to other, often disregarded, principles, such as mutual respect and tolerance, and to the idea that citizens

point of view does not rely on its own ability to 'persuade' reluctant interlocutors. Rather, it is based on the normative premises of democracy itself, on the reasons for these premises and on how social actors interpret these reasons as they experience the effects of democratic choice, suffer its distortions, or glimpse its potential.

A deliberative conception of democracy, then, invites us to conclude that a good democracy cannot be based on the tyranny of immediate preferences. Good democracy cannot result from the frantic rush to what *seems* to be the expression of a 'popular will' that is direct, *non-mediated*, and assumed as *given*, without any intervening process to make it more reflective, aware, open and forward-looking. This takes us back to a view that has accompanied us throughout this whole journey: what determines the quality and strength of a democracy is the quality of its *public discourse*: the 'public political culture' that prevails in society. This quality can in turn be produced only by the action of *actors* and *subjects*, *procedures* and *institutions*, that are not encumbered by the myth of an 'immediate' democracy.

The *public sphere* (as a place where *deliberative systems*, or *discourse networks*, built on the issues relevant to the future of a political community, are produced) can be left to itself and prove to be 'invertebrate', so to speak, devoid of a strong internal structure; experiencing varied and random waves of opinions; exposed to the domination of the most powerful interests, and, at the same time, to the proliferation of minor interests, contingent subjectivities, 'powers' and 'micro-powers', each trying to assert its 'will to power'. A *critical* public sphere, able to exercise a democratic function in its interaction with the institutions of representative democracy, needs *individuals*, *organisations* and an *associative network* that are able to offer ideas and references. It also needs *political parties* that are able to reinvent themselves without losing their role as collective actors that contribute to the formation and structuring of public discourse and are further able themselves to be agents of and spaces of participation and deliberation. Perhaps, as seems to be happening now, this critical public sphere also needs *new institutions, instruments* and *models of participation and public deliberation*, through which to construct and experiment with new spaces in which public discourse can be formed and articulated as well as new ways in which to 'connect' the sphere of discourses to the power of making decisions. A good democracy is not based simply on 'listening' and 'acknowledging' what 'people say', or on being able to watch and control what powerful people are up to. Rather, it is based on a deliberative politics able to *transform* and *enrich*, to make more critical and aware, the interpretive schemes by which citizens understand and experience the problems of their political community.

We have seen how the original idea of deliberative democracy relied on one of the foundational texts of modern representative democracy: *Federalist* 10,

---

constitute a collective body, divided on the level of values and interests, but nonetheless willing to live together. In deliberation, we see the reappearance of the idea of a common good at least as a normative ideal, and of democracy as a principle of pluralistic cohabitation' (2012: 229). For negotiation as including compromise but also providing alternatives to it, *see* Warren and Mansbridge *et al.*, 2015.

written by James Madison. Even today, this text can help measure the innovative challenge that democracy is facing. In Madison's view, the task of 'refining and enlarging' *public views* was entrusted to the wisdom of a 'select group' of citizens, able to transcend the partiality and immediacy of popular passions and to fight the (unavoidable) evil of factions. This *mediation*, he believed, would be able to express 'the public voice', and pursue the common good, better than a direct 'pronouncement' of people 'convened for the purpose', that is, gathered to express their views in this regard. Today we no longer think that only 'a select group' of citizens should exercise this function; the *public voice* has, and should have, many other ways to express itself. However, the need for *mediation* that we find expressed at the beginning of modern democracy has lost none of its relevance.

Bibliography

Aboulafia, M., Bookman, M. and Kemp, C. (eds) (2002) *Habermas and Pragmatism*, London, UK: Routledge.

Ackerman, B. (1980) *Social Justice in the Liberal State*, New Haven, CT and London, UK: Yale University Press.

— (1984) 'Discovering the constitution', *Yale Law Journal* 93(6): 1013–72.

— (1989) 'Constitutional politics/constitutional law', *Yale Law Journal* 99(3): 453–547.

— (1991) *We the People*, vol. 1 *Foundations*, Cambridge, MA and London, UK: Belknap Press of Harvard University Press.

— (1998) *We the People*, vol. 2 *Transformations*, Cambridge, MA and London, UK: Belknap Press of Harvard University Press.

— (2014) *We the People*, vol. 3 *The Civil Rights Revolution*, Cambridge, MA and London, UK: Belknap Press of Harvard University Press.

Ackerman, B. and Fishkin, J. (2004) *Deliberation Day*, New Haven, CT and London, UK: Yale University Press.

Akkerman, T., Hajer, M. and Grin, J. (2004) 'The interactive state: democratisation from above', *Political Studies* 52: 82–95.

Allegretti, U. (2011) 'Democrazia partecipativa', in *Enciclopedia del diritto*, Annali IV, Milan, IT: Giuffrè.

— (2015) 'Participatory democracy in multi-level states', in C. Fraenkel-Haberle, S. Kropp, F. Palermo and K.-P. Sommermann (eds) *Citizen Participation in Multi-Level Democracies*, Leiden, NL and Boston, MA: Brill Nijoff.

Almond, G. A. (1950) *The American People and Foreign Policy*, New York, NY: Harcourt, Brace & Co.

Almond, G. A. and Verba, S. (1963) *The Civic Culture: Political attitudes and democracy in five nations*, Princeton, NJ: Princeton University Press.

Alonso, S., Keane, J. and Merkel, W., with M. Fotou (eds) (2011) *The Future of Representative Democracy*, Cambridge, UK: Cambridge University Press.

APSA (American Political Science Association) Committee on Political Parties (1950) *Toward a More Responsible Two Party System*, New York, NY: Rinehart.

Arendt, H. (1958) *The Human Condition*, Chicago, IL: University of Chicago Press.

— (1963) *On Revolution*, New York, NY: Viking Press.

Aristotle (2009) *The Nicomachean Ethics*, trans, D. Ross, rev. and with Introduction and Notes by L. Brown, Oxford, UK and New York, NY: Oxford University Press.

— (2006) *On Rhetoric*, trans. G. A. Kennedy, Oxford, UK: Oxford University Press.

Arnstein, S. H. (1969) 'A ladder of citizen participation', *Journal of the American Institute of Planners* 35(4): 216–24.

Avritzer, L. (2009) *Participatory Institutions in Democratic Brazil*, Baltimore, MD: Johns Hopkins University Press.

Austin, J. L. (1962) *How To Do Things with Words*, Oxford, UK: Clarendon Press.

Bachrach, P. (1967) *The Theory of Democratic Elitism: A critique*, Boston, MA: Little, Brown.

Bachrach, P. and Baratz, M. S. (1962) 'Two faces of power', *American Political Science Review* 56(4): 947–52. Reprinted in W. E. Connolly (ed.) (1969a) *The Bias of Pluralism*, New York, NY: Atherton Press, pp. 51–64.

— (1963) 'Decisions and nondecisions: an analytical framework', *American Political Science Review* 57(3): 632–42.

— (1970) *Power and Poverty: Theory and practice*, London, UK and New York, NY: Oxford University Press.

Bächtiger, A., Niemeyer, S., Neblo, M., Steenberger, M. R. and Steiner, J. (2010) 'Disentangling diversity in deliberative democracy: competing theories, their blind spots, and complementarities', *Journal of Political Philosophy* 18(1): 32–63.

Bächtiger, A., Dryzek, J., Mansbridge, J. and Warren M. (2017, forthcoming) (eds) *Oxford Handbook of Deliberative Democracy*, Oxford: Oxford University Press.

Bacqué, M.-H. and Sintomer, Y. (eds) (2011) *La démocratie participative: Histoire et genéalogie*, Paris, FR: Editions La Découverte.

Bacqué, M.-H., Rey, H. and Sintomer, Y. (eds) (2005) *Gestion de proximité et démocratie participative: Une perspective comparative*, Paris, FR: Editions La Découverte.

Baiocchi, G. (2003) 'Participation, activism, and politics: The Porto Alegre experiment in deliberative democracy theory', in A. Fung and E. O. Wright (eds) *Deepening Democracy: Institutional innovations in empowered participatory governance*, London, UK and New York, NY: Verso.

— (2005) *Militants and Citizens: The politics of participatory democracy in Porto Alegre*, Palo Alto, CA: Stanford University Press.

Baiocchi, G. and Ganuza, E. (2015) 'Becoming a best practice: neoliberalism and the curious case of participatory budgeting', in C. W. Lee, M. McQuarrie and E. T. Walker (eds) *Democratizing Inequalities: Dilemmas of the new public participation*, New York, NY and London, UK: New York University Press, pp. 187–203.

Barber, B. (1984) *Strong Democracy: Participatory politics for a new age*, Berkeley, CA, Los Angeles, CA and London, UK: University of California Press.

Baritono, R. (2001) *La democrazia vissuta: Individualismo e pluralismo nel pensiero di Mary Parker Follett*, Turin, IT: La Rosa editrice.

Baynes, K. (1992) *The Normative Grounds of Social Criticism: Kant, Rawls and Habermas*, Albany, NY: State University of New York, NY Press.

— (1995) 'Democracy and the Rechtstaat: Habermas's Faktizität und Geltung', in S. K. White (ed.) *The Cambridge Companion to Habermas*, Cambridge, UK: Cambridge University Press, pp. 201–32.

— (2015) *Habermas*, London, UK: Routledge.

Beard, C. A. (1986 [1913]) *An Economic Interpretation of the Constitution of the United States*, intr. F. McDonald, New York, NY: Free Press.

Benhabib, S. (1994) 'Deliberative rationality and models of democratic legitimacy', *Constellations* 1: 26–51.

— (ed.) (1996a) *Democracy and Difference: Contesting the boundaries of the political*, Princeton, NJ: Princeton University Press.

— (1996b) 'Towards a deliberative model of democratic legitimacy', in S. Benhabib (ed.) *Democracy and Difference: Contesting the boundaries of the political*, Princeton, NJ: Princeton University Press, pp. 67–94.

— (2006) *Another Cosmopolitanism*, Oxford, UK: Oxford University Press.

Berelson, B. R., Lazarsfeld, P. F. and MacPhee, W. N. (1954) *Voting: A study of opinion formation in a presidential campaign*, Chicago, IL: University of Chicago Press.

Berle, A. A. (1959) *Power without Property: A new development in American political economy*, New York, NY: Harcourt.

Bernstein, R. J. (2010) *The Pragmatic Turn*, Malden, MA: London, UK: Polity Press.

Bessette, J. M. (1980) 'Deliberative democracy: the majority principle in republican government', in R. A. Goldwin and W. A. Schambra (eds) *How Democratic is the Constitution?*, Washington, DC and London, UK: American Enterprise Institute for Public Policy Research.

— (1994) *The Mild Voice of Reason: Deliberative democracy and American national government*, Chicago, IL: University of Chicago Press.

Besson, S. and Martì, J. L. (eds) (2006) *Deliberative Democracy and its Discontents*, Aldershot, UK and Burlington, VT: Ashgate.

Bevir, M. (2006) 'Democratic governance: systems and radical perspectives', *Public Administration Review* 66(3): 426–36

— (2009) (ed.) *Key Concepts in Governance*, London, UK: Sage.

— (2010) *Democratic Governance*, Princeton, NJ: Princeton University Press.

— (2011a) 'The contextual approach', in G. Klosko (ed.) *The Oxford Handbook of the History of Political Philosophy*, Oxford, UK: Oxford University Press, pp. 11–23.

— (2011b) 'Governance and governmentality after neoliberalism', *Policy & Politics* 39(4): 457–471.

— (2013) *A Theory of Governance*, Berkeley, CA: University of California Press.

Bickel, A. (1962) *The Least Dangerous Branch: The Supreme Court at the bar of politics*, New Haven, CT: Yale University Press.

Blondiaux, L. (2008a) *Le nouvel esprit de la démocratie: Actualité de la démocratie participative*, Paris, FR: Seuil.

— (2008b) 'Démocratie délibérative vs. démocratie agonistique? Le statut du conflit dans les théories et les pratiques de participation contemporaines', *Raisons politiques* 30: 131–47.

Blondiaux, L. and Forniau, J.-M. (2011) 'Un bilan des recherches sur la participation du public en démocratie: beaucoup de bruit pour rien'?, *Participations* (1): 8–35.

Bobbio, L. (ed.) (2004) *A più voci: Amministrazioni pubbliche, imprese, associazioni e cittadini nei processi decisionali inclusivi*, Naples and Rome, IT: Edizioni Scientifiche Italiane.

— (2005) 'La democrazia deliberativa nella pratica', *Stato e Mercato* 73(1): 67–88.

— (2008) (eds) *Amministrare con i cittadini: Viaggio tra le pratiche di partecipazione in Italia*, Soveria Mannelli, IT: Rubbettino.

— (2010a) 'Il dibattito pubblico sulle grandi opere: ill caso dell'autostrada di Genova', *Rivista Italiana di Politiche pubbliche* 1: 119–46.

— (2010b) 'Types of deliberation', *Journal of Public Deliberation* 6(1), article 1.

— (2013) (ed.) *La qualità della deliberazione: Scelte pubbliche e cittadinanza*, Rome, IT: Carocci.

Bobbio, L. and Melé, P. (2015) 'Les relations paradoxales entre conflit et participation', *Participations* 3: 7–34.

Bobbio, L. and Pomatto, G. (2007) 'Il coinvolgimento dei cittadini nelle scelte pubbliche', *Meridiana* 58: 45–68.

Bobbio, N. (1987) *The Future of Democracy: A defence of the rules of the game*, trans. R. Griffin, ed. R. Bellamy, Cambridge, UK: Cambridge University Press. [Or. edn (1984) *Il futuro della democrazia*, Turin, IT: Einaudi.]

Bohman, J. (1994) 'Complexity, pluralism, and the constitutional state: on Habermas's Faktizität und Geltung', *Law & Society Review* 28(4): 897–930.

— (1996) *Public Deliberation: Pluralism, complexity, and democracy*, Cambridge, MA and London, UK: MIT Press.

— (1998) 'The coming of age of deliberative democracy', *Journal of Political Philosophy* 6(4): 400–25.

— (2004) 'Realizing deliberative democracy as a mode of inquiry: pragmatism, social facts, and normative theory', *Journal of Speculative Philosophy* 18(1): 23–43.

— (2007) *Democracy Across Borders: From demos to demoi*, Cambridge, MA: MIT Press.

Bohman, J. and Rehg, W. (eds) (1997) *Deliberative Democracy*, Cambridge, MA and London, UK: MIT Press.

Bouvier, A. (2007) 'Démocratie délibérative, démocratie débattante, démocratie participative', *Revue européenne des sciences sociales* XLV–136: 5–34.

Brooks, T. and Nussbaum, M. C. (eds) (2015) *Rawls's Political Liberalism*, New York, NY: Columbia University Press.

Brown, M. B. (2006) 'Survey article: citizen panels and the concept of representation', *Journal of Political Philosophy* 14(2): 203–25.

Brown, W. (2006) 'Power after Foucault', in J. S. Dryzek, B. Honig and A. Phillips (eds) *The Oxford Handbook of Political Theory*, Oxford, UK: Oxford University Press, pp. 64–84.

Brunkhorst, H. (2006) *Habermas*, Leipzig, DE: Reclam.

Burnham, W. D. (1982) *The Current Crisis in American Politics*, Oxford, UK: Oxford University Press.

Button, M. and Ryfe, D. M. (2005) 'What can we learn from the practice of deliberative democracy?', in J. Gastil and P. Levine (eds) *The Deliberative Democracy Handbook: Strategies for effective civic engagement in the 21st century*, San Francisco, CA: Jossey-Bass, pp. 20–33.

Calhoun, C. (ed.) (1992) *Habermas and the Public Sphere*, Cambridge, MA and London, UK: MIT Press.

Carson, L. and Martin, B. (1999) *Random Selection in Politics*, Westport, CT: Praeger Publishing.

Carson, L., Gastil, J., Hartz-Kapp, J. and Lubensky, R. (eds) (2013) *The Australian Citizens' Parliament and the Future of Deliberative Democracy*, University Park, PA: Pennsylvania State University Press.

Castiglione, D. (2005) 'Republicanism and its legacy', *European Journal of Political Theory* 4(4): 453–65.

Cartocci, R. (2011) 'Political culture', in B. Badie, D. Berg-Schlosser and L. Morlino (eds) *International Encyclopedia of Political Science*, vol. vi, London, UK: Sage, pp. 1949–62.

Chambers, S. (1996) *Reasonable Democracy: Jürgen Habermas and the politics of discourse*, Ithaca, NY: Cornell University Press.

— (2003) 'Deliberative democratic theory', *Annual Review of Political Science* 6: 307–26.

— (2004) 'Behind closed doors: publicity, secrecy, and the quality of deliberation', *Journal of Political Philosophy* 12(4): 389–410.

— (2009) 'Rhetoric and the public sphere: has deliberative democracy abandoned mass democracy?', *Political Theory* 37(3): 323–50.

Christiano, T. (1993) *Social Choice and Democracy*, in D. Copp, J. Hampton and J. E. Roemer (eds) *The Idea of Democracy*, Cambridge, UK: Cambridge University Press, pp. 173–195.

Clarke, J. (2010) 'Enrolling ordinary people: governmental strategies and the avoidance of politics?', *Citizenship Studies* 14(6): 637–650.

Cohen, J. L. and Arato, A. (1992) *Civil Society and Political Theory*, Cambridge, MA: MIT Press.

Cohen, J. (1986a) 'An epistemic conception of democracy', *Ethics* 97(1): 26–38.

— (1986b) 'Autonomy and democracy: reflections on Rousseau', *Philosophy & Public Affairs* 15(3): 275–97.

— (1989) 'Deliberation and democratic legitimacy', in A. Hamlin and P. Pettit (eds) *The Good Polity*, Oxford, UK: Blackwell, pp. 17–34. Reprinted in J. Bohman and W. Rehg, (eds) (1997) *Deliberative Democracy*, Cambridge,

MA and London, UK: MIT Press, pp. 67–92. Also reprinted in J. Cohen (2009a) *Philosophy, Politics, Democracy*, Cambridge, MA and London, UK: Harvard University Press.

—— (1991) '... Institutional argument ... is diminished by the limited examination of the issues of principle... ', *Review Symposium on Dahl's Democracy and Its Critics, Journal of Politics* 53(1): 221–25.

—— (1993) 'Moral pluralism and political consensus', in D. Copp, J. Hampton and J. E. Roemer (eds) (1993) *The Idea of Democracy*, Cambridge, UK: Cambridge University Press, pp. 270–91. Reprinted in J. Cohen (2009a) *Philosophy, Politics, Democracy*, Cambridge, MA and London, UK: Harvard University Press, pp. 38–60.

—— (1994) 'A more democratic liberalism', *Michigan Law Review* 92(6): 1503–46.

—— (1996) 'Procedure and substance in deliberative democracy', in S. Benhabib (ed.) (1996a) *Democracy and Difference: Contesting the boundaries of the political*, Princeton, NJ: Princeton University Press, pp. 95–119. Reprinted in J. Bohman and W. Rehg (eds) (1997) *Deliberative Democracy*, Cambridge, MA and London, UK: MIT Press, pp. 407–437; and in J. Cohen (2009a) *Philosophy, Politics, Democracy*, Cambridge, MA and London, UK: Harvard University Press, pp. 154–80.

—— (1998a) *Deliberative Democracy* (ed.) Cambridge, UK: Cambridge University Press.

—— (1998b) 'Democracy and liberty', in J. Elster (ed.) *Deliberative Democracy*, Cambridge, UK: Cambridge University Press, pp. 185–231. Reprinted in J. Cohen (2009a) *Philosophy, Politics, Democracy*, Cambridge, MA and London, UK: Harvard University Press, pp. 223–67.

—— (1999) 'Reflections on Habermas on democracy', *Ratio Juris* 12(4): 385–416. Reprinted in J. Cohen (2010a) *The Arc of the Moral Universe and Other Essays*, Cambridge, MA and London, UK: Harvard University Press, pp. 260–96.

—— (2003) 'For a democratic society', in S. Freeman (ed.) *The Cambridge Companion to Rawls*, Cambridge, UK: Cambridge University Press, pp. 86–13.

—— (2009a) *Philosophy, Politics, Democracy: Selected essays*, Cambridge, MA and London, UK: Harvard University Press.

—— (2009b) 'Reflections on deliberative democracy', in T. Christiano and J. Christman (eds) *Contemporary Debates in Political Philosophy*, Oxford, UK: Blackwell, pp. 247–63. Reprinted in J. Cohen (2009a) *Philosophy, Politics, Democracy*, Cambridge, MA and London, UK: Harvard University Press, pp. 326–47.

—— (2010a) *The Arc of the Moral Universe and Other Essays*, Cambridge, MA and London, UK: Harvard University Press.

—— (2010b) *Rousseau: A free community of equals*, Oxford, UK: Oxford University Press.

Cohen, J. and Fung, A. (2004) 'Radical democracy', *Swiss Journal of Political Science* 10(4): 23–34.

Cohen, J. and Rogers, J. (1993) 'Associations and democracy', *Social Philosophy and Policy* 10(2): 282–312. Reprinted in J. Cohen (2009a) *Philosophy, Politics, Democracy*, Cambridge, MA and London, UK: Harvard University Press, pp. 61–97.

Cohen, J. and Sabel, C. (1997) 'Directly deliberative polyarchy', *European Law Journal* 3(4): 313–42. Reprinted in J. Cohen (2009a) *Philosophy, Politics, Democracy*, Cambridge, MA and London, UK: Harvard University Press, pp. 181–222.

— (2005) 'Global democracy?', *Journal of International Law and Politics* 37(4): 763–97.

Connolly, W. E. (ed.) (1969a) *The Bias of Pluralism*, New York, NY: Atherton Press.

— (1969b) (ed.) 'The challenge to pluralistic theory', in *The Bias of Pluralism*, New York, NY: Atherton Press, pp. 3–34.

Cooke, M. (2000) 'Five arguments for deliberative democracy', *Political Studies* 48(5): 947–69.

Copp, D., Hampton, J. and Roemer J. E. (eds) (1993) *The Idea of Democracy*, Cambridge, UK: Cambridge University Press.

Corchia, L. (2013) *Jürgen Habermas: A bibliography – Works and studies (1952–2012)*, with an introduction by Stefan Müller-Doohm, Pisa, IT: Il Campano-Arnus University Books.

Crosby, N., Kelly J. M. and Shafer, P. (1986) 'Citizen panels: A new approach to citizen participation', *Public Administration Review* 46(2): 170–8.

Crosby, N. and Nethercut, D. (2005) 'Citizens juries: creating a trustworthy voice of the people', in J. Gastil and P. Levine (eds) (2005) *The Deliberative Democracy Handboook: Strategies for effective civic engagement in the 21st century*, San Francisco, CA: Jossey-Bass, pp. 111–19.

Crozier, M., Huntington, S. P. and Watanuki, J. (1975) *The Crisis of Democracy: Report on the governability of democracies to the Trilateral Commission*, New York, NY: New York University Press.

Cunningham, F. (2002) *Theories of Democracy: A critical introduction*, London, UK: Routledge.

Dagger, R. (2004) 'Communitarianism and republicanism', in G. F. Gaus and C. Kukathas (eds) *Handbook of Political Theory*, London, UK: Sage.

Dahl, R. A. (1956) *A Preface to Democratic Theory*, Chicago, IL: University of Chicago Press.

— (1961) *Who Governs?*, New Haven, CT: Yale University Press.

— (1966) 'Further reflections on "the elitist theory of democracy"', *American Political Science Review* 60(2): 296–305.

— (1982) *Dilemmas of Pluralist Democracy*, New Haven, CT and London, UK: Yale University Press.

— (1985) *Controlling Nuclear Weapons: Democracy versus guardianship*, Syracuse, NY: Syracuse University Press.

—   (1989a) *Democracy and Its Critics*, New Haven, CT and London, UK: Yale University Press.

—   (1989b) 'The pseudodemocratization of the American presidency', *Tanner Lectures on Human Values X* (Harvard, 11–12 April 1988), Cambridge, UK: Cambridge University Press and Salt Lake City, UT: University of Utah Press, pp. 35–71.

—   (1991) 'A rejoinder, Review Symposium on *Democracy and Its Critics*', *Journal of Politics* 53(1): 226–31.

—   (1992) 'The problem of civic competence', *Journal of Democracy* 3(4): 45–59. Reprinted in R. A. Dahl (1997) *Toward Democracy: A journey*, Berkeley, CA: University of California Press.

Dahl, R. A. and Lindblom, C. (1953) *Politics, Economics, and Welfare*, New York, NY: Harper & Row.

Dahl, R. A. and Tufte, E. R. (1973) *Size and Democracy*, Stanford, CA: Stanford University Press.

Della Porta, D. (2005) 'Deliberation in movements: why and how to study deliberative democracy and social movements', *Acta Politica* 40: 336–50.

—   (2013) *Can Democracy Be Saved?*, Cambridge: Polity Press.

Delli Carpini, M. X., Cox, F. L. and Jacobs, L. R. (2004) 'Public deliberation, discursive participation, and citizen engagement: a review of the empirical literature', *Annual Review of Political Science* 7: 315–44.

Dewey, J. (1984 [1927]) 'The public and its problems: an essay in political inquiry', in J. A. Boydston (ed.) *John Dewey: The later works, vol. 2: 1925–1927*, intr. J. Gouinlock, Carbondale and Edwardswill, IL: Southern Illinois University Press, pp. 235–372.

Dienel, P. C. (2002) *Die Plannungzelle: Der Bürger als Chance*, Berlin: Springer.

Dorf, M. C. and Sabel, C. (1998) 'A constitution of democratic experimentalism', *Columbia Law Review* 98(2): 267–473.

Downs, A. (1957) *An Economic Theory of Democracy*, New York, NY: Harper & Row.

Dreben, B. (2003) 'On Rawls and political liberalism', in S. Freeman (ed.) *The Cambridge Companion to Rawls*, Cambridge, UK: Cambridge University Press.

Drucker, P. F. (1995) 'Introduction: Mary Parker Follett: prophet of management', in P. Graham (ed.) *Mary Parker Follett: Prophet of Management – A celebration of writings from the 1920s*, Boston, MA: Harvard Business School Press.

Dryzek, J. S. (1987) 'Discursive designs: critical theory and political institutions', *American Journal of Political Science* 31(3): 656–679.

—   (1989) 'Policy sciences of democracy', *Polity* 22(1): 97–118.

—   (1990) *Discursive Democracy: Politics, policy and political sciences*, Cambridge, UK: Cambridge University Press.

—   (2000) *Deliberative Democracy and Beyond: Liberals, critics, contestations*, Oxford, UK: Oxford University Press.

—   (2010) *Foundations and Frontiers of Deliberative Governance*, Oxford, UK: Oxford University Press.

Dryzek, J. S. and List, C. (2003) 'Social choice theory and deliberative democracy: a reconciliation', *British Journal of Political Science* 33(1): 1–28.

Dryzek, J. S. and Niemeyer, S. (2006) 'Reconciling pluralism and consensus as political ideals', *American Journal of Political Science* 50(3): 634–49. Reprinted in J. S. Dryzek (2010) *Foundations and Frontiers of Deliberative Governance*, Oxford, UK: Oxford University Press, pp. 85–113.

Dworkin, R. (1985) *A Matter of Principle*, Oxford, UK: Oxford University Press.

Eckstein, H. (1961) *A Theory of Stable Democracy*, Princeton, NJ: Princeton University Press.

Elster, J. (1979) *Ulysses and the Sirens*, Cambridge, UK: Cambridge University Press.

— (1983) *Sour Grapes*, Cambridge, UK and Paris, FR: Cambridge University Press and Editions de la maison des sciences de l'homme.

— (1986) 'The market and the forum: three varieties of political theory', in J. Elster and A. Hylland (eds) (1986) *Foundations of Social Choice Theory*, Cambridge, UK: Cambridge University Press, pp. 103–33.

— (1989) *The Cement of Society: A study of social order*, Cambridge, UK: Cambridge University Press.

— (1997) 'The market and the forum: three varieties of political theory' in J. Bohman and W. Rehg (eds) *Deliberative Democracy*, Cambridge, MA and London, UK: MIT Press, pp. 3–33.

— (1998a) (ed.) *Deliberative Democracy*, Cambridge, UK: Cambridge University Press.

— (1998b) 'Deliberation and constitution making', in J. Elster (ed.) (1998a) *Deliberative Democracy*, Cambridge, UK: Cambridge University Press, pp. 97–122.

— (2000) 'Arguing and bargaining in two constituent assemblies', *University of Pennsylvania Journal of Constitutional Law* 2 (1999–2000): 345–421. First published as J. Elster and J.-F. Baillon (1994), 'Argumenter et négotier dans deux assemblées constituantes', *Revue française de science politique* 44(187): 87–256.

Elster, J. and Hylland, A. (eds) (1986) *Foundations of Social Choice Theory*, Cambridge, UK: Cambridge University Press.

Elstub, S. (2010) 'The third generation of deliberative democracy', *Political Studies Review* 8(3): 291–307.

— (2014) 'Mini-publics: Issues and cases', in S. Elstub and P. McLaverty (eds) *Deliberative Democracy: Issues and cases*, Edinburgh, UK: Edinburgh University Press, pp. 166–88.

— (2015) 'A genealogy of deliberative democracy', *Democratic Theory* 2(1): 110–17.

Elstub, S. and McLaverty, P. (eds) (2014) *Deliberative Democracy: Issues and cases*, Edinburgh, UK: Edinburgh University Press.

Ely, J. H. (1980) *Democracy and Distrust: A theory of judicial review*, Cambridge, MA and London, UK: Harvard University Press.

Estlund, D. (1993) 'Who's afraid of deliberative democracy? On the strategic/ deliberative dichotomy in recent constitutional jurisprudence', *Texas Law Review* 71: 1437–77.

—— (1997) 'Beyond fairness and deliberation: the epistemic dimension of democratic authority, in J. Bohman and W. Rehg (eds) (1997) *Deliberative Democracy*, Cambridge, MA and London, UK: MIT Press, pp. 173–204.

—— (2008) *Democratic Authority: A philosophical framework*, Princeton, NJ: Princeton University Press.

Felicetti, A., Niemeyer, S. and Curato, N. (2016) 'Improving deliberative participation: connecting mini-publics to deliberative systems', *European Political Science Review* 8(3): 427–48.

Ferrara, A. (1987) 'A critique of Habermas's consensus theory of truth', *Philosophy & Social Criticism* 13(1): 39–67.

—— (1999) *Justice and Judgment: The rise and the prospect of the judgment model in contemporary political philosophy*, London, UK: Sage.

—— (2001) 'Of boats and principles: reflections on Habermas's "constitutional democracy"', *Political Theory* 29(6): 782–91.

—— (2008) *The Force of the Example: Explorations in the paradigm of judgment*, New York, NY: Columbia University Press.

—— (2014) *The Democratic Horizon: Hyperpluralism and the renewal of political liberalism*, Cambridge, UK and New York, NY: Cambridge University Press.

Finlayson, J. G. and Freyenhagen, F. (eds) (2011a) *Habermas and Rawls: Disputing the political*, New York, NY and London, UK: Routledge.

—— (2011b) 'Introduction: the Habermas–Rawls Dispute. Analysis and re-evaluation', in J. G. Finlayson and F. Freyenhagen (eds) (2011a) *Habermas and Rawls: Disputing the political*, New York, NY and London, UK: Routledge, pp. 1–25.

Fischer, F. and Forester, J. (eds) (1996) *The Argumentative Turn in Policy Analysis and Planning*, London, UK: UCL Press.

Fishkin, J. S. (1979) *Tyranny and Legitimacy: A critique of political theories*, Baltimore, MD and London, UK: John Hopkins University Press.

—— (1983) *Justice, Equal Opportunity and the Family*, New Haven, CT and London, UK: Yale University Press.

—— (1991) *Democracy and Deliberation: New directions in democratic reform*, New Haven, CT: Yale University Press.

—— (1995) *The Voice of the People: Public opinion and democracy*, New Haven, CT: Yale University Press.

—— (2009) *When the People Speak: Deliberative democracy and public consultation*, Oxford, UK: Oxford University Press.

—— (2014) 'Deliberative democracy in context: reflections on theory and practice', in K. Grönlund, A. Bächtiger and M. Setälä, *Deliberative Mini-Publics: Involving citizens in the democratic process*, Colchester, UK: ECPR Press, pp. 27–40.

Fishkin, J. S. and Laslett, P. (eds) (2003) *Debating Deliberative Democracy*, Oxford, UK: Blackwell.

Fishkin, J., He, B., Luskin, R. C. and Siu, A. (2010) 'Deliberative democracy in an unlikely place: deliberative polling in China', *British Journal of Political Science* 40(2): 435–48.

Floridia, A. (2008) 'Democrazia deliberativa e processi decisionali: la legge della Regione Toscana sulla partecipazione', *Stato e Mercato* 1: 83–110.

— (2012) *La democrazia deliberativa: teorie, processi e sistemi*, Roma: Carocci.

— (2013) 'Le "buone ragioni" di una legge: dilemmi e argomenti sul senso della partecipazione (e sui modi del governare)', in M. Morisi and C. Perrone (eds) *Giochi di potere: Partecipazione, piani e politiche territoriali*, Turin: UTET, pp. 17–68.

— (2015) 'La democrazia deliberativa e i partiti: un incontro impossibile?', *Teoria politica*, Nuova Serie/Annali V, pp. 389–420.

Follett, M. P. (1998 [1918]) *The New State, Group, Organizations: The solution of popular government*, Prefaces by B. Barber and J. Mansbridge, intr. K. Mattson, University Park, PA: Penn State University Press.

Foner, E. (1998) *The History of American Freedom*, New York, NY: Norton & Company.

Forester, J. (1985a) 'Critical theory and planning practice', in J. Forester (ed.) *Critical Theory and Public Life*, Cambridge, MA and London, UK: MIT Press, pp. 202–30. Also published (1979) by Dept. of City and Regional Planning in conjunction with the Program in Urban and Regional Studies, Cornell University, Ithaca, NY and (1980) *Journal of the American Planning Association* 46(3): 275–86.

— (1985b) (ed.) *Critical Theory and Public Life*, Cambridge, MA and London, UK: MIT Press.

— (1989) *Planning in the Face of Power*, Berkeley, CA: University of California Press.

— (1993) *Critical Theory, Public Policy, and Planning Practice*, Albany, NY: State University of New York Press.

— (1999) *The Deliberative Practitioner: Encouraging participatory planning processes*, Cambridge, MA and London, UK: MIT Press.

Forst, R. (2001) 'The rule of reasons: three models of deliberative democracy', *Ratio Juris* 14(4): 345–78.

— (2012) *The Right to Justification*, trans. J. Flynn, New York, NY: Columbia University Press. [Original edn (2007) *Recht auf Rechtfertigung*, Frankfurt a. M., DE: Suhrkamp Verlag.]

Fournier, P., van der Kolk, H., Kenneth Carty, R., Blais, A. and Rose, J. (2010) *When Citizens Decide: Lessons from citizens' assemblies on electoral reforms*, Oxford, UK: Oxford University Press.

Fraser, N. (1991) 'Struggles over needs', in N. Fraser (ed.) *Unruly Practices: Power, discourse and gender in contemporary social theory*, Oxford, UK: Oxford University Press.

— (1992) 'Rethinking the public sphere: a contribution to the critique of actually existing democracy', in C. Calhoun (ed.) *Habermas and the Public Sphere*, Cambridge, MA and London, UK: MIT Press, pp. 109–42.

Freeden, M. (2004) 'Ideology, political theory and political philosophy', in G. F. Gaus and C. Kukathas (eds) *Handbook of Political Theory*, London, UK: Sage, pp. 3–17.

Freeman, S. (1992) 'Original meaning, democratic interpretation, and the Constitution', *Philosophy & Public Affairs* 21(1): 3–42.

— (1994) 'Political liberalism and the possibility of a just constitution', *Chicago-Kent Law Review* 69(3): 301–50. Reprinted in S. Freeman (ed.) (2007b) *Justice and the Social Contract: Essays on Rawlsian political philosophy*, Oxford, UK: Oxford University Press.

— (2000) 'Deliberative democracy: a sympathetic comment', *Philosophy & Public Affairs* 29(4): 371–418.

— (2003a) (ed.) *Cambridge Companion to Rawls*, Cambridge, UK: Cambridge University Press.

— (2003b) 'Introduction', in S. Freeman (ed.) *Cambridge Companion to Rawls*, Cambridge, UK: Cambridge University Press, pp. 1–61.

— (2007a) *Rawls*, London, UK and New York, NY: Routledge.

— (2007b) *Justice and the Social Contract: Essays on Rawlsian political philosophy*, Oxford, UK: Oxford University Press.

Friedrich, C. J. (1963) *Man and His Government: An empirical theory of politics*, New York, NY: McGraw-Hill.

Fung, A. (2003) 'Survey article: recipes for public spheres. Eight institutional design choices and their consequences', *Journal of Political Philosophy* 11(3): 338–67.

— (2004) *Empowered Participation*, Princeton, NJ: Princeton University Press.

— (2005) 'Deliberation before revolution: toward an ethics of deliberative democracy in an unjust world', *Political Theory* 33(3): 397–419.

Fung, A. and Wright, E. O. (eds) (2003) *Deepening Democracy: Institutional innovations in empowered participatory governance*, London, UK and New York, NY: Verso.

Gadamer, H.-G. (1975) *Wahrheit und Methode: Grundzüge einer philosophischen Hermeneutik* 4th edn, Tübingen, DE: Mohr.

Garsten, B. (2006) *Saving Persuasion: A defense of rhetoric and judgment*, Cambridge, MA: Harvard University Press.

— (2011) 'The rhetoric revival in political theory', *Annual Review of Political Theory* 14: 159–80.

Gastil, J., Fung, A. and Levine, P. (2005) 'Future directions for public deliberation', in J. Gastil and P. Levine (eds) *Deliberative Democracy Handbook: Strategies for effective civic engagement in the 21st century*, San Francisco, CA: Jossey-Bass, pp. 271–88.

Gastil, J. and Levine, P. (eds) (2005) *The Deliberative Democracy Handbook: Strategies for effective civic engagement in the 21st century*, San Francisco, CA: Jossey-Bass.

Gastil, J. and Keith, W.-M. (2005) 'A nation that (sometimes) likes to talk: A brief history of public deliberation in the United States', in J. Gastil and P. Levine (eds) (2005) *Deliberative Democracy Handbook: Strategies for effective civic engagement in the 21st century*, San Francisco, CA: Jossey-Bass, pp. 3–19.

Geissel, B. (2009) 'How to improve the quality of democracy? Experiences with participatory innovations at the local level in Germany', *German Politics & Society* 27(4): 51–71.

Geuna, M. (1998) 'La tradizione repubblicana e i suoi interpreti: famiglie teoriche e discontinuità concettuali', *Filosofia politica* XII(1): 101–32.

Geuss, R. (1981) *The Idea of a Critical Theory*, Cambridge, UK: Cambridge University Press.

Girard, C. (2009) 'Raison publique rawlsienne et démocratie délibérative: deux conceptions inconciliables de la légitimité politique?', *Raisons politiques* 34(2): 73–99.

Girard, C. and Le Goff, A. (2010a) 'Introduction', in C. Girard and A. Le Goff (eds) *La démocratie délibérative: anthologie de textes fondamentaux*, Paris, FR: Hermann.

—— (2010b) (eds) *La démocratie délibérative: anthologie de textes fondamentaux*, Paris, FR: Hermann.

Goldwin, R. and Shambra, W. (eds) (1980) *How Democratic is the Constitution?*, Washington, DC and London, UK: American Enterprise Institute for Public Policy Research.

Goodin, R. E. (1986) 'Laundering preferences', in J. Elster and A. Hylland (eds) *Foundations of Social Choice Theory*, Cambridge, UK: Cambridge University Press, pp. 75–102.

—— (2003) *Reflective Democracy*, Oxford, UK: Oxford University Press.

—— (2008) *Innovating Democracy: Democratic theory and practice after the deliberative turn*, Oxford, UK: Oxford University Press.

Goodin, R. E. and Dryzek, J. S. (2006) 'Deliberative impacts: the macro-political uptake of "minipublics"', *Politics & Society* 34(2): 219–44. Reprinted in R. E. Goodin (2008) *Innovating Democracy: Democratic theory and practice after the deliberative turn*, Oxford, UK: Oxford University Press, pp. 11–37.

Gourgues, G., Rui, S. and Topçu, S. (2013) 'Gouvernementalité et participation. Lectures critiques', *Participations* 2: 7–33.

Graham, P. (ed.) (1995) *Mary Parker Follett: Prophet of Management – A celebration of writings from the 1920s*, Boston, MA: Harvard Business School Press.

Gramsci, A. (1971) *Prison Notebooks*, Q. Hoare and G. Nowell Smith, (eds and trans.), New York, NY: International.

Green, J. E. (2010) *The Eyes of the People: Democracy in an age of spectatorship*, New York, NY: Oxford University Press.

Gret, M. and Sintomer, Y. (2005) *The Porto Alegre Experiment: Learning lessons for better democracy*, New York, NY: Zed Books.

Grönlund, K., Bächtiger A. and Setälä, M. (2014) *Deliberative Mini-Publics: Involving citizens in the democratic process*, Colchester, UK: ECPR Press.

Gutmann, A. and Thompson, D. (1990) 'Moral conflict and political consensus', *Ethics* 101(1): 64–88. Reprinted in A. Gutmann and D. Thompson (2004) *Why Deliberative Democracy?*, Princeton, NJ and Oxford, UK: Princeton University Press, pp. 64–94.

— (1996) *Democracy and Disagreement*, Cambridge, MA and London, UK: Belknap Press of Harvard University Press.

— (2004) *Why Deliberative Democracy?*, Princeton, NJ and Oxford, UK: Princeton University Press.

Habermas, J. (1970) 'Towards a theory of communicative competence: Patterns of communicative behaviour', in H. P. Dreitzel (ed.) *Recent Sociology No2: Patterns of communicative behaviour*, New York, NY: MacMillan, pp. 115–48. First published in *Inquiry* 13(1–4): 360–75.

— (1971a) *Knowledge and Human Interests*, trans. J. J. Shapiro, Boston, MA: Beacon Press. [Original edn (1968) *Erkenntnis und Interesse*, Frankfurt a. M., DE: Suhrkamp Verlag.]

— (1971b) 'Vorbereitende Bemerkungen zu einer Theorie der kommunikativen Kompetenz', in J. Habermas and N. Luhmann (eds) *Theorie der Gesellshaft oder Sozialtechnologie*, Frankfurt a. M., DE: Suhrkamp Verlag.

— (1973) *Theory and Practice*, trans. J. Viertel, Boston, MA: Beacon Press. Reprinted (1974) London, UK: Heinemann. [Original edn (1971) (2nd edn) *Theorie und Praxis*, Frankfurt a. M., DE: Suhrkamp Verlag.]

— (1975) *Legitimation Crisis*, trans. and intr. T. McCarthy, Boston, MA: Beacon Press. [Original edn (1973) *Legitimationsprobleme in Spätkapitalismus*, Frankfurt a. M., DE: Suhrkamp Verlag.]

— (1979) *Communication and the Evolution of Society*, trans. and intr. T. McCarthy, Boston, MA: Beacon Press. [Original edn (1976) *Zur Rekonstruktion des historischen Materialismus*, Frankfurt a. M., DE: Suhrkamp Verlag.]

— (1982) 'A reply to my critics', in J. B. Thompson and D. Held (eds) *Habermas: Critical debates*, London, UK and Basingstoke, UK: Macmillan, pp. 219–83.

— (1984–1987) *The Theory of Communicative Action*, 2 vols, T. McCarthy (ed. and trans.), Boston, MA: Beacon. [Original edn (1981) *Theorie des kommunicakativen Handelns*, Frankfurt a. M., DE: Suhrkamp Verlag.]

— (1985) 'Modern and postmodern architecture', in J. Forester (ed.) *Critical Theory and Public Life*, Cambridge, MA and London, UK: MIT Press, pp. 317–30.

—   (1987) *The Philosophical Discourse of Modernity: Twelve lectures*, trans. F. Lawrence, Cambridge, MA: MIT Press. [Original edn (1985) *Der philosophische Diskurs der Moderne: Zwölf Vorlesungen*, Frankfurt am M., DE: Suhrkamp Verlag.]

—   (1989) *The Structural Transformation of the Public Sphere: An Inquiry into a category of bourgeois society*, trans. T. Burger and F. Lawrence, Cambridge, UK: Polity Press. [Original edn (1962) *Strukturwandel der Öffentlichkeit: Untersuchungen zu einer Kategorie del bürgerlichen Gesellschaft*, Frankfurt am M., DE: Suhrkamp Verlag.]

—   (1990a) *Moral Consciousness and Communicative Action*, trans. C. Lenhardt and S. Weber Nicholsen, intr. T. McCarthy, Cambridge, MA: MIT Press. [Original edn (1983) *Moralbewußtsein und kommunikatives Handelns*, Frankfurt am M., DE: Suhrkamp Verlag.]

—   (1990b) 'Vorwort zur Neueflage' to *Strukturwandel der Öffentlichkeit*, Frankfurt am M., DE: Suhrkamp Verlag, pp. 11–50.

—   (1992a) 'Further reflections on the public sphere', in C. Calhoun (ed.) *Habermas and the Public Sphere*, Cambridge, MA and London, UK: MIT Press, pp. 421–61.

—   (1992b) *Postmetaphysical Thinking: Philosophical essays*, trans. W. M. Hohengarten, Cambridge MA: MIT Press. [Original edn (1988) *Nachmetaphisysches Denken: Philosophische Aufsätze*, Frankfurt am M., DE: Suhrkamp Verlag.]

—   (1993a) 'On the pragmatic, the ethical, and the moral employments of practical reason', trans. C. Cronin, in J. Habermas (1993) *Justification and Application: Remarks on discourse ethics*, Cambridge, MA: MIT Press, pp. 1–18. First appeared as 'Vom pragmatischen, ethischen und moralischen Gebrauch de praktischen Vernunft', Howison Lecture, Berkeley, University of California, 7 September 1988. Reprinted in J. Habermas (1991) *Erläuterungen zur Diskursethik*, Frankfurt am M., DE: Suhrkamp Verlag, pp. 100–18.

—   (1993b) *Justification and Application: Remarks on discourse ethics*, trans. C. Cronin, Cambridge, MA: MIT Press. [Original edn (1991) *Erläuterungen zur Diskursethik*, Frankfurt am M., DE: Suhrkamp Verlag.]

—   (1995) 'Reconciliation through the public use of reason: remarks on John Rawls's political liberalism', *Journal of Philosophy* 92(3): 109–131. Reprinted in J. Habermas (1998) *The Inclusion of the Other: Studies in political theory*, Cambridge, MA: MIT Press, pp. 49–74.

—   (1995–6) 'Reply to Symposium participants, Benjamin N. Cardozo School of Law', *Cardozo Law Review* 17: 1477–1577. Reprinted in M. Rosenfeld and A. Arato (eds) (1998) *Habermas on Law and Democracy: Critical exchanges*, Berkeley, CA: University of California Press, pp. 381–452.

—   (1996) *Between Facts and Norms: Contributions to a discursive theory of law and democracy*, trans. W. Rehg, Cambridge, MA: MIT Press. [Original edn (1992) *Faktizität und Geltung. Beiträge zur Diskurtheorie des Rechts und des demokratischen Rechtsstaats*, Frankfurt am M., DE: Suhrkamp Verlag.]

— (1997a) 'Popular sovereignty as procedure', in J. Bohman and W. Rehg (eds) (1997) *Deliberative Democracy*, Cambridge, MA and London, UK: MIT Press, pp. 35–65. [Original edn (1988) 'Ist der Herzschlag der Revolution zum Stillstand gekommen? Volkssouveränität als Verfahren. Ein normativer Begriff der Öffentlichkeit', in Bad Homburg Forum für Philosophie, Die Ideen von 1789 in der deutschen Rezeption, Frankfurt am M., DE: Suhrkamp Verlag, pp. 7–36.] Reprinted (1998) in *Vorstudien and Ergänzungen*, paperback edn of *Faktizität und Geltung*, Frankfurt am M., DE: Suhrkamp Verlag.

— (1997b) 'A conversation about questions of political theory', in J. Habermas (1997) *A Berlin Republic: Writings on Germany*, trans. S. Rendall, intr. P. U. Hohendahl, Lincoln, NE: University of Nebraska Press, pp. 131–60. Reprinted in R. Von Schomberg and K. Baynes (eds) (2002) *Discourse and Democracy: Essays on Habermas's Between Facts And Norms*, Albany, NY: State University of New York Press, pp. 241–58. [Original pub. in Swedish as J. Habermas (1994) 'En ur förtvivlan född förhoppning', interview by M. Carleheden and R. Gabriels, *Res Publica* 3: 36–58.] Reprinted in J. Habermas (1995) *Die Normalität einer Berliner Republik: Kleine Politische Schriften VIII*, Frankfurt am M., DE: Suhrkamp Verlag, pp. 135–64.

— (1998a) *The Inclusion of the Other: Studies in political theory*, C. Cronin and P. De Greiff (eds), Cambridge, MA: MIT Press. [Original edn (1996) *Die Einbeziehung des Anderen*, Frankfurt am M., DE: Suhrkamp Verlag.]

— (1998b) ' "Reasonable" versus "true", or the morality of worldviews', in J. Habermas, *The Inclusion of the Other: Studies in political theory*, C. Cronin and P. De Greiff (eds), Cambridge, MA: MIT Press, pp. 75–101. Reprinted in G. J. Finlayson and F. Freyenhagen (eds) (2011), *Habermas and Rawls: Disputing the political*, London, UK: Routledge, pp. 92–114.

— (2001) 'Constitutional democracy – a paradoxical union of contradictory principles?', trans. W. Rehg, *Political Theory* 29(6): 766–781. Reprinted in J. Habermas (2006) *Time of Transitions*, Cambridge, UK: Polity Press, pp. 113–128.

— (2002) 'Postscript: some concluding remarks', in M. Aboulafia, M. Bookman and C. Kemp (eds) (2002) *Habermas and Pragmatism*, London, UK: Routledge, pp. 223–33.

— (2003a) *Truth and Justification*, B. Fultner (ed. and trans.), Cambridge MA: MIT Press. [Original edn (1999) *Wahrheit und Rechtfertigung: Philosophische Aufsätze*, Frankfurt am M., DE: Suhrkamp Verlag.]

— (2003b) 'On law and disagreement: Some comments on "interpretative pluralism"', *Ratio Juris* 16(2): 187–94.

— (2005) 'Concluding comments on empirical approaches to deliberative politics', *Acta Politica* 40(3): 384–92.

—   (2006) 'Political communication in media society: does democracy still enjoy an epistemic dimension?', *Communication Theory* 16(4): 411–26. Reprinted in J. Habermas (2009) *Europe: The faltering project*, trans. C. Cronin, Cambridge, MA: MIT Press, pp. 138–83. [Original edn (2008) *Ach, Europa. Kleine Politischen Schriften XI*, Frankfurt am M., DE, Suhrkamp Verlag.]

—   (2009 [1973]) 'Wahreitstheorien', in J. Habermas *Rationalitäts- und Sprachtheorie, Philosophische Texte*, Band 2, Frankfurt am M., DE: Studienausgabe Suhrkamp Verlag, pp. 208–69.

—   (2011) 'Reply to my critics', in J. G. Finlayson and F. Freyenhagen *Habermas and Rawls: Disputing the political*, New York, NY and London, UK: Routledge, pp. 283–304.

—   (2013) 'Prefazione alla presente edizione italiana', in J. Habermas *Fatti e norme*, trans. L. Ceppa, Bari and Rome: Laterza, pp. v–xi.

Habermas, J. and Luhmann, N. (1971) *Theorie der Gesellshaft oder Sozialtechnologie*, Frankfurt am M., DE: Suhrkamp Verlag.

Hajer, M. A. and Wagenaar, H. (eds) (2003) *Deliberative Policy Analysis: Understanding governance in the network society*, Cambridge, UK: Cambridge University Press.

Hamlin, A. P. and Pettit, P. (eds) (1989) *The Good Polity*, Oxford, UK: Oxford University Press.

Hardin, R. (1993) 'Public choice versus democracy', in Copp, D., Hampton, J. and Roemer, J. E. (eds) *The Idea of Democracy*, Cambridge, UK: Cambridge University Press, pp. 157–172.

—   (2002) 'Street–level epistemology and democratic participation', *Journal of Political Philosophy* 10(2): 212–29. Reprinted in J. Fishkin and P. Laslett (eds) (2003) *Debating Deliberative Democracy*, Oxford, UK: Blackwell, pp. 163–81.

Hartz, L. (1955) *The Liberal Tradition in America: An interpretation of American political thought since the Revolution*, New York, NY: Harcourt.

Hayat, S. (2011) 'Démocratie participative et imperatif délibératif : enjeux d'une confrontation', in M.-H. Bacqué and Y. Sintomer (eds) *La démocratie participative. Histoire et généalogie*, Paris, FR: Editions La Découverte, pp. 102–12.

He, B. (2014) 'Deliberative Culture and Politics: The Persistence of Authoritarian Deliberation in China', *Political Theory*, 42(1): 58–81.

He, B. and Warren, M. (2011) 'Authoritarian deliberation: the deliberative turn in Chinese political development', *Perspectives on Politics* 9(2): 269–89.

Healey, P. (1997) *Collaborative Planning: Shaping places in fragmented societies*, London, UK: Palgrave.

—   (2003) *Città e istituzioni: Piani collaborativi in società frammentate*, Postscript D. Borri, Bari, IT: Dedalo.

Heath, J. (2011) 'Transcendental not metaphysical', in J. G. Finlayson and F. Freyenhagen (eds) *Habermas and Rawls: Disputing the political*, New York, NY and London, UK: Routledge.

Held, D. (2006 [1987]) *Models of Democracy*, Cambridge, UK and Malden, MA: Polity.

Heller, P. and Rao, V. (2015) (eds) *Deliberation and Development: Rethinking the role of voice and collective action in unequal societies*, Washington D.C.: The World Bank Group.

Hendriks, C. M. (2006) 'Integrated deliberation: reconciling civil society's dual role in deliberative democracy', *Political Studies* 54: 486–508.

— (2015) 'Coupling citizens and elites in deliberative systems: the role of institutional design', *European Journal of Political Research* 55(1): 43–60.

Hendriks, C. M., Dryzek, J. and Hunold, C. (2007) 'Turning up the heat: partisanship in deliberative innovation', *Political Studies* 55: 362–83.

Hibbing, J. R. and Theiss-Morse, E. (2002) *Stealth Democracy: Americans' beliefs about how government should work*, Cambridge, UK: Cambridge University Press.

Hirschman, A. O. (1982) *Shifting Involvements: Private interest and public action*, Princeton, NJ: Princeton University Press.

Holmes, S. (1988a) 'Gag rules or the politics of omission', in J. Elster and R. Slagstad (eds) *Constitutionalim and Democracy*, Cambridge, UK: Cambridge University Press, pp. 19–58. Reprinted in S. Holmes (1995) *Passions and Constraint: On the theory of liberal democracy*, Chicago, IL: University of Chicago Press, pp. 202–35.

— (1988b) 'Precommittment and the paradox of democracy', in J. Elster and R. Slagstad (eds) *Constitutionalism and Democracy*, Cambridge, UK: Cambridge University Press, pp. 195–240.

— (1995) *Passions and Constraint: On the theory of liberal democracy*, Chicago, IL: University of Chicago Press.

Holzinger, K. (2004) 'Bargaining through arguing: an empirical analysis based on speech act theory', *Political Communication* 21: 195–222.

Johnson, J. (1993) 'Is talk really cheap? Prompting conversation between critical theory and rational choice', *American Political Science Review* 87(1): 74–86.

— (2006) 'Political parties and deliberative democracy?', in R. S. Katz and W. Crotty (eds) *Handbook of Party Politics*, London, UK: Sage.

Kaufman A. S. (1960) 'Human nature and participatory democracy', in C. J. Friedrich (ed.) *Responsibility*, NOMOS III, New York, NY: Liberal Art Press, pp. 266–89. Reprinted, with an extension, 'Ten years later', in W. E. Connolly (ed.) (1969) *The Bias of Pluralism*, New York, NY: Atherton Press, pp. 178–212.

— (1968) *The Radical Liberal: New man in American politics*, New York, Atherton Press.

Kateb, G. (1992) *The Inner Ocean: Individualism and democratic culture*, Ithaca, NY and London, UK: Cornell University Press.

Keim D. W. (1975) 'Participation in contemporary democratic theories', in R. J. Pennock and J. W. Chapman (eds) *Participation in Politics*, New York, NY: Lieber & Atherton, pp. 1–38.

Kelsen, H. (2013) *The Essence and Value of Democracy*, N. Urbinati and C. Invernizzi Accetti (eds and intro.), trans. B. Graf, New York, NY: Rowman & Littlefield Publishers. [Original edn (1929) *Vom Wesen und Wert der Demokratie*, Tübingen, DE: J. H. B. Mohr.]

Keith, W. (2011) 'Façonner un public délibérante: les forums comme outils d'éducation civique dans l'histoire des États-Unis', in M.-H. Bacqué and Y. Sintomer (eds) (2011) *La démocratie participative: Histoire et généalogie*, Paris, FR: Editions La Découverte, pp. 211–27.

Kemp, R. (1985) 'Planning, public hearings, and the politics of discourse', in J. Forester (ed.) *Theory and Public Life*, Cambridge, MA and London, UK: MIT Press, pp. 177–201.

Kendall, W. (1971) 'The two majorities', in R. C. Moe (ed.) *Congress and the President*, Pacific Palisades, CA: Goodyear Publishing Company.

Key, V. O. (1961) *Public Opinion and American Democracy*, New York, NY: Knopf.

Knight, J. and Johnson, J. (1994) 'Aggregation and deliberation: on the possibility of democratic legitimacy', *Political Theory* 22(2): 277–96.

Kuhn, T. S. (1962) *The Structure of Scientific Revolutions*, Chicago, IL: University of Chicago Press.

Laborde, C. (2013) 'Republicanism', in M. Freeden, L. T. Sargent and M. Stears (eds) *Oxford Handbook of Political Ideologies*, Oxford: Oxford University Press, pp. 513–35.

Landemore, H. (2013) *Democratic Reason: Politics, collective intelligence, and the rule of the many*, Princeton, NJ: Princeton University Press.

—— (2015) 'Inclusive constitution-making: the Icelandic experiment', *Journal of Political Philosophy* 23(2):166–191.

Landemore, E. and Elster, J. (eds) (2012) *Collective Wisdom: Principles and mechanisms*, Cambridge, UK: Cambridge University Press.

Landwehr, C. (2009) *Political Conflict and Political Preferences: Communicative interactions between facts, norms and interests*, Colchester, UK: ECPR Press.

Larmore, C. (1987) *Patterns of Moral Complexity*, Cambridge: Cambridge University Press.

—— (1990) 'Political liberalism', *Political Theory* 18: 339–60.

—— (1999) 'The moral basis of political liberalism', *Journal of Philosophy* 96(12): 599–625.

—— (2003) 'Public reason', in S. Freeman (ed.) *The Cambridge Companion to Rawls*, Cambridge, UK: Cambridge University Press, pp. 368–93.

Lasswell, H. D. and Kaplan, A. (1950) *Power and Society*, New Haven, CT: Yale University Press.

Lee, C. W., McQuarrie, M. and Walker, E. T. (eds) (2015) *Democratizing Inequalities: Dilemmas of the new public participation*, New York, NY and London, UK: New York University Press.

Lewanski, R. (2013) 'Institutionalizing deliberative democracy: the "Tuscany laboratory"', *Journal of Public Deliberation* 9(1), article 10.

Lipset, S. M. (1960) *Political Man: The social bases of politics*, New York, NY: Anchor Books.

Lowi, T. J. (1967) 'The public philosophy: interest-group liberalism', *American Political Science Review* 61(1): 5–24.

— (1979 [1969]) *The End of Liberalism: The second republic of the United States*, New York, NY and London, UK: Norton & Company.

Lowndes, V., Pratchett. L. and Stoker, G. (2001a) 'Trends in public participation. Part 1– local government perspectives', *Public Administration* 79(1): 205–22.

— (2001b) 'Trends in public participation. Part 2 – citizens' perspectives', *Public Administration* 79(2): 445–55.

Lukensmeyer, J., Goldman, J. and Brigham S. (2005) 'A town meeting for the twenty-first century', in J. Gastil and P. Levine (eds) (2005) *Deliberative Democracy Handbook: Strategies for effective civic engagement in the 21st century*, San Francisco, CA: Jossey-Bass, pp. 154–63.

Luskin, R. C., Fishkin, J. S. and Jowell, R. (2002) 'Considered opinions: deliberative polling in the UK', *British Journal of Political Science* 32(3): 455–87.

Macedo, S. (ed.) (1999) *Deliberative Politics*, Oxford, UK: Oxford University Press.

MacIntyre, A. (1981) *After Virtue: A study in moral theory*, Notre Dame, IN: University of Notre Dame Press.

Macpherson, C. B. (1977) *The Life and Times of Liberal Democracy*, Oxford, UK: Oxford University Press.

Maffettone, S. (2010) *John Rawls: An introduction*, Cambridge, UK: Polity.

Magnaghi, A. (2005) *The Urban Village: A charter for democracy and local self-sustainable development*, London, UK: Zed Books.

Maia, R. C. M. (2012) *Deliberation, the Media and Political Talk*, New York, NY: Hampton Press.

Majone, G. (1990) 'Policy analysis and public deliberation', in R. Reich (ed.) *The Power of Public Ideas*, Cambridge, MA: Harvard University Press, pp. 157–78.

Mandle, J. and Reidy, D. A. (eds) (2013) *Companion to Rawls*, Hoboken, NJ: Wiley-Blackwell.

— (eds) (2015) *Cambridge Rawls Lexicon*, Cambridge, UK: Cambridge University Press.

Manin, B. (1987) 'On legitimacy and political deliberation', *Political Theory* 15(3): 338–68.

— (1994) 'Checks, balances and boundaries: the separation of powers in the constitutional debate of 1787', in B. Fontana (ed.) *The Invention of the Modern Republic*, Cambridge, UK: Cambridge University Press, pp. 27–62.

— (1997) *The Principles of Representative Government*, Cambridge, UK: Cambridge University Press.

— (2002) 'L'idée de démocratie délibérative dans la science politique contemporaine. Introduction, généalogie et éléments critiques. Entretien avec Bernard Manin', [interview of Manin, by L. Blondiaux], *Politix* 15(57): 37–55.

— (2011) 'Comment promouvoir la délibération démocratique? Priorité du débat contradictoire sur la discussion', *Raisons Politiques* 42: 83–112.

Mansbridge, J. J. (1975) 'The limits of friendship', in R. J. Pennock and J. W. Chapman (eds) *Participation in Politics*, New York, NY: Lieber-Atherton, pp. 246–75.

— (1983 [1980]) *Beyond Adversary Democracy*, with revised Preface, Chicago, IL and London, UK: University of Chicago Press.

— (1987) Untitled review of Barber's *Strong Democracy*, *American Political Science Review* 81(4): 1341–2.

— (1990) 'The rise and fall of self-interest in the explanation of political life', in J. Mansbridge (ed.) *Beyond Self-Interest*, Chicago, IL: University of Chicago Press.

— (1999) 'Everyday talk in the deliberative system', in S. Macedo (ed.) *Deliberative Politics: Essays on democracy and disagreement*, Oxford, UK and New York, NY: Oxford University Press, pp. 211–39.

— (2003a) 'Practice–thought–practice', in A. Fung and E. O. Wright (eds) (2003) *Deepening Democracy: Institutional innovations in empowered participatory governance*, London, UK and New York, NY: Verso, pp. 175–99.

— (2003b) 'Rethinking representation', *American Political Science Review* 97(4): 515–28.

— (2007) '"Deliberative democracy" or "democratic deliberation"?', in S. W. Rosenberg (ed.) *Deliberation, Participation and Democracy: Can the people govern?*, Basingstoke, UK and New York, NY: Palgrave Macmillan, pp. 251–71.

— (2009) 'Deliberative and non-deliberative negotiations', Harvard Kennedy School, Faculty Research Working Papers Series, April.

Mansbridge, J. J., Bohman, J., Chambers, S., Estlund, D., Føllesdal, A., Fung, A., Lafont, C., Manin, B. and Martí, J.-L. (2010) 'The place of self-interest and the role of power in deliberative democracy', *Journal of Political Philosophy* 18(1): 64–100.

Mansbridge, J. J., Bohman, J., Chambers, S., Christiano, T., Fung, A., Parkinson, J., Thompson, D. E. and Warren, M. E. (2012) 'A systemic approach to deliberative democracy', in J. Parkinson and J. J. Mansbridge (eds) *Deliberative Systems: Deliberative democracy at the large scale*, Cambridge, UK: Cambridge University Press.

Martí, J. L. (2006) *La repùblica deliberativa: Una teoria de la democracia*, Barcelona, ES: Marcial Pons.

Mastropaolo, A. (2012) *Is Democracy a Lost Cause? Paradoxes of an imperfect invention*, trans. C. Tame, Colchester, UK: ECPR Press. [Original edn *La democrazia è una causa persa? Paradossi di un'invenzione imperfetta*, Turin, IT: Bollati Boringhieri, 2011.]

Mattson, K. (1998) *Creating a Democratic Public: The struggle for urban participatory democracy during the progressive era*, University Park, PA: Penn State University Press.

— (2011) 'Consolider les fondements de la démocratie: le mouvement des centre sociaux aux USA durant l'ère progressiste', in M.-H. Bacqué and Y. Sintomer (eds) *La démocratie participative: Histoire et genéalogie*, Paris, FR: Editions La Découverte, pp. 191–209.

McCarthy, T. (1975) 'Translator's Introduction', in J. Habermas, *Legitimation Crisis*, trans. and intr. T. McCarthy, Boston, MA: Beacon Press, pp. vvi–xxiv.

— (1994) 'Constructivism and reconstructivism: Rawls and Habermas in dialogue', *Ethics* 105(1): 44–63.

— (1995–6) 'Legitimacy and diversity: dialectical reflections on analytical distinctions', *Cardozo Law School Review* 17: 1083–1125.

Mead, G. H. (1934) *Mind, Self and Society, from the standpoint of a social behaviourist*, Chicago, IL: University of Chicago Press.

Meiklejohn, A. (1948) *Free Speech and Its Relation to Self-Government*, New York, NY: Harper Bros. Reprinted in A. Meiklejohn (1960) *Political Freedom: The constitutional powers of the people*, New York, NY: Harper.

Michelman, F. I. (1986) 'Foreword: traces of self–government', *Harvard Law Review* 100: 4–77.

— (1988a) 'Law's republic', *Yale Law Journal* 98: 1493–537.

— (1988b) 'Political truth and the rule of law', *Tel Aviv University Studies in Law* 8: 281–91.

— (1989a) 'Conceptions of democracy in American constitutionalism. Argument: voting rights', *Florida Law Review* 51: 443–90.

— (1989b) 'Conceptions of democracy in American constitutionalism. Argument: the case of pornography regulation', *Tennessee Law Review* 56: 291–319.

— (1989c) 'Bringing the law to life: a plea for disenchantment', *Cornell Law Review* 74: 256–69.

— (1995–6) 'Family quarrel', *Cardozo Law Review* 17: 1163–77.

— (1997) 'How can the people ever make the laws? A critique of deliberative democracy', in J. Bohman and W. Rehg (eds) *Deliberative Democracy*, Cambridge, MA and London, UK: MIT Press, pp. 145–72.

— (1999) *Brennan and Democracy*, Princeton, NJ: Princeton University Press.

— (2004) 'Introduzione all'edizione italiana', in G. Bongiovanni and G. Palombella (eds) *La democrazia e il potere giudiziario: dilemma costituzionale e il giudice Brennan*, Bari, IT: Dedalo.

— (2003) 'Rawls on constitutionalism and law', in S. Freeman (ed.) *Cambridge Companion to Rawls*, Cambridge, UK: Cambridge University Press, pp. 394–425.

Milbrath, L. W. (1965) *Political Participation: How and why people get involved in politics*, Chicago, IL: McNally & Co.

Mill, J. S. (1977 [1861]) 'Considerations on representative government', in J. M. Robson and A. Brady (eds) *Collected Works of John Stuart Mill, vol. XIX, Essays on Politics and Society*, Toronto, ON: University of Toronto Press and London, UK: Routledge & Kegan Paul.

Miller, D. (1992) 'Deliberative democracy and social choice', *Political Studies* 40: 54–67. Reprinted in J. Fishkin and P. Laslett (eds) (2003) *Debating Deliberative Democracy*, Malden, MA and Oxford, UK: Blackwell, pp. 182–99.

Miller, J. (1987) *Democracy in the Streets: From Port Huron to the siege of Chicago*, New York, NY: Simon & Schuster.

Montanaro, L. (2012) 'The democratic legitimacy of self-appointed representatives', *The Journal of Politics* 74(4): 1094–1107.

Morisi, M. and Perrone, C. (eds) (2013) *Giochi di potere: Partecipazione, piani e politiche territoriali*, Turin, IT: UTET.

Mouffe, C. (2005) *On the Political*, London, UK: Routledge.

Muirhead, R. (2010) 'Can deliberative democracy be partisan?', *Critical Review* 22(2): 129–57.

—— (2014) *The Promise of Party in a Polarized Age*, Cambridge, MA and London, UK: Harvard University Press.

Muirhead, R. and Rosenblum, N. L. (2006) 'Political liberalism vs "The Great Game of Politics": the politics of political liberalism', *Perspectives on Politics* 4(1): 99–108.

Mulhall, S. and Swift, A. (eds) (1996) *Liberals and Communitarians*, Hoboken, NJ: Wiley-Blackwell.

Mutz, D. C. (2008a) *Hearing the Other Side: Deliberative vs. participatory democracy*, Cambridge, UK and New York, NY: Cambridge University Press.

—— (2008b) 'Is deliberative democracy a falsifiable theory?', *Annual Review of Political Science* 11: 522–38.

Nagel, T. (2003) 'Rawls and liberalism', in S. Freeman (ed.) *Cambridge Companion to Rawls*, Cambridge, UK: Cambridge University Press, pp. 62–85.

Neblo, M. A. (2015) *Deliberative Democracy Between Theory and Practice*, Cambridge, UK and New York, NY: Cambridge University Press.

Nino, C. S. (1996) *The Constitution of Deliberative Democracy*, New Haven, CT and London, UK: Yale University Press.

Obama, B. (2006) *The Audacity of Hope*, New York, NY: Crown Publishing Group.

Ober, J. (2008) *Democracy and Knowledge: Innovation and learning in classical Athens*, Princeton, NJ: Princeton University Press.

Offe, C. (1984) *Contradictions of the Welfare State*, Cambridge, MA: MIT Press.

O'Flynn, I. (2006) *Deliberative Democracy and Divided Societies*, Edinburgh, UK: Edinburgh University Press.

O'Flynn, I. and Sood, G. (2014) 'What would Dahl Say? An appraisal of the democratic credentials of deliberative polls and other mini-publics', in K. Grönlund, A. Bächtiger and M. Setälä (eds) (2014) *Deliberative Mini-Publics: Involving citizens in the democratic process*, Colchester, UK: ECPR Press, pp. 41–58.

O'Neill, O. (1989) *Constructions of Reason: Explorations of Kant's practical philosophy*, Cambridge, UK: Cambridge University Press.

Ottonelli, V. (2012) *I principi procedurali della democrazia*, Bologna, IT: Il Mulino.

Owen, D. and Smith, G. (2015) 'Survey article: deliberation, democracy, and the systemic turn', *Journal of Political Philosophy* 23(2): 213–34.

Outhwaite, W. (1994) *Habermas: A critical introduction*, Cambridge, UK: Polity Press.

Palumbo, A. (2012) 'Epistemic turn or democratic U–turn? On the tension between philosophical reasoning and political action in deliberative democracy', *Teoria politica*, Annali II, pp. 269–91.

— (2015) *Situating Governance: Context, content, critique*, Colchester, UK: ECPR Press.

Papadopoulos, Y., and Warin, P. (2007) 'Are innovative, participatory and deliberative procedures in policy making democratic and effective?', *European Journal of Political Research* 46(4): 445–72.

Parkinson, J. (2004) 'Why deliberate? The encounter between deliberation and new public managers', *Public Administration* 82(2): 377–95.

— (2006) *Deliberating in the Real World: Problems of legitimacy in deliberative democracy*, Oxford, UK: Oxford University Press.

Parkinson, J. and Mansbridge, J. J. (eds) (2012) *Deliberative Systems: Deliberative democracy at the large scale*, Cambridge, UK: Cambridge University Press.

Pateman, C. (1970) *Participation and Democratic Theory*, Cambridge, UK: Cambridge University Press.

— (1974) 'Criticizing empirical theorists of democracy', *Political Theory* 2: 215–18.

— (1982) 'Introduction' in R. Mason (ed.) *Participatory and Workplace Democracy: A theoretical development in the critique of liberalism*, Carbondale, IL: Southern Illinois University Press.

— (2012) 'Participatory democracy revisited', APSA Presidential Address, *Perspectives on Politics* 10(1): 7–19.

Pellizzoni, L. (2001) 'The myth of the best argument: power, deliberation and reason', *British Journal of Sociology* 52(1): 59–86.

— (2009) 'Deliberative democracy stage four', *Sociologica* 2(3): 1–9.

— (2013) 'Une idée sur le declin? Evaluer la nouvelle critique de la déliberation publique', *Participations* 1: 87–118.

— (2015) 'Bridging promises and (dis)illusions: deliberative democracy in an evolutionary perspective', in R. Beunen, K. Van Assche and M. Duineveld (eds) *Evolutionary Governance Theory: An introduction*, New York, NY: Springer International Publishing, pp. 215–32.

Pennock, R. J. and Chapman, J. W. (eds) (1975) *Participation in Politics*, New York, NY: Lieber-Atherton.

Perelman, C. and Olbrechts-Tyteca, L. (1969) *The New Rhetoric: A treatise on argumentation*, trans. J. Wilkinson and P. Weaver, Notre Dame, IN: University of Notre Dame Press. [Original edn (1958) *Traité de l'argumentation: La nouvelle rhétorique*, Paris, FR: Presses Universitaire de France.]

Perrone, C. (2010) *DiverCity: Conoscenza, pianificazione, città delle differenze*, Milan, IT: Franco Angeli.

—— (2011) 'What would a "DiverCity" be like? Speculation on difference-sensitive planning and living practices', in C. Perrone, G. Manella and L. Tripodi (eds) *Everyday Life in the Segmented City*, Research in Urban Sociology, vol. 11, Bingley, UK: Emerald, pp. 1–25.

Pettit, P. (1997) *Republicanism: A theory of freedom and government*, Oxford, UK: Clarendon Press.

—— (2003) 'Deliberative democracy, the discursive dilemma, and republican theory', in J. S. Fishkin and P. Laslett (eds) *Debating Deliberative Democracy*, Oxford, UK: Blackwell, pp. 138–62.

—— (2004) 'Depoliticizing democracy', *Ratio Juris* 17(1): 52–65.

Pitkin, H. F. (1967) *The Concept of Representation*, Berkeley, CA, Los Angeles, CA and London, UK: University of California Press.

Piore, M. J. and Sabel, C. (1984) *The Second Industrial Divide: Possibilities for prosperity*, New York, NY: Basic Books.

Pocock, J. G. A. (1975) *The Machiavellian Moment: Political thought and the Atlantic republican tradition*, Princeton, NJ: Princeton University Press.

—— (1981) 'Virtues, rights and will in the origins of American constitutionalism', *Political Theory* 9(3): 353–68.

Polletta, F. (2015) 'Public deliberation and political contention', in C. W. Lee, M. McQuarrie and E. T. Walker (eds) *Democratizing Inequalities: Dilemmas of the new public participation*, New York, NY and London, UK: New York University Press, pp. 222–43.

Pomatto, G. (2011) *Gioco strategico e deliberazione. Il dibattito pubblico sulla Gronda di Genova*, Dipartimento di Studi politici, Università di Torino, Turin: SPS University Press.

—— (2013) 'Anche senza accordo: processi inclusivi e trasformazione dei conflitti territoriali', *Stato e Mercato* 99: 455–84.

—— (2015) 'Interprétations agonistiques, dialogiques et élitistes: participation et conflit dans trois cas en Italie', *Participations* 13(3): 35–61.

Post, R. C. (1987) 'Between governance and management: the history and theory of the public forum', *University of California Law Review* 34: 1713–1835.

—— (2014) *Citizens Divided: Campaign finance reform and the Constitution*, with comments by P. S. Karlan, L. Lessig, F. I. Michelman and N. Urbinati, Cambridge, MA and London, UK: Harvard University Press.

Putnam, R. D. (1993) *Making Democracy Work: Civic traditions in modern Italy*, Princeton, NJ: Princeton University Press.

—— (2000) *Bowling Alone: The collapse and revival of American community*, New York, NY: Touchstone and Simon & Schuster.

Ragazzoni, D. (2013) 'Book review of J. E. Green, *The Eyes of the People: Democracy in an age of spectatorship*', *Interpretation. A Journal of Political Philosophy* 40(1): 127–134.

Rasmussen D. A. (ed.) (1990) *Universalism vs. Communitarianism: Contemporary debates in ethics*, Boston, MA: MIT Press.

— (1996) (ed.) *Handbook of Critical Theory*, Oxford, UK and Malden, MA: Blackwell.

Ravazzi, S. and Pomatto, G. (2014) 'Flexibility, argumentation and confrontation: how deliberative minipublics can affect policies on controversial issues', *Journal of Public Deliberation* 10(2): article 10.

Rawls, J. (1971) *A Theory of Justice*, Cambridge, MA: Belknap Press of Harvard University Press.

— (1985) 'Justice as fairness: political not metaphysical', *Philosophy & Public Affairs* 14(3): 223–52. Reprinted in S. Freeman (ed.) (1999) *John Rawls, Collected Papers*, Cambridge, MA and London, UK: Harvard University Press, pp. 388–414.

— (1982) 'The basic liberties and their priority', Tanner Lectures in Human Values, 3, Salt Lake City, UT: University of Utah Press, pp. 3–87.

— (1987) 'The idea of an overlapping consensus', *Oxford Journal of Legal Studies* 7(1): 1–25. Reprinted in J. Rawls (2005) *Political Liberalism*, New York, NY: Columbia University Press, pp. 133–72.

— (1995) 'Political liberalism: reply to Habermas', *Journal of Philosophy* 92(3): 132–180. Reprinted in J. Rawls (2005) *Political Liberalism*, New York, NY: Columbia University Press, pp. 340–399.

— (1997) 'The idea of public reason revisited', *University of Chicago Law Review* 64(3): 765–807. Reprinted in S. Freeman (ed.) (1999) *John Rawls, Collected Papers*, Cambridge, MA and London, UK: Harvard University Press and in J. Rawls (1999) *The Law of Peoples*, Cambridge, MA: Harvard University Press.

— (1999) *John Rawls, Collected Papers*, S. Freeman (ed.), Cambridge, MA and London, UK: Harvard University Press.

— (2001) *Justice as Fairness: A reformulation*, E. Kelly (ed.), Cambridge, MA and London, UK: Belknap Press of Harvard University Press.

— (2005 [1993]) *Political Liberalism* (3rd edn, expanded), New York, NY: Columbia University Press.

Raz, J. (1990) 'Facing diversity: the case of epistemic abstinence', *Philosophy & Public Affairs* 19(1): 3–46.

Rehg, W. (1994) *Insight and Solidarity: A study in the discourse ethics of Jürgen Habermas*, Berkeley, CA, Los Angeles, CA and London, UK: University of California Press.

— (1996) 'Habermas's discourse theory of law and democracy: an overview of the argument', in D. M. Rasmussen (ed.) *Handbook of Critical Theory*, Cambridge, MA: Blackwell, pp. 166–89.

Reuchamps, M. and Suiter, J. (2016) (eds) *Constitutional Deliberative Democracy in Europe*, Colchester, UK: ECPR Press.

Revel, M., Blatrix, C., Blondiaux, L., Fourniau, J.-M., Dubreuil, B. H. and Lefebvre, R. (2007) (eds) *Le Débat Public: Une expérience française de démocratie participative*, Paris, FR: Editions La Découverte.

Rhodes, R. A. W. (1997) *Understanding Governance*, Buckingham, UK: Open University Press.

Riker, W. H. (1982) *Liberalism Against Populism*, Prospect Heights, IL: Waveland Press.

Rosanvallon, P. (2008) *Counter-Democracy: Politics in an age of distrust*, trans. A. Goldhammer, Cambridge, UK: Cambridge University Press. [Original edn (2006) *La contro-démocratie. La politique à l'âge de la défiance*, Paris, FR: Seuil.]

Rosenberg, S. W. (ed.) (2007) *Deliberation, Participation and Democracy. Can the people govern?*, Basingstoke, UK and New York, NY: Palgrave Macmillan.

Rosenblum, N. L. (2008) *On the Side of the Angels: An appreciation of parties and partisanship*, Princeton, NJ and Oxford, UK: Princeton University Press.

Rosenfeld, M. and Arato, A. (eds) (1998) *Habermas on Law and Democracy: Critical exchanges*, Berkeley, CA: University of California Press.

Rousseau, J.-J. (2012) *The Social Contract and Other Political Writings*, C. Bertram (ed.), trans. Q. Hoare, Penguin Classics series, London, UK: Penguin Books.

Rowe, G. and Frewer, L. J. (2000) 'Public participation methods: a framework for evaluation', *Science, Technology, & Human Values* 25(1): 3–29.

Ryan, M. and Smith, G. (2014) 'Defining mini-publics', in K. Grönlund, A. Bächtiger and M. Setälä, *Deliberative Mini-Publics: Involving Citizens in the Democratic Process*, Colchester, UK: ECPR Press, pp. 9–26.

Ryfe, D. M. (2005) 'Does deliberative democracy work?', *Annual Review of Political Science* 8: 49–71.

Sabel, C. (2012) 'Dewey, democracy, and democratic experimentalism', *Contemporary Pragmatism* 9(2): 35–55.

Sabel, C., De Búrca, G. and Keohane, R. O. (2013) 'New modes of pluralist global governance', *Journal of International Law and Politics* 45: 723–86.

Sabel, C. and Zeitlin, J. (eds) (1997) *World of Possibilities: Flexibility and mass production in Western industrialization*, Cambridge, UK and New York, NY: Cambridge University Press.

— (2010) 'Learning from difference: the new architecture of experimentalist governance in the EU', in C. Sabel and J. Zeitlin (eds) *Experimentalist Governance in the European Union: Towards a new architecture*, Oxford, UK and New York, NY: Oxford University Press.

— (2012a) 'Experimentalism in the EU: common ground and persistent differences', *Regulation & Governance* 6(3): 410–26.

— (2012b) 'Experimentalist governance', in D. Levi–Faur (ed.) *Oxford Handbook of Governance*, Oxford, UK: Oxford University Press, pp. 179–85.

Sabel, C., De Búrca, G. and Keohane, R. O. (2013) 'New modes of pluralist global governance', *Journal of International Law and Politics* 45: 723–86.

Sale, K. (1973) *SDS: The rise and development of the Students for a Democratic Society*, New York, NY: Random House.

Sandel, M. (1982) *Liberalism and the Limits of Justice*, Cambridge, UK: Cambridge University Press.

Sanders, L. (1997) 'Against deliberation', *Political Theory* 25(3): 347–76.

Santos, B. de Sousa (1998) 'Participatory budgeting in Porto Alegre: toward a redistributive democracy', *Politics and Society* 26(4): 461–510.

Sartori, G. (1962) *Democratic Theory*, Detroit, MI: Wayne State University Press.

— (1987) *The Theory of Democracy Revisited*, Chatham, NJ: Chatham House Publishers.

— (1989) 'Video power', *Government and Opposition* 24(1): 39–53.

— (2005 [1976]) *Parties and Party Systems: A framework for analysis*, Colchester, UK: ECPR Press.

Scanlon, T. M. (2003) 'Rawls on justification', in S. Freeman (ed.) (2003a) *Cambridge Companion to Rawls*, Cambridge, UK: Cambridge University Press, pp. 139–67.

Schelling, T. C. (1960) *The Strategy of Conflict*, Cambridge, MA and London, UK: Harvard University Press.

Schattschneider, E. E. (1960) *The Semi-Sovereign People: A realist's view of democracy in America*, New York, NY: Holt, Rinehart & Winston.

Scheuerman, W. E. (1999) 'Between radicalism and resignation: democratic theory in Habermas's "Between Facts and Norms"', in P. Dews (ed.) *Habermas: A critical reader*, Oxford, UK: Blackwell, pp. 153–77.

Schmidt, V. (2008) 'Discursive institutionalism: the explanatory power of ideas and discourse', *Annual Review of Political Science* 11: 303–26.

— (2011) 'Speaking of change: why discourse is key to the dynamics of policy transformation', *Critical Policy Studies* 5(2): 106–26.

Schmitt, C. (1988) *The Crisis of Parliamentary Democracy*, E. Kennedy (ed.), Cambridge, MA and London, UK: MIT Press. [Original edn (1923) *Die geistesgeschichtliche Lage des heutigen Parlamentarismus*, Berlin: Duncker & Humblot.]

Searle, J. R. (1969) *Speech Acts: An essay in the philosophy of language*, Cambridge, UK: Cambridge University Press.

Sen, A. (1986) 'Foundations of social choice theory: an epilogue', in J. Elster and A. Hylland (eds) *Foundations of Social Choice Theory*, Cambridge, UK: Cambridge University Press, pp. 213–48.

— (2009) *The Idea of Justice*, London, Penguin Books.

Simon, H. (1983) *Models of Bounded Rationality*, Cambridge, MA: MIT Press.

Sintomer, Y. (2007) *Le pouvoir au people: Jurys citoyens, tirage au sort et démocratie participative*, Paris, FR: Editions La Découverte.

— (2011a) 'Délibération et participation: affinité élective ou concepts en tension?', *Participations* 1(1): 239–26.

— (2011b) 'Démocratie participative, démocratie délibèrative: l'histoire contrastée de deux catègories émergentes', in M.-H. Bacqué and Y. Sintomer (eds) *La démocratie participative: Histoire et genéalogie*, Paris, FR: Editions La Découverte, pp. 113–34.

Sintomer, Y., Herzberg, C. and Allegretti, G. (2010) *Learning from the South*, Bonn, DE: InWEnt GmbH.

Sintomer, Y., Herzberg, C. and Röcke, A. (2008) *Les budgets participatifs en Europe*, Paris, FR: Editions La Découverte.

Sintomer, Y. and Talpin, J. (2011) 'La démocratie délibérative face au défi du pouvoir', *Raisons politiques* 42(2): 5–13.

Skinner Q. (1969) 'Meaning and understanding in the history of ideas', *History and Theory* 8(1): 3–53. Reprinted and revised in J. Tully (ed.) *Meaning and Context: Quentin Skinner and his critics*, Cambridge, UK: Cambridge University Press, 1988, pp. 29–67.

—— (1972) 'Motives, intentions and the interpretation of texts', *New Literary History*, 3(2): 93–408. Reprinted and revised in J. Tully (ed.) *Meaning and Context: Quentin Skinner and his critics*, Cambridge, UK: Cambridge University Press, 1988.

—— (1973) 'The empirical theorists of democracy and their critics: a plague on both their houses', *Political Theory* 1(3): 287–306.

—— (1978) *The Foundations of Modern Political Thought: The Renaissance*, Cambridge, UK: Cambridge University Press.

—— (1998) *Liberty Before Liberalism*, Cambridge, UK: Cambridge University Press.

—— (2002) *Visions of Politics: Renaissance virtues*, Cambridge, UK: Cambridge University Press.

Smith, G. (2009) *Democratic Innovation: Designing institutions for citizen participation*, Cambridge, UK: Cambridge University Press.

Smith, G. and Wales, C. (2000) 'Citizens' juries and deliberative democracy', *Political Studies* 48(1): 51–65.

Steiner, J. (2008) 'Concept stretching: the case of deliberation', *European Political Science* 7(2): 186–190.

—— (2012) *The Foundations of Deliberative Democracy: Empirical research and normative implications*, Cambridge, UK: Cambridge University Press.

—— (2014) 'Sequencing deliberative democracy to promote public openness', in S. Elstub and P. McLaverty (eds) *Deliberative Democracy: Issues and cases*, Edinburgh, UK: Edinburgh University Press, pp. 137–48.

Steiner, J., Bächtiger, A., Spörndli, M. and Steenbergen, M. (2003) 'Measuring political deliberation: a discourse quality index', *Comparative European Politics* 1(1): 21–48.

—— (2004) *Deliberative Politics in Action: Crossnational study of parliamentary debates*, Cambridge, UK: Cambridge University Press.

Steiner, J., Jaramillo, M. C., Maia, R. and Mameli, S. (2017) *Deliberation Across Deeply Divided Societies, Transformative Moments*, Cambridge, UK: Cambridge University Press.

Streeck, W. (2014) *Buying Time: The delayed crisis of democratic capitalism*, New York, NY and London, UK: Verso Books. [Original edn (2013) *Gekaufte Zeit*, Berlin: Suhrkamp Verlag.]

Sunstein C. R. (1984) 'Naked preferences and the constitution', *Columbia Law Review* 84(7): 1689–1732.

— (1985) 'Interest groups in American public law', *Stanford Law Review* 38(1): 29–87.

— (1986) 'Legal interference with private preferences', *University of Chicago Law Review* 53(4): 1129–1184.

— (1988a) 'Beyond the republican revival', Symposium: The Republican Civic Tradition, *Yale Law Journal* 97(8): 1539–1590.

— (1988b) 'Constitutions and democracies: an epilogue', in J. Elster and R. Stagstad (eds) *Constitutionalism and Democracy*, Cambridge, UK: Cambridge University Press, pp. 327–53.

— (1990) *After the Rights Revolution*, Cambridge, MA: Cambridge University Press.

— (1991) 'Preferences and politics', *Philosophy and Public Affairs* 20(1): 3–34.

— (1993a) 'Democracy and shifting preferences', in D. Copp, J. Hampton and J. E. Roemer (eds) *The Idea of Democracy*, Cambridge, UK: Cambridge University Press, pp. 196–230.

— (1993b) *The Partial Constitution*, Cambridge, MA: Harvard University Press.

— (1995) 'Incompletely theorized agreements', *Harvard Law Review* 108(7): 1733–72.

— (1999) 'Agreement without theory', in S. Macedo (ed.) *Deliberative Politics*, Oxford, UK: Oxford University Press, pp. 123–150.

— (2001) *Designing Democracy: What constitutions do*, Oxford, UK: Oxford University Press.

— (2002a) 'The law of group polarization', *Journal of Political Philosophy* 10(2): 175–195. Reprinted in J. Fishkin and P. Laslett (eds) (2003) *Debating Deliberative Democracy*, Oxford, UK: Blackwell, pp. 80–101.

— (2002b) *Republic.com 2.0*, Princeton, NJ: Princeton University Press.

Susskind, L. and Cruikshank, J. (1987) *Breaking the Impasse: Consensual Approaches to Resolving Public Disputes*, New York: Basic Books.

Susskind, L., McKearnan, S. and Thomas-Larmer, J. (eds) (1999) *The Consensus Building Handbook: A comprensive guide to reaching agreement*, Thousand Oaks, CA, London, UK and New Delhi, India: Sage Publications.

Talisse, R. B. (2012) 'Deliberation', in D. Estlund (ed.) *Oxford Handbook of Political Philosophy*, Oxford, UK and New York, NY: Oxford University Press, pp. 204–22.

Taylor, C. (1989) 'Cross-purpose: the liberal-communitarian debate', in N. Rosenblum (ed.) *Liberalism and the Moral Life*, Cambridge, MA: Harvard University Press, pp. 159–82.

Thompson, D. F. (2008) 'Deliberative democratic theory and empirical political science', *Annual Review of Political Science* 11: 497–520.

Thompson, J. B. (1982) 'Universal pragmatics', in J. B. Thompson and D. Held (eds) *Habermas: Critical debates*, London and Basingstoke, UK: MacMillan Press, pp. 116–133.

Thompson, J. B. and Held, D. (eds) (1982) *Habermas: Critical debates*, London and Basingstoke, UK: MacMillan Press.

de Tocqueville, A. (1969) *Democracy in America*, New York, NY: Anchor Books.

Truman, D. B. (1951) *The Governmental Process: Political interests and public opinion*, New York, NY: Knopf.

Uhr, J. (1998) *Deliberative Democracy in Australia: The changing place of Parliament*, Cambridge, UK: Cambridge University Press.

Urbinati, N. (2002) *Mill on Democracy: From the Athenian polis to representative government*, Chicago, IL: University of Chicago Press.

—— (2006) *Representative Democracy: Principles and genealogy*, Chicago, IL: University of Chicago Press.

—— (2009) *Individualismo democratico: Emerson, Dewey e la cultura politica americana*, Rome, IT: Donzelli.

—— (2010) 'Unpolitical democracy', *Political Theory* 38(1): 65–92.

—— (2011) 'Representative democracy and its critics', in S. Alonso, J. Keane and W. Merkel, with the collaboration of Maria Fotou, (eds) *The Future of Representative Democracy*, Cambridge, UK: Cambridge University Press, pp. 23–49.

—— (2012) 'Competing for liberty: the republican critique of democracy', *American Political Science Review* 106(3): 607–21.

—— (2014) *Democracy Disfigured: Opinion, truth, and the people*, Cambridge, MA and London, UK: Harvard University Press.

Urbinati, N. and Warren, M. (2008) 'The concept of representation in contemporary democratic theory', *Annual Review of Political Science* 1: 387–412.

Urbinati, N. and Zakaras, A. (eds) (2007) *J. S. Mill's Political Thought: A bicentennial reassessment*, Cambridge, UK: Cambridge University Press.

Urfalino, P. (2007) 'La décision par consensus apparent. Nature et propriétés', *Revue européenne des sciences sociales* LXV–136: 47–70.

—— (2014) 'The rule of non-opposition: opening up decision-making by consensus', *Journal of Political Philosophy* 22(3): 320–41.

Van Mill, D. (1996) 'The possibility of rational outcomes from democratic discourse and procedures', *Journal of Politics* 58(3): 734–52.

Von Schomberg, R. and Baynes, K. (eds) (2002) *Discourse and Democracy: Essays on Habermas's Between Facts and Norms*, Albany, NY: State University of New York Press.

Walker, J. L. (1966) 'A critique of the elitist theory of democracy', *American Political Science Review* 60(2): 285–95.

Walzer, M. (1999) 'Deliberation, and what else?', in S. Macedo (ed.) *Deliberative Politics*, Oxford, UK: Oxford University Press, pp. 58–69. Reprinted in M. Walzer (2004) *Politics and Passion: Toward a more egalitarian liberalism*, New Haven, CT and London, UK: Yale University Press.

Warren, M. E. (2009) 'Governance-driven democratization', *Critical Policy Analysis* 3(1): 3–13.

Warren, M. E, and Mansbridge, J. *et. al.* (2015) *Deliberative Negotiation*, in J. Mansbridge and C. J. Martin (eds) *Political Negotiation: A Handbook*, Washington D.C.: Brookings Institute Press, pp. 140–196.

Warren, M. E. and Pearse, H. (eds) (2008) *Designing Deliberative Democracy: The British Columbia citizens' assembly*, Cambridge, UK: Cambridge University Press.

Wellmer, A. (1974) 'The linguistic turn of critical theory', in H. P. Birne *et al.* (eds) *Critical Theory, Philosophy and Social Theory: A Symposion*, Chelmsford, UK: Stony Brook, pp. 74–101.

—— (1977) 'Kommunikation und Emanzipation. Überlegungen zur "sprachanalyische Wende" der Kritischen Theorie', in U. Jaeggi and A. Honneth (eds) *Theorien des Historischen Materialismus*, Frankfurt am M., DE: Suhrkamp Verlag.

West, C. (1989) *The American Evasion of Philosophy: A genealogy of pragmatism*, London, UK: Macmillan.

Westbrook, R. B. (1991) *John Dewey and American Democracy*, Ithaca, NY and London, UK: Cornell University Press.

Whitman, W. (1949 [1871]) *Democratic Vistas*, New York, NY: Little Library of Liberal Arts.

White, J. and Ypi, L. (2011) 'On Partisan Political Justification', *American Political Science Review* 105(2): 381–396.

Wiebe, H. R. (1995) *Self-Rule: A cultural history of American democracy*, Chicago, IL: University of Chicago Press.

Wolkenstein, F. (2016) 'A deliberative model of intra-party democracy', *Journal of Political Philosophy* 24(3): 297–320.

Wright Mills, C. (1956) *The Power Elite*, New York, NY: Oxford University Press.

Young, I. M. (2000) *Inclusion and Democracy*, Oxford, UK: Oxford University Press.

—— (2001) 'Activist challenges to deliberative democracy', *Political Theory* 29(5): 670–90. Reprinted in J. S. Fishkin and P. Laslett (eds) (2003) *Debating Deliberative Democracy*, Oxford, UK: Blackwell, pp. 102–20.

Zakaras, A. (2007) 'John Stuart Mill, individuality, and participatory democracy', in N. Urbinati and A. Zakaras (eds) (2007) *J. S. Mill's Political Thought: A bicentennial reassessment*, Cambridge, UK: Cambridge University Press, pp. 200–20.

Index

Index of Names

Lightning Source UK Ltd.
Milton Keynes UK
UKOW06n0849111017

310800UK00003B/118/P

9 781785 522420